PN

B4T 5633 4/93

THE APPLAUSE / BEST PLAYS

THEATER YEARBOOK OF 1991-1992

FEATURING

THE TEN BEST PLAYS

OF THE SEASON

THE APPLAUSE / BEST PLAYS

THEATER YEARBOOK
OF 1991-1992

featuring the Ten Best Plays of the Season

EDITED BY OTIS L. GUERNSEY JR.
AND JEFFREY SWEET

*Illustrated with photographs and
with drawings by* HIRSCHFELD

APPLAUSE
NEW YORK • LONDON

Copyright © 1992 by Applause Theatre Book Publishers
ISBN: 1-55783-146-7 (cloth)
ISBN: 1-55783-147-5 (paper)
ISSN: 1063-620X
Printed in the United States of America

A catalogue record for this book is available from the British Library.

EDITOR'S NOTE

INFORMATION about the American theater in all its glittering facets is the primary aim of each succeeding yearbook in the Best Plays series published for 68 years by Dodd, Mead and for the last five years by Glenn Young's Applause Theatre Books. The present volume, the *Applause/Best Plays 1991-92 Theater Yearbook*, mixes, as always, pleasure with business by communicating the literary essence and impact of our theater's best new work, and in the entertaining reviews of the Broadway and off-Broadway seasons by Jeffrey Sweet (whose play *American Enterprise* won an American Theater Critics Association citation this year) and the highlights of the off-off-Broadway season by Mel Gussow, distinguished drama critic of the New York *Times*.

But the heart of our matter is our detailed and comprehensive factual summaries of each theater year as it develops on the stages in New York and across the country. Our Best Plays contributors continue to give this their full attention. That there are so few errors in this complex coverage is the achievement not only of those who prepare it but also of Jonathan Dodd and the editor's wife who check and backstop every aspect of every volume. Camille Croce (off off Broadway) and Sheridan Sellers (regional theater) make major annual contributions with their extensive listings of new-play programs, as does Rue E. Canvin in charge of publications and necrology. And we point with special pride to our section devoted to the American Theater Critics Association's citation of outstanding new plays in 1991-92 regional theater production. ATCA makes it possible for us to highlight the best theater from coast to coast, which no single publication could do from any but ATCA's broad-based, expert viewpoint, focused by a play selection committee chaired by T.H. McCulloh of the Los Angeles *Times*.

No one sees as deeply into the spirit of the theater as does Al Hirschfeld, who shares his insight in the form of drawings which are the star of any publication in which they appear, including this one. Additionally, our 1991-92 graphics include examples of outstanding scene and costume designs in original drawings graciously provided to us by Jane Greenwood, William Ivey Long, Joe Vanek and Tony Walton; a Best Play (*Crazy for You*) synopsized in photos by Joan Marcus; and a bounteous sampling of the year's productions on New York and cross-country stages in the photos by Martha Swope and her associates (Carol Rosegg and William Gibson), Joan Marcus for the photos synopsizing *Crazy for You* and Chris Bennion, T.L. Boston, Marc Bryan-Brown, Jim Caldwell, Marvin Einhorn, T. Charles Erickson, Matthew Gilson, Wojciech Glinka, Gerry Goodstein, Nathaniel Kramer, Bob Lapin, Tom Lawlor, Robin Macgregor, Dan Rest, William Rivelli, Jonathan Slaff, Richard Termine, Jay Thompson and Thomas A. Werner.

And the hundreds of pages of information which this volume provides would be impossible to assemble without the diligent help and oft-taxed friendship of the men and women in the theater's press offices; or the special contributions of Sally Dixon Wiener (two Best Play synopses), William Schelble (Tony Awards listing), Thomas T. Foose (historical footnotes), Michael Kuchwara (Critics Circle voting), Dan Sullivan and Jonathan Abarbanel (ATCA citations), Henry Hewes (former Best Plays editor and present friend in need), Ralph Newman of the Drama Book Shop and Glenn Poppleton of American Theater Productions.

And then there is the dramatist, the founder of this feast, who confronts the blank paper or music sheet with his imagination and creates the magic that turns into all of the song and story—the best and the worst—of any theater year. We members of the audience are exceedingly grateful that the playwrights, lyricists, composers and librettists, all of them, keep on writing the plays and musicals with the incredible courage of their convictions. This series of Best Plays yearbooks annually proves that their efforts are not in vain. More than anything else, it stands on the library shelf as a tribute to and appreciation of their well-placed devotion to the living stage.

OTIS L. GUERNSEY Jr.
Editor

September 1, 1992

CONTENTS

Drawings by HIRSCHFELD

THE APPLAUSE / BEST PLAYS

THEATER YEARBOOK OF 1991-1992

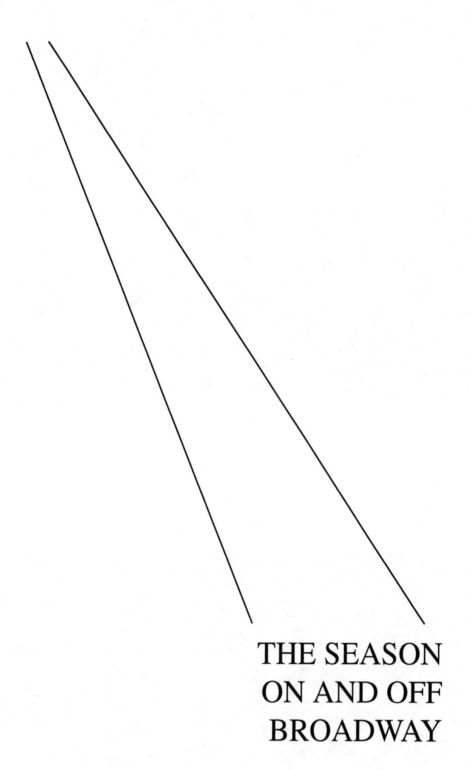

THE SEASON
ON AND OFF
BROADWAY

1991-92, A FRANK LOESSER YEAR—Among the season's most distinguished revivals were *Guys and Dolls* (pictured *above* with Faith Prince as Miss Adelaide and the Hot Box Girls in the "A Bushel and a Peck" number and *below right* with Nathan Lane as Nathan Detroit, *at left*, and Peter Gallagher as Sky Masterson); and *The Most Happy Fella* (pictured *below left* with Spiro Malas as Tony and Sophie Hayden as Rosabella in one of the year's two major productions of that musical). Loesser was the author of the *Guys and Dolls* score, and the book, music and lyrics for *The Most Happy Fella*

BROADWAY AND OFF BROADWAY

By Jeffrey Sweet

SUCH is the nature of the theater that the accomplishments of some of its legendary figures are difficult to make vivid to later generations. Theatrical accomplishments are, by definition, evanescent.

Dramatists have the best shot at remaining fresh in memory—their work may be encountered directly and anew through revival, publication and recordings. Actors, too, have a fair chance of maintaining some presence in public consciousness— many of the leading players of the stage get the chance to show some echo of their stuff on film or videotape. The names of the stage's directors and producers from decades past are less likely to stimulate vivid impressions. Those relatively few of today's theater audience who know Jed Harris's name are more likely to recall anecdotes about his notorious character than the excellences of the classic productions he produced and/or directed.

How then, will those of us who came of age in the 1960s and the 1970s be able to summon up for our children and grandchildren the importance of Joseph Papp, and the shock we felt when the front page of the New York *Times* reported that the artistic director of the New York Shakespeare Festival had died at age 70 on October 31? The sheer volume of the productions opened under his aegis can be gleaned from the pile of programs bearing the Festival's logo, and some sense of his influence can be felt by cataloguing the names of the impressively diverse artists these programs contain. But programs, recordings, and the film and television work he left behind will offer little sense of the juice of the man or what it felt like to be working in the theater during his time.

He was indeed one of that small handful of figures who define an era. Most significant in my mind was his position at the forefront of a movement which saw a profound shift in the development of the major efforts in the American theater. When Papp came onto the scene in the 1950s, Broadway was still where most of the action was. Most of the plays and musicals we hold up as representative of the best of the American stage were introduced as commercial enterprises within shouting distance of Times Square. The New York Shakespeare Festival was among the earliest, hardiest and most consistent non-commercial producing entities to champion new work. By the end of Papp's reign, and largely under his leadership, as a matter of course we came to expect that virtually all new work of consequence would originate in such non-commercial houses. In fact, the longest-running musical in the history of Broadway, *A Chorus Line*, began as a workshop under Papp's sponsorship at the Public. Not a few commentators noted the irony

3

The 1991–92 Season on Broadway

PLAYS (8)

Search and Destroy
Park Your Car in Harvard Yard
Lincoln Center:
Two Shakespearean Actors
Four Baboons Adoring the Sun
Crazy He Calls Me
Jake's Women
CONVERSATIONS WITH MY FATHER
TWO TRAINS RUNNING

MUSICALS (5)

Nick & Nora
CRAZY FOR YOU
Five Guys Named Moe
Metro
Jelly's Last Jam

REVUES (2)

Catskills on Broadway
The High Rollers Social and Pleasure Club

FOREIGN PLAYS IN ENGLISH (4)

DANCING AT LUGHNASA
Death and the Maiden
Shimada
A Small Family Business

HOLDOVERS WHICH BECAME HITS IN 1991-92 (2)

Lost in Yonkers
Miss Saigon

REVIVALS (17)

Circle in the Square:
Getting Married
On Borrowed Time
NYC Opera:
The Most Happy Fella
Brigadoon
Roundabout:
The Homecoming
The Visit
Hamlet
Peter Pan
Nat'l Actors Theater:
The Crucible
A Little Hotel on the Side
The Master Builder
The Most Happy Fella
Private Lives
A Streetcar Named Desire
Guys and Dolls
Man of La Mancha
Falsettos

SPECIALTIES (6)

Andre Heller's Wonderhouse
Moscow Circus
Radio City Music Hall: Christmas Spectacular
Easter Show
A **Christmas** Carol (one-actor perf.)
Bunraku

FOREIGN LANGUAGE PRODUCTIONS (1)

Gypsy Passion

Categorized above are all the new productions listed in the Plays Produced on Broadway section of this volume.
Plays listed in CAPITAL LETTERS have been designated Best Plays of 1991-92.
Plays listed in *italics* were still running June 1, 1992.
Plays listed in **bold face type** were classified as hits in *Variety's* annual estimate published June 8, 1992.

that this show—emblematic of Broadway razzmatazz—was created in an environment which grew up as a response to and, indeed, an implicit criticism of Broadway values. There was a nice irony, too, that much of the box office from that show went to support a good deal of work which would never have seen light of stage under a Broadway management.

So thoroughly did Papp and his colleagues in other non-profit companies transform the theater that all but one of the works selected as this year's Best Plays reached New York via institutional venues either in this country or abroad; one of them, *Fires in the Mirror*, at the Joseph Papp Public Theater. Three Best Plays, *Lips Together, Teeth Apart, Sight Unseen*, and *The Extra Man,* were produced at the Manhattan Theater Club (though the latter two originated at the South Coast Repertory Theater, as did *Search and Destroy*). *Conversations With My Father* originated at the Seattle Repertory Theater (where *The End of the Day* also was workshopped); *Marvin's Room* at the Goodman Theater; *Two Trains Running* at the Yale Repertory Theater (with stops at several other regionals on the way to New York); *Dancing at Lughnasa* at Dublin's Abbey Theater; and *Mad Forest* at London's Central School of Speech and Drama, then on to the New York Theater Workshop.

Among the other theaters whose work was imported to Broadway or full off-Broadway contracts this season were the Center Theater Group of Los Angeles (*Jelly's Last Jam*); Chicago's Victory Gardens Theater (*Beau Jest* and *Hauptmann*); the Pasadena Playhouse (*The Baby Dance*); Houston's Alley Theater (*The Baltimore Waltz*); Actors Theater of Louisville (*A Piece of My Heart*); London's Royal Court Theater (*Death and the Maiden*), Royal National Theater (*A Small Family Business*) and Royal Shakespeare Company (*Two Shakespearean Actors*); the Melbourne Theater Company (*Shimada*); Alberta Theater Projects (*Unidentified Human Remains and the True Nature of Love*); and off off Broadway's New Federal Theater Company (*From the Mississippi Delta*), WPA Theater (*Red Scare on Sunset*) and Jewish Repertory Theater (*Shmulnik's Waltz*).

The one Best Play which originated in the commercial arena is *Crazy for You*, an entertainment featuring mostly familiar Gershwin songs supported by a new book by Ken Ludwig. *Crazy for You* is also the only musical cited, though many were enthusiastic about *Jelly's Last Jam*, playwright-director George C. Wolfe's ambitious depiction of jazz pioneer Jelly Roll Morton. The season's best musical new to Broadway, *Falsettos,* in fact is comprised of two one-act off-Broadway musicals from seasons past—*March of the Falsettos* and *Falsettoland*—spliced together and slightly revised. (*Falsettoland* was one of last year's Best Plays.)

Much of the glitter of Broadway this season was provided by stars, including more than the usual number of bona fide movie and TV icons—Glenn Close, Richard Dreyfuss, Jessica Lange, Alec Baldwin, Joan Collins, Patrick Stewart, Judd Hirsch, George C. Scott, and Ellen Burstyn. Particularly pleasing were the returns of Gene Hackman, Alan Alda and Ben Gazzara, none of whom had appeared in New York productions in a dozen years or more. (Their returns

The season's outstanding straight-play costume designs were those of Jane
Greenwood for *Two Shakespearean Actors*, samples of which are shown above

would have been even more pleasing if the plays they honored were of higher
caliber.)

Welcome, too, were performers who, having distinguished themselves in past
seasons, further enhanced their reputations with excellent work this season—most
notably Faith Prince, Nathan Lane, Laura Esterman, Dennis Boutstikaris, Deborah
Hedwall, Cherry Jones, Lindsay Crouse, Jane Alexander, Anthony Heald, Brian
Bedford, Victor Garber, Roscoe Lee Browne, Stockard Channing, James Naughton,
Dana Ivey, John Mahoney, Joanna Gleason, Christine Baranski, Harry Groener,
Bruce Adler, Swoosie Kurtz, Paxton Whitehead, Mary Beth Hurt, Boyd Gaines,
Adam Arkin, Laila Robins, John Slattery, Roger Rees, Nancy Marchand, Mike
Nussbaum, W.H. Macy, Michael Rupert, Chip Zien, Maryann Plunkett, Fritz
Weaver, Campbell Scott, and Christopher Walken.

And there were special thrills to be had in encountering new (though not
necessarily young) faces which will undoubtedly grace our stages again—Denis
O'Hare, Larry Fishburne, Anna Deavere Smith, Cynthia Martells, Barbara Walsh,
Sophie Hayden, Spiro Malas and Liz Larsen.

Several big name directors came through with hits—notably Jerry Zaks (*Guys
and Dolls*), Mike Ockrent (*Crazy for You*), George C. Wolfe (*Jelly's Last Jam*),

Lloyd Richards (*Two Trains Running*), Daniel Sullivan (*Conversations With My Father*), James Lapine (*Falsettos*), and John Tillinger (*Lips Together, Teeth Apart*). Such established talents as Peter Hall, Edwin Sherin, Harold Prince, Mike Nichols and Gregory Mosher did not fare well, however, with their choices (*Four Baboons Adoring the Sun*, *The Visit*, *Grandchild of Kings*, *Death and the Maiden* and *A Streetcar Named Desire*, respectively). As is sadly usual, only a handful of women had directing credits this season—JoAnne Akalaitis (*'Tis Pity She's a Whore*), Anne Bogart (*In the Jungle of Cities* and *The Baltimore Waltz*), Melia Bensussen (*Blood Wedding*), Lynne Meadow (*A Small Family Business*), Elizabeth Swados (*Groundhog*), Jenny Sullivan (*The Baby Dance*). (Three of these were employed by the Public Theater and two by Manhattan Theater Club; two of these—Akalaitis and Meadow—are the artistic directors of the Public Theater and the Manhattan Theater Club.)

Tony Walton was the most visible designer of the season. Most admired was his Tony Award-winning vision of a bygone Times Square for *Guys and Dolls*. He was also represented by designs for *Four Baboons Adoring the Sun*, *Conversations With My Father*, and *Death and the Maiden*. Robin Wagner summoned up more images of a romanticized New York, juxtaposed with a poky Western town, for *Crazy for You*, which, like *Guys and Dolls*, featured costumes by William Ivey Long and lighting by Paul Gallo. Among the non-musicals, Joe Vanek's design of the kitchen of a small house in Ireland and a taste of the fields beyond in *Dancing at Lughnasa* was widely praised. I was particularly impressed by the ingenuity with which Loy Arcenas (*The Extra Man*) and James Youmans (*Sight Unseen*) managed to accommodate productions at Manhattan Theater Club requiring frequent shifts of setting. Much of the impact of two of the Shakespeare Festival productions was owed to Derek McLane and Peter Kaczorowski (set and lighting designers of *Blood Wedding*) and John Arnone and Frances Aronson (set and lighting designers of *Pericles*).

In most cases, the opportunities for the above-named artists to shine began with writers facing bare pages (or blank computer screens). Which brings us back to the central concern of this volume—saluting the dramatists who introduced the most distinguished new works of the season, the ten Best Plays. To quote Otis L. Guernsey Jr. in past volumes, "The choice is made without any regard whatever to the play's type—musical, comedy or drama—or origin on or off Broadway, or popularity at the box office or lack of same.

"We don't take the scripts of bygone eras into consideration for Best Play citation in this one, whatever their technical status as American or New York 'premieres' which didn't have a previous production of record. We draw the line between adaptations and revivals, the former eligible for Best Play selection but the latter not, on a case-by-case basis. If a script influences the character of a season, or by some function of consensus wins the Critics, Pulitzer or Tony Awards, we take into account its future historical as well as present esthetic importance. This is the only special consideration we give, and we don't always tilt in its direction, as the record shows."

Our choices for the Best Plays of 1991-92 are listed below in the order in which they opened in New York (a plus sign + with the performance number signifies that the play was still running on June 1, 1992).

Lips Together, Teeth Apart
  (Off B'way, 388+ perfs.)

Dancing at Lughnasa
  (B'way, 253+ perfs.)

Mad Forest
  (Off Off B'way, 54 perfs.)

Marvin's Room
  (Off B'way, 206+ perfs.)

Sight Unseen
  (Off B'way, 150+ perfs.)

Crazy for You
  (B'way, 117+ perfs.)

Conversations With My Father
  (B'way, 73+ perfs.)

Two Trains Running
  (B'way, 56+ perfs.)

Fires in the Mirror
  (Off B'way, 24+ perfs.)

The Extra Man
  (Off B'way, 16+ perfs.)

JAKE'S WOMEN—Kate Burton, Alan Alda and
Tracy Pollan in a scene from the play by Neil Simon

New Plays

Actresses commonly and justifiably complain that a disproportionate number of leading parts are written for men. This season saw the production of several new plays which, if nothing else, gave the edge to the women in their casts.

Heading this list was Brian Friel's extraordinary Best Play, *Dancing at Lughnasa*, a portrait drawn from the playwright's memory of five of his aunts. Quite a few critics made appropriate comparison between Friel's play and Chekhov's *Three Sisters*, noting that each deals with women whose spirits are held in check by the unspoken prohibitions of their society. In *Dancing at Lughnasa*, the society in question is Catholic Ireland in 1936. Friel introduces us to the five in the last few weeks of their life together, sharing a house in the country and eking out precarious livelihoods, only dimly aware of the forces which will soon disrupt the delicate balance of their collective household and atomize their family.

It is a play not of plot but of evocative incident. The most celebrated moment

The 1991–92 Season Off Broadway

PLAYS (33)

Mr. Gogol and Mr. Preen
Selling Off
Red Scare on Sunset
Circle Repertory:
The Balcony Scene
Babylon Gardens
The Rose Quartet
The Baltimore Waltz
Empty Hearts
Manhattan Theater Club:
LIPS TOGETHER, TEETH APART
Beggars in the House of Plenty
A Piece of My Heart
SIGHT UNSEEN
THE EXTRA MAN
Playwrights Horizons:
Young Playwrights Festival
MARVIN'S ROOM
The End of the Day
Beau Jest
The Baby Dance
Servy-n-Bernice 4Ever
From the Mississippi Delta
The Dropper
Willie & Esther

Raft of the Medusa
Grandchild of Kings
The Substance of Fire (return engagement)
Papp Public Theater:
The Home Show Pieces
Homo Sapien Shuffle
Before It Hits Home
Bert Sees the Light
Shmulnik's Waltz
Lotto
Zora Neale Hurston (retun engagement)
Hauptmann

FOREIGN PLAYS IN ENGLISH (3)

Unidentified Human Remains and the True Nature of Love
Iron Bars
MAD FOREST

MUSICALS (7)

Prom Queens Unchained
Return to the Forbidden Planet
Cinderella
Just a Night Out
Groundhog
Ruthless!
Eating Raoul

REVUES (6)

Forbidden Broadway 1991½
Cole Porter at the Kaufman
I Won't Dance
Finkel's Follies
Big Noise of '92
Forbidden Broadway 1992

REVIVALS (10)

Safe Sex
Shakespeare Marathon:
Othello
Pericles
The Matchmaker
Papp Public Theater:
In the Jungle of Cities
'Tis Pity She's a Whore
Blood Wedding
The Shadow of a Gunman
Boesman and Lena
Chess

ONE-ACTOR PERFORMANCES (7)

Mambo Mouth (return engagement)
At Wit's End
Reno Once Removed
FIRES IN THE MIRROR
Julie Halston's Lifetime of Comedy
The Other Side of Paradise
Dancing on the White House Lawn

SPECIALTIES (4)

Penn & Teller Rot in Hell
The Radiant City
Tubes
Moving Beyond the Madness

FOREIGN LANGUAGE PRODUCTIONS (7)

Bergman on Stage:
Miss Julie
Long Day's Journey Into Night
A Doll's House
State Theater, Lithuania:
Uncle Vanya
The Square
Festival Latino:
A Midsummer Night's Dream
The Tempest

Categorized above are all the new productions listed in the Plays Produced Off Broadway section of this volume.
Plays listed in CAPITAL LETTERS have been designated Best Plays of 1991-92.
Plays listed in *italics* were still running June 1, 1992.

shows the five briefly prompted by a folk tune over the wireless to put aside their repressed ways and break into the freedom of a wild dance of whooping and stomping. The radio's fizzling aborts their revel in mid-step, but for a brief time the vitality of their natures has slipped the bonds of inhibition. The effect is simultaneously exhilarating and poignant, dramatizing both the women's potential for joy and the bitter truth that that joy is rarely to be touched in lives circumscribed by custom and religious stricture. Other, more understated sequences are as haunting, most notably the heartbreaking *pas de deux* by one sister with the charming but hopelessly undependable father of her illegitimate son as a second sister looks on yearningly.

The production, which originated at the Abbey Theater in Dublin under the direction of Patrick Mason, matched the excellences of Friel's text. Catherine Byrne as Chris, the unwed mother, and Dearbhla Molloy as Maggie, the most outspoken of the clan, were particularly affecting, but Brid Brennan as Agnes, Rosaleen Linehan as Kate and Brid Ni Neachtain as Rose all had opportunities to shine. Robert Gwilym as Chris's sometimes lover, Donal Donnelly as a disoriented former missionary brother and Gerard McSorley as the narrator, Chris's adult son, whose memories frame the play, rounded out the flawless cast. The cumulative impression was of the definitive production of a play likely to become a classic of the world stage.

Sisters again were central characters in Scott McPherson's Best Play, *Marvin's Room*. Having spent her life caring for her bedridden father and an invalid aunt to the exclusion of much by way of an emotional life, middle-aged Bessie learns that she has leukemia and her chief hope for survival is a bone marrow transplant from her sister, Lee, or Lee's sons Hank and Charlie. This is the catalyst for the first encounter between the two in years. The cause for the estrangement is immediately apparent—Lee's impatience and casual indifference to ethical niceties stand in sharp contrast to Bessie's self-sacrifice and seemingly limitless altruism. Still, temperamental difference or not, the bonds of family bring Lee and her children to Bessie's home in Florida to be tested for compatibility. Though the medical results ultimately testify that they are physically incompatible, the action of the play moves the sisters and their damaged family to a new emotional compatibility.

McPherson dramatizes the double set of relations which exists between his characters—the biological relationships and the set of relationships determined by the family's various illnesses and incapacities. In the case of Bessie and her father, the child has become caretaker of the parent. In the case of Bessie and her rebellious and mentally unstable nephew Hank, the aunt becomes a truer mother than the biological mother.

All of this may sound like heavy going, but, though dealing with somber subject matter, *Marvin's Room* is written with a bracing dollop of black humor to counteract any sentimental tendencies. In production, McPherson's script was blessed with Laura Esterman and Lisa Emery in the roles of the sisters, Emery as the incendiary Lee and Esterman making the saintly Bessie human and credible. A few seasons back, Esterman gave a dazzling though largely unnoticed performance in the short-lived Best Play *Kvetch*. As the central figure in a critically-embraced hit, she made a well-deserved splash, re-establishing herself as an actress of finely-tuned gifts. Mark Rosenthal also impressed as the pyromaniac nephew with untapped sensitivity.

Both *Dancing at Lughnasa* and *Marvin's Room* were written by male dramatists. Three of the other plays with virtuoso roles for actresses were composed by female playwrights. Two, *From the Mississippi Delta* and *A Piece of My Heart*, were derived from fact, each portraying women in the middle of the turmoil of the 1960s.

Shirley Lauro's *A Piece of My Heart*, suggested by Keith Walker's book of the same name, follows the experiences during the Vietnam War of six American women—four nurses, a black intelligence officer and a singer who tours bases entertaining the troops. The piece is structured in three parts: first, the introduction of the idealistic women prior to going overseas, second, vignettes of their largely horrifying and disillusioning experiences in Southeast Asia, and third, scenes describing their difficulty adjusting to American society after their return home. Though there were many passages which showed the production's strong cast to advantage, the piece was too dramatically diffuse to be persuasive as a fully-realized play. It also suffered somewhat in contrast to *China Beach,* the remarkable television series which covered similar territory in greater depth.

From the Mississippi Delta is an autobiographical account by Dr. Endesha Ida Mae Holland of her journey from a young, black prostitute in the deep South to an associate professorship. The best passages of the play tell stories of her childhood and the eccentric characters who peopled it, bringing to mind Samm-Art Williams's Best Play *Home*. Disappointingly, the central event of the play, the transformation of the central character, is under-dramatized. Newspaper pieces on Dr. Holland indicated that the arrival of the civil rights movement in her town triggered her political awakening; one article described how, having been tossed into the local jail many times for solicitation, young Endesha was able to act as a comforting guide to the civil rights workers with whom she was jailed after a protest. This key scene in her story is not represented onstage, and none of the individuals who presumably encouraged her to change her life is characterized with any specificity. Additionally, by having the production's three splendid actresses (Cheryl Lynn Bruce, Sybil Walker and Jacqueline Williams) play the various characters in relays, it was sometimes hard to follow who was doing what. Ultimately, in performance the rousing humor and humanity of many of the episodes overcame the play's weaknesses, but I couldn't help regretting that the powerful and inspiring story hadn't been told to full advantage.

The press was sharply divided on Jane Anderson's *The Baby Dance*, Frank Rich of the *Times* weighing in with an opinion which was one withering insult, and Clive Barnes of the *Post* and Edith Oliver of *The New Yorker* registering enthusiastic appraisals. The plot concerns a poor, white working-class married woman named Wanda who has entered into an agreement with an upper middle-class woman named Rachel under which, in return for Rachel and her husband Richard covering the medical expenses and a little more, Wanda is to carry her unplanned baby to

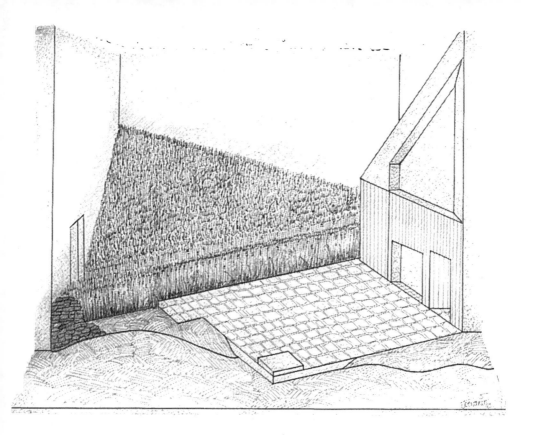

Pictured on this page are examples of Joe Vanek's sketches for his outstanding designs for Brian Friel's *Dancing at Lughnasa*: *above*, the setting; *below*, the costumes for Maggie (*left*), Gerry (*center*) and Kate (*right*)

term and then turn the newborn over to Rachel and Richard for adoption. In the first act, Rachel visits Wanda's trailer park home, trying to maintain a friendly if businesslike attitude while choking back her disdain for Wanda's lifestyle. In the second act, set in the hospital, legal and financial wrangling run in counterpoint to Wanda's giving birth.

The premise of *The Baby Dance* had the potential of being a superficial TV movie, but Anderson uses it to explore pregnancy as a fault line between classes. Anderson views wealth not merely as the ability to surround oneself with material goods but to purchase options in life. Money doesn't shield Rachel and Richard from sadness and disappointment, but it gives them some recourse. In contrast, at the end of the play, Wanda and Al, faced with the tragedy of a brain-damaged child who no longer is an attractive adoption prospect, have no shields between them and their misery. The script has its flaws—Anderson takes too many easy shots at Wanda and Al's so-called white trash world, and Rachel and Richard are similarly too easily typed as Southern Californians addicted to trends and status symbols. Eventually, though, the play transcends these lapses and engages the moral issues unflinchingly. Under Jenny Sullivan's direction, Linda Purl and Stephanie Zimbalist gave exemplary performances as Wanda and Rachel, respectively. Incidentally, rather than merely complain about the paucity of good women's roles, Purl and Zimbalist demonstrated admirable gumption by commissioning Anderson to write *The Baby Dance* for them in the first place. Purl, Zimbalist and Anderson surely will be owed thanks by actresses around the country who will play these roles in the future.

Terrence McNally is an extremely proficient writer of one-act plays who, to my taste, has had less success with full-length works. The first acts of *Frankie and Johnny in the Clair de Lune* and *The Lisbon Traviata* (both produced at his artistic home, the Manhattan Theater Club) were complete and satisfying unto themselves; their second acts less gratifying, giving the impression of addenda rather than developments of the firsts. What a pleasure it is, then, to encounter his Best Play *Lips Together, Teeth Apart*, a fully persuasive three-act work which deepens after each intermission. Set during a Fourth of July weekend, the play introduces us to two married couples sharing a beach house on Fire Island. (The brother of one of the wives has died recently of AIDS, and the occasion of the visit involves estate business.) McNally cannily highlights their tensions and insecurities by placing the couples, accustomed to being in environments in which heterosexuality is dominant, in a gay enclave in which they can't help feeling in the minority. The action of the play touches on such expected issues as alienation, adultery and mortality, but with McNally's characteristic mixture of irony, outrageous humor and sympathy. Under the direction of McNally's frequent collaborator, John Tillinger, a cast largely made up of alumni from McNally's previous plays— Christine Baranski, Anthony Heald, Swoosie Kurtz and Nathan Lane—sensitively negotiated the reefs and shoals of the two troubled marriages. All in all, I found it to be the most successful American drama on marriage since Lanford Wilson's underestimated *Serenading Louie* (which John Tillinger also directed memorably in revival some years back).

Donald Margulies's Best Play *Sight Unseen* may be viewed as a companion piece to his previous Best Play, *The Loman Family Picnic*. In the earlier work, Margulies drew a harrowing portrait of a Jewish family in Brooklyn in the early 1960s. It is not too hard to imagine *Sight Unseen*'s protagonist as being the product of a similar family. Jonathan Waxman is a successful painter who decries a critic's characterization of him as a Jewish artist as an act of cultural ghettoization and simultaneously reveals the effects of having been brought up in a virtual ghetto in both his art and his life. The play has an unconventional shape, being comprised of eight scenes in distinctly unchronological order. Half of the scenes occur in an English farmhouse where Jonathan has imposed himself as the overnight guest of a former lover, Patricia, and her eccentric archeologist husband, Nick. Nick at first appears painfully diffident, but behind that reserve is an abundance of contempt for Jonathan's art and values as well as resentment for the hold the memory of the artist's relationship with Patricia still has on her. Intercut with these scenes are two scenes of a German interviewer grilling Jonathan about the influence of his background on his work, a grilling which the irritated artist ascribes to anti-Semitism. Each act ends with an episode from Patricia and Jonathan's past—the first, detailing the end of their affair, the second, its beginning. And yes, Patricia's status as a non-Jew has a great deal to do with both.

BEAU JEST—Laura Patinkin and Tom Hewitt in James Sherman's play

Margulies serves up much incisive commentary about the art scene and what it means to be anointed by the arbiters. But *Sight Unseen* is about something larger than celebrity. It is about cultural identity as both a fortress and a prison. Through the example of his protagonist, Margulies implies that the same tribalism which has helped protect Jews in hostile environments also discourages bridging differences with non-Jews. Jonathan's background inculcated him with values which led him to the arts and out to a wider, more cosmopolitan world, but they also lead him to view this world with chronic suspicion and, in self-fulfilling prophecy, to trigger constant antagonism. Under Michael Bloom's direction, the cast—Dennis Boutsikaris as Jonathan, Deborah Hedwall as Patricia, Jon De Vries as Nick and Laura Linney as the disquieting interviewer—gave a quartet of superb performances.

Another Best Play, Herb Gardner's *Conversations With My Father,* also deals with the contradictions of the American-Jewish experience. At the beginning, Charlie—the successful author of a series of novels about a lovable, colorful Jewish bar owner—is making a final visit with his son to the Canal Street bar his late father Eddie ran for years. The visit triggers memories of colorful but not particularly lovable Eddie. For most of the play, Charlie sits to the side, providing commentary and transitions between the series of scenes which take Eddie and his sons from 1936 to 1976. The play's central concern is the fight in Eddie's soul between his Jewish background and his desire to assimilate. Eddie has worked hard to neutralize his accent, he has changed his name from Goldberg to Ross, and he constantly re-invents his bar under new names proclaiming American values and imagery. But, despite his assimilationist gestures, he remains, at heart, an angry and defiant man. The anger and defiance are a mixed legacy for his sons. On the one hand, they carry with them his determination not to be beaten down. On the other hand, the habitual contentiousness is spiritually brutalizing, resulting in alienation and hostility to much of the outside world as well as intimates. (In a particularly revealing moment, we see Charlie unwittingly re-enact with his son a clash he had had decades before with his father. As much distance as he has tried to put between himself and his father's values, Charlie is mortified to discover that his father is so firmly entrenched inside him that, when provoked, Eddie's voice barks from his throat.)

Gardner is dramatizing a substantial chunk of the American-Jewish experience—sequences deal with Eddie trying to come to terms with the pogroms he left behind him, Mafia thugs leaning on him for protection, the holocaust, and domestic anti-Semitism, in addition to conflicts between family members. Probably the play takes on *too* much to keep from being lumbering and ungainly, but what it lacks in structural grace it more than makes up for in the richness of characterization of its principal characters and the sense of history made vivid.

Early in the play, in an address to the audience, Charlie has an extended speech in which he demonstrates English's poverty of expression when compared to Yiddish. Ironically, Gardner spends the rest of the play demonstrating how very expressive and lyrical colloquial English can be. There is nothing mingy about Gardner's language. His is not a world of understatement. Rather he unleashes aria after glorious aria without sounding like a showoff. Under Daniel Sullivan's direction, the cast—led by Judd Hirsch as Eddie, Tony Shalhoub and David Krumholtz as Charlie at different ages, and David Margulies as a Yiddish actor who is a regular in the bar—met Gardner's challenges with brio. All in all, *Conversations With My Father* is not only a Best Play, it is probably Gardner's best play.

Two other plays offered gentler views of the American-Jewish experience. James Sherman's *Beau Jest* is a charming comedy about a young woman who hires a non-Jewish actor to pretend for her parents' sake to be her perfect Jewish suitor. Sherman is an alumnus of Chicago's Second City, and true to his background, most of the humor is rooted in well-observed behavior rather than wisecrack. Allan Knee's *Shmulnik's Waltz* borrows elements of *Cyrano de Bergerac* and *The Shop Around the Corner* in its tale of a poor Russian-Jewish immigrant who finds himself hired by a rich illiterate to ghost-write love letters to the woman he himself loves. Ultimately the title character inadvertently ends up winning the heart of the woman's intellectual sister, who has fallen in love with the author of the letters without realizing his true identity. Directed with easy grace by Gordon Hunt, the production featured an especially appealing performance by Ilana Levine as the sister, Feyla.

John Guare's extraordinary Best Play from the 1990-91 season, *Six Degrees of Separation*, had its genesis in a compelling story based in fact, the telling of which suggested several levels of meaning. In his *Four Baboons Adoring the Sun*, I have the sense that he began with what the play was supposed to mean, then tried to build a story to accommodate his theme—something to do with the presence of the mythic in contemporary life. The action concerns a newly-married pair of archeologists and their attempts to meld the children from their previous marriages into a family while working on a dig in Sicily. As usual with any Guare play, there are marvelous passages on the attempt to make spiritual connection in a largely oblivious world. But the characters—even as played by such able actors as Stockard Channing and James Naughton—don't feel like full human beings but rather vessels for Guare's verbal flights. But then Guare is a daring playwright, and part and parcel with taking the chances is the probability that occasionally his aspiration will outrun his execution. Never mind. Even when he doesn't pull off what he attempts, he commands interest and respect.

Last season, the competition for the major play awards was between Guare's *Six Degrees* and Neil Simon's *Lost in Yonkers*. This year, Simon, too, disappointed. The structure of *Jake's Women* is rather similar to Stephen Sondheim's, George Furth's, and Hal Prince's *Company*. In both, men in crisis try to sort through their fear of intimacy by invoking memories and fantasies of figures in their lives. In *Company*, the figures are married couples and a few girl friends of the central character's acquaintance. In *Jake's Women*, Jake—a stand-in for Simon—summons up two wives, two versions of his daughter, a girl friend, his sister and his analyst. Just as in *Company*, the action of Simon's play moves to the central character reaching a catharsis which makes it possible for him to extend himself to another.

Unfortunately, though there is the expected quotient of zippy lines, Simon doesn't come through with anything profound about the human heart. Simon sticks a lot of homilies into the mouth of his alter ego, but the philosophizing sounds hollow. The play does, however, include one passage of classic Simon—a sequence in which a hyperactive Jake spews out a torrent of plans for hypothetical trips with a bewildered girl friend. His frenetic behavior makes manifest better than any overtly articulated speech could the conflicting impulses to which he is subject. It was a pleasure to see Alan Alda—all of his skill and charm intact—on the Broadway stage again. Though I had problems with the script, Simon certainly offered most of the ladies in his company ample material to score, most notably Helen Shaver, Brenda Vaccaro, Joyce Van Patten and a radiant Kate Burton as the memory of Jake's wife. The play was directed by his frequent collaborator, Gene Saks.

Another familiar playwright-director team—August Wilson and Lloyd Richards—returned to Broadway with the latest in Wilson's series of plays illuminating different eras of the American black experience. This one, Best Play *Two Trains Running*, is set in the most recent past of any of his works—1969. Having already given good account of his version of the boarding house play (*Joe Turner's Come and Gone*, also a Best Play), Wilson here takes on the diner play, using a hash house as the meeting place of a community of characters each of whom is affected by the turmoil and promise of the 1960s.

Two Trains Running is the most languorous of Wilson's works; the first act is comprised mostly of members of the ensemble holding forth in a series of setpieces. Wilson's language is rich and poetic, but there is little sense of urgency. The first act ends with no pressing question compelling a return for the second. The second act, however, is a considerable improvement as the various characters face choices of some dramatic weight. Happily, too, unlike in *Joe Turner's Come and Gone* and *The Piano Lesson*, Wilson has managed to construct a persuasive conclusion without recourse to a spiritual or supernatural *deus ex machina*. *Two Trains Running* also is the first of Wilson's plays to suggest hope of the tide turning for blacks in white-dominated America; through persistence, the black owner of the diner whose building has been targeted for purchase and demolition by white politicians ends up being compensated with more than he'd dreamed of realizing.

As usual with Richards's productions of Wilson's work, the actors made the most of their opportunities. Larry Fishburne won a Tony for his performance as a young hothead fresh out of prison and looking for a new life; there was also very strong work from Cynthia Martells as the proud waitress who attracts his attention, Roscoe Lee Browne as an elderly man of philosophical bent with a faith in magic, and Sullivan Walker as a half-mad character obsessed with the ham he feels he was cheated out of for work done years ago.

The past is also an important element of Jill Shearer's *Shimada*, concerning an Australian's growing conviction that the Japanese businessman angling to take over the bicycle company he manages was the officer who brutalized him and murdered one of his friends in a P.O.W. camp in World War II. Shearer's avowed intention was to dramatize the necessity of coming to terms with the pain of the past so as to be able to cope with the future. But, between the muddled flashbacks and awkward exposition, even a good cast featuring Ben Gazzara, Ellen Burstyn, Mako, Estelle Parsons, Tracy Sallows and Robert Joy couldn't make the material involving.

Charles Busch wrote and starred in another play dealing with history, *Red Scare on Sunset*. As in his *The Lady in Question*, cross-dressing Busch played a performer going through her political baptism. In *Lady*, she was a concert pianist getting wise to the Nazi menace; in *Red Scare*, a movie star battling Communist infiltration in Hollywood. Both plays draw their inspirations from the conventions of movie melodramas; in parodying popular culture's reaction to serious issues, Busch mocks the values on which those films were based. *Red Scare* struck me as a better sustained effort than its predecessor, but at more than two hours, it was still a good deal longer than was necessary to make its satiric points.

John Logan's *Hauptmann* deals more starkly with American hysteria. The thesis of his play is that the title character's conviction and execution for the kidnapping and murder of Charles and Anne Morrow Lindbergh's baby boy were the results of the same strain of xenophobia which would later fuel McCarthyism. Lindbergh exemplified the American ideal; Hauptmann, with his strong German accent and his off-putting manner—a combination of whininess and arrogance—represented the threatening alien. The question Logan so effectively poses is not so much whether Hauptmann was guilty (though the evidence presented sounds far from conclusive), but whether in the atmosphere of the times there was any chance of him receiving a fair trial. Denis O'Hare gave one of the season's most complex and riveting performances as Hauptmann.

Early in 1991, playwright Caryl Churchill, director Mark Wing-Davey and students from London's Central School of Speech and Drama journeyed to Romania in the belief that there was a play to be made out of the events of the previous several months. The first act of the work they built, Best Play *Mad Forest*, focuses on Romanian life under the Ceausescus' regime, the second on the regime's overthrow, the third on the attempt to find a new equilibrium in the unsteadiness of the first post-Communist months.

The play is a dramatic patchwork. Much of the text is made up of short, documentary-style vignettes, e.g., a man standing on line grumbles an anti-government sentiment and the people on either side of him edge away so as to distance themselves from any taint of supposed association. Other scenes have a more fantastic quality; a vampire and a starved dog engage in a dark dialogue about the Romanian character. The overthrow itself is presented with the cast placed in stationary positions around the stage, directly addressing the audience in a series of monologues contrasting different participants' perspectives.

Giving the work dramatic shape is the story of two Romanian families—one upper middle class, the other working class. Under the Communist regime, both families live in fear of spies and reprisals. (One memorable scene depicts an evening at home with the working class family. Afraid of being overheard by bugging devices, the tensions between the father, mother and the children are mostly played out wordlessly through their negotiations over black market

DEATH AND THE MAIDEN—Gene Hackman, Richard Dreyfuss and Glenn
Close in a scene from the play by Ariel Dorfman, directed by Mike Nichols

cigarettes and eggs.) After the overthrow, a girl from one family marries a boy from
another. At the wedding, what should be a celebration of the linking of two families
instead turns into a donnybrook. It is easy to see this ceremony gone awry as
representative of life in many of the post-Communist states. Freed from
totalitarianism, people one would hope would unite and cooperate in building a new
future instead are turning on each other, the result being the civil wars and ethnic
and class animosities rending Eastern Europe today.

The New York production, directed by Mark Wing-Davey and employing a
company of 11 versatile American actors, was a major critical success in its run at
the off-off-Broadway New York Theater Workshop. Despite the attention it
received and its sold-out houses, no commercial management was willing to step
forward and move the play to the extended run it clearly merited.

Although, like Churchill's play, Anna Deavere Smith's *Fires in the Mirror* has a
large *dramatis personae*, Smith's requires only one actor; in its premiere run, that
single performer was Smith herself. Encouraged by dramatist-director George C.
Wolfe, she interviewed dozens of people in an attempt to explore the tensions
which erupted in the Crown Heights area of Brooklyn in the fall of 1991 after an
elderly Jewish driver killed a young black boy in a traffic accident. Within hours of

the accident, in an action widely viewed as retaliation, a group of 20 blacks assaulted a young Hasidic scholar; that night he died. The weeks following saw Crown Heights torn by confrontation and violence.

Smith's text is derived from her interviews. In performance, she played the interviewees, shifting sexes, ages, classes and colors. Part of the marvel of the evening was in watching this attractive slim black woman in her 30s so persuasively slip into the skins, speech patterns and logics of such a diverse group of people. No less marvelous than the pyrotechnics of the performance is the skill with which Smith organized her material, never speaking directly in her own voice, but juxtaposing what she insists are verbatim excerpts of her subjects' observations. Physicists tell us that when two tuning forks of different pitches are sounded in proximity, the interplay of their frequencies will produce a third frequency. Something similar happens here, the very different voices Smith introduces resonating off each other and producing new overtones. Rather than impose her own conclusions, Smith allows the audience the privilege of interpreting for themselves.

I find it particularly interesting that the two Best Plays by women this year are in sharp contrast to what one conventionally expects of female dramatists. Instead of drawing on intimate personal impulses, Churchill and Smith, like reporters, have ventured into alien milieus and brought back vivid impressions of their journeys. I have long believed that the theater began out of a journalistic impulse, the desire to share with one's community stories necessary for the community to understand itself and the outside world. Certainly, in these two extraordinary works, Churchill and Smith have satisfied both journalistic and theatrical imperatives.

Another solo performance dazzled this season—that of Patrick Stewart narrating and playing all the roles in his condensation of Charles Dickens's *A Christmas Carol*. After years of stage, film and TV adaptations, it was wonderful to see a version minus the usual props, sets, and special effects, resting instead on Dickens's language. All of the familiar characters were there, of course—Scrooge, the ghosts, Tiny Tim and his family—essayed with great passion and specificity by Stewart. The particular treat of the performance were the less-familiar descriptive passages, now sketching vivid impressions of passing characters, now summoning up large chunks of Victorian London. This deserves to become a perennial offering.

Harold Prince used considerably more resources to summon up the Dublin of Sean O'Casey in *Grandchild of Kings*. Employing members of the Irish Repertory Theater to clamber, brawl, keen and carouse over an environmental set, Prince as director displayed his usual gift for creating stage pictures. The problem with the evening lay with the text, Prince's own adaptation of O'Casey's autobiographic writings. Though scene by scene Prince displayed admirable craft, he never offered a compelling reason to be seriously invested in O'Casey's journey from birth into adulthood. This is the first of a proposed three-part effort. One hopes that the older O'Casey will register as a more dynamic figure in the parts to come.

Mike Nichols's staging of Ariel Dorfman's *Death and the Maiden* featured the return to the stage of a trio of our finest actors, Glenn Close, Richard Dreyfuss and

Gene Hackman. The story, set "in a country that is probably Chile," concerns a woman who holds prisoner in her house a doctor whom she believes raped and tortured her during the years of dictatorship from which her nation has only recently emerged. Her husband, appalled at her threat to kill the doctor, works to save this man whom we gradually grow to believe is indeed guilty of her charges. The form is melodramatic. The intention is to dramatize the battle between humanistic impulses and the cruelties to which all parties are prone during bitterly fought political conflicts. The intention is noble, but, at least in this production, not esthetically successful. I found the script too predictable. Once the situation is in place, it is hard to imagine any reasonably sophisticated member of the audience not anticipating the logic of whole scenes to come. Finally, near the end of the second act, Dorfman gives the doctor a long, understated speech about how he slipped into collaborating with torturers and the effects of his complicity on his conscience. As performed by Hackman, it was the one genuinely stirring and surprising passage in an earnest but curiously inert evening.

Hackman's character—a man of decent impulses who hadn't sufficient strength to resist the evil of his environment—had many brothers onstage this year. Moral deterioration was the central theme of Howard Korder's *Search and Destroy*, Jon Robin Baitz's *The End of the Day* and Alan Ayckbourn's *A Small Family Business*.

Search and Destroy concerns a naive huckster named Martin Mirkheim who adopts illegitimate means in his attempt to make a movie to trumpet the moral vision of a more spectacular huckster. His path leads to cocaine, murder and ultimately great success in Hollywood. Korder continues to write in a style so reminiscent of David Mamet as to be distracting; Martin Mirkheim's philosophizing to a tax auditor at the beginning of *Search and Destroy* has the same pattern of outbursts, hesitations and specious logic that Mamet practically trademarked with Ricky Roma's extraordinary monologue in *Glengarry Glen Ross*. There is an undeniable theatrical intelligence at work here, but Korder needs to find his own distinct voice.

Baitz's play, *The End of the Day*, tells the tale of Dr. Graydon Massey, a naturalized American of English background who, as a gesture of expiation, has volunteered to work in an underfunded clinic in Los Angeles's inner city. A threat from his Mafia-connected former father-in-law, Hilly, sends him back to London to beg his corrupt upper-class family for emergency cash. Ultimately, Massey discovers links between his family's corruption and Hilly's criminal enterprises. His response? Not only to accept the pervasive evil but to embrace it. This leads to—yes—cocaine, murder and great success in Hollywood. I admire Baitz's extraordinary precision of language and irony (which was so evident in his Best Play of last year, *The Substance of Fire*), but overall the play is too facile in its cynicism. The production, under the smartly-timed direction of Mark Lamos, featured a delicious performance by Nancy Marchand as two powerful women in the doctor's life—his tough and principled boss at the clinic and his appallingly unprincipled mother.

It was back to cocaine and murder (though not great success in Hollywood) in

Alan Ayckbourn's *A Small Family Business*. Jack McCracken has been brought in to take over management of the furniture business founded by and employing his wife's family. He begins with a declaration of principles, announcing his intention to run the company on the highest moral plane. The play chronicles his attempt to root out the corruption in the company. It turns out, however, that all of the corruption can be traced to the family. By the end of the play, even as he self-deludingly claims to have contained and resolved the scandals, he is colluding in a plan which, one understands, will probably end up unwittingly helping to import drugs his own daughter will ingest. Unfortunately, much of the time Ayckbourn takes on his way to this powerful conclusion seems to be occupied by filler. (Someone should tell him he should stop making jokes about inept cooks; after *Season's Greetings* and *A Woman in Mind*, he's mined that particular vein to the point of exhaustion.) Lynne Meadow directed a strong cast headed by Brian Murray as Jack McCracken and featuring a bravura comic turn by Anthony Heald as a creepy detective, but their good work was in the service of a script a draft or two shy of fulfilling its potential.

Every year, though it is not the specific intention of the editors, this volume includes one selection of a Best Play that is viewed by many in the critical community as, well, eccentric. This year, I suspect, that buzz-mumble will be over the choice of Richard Greenberg's *The Extra Man*, which was produced by the Manhattan Theater Club. It is a play that I believe was widely misunderstood and underestimated. The title character, Keith, at first seems a blandly agreeable fellow eager to lend a sympathetic ear to his friends. Gradually, one becomes aware that he is trying to instigate an affair between Laura and Jess. Laura is an editor married to Daniel, another of Keith's friends; Jess is a chronically lovelorn film critic. The relationship does indeed begin, but then Laura grows suspicious of Keith's part in encouraging the romance, which further leads her to question the basis of the romance itself. When the affair finally ends, it has taken an enormous toll on Laura, Jess and Daniel; and Keith, as ever, is there to offer sympathy.

Many of those who dislike *The Extra Man* seem to be at a loss to understand 1) Keith's motivation for wreaking havoc in his friends' lives and 2) why we should care anyway. The leading theories advanced to address the former—that Keith is expressing crypto-homosexual tendencies by upsetting the lives of his heterosexual friends, or is secretly in love with Laura himself—I think trivialize the play.

In his review for the New York *Times*, Frank Rich compared Keith to Iago, but, whereas Iago is clearly fueled by malice, Keith's manipulations are devoid of animosity. There is no evidence that Keith is trying to destroy Laura and Daniel's marriage or to devastate Jess emotionally. So why, if he has no malign intent, does Keith behave as he does?

We are accustomed to drama in which characters who do evil have clearly delineated motivations for the violence they do others. Either they are possessed by one of the classic vices—envy, greed, lust—or they are driven by the desire to work out some psychic injury done to them prior to the beginning of the play. What is so disturbing about Keith is we don't have recourse to these convenient explanations.

Greenberg is presenting a character who does evil, blithely unaware that he is doing so.

I believe that a desire to have some effect on the world is basic to human nature. The initial impulse is to have a positive effect, but those frustrated in their attempt to do something positive frequently rechannel their energies into negative outlets. It is significant that Keith, who had published a collection of short stories a number of years before, has been unable to produce anything since. Blocked from being able to make things happen on a page, he looks for some other arena in which to matter. Feeling effectless, he siezes opportunities to do something, to make something happen. He bears no antagonism toward Laura, Jess and Daniel. Indeed, by the end of the play, he undoubtedly still believes himself to be a true friend to all of them. But that doesn't keep him from having done them all serious damage.

As to why an audience should care—we are constantly being told by psychologists and sociologists that many in our society feel powerless and ineffectual. For such people, the phrase "Don't just stand there, do something!" has particular appeal. The implication is that action—any action—is better than none at all, the corollary being that the various options are morally indistinguishable. In what is seemingly an anecdote about an enclave of New York literati, Greenberg is warning

THE END OF THE DAY—Nancy Marchand and Roger Rees
in a scene from the play by Jon Robin Baitz at Playwrights Horizons

about the dangers of a society in which the effective is held to count for more than the good.

Another Manhattan Theater Club production, *Beggars in the House of Plenty*, written and directed by John Patrick Shanley, offered a portrait of a bitterly dysfunctional Irish-American family raised to mythic intensity. I found its nearly relentless bellowing to be numbing; a substantial portion of the critical community admired it a great deal more than I.

For years, Circle Rep has held the image of being the home of lyrical plays frequently set on country front porches. This season, the company was firmly focused on the urban ethos, three of their offerings concerning the difficulty of establishing and maintaining constructive human relationships surrounded by the noise and cruelty of the city. Thomas Cumella's *The Rose Quartet* and Wil Calhoun's *The Balcony Scene* describe tentative courting in the upper reaches of apartment buildings. Both are more interesting for nicely observed small negotiations than persuasive as full-length plays. Timothy Mason's *Babylon Gardens* attempts to correlate the deterioration of a marriage to the deterioration of the quality of life in New York but, despite strong work by Timothy Hutton and Mary-Louise Parker as the couple in question, it struck me as overwrought. A fourth play, *Empty Hearts*, written and directed by John Bishop, was a sort of whydunnit, alternating scenes of a murder trial with flashbacks of the affair and subsequent marriage that led to a woman's death at the hands of her love-obsessed husband. Mel Harris and Cotter Smith are compelling performers, and there was pleasure in watching the integrity of their work together on a scene-by-scene basis, but ultimately Bishop was unsuccessful in making the characters' private miseries sustain a full evening.

Circle Rep's most successful production of the season was of Paula Vogel's *The Baltimore Waltz*, in which a grade school teacher named Anna, learning she has a fatal malady called ATD (Acquired Toilet Disease), a sickness caught from sharing bathroom facilities with her pupils, goes on a trip to Europe with her gay brother Carl. While she has a series of assignations with men of various nationalities, Carl has a series of encounters with shady characters who hold out the promise of unorthodox drugs to combat her disease. At the end of the piece, it is revealed that the bulk of the play has been a dream. It is Carl, not Anna, who dies, and not of a fictional affliction, but of AIDS. At his bedside in his Baltimore hospital room is a stack of brochures touting European sights, a stack acquired in anticipation of a vacation he and his sister never got around to taking together. Thinking back over the European adventure, one realizes that it was an empathetic fantasy in which Anna has metaphorically put herself into her brother's grim situation.

Vogel's idea is an original one; her execution is erratic. The caricatures of European men are rather familiar from years of Second City and Saturday Night Live scenes, and the parody of *The Third Man*'s world of black market drugs isn't sufficiently developed to register as much more than a wink to film fans. But the heart of the play—the relationship between sister and brother—is sensitively written and, under Anne Bogart's direction, was sensitively played by Cherry Jones and Richard Thompson.

As in recent seasons, AIDS influenced much of the other dramatic writing of the season. Scott McPherson, himself diagnosed HIV positive, explicitly stated that *Marvin's Room* is intended to reflect on the epidemic; and, as noted previously, the death of a gay brother by AIDS is an element in the backstory of McNally's *Lips Together, Teeth Apart*. The effect of the epidemic was brought center stage in Joe Pintauro's *Raft of the Medusa*, a dramatization of a therapy group for those infected with the virus. The characters are intended to be a cross-section of the AIDS-infected community—many gay or drug users, but also two straight, non-using women. The play suffers from being too calculated—confrontations escalating to violence seem contrived for the sake of creating dramatic climaxes rather than earned—but the play deserves its hearing for making vivid the plights of people among us coping, largely anonymously, with despair.

Though it employs the names of 19th-century stars Edwin Forrest and William Charles Macready and contains in its action the famous riot engendered by their theatrical rivalry, my friend Michael Feingold informs me that Richard Nelson's *Two Shakespearean Actors* is a thorough distortion of history. I am less offended by this than is Michael, remembering that the dramatist whose work the title characters enacted also played fast and loose with historical fact in pursuit of compelling drama (as those attempting to rehabilitate Richard III's reputation will tell you). Unfortunately, Nelson's play is not compelling drama. Underneath the period references, *Two Shakespearean Actors* is little more than a character study of two amiably egomaniacal performers, more concerned with their transitory glory onstage than so-called real life. There is no denying the grace in the writing, and there are passing references to issues which have contemporary reverberations, but with a cast of 27 and a running time of more than two and a half hours, I felt that too many resources were employed in the pursuit of too little matter. Still, no evening that offered Victor Garber and Brian Bedford ample excuse to strut and preen and fulminate so engagingly could be counted a loss.

Another play produced by Lincoln Center is built on the dynamic of two male leads, which, come to think of it, is about all they have in common. Elaine May's *Mr. Gogol and Mr. Preen* concerns an eccentric elderly Jew named Gogol who virtually kidnaps a younger non-Jewish vacuum cleaner salesman named Preen in order to have company. The piece is devoid of real dramatic development, and the death of Gogol wallows in unearned sentiment and appears to occur only so as to bring the play to a close. In short, as drama, it is pretty woeful. But several passages in which the intellectually-limited title characters attempt to debate philosophical issues recall the classic "Pete and Dud" dialogues of Peter Cook and Dudley Moore and are pure comic gold. With engagingly deadpan performances by Mike Nussbaum and William H. Macy in the title roles, and some inspired bits of slapstick orchestrated by director Gregory Mosher, *Mr. Gogol and Mr. Preen* made me laugh harder than most of the season's better plays.

I can't help feeling for the actors required to simulate sexual activity in front of crowds of strangers, particularly when the writing is wanting. Theoretically I suppose it is possible to write a dramatically valid scene about a handjob, but Abraham Tetenbaum didn't supply one for Polly Draper and Barry Miller in the short-lived *Crazy He Calls Me*. (In fairness, some of the early scenes concerning the courtship of a couple in postwar Brooklyn indicate Tetenbaum has a talent for dialogue which might be shown to better advantage in a more sturdily-conceived play.) Virtually everyone in the cast of *Unidentified Human Remains and the True Nature of Love* at one point or another stripped down and pretended to go at it with someone else, but the artificial lather they worked up didn't obscure the impression that author Brad Fraser's script resembles David Mamet's *Sexual Perversity in Chicago* minus the wit plus some pretentious moralizing about the equivalence of casual sex to serial killing. David Greenspan couldn't complain about the author of *The Home Show Pieces* compelling him to masturbate onstage under a cover as he was the author. I continue to be mystified by the enthusiasm Mr. Greenspan elicits from some of my more knowledgeable friends in the theater.

And then there were the works which, if not particularly distinguished as plays, nevertheless gave talented actors opportunities to register strong impressions. Seth Zvi Rosenfeld's *Servy-n-Bernice 4Ever*, a rambling and sentimental portrait of a young black woman and her parole-violating white lover, let Lisa Gay Hamilton and Ron Eldard frolic and slam about the stage in a style popularized by Chicago's Steppenwolf Theater (not surprising, given that it was directed by a member of the Steppenwolf company, Terry Kinney). Similarly, Jason Robards and Judith Ivey, by sheer force of personality, were able to counteract much of the contrivances and cutenesses of Israel Horovitz's *Park Your Car in Harvard Yard*, a two-hander about an aging music teacher and a newly-hired housekeeper who comes to his house for revenge and stays to appreciate the glories of the great composers.

Here's where we list the *Best Plays* choices for the outstanding straight play achievements of 1991-92 in New York, on and off Broadway. In the acting categories, clear distinction among "starring," "featured" or "supporting" players can't be made on the basis of official billing, which is as much a matter of contracts as of esthetics. Here in these volumes we divide acting into "primary" or "secondary" roles, a primary role being one which might some day cause a star to inspire a revival in order to appear in that character. All others, be they vivid as Mercutio, are classed as secondary. Furthermore, our list of individual standouts makes room for more than a single choice when appropriate. We believe that no useful purpose is served by forcing ourselves into an arbitrary selection of a single best when we come upon multiple examples of equal distinction.

PLAYS

BEST PLAY: *Dancing at Lughnasa* by Brian Friel

BEST AMERICAN PLAY: *Conversations With My Father* by Herb Gardner; *Sight Unseen* by Donald Margulies

BEST REVIVAL: *The Subject Was Roses* by Frank D. Gilroy

BEST ACTOR IN A PRIMARY ROLE: Patrick Stewart in *A Christmas Carol*

BEST ACTRESS IN A PRIMARY ROLE: Laura Esterman as Bessie in *Marvin's Room*; Deborah Hedwall as Patricia in *Sight Unseen*

BEST ACTOR IN A SECONDARY ROLE: Larry Fishburne as Sterling in *Two Trains Running*; Paxton Whitehead as Mathieu in *A Little Hotel on the Side*

BEST ACTRESS IN A SECONDARY ROLE: Mary Beth Hurt as Emelia in *Othello*; Nancy Marchand as Rosamund Brackett and Jocelyn Massey in *The End of the Day*; Dearbhla Molloy as Maggie in *Dancing at Lughnasa*

BEST DIRECTOR: Patrick Mason for *Dancing at Lughnasa*

BEST SCENERY: Joe Vanek for *Dancing at Lughnasa*

BEST COSTUMES: Jane Greenwood for *Two Shakespearean Actors*

BEST LIGHTING: Frances Aronson for *Pericles*; Jules Fisher for *Two Shakespearean Actors*

SPECIAL CITATION: The State Theater of Lithuania for *Uncle Vanya*

JELLY'S LAST JAM—Savion Glover and Gregory Hines in a scene
from the musical about the life and times of Jelly Roll Morton

Musicals, Revues and Special Attractions

Were the turf this book covers less strictly defined, I would have no hesitation
applauding *The Ghosts at Versailles*—featuring music by John Corigliano and text
by William H. Hoffman (author of the Best Play *As Is*)—as the musical theater
triumph of the season. The work's premise gathers the ghosts of the court of Louis
XVI to watch the premiere of Beaumarchais's latest play featuring Figaro, the wily
servant, in a plot to save the life of Marie Antoinette. At a crucial moment, Figaro
refuses to do as Beaumarchais commands, so the author enters the world of his own
work in an attempt, motivated by love for his queen, to change history. The result is
a musical and intellectual treat, shifting gears gracefully between operatic parody
and genuinely poignant drama as Hoffman's libretto explores the relative powers of
art and history.

The best new musical theater piece to be introduced this year, or, indeed, in
many years, *The Ghosts at Versailles* premiered at the Metropolitan Opera House.
In the classification process necessary to keep the items considered for this volume
within the boundaries of the show-business area known familiarly as "theater," this
highly dramatic and theatrical work was offered as an opera and therefore was off
limits for selection as a Best Play.

The best of what's left for consideration offers pleasures of a milder kind. The
single new musical named as a Best Play this season is *Crazy for You*, though one

could well debate how "new" this new musical is. The score is a compendium of mostly well-known songs by George and Ira Gershwin, and the script, by Ken Ludwig, recycles the central premise of Ludwig's Best Play, *Lend Me a Tenor*. In that farce, a young lady, who has resisted the advances of a love-struck singer, falls for a visiting opera star, not realizing that, in fact, what she thinks is the opera star is the singer in disguise. In *Crazy for You*, the young lady is a cowgirl and the visiting opera star is transformed into a Ziegfeld-like producer putting together a show in her town of Deadrock, Nevada in order to help her and her father to save their theater. In reality (though what the word "reality" has to do in a discussion of this is a good question), the producer is a young millionaire hoofer from New York who has made himself up to impersonate the producer after she has spurned him as himself.

The point of the evening is to create a 1990s version of the cheerfully mindless shows of the 1930s featuring lots of songs, elaborate dance routines, fast-paced comic bits and an attractive chorus. In this, Ludwig and director Mike Ockrent succeeded handsomely. Top-billed Harry Groener, Jodi Benson and Bruce Adler performed their song-and-dance duties as hoofer, heroine and producer with aplomb (all three were nominated for—though did not win—Tony Awards), but the star of the show was generally deemed to be Susan Stroman, who built dazzling razzmatazz numbers based on the props at hand (and earned a richly-deserved Tony for her work).

The whole enterprise zipped along wonderfully well. If I am a shade less than totally enthusiastic, it's because, after years of hearing such songs as "Embraceable You" and "They Can't Take That Away From Me" plumbed for real depth by generations of song stylists, it's somewhat disconcerting to hear them diminished to tuneful musical intervals which, in the mouths of farcical characters, have little emotional punch.

Our consulting historian, Thomas T. Foose, declares flatly that "*Crazy for You* is not a revival of *Girl Crazy*. The closest relationship between these shows is in the songs, for *Crazy for You* uses five of the 13 songs in *Girl Crazy*: 'Bidin' My Time,' 'But Not for Me,' 'Could You Use Me?' 'Embraceable You' and 'I Got Rhythm.' Other songs by the Gershwins were added to the score for *Crazy for You*: 'The Real American Folk Song (Is a Rag)' from *Ladies First* (1918), 'Naughty Baby' from the London musical *Primrose* (1924, lyrics by Ira Gershwin and Desmond Carter), 'Someone to Watch Over Me' from *Oh, Kay!* (1928), 'K-ra-zy for You' and 'What Causes That?' from *Treasure Girl* (1928), 'Tonight's the Night' written for *Show Girl* but dropped prior to the New York opening (1929, lyrics by Ira Gershwin and Gus Kahn); and 'I Can't Be Bothered Now,' 'Nice Work if You Can Get It,' 'Stiff Upper Lip' and 'Things Are Looking Up' from the movie *Damsel in Distress* (1937); and 'Shall We Dance?' and "Slap That Bass' from the movie *Shall We Dance* (1937),"

As I mentioned, *Crazy for You* is about putting on a show. In one way or another, every new musical or musical entertainment (including the Polish musical *Metro*, which I didn't get to see because it closed so swiftly) touched on show business.

Nick & Nora is an attempt to bring to the musical stage Nick and Nora Charles, the married crime-solving couple created by Dashiell Hammett in his novel *The Thin Man* and popularized in a series of films starring William Powell and Myrna Loy. Like *Crazy for You*, it is set in a showbiz capital in the 1930s, this time in Hollywood.

There are two main problems with the piece. One is that a truly intriguing mystery requires that adequate time be spent introducing the various suspects and exploring their possible motives. The book of a musical is about half the length of a conventional script, so librettist Arthur Laurents had to cram an enormous amount of matter into very little space. Ultimately, there are too many clues and too many theories of the crime to assimilate, much less care about. (In fact, in performance, the only character to work up much audience enthusiasm was the murder victim played by Faith Prince; as various theories of the murder were enacted, she got killed off comically several times during the course of the evening and suffered repetitive demise with infectious good cheer.)

The second problem involves the title characters. In order to generate some kind of emotionally-charged question for Nick and Nora to play, Laurents had to put their marriage into jeopardy. But Laurents doesn't dramatize a credible basis for the strain in their relationship, so the effort seems half-hearted.

Though the show as a whole doesn't work, there is a good deal of craft evident in individual elements. I trust that when the album is released and the score is isolated from the dramatic machinery which surrounds it, Charles Strouse's tuneful music and Richard Maltby Jr.'s inventive lyrics will be better appreciated.

Three Broadway offerings explored the black musical experience and derived much of their music from pre-existent sources. *Five Guys Named Moe* drew its songs from the repertory of the late band leader, Louis Jordan. *The High Rollers Social and Pleasure Club* featured its band leader, Allen Toussaint, onstage, as he led the cast through a program mostly made up of old numbers by himself and others. Both featured ensembles of talented singers and dancers putting over song after song with daunting energy. Although individual numbers were stirring, in both cases two hours were one hour too many. These songs, as good as many of them were individually, did not cohere into scores which served larger theatrical purposes.

A substantial chunk of *Jelly's Last Jam*'s score features music by its subject, black jazz composer and pianist Jelly Roll Morton. Although the show celebrates Morton's music, it finds little to applaud about his character. As book writer and director George C. Wolfe sees it, Morton drew on his heritage in creating his music, but tried to deny any responsibility to or kinship with fellow blacks, going so far as to claim he was not black but Creole.

The work begins with the composer's death. An MC figure called the Chimney Man leads Morton back over his life to face his accomplishments and contradictions. In between numbers, Morton roams about, being abusive to virtually everyone he encounters, going into a tailspin when his style of piano falls out of fashion, and ending his life in bitterness and obscurity. By a not terribly persuasive theatrical coup, he has a post-death epiphany, is spiritually rehabilitated and joins the ranks of other great black musical talents.

The idea of the show is more intriguing than its execution. The problem isn't just Morton's unappealing character; it's the lack of relationship between his character and his fate. According to Wolfe, Morton didn't fall out of favor for any reason relating to the way he dealt with others. Certainly, there is no indication that if he had been nicer to fellow blacks on the way up, he could have prevented his decline. So what *is* the dramatic point of painting such an unflattering picture? And why, aside from the desirability of ending a musical with an up number, is Jelly granted forgiveness after his death? Or is Wolfe trying to say that it's ultimately okay to be a miserable human being if you have enough talent?

Part of the irony of *Jelly's Last Jam* is that this disagreeable man is played by one of the musical theater's most ingratiating performers, Gregory Hines. (Let's not look too closely at the logic of having a virtuoso pianist played by a dancer.) Hines is an actor of considerable ability, and he lent Morton his compelling presence, but the high points of the production were those moments when Hines put aside Morton's meanness and let his feet loose to Morton's music. (Hines co-choreographed the show with Ted L. Levy and Hope Clarke.) There were several other, considerable pluses to the evening—Susan Birkenhead's sassy lyrics, Luther Henderson's arrangements and additional scoring, and performances by Savion Glover as Jelly as a young man and Tonya Pinkins as the woman who could have been the love of Jelly's life, had he been worthy of love. All in all, an exciting if unfulfilled evening.

At the opposite end of the production scale, Stan Freeman played another pianist with a personality disorder in *At Wit's End*, a simulation of an evening with Oscar Levant. Writer Joel Kimmel has Levant telling a series of tales about the musical and film figures with whom Levant associated, peppering most with flashes of mordant wit, reserving his most scathing comments for himself. An evening with the real Levant in this mode would probably have been too much, but Freeman leavened the bile with an appealing vulnerability. An extra attraction was Freeman's virtuoso interpretations of music ranging from Gershwin to Scarlatti to Shostakovitch. In *I Won't Dance*, another gentleman at another piano, Steve Ross, played and sang a program of music associated with Fred Astaire. I gather Ross has a following as a singer in the cabaret circuit, but most of my favorite moments were those when he let his pianistic skills dominate.

Strong elements of camp dominated three off-Broadway musicals, *Return to the Forbidden Planet*, *Eating Raoul* and *Ruthless!*. *Return to the Forbidden Planet*, a British import, is loosely based on *Forbidden Planet*, a film about a space team fighting a monster on an alien planet, which was itself loosely based on Shakespeare's *The Tempest*. Writer-director Bob Carlton's inspiration (if that is the word) was to combine a parody of the cheerfully trashy conventions of 1950s science-fiction movies with shards of mangled Shakespeare, inter-rupting frequently with old rock'n'roll songs of dubious relevance. My ten-year-old son had a wonderful time.

Book writer Paul Bartel takes his swipes at the 1960s with *Eating Raoul*, a musical adaptation of the cult film Bartel wrote, directed and starred in. The lead characters, Paul and Mary Bland, are a repressed couple who simultaneously express their disgust for the sexual revolution of the 1960s and work to finance their dream of opening a family-style restaurant by luring swingers into their apartment, murdering them and banking the money found in their victims' wallets. The way much of the New York press reacted, you'd think they'd been assaulted. Though I wish less time had been given to the showbiz aspirations of the Blands' lascivious Latino henchman (the Raoul of the title), I enjoyed much of the evening. The score by composer Jed Feuer and lyricist Boyd Graham was of erratic quality, but the best gave promise of better to come. Most impressive was Courtenay Collins, giving the most appealing performance of a murderous comic heroine since Angela Lansbury lifted her rolling pin as Mrs. Lovett in *Sweeney Todd*.

She had some competition in this category from young Laura Bundy, who in *Ruthless!* played a grade school actress willing and able to kill a schoolmate in order to take over the lead in a musical version of *Pippi Longstocking*. Miss Bundy was terrifyingly proficient in the role, but even more fun was Donna English as her mousy homemaker-mother trying to suppress a genetic inclination toward show business. The first act, played out in the suburbs, was more successful than the second, which turned into the umpteenth parody of *All About Eve*. As entertaining and crowd-pleasing as *Ruthless!* is, I look forward to book writer-lyricist Joel Paley and composer Marvin Laird tackling subject matter less frequently satirized than

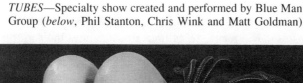

TUBES—Specialty show created and performed by Blue Man Group (*below*, Phil Stanton, Chris Wink and Matt Goldman)

the murderous egos of those who would be stars.

The season's most daring musical was *Groundhog*, written and composed by Elizabeth Swados. I can't pretend to have ever been a fan of Swados's song writing; her approach to musical theater strikes me as adding music indiscriminately to any text. But, unlike any of her shows I have previously seen, *Groundhog* has something approaching a book, and much of it is provocative. The story deals with the troubled relationship between a half-mad homeless character whose nickname gives the show its title and his sister Gila, a relationship which echoes Swados's relationship with her own brother, who died after a life on the streets. It is notoriously difficult for writers to make characters based on themselves interesting. Torn by her desire to see her brother protected against himself in an institution and her hope that he manages to maintain sufficient equilibrium to remain independent, Gila is the most complex figure in the piece and, under Swados's direction, was beautifully played and sung by Anne Bobby.

Even as seriously intended a piece as *Groundhog* spends a substantial chunk of its running time with show business on its mind (much of it deals with *Groundhog*'s reveling in the celebrity status conferred upon him by the media's interest in his case). How nice it would have been be if at least one writing team of the season had demonstrated some interest in subject matter that didn't either invoke or parody some aspect of the media or performing arts. There is a whole world of people who do not aspire to celebrity or to put on a show. Great musicals of the past have featured teachers, cowboys, legislators, sailors, kings, barbers and even a milkman. It's time for our librettists and song writers to make the acquaintance of a wider range of humanity lest we be reduced to a steady diet of recycled Broadway and Hollywood.

Since Jackie Mason's successes on Broadway, stand-up comedy has increasingly found its way to the legitimate stages (though sometimes the performers prefer to be called "performance artists"). Under the title *Catskills on Broadway*, four veterans of comedy rooms in the mountains—Dick Capri, Freddie Roman, Marilyn Michaels and Mal Z. Lawrence—took turns piling joke on joke primarily around the topics of food and sex. Subtle, sophisticated? No. Funny? Yes, very. *Reno Once Removed* featured the mononymed performer Reno mining humor out of her outrage at the current political and social scene. In *Julie Halston's Lifetime of Comedy,* Halston drew on her personal experiences, telling the tale of her Catholic upbringing, her failed early marriage and her apprenticeships in show business with cheerfully self-deprecating humor.

The Blue Man Group, made up of three men with shaved, blue-painted heads, were a major hit off Broadway with a program of inspired nonsense called *Tubes*. If you were looking for meaning you could see the show as a critique of pretension in the art scene. My son was not looking for meaning. He just enjoyed the spectacle of three weird grown-ups biting into eggs filled with paint and spitting the contents out onto whirling canvases. And rigging up suits which made it look as if food were exploding out of the centers of their chests. And sending cascades of toilet paper in huge waves over the heads of the audience; an entertainment for those who think that "Gross!" can be a compliment.

Andre Heller's Wonderhouse served up a variety show made up of European acts emphasizing bizarre skills—among them, Baroness Jeanette Lips Von Lipstrill, who whistles intricate and baroque arrangements of the classics, Macao, who renders flamboyant creations out of swiftly ripped paper, a black light illusionist under the name of Omar Pasha, and the slapstick comedy dance team of Marion and Robert Konyot. Perhaps the evening might have met with a warmer reception had it been performed in a cabaret environment rather than the Broadhurst Theater, but, in contrast with most of the press, I shared the audience's delight at this slightly motley collection of offbeat artistes.

A more soberly-intended special attraction, *The Radiant City*, chronicled the reign of Robert Moses—the man who, through a variety of government positions, shaped much of the face of modern New York. (In fact, Joseph Papp gained early attention by being one of the few to challenge Moses's authority. Papp wanted free Shakespeare in Central Park and Moses didn't. There is free Shakespeare in the park.) The story of this complex man, subject to both authoritarian and populist impulses, should have made for a compelling work. Theodora Skipitares, who conceived the piece, specializes in creating stage images out of puppets, mechanical constructions and sculpture. Though the occasional image was arresting, the piece, with its severe score by Christopher Thall and its didactic lyrics by Andrea Balis, was slow-paced and remote. Someone should take another crack at staging this story.

To end on the most positive note, here's where we list the *Best Plays* choices for the musical and revue bests of 1991-92.

MUSICALS, REVUES AND SPECIAL ATTRACTIONS

BEST MUSICAL OR REVUE: *Crazy for You*

BEST REVIVAL: *Falsettos*; *Guys and Dolls*

BEST BOOK: Ken Ludwig for *Crazy for You*

BEST MUSIC: Charles Strouse for *Nick & Nora*

BEST LYRICS: Susan Birkenhead for *Jelly's Last Jam*; Richard Maltby Jr. for *Nick & Nora*

BEST ACTOR IN A PRIMARY ROLE: Gregory Hines as Jelly in *Jelly's Last Jam*; Spiro Malas as Tony in *The Most Happy Fella*

BEST ACTRESS IN A PRIMARY ROLE: Faith Prince as Adelaide in *Guys and Dolls*

BEST ACTOR IN A SECONDARY ROLE: Bruce Adler as Bela Zangler in *Crazy for You*

BEST ACTRESS IN A SECONDARY ROLE: Faith Prince as Lorraine Bixby in *Nick & Nora*; Michele Pawk as Irene Roth in *Crazy for You*

BEST DIRECTOR: Jerry Zaks for *Guys and Dolls*

BEST CHOREOGRAPHY: Christopher Chadman for *Guys and Dolls*; Susan Stroman for *Crazy for You*

BEST SCENERY: Tony Walton for *Guys and Dolls*; Robin Wagner for *Crazy for You*

BEST COSTUMES: William Ivey Long for *Crazy for You* and *Guys and Dolls*

BEST LIGHTING: Paul Gallo for *Crazy for You* and *Guys and Dolls*

SPECIAL CITATIONS: Matt Goldman, Phil Stanton and Chris Wink for *Tubes*

A STREETCAR NAMED DESIRE—Jessica Lange as Blanche DuBois in the Broadway revival of Tennessee Williams's drama

Revivals

Two works many would name as candidates for the best American play and the best American musical were revived this season to strikingly different effect.

Those who believe that a great script is actor-proof would have found the theory challenged by the production of Tennessee Williams's *A Streetcar Named Desire* which opened for a limited run at the Ethel Barrymore (the same theater where it had premiered in 1947). On paper, the project looked promising: Jessica Lange, with a gallery of fine film performances to her credit, making her Broadway debut as Blanche; Alec Baldwin, who did such moving work off Broadway in Craig Lucas's *Prelude to a Kiss*, as Stanley; and the vibrant Amy Madigan, seemingly a natural for Stella. The promises on paper were not realized on stage. At the performance I saw, Lange was a curiously reserved Blanche, Baldwin played Stanley as a large, good-hearted puppy who occasionally misbehaved on the carpet, and Madigan's Stella seemed walled up behind a broad accent that bore little relationship to Blanche's. What was particularly surprising about this production is that it was directed by Gregory Mosher who, in stagings of plays by David Mamet, Thornton Wilder and Elaine May, has demonstrated a keen sense of how to shape scenes. This *Streetcar*, however, seemed amorphous. The confrontations between Blanche and Stanley did not build. When Stanley bellowed at Blanche, "Now let's cut the re-bop!", my instant reaction was, "What re-bop?" Lange had been playing nothing for Baldwin to overwhelm. As for pacing, you know something is wrong with a *Streetcar* when, even after cutting back to one intermission, the play's running time tops three hours. It was a disappointment from a team of indisputable talent.

Guys and Dolls, on the other hand, was deservedly the smash hit of the season. As soon as the lights came up on Tony Walton's glorious riot of billboards, lights and dives, and a trio of horseplayers launched into Frank Loesser's ingenious marriage of the classical and the crass, "Fugue for Tinhorns," we knew we were in confident hands. Under Jerry Zaks's direction, the emphasis was on the comedy, the show having a special sparkle whenever Nathan Detroit and/or his long-standing (and long-waiting) fiancee Adelaide took the stage. Nathan Lane capped a busy and varied season (also including *Lips Together, Teeth Apart* and *On Borrowed Time*) as Nathan, marshaling his formidable arsenal of shtick in a virtuoso display of Broadway clowning. In contrast to Lane's full-tilt, helter-skelter attack, Faith Prince's Adelaide got many of her biggest laughs out of the economy of her performance—a shift of the eyes or an unexpected inflection. The highest point of a show rich with high points came when the two teamed up for "Sue Me" late in the second act, bringing the audience to applause with a shared, stubborn sustained note that had gone unmined in other productions I've seen. (If only the original Nathan Detroit, Sam Levene, had been a better singer—or, for that matter, any kind of a singer—more songs might have been written for the character, and Lane would have had more opportunity to shine musically.)

Among a strong supporting cast, Walter Bobbie was an engaging Nicely-Nicely Johnson, and Scott Wise an acrobatic marvel as one of the dancing crapshooters. A perfect *Guys and Dolls*? Not quite. Though Peter Gallagher and Josie de Guzman sang their songs well (and de Guzman had a sweet loopy quality in the Havana scenes), the romance of Sky Masterson and Sarah Brown carried little weight and so provided little emotional ballast to the evening. Never mind. Featuring revised orchestrations by Michael Starobin, *Guys and Dolls* brought vintage Broadway pizzazz back to Broadway.

The emotional side of Loesser that was subdued in this *Guys and Dolls* was brought to the fore in a production of another of his extraordinary works, *The Most Happy Fella*. Based on Sidney Howard's play *They Knew What They Wanted*, it tells the story of the courtship by mail and the subsequent December-May marriage of Tony, the immigrant owner of a California vineyard, and the waitress he calls Rosabella, complicated by her pregnancy by another man. If *Guys and Dolls* is Loesser at his jauntiest, *The Most Happy Fella* is him at his most heartfelt. Virtually an opera (in fact, this season it was also given a well-regarded production by the New York City Opera), it contains an almost endless stream of melody with a nod to Puccini. Sophie Hayden gave Rosabella an initial toughness which made her later emotional blossoming all the more touching; and Spiro Malas, unaccountably overlooked by the Tony Award nominators, sang beautifully and made Tony a moving mixture of pride and vulnerability. Though the comedic couple of Cleo and Herman don't quite seem to inhabit the same world—musically or dramatically—as Rosabella and Tony, Liz Larsen and Scott Waara, aided by a couple of Loesser's show stoppers ("Big D" and the politically-incorrect but exuberant "Standin' on the Corner"), offered welcome sass and spunk to contrast with and highlight the more lyrical material.

Originally scored for an orchestra of 35, this production was accompanied by two pianos. This instrumentation revealed a good deal of charming detail in the score; but, without the strings and horns, some of the bigger musical moments (notably the end of the first act) sounded skimpy. Still, under the inventive direction of Gerald Gutierrez, *The Most Happy Fella* offered melody, heart and humor in portions Broadway musicals rarely serve up these days.

With *The Most Happy Fella*, Frank Loesser joined the small fraternity of dramatists who have written not only the music and lyrics but also the books of musicals. (Offhand, I can think of only a few others who successfully managed these triple credits—Meredith Willson with *The Music Man*, Rick Besoyan with *Little Mary Sunshine*, Rupert Holmes with *The Mystery of Edwin Drood* and Noel Coward.) With *Falsettos*, William Finn became the latest triple-threat to arrive on Broadway (he shared credit for the book with director James Lapine). Like *The Most Happy Fella*, *Falsettos* contains so much music that one is tempted to call it an opera. In fact, the show is a combination, with some revisions, of two shows— *March of the Falsettos* and *Falsettoland*, the first of which premiered in 1981, the second last season. The first act introduces neurotic New Yorker Marvin and the circle of characters whose lives are changed when he leaves his wife Trina and son Jason for a male lover named Whizzer. In the second act, which takes place two years later, Trina has remarried (to Marvin's psychiatrist Mendel), and the two households stumble their way into an awkward but workable relationship prompted by the necessity of cooperating on arrangements for Jason's bar mitzvah. As Jason's symbolic entrance into manhood approaches, Whizzer comes down with an illness we with the benefit of hindsight recognize to be AIDS. The two households (plus a lesbian couple who live in the same building as Trina, Jason and Mendel) band together to cope with the intersection of celebration and grief. As I mentioned in my essay last year, I find this piece particularly moving in part because (whether or not Finn and Lapine so intended) it is a fantasy of how well people ultimately can behave. In reality, in the early days of AIDS, when ignorance amplified fear, there was very little of the harmony and generosity of spirit represented here. But then so much of the appeal of musical theater is rooted in the projection of romantic myth.

Approaching this incarnation, my biggest apprehension had to do with whether the uniting of the two shows might be too much of a good thing; *Falsettoland* by itself, a Best Play last season, although barely more than an hour in running time, had been such a full experience. My fears were unfounded. In fact, resting on the foundation of the first, the second act gained in poignancy. The cast, including several veterans of past stagings, was exemplary. Particularly welcome was Barbara Walsh, who had played Trina in another assemblage of the "Marvin" material under the direction of Graciela Daniele at the Hartford Stage Company. The only reservation I have about the show is that I have no idea of what the hell the word "falsetto" is supposed to mean. Some critics have suggested that it's meant to represent gay men. If so, why do Mendel and Jason, who are not gay (perhaps it's

Pictured on these pages are examples
of the outstanding designs for this
season's *Guys and Dolls*: *on this page*,
Tony Walton's models for his set
designs of Times Square (*above*), the
Save-a-Soul Mission (*left*) and the Ho.
Box night club (*below*); *on opposite
page*, samples of William Ivey Long's
sketches for his costume designs

too early to tell about Jason), participate in the first act's "March of the Falsettos"? (Besides which, the idea of gay men being falsettos—bringing to mind castrati— carries with it the disquieting implication that they are less than men for being gay. Oh, the dangers of imprecise metaphors!)

Besides *Streetcar*, the only commercially-produced revival of a non-musical this season was of Noel Coward's *Private Lives*, fitted out under the direction of Arvin Brown as a vehicle for glamour queen Joan Collins. Those who were expecting her to fall on her pretty face were disappointed. If the undercurrent of sadness, waste and regret which informs the best productions of *Private Lives* was in short supply, Collins and her co-star Simon Jones proved to be deft at keeping the verbal ball in the air.

Otherwise, it fell to non-profit managements to offer revivals. The Manhattan Theater Club had a critical success with a production of *Boesman and Lena* directed by Athol Fugard. For Circle in the Square, George C. Scott directed and starred in *On Borrowed Time*, Paul Osborn's mild whimsy about an old man keeping death (played by Nathan Lane) up a tree. Circle in the Square had more luck with the first half of George Bernard Shaw's *Getting Married*, a virtually plotless convocation of characters who, in anticipation of a wedding, discuss the pros and cons of matrimony. Unfortunately, in the second half of the script, Shaw brings on a character named Mrs. George who slips into a mystical state and speaks a great deal of semi-coherent stuff in the name of Woman. The play never recovers from this confusion; but, under the direction of Shaw veteran Stephen Porter, the playable material played at a very high level indeed.

Realizing a long-held dream to form an American company devoted to the classics, Tony Randall opened his National Actors Theater for a season at the Belasco. I didn't see the reason for presenting another production of Arthur Miller's *The Crucible* so shortly after the solid revival by the Roundabout. Under the direction of Yossi Yzraely, it proved to be a murky affair. The most satisfying elements were the performances of Maryann Plunkett as Elizabeth Proctor and Fritz Weaver, the epitome of self-righteous malevolence as Deputy-Governor Danforth. John Mortimer's adaptation from Feydeau, *A Little Hotel on the Side*, provided a change of pace. Again Maryann Plunkett stood out as a nervous wife contemplating adultery. Most memorable was Paxton Whitehead as a father who inadvertently has chosen a hotel of questionable repute in which to spend the night with his four young daughters. Whitehead has long been one of our most expert players of farce, partially because he plays the ridiculous with such dead seriousness. Others in the company could have learned from his example. The critical drubbing received by these productions and a third, Randall's staging of Ibsen's *The Master Builder*, hasn't discouraged Randall. He will return with a new season of plays next year, and more power to him.

The Roundabout began the 1991-92 season with two productions in their old off Broadway home, the Haft Theater, and then moved into their new digs on Broadway at the Criterion Center Stage Right. Their last production downtown, Thornton Wilder's *The Matchmaker*, did not fare well, but the one prior to that,

Frank D. Gilroy's *The Subject Was Roses*, ranked with the best of their work. For those who thought Gilroy's Pulitzer Prize-winning, three-character play about an Irish-American family might prove, to contemporary eyes, to be a tired entry in the postwar kitchen sink genre, Jack Hofsiss's sturdy production came as a firm rebuke. No apologies for the script's age or genre are required; it holds up as a perceptive and psychologically-precise study of family dynamics. One could hardly hope for the parts of the father and mother to be better cast than with John Mahoney and Dana Ivey. As the son, Patrick Dempsey, familiar to movie audiences as something of a teenage heart-throb, proved to fully deserve his place with his stage parents. (Since *The Subject Was Roses* opened for the Roundabout's subscription audiences May 15, 1991, it was listed in the Plays Produced Off Broadway section as a 1990-91 production in last year's *Best Plays* volume; but the critics were not invited to review the production until after this season's June 5, 1991 performance.)

On Broadway, the Roundabout took on two European post-war classics about the unpleasant consequences of revisiting one's roots; Friedrich Duerrenmatt's *The Visit* and Harold Pinter's *The Homecoming*. I admired Jane Alexander's performance as Claire Zachanassian, the richest woman in the world who returns to the town where she was born to bribe the townspeople to take violent revenge on the man who dishonored her when she was young. I was less taken with Ed Sherin's production, which, perhaps for economic reasons, called for a small ensemble to play multiple parts behind masks. I was also disappointed by the awkward work which usually good actor Harris Yulin did as Anton Schill, Claire's victim and former lover; how I would have loved to have seen Alexander's Claire matched with the extraordinary Anton of Josef Sommer in the Goodman Theater's 1991 production! Director Gordon Edelstein did better by Harold Pinter's *The Homecoming*. Led by an alluring Lindsay Crouse as Ruth, and featuring Daniel Gerroll and Roy Dotrice as two of her hypnotically-repellent in-laws, the play continues to disturb as a black comic nightmare of the underside of family life.

The least successful of the Roundabout's Broadway offerings was Stephen Lang's attempt of *Hamlet*, which reduced the character from tragic stature to peevishness. The most impressive Shakespeare of the year was the Shakespeare Festival's Central Park production, under Joe Dowling's direction, of *Othello*. Raul Julia was a little shy of the stature and grace for an optimum Moor, but Christopher Walken made a memorable rock'n'roll Iago, suggesting that Iago's hostility might have its root in being born out of his time. He was matched by the unusually spunky, clear-sighted and funny Emilia of Mary Beth Hurt. The Festival also sponsored a Brazilian production, in Portuguese under the direction of Caca Rosset, of *A Midsummer Night's Dream*, which was mostly talked about for the nudity of the fairies (very pretty, thank you), but also featured some well-integrated circus skills.

The Shakespeare Festival's other Shakespeare was Michael Greif's staging of the infrequently-seen *Pericles*. The text is made up of a series of episodes as Pericles travels from land to land, and Greif, in association with his set designer Jon Arnone, decided to emphasize the episodic nature by staging each section in a different style. The problem Greif played into by lurching from style to style was in signaling conflicting audience responses to the story. In one scene, staged virtually as a cartoon with large cutouts representing additional characters, Pericles meets and marries the princess Thaisa; the cartooniness undercut an emotional investment in the marriage, an investment necessary to make Thaisa's subsequent rescue from drowning moving. Later, a large chunk of time during which a despairing Pericles ages was represented by a laugh-producing black and white silent film, which undercut what should have been a touching reunion with his wife and daughter. In the midst of all this, Campbell Scott was an impressive and heroic Pericles.

Generally the Shakespeare Festival's other revivals placed heavy emphasis on the directors' visual ingenuity. JoAnne Akalaitis's version of John Ford's Jacobean tragedy *'Tis Pity She's a Whore* was filled with strikingly surrealist imagery, but it was as if the production and the text were two trains running on parallel tracks with parties from the production train occasionally waving hello to the other but never linking up. From our consulting historian's viewpoint, however, *'Tis Pity She's a Whore* was "the most interesting revival of the 1991-92 season." Thomas T. Foose informs us further, "The Joseph Papp Public Theater staging is the first major professional production in New York City and one of the few productions of any sort here. What may have been the first New York City staging was in 1925-26 by an amateur group, the Lenox Hill Players. There was a solid New York City production in 1958-59, the only one of any importance prior to the 1992 staging. This ran for 204 performances, opening at the Orpheum Dec. 5, 1958 and moving to the Players on Jan. 13." Parenthetically, Louis Kronenberger mentions this one *en passant* in *The Best Plays of 1958-59*, with the comment that it "ran into amusing problems because of its title." Mr. Foose concludes on this subject: "The other New York City productions were in 1970-71 (by The Assembly), 1982-83 (by Meat and Potatoes) and 1985-86 (by Juilliard Theater Center). In 1989-90 in Chicago the Goodman Theater offered *'Tis Pity She's a Whore*, and the Public Theater production stemmed directly from this Goodman staging. Both had the same director, sets, costumes, music, choreography and fight staging, and even vocal coach. And three male actors played the same parts both in Chicago and New York: Erick Avari, Ross Lehman and Daniel Oreskes."

Anne Bogart's production of Bertolt Brecht's *In the Jungle of Cities* was heavy on oppressive atmosphere but short on coherent storytelling. More successful was Melia Bensussen's staging of Langston Hughes's translation of Lorca's *Blood Wedding*, which wove a flamenco-flavored score by Michele Navazio and choreography by Donald Byrd into a haunting tale of obsessive love, with Elizabeth Peña particularly striking as the doomed bride. (Interesting that the Shakespeare Festival should present three plays, *Pericles*, *'Tis Pity* and *Blood Wedding* in which marriages serve as prologues to tragedy. Are the people at the Public trying to tell us something?)

The most exciting directorial reinterpretation of a classic I saw was the State Theater of Lithuania's *Uncle Vanya*. Even though the evening topped three and a quarter hours and had to be watched with one ear glued to a headphone for simultaneous translation, Eimuntas Nekrosius's audaciously expressionistic staging held the audience spellbound. The most vivid sequence came in an extended scene between the doctor, Astrov, and Soyfa, who suffers so from her unrequited love for him. At one point, as he reaches for a decanter of vodka to further obliterate his senses, her yelp of protest so surprises him that he tips the open square-shaped decanter over on its side on the high shelf where it's kept. As the two stand frozen in position, all of the liquor spills out into a small lake on the floor. Then, placed on either side of the open-sided cabinet, Astrov quietly bares his self-disgust to Soyfa in a stage picture bringing to mind a confessional. The combination of intimacy and isolation was moving beyond any experience I've previously had with Chekhov. It is my most indelible memory of the season.

Offstage

"It was a season that began in the doldrums and ended in a blaze of activity," said Harvey Sabinson, executive director of the League of American Theaters and Producers. According to League figures, theatergoers spent a record high of $292 million in 1991-1992, in contrast to 1990-1991's $267 million. Among the factors, a slight rise in the attendance (to 7,352,005) and an increase in the number of new Broadway presentations (from 28 last year to 37 by their count; from 27 to 44 by ours).

Every season has its big winner. This season that winner was *Guys and Dolls*. There was the unmistakable undercurrent of celebration in the reports that this home-grown revival of a classic American musical broke the cycle of imported British megahits. In his *New York* magazine cover story on the "phenomenon" of the show (not just a show, but a phenomenon!), Ross Wetzsteon reported sales on the day following opening night unseated the *The Phantom of the Opera* record by more than $35,000, the box office taking in $396,709.50.

In addition to *Guys and Dolls*, healthy Broadway grosses were reported for two other musicals seemingly on their way to hit status, *Crazy for You* and *Jelly's Last Jam*. Among the straight plays, another revival of an American classic, *A Streetcar Named Desire*, posted strong box office (despite generally gloomy reviews). In the meantime, *Miss Saigon*, *The Phantom of the Opera* and *Cats* continued to rumble along, registering strong box office and keeping scores of New York actors employed.

Not all of the ticket sales are through the box offices of the theaters which host the shows; the Theater Development Fund's discount TKTS booth accounts for a significant percentage of sales. From its inception, the booth has offered admissions to unsold theater seats on the day of sale at 50 percent off plus a service charge. This season that formula shifted to a two-tier discounting policy. Under the new arrangement, some shows are still sold at the old rate; what the producers see as more desirable offerings are sold at 25 percent off. Theoretically, the move was designed to broaden the range of fare offered and increase the take of the more popular shows. Additionally, Ticketmaster, through an outlet at Bloomingdale's department store, began selling seats to Nederlander shows at discounts ranging from 10 to 75 percent.

The biggest budgets of the season, as usual, were those for the big musicals, *Guys and Dolls* and *Jelly's Last Jam* both reporting capitalizations of $5.5 million. (Hefty sums, to be sure, but nowhere near the $10 million *Miss Saigon* required for its launching.) *The High Rollers Social and Pleasure Club*, a more modest musical undertaking, required $1 million. Of course, though its investors forked out less, those who rolled with *High Rollers* won't see much if anything back, whereas luck is being a lady for investors in *Guys and Dolls* and *Jelly's Last Jam*.

Luck was not ladylike for *Crazy He Calls Me*. This was the third show to be produced under the Broadway Alliance contract, which offers producers salary concessions by the various guilds and unions in the hope of stimulating new straight play production on Broadway. It was also the third to lose money. (The previous two were last season's *The Speed of Darkness* and *Our Country's Good*, a Best Play.) Supporters of the contract maintained that the failure spoke not to flaws in the plan, but to the audience's indifference to the material produced under it.

Off Broadway, budgets continued to be comparable to what Broadway budgets used to be not so many years ago. The commercial transfer of *Marvin's Room* cost $400,000, and the musical *Eating Raoul* ate up about a million. The number of offerings held fairly steady—77 this year as compared with 79 in 1990-91—but this total included 7 fewer new plays and 5 fewer new musicals on a schedule filled out with visiting foreign-language troupes, one-acter performances and revues.

The news on ticket prices for Broadway straight plays was that they went up from a $45 top to $50. (Anyone surprised?) The reason the producers gave for the increase was the need to pay big-name movie and TV stars such as Alec Baldwin, Jessica Lange, Glenn Close, Richard Dreyfuss, Gene Hackman and Alan Alda. The reason the producers thought audiences would pay the extra $5—the opportunity to see big-name movie and TV stars. And, despite mixed notices, the star vehicles generally did do good business.

The top musical ticket price, on the other hand, went down, though only because *Miss Saigon* shaved its $100 top to $65, on a par with the tops of *The Phantom of the Opera* and *Crazy for You*.

Election year politics had their influence on the arts. Backers of conservative Republican Presidential challenger Patrick Buchanan attacked the National Endowment for the Arts with a television advertisement claiming, "In the last three years, the Bush administration has wasted our tax dollars on pornographic and blasphemous art too shocking to show. This so-called art has glorified homosexuality, exploited children and perverted the image of Jesus Christ. Even after good people protested, Bush continued to fund this kind of art. Send Bush a message." (Never mind that President Bush had nothing to do with the Endowment's choices; never mind that the amount of the percentage of funding which went to so-called controversial art would require an economic microscope to discern.)

Evidently Bush considered Buchanan's strong showing in the New Hampshire primary to be a message he couldn't afford to ignore; he swiftly fired N.E.A. chairman John Frohnmayer. During the earlier days of his two and a half years in the post, Frohnmayer had been perceived as a less-than-staunch defender of artistic freedom, supporting, among other things, a provision which would have required artists receiving federal funding to sign a statement promising not to produce offensive art. In his later days, Frohnmayer had grown stronger in his defense of the funded artist's right to creative autonomy. His increased outspokenness made him a convenient scapegoat.

He was replaced by an acting chairman, Anne-Imelda Radice, who swiftly dove into controversy by overruling a panel's recommendations and refusing to fund two visual arts projects involving sexual imagery. That panel resigned in protest, and a

METRO—The Polish company in a scene from this imported musical with its Tony-nominated score, in a very short Broadway run

panel assigned to recommend grants to solo theater artists was disbanded under disputed circumstances. Playwright Jon Robin Baitz, who had just been selected to receive a playwriting fellowship from the Endowment, announced he would sign over his entire $15,000 check in support of the visual arts projects to which Radice had objected. He was joined in this by the rock group Aerosmith.

Composer-lyricist Stephen Sondheim registered his dismay by refusing to accept the N.E.A.-administered National Medal for the Arts President Bush had planned to award him in July. In a letter he made public, Sondheim characterized the N.E.A. under the Bush administration as "a symbol of censorship and repression rather than encouragement and support" and stated that for him to accept the award "would be an act of the utmost hypocrisy." Author Wallace Stegner, too, refused to accept a medal, in protest of "the political controls placed upon the agency."

Some conservative figures, such as George Will and Republican Party chief Rich Bond, want the government to retreat entirely from involvement in the arts, calling for the complete abolishment of the N.E.A. Buchanan, Bond and Will may (or may not) have been surprised to learn from a survey conducted by Louis Harris that a majority of Americans apparently support both federal funding of the arts and creative autonomy for funded artists. In fact, a majority of respondents to the poll favored increased government funding.

The loss of public funding of the arts would certainly mean a hardship (possibly insurmountable) to the non-profit theater companies, some of which were battling more frantically than usual for survival. At season's end, several New York non-profits with estimable production records had either closed or were in serious jeopardy, among them the Negro Ensemble Company, Manhattan Punch Line and Amas. Ellen Stewart, the founder and director of the internationally-acclaimed off-off-Broadway La Mama company nearly canceled much of its season for want of $150,000. Happily, a number of La Mama's better-heeled alumni responded and pitched in to keep the doors open. The necessary lesson: New York's treasured companies cannot be taken for granted.

Another political issue familiar from seasons past—minority casting—also reared its head. The *dramatis personae* of Ariel Dorfman's *Death and the Maiden* have Latin names, but nobody in the cast came from a Latin background. Actors' Equity and the Hispanic Organization of Latin Actors protested and threatened to demonstrate at the theater. Ultimately, the controversy was resolved by the producers' agreement to "actively search for Hispanic talent as replacements and understudies for Broadway as well as principals for touring and regional productions." The first move was to hire Patricia Mauceri as a standby for Glenn Close.

The *Times*'s influence over the theater scene was debated yet again, though this year the discussion took a decidedly personal tone. First-string critic Frank Rich is married to Alex Witchel, who, in addition to writing feature articles on theatrical subjects, contributed a column of news of the stage for the *Times*'s Friday edition through the end of the 1991-92 season. Robert Brustein, artistic director of Boston's American Repertory Theater and a theater critic himself, penned an article attacking them in *The New Republic*. Other articles critical of the couple, suggesting that Witchel plugged shows that Rich praises and Rich praises actors about whom Witchel has written favorably-slanted pieces, appeared in various tabloids and magazines such as *TheaterWeek*. Readers who get their news on the theater only from the *Times* would have had no idea there was any controversy; not a word on the subject was printed in the paper for which they write. The *Times* also didn't mention Glenn Close's wisecrack about them in her acceptance speech when she collected her Tony Award for best actress. (Close reportedly wasn't pleased either with Rich's review of her performance or Witchel's column suggesting that Close would win because she had little real competition from the other nominees in her category.)

The Tony Awards, too, were the center of controversy. There was some head-scratching about the nominations. Some wondered why *Conversations With My Father* wasn't nominated rather than *Four Baboons* or *Two Shakespearean Actors*. Others wondered why Spiro Malas, who was so enthusiastically praised for his performance as Tony in *The Most Happy Fella*, was overlooked. The fact that there were some unexpected choices and omissions was evidence of the independence of the Tony nominating committee. Apparently they were too independent for the taste of the League of American Theaters and Producers and the American Theater Wing, members of which make up the administration committee. There was much speculation that producers in the League were miffed that so many of the nominations went to shows that had already closed; given the economic boost a Tony nomination is supposed to confer, these producers were said to be disgruntled that these nominations were wasted, insisting they should instead have gone to support shows still open. Whatever the motives, the administration committee canned nine of the 12 members of the nominating committee. (Some nominators found out about their dismissal from the *Times*. Considerate touch, that.)

It was the second year in a row that the majority of the nominators were dismissed for reportedly being too independent. (I can still feel the bootmark on my rump from the previous season's purge.) The League's official line was that certain changes in the process—expanding the number of nominators, limiting to three the number of years a nominator could serve and drawing more panelists from the world of the working theater—"would make for a more balanced slate of nominees." The League also continued to claim that it wanted a genuinely independent nominating committee—which raises the question of whether the new and assumedly genuinely independent nominating committee will be in trouble at the end of next season if *it* doesn't select "a more balanced slate of nominees." Observers also noted, with some irony, that the bulk of the nine dismissed from the committee *were* in fact from the world of the working theater, and the three who were held over were not.

More Tony controversy was stirred up by an article by *Variety*'s Jeremy Gerard questioning the integrity of the voting of the awards. Tony rules put voters on their honor to vote only in categories in which they have seen all of the nominees. Gerard questioned whether, for instance, everyone who voted in the category of "best score" had heard the nominated score of *Metro*, which closed so fast that much of the post-opening night press (myself included) didn't even get to see it. Whenever nominees come from a show which either has had only a brief run or has closed before the nominations are issued, the assumption is that a substantial percentage of the Tony voters won't be able truthfully to claim to have seen everyone eligible. This evidently doesn't keep many from voting, despite the rules.

The importance of Tony nominations and awards to the economic life of a show is now influencing the shape of the season. Increasingly, the bulk of the productions opening on Broadway do so in the spring, close to the eligibility cutoff date. As I write this, very few productions are scheduled to open in the fall. The likelihood is, there will be a lot of empty theaters in the Times Square neighborhood for much of the season, until the annual spring log jam.

The surprise winner of the Pulitzer Prize for drama was *The Kentucky Cycle* by Robert Schenkkan, a six-and-one-half-hour, nine-play cycle covering 200 years in the lives of three Appalachian families. The award was particularly notable because, unlike previous winners, Schenkkan's play had neither opened in New York nor been set for New York production when the award was announced. (It began its life at Seattle's Intiman Theater and then had a run in Los Angeles at the Mark Taper Forum.) At season's end, a New York production still hadn't been set.

The various end-of-season prizes for straight plays on and off Broadway were distributed among *Dancing at Lughnasa* (Tony, the Drama Critics Circle and Outer Critics Circle Awards), *Marvin's Room* (Drama Desk), and *Sight Unseen* (Obie).

Poised at the beginning of the 1992-1993 season, we're faced with a number of questions: Will economics further impinge on New York's ability to showcase the best of American theater? Will the musical be able to disenthrall itself from its obsession with showbiz conventions and become as genuinely reflective of the present as the best of the straight plays?

And who will come forward to pick up the leadership standard which death pried from Joseph Papp's hands?

A GRAPHIC GLANCE

Jodi Benson, Harry Groener, The Manhattan Rhythm Kings, Jane Connell and Showgirls in the new Gershwin (Ira *and* George *at top*) musical *Crazy for You*

Al Pacino in *Salome*

Nathan Lane, Christine Baranski, Swoosie Kurtz
and Anthony Heald in *Lips Together, Teeth Apart*

Barry Bostwick, Joanna Gleason and Christine Baranski in *Nick & Nora*

Alec Baldwin and Jessica Lange in *A Streetcar Named Desire*

Joan Collins in *Private Lives*

(*Top row*) Michael Rupert, Heather Mac Rae, Carolee Carmello, (*bottom row*),
Chip Zien, Barbara Walsh, Stephen Bogardus and Jonathan Kaplan in *Falsettos*

Stephen Lang in *Hamlet*

Christopher Walken and Raul Julia in *Othello*

Brenda Vaccaro, Helen Shaver, Genia Michaela, Kate Burton, Tracy Pollan, Joyce Van Patten, Talia Balsam and (*center*) Alan Alda in *Jake's Women*

Richard Dreyfuss, Gene Hackman and Glenn Close in *Death and the Maiden*

Angela Goethals, Will Horneff, Stockard Channing, James Naughton, more children and (*in background*) Eugene Perry in *Four Baboons Adoring the Sun*

Nathan Lane, "the Dolls," Faith Prince, "the Guys,"
Peter Gallagher and Josie de Guzman in *Guys and Dolls*

(*Top row*) Tonya Pinkins, Stanley Wayne Mathis, Keith David (*bottom row*) Savion Glover, Allison M. Williams, Stephanie Pope, Mamie Duncan-Gibbs, Brenda Braxton and (*center*) Gregory Hines in *Jelly's Last Jam*

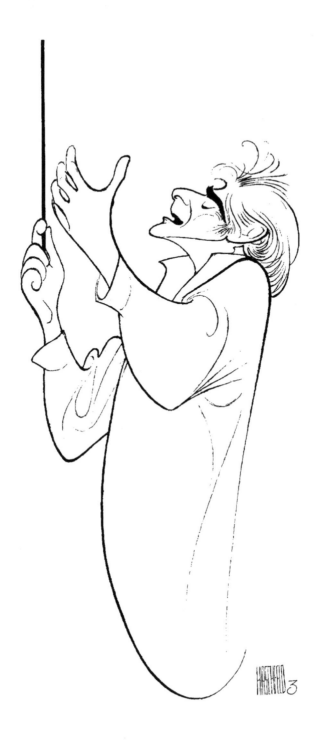

Leonard Bernstein

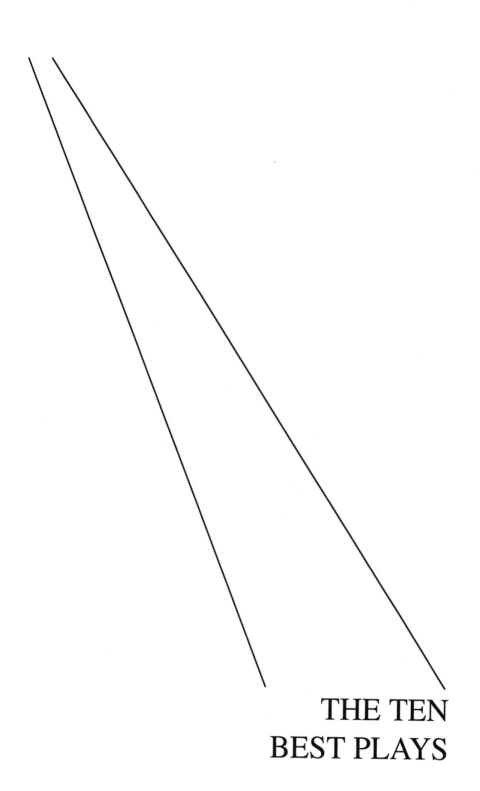

THE TEN
BEST PLAYS

Here are details of 1991-92's Best Plays—synopses and biographical sketches of authors. By permission of the publishing companies that own the exclusive rights to publish these scripts in full in the United States, most of our continuities include substantial quotations from crucial pivotal scenes in order to provide a permanent reference to style and quality as well as theme, structure and story line.

In the case of such quotations, scenes and lines of dialogue, stage directions and descriptions appear exactly as in the stage version or published script unless (in a very few instances, for technical reasons) an abridgement is indicated by five dots (. . . . .). The appearance of three dots (. . .) is the script's own punctuation to denote the timing of a spoken line.

LIPS TOGETHER, TEETH APART

A Play in Three Acts

BY TERRENCE McNALLY

Cast and credits appear on page 325

TERRENCE McNALLY was born in St. Petersburg, Fla., November 3, 1939 and grew up in Corpus Christi, Texas. He received his B.A. in English at Columbia where in his senior year he wrote the varsity show. After graduation he was award-ed the Harry Evans Travelling Fellowship in creative writing. He made his profes-sional stage debut with The Lady of the Camellias, *an adaptation of the Dumas story produced on Broadway in 1963. His first original full-length play,* And Things That Go Bump in the Night, *was produced on Broadway in 1965 following a production at the Tyrone Guthrie Theater in Minneapolis.*

McNally's short play Tour *was produced off Broadway in 1968 as part of the* Collision Course *program. In the next season, 1968-69, his one-acters were pro-duced all over town:* Cuba Si! *off Broadway in the ANTA Matinee series;* Noon *on the Broadway program* Morning, Noon and Night; Sweet Eros *and* Witness *off Broadway that fall, and in early winter* Next *with Elaine May's* Adaptation *on an off-Broadway bill that was named a Best Play of its season.*

McNally's second Best Play, Where Has Tommy Flowers Gone?, *had its world premiere at the Yale Repertory Theater before opening on Broadway in 1971. His third,* Bad Habits, *was produced OOB in 1973 by New York Theater Strategy, directed then and in its off-Broadway and Broadway phases in the 1973-74 season by Robert Drivas. His fourth,* The Ritz, *played the Yale Repertory Theater as* The Tubs *before opening on Broadway January 20, 1975 for a run of 400 performances. His fifth,* It's Only a Play, *was produced in a pre-Broadway tryout under the title* Broadway, Broadway *in 1978 and OOB under the new title by Manhattan Punch Line in 1982. It finally arrived in the full bloom of an off-Broadway production—and Best Play designation—January 12, 1986, for 17 performances at Manhattan Theater Club. This organization has produced most of his recent work including his sixth Best Play,* Lips Together, Teeth Apart, *which came onto the scene early this season on June 25.*

Other notable McNally presentations in one of the most active and successful playwriting careers in his generation have included Whiskey *(1973, OOB); the book for the John Kander-Fred Ebb musical* The Rink *(1984, Broadway);* The Lisbon Traviata *(1985, OOB; 1989, off Broadway at MTC);* Frankie and Johnny in the Clair de Lune *(1987, off Broadway by MTC for 533 performances); sketch material for MTC's musical revue* Urban Blight, *1988; in 1989,* Prelude and Liebestod *and* Hope *OOB and* Up in Saratoga *in regional theater at the Old Globe in San Diego; and in 1990, a revival at MTC of his* Bad Habits *and the book of the musical* Kiss of the Spider Woman *produced at SUNY Purchase, N.Y., in the short-lived New Musicals Program.*

McNally adapted his own The Ritz *for the movies and is the author of a number of TV plays. He has been the recipient of Obies, Hull-Warriner Awards (for* Bad Habits *and* The Lisbon Traviata*); fellowships from CBS, Rockefeller and two from the Guggenheim Foundation; and a citation from the American Academy of Arts and Letters. He lives in Manhattan and has served as vice president of the Dramatists Guild, the organization of playwrights, composers, lyricists and librettists, since 1981.*

Time: The present, a Fourth of July Weekend

Place: A summer beach house

ACT I

SYNOPSIS: The rooms of a Long Island beach house (living room and kitchen flanked by bedrooms) are clearly visible through sliding glass panels which give out onto a wooden deck furnished for summer pleasures and including a shower area and a bug lamp to zap mosquitoes. The beach is accessible from both ends of the deck, and directly downstage the deck adjoins the end of a swimming pool. A steady sea breeze is evident throughout the action and will sometimes disrupt objects on the deck.

The tableau at curtain rise shows Sally Truman painting at an easel; her husband

Sam Truman (a self-employed business man) testing the pool's chlorine level; John Haddock (head of admissions at a boys' prep school) reading a newspaper; and his wife Chloe (who is also Sam Truman's older sister) standing indoors at the kitchen sink. The characters come to life and movement accompanied by "The Farewell Trio" from Mozart's *Cosi Fan Tutte.*

Chloe asks if anyone is still hungry and catalogues the breakfast delights available from the kitchen. Sam judges that the pool is clean. John announces that the New York *Times* has informed him that only 11 percent of the U.S. population is black. Sally adjusts to the changes in the light as she tries to paint a sea scene. Chloe comes out onto the deck, comments on the painting ("Abstract expressionism? Pop? Cubism? What?") then speaks to the men.

CHLOE: . . . . . Have we seen our neighbors yet?

SAM: You mean the boys from Ipanema next door? No. They're still getting their beauty sleep.

CHLOE: I'm sure they'll be very nice. I did a little research: it's strictly *creme de la creme* here. We should all have a wonderful brother like David to leave us something like this.

Sam pulls something on a string out of the pool.

SAM: According to this gauge, the water is perfect. The question is: do we trust a gauge? I'm sorry, but I'm very sensitive about pools. Our mother was very big on polio. And this was after they'd come up with a cure for it. She was ready for it to make a big comeback. Grow up like that and you view a pool or a public toilet seat as a natural enemy.

CHLOE: Can we not talk about toilet seats right after breakfast? Thank you. I just hope you're all going to get into that pool—that includes you too, Sally!—and stay there all weekend. If I weren't allergic to chlorine, you'd never get me out of that thing . . . . .

The group plans to spend the day with no particular agenda, just relaxing in various ways. It seems that this place belongs to Sam and Sally, though Chloe is managing the kitchen this weekend, commenting that Sally is "a woman who doesn't cook." She goes to the kitchen to get the others fresh coffee, a special blend purchased at a New Canaan specialty shop, giving Sam the opportunity to comment to John that Chloe seems "unusually hyper, even for her." John assures Sam that all is O.K. with Chloe and their marriage, which he describes as "fecund."

Sam is annoyed that John keeps on reading the paper while they are talking.

JOHN: I'm not really reading. I'm more like skimming. Besides, I can do both. You think your sister seems a little extra hyper, even by her own high standards, and I'm being told by that book reviewer whose name I can never pronounce that we should all be home reading a new biography of Melville this weekend. Apparently, the whale isn't a metaphor, it's a whale. You have my complete attention, Sam.

He turns the page.

SAM: It's very unpolite.

JOHN: Impolite. I'm sorry.

SAM: I'd like you to stop it.

JOHN: Why?

SAM: I don't like it.

He pulls the paper away from John.

Look at me when I speak to you.

JOHN: All right.

SAM: That's more like it.

JOHN: What do you want to say?

SAM: It's very rude to read while people are speaking to you.

JOHN: I can see that.

SAM: It makes them feel unimportant.

JOHN: That was not my intention.

SAM: Well, that's how it comes across.

He hands paper back to John.

Don't let me interrupt you. I've made my point.

John resumes reading, while Sam goes to his wife Sally and remarks that this is the last weekend they'll invite the others down here and asks her what "fecund" means. But Sally is preoccupied, watching a swimmer way out off the beach. He was sitting on the sand looking out to sea in early morning when Sally started painting. Finally he rose, waved to someone—"It was like a salute or a farewell"—plunged in and swam straight out. It was like that scene in *A Star Is Born* with James Mason, Sally and Sam decide. The swimmer has left his robe on the beach, and he went into the water naked—"He had a beautiful body," Sally remembers, and Sam adds, "I'm sure he did. Most of them do. It's one of their requirements." Sally can still see him out there—too far out for a lone swimmer.

Chloe brings in a tray loaded with coffee and breakfast cakes. Sam reassures Sally that the swimmer will be O.K. Chloe calls their attention to a young man in a red bikini in the house next door—"*Tres, tres* fetching." John proceeds to do the *Times* puzzle. He refuses the offered food, but Chloe insists that he must have a muffin and takes one inside to toast for him.

Again we will watch Chloe working in the kitchen and again we will be able to hear her singing to herself. Chloe is almost never silent. She also almost never stops working.

SAM: You don't call that hyper?

JOHN : I barely listen any more, Sam.

SAM: She hasn't shut up since we got here.

JOHN: She's happy to see you.

SAM: Shit!

JOHN: What's the matter?

SAM: That guy in the red bikini is looking down here.

JOHN: Ignore him.

SAM: I'm trying to. He waved at me.

JOHN: So wave back.

SAM: You wave back. Imagine if they thought we were queer. I'm gonna sit with my legs apart and smoke a cigar all weekend. Why do these houses have to be so close together?

JOHN: Beach property is expensive.

SAM: The first thing we're going to do if we keep this place is build a deck higher than theirs. I don't want people looking down at me. Right, honey?

But Sally is obsessed with the swimmer—she can't see him any longer, and he hasn't come in, because his robe is still on the beach. Sam decides to go rummage around for binoculars, just as Sally asks him why he wanted to know about "fecund"—he can't remember. Talking to herself as though Sam were listening (he isn't; time has stopped for all the others while Sally is speaking), Sally goes on, "I don't know whether to tell you I'm pregnant. I've disappointed you so many times. The last one would have been a boy. No, was a boy. He was a boy. You think I'm crazy to find out about their sexes. You think it just makes losing them more painful. It probably does for you, but I want to know what they would have been. It helps me to believe there's some reason we're having this trouble."

As the activity continues, Sam comes in with a large carton he has found.

SAM: I hit the jackpot. There's a closet in there filled with all sorts of things.

SALLY: I don't think we should be doing this. I think we should ask Aaron first.

> *During the following exchange, Sam will continue to remove various items from the carton, finally finding a safety deposit box in the bottom.*

SAM: It's our house now. Everything left is ours. I'm sure all the really good stuff is gone.

SALLY: Aaron wouldn't take anything that wasn't his.

SAM: Don't be so naive.

SALLY: He was my brother's friend.

SAM: He was your brother's boyfriend. I'm sure he took what he wanted. Wake up and smell the coffee.

SALLY: I hate it when you talk like that.

> *He's found the safety deposit box at the bottom of the carton.*

SAM: Double bingo! Talk like what?

SALLY: I don't want to know any more of my brother's secrets.

SAM: I think you found out the big one a long time ago . . . . .

Sam goes to look for something with which to pry the box open. In passing, he comments to himself—unheard by the others, removed from real time—that he's

Nathan Lane as Sam Truman, Swoosie Kurtz as Sally Truman, Christine Baranski as Chloe Haddock and Anthony Heald as John Haddock in a scene from Terrence McNally's *Lips Together, Teeth Apart*

always known that people talk about him whenever he leaves a room. Likewise John, unheard and removed from real time, speaks his thoughts as though talking to Sally, who of course cannot hear him: "I have cancer, Sally. It's only a little speck now, a microscopic dot of pain and terror, but they tell me it will soon grow and ripen and flower in this fertile bed of malignancy that has somehow become my body. I never meant it to. When it blossoms and when and if they cut it from me, all will marvel at its size, dark beauty and malevolence. They will then take this enormous cancer and give it to a medical university—Johns Hopkins or Cornell— and it will be displayed there in a Cancer Hall of Fame for generations of young doctors to study and marvel at. No cancer will be worse than mine, Sally, nor none more virulent, more horrendous, more agonizing. I am scared, Sally. I am very, very scared."

Chloe comes back with her tray, wondering why they're not all in the pool. She kisses her husband on top of his head and then waves and shouts "Good morning!"

offstage to the neighbors, to John's dismay. She chats with Sally about the joys of performing in little theater (which she does) and painting, which Sally takes so seriously it seems to be a burden to her. When John makes a caustic comment about the muffin she brought him, Chloe warns him, "I can take your little barbs. After fourteen years, I'm like an archery target! But I don't think other people understand or appreciate them. 'Nuff said?"

Chloe, enjoying the sound of Schubert being played next door, returns to the kitchen. John, doing the *Times* crossword puzzle, thinks to himself that the others must know about him and Sally, just from the way he and Sally look at each other. And Sally is thinking about her brother David and her mother, who once hurt David's feelings by telling him he couldn't understand the nature and depth of affection between a man and a woman.

Chloe, checking the house's inventory (which Sally wishes she wouldn't do), has found that they have no Kahlua for Black Russian drinks after supper, but she's ready to make Bloody Marys for all. Down below, Sam exclaims that he's found a snake. Chloe warns him not to bring it upstairs and goes to the kitchen, salting her conversation with French words and expressions.

JOHN: I'm married to Edith Piaf.
SALLY: She's a very nice woman.
JOHN: I know. Believe me, I know.
SAM (*from below*): I think it's a copperhead.
JOHN: Have you thought about what happened?
SALLY: Of course I have.
JOHN: You haven't even looked at me.
SALLY: That's not true.
JOHN: You said you would call.
SALLY: She's right inside.
CHLOE (*from the kitchen*): Did you say something, darling?
JOHN: Are you going to be like this all weekend?
SALLY: I knew this would happen.
SAM (*from below*): It's too big for a coral snake.
CHLOE (*from the kitchen*): There's no Smirnov. They've got Stoly and Absolut.
SAM (*from below*): I'm going to kill it.
> *We hear the sounds of a spade striking the sand from under the house. It will continue for maybe 30 seconds while the action on the deck continues.*
Ugh .
> *John has kissed Sally. She slaps him.*

Sally promises that they'll talk, but John fears that "He follows you around like a dog." Chloe puts an end to this exchange by appearing with a tray of drinks. Sam enters carrying tools in a gardener's basket, and of course he has brought the dead snake to frighten Chloe, which it does. When it doesn't get a reaction from either John or Sally, he throws it into the neighbors' grass. John calls to Chloe, "It's okay, Petal!", to tell her the coast is now clear, and she comes back dismissing the incident as "brother-sister stuff."

The voice of Joan Sutherland is heard in full volume from the speakers next door. John calls to the neighbors to turn down the volume, then calls them a rude name under his breath.

CHLOE (*to others*): He doesn't mean it. We have three gay men and one lesbian in administration at Sturman. God only knows how many on faculty. One of the men in admissions right under John has AIDS. John has been terrific about it.

JOHN: Shut up, Chloe.

SAM: John.

CHLOE: It's all right. I need it. I want it, in fact. I tend to run on. John keeps me in line.

She kisses John on the top of his head.

He's my knight in shining armor!

JOHN: Chloe, you know I hate it when you do that.

CHLOE: So spank me, Daddy. Spank me right out here in total daylight. (*To Sam and Sally.*) You know, I'm not usually like this. You know what this is? It's grown-up time. We can behave like grown-ups! . . . . .

To prove her point, Chloe launches into a recitation of obscene words but finally winds down and decides to sun herself in silence for a while.

Sam admires Sally's painting, and as though talking to her while real time stops, Sam reveals that he is a bundle of insecurities: "Three days ago I was standing in front of our bathroom mirror in terror because I couldn't knot my tie . . . . . No one wants to listen to who we really are. Know somebody really. Know you leave shit stains in your underwear and pick your nose. Tell a woman you've forgotten how to swallow your food, and she's in her car and out of your life before you can say, 'Wait, There's more. Sometimes I have to think about someone else when I'm with you because I'm afraid I won't stay hard if I don't . . . How my father takes all the air out of the room and I can't breathe when I'm with him. How if I could tear my breast open and rip out my heart and feed it to these seagulls in little raw pieces, that pain would be nothing to the one I already feel, the pain of your betrayal! How most afraid I am of losing you.' How can I tell you these things and there be love?"

Sally sees someone, not the swimmer, retrieving the robe from the beach. This upsets her, but she obeys Sam's admonition not to become involved. Sam breaks the lock on the safety deposit box. Chloe waves offstage at a man in a blue bikini and then exclaims to Sally, "You compare that or your brother or your neighbors next door with the hi-fi to our two, and you have to ask yourself something: don't straight men think we have eyes? Don't they occasionally look at themselves in the mirror? God knows, they expect us to." Chloe declares her need for John to make love to her, "Big love! Last night was *petit*. I'm talking about *l'amour grand*!"

A recorded Broadway score is heard from next door, driving John to his room to read, though the neighbors turn the volume down before they are requested to do so.

Chloe goes into the bedroom to give John a massage.

SAM: I'm sorry. It was a bad idea. We shouldn't have done this. I just didn't think we wanted to spend a long weekend together in a strange beach house. I didn't know what we'd be getting into out here.

SALLY: They could have brought the children.

SAM: Any place but this and they probably would have. They're going through a patch. I should talk! We're going through a patch. Every marriage does. As long as there's no one else, we'll work it out.

   Pause.

I said, as long as there's no one else, we'll work it out.

SALLY: I heard you.

SAM: Is there someone else?

SALLY (*after another pause*): No.

SAM: Then we'll work it out. Weren't you going to see Sugarman this week? (*Sally nods.*) What did he say?

SALLY: No.

SAM: Have you been—?

SALLY: Yes, everything he tells me to do.

SAM: I'm not—

SALLY: I didn't say you were.

SAM: It's nobody's fault.

SALLY: Yes, it is.

Looking into the safety deposit box, Sam finds legal papers and some old photos of Sally's brother David with their father, at a time before the pool was installed. There are cuff links and a ring, which gets away from Sam and rolls into the pool. Sally recognizes it as David's ring, and Sam promises to retrieve it.

John comes onto the deck, to the accompaniment of soothing music from Gluck's *Orfeo* next door which soon has him "blissing out." Chloe comes onto the deck, on her way to the kitchen for refills. Sam is reading an old postcard, and Sally is looking out at the ocean.

SALLY: I think I see—! There! Please, God, let it be him!

   She stares at the horizon line, not moving now. Sam continues to read,
   his lips moving. Chloe is the only one still animated.

CHLOE (*from within*): Don't worry, everybody. I can manage this time.

   She struggles to open the door with her foot.

Oh!!

She drops the tray. Everything shatters. She is still behind the sliding screen door. She calls out to the others on the deck.

It's all right. Don't get up. I'll handle it.

She begins to clean up. As she works, her movements become slower and slower until she is still. Lights fade down except for special lamps on our four characters. They are isolated by them. They do not move. The Gluck continues to the end of the piece. There is a brief pause. We hear the ocean, maybe a gull. The lights snap off. Curtain.

ACT II

At noon of this sunny day, music is coming from both neighboring houses while Chloe cooks hamburgers on the deck. Sally is dangling her feet in the pool, John is flying a kite and Sam is fiddling with an astronomical telescope he's found in the closet.

Sally is still worried about the swimmer. Chloe deplores her allergy to chlorine because she so loves to swim; she remembers how she and John were swimming naked at St. Bart's on their honeymoon and making love, and then bumped into another couple enjoying the same thing. They hid behind a dinghy named Petal. Sam realizes that's where John's pet name for Chloe came from; he wishes he and Sally had pet names for each other. A seagull attacks John's kite, and Sam comments that they could feed a lot of people with seagulls if they were allowed to eat them. John is taking a childish pleasure in the kite.

JOHN: Hah! Did you see that maneuver? The Red Baron flies again!
SAM: Can I try it awhile?
JOHN: No.
SAM: No?
JOHN: Get your own kite.
SAM: That was the only one in there.
JOHN: Then you should have put it up.
SAM: I didn't know it would be so much fun.
JOHN: Monkey see, monkey do.
SAM: Just for a few minutes.
JOHN: No!
SAM: Please!
JOHN: When I'm done.
SAM: When will that be?
JOHN: When I'm done. Jesus!
SAM: Pig. Kite hog!
SALLY: Sam!
She motions him to join her sitting at the edge of the pool . . . . .

SAM (*to Sally*): This is their first and last weekend.
   He sits at the pool's edge next to Sally.

Chloe suggests that if Sally and Sam are going to keep this place they screen out their neighbors with landscaping. Sally finds that Sam has quite a sunburn and applies sunblock. Sam, still fuming at John, mutters, "He thinks he's such a hot shit because he's the director of admissions at a swanky prep school and they're members of a fucking country club," then blurts out, "I know you've slept with him." Sally denies this categorically, but Sam doesn't believe her. As the others start to get their hamburgers (John tying his kite to the picnic table), Sally tells herself, "It's gone, that moment to speak the truth. He'll ask again, I'll lie again. The truth is, I don't want him to know."

Chloe kisses John on top of his head and gets into a brief, casual exchange with the neighbors offstage, who apparently ask about Aaron. Sam worries that if Chloe keeps this up, the neighbors "will think we want to be friends. They'll be over here all the time now."

Sally, joining the others, wonders whether she shouldn't just give the place to Aaron.

JOHN: . . . . . Why would you give something worth maybe close to a million dollars to a total stranger?

SALLY: He's not a total stranger.

SAM: He's black, y'know.

SALLY: He was wonderful to David. He took extraordinary care of him. Never left his side, slept in the hospital, everything one person can possibly do for another.

SAM: Did you both know he was black? Black, black. Very African, that kind of black. Nothing white about him.

SALLY: There should be some way to acknowledge that kind of devotion.

SAM: I agree. Thank you. Thank you very much. You want the TV set? The books, the records? Take what you want. But an 800,000 dollar beach house? I'm sorry.

SALLY: I keep thinking David would want me to give it to Aaron.

SAM: Then why did he leave it to you?

SALLY: I don't know. I really don't know.

SAM: He got the apartment, for Christ's sake.

SALLY: I don't think we'd ever feel really comfortable here . . . . . I don't think I have anything against gay men. I just don't want to be the only non-gay people here.

CHLOE: You don't want to be a token anything. I hear you. Who wants to feel everyone's staring at them?

John advises them to hold on to it—the waterfront is all developed, Maine to

Florida, and in ten years this place'll be worth $2 million. Let it if need be. "I'm totally comfortable here," Chloe remarks, "but then of course I'm in the theater. Lesbians make me a little nervous, but I've never had a problem with the men." It's even easy for Chloe and John to get here—just a trip across Long Island Sound— but for Sally and Sam it means coping with the New Jersey Turnpike and all its woes. Chloe's chatter is depressing Sally, so John sentences Chloe to six hours of silence, until 7:30 p.m. Obediently, Chloe moves toward her room, but before exiting she lets the others know exactly where she stands: "I think it is precisely the small things I run on about and that seem to annoy you so, the little day-to-day details, the nuances, that give our lives some zip and some meaning. I care about cooking the burgers so each of you gets exactly what you ask for. I worry about who's driving the children's car pool that particular week. I notice what's going on around me, every detail. I don't miss a thing. I've got all your numbers. I talk too much, probably because it's too horrible to think what's really going on. You should try it, Miss Broody-Woody, Miss High Falutin! You think you're so superior. Well, maybe you are. But to whom? Me? Honey, just about anyone is superior to me. You're going to have to do a lot better than that if you want to keep that attitude up . . . . ."

Chloe assures them she's not really angry at them, then goes to her room and lies down on the bed. Sam is a little worried about his sister, but John assures him everything's fine. Sam persists, and when John calls him a fighting name— "puerile"—Sam puts up his fists and starts punching John on the arm. John rises to face him, while Sally calls for Chloe and asks her to stop them. "Stop them?" Chloe replies, at the door of her room, "Honey, I want the cable rights to this."

> *Sally grabs hold of Sam's arm. He pulls violently away, the force of his gesture sending her reeling.*

SAM: I'm going to fucking kill you.

CHLOE: All right, that's enough. Break it up. Both of you!

JOHN: You miserable little asshole.

> *By now we should realize the men are deadly serious.*

CHLOE: John, people are looking from the other deck.

> *She waves.*

Will you gentlemen please tell them how silly they look?

> *John and Sam keep circling each other, dukes up. Punches have been thrown, but none landed.*

JOHN: Come on, big shot. You started something, now let's finish it.

> *John swings at Sam and misses. Sam swings at John and misses.*

SALLY: Sam, you're going to hurt yourself.

SAM: I'll kill the bastard.

CHLOE: Don't rip his shirt, Sam. I just bought it—

JOHN: Fight fair.

> *Sally picks up Chloe's large glass container for making sun tea.*

SALLY: Okay, that's it!

Sally throws the container of tea at them. It drenches both men, but instead of parting they leap at each other and start grappling.

John twists Sam's arm tighter and tighter until he makes Sam say, "I give up, John." John doesn't relax his hold and demands that Sam add, "I admit I'm a stupid piece of shit." Sam refuses, challenging John to break his arm. Appalled at what he has been doing, John lets Sam go, apologizes and beats a shameful retreat to his room and throws himself on the bed.

The women soothe Sam. Chloe calls over to the offstage neighbors that the men were just rehearsing *West Side Story*. Sally resents Chloe's interference in their relations with the neighbors, sending Chloe to her room in tears.

Sam tells Sally why and how much he dislikes John, winding up with, "I hate waves. I hate the beach. I like New Jersey." While Sally comforts him, John comes out and stands facing outward, confessing to himself that his loss of control has not only ruined the weekend—"The four of us can never look at each other the same way again"—but also alarms him because these surges of mindless fury happen to him often. He remembers a baby picture of himself and thinks out loud, " . . . . . I just wish I knew the precise moment I stopped being that laughing child with apple and turned into this. I would go back there again and again until I understood it. I know the precise moment I almost broke my brother-in-law's arm . . . . . Sally will never let me fuck her again. That pisses me off as well as it saddens me. We gave each other great pleasure. We can never talk about these things the way they really happened and what they really meant. There's no apology deep enough to undo what I did to Sam. None. I will say, 'I'm sorry,' and he will accept my apology, but they will just be words and lies to get us through the business of living."

John apologizes (Sam's reaction is, "Let's not ruin the girls' weekend because of us"). But Sam is obviously still hostile. John offers to leave. Sally doesn't care whether they stay or go, but Sam doesn't want his bad humor to spoil the others' party mood. "No one's in a good mood, Sam," Sally reassures him.

Changing the subject, Sam expresses the wish that he could jump right into the pool—but he can't, he says, because he and Chloe were trained to wait an hour after eating before going in swimming. Sally remembers that she learned to swim because her father threw her off the end of a pier.

SALLY: . . . . . All of a sudden we heard him saying, "All children can swim, it's a natural instinct," and the next thing we knew he was picking us up and dropping us off the end. Plop, plop!

CHLOE: How old were you?

SALLY: Six or seven. David was two years younger.

CHLOE: Your father dropped a four-year-old child off the end of a pier?

SALLY: Maybe he was five. I don't remember exactly.

JOHN: What happened?

SALLY: I guess I instinctively knew what to do. I started paddling like a little dog, but David went right down to the bottom like a stone.

CHLOE: Did he drown? I mean, did he start to drown?

SALLY: He would have. Our father dove in and brought him up.

JOHN: That was big of him.

CHLOE: John hates his father.

JOHN: I do not.

CHLOE: Yes you do, darling. Don't interrupt.

SALLY: He just ignored David, like it had never happened, and went back to drinking with his friends, but you could see he was disappointed in his son. Poor David. He looked so sad.

CHLOE: I wonder why. That's a terrible story. It sounds like your brother never had a chance.

SALLY: At what?

CHLOE: I know I'm not supposed to say "normal." "Straight" is the word I'm supposed to use. I hate it. It sounds like a ruler. And "heterosexual" is just plain ugh-y! I hate all those "o" words.

SALLY: I think the causes of our sexuality run a little deeper and are a hell of a lot more mysterious than being thrown off a pier.

CHLOE: It's entirely the parents' fault. If any of our three turned out that way, I would feel like killing myself. I probably wouldn't do it, actually, it is a mortal sin, after all, for those of us who still practice the faith of our fathers—

SAM: Don't start, Chloe!

CHLOE: —but I would feel like doing it. It's such a rejection. Can we change the subject? This is very depressing.

JOHN: You brought it up, Chloe.

CHLOE: I dredge everything up sooner or later. I'm a walking nerve end. I think these are very difficult times to be a parent in.

SALLY: I think these are very difficult times to be anything in.

JOHN: I'll drink to that.

Sam goes to the outdoor waist-high enclosed shower to wash off the tea. When Chloe asks him why he doesn't just jump into the pool, Sam replies, "We've been through that." One of the neighbors calls over to tell Sally that David's funeral (which they attended) was "beautiful" and to invite them all next door to watch tonight's fireworks. They are hesitant to accept, so Sally calls over, "Unfortunately, we have other plans." While Sam complains that the water is coming out too hot and John and Chloe exchange remarks about the people next door, Sally continues her shouted conversation, now on the subject of the missing swimmer (the neighbors don't seem to know anything about it but agree that the ocean can be dangerous).

Chloe prepares to rehearse for her next show, *Guys and Dolls*.

SAM: Ow!! Goddammit, someone's flushing a toilet . . . . .

SALLY: No one's flushing a toilet . . . . .

CHLOE (*to someone next door*): I hope you boys don't mind a little show.

SALLY: Don't call them boys, Chloe.

JOHN: Leave them alone, Chloe.

CHLOE (*to someone next door*): If you like what you see, send money. If you don't, I don't want to know. I have very thin skin.

SALLY: Chloe, they were only asking us over for drinks tonight. They weren't requiring a floor show.

CHLOE: Drinks? That's so nice of them! (*To someone next door.*) I'll bring some dip!

SAM: Will someone bring me a towel?

SALLY: I just got through telling them no.

JOHN: The word isn't in her vocabulary.

CHLOE: That's not true. (*To Sally.*) So we're not going over?

SAM: A towel, someone!

SALLY: I think it's best.

CHLOE: It's your house. (*To someone next door.*) I'll still send some dip over!

John gets a towel for Sam. Chloe sets up her cassette player. John comments on a mole on Sam's skin, embarrassing him: "I'm not real good at this locker room stuff." Sam asks John to go fetch him some clean clothes. Chloe astonishes Sam by coming over and asking to see his male equipment, reminding him that she didn't make a fuss when little Sam and a friend wanted to look at her, years ago. Reluctantly, Sam lets her have a look, and she comments, "I'm impressed . . . . . It's much bigger than you-know-who's, certainly in that state of flaccidity . . . . . My compliments to our parents."

They hear Sally and John laughing inside the house, and Sam wonders what they're doing.

CHLOE: Right now it looks like he's got her legs over her head in some Kama Sutra position we learned at the Club Med.

> *Sam emerges from the shower with a towel around his waist and crosses to Chloe.*

SAM: That's not funny.

CHLOE: I know.

SAM: Then you know?

CHLOE: I only know what I read in the paper.

SAM: He's fucking her.

CHLOE: He fucked her. It's over.

SAM: How do you know?

CHLOE: He told me.

SAM: And you believe him?

CHLOE: Yes.

SAM: Why?

CHLOE: I want to.

SAM: That's a wonderful reason.

CHLOE: You got a better one?

SAM: The truth.

CHLOE: That word has gotten more people into more trouble than all the lies that were ever told. Fuck the truth. It's more trouble than it's worth.

She goes back to her cassette and rewinds it to the beginning.

If I don't believe the son of a bitch, I've only got one option as I see it.

SAM: What's that?

CHLOE: Wait till he's sound asleep, take a hammer and bludgeon him to death.

Sam stubs his toe on the deck and runs a splinter into his foot. John gets his kit and Sally holds Sam's foot while John extracts a two-inch splinter (and Chloe rehearses her song, admitting "I can't deal with any kind of puncture of the human flesh"). John means to probe the wound, for slivers, in spite of Sam's vociferous protests. For one thing, Sam doesn't want John rummaging around in his medicine cabinet looking for iodine—"I don't want some stranger knowing certain things about me"—but John goes inside and returns with iodine and a pin. They sterilize the pin with a match. Sam wants Sally to do the probing. She works on Sam's foot while Chloe continues with her rehearsal.

> *John moves apart from the others. He looks at Chloe practicing her number.*

JOHN: You're looking good, Petal!

CHLOE: Give me five more weeks! Can we call the kids tonight? I gave Mima the number here, but you know how cheap she is.

JOHN: I'll tell mother you said so. Yes, we'll call! Hey! I love you.

CHLOE: What?

JOHN: You heard me.

> *He goes to the egde of the deck and looks out to the ocean.*

SALLY: When did your feet get so callused and bunioned and corny?

SAM: Those aren't bunions. Old people have bunions. Stick to the splinter. Ow!

SALLY: I'm sorry.

SAM: Ow!!

SALLY: I said I was sorry!

SAM: That's enough.

> *Sam takes the pin away from Sally and begins to work on his own foot. The lights are coming down on Chloe silently singing and dancing, John watching her, and Sam bent over his foot. Sally stands and looks out to sea, very strong light on her. Her eyes tell us that she has seen something on the shore.*

SALLY: Oh my God. Drowned.
> *The light snaps off. Curtain.*

ACT III

That night, under a full moon, with swimming pool and bug lamp alit, and with loud parties going on to the right and left, Sam is looking at the stars through his telescope, Sally is washing dishes, Chloe is dressing, while John talks on the phone to his children back home. They want to go hayriding in the rain. Their sitter, John's mother, is at a meeting. John is more concerned by the fact that his kite has fallen, there being no wind in the evening calm to hold it up. He passes the phone to Sam, who passes it along to Sally. Sally explains to the children that a hayride in the rain might be dangerous because of lightning, but she doesn't stop there. She keeps on talking on the phone to the children, telling them that they are loved and protected by their parents.

SALLY: . . . . . If I had children, they would be so safe. They would never be alone. I would never let them go.
> *John puts his hand on her arm*

Don't touch me.

JOHN: I'm sorry.

SALLY: I'm feeling very sad and angry and unlistened to right now. That's why it's so important you understand me. I saw a terrible thing this afternoon. I saw what happens when we're not loved and protected and we feel so alone.

JOHN: You're not alone, Sally.

SALLY: I saw a man who drowned in the ocean.

JOHN: Jesus, Sally, don't—

SALLY: He was very young. Even though his features were swollen from the water, he was very handsome. Nobody wanted to look at him like this, but I made myself.

JOHN: We all told you not to go down there.

SALLY (*into phone*): I wanted to see what death looks like and not be afraid of it.

JOHN: What kind of thing is that to say to a child?

SALLY (*into phone*): Oh, he could swim all right, Megan. He could swim too well too far. I saw him swim out this morning. I knew he wouldn't come back, and I didn't do anything.

JOHN: Jesus, Sally, you're scaring them.
> *John takes the phone from her.*

SALLY: Our eyes had met.

JOHN: Children, this is your father again.

SALLY: His wave did acknowledge me.

JOHN: Now settle down.

SALLY: I let him swim out, never to return.

JOHN: Aunt Sally's still upset by what happened. We all are.

He continues, but we don't hear him. Special light on Sally.

SALLY: My eyes didn't say, "Stay, life is worth living." They said, "Go, God speed, God bless." My wave didn't say, "Hurry back, young man, happiness awaits you ashore." It said, "Goodbye, I know where you're going. I've wanted to go there too." I knew his secret, and he knew mine. Even from a great distance we know so much about each other but spend our lives pretending we don't. He wanted to die, and I helped him. Oh children, children, such perils await you, such pain and no one to protect us.

She touches her stomach.

Don't you leave me. Stick around this time.

Chloe comes in, showing off a new outfit, and John hands her the phone. Chloe simply tells the children no, they can't go hayriding in the rain. In the meantime, John is worried about Sally's behavior and tries to find out what's wrong, but Sally won't talk to him.

Sam comes in to show Sally a picture of a stinging jellyfish in a magazine. Chloe is trying to soothe the children and asks Sally to tell them she's sorry for what she said, but Sally won't. "It scared them!" Chloe protests, and Sally replies, "Good. I want to scare everyone tonight." Chloe begs Sally to tell the children they're loved and safe, but she won't do it. Instead, she sits at the edge of the pool

Nathan Lane and Anthony Heald in *Lips Together, Teeth Apart*

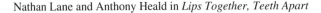

with her feet in the water. Chloe has to be satisfied with telling the children herself that their Aunt Sally didn't mean what she said, and then she hands the phone over to John, who finds that his mother has returned from her Weight Watchers meeting and is now in charge again.

Sam sits with Sally and assures her they all feel badly about the drowned swimmer, whose identity is till a mystery—nobody in any of the houses knows who he was. John joins them at the pool's edge, feet in the water.

SAM: Why don't you go in?

JOHN: Maybe later. Why don't you and Sally?

SAM: I still feel that steak and baked potato and corn on the cob and strawberry shortcake with real whipped cream right here. I'd sink like a rock.

SALLY: None of us are ever going to go into that pool, so can we just stop talking about it?

CHLOE (*from within*): Did somebody say something?

SALLY: We all think it's infected. We all think it's polluted. We all think we'll get AIDS and die if we go in.

JOHN: That's not quite true, Sally.

SALLY: One drop of water in your mouth or on an open sore, and we'll be infected with my brother and his black lover and God knows who else was in here. Pissing, ejaculating. I think we're very brave to dangle our feet like this. They may fall off.

CHLOE (*from within*): If you have something to say to me, John, come in here and say it. I cannot hear through walls or screens or whatever they are! Partitions!

JOHN: When did you develop this uncanny ability of yours to say absolutely the most inappropriate thing you could think of?

SALLY: Everybody's thinking them. I've merely decided to say them.

She splashes John.

JOHN: Stop that!

SALLY: Close your mouth!

JOHN: Sally, stop it, I said!

SAM: Sally!

SALLY: You afraid of the water?

She splashes Sam too.

Everybody's afraid of dying around here!

JOHN: If you can't control your wife, Sam! . . . . .

SALLY: Come on, Sam, you heard the man. Control me! Your wife is out of control. Do something!

She splashes him.

It's your last chance to be a man!

She stops splashing him and scoops up water from the pool in the palm of her hand and drinks it.

Then let's all get AIDS and die!

> *Sam knocks her hand away from her mouth. He grabs and holds her right wrist. She pulls him to her with her other hand and kisses him very hard and long on the mouth.*

I love you.

SAM: Jesus, Sally, what's gotten in to you?

SALLY: Thank you for not being a man. Thank you for not controlling your wife. *She kisses him again. He pulls away from her and tries to clear his mouth. Clearly, he is not comfortable with the taste of her mouth in his. He gets up from the edge of the pool.*

SAM: Stop that! I don't want to kiss you. I'm sorry your brother died, but it's not my fault. I didn't kill him. I don't know about pools and AIDS and homosexuals. I don't want to. It frightens me, all right? All of this! I'm sorry, I can't help it, it's who I am. Excuse me.

Sam goes into the house. Sally explains to John that she would hate being married to anyone—John included—who wants to "control" his wife. She confesses she needed John badly that weekend they made love but otherwise has been almost entirely faithful to Sam. John never gives all of himself away, Sally has noticed. He admits he's afraid that to know him completely would be to dislike him.

They see Sally's brother's ring at the bottom of the pool, and John offers to retrieve it; he doesn't regard AIDS as the only danger "on God's miraculous planet." Chloe joins them dressed in still another outfit and assures Sally she's decided not to be mad at her. Meanwhile, John goes into the pool to get the ring, to Chloe's astonishment. She's alarmed when John splashes water on her, but John has decided that they should all behave with Sally's defiance of AIDS. He puts his head under and plays dead. When Sam pulls him out and Chloe leans over him, John spurts her with a stream of water from his mouth—and Chloe doesn't flinch.

"Now we're all infected," John remarks, and Chloe replies, "Just as long as you're all right. You're my life." John kisses her fingers. Sally remembers that her brother David, in the hospital, having lost his sight, would touch her face with his fingers to help him remember what she looked like. She loved her brother David, hated what had happened to him. Meanwhile, Chloe leads off a series of introspective comments with, "I'm as close to love as he's ever going to get, and that suffices. It shouldn't, but it does." Sam is watching two men having sex outdoors in what appears to be a patch of poison ivy, and his comment is, "I see huffing and puffing and biting and licking and kissing and hugging and grunting and groaning, but I don't hear anyone say, 'I love you.'" Sally recalls David introducing Aaron to her, when she realized that she could no longer count herself as her brother's best friend. Sam finally hears one of the men say, "I love you," and this series of introspective comments is interrupted by the beginning of the fireworks.

Chloe continues attentive to John, fetching a towel and drying his hair for him. The neighbors call over, wondering if they have any flags to wave. Finding they don't, the neighbors throw over a packet of small American flags, which John distributes. They wave them, singing "America the Beautiful," which is finally drowned out by the climax of noise from the fireworks. In the silence that follows, they exchange greetings with the neighbors, and Chloe sets about fixing a round of drinks. John goes into his room and draws the drapes. Sally is still weeping quietly from the emotion of the song.

SALLY: Look, they're dancing up there. Both houses.

SAM: That's not all some of them are doing.

SALLY: I wish I had a better opinion about all this.

SAM: I know. It's hard.

SALLY: Seeing them touching sort of sickens me. I can't help it. I was glad I never saw my brother dancing with another man, and now I never will.

She breaks down and cries. Sam comforts her.

SAM: I'm right here.

SALLY: And yet if we had a child and they grew up that way, I know I would love them all the same. I know I would, I know it. But my love stops right there. It can't go any further.

SAM: It's O.K., nobody's judging you.

SALLY: I'm judging myself.

SAM: If we had a child, he wouldn't grow up that way. I know it, I just know it. We would do everything right, so he wouldn't, and then even if he did, or her, you're right, we would love them all the same. But it won't happen. I'd be willing to bet my life on it.

Sally and Sam each have something to tell the other (they say), but not now, when Chloe comes in with her tray of drinks and calls for John to come out and join them. Sam goes to John's room to summon him to the deck. He enters without knocking and then comes out apologizing. He didn't mean to intrude, but he embarrassed John by blundering in on him while he was coping with an array of pills. Chloe explains, "John was diagnosed with cancer of the esophagus six weeks ago. We don't talk about it. We're going to fight it. They don't think they can operate. The pills are aggressive therapy. Don't ask me what that means. We're going to fight and hope. Hope and fight."

This is supposed to be a secret, says Chloe, succumbing to tears, and Sam and Sally mustn't let on that they know. John comes out onto the deck with a bitter comment, showing that he assumes they all know about his illness now. Chloe insists on continuing a game of charades they had started. It's Sally's turn, and she has chosen a song title, but she can't seem to get started pantomiming the individual words. She finally has to tell the others that she had chosen "There's No Business Like the Show Business." Sam argues that there shouldn't be any "the" in that title. The others agree with Sally. Sam appeals to the neighbors, but they can't hear him over the music. Sam is being stubborn, John remarks, and Sally agrees: Sam is so stubborn he grinds his teeth in his sleep. Chloe insists on looking into

Sam's mouth and agrees, he's grinding his teeth down. The dentist has advised Sam to fall asleep saying "Lips together, teeth apart," over and over, to help him stop grinding in his sleep.

SAM: I don't grind my teeth.

SALLY: He won't even try it. I'm the one who falls asleep saying it for him, "Lips together, teeth apart."

JOHN: I believe you do. That sounds very loving. I'm jealous.

CHLOE: Do you want to fall asleep with me saying that? "Lips together, teeth apart." I'll do it, lover. I guess this means the end of charades?

SALLY: Please, Chloe. We're all dreadful at them.

SAM: Speak for yourself.

JOHN: Look, I don't want my health to be an issue this weekend or any other. With or without cancer, I'm still the same person, so there's no reason to change your opinion of me. I mean, riddled with the stuff, I'm still going to be the same rotten son of a bitch. I wish I could change. I really, really, really do. Profoundly. I can't. I just can't. I apologize to all of you. I think maybe you, Sam, the most.

SAM: Why me? Why most of all me?

JOHN: You seem the least defended of all of us.

SAM: I've got Sally.

SALLY: You certainly do.

At the neighbors' they are all dancing, and Sam asks Chloe to dance. John joins Sally, watching the brother and sister, who dance very well together. Sally tells John what she hasn't yet told Sam: she's pregnant again. John asks, "It's his?" Sally replies, "Of course." They agree that their spouses both know about their fling but make no further comment on this subject. They discuss the zapping of the bugs dying in contact with the bug lamp and find the repeated sound comforting.

SALLY: Zap. It's all over. Zap. Peace. Zap. No more pain.

JOHN: The end. *La commedia e finita.*

SALLY: I can hear our neighbors' even when I'm in bed. They leave it on all night. No mosquitoes on their property! We're swarming with 'em, of course. I think they can see the property line. Sam's grinding his teeth, the neighbors' bug lamp is zapping the mosquitoes, God's in His heaven, or at least our neck of New Jersey, and all's right with the world. I helped David to die. Sam doesn't know that. I don't want him to, ever.

JOHN: You've got it.

SALLY: How sick are you?

JOHN: Very.

SALLY: I'm sorry.

JOHN: Zap.

SALLY: Zap.

> *They sit quietly and look out to the sea. Sam and Chloe are dancing a*
> *slow fox trot now.*

SAM: Sis, I don't want to have children. Don't say anything. I know that's hard for you, but just listen: I'm scared they won't love me. I'm scared I won't know how to raise them. Two little eyes looking up at me! Needing me, trusting me. I don't want that responsibility. I don't believe in enough to be a father. I don't have anything to give or teach. I'm empty. I'm just coasting. You don't love "empty." Please, I don't want you to say anything. This isn't about answers.

CHLOE: They would love you. You would be a wonderful father.

SAM: I wish I could believe that. How am I going to tell Sally?

CHLOE: I hope you never will.

> *They stop dancing.*

JOHN: Zap.

SALLY: Zap.

SAM: Maybe you're right, honey. Maybe we should get one of these lamps.

SALLY: Zap.

JOHN: Zap.

SAM: Zap.

CHLOE (*sees a shooting star on the horizon*): Look! A shooting star!

SAM: Where?

CHLOE: There!

SAM: Oh!

SALLY: Oh!

JOHN: Oh!

> *They freeze. The opening music, the trio from Mozart's* Cosi Fan Tutte
> *is heard again, only this time it comes from all over the theater. It*
> *begins slowly but will get louder and louder. As it gets louder, both the*
> *stage lights and the house lights will come up to full intensity. The*
> *actors still have not moved. Their eyes are fixed on that distant star,*
> *their fingers pointing to it. The stage and the theater are blazing.*
> *Audience and actors are in the same bright light. The music reaches a*
> *climax. All the lights snap off. Curtain.*

DANCING AT LUGHNASA

A Play in Two Acts

BY BRIAN FRIEL

Cast and credits appear on pages 291-292

BRIAN FRIEL was born January 9, 1929 in Omagh County, Tyrone. Educated at St. Patrick's, Maynouth, he became a schoolteacher but since 1960 has devoted himself entirely to writing. His short stories have appeared in The New Yorker *and have been collected in volumes entitled* The Saucer of Larks *and* The Gold in the Sea.

Friel's first produced play was The Francophile *in 1958 in Belfast, followed by* This Doubtful Paradise, The Enemy Within *and* The Blind Mice *in Dublin, Belfast and London. His first far-flung international hit was* Philadelphia, Here I Come!, *produced in Dublin in September 1964, on Broadway Feb. 16, 1966 for 326 performances and a citation as Friel's first Best Play, and since then in every major theater center in Europe and America. A program of Friel one-acts,* Lovers, *was named his second Best Play at the time of its Lincoln Center engagement July 25, 1978 for 148 performances, and his third was* Translations, *produced off Broadway for 48 performances by Manhattan Theater Club April 7, 1981 after its premiere in Derry at the Field Day Theater Company, of which Friel was a co-founder with Stephen Rea.* Aristocrats, *his fourth Best Play, was written in 1979 but did not reach New York until April 25, 1989, in a Manhattan Theater Club production for*

186 performances. His fifth Best Play is Dancing at Lughnasa, *which came to Broadway in the Abbey Theater production October 24, 1991, via Dublin and London's West End where it won the Olivier Award as the best play of 1991.*

The succession of Friel's distinguished plays produced over the decades in Europe and America has included The Loves of Cass McGuire *(1967, reaching Broadway for 20 performances),* Crystal and Fox *(1969, reaching Los Angeles in 1970 and off Broadway in 1973),* The Mundy Scheme *(1969, reaching Broadway for 4 performances after a Dublin production),* The Gentle Island *(1972),* The Freedom of the City *(which premiered simultaneously at the Royal Court and Abbey Theaters and was produced by the Goodman Theater in Chicago and on Broadway Feb. 17, 1974 for 9 performances),* Volunteers *(1975),* Living Quarters *(1977, OOB 1983) and* Faith Healer *(world premiere on Broadway for 20 performances April 5, 1979), a translation of Chekhov's* Three Sisters *(1981),* The Communication Cord *(1982), an adaptation of Turgenev's novel* Fathers and Sons *(1987) and* Making History *(1988).*

As his writing career began, Friel provided radio plays to the Belfast arm of the BBC, and in 1963 he spent six months with Tyrone Guthrie at the latter's regional theater in Minneapolis. Among his many awards is that of the Irish-American Cultural Institute in 1980 for his work on the Irish stage, an honor bestowed annually but seldom to a dramatist. He lives in Ireland, and he and his wife, married for more than 40 years, are the parents of four daughters and a son.

As in the case of other Best Plays where atmosphere and characterization—the mood and style of the work—are more telling than the sequence of events, we represent Dancing at Lughnasa *in these pages with blocks of dialogue rather than a closely detailed synopsis, so that the author's purposes may be served as faithfully as possible in our text.*

Time: A warm day in August, 1936

Place: The home of the Mundy family two miles outside the village of Ballybeg, County Donegal, Ireland

ACT I

SYNOPSIS: Michael, son of one of the five Mundy sisters (Chris), speaks to the audience of his memories of the year 1936—the summer they installed a battery-operated radio (they called it the "Marconi") in the kitchen; the summer that the Mundy brother, Father Jack, came back home after 25 years of service in an African leper colony; the summer that Michael's father, Gerry Evans, visited the Mundy home on two occasions, so that his son had a chance to make his acquaintance.

As Michael finishes his narration, the characters are animated at their busy tasks in and around the Mundy kitchen and outside in the garden. Maggie is preparing fodder for hens, Agnes knits gloves, Rose brings in a basket of turf for the fire, Chris is doing her ironing at the kitchen table. The seven-year-old boy Michael is present only in imagination, but the others sometimes address him as though he were here in the flesh like themselves. While the others go about their chores, the boy is imagined as lying on the ground making kites. Maggie jumps and screams because the boy pretends he sees a rat.

The oldest sister, Kate, comes in with shopping bags, whose contents include a new library book for the boy. She reports that the whole village is talking about the forthcoming dance celebrating the harvest festival of Lughnasa. Agnes wonders why they don't all of them go to the dance, Kate is doubtful—but wavers—and the others are determined. Agnes has enough money saved to pay the admission fees for them all.

> *Rose kisses Agnes impetuously, flings her arms above her head, begins singing "Abyssinia" and does the first steps of a bizarre and abandoned dance. At this, Kate panics.*

KATE: No, no, no! We're going nowhere!

CHRIS: If we all want to go—

KATE: Look at yourselves, will you! Just look at yourselves! Dancing at our time of day? That's for young people with no duties and no responsibilities and nothing in their heads but pleasure.

AGNES: Kate, I think we—

KATE: Do you want the whole countryside to be laughing at us?—women of our years?—mature women, *dancing*? What's come over you all? And this is Father Jack's home—we must never forget that—ever. No, no, we're going to no harvest dance.

ROSE: But you just said—

KATE: And there'll be no more discussion about it. The matter's over. I don't want it mentioned again.

> *Silence. Maggie returns to the garden from the back of the house. She has the hen bucket on her arm, and her hands are cupped as if she were holding something fragile between them. She goes to the kite materials.*

MAGGIE: The fox is back.

(BOY, *an imaginary presence whose lines are spoken by Michael—the boy grown up—the narrator in whose memory the events of this play take place*: Did you see him?)

MAGGIE: He has a hole chewed in the henhouse door.

(BOY: Did you get a look at him, Aunt Maggie?)

MAGGIE: Wasn't I talking to him. He was asking for you.

(BOY: Ha-ha. What's that you have in your hands?)

MAGGIE: Something I found.

(BOY: What?)

MAGGIE: Sitting very still at the foot of the holly tree.

(BOY: Show me.)

MAGGIE: Say please three times.

(BOY: Please-please-please.)

MAGGIE: In Swahili.

(BOY: Are you going to show it to me or are you not?)

MAGGIE (*crouching down beside him*): Now, cub, put your ear over here. Listen.
Shhh. D'you hear it?

(BOY: I think so . . . yes.)

MAGGIE: What do you hear?

(BOY: Something.)

MAGGIE: Are you sure?

(BOY: Yes, I'm sure. Show me, Aunt Maggie.)

MAGGIE: All right. Ready? Get back a bit. Bit further. Right?

(BOY: Yes.)

> *Suddenly she opens her hands, and her eyes follow the rapid and imag-
> inary flight of something up to the sky and out of sight. She continues
> staring after it.*

(What was it?)

MAGGIE: Did you see it?

(BOY: I think so . . . yes.)

MAGGIE: Wasn't it wonderful?

(BOY: Was it a bird?)

MAGGIE: The colors are so beautiful. (*She gets to her feet.*) Trouble is—just one
quick glimpse—that's all you ever get. And if you miss that . . .

> *She moves off toward the back door of the kitchen.*

(BOY: What was it, Aunt Maggie?)

MAGGIE: Don't you know what it was? It was all in your mind. Now we're quits.

KATE (*unpacking*): Tea . . . soap . . . Indian meal . . . jelly . . .

MAGGIE: I'm sick of that white rooster of yours, Rosie. Some pet that. Look at
the lump he took out of my arm.

ROSE: You don't speak to him right.

MAGGIE: I know the speaking he'll get from me—the weight of my boot. Would
you put some turf on that fire, Chrissie; I'm going to make some soda bread.

> *Maggie washes her hands and begins baking.*

ROSE (*privately*): Watch out. She's in one of her cranky moods.

KATE: Your ten Wild Woodbine, Maggie.

MAGGIE: Great. The tongue's out a mile.

ROSE (*privately*): You missed it all, Maggie.

MAGGIE: What did I miss this time?

ROSE: We were all going to the harvest dance—like the old days. And then
Kate—

Pictured here is the Irish cast playing the five Mundy sisters in Brian Friel's prizewinning play *Dancing at Lughnasa*: Dearbhla Molloy (Maggie), Catherine Byrne (Chris), Rosaleen Linehan (Kate), Brid Ni Neachtain (Rose) and Brid Brennan (Agnes)

KATE: Your shoes, Rose. The shoemaker says, whatever kind of feet you have, only the insides of the soles wear down.

ROSE: Is that a bad thing?

KATE: It is neither a bad thing nor a good thing, Rose. It's just—distinctive, as might be expected. (*Rose grimaces behind Kate's back.*) Cornflour . . . salt . . . tapioca—it's gone up a penny for some reason . . . sugar for the bilberry jam—if we ever get the bilberries . . .

   Agnes and Rose exchange looks.

MAGGIE (*privately, to Rose*): Look at the packet of Wild Woodbine she got me.

ROSE: What's wrong with it?

MAGGIE: Only nine cigarettes in it. They're so wild, one of them must have escaped on her.

They laugh secretly.

CHRIS: Doesn't Jack sometimes call you Okawa, too, Maggie?

MAGGIE: Yes. What does it mean?

CHRIS: Okawa was his house boy, Kate says.

MAGGIE: Dammit, I thought it was Swahili for gorgeous.

AGNES: Maggie!

MAGGIE: That's the very thing we could do with here—a house boy.

KATE: And the battery. The man in the shop says we go through these things quicker than anyone in Ballybeg.

CHRIS: Good for us. (*Takes the battery and leaves it beside Marconi.*)

KATE: I met the parish priest. I don't know what has happened to that man. But ever since Father Jack came home he can hardly look me in the eye.

MAGGIE: That's because you keep winking at him, Kate.

CHRIS: He was always moody, that man.

KATE: Maybe that's it. The paper . . . candles . . . matches . . . The word's not good on that young Sweeney boy from the back hills. He was anointed last night.

MAGGIE: I didn't know he was dying?

KATE: Not an inch of his body that isn't burned.

AGNES: Does anybody know what happened?

KATE: Some silly prank up in the hills. He knows he's dying, the poor boy. Just lies there, moaning.

CHRIS: What sort of prank?

KATE: How would I know?

CHRIS: What are they saying in town?

KATE: I know no more than I've told you, Christine.

    Pause.

ROSE (*quietly, resolutely*): It was last Sunday week, the first night of the Festival of Lughnasa; and they were doing what they do every year up there in the back hills.

KATE: Festival of Lughnasa! What sort of—

ROSE: First they light a bonfire beside a spring well. Then they dance around it. Then they drive their cattle through the flames to banish the devil out of them.

KATE: Banish the—! You don't know the first thing about what—

ROSE: And this year there was an extra big crowd of boys and girls. And they were off their heads with drink. And young Sweeney's trousers caught fire, and he went up like a torch. That's what happened.

KATE: Who filled your head with that nonsense?

ROSE: They do it every Lughnasa. I'm telling you. That's what happened.

KATE (*very angry, almost shouting*): And they're savages! I know those people from the back hills! I've taught them! Savages—that's what they are! And what pagan practices they have are no concern of ours—none whatever! It's a sorry day to hear talk like that in a Christian home, a Catholic home! All I can say is that I'm shocked and disappointed to hear you repeating rubbish like that, Rose!

ROSE (*quietly, resolutely*): That's what happened. I'm telling you.
> *Pause.*

MAGGIE: All the same, it would be very handy in the winter time to have a wee house boy to feed the hens: "Tchook-tchook-tchook-tchook-tchook-tchook-tchook-tchookee . . . "

> *Father Jack enters by the back door. He looks frail and older than his fifty-three years. Broad-brimmed black hat. Heavy gray topcoat. Woolen trousers that stop well short of his ankles. Heavy black boots. Thick woolen socks. No clerical collar. He walks—shuffles quickly—with his hands behind his back. He seems uneasy, confused. Scarcely any trace of an Irish accent.*

JACK: I beg your pardon . . . the wrong apartment . . . forgive me . . .

KATE: Come in and join us, Jack.

JACK: May I?

MAGGIE: You're looking well, Jack.

JACK: Yes? I expected to enter my bedroom through that . . . what I am missing—what I require . . . I had a handkerchief in my pocket, and I think perhaps I—

CHRIS (*taking one from the ironing pile*): Here's a handkerchief.

JACK: I thank you. I am grateful. It is so strange: I don't remember the—the architecture?—the planning?—what's the word?—the layout!—I don't recollect the layout of this home . . . scarcely. That is strange, isn't it? I thought the front door was there. (*To Kate.*) You walked to the village to buy stores, Agnes?

KATE: It's Kate. And dozens of people were asking for you.

JACK: They remember me?

KATE: Of course they remember you! And when you're feeling stronger they're going to have a great public welcome for you—flags, bands, speeches, everything!

JACK: Why would they do this?

KATE: Because they're delighted you're back.

JACK: Yes?

KATE: Because they're delighted you're home.

JACK: I'm afraid I don't remember them. I couldn't name ten people in Ballybeg now.

CHRIS: It will all come back to you. Don't worry.

JACK: You think so?

AGNES: Yes, it will.

JACK: Perhaps . . . I feel the climate so cold . . . if you'll forgive me . . .

AGNES: Why don't you lie down for a while?

JACK: I may do that . . . thank you . . . you are most kind . . .

> *He shuffles off. Pause. A sense of unease, almost embarrassment.*

KATE (*briskly*): It will be a slow process, but he'll be fine . . .

Maggie reminisces about sneaking off to a dance contest when she was 16 and coming in second, much to the chagrin of her friends, who placed third.

Meanwhile, Chris switches on Marconi. Maggie begins to dance, surrendering herself to the rhythm. Kate protests, but Agnes, Rose and Chris join Maggie in a sort of circle. Unable to contain herself, Kate shouts "Yaaah!" and goes into a solo that takes her out into the garden. The sisters are so enrapt in their dancing that they keep on for a few seconds after fickle Marconi, never entirely reliable, suddenly shuts off itself and the music.

The sisters are complaining about the radio, when their attention is arrested by the sight of Gerry Evans approaching the house—Gerry is the father of Chris's boy Michael. Chris doesn't know what she will say to him; Kate advises her to send him away. Chris goes to the garden to meet Gerry and reminds him that she hasn't seen him in 13 months. They make small talk, Gerry describing his experiences as a ballroom dancing teacher and then asking after his son Michael (and the sisters are observing this meeting from the kitchen and exchanging comments about it).

Gerry, a Welshman, considers Ireland his home but is now planning to go to Spain to fight with the International Brigade. Chris and Gerry are both aware that their son is watching them—the boy must be very curious about his father, whom he scarcely knows. The radio in the kitchen plays "Dancing in the Dark," and Gerry takes Chris in his arms and dances her across the garden (and even Kate, watching, has to admit that Evans could always dance well, and they make a good-looking couple). While dancing, Gerry proposes that Chris marry him when he comes back here in a couple of weeks. Chris turns him down—she just wants Gerry to keep dancing her down the lane, which he does, and they exit dancing.

In the kitchen, Kate's and Agnes's worries about Chris cause them to go at each other. Maggie tries to reassure Kate, who fears that the world she works so hard to hold together is showing cracks, breaking up.

KATE: . . . . . Mr. Evans is off again for another twelve months, and next week or the week after Christina'll collapse into one of her depressions. Remember last winter? —all that sobbing and lamenting in the middle of the night. I don't think I could go through that again. And the doctor says he doesn't think Father Jack's mind is confused but that his superiors probably had no choice but send him home. Whatever he means by that, Maggie. And the parish priest did talk to me today. He said the numbers in the school are falling and that there may not be a job for me after the summer. But the numbers aren't falling, Maggie. Why is he telling me lies? Why does he want to get rid of me? And why has he never come out to visit Father Jack? (*She tries to laugh.*) If he gives me the push, all five of us will be at home together all day long—we can spend the day dancing to Marconi.

Now she cries. Maggie puts her arm around her. Michael enters left.
But what worries me most of all is Rose. If I died—if I lost my job—if this house were broken up—what would become of our Rosie?

MAGGIE: Shhh.

KATE: I must put my trust in God, Maggie, mustn't I? He'll look after her, won't He? You believe that, Maggie, don't you?

MAGGIE: Kate . . . Kate . . . Kate, love . . .

KATE: I believe that, too . . . I believe that . . . I do believe that . . .

> *Maggie holds her and rocks her. Chris enters quickly, hugging herself.*
> *She sees the boy at his kites, goes to him and gets down beside him. She*
> *speaks eagerly, excitedly, confidentially.*

CHRIS: Well. Now you've had a good look at him. What do you think of him? Do you remember him?

(BOY, *bored*: I never saw him before.)

CHRIS: Shhh. Yes, you did; five or six times. You've forgotten. And he saw you at the foot of the lane. He thinks you've got very big. And he thinks you're handsome!

(BOY: Aunt Kate gave me a spinning-top that won't spin.)

CHRIS: He's handsome. Isn't he handsome?

(BOY: Give up.)

CHRIS: I'll tell you a secret. The others aren't to know. He has got a great new job. And he's wonderful at it!

(BOY: What does he do?)

CHRIS: Shhh. And he has bought a bicycle for you—a black bike—a man's bike, and he's going to bring it with him the next time he comes.

> *She suddenly embraces and hugs him.*

(BOY: Is he coming back soon?)

CHRIS (*eyes closed*): Maybe—maybe. Yes! Yes, he is!

(BOY: How soon?)

CHRIS: Next week—the week after—soon—soon—soon! Oh, yes, you have a handsome father. You have a handsome father. You are a lucky boy and I am a very, very lucky woman.

> *She gets to her feet, then bends down again and kisses him lightly.*

And another bit of good news for you, lucky boy: you have your mother's eyes!

> *She laughs, pirouettes flirtatiously before him and dances into the*
> *kitchen.*

And what's the good news here?

MAGGIE: The good news here is . . . that's the most exciting turf we've ever burned!

KATE: Gerry's not gone, is he?

CHRIS: Just this minute.

> *Agnes enters through the back door. She is carrying some roses.*

He says to thank you very much for the offer of the bed.

KATE: Next time he's back.

CHRIS: That'll be in a week or two—depending on his commitments.

KATE: Well, if the outside loft happens to be empty.

CHRIS: And he sends his love to you all. His special love to you Aggie; and a big kiss.

AGNES: For me?

CHRIS: Yes! For you!

MAGGIE (*quickly*): Those are beautiful, Aggie. Would Jack like some in his room? Put them on his windowsill with a wee card—"Roses"—so that the poor man's head won't be demented looking for the word. And now, girls, the daily dilemma: what's for tea?

CHRIS: Let me make the tea, Maggie.

MAGGIE: We'll both make the tea. Perhaps something thrilling with tomatoes? We've got two, I think. Or if you're prepared to wait, I'll get that soda-bread made.

AGNES: I'm making the tea, Maggie.

CHRIS: Let me, please. Just today.

AGNES (*almost aggressively*): I make the tea every evening, don't I? Why shouldn't I make it this evening as usual?

MAGGIE: No reason at all. Aggie's the chef . . . . . (*Now at the radio.*) Marconi, my friend, you're not still asleep, are you?

> *Father Jack enters. He shuffles quickly across the kitchen floor, hands behind his back, eyes on the ground, as if he were intent on some engagement elsewhere. Now he becomes aware of the others.*

JACK: If anybody is looking for me, I'll be down at the bank of the river for the rest of the . . . (*He tails off and looks around. Now he knows where he is. He smiles.*) I beg your pardon. My mind was . . . it's Kate.

KATE: It's Kate.

JACK: And Agnes. And Margaret.

MAGGIE: How are you, Jack?

JACK: And this is—?

CHRIS: Chris. Christina.

· JACK: Forgive me, Chris. You were only a baby when I went away. I remember Mother lifting you up as the train was pulling out of the station and catching your hand and waving it at me. You were so young you scarcely had any hair. But she managed to attach a tiny pink—a tiny pink—what's the word?—a bow!—a bow!— just about here; and as she waved your hand, the bow fell off. It's like a—a picture?—a camera-picture?—a photograph!—it's like a photograph in my mind.

CHRIS: The hair isn't much better even now, Jack.

JACK: And I remember you crying, Margaret.

MAGGIE: Was I?

JACK: Yes, your face was all blotchy with tears.

MAGGIE: You may be sure—beautiful as ever.

JACK (*to Agnes*): And you and Kate were on Mother's right, and Rose was between you; you each had a hand. And Mother's face, I remember, showed nothing. I often wondered about that afterwards.

CHRIS: She knew she would never see you again in her lifetime.

JACK: I know that. But in the other life. Do you think perhaps Mother didn't believe in the ancestral spirits?

KATE: Ancestral—! What are you blathering about, Jack? Mother was a saintly woman who knew she was going straight to heaven. And don't you forget to take your medicine again this evening. You're supposed to take it three times a day.

JACK: One of our priests took so much quinine that he became an addict and almost died. A German priest: Father Sharpeggi. He was rushed to the hospital in Kampala, but they could do nothing for him. So Okawa and I brought him to our local medicine man, and Karl Sharpeggi lived until he was eighty-eight! There was a strange white bird on my windowsill when I woke up this morning.

AGNES: That's Rosie's pet rooster. Keep away from that thing.

MAGGIE: Look what it did to my arm, Jack. One of these days I'm going to wring its neck.

JACK: That's what we do in Ryanga when we want to please the spirits—or to appease them: we kill a rooster or a young goat. It's a very exciting exhibition— that's not the word, is it?—demonstration?—no—show? No, no; what's the word I'm looking for? Spectacle? That's not it. The word to describe a sacred and myste-rious . . . ? (*Slowly, deliberately.*) You have a ritual killing. You offer up sacrifice. You have dancing and incantations. What is the name for that whole—for that—? Gone. Lost it. My vocabulary has deserted me. Never mind. Doesn't matter . . . I think perhaps I should put on more clothes . . .

> *Pause.*

MAGGIE: Did you speak Swahili all the time out there, Jack?

JACK: All the time. Yes. To the people. Swahili. When Europeans call, we speak English. Or if we have a—a visitor?—a visitation!—from the district commission-er. The present commissioner knows Swahili, but he won't speak it. He's a stub-born man. He and I fight a lot, but I like him. The Irish Outcast, he calls me. He is always inviting me to spend a weekend with him in Kampala—to keep me from "going native," as he calls it. Perhaps when I go back. If you cooperate with the English they give you lots of money for churches and schools and hospitals. And he gets so angry with me because I won't take his money. Reported me to my supe-riors in Head House last year; and they were very cross—oh, very cross. But I like him. When I was saying goodbye to him—he thought this was very funny!—he gave me a present of the last governor's ceremonial hat to take home with— Ceremony! That's the word! How could I have forgotten that? The offering, the rit-ual, the dancing—a ceremony! Such a simple word. What was I telling you?

AGNES: The district commissioner gave you this present.

JACK: Yes, a wonderful triangular hat with three enormous white ostrich plumes rising up out of the crown. I have it in one of my trunks. I'll show it to you later. Ceremony! I'm so glad I got that. Do you know what I found very strange? Coming back in the boat there were days when I couldn't remember even the sim-plest words. Not that anybody seemed to notice. And you can always point, Margaret, can't you?

MAGGIE: Or make signs.

JACK: Or make signs.

MAGGIE: Or dance.

KATE: What you must do is read a lot—books, newspapers, magazines, anything. I read every night with young Michael. It's great for his vocabulary.

JACK: I'm sure you're right, Kate. I'll do that. (*To Chris.*) I haven't seen young Michael today, Agnes.

KATE: Christina, Jack.

JACK: Sorry, I—

CHRIS: He's around there somewhere. Making kites, if you don't mind.

JACK: And I have still to meet your husband.

CHRIS: I'm not married.

JACK: Ah.

KATE: Michael's father was here a while ago . . . Gerry Evans . . . Mr. Evans is a Welshman . . . not that that's relevant to . . .

JACK: You were never married?

CHRIS: Never

MAGGIE: We're all in the same boat, Jack. We're hoping that you'll hunt about and get men for all of us.

JACK (*to Chris*): So Michael is a love-child?

CHRIS: I—yes—I suppose so . . .

JACK: He's a fine boy.

CHRIS: He's not a bad boy.

JACK: You're lucky to have him.

AGNES: We're all lucky to have him.

JACK: In Ryanga, women are eager to have love-children. The more love-children you have, the more fortunate your household is thought to be. Have you other love-children?

KATE: She certainly has not, Jack; and strange as it may seem to you, neither has Agnes nor Rose nor Maggie nor myself. No harm to Ryanga, but you're home in Donegal now, and much as we cherish love-children here they are not exactly the norm. And the doctor says if you don't take exercise your legs will seize up on you; so I'm going to walk you down to the main road and up again three times, and then you'll get your tea, and then you'll read the paper from front to back, and then you'll take your medicine, and then you'll go to bed. And we'll do the same thing tomorrow and the day after and the day after that until we have you back to what you were. You start off, and I'll be with you in a second. Where's my cardigan?

Jack goes out to the garden. Kate gets her cardigan.

MICHAEL: Some of Aunt Kate's forebodings weren't all that inaccurate. Indeed, some of them were fulfilled before the Festival of Lughnasa was over. She was right about Uncle Jack. He had been sent home by his superiors not because his mind was confused, but for reasons that became clearer as the summer drew to a close. And she was right about losing her job in the local school. The parish priest didn't take her back when the new term began; although that had more to do with Father Jack than with falling numbers. And she had good reason to be uneasy about Rose—and, had she known, about Agnes, too. But what she couldn't have foreseen was that the home would break up quite so quickly and that when she would wake up one morning in early September both Rose and Agnes would have left forever.

> *At this point in Michael's speech Jack picks up two pieces of wood, portions of the kites, and strikes them together. The sound they make pleases him. He does it again—and again—and again. Now he begins to beat out a structured beat whose rhythm gives him pleasure. And, as Michael continues his speech, Jack begins to shuffle-dance in time to his tattoo—his body slightly bent over, his eyes on the ground, his feet moving rhythmically. And as he shuffle-dances, he mutters—sings— makes occasional sounds that are incomprehensible and almost inaudible. Kate comes out to the garden and stands still, watching him. Rose enters. Now Rose and Maggie and Agnes are all watching him—some at the front door, some through the window. Only Chris has her eyes closed, her face raised, her mouth slightly open; remembering. Michael continues without stopping.*

But she was wrong about my father. I suppose their natures were so out of tune that she would always be wrong about my father. Because he did come back in a couple of weeks as he said he would. And although my mother and he didn't go through a conventional form of marriage, once more they danced together, witnessed by the unseen sisters. And this time it was a dance without music; just there, in ritual circles round and round that square and then down the lane and back up again; slowly, formally, with easy deliberation. My mother with her head thrown back, her eyes closed, her mouth slightly open. My father holding her just that little distance away from him so that he could regard her upturned face. No singing, no melody, no words. Only the swish and whisper of their feet across the grass. I watched the ceremony from behind that bush. But this time they were conscious only of themselves and of their dancing. And when he went off to fight with the International Brigade, my mother grieved as any bride would grieve. But this time there was no sobbing, no lamenting, no collapse into a depression.

> *Kate now goes to Jack and gently takes the sticks from him. She places them on the ground.*

KATE: We'll leave these back where we found them, Jack. They aren't ours. They belong to the child.

> *She takes his arm and leads him off.*

Now we'll go for our walk.

> *The others watch with expressionless faces. Curtain.*

ACT II

Three weeks later, Maggie carries two buckets of water into the kitchen, where the boy (his two kites finished and leaning against the garden seat outside) is supposedly sitting, writing a letter to Santa asking for a bell for the bike his father has promised him (Michael, observing from downstage left, speaks the boy's lines as usual). Jack enters, wearing one of his sisters' sweaters, feeling stronger now, headed for his fourth walk of the day. Kate comes in with clothes from the line and, noting Jack's improvement, suggests that he might start celebrating Mass again, right here in the house. This jogs Jack into remembering how he enjoyed Ryanga, with his house boy Okawa beating an iron gong to summon hundreds to outdoor ceremonies—pagan ones with wine and several days of dancing.

After Jack leaves for his walk, Kate shows her despair at her brother's admiration of the religious-secular celebrations of the African tribes. Maggie takes it with a dose of humor. Chris and Gerry Evans come in, having been dancing up and down the lane. Gerry has signed on as a dispatch writer for the International Brigade, and his mechanical expertise is sought in aid of ailing Marconi. He goes to adjust the aerial, while Chris tells Maggie that there is to be no more market for Agnes's and Rose's hand-knitted gloves, too expensive now in competition with the factory-made product.

Agnes comes in, leaving two pails of blackberries outside, and it is soon obvious that Rose has been missing for some three hours. Rose wasn't feeling well (Agnes tells the others) and decided to head home to rest. Maggie suggests Rose may have gone looking for a man named Danny Bradley who Rose imagines is in love with her. But suddenly Rose appears, carrying a poppy and walking across the garden, staining her face and clothes with a handful of berries from one of the buckets, as calm as though nothing out of the ordinary had happened.

Kate demands to know where Rose has been. Rose admits straightforwardly that she'd arranged to meet Danny Bradley at the quarry. They picnicked, went for a walk through the hills, and Danny called her his "Rosebud." Danny walked her as far as the workhouse, and she then came home by herself. And that—Rose declares adamantly—is all she's ever going to tell them about how and where she spent the afternoon.

Michael now reports to the audience how the glove buyer came over to explain why she couldn't market hand-knitted gloves any more. Agnes and Kate decided not to apply for jobs at the factory, Michael tells the audience, and on Michael's first day at school the two sisters disappeared, leaving a note asking the others not to try to find them. (Michael did, 25 years later, in London; they'd scraped a living for a while but gravitated downward from penury to drunken homelessness; now Agnes was dead and Rose was dying in a poorhouse.)

Father Jack recovered his faculties (Michael explains) but never said Mass again and never lost his fondness for Ryanga and its pagan ways, until he died of a heart attack the following year. Michael's father came back from Spain with a wound (he had fallen off his motorbike), and his visits became less and less frequent and finally stopped altogether—and he never gave Michael the promised bike. Years later, Michael got a letter from a half-brother in Wales, also called Michael Evans, telling of their father's death, leaving a wife and three more grown children. Irish Michael never told his mother of that letter.

In the kitchen the women resume their tasks. Maggie suggests that Agnes turn her hand to dressmaking in place of gloves, which Agnes receives without enthusiasm. Jack comes in and assures his sisters if they came to Ryanga he'd acquire a husband for them all—one man for the four women, in the Ryanga way. Kate remarks reproachfully that such an arrangement would not receive Pope Pius XI's approval.

Marconi comes on with music from *Anything Goes*, as Gerry runs in, having fixed the aerial, and Jack goes to get his plumed hat. Gerry persuades Agnes to dance. They dance out into the garden (where Gerry kisses Agnes on the forehead, observed by Chris) and back again. Then Gerry asks Chris to dance but is icily refused. Maggie decides to give it a try, but when she begins to dance with Gerry, Chris stops the music by turning the radio off. Then she relents and turns it back on, but now something is wrong with it—no sound comes forth.

> *Rose enters the garden from the back of the house. At first nobody notices her . . . . . In her right hand she holds the dead rooster by the feet. It's feathers are ruffled, and it is stained with blood. Rose is calm, almost matter-of-fact. Agnes sees her first and goes to her. Chris and Gerry join the others in the garden.*

AGNES: Rosie, what is it, Rosie?

ROSE: My rooster's dead.

AGNES: Oh Rosie . . .

ROSE (*holding the dead bird up*): Look at him. He's dead.

AGNES: What happened to him?

ROSE: The fox must have got him.

AGNES: Oh, poor Rosie . . .

ROSE: Maggie warned me the fox was about again. (*To all.*) That's the end of my pet rooster. The fox must have got him. You were right, Maggie.

> *She places it carefully on the tablecloth in the middle of the garden.*

MAGGIE: Did he get at the hens?

ROSE: I don't think so.

MAGGIE: Was the door left open?

ROSE: They're all right. They're safe.

MAGGIE: That itself.

AGNES: We'll get another white rooster for you, Rosie.

ROSE: Doesn't matter.

MAGGIE: And I'll put manners on him early on.

ROSE: I don't want another.

MAGGIE (*quick hug*): Poor old Rosie. (*As she moves away.*) We can hardly expect him to lay for us now . . .

CHRIS: Where's that Michael fellow got to? Michael! He hears me rightly, you know. I'm sure he's jouking about out there somewhere, watching us. Michael!

> *Rose sits on the garden seat.*

MAGGIE: All right, girls, what's missing? Knives, forks, plates—(*She sees Jack coming through the kitchen.*) Jesus, Mary and Joseph!

> *Jack is wearing a very soiled, very crumpled white uniform . . . . One of the epaulettes is hanging by a thread, and the gold buttons are tarnished. The uniform is so large that it looks as if it were made for a much larger man: his hands are lost in the sleeves, and the trousers trail on the ground. On his head he wears a tricorn, ceremonial hat; once white like the uniform but now grubby, the plumage broken and tatty. He carries himself in military style, his army cane under his arm.*

JACK: Gerry, my friend, where are you?

GERRY: Out here, Jack.

JACK: There you are. (*To all.*) I put on my ceremonial clothes for the formal exchange. There was a time when it fitted me—believe it or not. Wonderful uniform, isn't it?

GERRY: Unbelievable. I could do with that for Spain.

JACK: It was my uniform when I was chaplain to the British army during the Great War.

KATE: We know only too well what it is, Jack.

JACK: Isn't it splendid? Well, it was splendid. Needs a bit of a clean up. Okawa's always dressing up in it. I really must give it to him to keep.

KATE: It's not at all suitable for this climate, Jack.

JACK: You're right, Kate. Just for the ceremony—then I'll change back. Now, if I were at home, what we do when we swap or barter is this. I place my possession on the ground—

> *He and Gerry enact this ritual.*

Go ahead. (*Of hat.*) Put it on the grass—anywhere—just at your feet. Now take three steps away from it—yes?—a symbolic distancing of yourself from what you once possessed. Good. Now turn round once—like this—yes, a complete circle—and that's the formal rejection of what you once had—you no longer lay claim to it. Now I cross over to where you stand—right? And you come over to the position I have left. So. Excellent. The exchange is now formally and irrevocably complete. This is my straw hat. And that is your tricorn hat. Put it on. Splendid! And it suits you! Doesn't it suit him?

CHRIS: His head's too big.

GERRY (*adjusting hat*): What about that? (*To Agnes.*) Is that better, Agnes?

AGNES: You're lovely.

> *Gerry does a Charlie Chaplin walk across the garden, his feet spread, his cane twirling.*

GERRY (*sings*):
"In olden days a glimpse of stocking
Was looked on as something shocking . . . "

JACK (*adjusting his hat*): And what about this? Or like this? Or further back on my head?

Pictured on this page are American replacements for the Irish cast playing the sisters in *Dancing at Lughnasa*: *above left*, Patricia Hodges (Kate) and Jaqueline Knapp (Maggie); *above right*, Miriam Healy-Louie (Rose); *right*, Jennifer Van Dyck (Chris) and Jan Maxwell (Agnes)

MAGGIE: Would you look at them! Strutting about like a pair of peacocks! Now—teatime!

AGNES: I'll make the tea.

MAGGIE: You can start again tomorrow. Let me finish off Lughnasa. Chrissie, put on Marconi.

CHRIS: I think it's broken again.

AGNES: Gerry fixed it. Didn't you?

GERRY: Then Chrissie got at it again.

CHRIS: Possessed, that thing, if you ask me.

KATE: I wish you wouldn't use words like that, Christina. There's still great heat in that sun.

MAGGIE: Great harvest weather.

KATE: I love September.

MAGGIE (*not moving*): Cooking time, girls.

KATE: Wait a while, Maggie. Enjoy the bit of heat that's left.

> *Agnes moves beside Rose.*

AGNES: Next Sunday, then. Is that all right?

ROSE: What's next Sunday?

AGNES: We'll get some more bilberries.

ROSE: Yes, yes. Whatever you say, Aggie.

GERRY (*examines the kites*): Not bad for a kid of seven. Very neatly made.

KATE: Look at the artwork.

GERRY: Wow-wow-wow-wow! That is unbelievable!

KATE: I keep telling his mother—she has a very talented son.

CHRIS: So there, Mr. Evans.

GERRY: Have you all seen these?

MAGGIE: I hate them.

GERRY: I think they're just wonderful. Look, Jack.

> *For the first time we all see the images. On each kite is painted a crude, cruel, grinning face, primitively drawn, garishly painted.*

I'll tell you something: This boy isn't going to end up selling gramophones.

CHRIS: Michael! He always vanishes when there's work to be done.

MAGGIE: I've a riddle for you. Why is a gramophone like a parrot?

KATE: Maggie!

MAGGIE: Because it . . . because it always . . . because a parrot . . . God, I've forgotten!

> *Maggie moves into the kitchen. Michael enters. The characters are now in positions similar to their positions at the beginning of the play—with some changes. Agnes and Gerry are on the garden seat. Jack stands stiffly to attention at Agnes's elbow. One kite, facing boldly out front, stands between Gerry and Agnes; the other between Agnes and Jack. Rose is upstage left. Maggie is at the kitchen window. Kate is downstage right. Chris is at the front door. During Michael's speech, Kate*

cries quietly. As Michael begins to speak, the stage is lit in a very soft, golden light, so that the tableau we see is almost but not quite, in a haze.

MICHAEL: As I said, Father Jack was dead within twelve months. And with him and Agnes and Rose all gone, the heart seemed to go out of the house. Maggie took on the tasks Rose and Agnes had done and pretended to believe that nothing had changed. My mother spent the rest of her life in the knitting factory—and hated every day of it. And after a few years of doing nothing, Kate got the job of tutoring the young family of Austin Morgan of the Arcade. But much of the spirit and fun had gone out of their lives; and when my time came to go away, in the selfish way of young men I was happy to escape.

Now fade in very softly, just audible, the music "It Is Time to Say Goodnight"—not from the radio speaker. And as Michael continues, everybody sways very slightly from side to side—even the grinning kites. The movement is so minimal that we cannot be quite certain if it is happening or if we imagine it.

And so, when I cast my mind back to that summer of 1936, different kinds of memories offer themselves to me. But there is one memory of that Lughnasa time that visits me most often; and what fascinates me about that memory is that it owes nothing to fact. In that memory, atmosphere is more real than incident, and everything is simultaneously actual and illusory. In that memory, too, the air is nostalgic with the music of the Thirties. It drifts in from somewhere far away—a mirage of sound—a dream music that is both heard and imagined; that seems to be both of itself and its own echo; a sound so alluring and so mesmeric that the afternoon is bewitched, maybe haunted, by it. And what is so strange about that memory is that everybody seems to be floating on those sweet sounds, moving rhythmically, langorously, in complete isolation; responding more to the mood of the music than to its beat. When I remember it, I think of it as dancing. Dancing with eyes half closed because to open them would break the spell. Dancing as if language had surrendered to movement—as if this ritual, this wordless ceremony, was now the way to speak, to whisper private and sacred things, to be in touch with some otherness. Dancing as if the very heart of life and all its hopes might be found in those assuaging notes and those hushed rhythms and in those silent and hypnotic movements. Dancing as if language no longer existed because words were no longer necessary . . .

Slowly bring up the music. Slowly bring down the lights. Curtain.

MAD FOREST

A Play in Three Acts

BY CARYL CHURCHILL

Cast and credits appear on page 343

CARYL CHURCHILL is a native Londoner, born there September 3, 1938, but went to school in Montreal at the Trafalgar School prior to receiving her B.A. at Lady Margaret Hall, Oxford, in 1960. The impressive roster of her stage credits began at Oxford in 1958 with Downstairs *and continued with productions in England of her* Having a Wonderful Time, Easy Death, Schreber's Nervous Illness *and* Owners, *her first major work, produced at the Royal Court Theater Upstairs in 1972 and off Broadway for 2 performances the following year. There followed* Perfect Happiness *(1974),* Moving Clocks Go Slow *(1975),* Objections to Sex and Violence *(Royal Court, 1975),* Vinegar Town *(Monstrous Regiment, a touring feminist group, 1976),* Light Shining in Buckinghamshire *(1976, presented February 12, 1991 for 39 OOB performances by New York Theater Workshop),* Traps *(1977, presented OOB in the 1987-88 season) and* Cloud 9 *(1979), a transatlantic hit produced by the Joint Stock Company at the Royal Court and off Broadway for 971 performances in independent production May 18, 1981, Churchill's first Best Play and first Obie citation for playwriting.*

Since then, New York audiences have seen a stream of Churchill plays produced off Broadway by the late Joseph Papp on his Public Theater schedules: Top Girls

December 29, 1982 for 40 performances, Fen *May 24, 1983 for 43 performances,* Serious Money *December 3, 1987 for 30 performances followed by a 15-performance Broadway engagement March 3, 1984, and the double bill of Churchill one-acts* Ice Cream With Hot Fudge *May 3, 1990 for 38 performances. This season's* Mad Forest, *subtitled A Play From Romania and based on Churchill's researches on a recent visit to that country, came to New York, after Bucharest and London premieres, as an OOB production by New York Theater Workshop, cited as Churchill's second Best Play in our policy of including outstanding OOB scripts which have established themselves on the national or international scene and are therefore "frozen" (indeed,* Mad Forest *has already been published) and in no sense experimental work-in-progress subject to revision.*

Churchill's long list of scripts produced in all dramatic media has included: for the theater, sketches for Floorshow *(1977),* Three More Sleepless Nights *(1980),* Softcops *and* A Mouthful of Birds *(written in collaboration); for radio,* The Ants; *for TV,* The Judge's Wife. *On this side of the Atlantic, she collected the second and third of her three authorship Obies for* Top Girls *and* Serious Money. *Churchill is married and lives in London.*

Place: Romania

ACT I: LUCIA'S WEDDING

1. Lucia has four eggs

SYNOPSIS: With the sound of stirring Romanian music coming from their radio, Bogdan (an electrician) and Irina (his wife, a tram driver) Vladu sit quietly, smoking Romanian cigarettes. Bogdan turns the volume up as Irina puts her head next to his and they argue, getting angry. Their words are inaudible. Finally they sit in silence which Bogdan is about to break when their daughters, Florina and Lucia, come in. The sisters' laughter stops when they get a good look at their parents.

Irina turns the radio down low.
Lucia produces four eggs with a flourish. Irina kisses her.
Bogdan ignores her.
Lucia produces a packet of American cigarettes.
Florina laughs.
Lucia opens the cigarettes and offers them to Irina. She hesitates, then puts out her cigarette and takes one. Florina takes one.
Bogdan ignores her.
Lucia offer a cigarette to Bogdan. He shakes his head.
Lucia takes a cigarette. They sit smoking.
Bogdan finishes his cigarette. He sits without smoking. Then he takes a cigarette.

Lucia and Florina laugh.
Bogdan picks up an egg and breaks it on the floor.
Irina gathers the other eggs to safety.
Lucia and Florina keep still.
Irina turns the radio up loud and is about to say something.
Bogdan turns the radio completely off. Irina ignores him and smokes.
Florina gets a cup and spoon and scrapes up what she can of the egg off the floor.
Lucia keeps still.

2. Who has a match?

At the home of the Antonescu family (*"noticeably better off than the Vladus"*) Mihai (an architect) is making notes, his wife Flavia (a school teacher) is correcting papers, and their son Radu (an art student) is drawing. Mother and father indicate they don't approve of the girl their son has been seeing, presumably one of the Vladu girls. Mihai tells his family that for the third time he's been ordered to change his building design.

3. She has a letter from the United States

Lucia shrugs off a question from Florina about Radu and shows her an airmail letter from Wayne, an American, whom evidently she loves.

4. The pupils listen to the lesson

FLAVIA (*speaks loudly and confidently to her pupils*): Today we are going to learn about a life dedicated to the happiness of the people and noble ideas of socialism. The new history of the motherland is like a great river with its fundamental starting point in the biography of our general secretary, the president of the republic, Comrade Nicolae Ceaucescu, and it flows through the open spaces of the important dates and problems of contemporary humanity. Because it's evident to everybody that linked to the personality of this great son of the nation is everything in the country that is most durable and harmonious, the huge transformations taking place in all areas of activity, the ever more vigorous and ascendant path towards the highest stages of progress and civilization. He is the founder of the country. More, he is the founder of man. For everything is being built for the sublime development of man and country, for their material and spiritual wellbeing. He started his revolutionary activity in the earliest years of his adolescence in conditions of danger and illegality, therefore his life and struggle cannot be detached from the most burning moments of the people's fight against fascism and war to achieve the ideals of freedom and aspirations of justice and progress. We will learn the biography under four headings: 1) village of his birth and prison, 2) revolution, 3) leadership, 4) the great personality of Comrade Nicolae Ceaucescu.

5. We are buying meat

> *Radu is in a queue of people with shopping bags. They stand a long time in silence. Someone leaves a bag with a bottle in it to mark the place and goes. They go on standing.*

RADU (*whispers loudly*): Down with Ceaucescu.

> *The woman in front of him starts to look round, then pretends she hasn't heard. The man behind pretends he hasn't heard and casually steps slightly away from Radu. Two people towards the head of the queue look round, and Radu looks round as if wondering who spoke. They go on queueing.*

6. Two men are sitting in the sun

A Securitate man chides Bogdan for giving his daughter Lucia permission to marry an American, and thus denying their country her future services as a primary school teacher. But people may believe Bogdan has sympathy for foreign values and thus may confide in him; so the Securitate man orders Bogdan to listen to them and report to him once a week.

7. Are you listening?

Lucia pays a doctor a large sum of money for an illegal abortion.

Garret Dillahunt as Ianos, Tim Nelson as Gabriel and Jake Weber as Radu in a scene from Caryl Churchill's *Mad Forest*

8. *The bottle of wine is on the table*

Radu, the Vladus' son Gabriel and Ianos, a friend, tell each other jokes denigrating the regime.

9. *The sky is blue*

A Priest discusses the political situation with an Angel. They agree that it's a function of the Romanian church to provide the sort of freedom that comes from escaping reality and "flying around in the blue" of thought and imagination.

ANGEL: Don't be ashamed . . . . . There's no question of taking a stand, it's not the job of the church.
PRIEST: Everyone will think we're cowards.
ANGEL: No no no. Flying about in the blue.
PRIEST: Yes yes.
    Pause.
You've never been political?
ANGEL: Very little. The Iron Guard used to be rather charming and called themselves the League of the Archangel Michael and carried my picture about. They had lovely processions. So I dabbled.
PRIEST: But they were fascists.
ANGEL: They were mystical.
PRIEST: The Iron Guard threw Jews out of windows in '37. My father remembers it. He shouted and they beat him up.
ANGEL: Politics, you see. Their politics weren't very pleasant. I try to keep clear of the political side. You should do the same.
    Pause.
PRIEST: I don't trust you any more.
ANGEL: That's a pity. Who else can you trust?
    Pause.
Would you rather feel ashamed?
    Pause.
Or are you going to take some kind of action, surely not?
    Silence.
PRIEST: Comfort me.

10. *This is our brother*

Although the radio can't be turned on to drown out his voice, Gabriel Vladu insists on telling his family about an incident at the office that day: they took him aside, mentioned his sister Lucia and questioned his patriotism. Fortunately, Gabriel remembered something Ceaucescu once said about hard, diligent work being a citizen's duty and told them, "Because I'm a patriot, I work so hard that I can't think about anything else." Thus he can't help them spy on his fellow workers. Lucia hopes this doesn't mean she won't be able to get her passport.

11. Look!

A rat runs loose in the street and is chased by a soldier and a waiter, soon joined by Radu, Ianos and Gabriel.

12. I am visiting my granddaughter

Flavia's grandmother pays her granddaughter a visit and reproaches her for living too much in the past and in the future—as though pretending the present isn't real.

13. What's the time?

Lucia and Ianos stand silently with their arms around each other, Lucia tries to check the time, but Ianos puts his hand over the face of her watch.

14. Where is the trolleybus?

Radu and Florina meet while waiting for a bus. Radu asks about her sister Lucia's wedding.

15. Irina has a headache

Irina helps her daughter Lucia try on her wedding dress.

16. Lucia has a golden crown

The priest marries Lucia and her American suitor Wayne, placing a crown alternately on the bride's and groom's heads, with Bogdan, Irina, Florina, Gabriel, Rodica and others as witnesses.
Music. Curtain.

ACT II: DECEMBER

A group of Romanians reports on the turbulent events of December 1989, each as he or she experienced them either first hand or in immediate hearsay, none of them characters which have been introduced in Act I. *"Each behaves as if the others are not there, and each is the only one telling what happened."*

PAINTER: My name is Valentic Barbat, I am a painter, I hope to go to the Art Institute. I like to paint horses. Other things too, but I like horses. On December 20 my girlfriend got a call, go to the Palace Square. People were wearing black armbands for Timicoara. There was plenty of people but no courage. Nothing hap-

Pictured above in an Act II scene from *Mad Forest* are Garret Dillahunt (Painter), Lanny Flaherty (Translator), Tim Nelson (Boy Student), Jake Weber (Soldier) and Randy Danson (Flowerseller, *far right*)

pened that day, and we went home . . . . .

TRANSLATOR: I'm Dimitru Constantinescu, I work as a translator in a translation agency. On the 21st we were listening to the radio in the office to hear Ceaucescu's speech. It was frightfully predictable. People had been brought from factories and institutes on buses, and he wanted their approval for putting down what he called the hooligans in Timicoara. Then suddenly we heard boos, and the radio went dead. So we knew something had happened. We were awfully startled. Everyone was shaking . . . . .

STUDENT 1: There were two camps, army and people, but nobody shooting. Some workers from the People's Palace come with construction material to make barricades. More and more people come, we are pushed together . . . . .

BULLDOZER DRIVER: In the square there is much army and tanks. My son is six years old. I am scared for him. I take him home, and we watch what happens on TV with my wife and daughter . . . . .

PAINTER: When we heard shooting we went out, and we stayed near the Intercontinental Hotel till nearly midnight. I had an empty soul. I didn't know who I was.

STUDENT 1: They shot tracer bullets with the real bullets to show they were shooting high. At first people don't believe they will shoot in the crowd again after

Timicoara.

PAINTER: I saw a tank drive into the crowd, a man's head was crushed. When people were killed like that, more people came in front of the tanks . . . . .

SECURITATE: In the night the army cleared the blood off the streets and painted the walls and put tar on the ground where there were stains from the blood, so everything was clean.

STUDENT 1: At six in the morning there is new tar on the road, but I see blood and something that is a piece of skin. Someone puts down a white cloth on the blood, and peoples throw money, flowers, candles, that is the beginning of the shrines . . . . .

DOCTOR: At the hospital no one knew what had happened, but there were fourteen dead and nineteen wounded. There were two kinds of wounds, normal bullet wounds and bullets that explode when they strike something and break bones in little pieces, there is no way of repairing them . . . . .

TRANSLATOR: I heard people shouting, "Down with Ceaucescu," for the first time. It was a wonderful feeling to say those words, "*Jos Ceaucescu.*"

GIRL STUDENT: Suddenly there was a huge crowd with young people. For the first time I saw the flag with the hole cut out of it. I began to cry, I felt ashamed I hadn't done anything. My father agreed to go on, but not with the crowd.

STUDENT 2: Then I saw students singing, with flags with holes in them, and I thought, "Surely this is the end." I walked on the pavement beside them, quickly looking to the side for an escape route, like a wild animal.

TRANSLATOR: I had promised my wife to take care. We were walking towards the tanks, and I was in a funk. But when you're with other people you keep walking on . . . . . then I saw there were flowers in the guns.

GIRL STUDENT: I saw a tank with a soldier holding a red carnation.

TRANSLATOR: Everyone was hugging and kissing each other, you were kissing a chap you'd never seen before.

GIRL STUDENT: And when I looked again the police had vanished . . . . .

SECURITATE: On the twenty-second the army went over to the side of the people. I gave my pistol to an army officer, and both magazines were full. That's why I'm here now. I had no more superiors, and I wanted to get home. I caught the train and stayed in, watching what happened on TV . . . . .

PAINTER: That night the terror shooting started. There was no quiet place.

TRANSLATOR: When the terror shooting started, I was at home and heard it. My legs buckled, I vomited, I couldn't go out. It took me weeks to get over that.

STUDENT 1: About seven o'clock we heard on the radio, "Help, our building is being attacked." So I went out again.

HOUSEPAINTER: At the radio station I am scared, my husband says, "Why you come then?" Terroristi shoot from a building, and my husband goes with men inside and catch them. There are many wounded, and I help. I am the only woman.

SOLDIER: They say us it is not Hungarians. It is terroristi. We guard the airport. We shoots anything, we shoots our friend. I want to stay alive.

PAINTER: They are asking on TV for people to defend the TV station. My girl friend and I go out. We stop a truck of young people and ask where they're going, they say, "We are going to die." They say it like that. We can do nothing there, everyone knows it . . . . .

SECURITATE: When I heard about the execution on the twenty-fifth I came at night with my father to the authorities to certify what I was doing during the event. I was detained three days by the army, then told to remain at home. I will say one thing. Until noon on the twenty-second we were law and order. We were brought up in this idea. I will never agree with unorder. Everyone looks at me like I did something wrong. It was the way the law was then and the way they all accepted it.

STUDENT 1: On the twenty-fifth we hear about the trial and their deaths. It is announced that people must return their weapons, so we go to the factory and give back our guns. Of the twenty-eight who had guns, only four are alive.

BULLDOZER DRIVER: I stay home with my family till the twenty-eighth, then I go to work. They say the time I was home will be off my holidays. There is no more work on the People's Palace, nobody knows if they finish it.

PAINTER: Painting doesn't mean just describing, it's a state of spirit. I didn't want to paint for a long time then.
    Curtain.

ACT III: FLORINA'S WEDDING

1. The dog is hungry

At night, outdoors, a man approaches a dog who is *"undecided between eagerness and fear."* The man is a vampire.

VAMPIRE: Good dog. Don't be frightened.
    Dog approaches, then stops. Growls. Retreats, advances. Growls.
No, no, no, no, no. You can tell, of course. Yes, I'm not a human being, what does that matter? It means you can talk to me.

DOG: Are you dead?

VAMPIRE: No, no, I'm not, unfortunately. I'm undead and getting tired of it. I'm a vampire, you may not have met one before, I usually live in the mountains, and you look like a dog who's lived on scraps in the city. How old are you?

DOG: Five, six.

VAMPIRE: You look older, but that's starvation. I'm over five hundred, but I look younger. I don't go hungry.

DOG: Do you eat dogs?

VAMPIRE: Don't be frightened of me, I'm not hungry now. And if I was, all I'd do is sip a little of your blood. I don't eat. I don't care for dogs' blood.

DOG: People's blood?

VAMPIRE: I came here for the revolution, I could smell it a long way off.

DOG: I've tasted man's blood. It was thick on the road, I gobbled it up quick, then somebody kicked me.

VAMPIRE: Nobody knew who was doing the killing, I could come up behind a man in a crowd . . . . .

DOG: You could feed me.

Dog approaches Vampire carefully.

VAMPIRE: I've no money to buy food for you, I don't buy food, I put my mouth to a neck in the night, it's a solitary—get off.

As the Dog reaches him, he makes a violent gesture, and the dog leaps away.

DOG: Don't throw stones at me, I hate it when they throw stones, I hate being kicked, please please, I'd be a good dog, I'd bite your enemies. Don't hurt me.

VAMPIRE: I'm not hurting you. Don't get hysterical.

Dog approaches again.

DOG: I'm hungry. You're kind. I'm your dog.

Dog is licking his hands.

VAMPIRE: Stop it, go away. Go. Go. Go away.

Dog slinks a little further off then approaches carefully.

DOG: I'm your dog. Nice. Yes? Your dog? Yes?

VAMPIRE: You want me to make you into a vampire? A vampire dog?

DOG: Yes please, yes, yes.

The Vampire explains how repetitive and lonely a vampire's existence can be, but the Dog persists, so the *"Vampire puts his mouth to the Dog's neck."*

2. Everyone hopes Gabriel will feel better soon

Gabriel Vladu, wounded in the fighting, is recovering in a hospital where his sister Florina is a nurse. Radu Antonescu, also a hero, comes looking for Florina, with whom he can freely associate now that the revolution has narrowed the wide gulf between their families.

A couple of weeks later, Gabriel is well on the way to recovery. A patient in a dressing gown comes over to talk to him.

PATIENT: Did we have a revolution or a putsch? Who was shooting on the twenty-first? And who was shooting on the twenty-second? Was the army shooting on the twenty-first, or did some shoot and some not shoot, or were the Securitate disguised in army uniforms? If the army were shooting, why haven't they been brought to justice? And were they still shooting on the twenty-second? Were they now disguised as Securitate? Most important of all, were the terrorists and the army really fighting, or were they only pretending to fight? And for whose benefit? And by whose orders? Where did the flags come from? Who put loudhailers in the square? How could they publish a newspaper so soon? Why did no one turn off the power at the TV? Who got Ceaucescu to call everyone together? And is he really dead? How many people died at Timicoara? And where are the bodies? And were they mutilated after they'd been killed, specially to provoke a revolution? By whom? For whose benefit? Or was there a drug in the food and water at Timicoara to make people more aggressive? Who poisoned the water in Bucharest?

GABRIEL: Please stop.

PATIENT: Why weren't we shown the film of the execution?

GABRIEL: He is dead.

PATIENT: And is the water still poisoned?

GABRIEL: No.

PATIENT: And who was shooting on the twenty-second?

GABRIEL: The army, which was on the side of the people, was fighting the terrorists, who were supporting Ceaucescu.

PATIENT: They changed clothes.

GABRIEL: Who changed clothes?

PATIENT: It was a fancy dress party. Weren't you there? Didn't you see them singing and dancing?

This conversation ends when Florina, Radu and Lucia (come over from the U.S.) arrive to visit Gabriel. Rodica, his wife, has been sitting by his bedside. Lucia tells them that the Americans are most enthusiastic about developments in Romania, and that her husband Wayne was too busy to take the trip with her. The Patient tries to resume his line of questioning with "Ceaucescu so quickly?" but is hushed and escorted off by Radu. And soon the others are echoing some of the Patient's questions among themselves.

3. Rodica is still having nightmares

Rodica has a strange dream of being dressed like a queen and interrogated by a couple of soldiers who apparently have come to help her escape in a helicopter but in exchange want everything she owns including her hands and feet.

4. When we went to visit our grandparents in the country it was a sunny day

Florina, Radu, Lucia and her lover Ianos visit the Vladu grandparents so that Radu can meet them before his wedding to Florina. The Grandmother notices with some consternation that Ianos is a Hungarian but is reassured by Lucia that he's their friend.

Lucia and Ianos go off to discuss their future in private. Ianos feels he owes her husband Wayne the money Wayne paid for Lucia's abortion, not knowing that Ianos was the father. Lucia considers leaving Wayne in America and staying in Romania to marry Ianos, whom she loves. She confesses she doesn't like America, anyhow. Ianos wonders whether her family will let her marry a Hungarian.

Meanwhile, Radu and Florina are talking politics.

RADU: Iliescu's going to get in because the workers and peasants are stupid.
>   *Pause.*

Not stupid, but they don't think. They don't have the information.
>   *Pause.*

I don't mean your family in particular.

FLORINA: You're a snob like your father. You'd have joined the party.

RADU: Wouldn't you?
>   *Silence. He touches her face.*

FLORINA: I used to feel free then.

RADU: You can't have.

FLORINA: I don't now and I'm in a panic.

RADU: It's because the Front tricked us. When we got rid . . .

FLORINA: It's because I couldn't keep everything out.
>   *Pause.*

RADU: But you didn't have me then.

FLORINA: No, but I thought you were perfect.

RADU: I am perfect.
>   *Silence.*

What?

FLORINA: Sometimes I miss him.

RADU: What? Why?

FLORINA: I miss him.

RADU: You miss hating him.

FLORINA: Maybe it's that.

RADU: I hate Iliescu.

FLORINA: That's not the same.

RADU: I hate him worse. Human face. And he'll get in because they're stupid
and do what they're told. Ceaucescu Ceaucescu. Iliescu Iliescu.

FLORINA: I don't have anyone to hate. You sometimes.

RADU: Me?

FLORINA: Not really.

RADU: Me?

Ianos, Radu, Lucia and Florina lie on the grass, separated, each considering
what he or she hopes for in the immediate future.

5. *Would you like some more cheese?*

Flavia Antonescu and her husband Mihai are eating cheese and salami and discussing their future. Mihai took no part in the events of the 22nd and will probably
be reassigned to some project by the new government. Flavia is worried about her
own situation.

FLAVIA: All I was trying to do was teach correctly. Isn't history what's in the history book? Let them give me a new book, I'll teach that.

MIHAI: Are you losing your job?

FLAVIA: I didn't inform on my pupils, I didn't accept bribes. Those are the people whose names should be on the list.

MIHAI: Are they not on the list?

FLAVIA: They are on the list, but why am I with them? The new head of department doesn't like me. He knows I'm a better teacher than he is. I can't stop teaching. I'll miss the children.

Silence, during which Radu comes in,

Why are you always out, Radu? Come and eat.

Radu is already making sandwiches.

MIHAI: I hope you're going to join us for a meal.

Radu goes on making sandwiches.

RADU: Have you noticed the way Iliescu moves his hands? And the words he uses?

MIHAI: He comes from a period when that was the style.

RADU: Yes he does, doesn't he.

MIHAI: Not tonight, Radu. Your mother's had bad news at work about her job.

FLAVIA: The new head of department—

RADU: There you are. It's because of me. No one who's opposed to the Front will get anywhere.

MIHAI: Radu, I don't know what to do with you. Nothing is on a realistic basis.

RADU: Please don't say that.

MIHAI: What's the matter now?

RADU: Don't say "realistic basis."

FLAVIA: It's true, Mihai, you do talk in terrible jargon from before, it's no longer correct.

MIHAI: The head of department is in fact a supporter of the liberals.

RADU: Is he?

FLAVIA: It may not come to anything.

RADU: You mean it's because of what you did before? What did you do?

MIHAI: Radu, this is not a constructive approach.

RADU: It won't come to anything, don't worry. It's five weeks since we made out our list of bad teachers. Nobody cares that the students and staff voted. It has to go to the Ministry.

FLAVIA: Do you want me to lose my job?

RADU: If you deserve to.

Flavia slaps Radu. Silence.

Do you remember once I came home from school and asked if you loved Elena Ceaucescu?

FLAVIA: I don't remember, no. When was that?

RADU: And you said yes. I was seven.

FLAVIA: No, I don't remember.

Pause

But you can see now why somebody would say what they had to say to protect you.

RADU: I've always remembered that.

FLAVIA: I don't remember that.

RADU: No, you wouldn't.

Mihai asks Radu to remember how he got into the Art Institute, suggesting that it was with the help of Mihai's connections. But when Radu goes, Mihai admits, "In fact, I didn't do anything," but Radu would never believe that if he told him. And Mihai believes that Flavia will come out all right in the present circumstances.

6. Gabriel is coming home tonight.

A group of friends celebrates Gabriel's homecoming from the hospital. In the flat where he and Rodica live, in honor of the occasion, they act out the trial of Nicolae and Elena Ceaucescu, with Radu and Florina playing the Ceaucescus and Ianos their judge. Florina (as Elena) and Radu (as Ceaucescu) refuse to recognize the existence of the court which has them in custody.

Mary Shultz (Rodica) and Tim Nelson in *Mad Forest*

RADU: The only judges I recognize are the ones I appointed myself.

SOMEONE: You're on trial for genocide.

FLORINA: These people are hooligans. They're in the pay of foreign powers. That one's just come back from America.

ALL: Who gave the order to shoot at Timicoara? What did you have for dinner last night? Why have you got gold taps in your bathroom? Do you shit in a gold toilet? Shitting yourselves now. Why did you pull down my uncle's house? (*Etc.*)

FLORINA: Where's the helicopter?

RADU: On its way.

FLORINA: Have these people arrested and mutilated.

RADU: Maybe just arrested and shot. They are our children.

FLORINA: After all we've done for them. You should kiss my hands. You should drink my bathwater.

ALL: That's enough trial. We find you guilty on all counts. Execution now.

FLORINA: You said there'd be a helicopter, Nicu.

IANOS: Stand up.

FLORINA: Sit down.

> *They are roughly pushed to another place.*

RADU: You can't shoot me. I'm the one who gives the orders to shoot.

FLORINA: We don't recognize being shot.

ALL: Gypsy. Murderer. Illiterate. We've all fucked your wife. We're fucking her now. Let her have it.

> *They all shoot Elena (Florina), who falls dead at once. Gabriel, who is particularly vicious through all this, shoots with his crutch. All make gun noises, then cheer. Ceaucescu (Radu) runs back and forth. They shout again.*

We fucked your wife. Your turn now. Murderer. Bite your throat out.

RADU (*pleading*): Not me, you've shot her, that's enough. I've money in Switzerland, I'll give you the number of my bank account, you can go and get my money—

IANOS: In his legs.

> *They shoot, and Radu falls over, still talking and crawling about.*

RADU: My helicopter's coming, you'll be sorry, let me go to Iran—

IANOS: In the belly.

> *They shoot. Radu collapses further but keeps talking.*

RADU: I'll give you the People's Palace—

IANOS: In the head.

> *They shoot again. He lies still. They all cheer and jeer.*

Radu starts to get up, but they indicate they want him to lie still so they can indulge in more cheering. Finally Radu and Florina get up; meanwhile, Gabriel hits at Ianos (who is hugging Lucia) with his crutch and orders him, "Get your filthy Hungarian hands off her," but suddenly shifts to "Just joking."

7. She had just finished work when Radu came

Radu meets Florina at the hospital, and soon they are quarreling about politics. Radu and his friends are planning a hunger strike. Florina accuses him of wanting to continue being a hero, Radu calls Florina a communist and stalks off, leaving Florina alone with the ghost of a riot victim who has just died of his wounds.

8. We wish you happiness

Florina and Radu's wedding party takes place at a hotel, with numerous guests enjoying a number of separate conversations about the relationships, connivances and some of the perils of post-revolutionary society. Bogdan Vladu observes that Romania needs a strong man to loosen up the traffic jams and now has one in the person of Iliescu. Flavia, hugging Florina, is planning to write a true history of recent events. Radu remarks, "Look at Gaby, crippled for nothing. They've voted the same lot in." Gabriel and Rodina can't find work. Irina advises Lucia to go back to America, to her husband. Bogdan calls Lucia a slut for keeping company with Ianos, a mere Hungarian. Lucia confesses to Florina that she loved Wayne when she first met him but married him only because she'd just lost her job and had no alternative.

After a while and a good many drinks, guests divide into two groups. Bogdan, drunk, tells one group he supports the Peasants Party and the other that he agreed with Ceaucescu that "We're all in the hands of foreign agents."

Mihai, Radu and Florina are joined by Flavia.

MIHAI: The Front wouldn't fix the vote because they knew they were going to win. Everyone appreciates the sacrifice made by youth. The revolution is in safe hands. This isn't a day for worrying, Florina and Radu, you take too much on your-selves. I wish you could let it all go for a little while. Please believe me, I want your happiness.

FLORINA: I know you do.

She kisses him.

RADU: Yes, I know. I appreciate that.

MIHAI: After all, I'm not a monster. Most of the country supports the Front. It's only in my own home it takes courage to say it. We have a government of reconcil-iation.

FLAVIA: Why don't the Front tell the truth and admit they're communists? Nothing to be . . .

MIHAI: Because they're not.

RADU: I don't care what they're called, it's the same people.

FLAVIA: . . . ashamed of in communism, nothing to be . . .

FLORINA: They should have been banned from . . .

MIHAI: That's your idea of freedom, banning people?

FLORINA: . . . standing in the election.

RADU: We've got to have another revolution.

FLAVIA: . . . ashamed of in planning the revolution if they'd just admit it. You never dared speak out against Ceaucescu, Mihai, and you don't dare speak out now. Say it, I'm a communist and so what. Say it, I'm a communist.

RADU: *Jos communismul, jos communismul. Jos Iliescu. Jos tiranul. Jos Iliescu. Jos Iliescu.*

FLORINA: Radu, don't be childish.

> *Bogdan joins in shouting, "Jos communismul," then turns his attention to the other group.*

GABRIEL: The only reason we need an internal security force is if Hungary tried to invade us. We'd need to be sure—

LUCIA: Invade? Are you serious?

IANOS: When we get Transylvania back it's going to be legally, because it's ours.

IRINA: You're not going to marry a Hungarian.

LUCIA: I'm married already.

IANOS: Gaby, the Hungarians started the revolution. Without us you'd still be worshipping Ceaucescu. And now the . . .

> *Gabriel jeers.*

LUCIA: We didn't worship him.

IRINA: Gaby's a hero, Ianos.

IANOS: . . . Romanians worship Iliescu. Who's the opposition? Hungarians.

GABRIEL: That's just voting for your language.

LUCIA: Why shouldn't they have their own schools?

IRINA: And lock Romanian children out in the street. If it wasn't bad enough you going to America, now a Hungarian, and Gaby crippled, and Radu's irresponsible, I worry for Florina.

GABRIEL: If they want to live in Romania they can . . .

LUCIA: In the riots on TV I saw a Hungarian on the . . .

GABRIEL: . . . speak Romanian.

IANOS: We can learn two languages, we're not stupid.

LUCIA: . . . ground and Romanians kicking him.

GABRIEL: That was a Romanian on the ground, and Hungarians—you think we're stupid?

IANOS: You were under the Turks so long, it made you like slaves.

LUCIA: You think I'm a slave? I'm not your slave.

> *Gabriel pushes Ianos, who pushes him back. Bogdan arrives.*

BOGDAN: Leave my son alone. Hungarian bastard. And don't come near my daughter.

IANOS: I'm already fucking your daughter, you stupid peasant.

> *Bogdan hits Ianos.*
> *Radu restrains Bogdan.*

Lucia attacks Bogdan.
Bogdan hits Radu.
Mihai pushes Bogdan.
Bogdan hits Mihai.
Flavia attacks Bogdan.
Ianos pushes Gabriel.
Irina protects Gabriel.
Gabriel hits Ianos.
Radu attacks Bogdan.
Mihai restrains Radu.
Radu attacks Mihai.
Florina attacks Radu.

Gabriel hits out indiscriminately with his crutch and accidentally knocks Bogdan to the floor. Stunned silence.

FLAVIA: This is a wedding. We're forgetting our program. It's time for dancing. *They pick themselves up, see if they are all right. Music—the lambada. Gradually couples form and begin to dance.*

Even the Vampire and the Angel are part of the group, with couples dancing, chatting and finally all talking at once in Rumanian, stating opinions they've stated before. The Vampire has the last words: *"Trebuie sa te misti din ce in ce mai repede"* ("You have to keep moving faster and faster"), as the curtain falls.

MARVIN'S ROOM

A Play in Two Acts

BY SCOTT McPHERSON

Cast and credits appear on pages 328-329

SCOTT McPHERSON was born in Columbus, Ohio October 13, 1959 in a family whose father was in sales and service. After college at Ohio University in Athens, he pursued a career in the theater as both actor and writer. In 1987 his first play, 'Til the Fat Lady Sings, *was produced by the Lifeline Theater in Chicago and won him a Joseph Jefferson Award citation for best new work. His one-act* Scraped *was put on at the Organic Theater, and then his second full-length,* Marvin's Room, *brought him into full cross-country prominence as a playwright. It opened at the Goodman Theater in a Chicago Theater Group production February 9, 1990, after development with the assistance of the Victory Gardens Theater, and was cited by the American Theater Critics Association as one of three outstanding new plays of the 1989-90 season in cross-country theater. It moved on to another production by the Hartford, Conn. Stage Company and to its New York debut at Playwrights Horizons December 5, 1991 and citation as its author's first Best Play.*

McPherson's writing credits also include TV shows for Fox, WGN-TV and NBC and an original screenplay for Norman Lear's Act III, and he prepared a screenplay of Marvin's Room *for Paramount. He was a recipient of a 1991 Whiting Writer's Award and an honorable mention in the 1991 National Arts Club Joseph*

Kesselring Prizes. He died in November of 1992 after a protracted illness.

The following synopsis of Marvin's Room *was prepared by Sally Dixon Wiener.*

Time: The present

Place: Various locations in Florida and a mental institution in Ohio.

ACT I

Scene 1

SYNOPSIS: The basic set is a lighted glass brick wall filling the upstage area and four free-standing lighted glass brick columns, two at stage right. A black door is in the center of the upstage wall, and the floor is also black. Props appear as needed for each scene. Music and sound design unobtrusively contribute to establishing and maintaining the tone of the play.

Bessie, "*a woman of 40 years,*" is in a doctor's examining room with Dr. Wally to have some blood tests to determine whether or not her fatigue and easy bruising are due to a vitamin deficiency. She has an almost naive air of youthful innocence and good will that belie her age. She is slender, attractive and attractively dressed. Dr. Wally, about the same age, is substituting for the vacationing Dr. Serat and is a deliberate caricature of an absent-minded, bumbling physician. He calls Bessie by two other names, including the name of his dog, during the brief scene. He can neither remember the name of the tourniquet or where it is—he's been sitting on it— and he's upset because the receptionist has just quit.

BESSIE: Janine quit?

DR. WALLY: Uh-huh. Did you know her?

BESSIE: Only from here. I bring my father Marvin and my Aunt Ruth in quite a bit to see Dr. Serat. Why did she quit? Is she getting married?

DR. WALLY: No, no. Unbeknownst to any of us, she was harboring a deep-seated phobia about cockroaches. She said she just couldn't work here any longer. It made her itch.

BESSIE (*looks around*): Oh?

DR. WALLY: I think I have seen you out front. Is your father fairly thin?

BESSIE: Dad's a bone. You could snap him like a twig.

DR. WALLY: He's somewhat pale?

BESSIE: He's as white as a bedsheet unless he's choking. Then he gets a little color.

DR. WALLY: He has trouble breathing?

BESSIE: No. He likes to put things in his mouth. I'll walk into his bedroom and he'll be lying there all blue in the face with the Yahtzee dice stuck down his throat . . . . .

DR. WALLY: And your aunt, now this is odd, but I remember she kept staring at my shoes.

BESSIE: Ruth has three collapsed vertebrae in her back.

DR. WALLY: Oh, I'm sorry.

BESSIE: I'm always lugging one of them in here for something or other.

DR. WALLY: I hope they are both all right for the moment.

BESSIE: Oh, they're fine. Dad's dying, but he's been dying for about twenty years. He's doing it real slow so I don't miss anything. And Dr. Serat has worked a miracle with Ruth. She's had constant pain from her back since she was born, and now the doctor had her get an electronic anesthetizer, you know, they put the wires right into the brain, and when she has a bad pain she just turns her dial. It really is a miracle.

DR. WALLY: That's wonderful.

BESSIE: If she uses it in the kitchen our automatic garage door goes up. But that's a small price to pay, don't you think?

DR. WALLY: It's amazing what they can do.

Dr. Wally sets up a number of glass vials for blood, has more in his pocket and looks for more in a drawer. It seems like a lot of blood to Bessie. It *is*, he assures her. He fumbles with the tourniquet, then opens a bag of cotton balls—sterile, he assures her, since the bag is still sealed—with his teeth. Bessie is still reluctant about the test, and he urges her just to look down at the floor. She does and sees a large cockroach. Dr. Wally finally hits it with a magazine. Bessie announces she might prefer to lie down, and Dr. Wally goes off to see if the room is free. Alone, Bessie hikes up her skirts and looks at the large bruise on her thigh. When Dr. Wally returns, he offers her the magazine he'd used to kill the cockroach. The room is free, but Bessie says she will remain seated for the tests.

Scene 2

"Bessie's home. Marvin lies in a bed behind the upstage wall, barely visible through glass bricks. Ruth, a woman of 70 years with a slight hunchback, sleeps in a chair. Bessie enters with groceries. Her arms are bruised from the doctor's attempts to draw blood."

Bessie places the groceries on the unit kitchen at stage left and goes to wake her Aunt Ruth, who is not supposed to sleep sitting up in her chair because it puts pressure on her lower spine. Ruth, a pleasant and cheerful-enough woman who is almost childlike in her dependency upon Bessie, blames herself for not knowing she was asleep and is also concerned that her control box is making a hole in her sweater.

Ruth is worried about Bessie, but Bessie says she just has a vitamin deficiency. "It's because you don't make stinky often enough," Ruth believes.

It seems Ruth has not only forgotten to give Marvin his 5 o'clock pill, but the 4 o'clock medication as well. Ruth blames it on her cure, the wires in her brain, but Bessie won't let her use that as an excuse. Ruth never forgets what time her soap opera program comes on.

RUTH: You usually give Marvin his pills.

BESSIE: Today I asked you to.

> *Bessie goes into Marvin's room to give him his pills while Ruth crosses to the kitchen to get her vitamins.*

I have been running all over today. Would you quit hogging the bed so I can sit down. Here. Take these now. We're a little off schedule today. Have you been pulling at your sheets? You've got them all twisted. That can't be very comfortable. What does that face mean? Mr. Innocent. How about some tomato soup? And some juice? Water? Juice? Which? Juice.

> *Reenters.*

He's confused. He doesn't know why he's getting his four o'clock at five thirty.

RUTH (*with pills*): Do you want to take one of mine for your deficiency?

BESSIE: I'll get some real vitamins later.

RUTH: These are real. They're just easier to swallow because I don't like to swallow things. Do you want Pebbles or Bam-Bam?

BESSIE: Ruth . . . . .

RUTH: I know you have things you have to do, and it's hard getting someone to come in, but I wish you wouldn't leave me at home alone.

BESSIE: Honey, you do fine.

RUTH: But I'm so useless. What if Marvin were to choke on something again? What if he gets hold of the Yahtzee dice or tries to kill himself with the Parcheesi men?

BESSIE: Dr. Serat explained this to you. He puts things in his mouth because it gives him pleasure. He likes the way it feels. You know how much he likes it when you bounce the light off your compact mirror? This is another thing he likes. He's not trying to choke himself.

RUTH: What if he dies while you're out of the house?

BESSIE: Then you'll call me and I'll come home.

> *Pause.*

You've got your cure now. There's no reason you can't help out around here. I don't ask you to do much.

RUTH: Do you want me to make the tomato soup?

BESSIE: No. You'd make a mess of it.

> *Bessie starts to make the soup.*

RUTH: I'll go bounce the light around Marvin's room.

BESSIE: That's a good idea. Why don't you do that. And later we'll watch some TV. All right?

Ruth is in Marvin's room bouncing the light around, as Bessie prepares the soup, reminiscing about the things her father used to like, flapjacks and bacon and eggs, grits and biscuits, roast beef, green beans, mashed potatoes and apple pie, and ice cream he churned himself. As the scene ends, *the bouncing light in Marvin's room is the last to go out.*

Scene 3

Bessie is alone in the doctor's office when Dr. Wally comes on with a bicycle wheel, not having been able to locate a place to lock his bike. She's nervous about the test results which they would not give her on the telephone—not their policy, Dr. Wally explains, and also he wanted to see her again, to run some other tests. It seems a vitamin deficiency has been ruled out. What Dr. Wally, in between ludicrous phone interruptions from the new receptionist (his brother, Bob, it is revealed), has in mind is to give her a local anesthetic and then remove a little bone marrow from her hip.

DR. WALLY: You won't really feel it. Maybe a slight pinching. Now, it will make a little noise so don't let that bother you.

BESSIE: You're going to take bone marrow out of my hip?

DR. WALLY: Just a little. There will be a crunching noise. If you've ever had your wisdom teeth pulled, you know the sound. And you also know that it sounds worse than it is.

BESSIE: I've never had my wisdom teeth out.

DR. WALLY: Really. Hmmmm. Maybe you should see someone.

BESSIE: I've never had a problem with them.

DR. WALLY: . . . . . Could you hike up your dress, please?

BESSIE: I don't mean to be nosey, but could you tell me why you're going to take bone marrow out of my hip?

DR. WALLY: There's not a lot of flesh on the hip.

BESSIE: But what is the test for?

DR. WALLY: Why don't you let me do the worrying for now?

BESSIE: I am probably thinking it's something much worse than it actually is.

DR. WALLY: I wouldn't waste your time thinking anything until we get the test results back.

BESSIE: Is it serious like a brain tumor?

DR. WALLY: No, no.

BESSIE: M.S.?

DR. WALLY: No.

BESSIE: Cancer?

    Pause.

Cancer?

Dr. Wally doesn't answer her question, but he does want to explain about her blood test. He has difficulty getting to the point, which is that her blood work shows abnormally low levels of red cells, platelets and mature white cells. Also, her spleen and liver, on her last visit, were slightly enlarged. One of the possibilities he hopes to rule out, he confesses, is leukemia. Bessie wonders if leukemia is still fatal. Dr. Wally asks what she means by that. She means, "Does it still kill you?" she tells him patiently. There are different kinds of leukemia and different treatments, he explains, including bone marrow transplants. He asks about her family; her file mentions a sister, Dr. Wally recalls. Bessie admits she does have a sister, Lee. Bob arrives with coffee for Bessie and exits. Dr. Wally tells her to drink it as he waits, needle in hand.

Scene 4

"*An institutional visiting room. There are three chairs. A doctor sits in one. Lee, a woman in her late 30s, sits in another.*" It is visiting day and Lee, Bessie's sister, has come to see her older son, Hank, at the mental institution where he is confined. Lee is tense. Despite the no-smoking rules, reiterated by the woman psychiatrist who is in charge of Hank's therapy, Dr. Charlotte, Lee lights up a cigarette and is smoking as she waits for Hank to arrive from occupational therapy in another building. She wants the psychiatrist to know, in order for her to help with his therapy, that Hank lies. Lee assumes Hank has been saying bad things about her. Dr. Charlotte, who produces an ashtray at Lee's request, wishes Lee would get involved in Hank's therapy and wants her to visit more often.

LEE: Doctor, can I be honest with you? What is your first name?
DR. CHARLOTTE: Charlotte.
LEE: Oh, my youngest boy's a Charlie.
DR. CHARLOTTE: Yes.
LEE: Charlotte. I've forced myself through school, and I'm about to get my degree. I'm very picky now about the kind of man I'll go with. I keep—I used to keep a very clean house. Hank makes fun of my degree in cosmetology. He terrorizes any man I'm interested in. This last one, Lawrence, Hank made fun of his being on parole, made fun of the way he held his liquor, made fun of his Pinto. The point is, Hank cost me a potentially good relationship. And as for my house . . . Hank is not something I can control, so what is the point of my visiting?
DR. CHARLOTTE: He says he misses you.
Hank enters. He is a big 17-year-old covered with motor grease.
HANK: Hey.
LEE: Look at you. You look like a pig.
HANK: I'm working on an engine.
LEE: Don't they let you shower?
HANK: They told me you were here and I was suppose to come here.
LEE: Don't sit down, Hank.
He sits.

You'll get the chair all greasy.
> *Slight pause.*

Are you behaving yourself?

HANK: They're not strapping me down anymore.

LEE: Well, don't abuse that privilege. You want an M & M? I got some in my purse.

HANK: Where's Charlie? He didn't come?

LEE: He has a class in geometry.

HANK: He's already taken remedial geometry.

LEE: This is a makeup class in remedial geometry. (*To the doctor.*) Charlie's not doing too well in school.

DR. CHARLOTTE: Mm-hmm.

LEE: They say it's because he reads too much. Do you want—
> *Lee holds out M & M bag.*

DR. CHARLOTTE: No, thank you.

LEE: So, are you behaving yourself?

HANK: I told you yes.

LEE: All right, I'm just asking.

Hank is curious as to why his mother is visiting, since she hasn't before. She doesn't have to have a reason, Lee insists, and besides she has been there before, but he'd been unconscious. Dr. Charlotte reports that he's off Thorizine now and would probably be alert any visiting day. Unfortunately, Saturday, the visiting day, is difficult for Lee. "We're still living in the basement of the church because of our house," she reports, and on Saturday she helps when the nuns make the Communion hosts.

Dr. Charlotte asks Lee if the nuns wouldn't understand if she said she needed to visit her son. She's there today, Lee defends herself. She puts another M & M in Hank's mouth and admits she's come to tell him something, although she was planning to come anyway. It isn't good news, Lee admits, but Hank's doctor has said it's all right to tell him, and anyway she hasn't any choice. It's his Aunt Bessie in Florida. She has leukemia, isn't doing well and might die. Hank doesn't know who Lee is talking about. Bessie is her sister, Lee reminds Hank, and finally Hank recalls Lee mentioning at Christmas how "it looks like Bessie didn't send a card this year either." Hank wants another M & M. Lee obliges, then goes on to explain that as Bessie's nearest relatives they are to be tested to see if their bone marrow is compatible because her life might be saved if they do a bone marrow transplant. They'd been supposed to go to Florida but couldn't afford it, so the tests will be done here and sent down. A simple test and not supposed to be too painful, Lee tells him. Hank doesn't know his aunt, he reminds Lee, and why should he let them do something to him?

LEE: This is my sister we are talking about. And maybe I haven't mentioned her to you before, but that doesn't mean that she isn't on my mind a lot, and we are not going to just let her die because you want to have one of your moods. Do you understand? Now they say they can do your test up here so . . .

> *Hank has walked away and turned his back.*

Well, I have to go. It's good to see you, Hank.

HANK: You coming next week?

LEE: I don't know. It's the Feast of the Ascension. It gets kind of busy.

DR. CHARLOTTE: Hank, is there anything you want to say to your mother?

LEE: Will it take long? Because I'm already late.

HANK: No, I just—well, I'm really sorry I burnt the house down.

LEE: Is that it? 'cause I am really late. Okay, Hank. Well, you be good now. I'd leave you these, but they're Charlie's. I just took them with me for the drive. Here, I'll leave you some here. Then when you get cleaned up you can come back for them.

> *She pours out some M & Ms on the seat of the chair.*

Okay, well, we'll see you, and Bessie's doctor should be calling you.

DR. CHARLOTTE: We'll be waiting.

When Lee goes off, Dr. Charlotte lights a cigarette, takes a deep puff, and remarks, "Good session."

Scene 5

Bessie, in a hospital bed, is wearing a wig. Ruth has come to visit her and sits in a chair next to the bed. Bessie is concerned at Ruth having come so far to see her and thinks she shouldn't make the long walk again. Ruth reminds Bessie she visited her every day when she was in the hospital for her cure. But she's needed at home, Bessie points out.

Bessie asks if her father misses her, and Ruth confesses she hasn't told Marvin that Bessie is in the hospital. She didn't know what to say. When he asks where Bessie is, Ruth tells him she's busy in the other room. When he goes to sleep and then wakes up, Ruth tells him Bessie's just been in his room. Bessie is put out at Ruth, but Ruth claims he would be upset if he knew.

There is a nurse at the house, and Bessie asks who her father thinks that is. Ruth pretends she doesn't notice the nurse, as if she didn't exist. As for what Bessie's father thinks, Ruth believes he thinks he is hallucinating. She was trying to tell him Bessie was in the hospital, but the nurse came in before she was ready to, so she didn't. He must be told, Bessie insists. Ruth claims he is used to it by now. He only seems bothered when the nurse carries him to the bath. "And I say oh look, Marvin, you're flying." Bessie's concerned that her father must think he is losing his mind. That's better than telling him, Ruth believes. Ruth would not know what to say.

BESSIE: Tell him that I'm going to be fine, and I'll be home soon, and there's no reason to be upset.

RUTH: You want me to tell him?

BESSIE: Yes. Because there's no reason to be upset. I'm going to be fine, Ruth. I know I am.

RUTH: Nothing happens that God doesn't have a reason for.

BESSIE: I'm sure He does.

RUTH: He tries to teach us things. He tries to reach down and shake us out of our ignorance.

BESSIE: I'm sure that's it.

RUTH: I know He made me crippled for a reason. He wants me to learn something. It may be patience or it may be forbearance or it may be how to dress without standing up. He doesn't tell you what it is, you just have to learn it.

BESSIE: I don't think it's how to dress.

RUTH: Oh, it wouldn't surprise me. I often ask Him why I'm crippled. I also ask Him why he let Marvin buy this house down here to take care of me, then strike Marvin with a stroke. Why? And then have him lose his colon to cancer. Why? And then lose the sight in one eye and the use of one kidney and yet keep a full head of hair. Why?

BESSIE: I don't know.

RUTH: But God knows. He has His reasons. And I'm not upset.

BESSIE: Then tell Dad his nurse is not a hallucination and that I am not in the other room.

RUTH: I think he's starting to enjoy flying.

BESSIE: And I don't want you to visit me again. It's too hard on you.

Bessie changes the subject to ask Ruth if she wouldn't like to see her soap opera, which Bessie's been watching, too, since she's been in the hospital. Bessie wants to see if Lance is going to propose to Coral. Ruth, getting up on the bed with Bessie, claims Lance and Coral really love each other. He *is* the one who raped Coral at some point, but "that was months ago. He's really a nice boy." "*The soap opera theme swells as the lights fade.*"

Scene 6

Bessie is in Marvin's room changing his sheets when Lee comes on, calling, with suitcases. Ruth, preoccupied with her television program, has failed to heed the doorbell. Bessie seems surprised that her sister seems much older. If Lee's that old, how old does it make her? she wonders. Lee assures Bessie she looks good and that she likes her hair. It's a wig, from the chemo, Bessie admits. Lee's wearing a fall, she confides.

When Bessie goes off briefly to put the sheets to soak, Lee goes to the entrance of Marvin's room and calls to him, telling him who she is, that they've come all the way from Ohio after all, because the nuns had a big bake sale for them to pay their way. She steps into the room briefly to greet him, then comes out, a little upset. She lights up a cigarette, which concerns Bessie. The oxygen tanks. Lee could smoke in the garage, or the yard. She doesn't have to smoke, Lee assures her. Upon learning that a nurse had been staying at the house while Bessie was in the hospital, Lee writes a check. Bessie demurs, saying they've "gotten by this long." But she's glad Lee is here now.

Bessie wonders if Lee was able to get Hank out of the mental institution for the trip. "We call it the looney bin or the nut house to show we've got a sense of humor about it," Lee apprises her. In any event, Hank and Charlie are here, outside, sitting in the car. Bessie goes off to dress her father and make him ready for Lee to see him, and Ruth comes in. Lee and Ruth great each other fondly. Ruth wants to get back to her program, but first wants a hug from Lee, then a bigger hug. But the second hug hurts Ruth, and as she turns her dial we hear the garage door going up.

Lee has brought cookies left over from the bake sale, but Ruth is not allowed sugar. Bessie is attempting to stay away from that now, too. Their father still has a

Laura Esterman as Bessie in *Marvin's Room*

sweet tooth, yes, but that makes "his diabetes all the more frustrating."

Hank's sitting out in the car is an example of his doing things to get attention, Lee explains to Bessie. And Lee has been told to ignore it or to give Hank an ultimatum. Bessie wonders about Charlie. It seems he "just goes along with Hank. Or he might be reading." Bessie suggests she could ask them to come in. Lee says no: "If we ask them in I have to be prepared to make him come in," and she's not feeling up to it. She also reveals that Hank has not yet agreed to be tested for the transplant. Bessie indicates her disappointment and doesn't think they can have Hank do something he doesn't want to do. Lee agrees, then says she will make him if she has to. Bessie points out Lee can't even make him come in from the driveway, and Lee goes off. Bessie sees the check, tears it up and puts the pieces on the counter top.

Lee returns and asks to use the phone to call the police. Bessie and Ruth, who's come on again, wonder what's happened. It's just that she had to give Hank an ultimatum, Lee explains. Couldn't she just tell him no television? Bessie wonders. He burned the television, Lee relates, and asks for the police number. It's on the list of emergency numbers, Bessie points out. As Lee dials, Hank and Charlie come in, Charlie engrossed in a book. Lee thanks Hank for coming in. Hank explains, "They were doing a top-ten countdown, and we wanted to hear number one." Why hadn't he said that? Lee wonders. Hank isn't sure, but she had been shouting and it hadn't "seemed like the time."

Bessie doesn't care if Hank is all grown up, she's his aunt and expects a big fat hug. Hank obliges and then hugs Ruth as well, and, as she mutters "Oh Jesus," she turns her dial, and we hear the garage again. Hank is upset until it's explained. Bessie greets Charlie, and they hug as well, but Charlie cautiously extends a hand to Ruth instead of hugging her.

They all go into Marvin's room, and we can hear Marvin muttering. Bessie tells him it's Lee, his daughter, and that the boys are his grandkids, and he shouldn't be frightened. It seems it's a bit much, and they leave the room, except for Ruth.

Bessie explains to Lee and the boys that she's in remission, "the best time for a transplant," and thanks them for coming, appreciative of the fact that it's a lot to ask of someone to donate bone marrow. Charlie allows as how it sounds fine to him, and Hank claims he's thinking about it, "That's all." Lee's appointment is at 3 p.m. Bessie points out to the boys that the chances are better that their mother would be a match, so she'll be tested first, and maybe they will not have to be tested.

CHARLIE (*disappointed*): Really?
>   *Hank picks up a potato chip out of a bowl.*
LEE: Hank, did Bessie offer you a chip yet?
BESSIE: Oh, that's what they're there for.
LEE: He has to wait to be asked, Bessie. Put the chip back, Hank.
>   *Pause.*

Put it back.
>   *Pause.*

Put back the chip.
>   *Pause. Lee crumbles the chip in Hank's hand.*

BESSIE: Lee, I put them out for the kids.

LEE: You have to understand, he has to wait to be asked.

BESSIE: Hank, would you like a chip?

HANK: No, thank you, Aunt Bessie. Not right now.

LEE: Your aunt offered you a chip, the polite thing to do would be to take it.

HANK: I don't want one right now.

LEE: Eat a chip or no Disney World.

HANK: I could give a fuck about Disney World.

LEE: That's it. Get out of my sight. I don't care where. Just so I can't see you.
>   *Hank exits the house. Pause.*

BESSIE: Charlie, would you like a chip?
>   *Charlie looks at his mom.*

LEE: Go ahead, honey, if you want one.

BESSIE: Take a bunch.
>   *Charlie grabs a handful.*

LEE: Not too many. You'll spoil your lunch.
>   *Charlie puts them all back but one. He is about to bite it.*

Don't make crumbs on your aunt's nice floor.
>   *Charlie sucks on the chip. Pause.*

CHARLIE: Can I go watch Grandpa breathe?

LEE: Charlie, don't word things that way.

BESSIE: Sure you can.

Charlie goes into Marvin's room. Ruth reminds Marvin who Charlie is and shows Charlie how to bounce the light around Marvin's wall.

Lee is apologetic, but she's doing what the doctor told her to do. She sees the torn-up check and is disappointed. Bessie again reminds her that she's glad she's there, but that they've been doing well by themselves for all this time, "Not because we wanted to"—that was Lee's choice.

As Lee looks out the window she sees Hank and screams "Hank, I can see you!!"

Scene 7

"Late at night in the back yard. Hank is examining tools in an old toolbox. Bessie enters with a cup of coffee." She is surprised to find Hank outside at such a late hour, but they strike up a tentative conversation. If she wants him to go inside, Hank will, he tells her. Bessie doesn't, as long as his mother doesn't care (his mother's asleep). Bessie asks him not to tell his Aunt Ruth that she goes outside at night, as it could make her nervous. Ruth is his great aunt, Bessie's aunt, and

Marvin's his grandfather—a whole new family, Hank remarks. Bessie repeats she's glad he is here. Hank replies with "Yeah, we should do it again in another seventeen years."

The Florida nights like this are nice, she muses, remembering it used to be possible to see a little of the Gulf from the yard before the elementary school was built. She rather shyly mentions that she and his mother haven't always gotten along. That's the reason she hasn't been in touch often.

Bessie commends Hank for the work he's done that afternoon. He was bored, Hank admits, but he managed to get the Monopoly hotels loose that were crammed into Marvin's respirator, making it rattle. Bessie wishes Hank could have known his grandfather before, that Marvin would have enjoyed having a boy around.

Hank asks Bessie if she ever wishes Marvin would die, upsetting Bessie. She asks Hank what he was doing with the tools. He was going to return them, he assures her. Bessie didn't think he was stealing them and offers them to him if he'd like to have them. He can't believe she would give these wonderful old implements to him. It was his grandfather's toolbox, and Bessie thinks Marvin would like Hank to have it. Hank is afraid they won't allow him to keep them—the hospital, he explains. Bessie reminds him that he won't be there forever. Hank reveals that when he gets back they're moving him to an adult place because he is turning 18 in three weeks.

BESSIE: Oh. Happy birthday.

HANK: Thanks. If the fire hadn't spread up the street it wouldn't be such a big deal.

BESSIE: Uh-huh.

HANK: Or if melting plastic didn't give off noxious fumes. Now they want to be sure I'm not a threat.

BESSIE: You're not a threat. I'm sure they'll see that. You're probably the best one there.

HANK: There's this one dude on my floor held a razor blade under his tongue for five hours. Talked to the orderlies and ate and everything.

BESSIE: Why on earth would he do that?

HANK: He was trying to break my record.

BESSIE: Hank. What do you want to be when you grow up?

HANK: I am grown up.

BESSIE: When I look at you I see a lost little boy.

HANK: Then get your eyes checked.

    Pause.

So Marvin liked to fix stuff?

BESSIE: Maybe that's where you get it from. He used to make your mom so mad. He'd leave the radio lying in pieces. She liked to turn it up and dance wild around the house.

HANK: Mom liked to dance?

BESSIE: You bet.

HANK (*taking photo from toolbox*): Hey, who is this?

BESSIE: Let me see.

    Looking at photo together.

That's your grandmother.

HANK: Looks kind of like Mom.

BESSIE: She takes after her. Your grandfather used to have this taped above his workbench.

HANK: She's young.

BESSIE: She was young. Do you want this too?

HANK: I don't care.

BESSIE: Then I'll keep it.

In answer to Hank's question as to whether Bessie had known his father, Bessie says she met him only once. She'd left Florida to go home to sell the rest of her things and went to her sister's, curious to meet him, but only saw him asleep on the couch. When Bessie left he was still sleeping.

Hank confesses he doesn't think he'll have the bone marrow test and wants Bessie's reaction. She wonders why he won't. He claims there's no reason.

BESSIE: Did Ruth thank you for fixing the garage door?

HANK: Yeah.

BESSIE: That was very nice of you.

HANK: Nobody ever does anything to be nice. That's what my therapist says.

BESSIE: He does?

HANK: People don't just do things. They get something for it.

BESSIE: He says that?

HANK: Yeah.

BESSIE: And you believe him?

HANK: Yeah.

BESSIE: Why have I spent the last twenty years of my life down here. Because I enjoyed it? Because I got something out of it?

HANK: Yeah, or you wouldn't do it.

BESSIE: No, Hank, no. Sometimes I can barely . . . no.

HANK: First time I hear from you is when you need something.

BESSIE: Hank—

HANK: Maybe you did it because maybe you thought you'd never land a husband. Or maybe you just wanted to hide out. When you're not around, a nursing home will do it for the cash.

BESSIE: Your mom wouldn't let them go to a home.

HANK: Why not? She doesn't give a shit about anybody.

Lee is calling Hank from off. Hank asks Bessie where she wants him to put the tools. She insists they're his. Before he goes off she tells him he's her nephew and she loves him no matter what he's decided about the test. She is alone in the yard as the scene ends. *Curtain.*

ACT II

Scene 1

"Bessie and Lee wait in the consulting room of a retirement home. A bowl of candies sits on the table." Their conversation is desultory as they await the return of the retirement home Director, a woman upscale in appearance and officious in manner.

DIRECTOR (*enters and joins Bessie and Lee*): Let me try to explain it again.

LEE: I understood what you were saying.

DIRECTOR: Then for your sister's benefit.

BESSIE: You're saying I couldn't afford to put Dad and Ruth in this nursing home even if I wanted to.

DIRECTOR: That's not what I'm saying.

LEE: It's not?

DIRECTOR: No.

LEE: What are you saying?

DIRECTOR: Let me say this, what does it matter what I'm saying if you have no interest in this institution?

LEE: I didn't say that.

DIRECTOR: She did.

LEE: She didn't mean it.

BESSIE: I think I did.

LEE: Where do you want them to end up, Bessie? At county? For recreation they push the wheelchairs into the hall and let you watch the medicine carts roll by. Here they have computer games. They have nerf basketball.

DIRECTOR: We have a video library. Sing-alongs. Date nights.

BESSIE: Who is Dad going to date?

DIRECTOR: You'd be surprised. Women outnumber men five to one.

LEE: This is the best place we've seen.

BESSIE: We can't afford it, so why are we talking?

DIRECTOR: I never said that.

BESSIE: What did you say?

DIRECTOR: Let me get something that might help.

    Exits.

While the Director is off again, Lee acknowledges that this is hard on her sister. Bessie shouldn't be depressed about Lee's results, because Lee is sure Charlie will match. Therefore Bessie will be fine, and none of this means anything.

Bessie must get Charlie to Dr. Wally's and also get to the drug store before it closes. There's time, Lee assures her, and Lee can take Charlie herself. Bessie has more energy than she does, Lee marvels. She wouldn't last a week having to handle their father and Ruth. Bessie claims it's not hard, but Lee insists she's done amazing things and ought to be proud. She's only done "what anybody would do," Bessie demurs. Lee will get her degree next quarter, and Bessie thinks she should be proud of that. Lee has had a free-lance job for a day doing hair for a television commercial. She asks Bessie to guess how much she made, and Bessie guesses three hundred dollars. Lee's disappointed. She'd hoped Bessie would pick a lower figure. But that's a lot of money, Bessie reassures her. Lee agrees and admits to feeling as if her life is finally beginning.

Lee asks Bessie if she'd like a candy, and then decides she'll take them all, for the boys. They've been kept waiting by the Director for so long it will serve her right, she believes. Bessie tries to dissuade Lee—"She'll notice they're gone." But Lee dumps the candies into her purse, claiming the director would be too embarrassed to accuse them of stealing them. Bessie is shocked and tries to get Lee to put them back.

Bessie remarks that Dad would never have approved of what they're considering, recalling how he cared for their mother. Lee insists they're doing the right thing by looking into their options. Why can't Lee take Dad and Ruth? Bessie wonders. Lee doesn't think the nuns would appreciate that. Lee could move to Florida, Bessie points out, and could have the house. Lee thinks not—she has Hank on her hands. Bessie claims he's unhappy where he is, and Lee could find a place for him in Florida. Lee could find work here, Bessie argues.

LEE: No.
BESSIE: Give me one good reason.
LEE: Just no.
BESSIE: Why?
LEE: Because I don't want to.
     Pause.
I made this decision once already. When Daddy had his first stroke, I made this decision then. I wasn't going to waste my life.
BESSIE: You think I've wasted my life?
LEE: Of course not.
BESSIE: I can't imagine a better way to have spent my life.
LEE: Then we both made the right decision.
BESSIE: You are the most . . .
LEE: Say it. You've been saying it a million different ways since I got down here.
BESSIE: I have not. I have bent over backwards to avoid having this conversation with you.

LEE: What conversation?
> *Pause. Bessie opens her purse and puts about a dollar's change in the candy bowl.*

What are you doing?

BESSIE: I'm paying her for them.

LEE: Put that back.

BESSIE: I'm not going to steal them. That's wrong.

LEE: It's not wrong.

BESSIE: Wrong is wrong.

LEE: It's your money.

The Director returns, telling them they don't qualify for any of the various aid programs available, but that only means they have to drop into a lower income bracket. They must deplete savings by spending them on non-asset acquisitions, including the home equity. They must spend savings and home equity on "something that has no resale value and cannot be considered an asset." Seventy per cent of the institution's residents have qualified in this manner. Lee is curious as to what they buy. For most of them, the perfect solution has been the purchase of elaborate tombstones.

Bessie leaves. Lee asks the Director if there is something she can take with her. *"The Director reaches to pick up a brochure off the table, sees the money in the candy bowl, and looks at Lee."*

Scene 2

Hank and Charlie are in the waiting room with Dr. Wally and his receptionist Bob. Charlie wants to be tested first and goes off with Dr. Wally. Bob has gone off as well when Bessie arrives. Lee, it is revealed, is visiting the mall. Hank admits to Bessie he will probably be tested, too. Bessie, making conversation, remarks that these are new offices, that bugs had infested the old ones. Bugs don't bother Hank, he brags, going on and on about one of his eleven roommates catching bugs and putting them on hair leashes. Increasingly carried away, he tells other stories, climaxing with one about doing an emergency tracheotomy with a piece of bark and a pen after a mudsliding accident. Bessie asks why he makes up the stories. He wasn't, Hank protests. And why did he put her through pretending he wasn't going to be tested. Why the lies?

Hank starts another story, and Bessie interrupts—if it's another tall tale she doesn't want to hear it. They look at magazines briefly. Hank finally mentions he was fourth in the pool tournament in his ward. Had his mother told Bessie that? No, Bessie says, but she thinks it's great. Gradually Hank begins to open up.

HANK: Most of the time I keep to myself. Most of the time I sit in my room. I've got a roommate, but most of the time he's got his face to the wall. Most of the time I think about not being there. I think what it would be like to be someone else.

Someone I see on the TV or in a magazine, or even walking free on the grounds. They can keep me as long as they want. It's not like a prison term. I've already been there longer than most. A lot of the time I think about getting this house with all this land around it. And I'd get a bunch of dogs, no little ones you might step on but big dogs, like a horse, and I'd let them run wild. They'd never know a leash. And I'd build a go-cart track on my property. Charge people to race around on it. Those places pull in the bucks. I'd be raking it in. And nobody would know where I was. I'd be gone. Most of the time I just want to be some place else.

BESSIE: Why aren't you?

HANK: Huh?

BESSIE: Why aren't you some place else?

HANK: What do you mean?

BESSIE: Do you want to be in there?

HANK: No way.

BESSIE: Then why are you?

HANK: I've got no choice.

BESSIE: You're the one who told me people only do what they want.

HANK: Yeah.

BESSIE: So you must want to be there.

HANK: No. No way.

BESSIE: Then show them you don't need to be in there.

HANK: It's not easy like that. People start thinking of you a certain way, and pretty soon, you're that way.

BESSIE: So there's nothing you can do?

HANK: It's hard, that's all.

BESSIE: I don't want you wasting your life in there.

HANK: Neither do I.

BESSIE: Then why are you still there?

HANK: They put me there.

BESSIE: Why'd they put you there?

HANK: 'Cause I burned down the house.

Bessie is asking Hank why he burned down the house when they are interrupted by Dr. Wally, who has come for Hank. As Dr. Wally goes off, Hank asks Bessie if she'll go with him.

Scene 3

"Bessie's home. Night. Charlie and Hank on the floor in sleeping bags." The boys' brief discussion, revealing they are looking forward to going to Walt Disney World, ends as Bessie comes into the kitchen area to get some coffee. Lee comes on, turns the light on and catches Bessie without her wig on. As Lee pours juice and vodka into a glass, Bessie hurries off, then returns, wearing her wig, and they chat quietly. Bessie has a way with Hank, Lee points out. She just talks to him,

Bessie claims. Lee wants to talk Bessie into letting her style her wig for her.

Bessie hopes that Lee has someone in her life. Lee claims there's no reason Bessie hasn't had love in hers—she's not ugly. Boys took an interest in her, but thought Bessie was "stuck up." She didn't encourage them, Lee nags. Bessie confesses she did have "a true love," and, yes, he did know it. It was not someone Lee knew. When Lee can't understand how she couldn't have known about this, Bessie finally reveals his name. He was only there during the summers, and Lee realizes it must have been a carny worker. "Daddy would have killed you," Lee remarks. That is why Bessie kept the relationship a secret. Lee admits there were some carny workers who were cute and wonders which one took Bessie's fancy. The one who usually ran the Ferris wheel, it seems.

BESSIE: He always said he probably came from England because of his name. Clarence James. He'd make a big deal out of his manners. He had the funniest laugh. He'd open his mouth real wide, and no sound would come out.

LEE: He was only there about three summers.

BESSIE: Four summers.

LEE: Then he stopped coming.

BESSIE: That's right.

> *Pause.*

LEE: What happened?

BESSIE: Nothing like you think.

LEE: What happened?

BESSIE: They always have a last picnic down by the river. This year there was a kind of a cold snap, so a lot of people were bundled up. But Clarence, he'll deny it, but he likes to be the center of attention. Clarence goes swimming anyway. And he knows everybody is watching him. Everybody is there, his family, his friends, me. And he bobs up out of the water, and he's laughing, making that monkey face, which gets all of us laughing, and he dunks under again and pops up somewhere else laughing even harder, which gets us laughing even harder. And he dives under again, and then he doesn't come up and doesn't come up and he doesn't come up. Laughing and choking looked the same on Clarence. He drowned right in front of us. Every time he came up for air, there we were chuckling and pointing. What could he have thought?

LEE: Bessie, you should have told me.

BESSIE: If I couldn't tell people I had a carny boyfriend, I couldn't tell people my carny boyfriend drowned.

LEE: You should have told me anyway.

BESSIE: We were never that close.

LEE: Weren't we?

BESSIE: No.

Again Lee asks if Bessie would like her to do something with the wig. Bessie is reluctant but finally gives Lee the wig, and Lee has a chance to see the effects of Bessie's chemotherapy. She tells Bessie she's glad they've made the trip down. They are interrupted by Ruth. Bessie ties a scarf over her head as Ruth comes in to explain that she'd gone to Bessie's room and found her gone and was upset. Bessie reassures her and Lee watches as Ruth and Bessie hug each other.

Scene 4

Hank is sitting on a bench at Walt Disney World when Lee comes on with two cokes which they drink as they talk, waiting for the others to join them. Lee remarks on how huge the Swiss Family Robinson tree house is and recalls taking the boys to the movie. Hank doesn't remember that but recalls that his father took them to *Planet of the Apes*. Lee says *she* took them to that movie, and Hank is surprised. It was a good movie, he then remarks. Lee's glad he liked it. She asks him if he's having a good time and also remarks that she's proud of him for getting tested for Bessie. Hank seems restless and announces that he and Charlie want to go to Space Mountain. Lee agrees they will, but Hank means they want to go by themselves.

LEE: No. Uh-uh. I've already gone back on my ultimatum just letting you come. I think you're doing really well this trip. I think everyone is going to hear how well you did. I think it will mean a lot to them. For the most part your behavior down here has made me very happy, but no.
    Pause.
That submarine ride. Now, that's a movie too.
    HANK: Did we see that one?
    LEE: Did you?
    She tries hard to remember.
I don't think so. I don't remember.
    HANK: With Dad?
    LEE: No, no, no, not with your dad. Do you like apes? Do you like animals?
    Hank stands and hurls his coke offstage. He sits.
Hank! You're not getting another one.
    Pause.
Do you want to know something about your dad? On Saturdays I worked, and your dad took care of you.
    HANK: He did?
    LEE: Yeah. And sometimes on Saturdays you'd get hurt. And I know you roughhoused too much. And I'd yell at you for roughhousing too much, but you'd still get hurt. And I started leaving my job early so I could get home, and . . . I'd yell at you and yell at you and beg you to please stop hurting yourself, because he was my husband, and I loved him and what was I supposed to do? Then Charlie came and I just . . .
    Pause.
My feelings for you, Hank, are like a big bowl of fish hooks. I can't just pick them

Laura Esterman (Bessie) and Lisa Emery (Lee) with Alice Drummond (Ruth, *in foreground*) in a scene from *Marvin's Room* by Scott McPherson

up one at a time. I pick up one, they all come. So I tend to leave them alone.

Charlie, in a Goofy cap, arrives, pushing Ruth in a wheelchair. Ruth is ecstatic, Mickey Mouse had pushed her chair for a bit. She enjoyed the Hall of Presidents— "It was so nice to see F.D.R. again." Lee starts to complain when Charlie begins reading a book, then tells him it doesn't matter. Bessie, who has been getting cokes for everyone, comes on in her newly-styled wig. She enjoyed the Hall of Presidents, too—"It was kind of fun to see J.F.K. again."

Ruth points out to Lee that one of the cartoon characters is nearby if she wants a picture taken with him. Lee thinks it might be Pluto. Hank doesn't want his picture taken with "some mutant." Lee sets off anyway to ask him to come over. Hank suggests to Charlie they go to Space Mountain, but Bessie doubts their mother would want them to go off alone. They argue, but Hank finally accedes to Bessie's wishes. Lee returns, complaining the cartoon character was rude and pretended not to understand what she wanted. The others are ready to go on, but Bessie begs off. She wants to sit in the sun for a while. She agrees to meet them in an hour at Space Mountain, and they go off.

"Bessie shuts her eyes and breathes deeply. She is not feeling well. The feeling passes. She sips her coke from a straw. It comes away bloody. She puts her finger in her mouth. More blood. She stares at it. She puts her hand to her mouth. There is blood in her mouth. It gets on her hand. She stands as if to go. A cartoon character enters as Bessie faints and falls to the ground. The cartoon character turns and walks toward the audience waving as the lights fade."

Scene 5

Bessie is lying asleep on a small bed in the Lost Children's hut at Walt Disney World. Lee is sitting near her in a tiny chair. When Bessie wakes up, Lee tells her where she is and reassures her that she's all right. Bessie is worried that they've only paid Marvin's nurse until 7 p.m. Ruth, who has come on, goes off to phone.

Lee tells Bessie that Dr. Serat, who has returned, and Dr. Wally will meet them at the hospital. Bessie is disappointed to think she has to go back to the hospital, but Lee claims they want to look at Bessie. If she feels well, there's no reason for her not to come home. Lee wants to know what happened. Bessie explained that she fainted—not from the heat, as Lee surmises, but because there was blood in her mouth. It isn't bleeding now.

One of the cartoon characters carried her into the hut, Lee reports, just assuming she'd fainted, not realizing she'd been bleeding as well. She might have been hungry, too, Lee opines, but Bessie claims she fainted because she was scared. She wants to know what's happening to her and reveals to Lee that she can't sleep because she's frightened she won't wake up. She keeps jerking herself awake and pouring herself coffee. She's trying to be brave, but she's frightened. They hug, and Lee comforts her. She shouldn't be frightened. Everything will be all right.

Lee is lucky to have Hank and Charlie, Bessie believes, and Lee agrees with her that they are good boys.

BESSIE: I'm lucky to have Dad and Ruth.
LEE: Mm-hmm.
BESSIE: I've had such love in my life. I look back, and I've had such love.
LEE: They love you very much.
BESSIE: I don't mean—I mean I love them. I am so lucky to have been able to love someone so much. I am so lucky to have loved so much. I am so lucky.

LEE: Yes, you are. You are.

BESSIE: We're fooling ourselves, Lee.

> *Hank appears in the doorway.*

LEE: How?

BESSIE: Hank and Charlie aren't going to match.

LEE: We don't know that.

BESSIE: They're my nephews. They're once removed.

LEE: It could still happen.

BESSIE: I don't want to pretend any longer. We have too many decisions to make before you leave.

LEE: We don't have to make them right now.

HANK: Is that true?

LEE (*notices Hank*): Hank, would you find me a wheelchair.

HANK: Charlie is.

LEE: Do you feel up to going to the car?

BESSIE: Oh, sure.

> *Bessie sits up. Charlie enters with a wheelchair and stops it next to the tiny chair. Hank picks Bessie up and puts her in the wheelchair. She looks at the tiny chair.*

I don't remember ever being that small.

Scene 6

"Night. Hank and Charlie are in their sleeping bags." Hank, having awakened Charlie by shining a penlight in his face, is lecturing his younger brother. Charlie does badly in school and ought to study more and pay attention more. He shouldn't let their mother buy his clothes—he looks like a geek. Meanwhile Hank is fascinated that Charlie's "eyes shrink" when he shines the penlight on them. Hank also wants to know how much money Charlie has. On learning that Charlie has fifteen dollars and thirty-six cents left, Hank asks him why he bought the Goofy cap. He liked it, Charlie declares. As the scene ends, Hank, obviously going to take Charlie's money and leave, tells Charlie, "If I ever take anything from you, you know I'll find a way to pay you back." When Charlie sounds curious about Hank's remark, Hank just tells him to go to sleep.

Scene 7

Ruth is all dressed up, as for an evening party. She is sitting in her chair, and on her lap is Lee's makeup kit. Charlie is standing over Ruth. She selects an eyeliner which she gives him, assuring him he won't poke her in the eye because he has a steady hand, which she doesn't. Ruth is aglow with excitement. She's dressed up because it's the day Coral and Lance are supposed to be getting married on her television program. "I haven't had reason to pretty myself up since I can't think when," she remarks, hoping something won't go wrong this time. The time before, the church caught on fire, she recalls.

Charlie finishes with the eyeliner, and Ruth commends him for doing a good job. She looks pretty, Charlie thinks. Ruth demurs. She wants Hank to move the television into Bessie's room so she can watch, too, but Charlie claims he can move it himself.

Lee comes on to see how Ruth looks and remarks that she looks beautiful. Ruth acts as if Lee is teasing her. Lee assures her she's not. Lee's come to get snacks to have during the program, and Ruth is impressed. Is everybody going to watch? she wonders. Lee isn't sure about Hank because she doesn't know where he is. Ruth will go find him. Lee is pleased that Ruth is up and around and remarks on how wonderful it must be to not have constant pain. Ruth, as she's going off, agrees, but adds that sometimes she misses it.

Lee is putting chips in a bowl. Charlie has come back on and started to read, when Bessie comes on. She's gotten up to give her father his one o'clock medicine. Lee thinks Bessie should be in bed taking it easy. When the phone rings, Lee answers. It is Dr. Serat, and he wants to speak to Bessie.

BESSIE: Hello. Oh, you did. Good. Um . . . uh, what is— I see. I see. Uh-huh. Then should I keep taking what I'm taking now? No, I understand. I'm not. Thank you, Doctor. Goodbye.
    Hangs up.
They got Hank and Charlie's test results back, and it looks like it didn't work out.
    LEE: Oh, Bessie.
    BESSIE: That's pretty much what we expected. We knew the odds were against it.
    LEE: Maybe we should do them again. Maybe they made a mistake.
    BESSIE: Maybe, but I don't . . . I'm supposed to continue with the therapies I'm doing right now and see what kind of luck I have.
    LEE: That's right. Those are good things to be doing.
    BESSIE: Where's Hank? We should tell Hank. I was in the middle of doing something. What was I . . . ? Oh, Dad.
    She reaches for the pills and knocks them onto the floor. The pills spill all over.
    LEE: Do you want to go lie down?
    BESSIE: No, I'm fine, I just . . .
    She starts picking up the pills.
    LEE: I can do that. Charlie.
    Charlie and Lee help pick up the pills.
    BESSIE: It's what we thought. It's not a surprise. It's what I always had in the back of my head. Now I don't have to think about it anymore. I can quit thinking about it. (*Sigh of relief.*) Oh, I can quit thinking about it. We should tell Hank.

When Lee goes off to look for Hank, Charlie reveals to Bessie that Hank is gone. He gives her the note Hank left for her the night before. Charlie hasn't read it. Bessie reads it to him. "Aunt Bessie, gone someplace else. Goodbye, good luck. I love you, too. Hank." Charlie reports that Hank was sorry that he could not wait. He and Bessie hug. They've got to tell Lee, she insists, but Charlie promised Hank he wouldn't tell her until night. Bessie is determined Lee should know and suggests Charlie go outside.

> *Charlie exits. Bessie reads the note again. She is overcome and begins to break down, when Marvin stirs in his room.*

BESSIE: Dad? What is it? What's wrong? It's just me. There's nothing to be afraid of.

> *Marvin calms down.*

There's nothing to be afraid of.

> *Leaves the note on the counter and goes into Marvin's room. Lee enters and . . . . . sees Hank's note and reads it to herself. After a few moments she crumbles the note, tosses it on the counter, and she begins to exit. Before she can leave, Hank enters with his bags. He does not see Lee. He crosses to the chair, drops his bags, goes to look into Marvin's room, stops, turns back to the chair and sees Lee. The two look at each other from across the room. Hank removes his bandana.*

RUTH (*off*): Hurry up, Charlie. The show's starting.

> *Hank crosses past Lee and exits.*

When Hank has gone off, Lee goes to the chair where Hank has put down his things. She picks them up and hugs them to her breast with the prolonged intensity of a mother holding her firstborn.

In Marvin's room, Bessie is talking to Marvin and then begins to bounce the light around the room. Lee goes off, and the lights are fading down to Bessie and Marvin. Then the lights become very bright in Marvin's room before fading down on Bessie and Marvin again. We hear Bessie and Marvin laughing. "*Then the lights fade completely out.*" Curtain.

SIGHT UNSEEN

A Play in Two Acts

BY DONALD MARGULIES

Cast and credits appear on pages 333-334

DONALD MARGULIES was born in Brooklyn September 2, 1954. His father was a salesman in a store selling wallpaper, and the future playwright showed an early interest, not in writing, but in the visual arts. After attending public school and John Dewey High School he studied graphic design at Pratt Institute and proceeded to SUNY Purchase where he received his B.F.A. in visual arts in 1977. But at SUNY he began to take an interest in playwriting—for no particular reason he can put his finger on now—and approached Julius Novick, who was teaching the subject there. Novick asked Margulies if he'd ever written a play, and Margulies replied frankly, "No." Novick nevertheless agreed to sponsor the young man in a playwriting tutorial, "a life-changing event," as Margulies looks back on it.

The first Margulies scripts were put on at SUNY, and in New York he first surfaced off off Broadway with Luna Park, *a one-act adaptation of a Delmore Schwartz short story, commissioned by Jewish Repertory Theater and staged by them February 5, 1982. There followed* Resting Place *OOB at Theater for the New City (1982),* Gifted Children *at JRT (1983) and finally the full-fledged off-Broadway production of* Found a Peanut *at New York Shakespeare Festival for 33 performances in June 1984.*

Later that season, Manhattan Theater Club produced Margulies's What's Wrong With This Picture? *in previews, but this one was withdrawn before opening and wasn't officially presented until 1988 in a revised version at the Back Alley Theater in Los Angeles, a city which also witnessed the premiere of his* The Model Apartment *at its Theater Center in 1989, winning a Drama-League Award and a New York State arts grant. This play was later produced in 1990 by JRT, and an off-Broadway staging is planned for 1993. Meanwhile in 1987, his* Zimmer *appeared on a JRT program. His one-acter* Pitching to the Star *is scheduled to receive its third OOB production at West Bank Cafe in the fall of 1992.*

Margulies's first Best Play, The Loman Family Picnic, *was produced by MTC on June 20, 1989, for 16 performances. His second Best Play,* Sight Unseen, *was commissioned and originally produced in 1991 by South Coast Repertory in Costa Mesa, Calif., after which MTC provided its New York debut in this production on January 20. It has won Margulies an Obie for playwriting and was nominated for all major awards including the New York Drama Critics, Pulitzer, Outer Critics Circle and Drama Desk best-play citations.*

Margulies is also the author of Women in Motion, *commissioned by the Lucille Ball Festival, and the recipient of a 1991 National Endowment for the Arts grant in playwriting. He is currently working on the film adptation of* Sight Unseen *for HBO Films; a TV film for NBC; a screen play based on the life of Robert Capa for Warner Brothers; and a new play commissioned by South Coast Repertory. He is a member of both New Dramatists and the Dramatists Guild and lives with his wife and son in New Haven, Connecticut, where he is a visiting lecturer at the Yale School of Drama.*

ACT I

Scene 1: A farmhouse in the English countryside

SYNOPSIS: Nick, an Englishman in his 40s, is chewing on a hard roll in the kitchen area of his cold farmhouse, while Jonathan, 35 to 40 years of age, an overnight bag hanging from his shoulder, stands in the doorway. The time is *in medias res*, as succeeding scenes will move backward and forward hours, days and years to significant moments in Jonathan's life.

Jonathan extends his hand to Nick who ignores it, obviously unenthusiastic about his visitor, who has come here at the invitation of Nick's wife Patricia. She has gone on an errand to fetch a roast for dinner, and Jonathan tries to open a conversation about Nick's work, archeology, but Nick busies himself with taking out bottles of wine to go with their meal.

Patricia, an American the same age as Jonathan, "*enters wearing a bulky sweater and carrying a bag bursting with groceries.*" After greeting Jonathan she orders Nick off to his office—he has work to do—and Nick exits.

Jonathan is obviously glad to see Patricia, she perhaps a little less so to see him.

She admits that her husband is "painfully shy," and Jonathan pretends that Nick wasn't stand-offish with him. Patricia puts the water on to boil for tea. Jonathan offers to help with the chores, but Patricia invites him to relax and make himself comfortable. When he decides to keep his coat on, Patricia is amused, as usual, by an American visitor's reaction to the chill of the British indoors.

Patricia has kept her American accent (Jonathan notices, remarking that she has turned her back on her home and past). She declares that she doesn't miss her homeland—not even Zabar's—though life here in England is relatively hard: "It shows on our faces, our hands. I haven't bought myself new clothes in years. We have to save for everything." And being an American licenses her to become aggressive, even rude, as a woman running the archeological dig. On balance, she likes it here.

PATRICIA: I *like* the struggle! I like surviving obstacles. Hell, I survived *you*, didn't I?
>   *He reaches for her hand, she pulls away. Pause.*
Who are you to talk about turning one's back?
JONATHAN: What do you mean?
PATRICIA: You with your shiksa wife in Vermont.
JONATHAN: Upstate.
PATRICIA: Whatever.
JONATHAN: I don't understand. What does my wife have to do . . .
PATRICIA (*over "have to do"*): You're an expatriate too, and you don't even know it.
JONATHAN: How?
PATRICIA: You made a choice. When you married your wife, you married her world. Didn't you? You can't exist in two worlds; you've got to turn your back on one of them.
JONATHAN: I hadn't thought of it like that.
PATRICIA: See? We're more alike than you thought. (*Pause.*) God, when I think of all the angst, all the—what's the word?—"cirrus?"
JONATHAN: Tsuris.
PATRICIA: After all the tsuris our young souls went through . . . Your wife should thank me.
JONATHAN: You're right. She should.
PATRICIA: I laid the groundwork. I was the pioneer.
JONATHAN: Yeah.
PATRICIA: The sacrificial shiksa.

Jonathan tells Patricia she looks beautiful, and she replies that he looks rich. Jonathan belittles his success, his fame and fortune as a painter, as "all timing and luck." He's a millionaire, he's "it," Patricia declares, but Jonathan protests that his peak is behind him. Patricia has read the *Times* Sunday magazine cover story

"Jonathan Waxman: The Art Scene's New Visionary," portraying him as "the very model of messy, Jewish intensity," but that was a couple of years ago. Her mother has been sending her clippings about Jonathan from various American publications, as though in reproach to her daughter for letting Jonathan slip through her fingers.

Jonathan has brought Patricia a catalogue from his London show, which is supposed to be a retrospective. Patricia still has a painting Jonathan did of her when he was 22, and she sends him to the living room doorway to see it hanging over the mantel. Jonathan is pleased to find that it is a good example of his early work. There's nothing from this period in the London show, which marks his European debut. He expects the press to eat him alive but acknowledges, "Press is press." He recalls his father's reactions to seeing his son's name in print: "My last name, after all, was *his* last name. Got such a kick out of it. Eight pages in the Sunday *Times*. He couldn't believe the New York *Times* could possibly have that much to say about *his* kid. 'All these words,' he said, 'are about *you*? What is there to say about you?' (*She laughs.*) He was serious; he wasn't just teasing. Oh, he was teasing, too, but it threatened him. No, it did. It pointed up the fact that he could be my father and still not know a thing about me. Not have a clue. What did the fancy-schmancy art world see that he didn't? What were those big dirty paintings about, anyway? So then when all the hype started . . . . . it didn't make him proud. It bewildered him. It alienated him. How could he have produced a 'visionary?' It shamed him somehow. I can't explain."

As a matter of fact (Jonathan informs Patricia), his father died only last week. With the London show being mounted, Jonathan didn't have time to sit shiva and doesn't claim to have been a very good son. When he went to pack up his father's possessions he found that a kind of shrine had been made by removing all the old family photos from the albums and covering a wall with them. His father had been very proud of this display but had inadvertently ruined the photos by stapling them, symbolizing for Jonathan a kind of destruction of his past.

Jonathan's wife Laura didn't come with him to England because she's pregnant with a boy and pretty far along. He shows Patricia a picture of Laura in her wedding dress a year ago. Patricia, who has been married to Nick for about nine years, wonders what prompted Jonathan to come so far out of his way to visit her.

JONATHAN: I wanted to see you again.
PATRICIA: Why?
JONATHAN: I don't know, it felt somehow . . . incomplete.
PATRICIA: What did?
JONATHAN: We did. I did. (*A beat.*) I came . . . I wanted to apologize.
PATRICIA (*smiling*): Not really.
JONATHAN: What did you think when I called?
PATRICIA: I don't know, I was nonplussed. I buried you years ago, then all of a sudden a call from London. You caught me off guard.

JONATHAN: So why did you invite me up?

PATRICIA: You caught me off *guard*, I said. I don't know, what *should* I have done?

JONATHAN: You could've said it was a bad time, you were busy, you had other plans . . .

PATRICIA: None of which was true.

JONATHAN: You could've said you had no interest in seeing me again. (*Pause.*) Patty . . .

> *He makes a conciliatory gesture. She rebuffs him.*

PATRICIA: I'll give you dinner and a place to spend the night, but, no, Jonathan, I won't forgive you.

Jonathan offers to leave, but Patricia wants him to stay and goes out to the garden to get supplies for dinner. Jonathan is studying the painting of Patricia over the mantel when Nick enters with the scotch bottle and comments, "I can't tell you how many nights I've stared at the fire and imagined that painting in the flames." He acknowledges that he wouldn't really damage it. Patricia looks at it sometimes, though Nick sees nothing in it. Nick knows that Jonathan is now rich and wonders how much the painting might be worth. Jonathan answers him casually—he lets his gallery worry about money—and guesses its value might be in the thousands. Tens of thousands, Nick would guess, for a work which Jonathan himself admits is seminal.

Nick has known Jonathan for years, he says, by means of a polaroid photo of Patricia and Jonathan in their co-ed days, dressed for a costume party, she as Miss America in a bathing suit, he as something Nick calls "a pimp" but, Jonathan tells him, is supposed to be a tourist dressed in loud plaids and carrying a camera. Nick asks if the costume was "Symbolic of your perception of yourself at that time, perhaps? A transient person? Dislocated?" And Nick has snooped in Patricia's keepsake box, finding there only a postcard, no letters. Jonathan explains that they were schoolmates who saw each other almost every day and had no need for added written correspondence. Nick had imagined that there must have been letters and that Patricia burned them ceremoniously, gleefully.

NICK: Then there are the stories. Tales of Waxman. The Jonathan stories. Faraway sounding, exotic. Like from the Old Testament, if you will. Patricia's voice becomes especially animated while telling a Jonathan story. She achieves a new range in a different key. A new tune, a new music entirely. Fascinating. I watch her face. The dimples that sprout! The knowing smiles! Remarkable behavioral findings.

> *A beat. He drags his chair closer.*

I've become a Waxmanologist, you see. A Waxmanophile. No, a Waxmanologist. It's my nature. Beneath this reticent exterior lies a probing, tireless investigator. A detective. An historian. And I'm good at my work. I'm compulsive. I'm meticulous. I study the past in order to make sense of the present.

JONATHAN: I understand.

NICK: You're smaller in person than I imagined. I held out for a giant. A giant among men. Instead, what's *this*? You're medium-sized. Compact. Razor burn on your neck. Pimple on your cheek. She said you were handsome; you're alright. Perhaps your appeal lies below the belt, but I doubt I'd be surprised.

Jon De Vries (Nick) Dennis Boutsikaris (Jonathan) and Deborah Hedwall (Patricia) in a scene from *Sight Unseen* by Donald Margulies

JONATHAN: Look, I think I'll— (*Pointing to the door.*)

NICK: Circumcision isn't common practice in the U.K., you know.

> *Jonathan stops.*

Jews still do it the world over, don't they. On religious grounds. Here the risk is too great. Too many accidents. Too many boy sopranos. Here we hold on to our overcoats.

> *Patricia returns with her basket filled with vegetables and herbs.*

PATRICIA: Oh. Good. You're getting acquainted.

> *Jonathan and Nick look at one another.*

Scene 2: An art gallery in London, four days later

After Jonathan's opening, Grete, "*an attractive, European new-wave-looking young woman,*" sets up a tape recorder on a table between two chairs. Jonathan enters, and they sit, as Grete congratulates him on a "provocative" exhibition. Jonathan is in somewhat of a hurry, so Grete gets to the questions.

GRETE: Your depiction of the emptiness and spiritual deadness of middle-class American life in the closing years of the twentieth century have earned you both accolades and astonishment in your own country. Your large, bold canvases of nude men and women who seem as alienated from one another as they do from their environment have been generating controversy in the art community in the United States for the better part of the last decade. They have also been commanding huge price tags in the art market. How do you reconcile the success of your work with its rather bleak subject matter?; and b), do you think your work speaks as effectively to the rest of the world?; or, like a joke that loses something in translation, is its popularity purely an American phenomenon?

JONATHAN (*a beat*): Your English is very good.

GRETE: Thank you. I was a year at N.Y.U.

JONATHAN: Ah. Now: Do I think my work is intrinsically American? Yes. Do I think that it's the equivalent of an inside joke that excludes the rest of the world? Definitely not. Whether the rest of the world likes it is another question. I'm not gonna worry too much about it.

Their conversation continues in this vein. Jonathan remarks that Grete is a German, and that German artists have been way ahead of Americans in politicized art, reflecting "the most horrible event of our time" in their terrifying work. Grete begins to argue that events like the Viet Nam war might have pushed American artists in the same direction, but Jonathan immediately insists that they change the subject.

Grete brings up a controversy over a Waxman painting called Walpurgisnacht showing a black man making love with a white woman. Some have called this a depiction of rape, but Jonathan argues that it is only the eye of the beholder that sees it that way. The lovemaking is taking place in a desecrated Jewish cemetery, and Jonathan insists it doesn't deserve the accusations of racism or of anti-feminism that have been aimed at it.

Grete brings up another painting, The Beginning, a seated figure, one of Jonathan's early student works, the only painting in the exhibition that belongs to the artist. Jonathan tells her he had supposed it was lost but came across it recently and found that it awakened in him the same excitement he remembers feeling on that special day when he painted it.

GRETE: What was it about that day?

JONATHAN: I don't know, it was one of those days artists kill for. The kind we always hope we're waking up to, but which rarely comes to pass. I wish I knew what I'd had for breakfast that day or what shirt I was wearing or what I'd dreamed the night before. Burning leaves; I remember the room smelled of burning leaves. Whatever it was, something clicked that day. I was born. My life began. I started seeing things I'd never seen before.

GRETE: There *is* a kind of . . . *openness*, yes?, present in this painting that is virtually absent in your later work. The way the model *engages* the viewer, for instance. Her penetrating, unwavering eye contact. Nowhere else in your work does one find that kind of . . . connection.

JONATHAN (*a beat; she's right*): Hm.

GRETE (*rhetorically*): I wonder about the model. Who *was* this woman? What role did *she* play? I wonder where she is today.

JONATHAN (*a beat*): I have no idea.

Scene 3: The Farmhouse, an hour before the start of Scene 1

Nick is making tea while Patricia sweeps up. They are talking about where Jonathan is to sleep, and Patricia is trying to persuade Nick to agree that it would be easier for them to give him their bed and sleep on a futon downstairs. He won't tell her whether he objects to giving up the bed, he merely comments, "It's only for one night."

Patricia hasn't seen Jonathan in 15 years and is worried about how the visit will go. She insists on going to fetch a roast for dinner, asking Nick to stay and entertain Jonathan while she's gone. Nick tells her it'd be more sensible for him to go to the butcher's and Patricia to wait for Jonathan—after all, he's her friend, not his.

PATRICIA: You're mad about the bed.

NICK: I am not mad about the bloody bed!

PATRICIA (*over "the bloody bed"*): If you don't want him to have our bed, *tell* me. *Tell* me you don't want him to!

        Pause.

NICK (*simply*): He has it already.

        Pause.

PATRICIA: Why didn't you tell me not to invite him?

NICK: Me? Tell you? What do you mean?

PATRICIA (*over "what do you mean?"*): Why didn't you forbid me from seeing him again?

NICK: Forbid you? How, Patricia? How could I forbid you? Why would I? I wouldn't presume to forbid you to do anything.

PATRICIA: Why? Why wouldn't you?

> *They look at one another. Pause. She starts to exit. He calls.*

NICK: Patricia.

> *She stops and turns. Pause.*

Come home soon.

Scene 4: Jonathan's bedroom in Brooklyn, 15 years earlier

In Jonathan's boyhood bedroom in his parents' home, Patricia comes in and looks over the books, commenting that one's choice of books, like archeology, "Let's you into all the secret places." Jonathan is wearing a suit and putting on his shoes while Patricia informs him that his father kissed her when she came in. She notices an incongruous piece of furniture—a sewing machine—which Jonathan's mother had moved into this room after the boys moved away. His mother has died, and his father is sitting shiva in the living room.

Patricia instinctively wants to do something to help Jonathan at this time—even offers him sex (they've been lovers for two years)—but he holds her at arm's length, declaring that in this situation he's beyond help. He didn't want her to attend his mother's funeral, and he feels that she shouldn't even be here now. Patricia and his mother never took to each other.

PATRICIA: Not that I ever did anything to *offend* the woman personally or anything. I just happened to be born a certain persuasion, a certain incompatible persuasion, even though I'm an atheist and I don't give a damn *what* religion somebody happens to believe in. But did she even bother to get to know me, even a little bit?

JONATHAN: Oh, Patty, this is—

PATRICIA: It's like I was invisible. Do you know how it feels to be invisible?

JONATHAN: What do you think?, my mother's dying wish was to keep that shiksa away from my funeral?! Come on, Patty! Grow up! Not everything is about you. I know that may be hard for you to believe, but not everything in the world—

PATRICIA (*over "in the world"*): Oh, great.

JONATHAN (*a beat*): Let's face it, Patricia, things haven't exactly been good between us for months.

PATRICIA: What do you mean? Your mother's been sick for months. How can you make a statement like that?

JONATHAN: What, this is a surprise to you what I'm saying?

PATRICIA: Hasn't your mother been dying for months?

JONATHAN: I don't really have the strength for this right now.

PATRICIA: Hasn't she? So how can you judge how things have been between us? Her dying has been weighing over us, over both of us, for so long, it's colored so much . . .

JONATHAN (*over "it's colored so much"*): Look . . . if you must know—

PATRICIA: What.

JONATHAN: If you *must* know . . . (*A beat.*) I was the one who didn't want you there. It wasn't out of respect to my mother or my father or my grandmother, it was me. I didn't want to see you. I didn't want you there, Patty. I didn't want to have to hold *your* hand and comfort *you* because of how cruel my mother was to you, I didn't want that . . . I didn't want to deal with your display of—

PATRICIA: Dis*play*?

JONATHAN: Your display of love for me. Your concern. It was all about you whenever I thought about how it would be if you were with me! I didn't want you there, Patty. I'm sorry. (*A beat.*) I guess when something catastrophic like this happens . . . You get to thinking.

PATRICIA: Yes? Well?

> *Pause.*

JONATHAN: I don't love you, Patty.

> *He smiles lamely and reaches for her as if to soothe her, as she goes to get her bag. She groans, punches his arm and goes. He stands alone for a long time before moving slowly over to the sewing machine. He clutches a pillow and gently rocks himself. As he begins to cry, lights fade to black. Curtain.*

ACT II

Scene 5: The farmhouse, a few hours after the end of Scene 1

Nick is leafing through Jonathan's show catalogue, while Patricia and Jonathan are still seated at the dinner table: "*The wine is nearly finished; they are all somewhat disinhibited.*" Jonathan invites Patricia to come to London with him to do museums as well as his show, and he includes Nick in the invitation; but Nick can't stand big cities, and Patricia won't come by herself. And they are both busy with their dig, having unearthed a Roman latrine and a late medieval rubbish heap, which declares everything about the culture which produced it: "What they wore, what they ate. It's a treasure trove. Tons of it."

Nick, looking through Jonathan's catalogue, is perplexed.

NICK: I mean, is this all it takes to set the art world ablaze?

PATRICIA: Nick's idea of art is the Mona Lisa.

NICK: My idea of art, in point of fact, Patricia, begins and ends with the Renaissance. Everything before it was ceremonial arts-and-crafts—hardly "art," really; everything since, well, everything since has been utter rubbish.

JONATHAN: Are you kidding? How can you say that? (*To Patricia.*) All of modern art, he's dismissing just like that?

NICK (*over "just like that"*): But it's all been done, hasn't it. The so-called modern age, as far as I can tell, has been one long, elaborate exercise, albeit a futile one, to reinvent what had already been perfected by a handful of Italians centuries ago.

JONATHAN: But the world is constantly reinventing *itself.* How can you say that Leonardo's world view expresses our world, or Picasso's even?

NICK: Picasso. Now there was an energetic little bloke.

JONATHAN: Am I supposed to shrink in the shadow of the great masters and pack it all in? Say the hell with it, why bother?

NICK: If you had any sense, yes.

Patricia laughs, as Nick adds that artists have too great a sense of their own importance—the world would lose little or nothing if they all disappeared. Returning his attention to the catalogue, Nick judges that if beauty is an aim of art, this work of Jonathan's is far from beautiful. It's pornography, Nick declares, "and not very good pornography, at that."

Nick points to the reproduction of Jonathan's Walpurgisnacht, calling it "a couple of mixed race fornicating in a cemetery." Jonathan claims it's an allegory, and Patricia observes that the woman is being raped, because her hands are fists.

NICK: They aren't necessarily fists; they're just poorly drawn hands.

JONATHAN: Jesus.

NICK: That's what I mean by the apparent disregard for basic traditions in art, like knowing the skeletal structure of the human hand.

JONATHAN: But you know what hands look like.

NICK: What?! Is that your response? I *know* what hands . . . ?

JONATHAN: What I'm saying is, it's not my job to photographically recreate the skeletal structure of the human hand.

NICK (*over "of the human hand"*): What *is* your job? You keep talking about what isn't your job; what *is* your job? Is it your job to paint well, or not?

JONATHAN: What do you mean by "paint well?" You obviously have very limited ideas about painting. I'm telling you, if you guys come down to London, I'll take you around, we'll look at art, I could *show* you . . .

Nick interrupts and turns to the subject of money—how much would he have to pay if he wanted to buy one of Jonathan's paintings? All those in the exhibition are already sold, Jonathan informs Nick, many to large corporations like Union Carbide or Mobil, and there is a waiting list for his forthcoming work, presold sight unseen whether customers happen to like the paintings or not, so long as they are genuine Waxmans: ten a year (Jonathan figures) at $250,000 apiece (Nick estimates). Jonathan refuses to apologize for his success, believing it his right to profit from a system "Gone haywire."

And Jonathan can't see why it should make any difference whether the hands in Walpurgisnacht are fists or not. Patricia tells him, "It makes a very big difference. It changes everything. If they're fists, then that suggests that she's being taken against her will. If they're not . . . Is the painting about a black man raping a white woman, or is it about a couple screwing in a cemetery?" If Jonathan is deliberately being confusing, satisfied merely to induce the viewer to think about it, then (Patricia concludes) the painting is intended merely as shock effect.

PATRICIA: . . . You can't *mean*, "What difference does it make?", Jonathan, that just isn't good enough.

JONATHAN (*over "isn't good enough"*): You know I don't entirely mean that. I mean, my intention is irrelevant; it's all about what you make of it.

NICK: Either way you look at it, it has about as much impact as a smutty photo in a porno mag.

JONATHAN: You can't get past the flesh, can you.

NICK: What?

JONATHAN: This is very interesting. All you see is the flesh. Of course! You surround yourself with *bones* all day. I mean, here you are, freezing your asses off . . .

PATRICIA: Jonathan . . .

JONATHAN: . . . buried in your rubbish pits and your Roman latrines . . . cataloguing bones whose flesh rotted away centuries ago! No wonder my paintings scare you.

NICK: Scare me, did you say?

JONATHAN: Yes. They're voluptuous, dangerous. They deal with unspeakable things, fleshy things. *That's* what's going on in my paintings. The lengths people go to, living people go to, in order to feel something. Today. Now.

After a pause, Patricia changes the subject and informs Jonathan they're going to turn their bedroom over to him. Jonathan protests that he'll be well enough down here, and Nick agrees with him. Nick goes to fetch bedding for their guest. In his absence, Patricia confesses to Jonathan, "I married Nick to stay in England" after she obtained her degree and her student visa expired. Jonathan can perceive clearly that Nick, on his part, is very much in love with Patricia. Patricia admits that she knows it.

JONATHAN: You were the "student of the world!" Remember? No, really, how do you . . . I mean, passion, sex, love . . . You just decided, what, you don't need those things any more? You just shut that part of you all out?

PATRICIA: Yes. Exactly. My "passion" nearly did me in, now, didn't it.

JONATHAN: Oh, come on, don't lay this on me. That's bullshit. You call yourself an expatriate? You're no expatriate, you're just hiding!

PATRICIA: Who the hell are you to judge my life—?!

JONATHAN: Why do you live with him?

PATRICIA: Why? He's my husband.

JONATHAN: That's not a reason. Why do you live with him if you don't love him?

PATRICIA: Who said I don't love him?

JONATHAN: You just said yourself, you married Nick . . .

PATRICIA: *This is the best I can do!*

> *Pause.*

JONATHAN: Don't say that. It isn't even true. I know you too well.

PATRICIA: *Knew* me. *Knew* me. You don't *know* who I am.

> *A beat. Nick appears with a bundle of bedding. They look at him. Pause.*

NICK: Um . . . Shall I . . . Would you like me to make your bed?

Scene 6: The gallery, continued from the end of Scene 2

Continuing their discussion of his work, Jonathan admits to Grete that he likes to startle people and "color their dreams," while Grete steers them to the subject of "good" art. Most people don't have the faintest idea of what "good" art is (Jonathan argues, giving as an example the middle-class throngs at a Van Gogh exhibition) unless the media tells them or Kirk Douglas acts it out on the screen. "See, there's this Hollywood packaging of the artist that gets me," Jonathan goes on, "The packaging of the mystique. Poor, tragic Vincent: he cut off his ear 'cause he was so misunderstood, but still he painted all those pretty pictures. So ten bodies deep they lined up in front of the paintings. More out of solidarity for Vincent (or Kirk) than out of any kind of love or passion for 'good art.' Hell, some art lovers were in such a hurry to get to the postcards and prints and souvenir place mats, they strode past the paintings and skipped the show entirely! Who can blame them? You couldn't *experience* the paintings anyway, not like that. You couldn't *see any-thing.* The art was just a backdrop for the *real* show that was happening. In the gift shop!"

Jonathan insists that every painting he does is an attempt to come up with some kind of an answer that will serve the masses, but it's the media who direct the traffic of so-called art lovers. "You seem to have such contempt," Grete observes, but Jonathan thinks his remarks are fair criticism. He remembers a time when he painted apartments for a living and did his own serious work at night; then he had a gallery show at which the public discovered him. He found that "When you take your art out of your little room and present it to the public, it's not yours any more, it's *theirs,* theirs to see with their own eyes. And for each person who sees your work for the first time, you're discovered all over again. That begins to take its toll. You can't be everybody's discovery. That gets to be very demanding. Who are these people who are suddenly throwing money at you and telling you how wonderful and talented you are? What do they know? You begin to believe them. They begin to want things from you. They begin to expect things. The work loses its importance, the importance becomes 'Waxman.'"

Yet—Jonathan admits to Grete—it can be cold and lonely on the outside looking in. Grete is reminded of Groucho Marx's joke about not wanting to join a club
that would take him as a member, and she annoys Jonathan by labeling it a
"Jewish" joke. She claims that it characterizes the problem Jews have, of being
"very much on the inside" while considering themselves outsiders. Jonathan is
offended. Grete tries to explain.

GRETE: All I am suggesting, Mr. Waxman, is that the artist, like the Jew, prefers
to see himself as alien from the mainstream culture. For the Jewish *artist* to   •
acknowledge that the *contrary* is true, that he is *not* alien, but rather, *assimilated*
into that mainstream culture—

JONATHAN (*over "mainstream culture"*): Wait a minute, wait a minute. What is
this *Jewish* stuff creeping in here?

GRETE: You are a Jew, are you not?

JONATHAN: I don't see what that—

GRETE (*over "what that"*): Are you?

JONATHAN: Yeah; so?

GRETE: I am interested in the relationship between the artist and the Jew, as
Jonathan Waxman sees it.

JONATHAN: Who *cares* how Jonathan Waxman sees it? I'm an American
painter. *American* is the adjective, not *Jewish*. *American*.

GRETE: Yes, but your work calls attention to it.

JONATHAN: How?

GRETE: The Jewish cemetery in Walpurgisnacht.

JONATHAN: *One* painting.

GRETE: One *important* painting—the depictions of middle-class life, obviously
Jewish.

Grete qualifies herself as an expert on this subject: she's studied Jonathan's
work, researched his background and upbringing and has written often for arts publications. She asks Jonathan about the importance of autobiography in his paintings. He admits they're probably based on his life experiences and reactions, but
argues that they're not therefore necessarily Jewish in subject.

Grete has one more question: isn't it true that Jonathan hired a public relations
firm to promote his work? Jonathan explains, irritably, that PR people take care of
all the public and social responsibilities which would otherwise overwhelm an
artist who becomes popular. Grete asks him if it's true that he hired PR two years
before he had his first success.

JONATHAN: What are you saying? I bought my career? I bought my reputation,
what?

GRETE: Mr. Waxman . . .

Laura Linney (Grete) and Dennis Boutsikaris in *Sight Unseen*

JONATHAN (*continuous*): What about the work? Why aren't we talking about the work? Why must it always come down to business? Huh? *I'm* not doing it, and yet you accuse me . . .

GRETE (*over "and yet you accuse me"*): *Is* it true or is it *not* true?

JONATHAN: That's irrelevant. True or not, who cares?

GRETE (*over "who cares"*): It *is* relevant. It is relevant if you espouse to be a visionary of truth.

JONATHAN (*over "visionary of truth"*): I espouse nothing! What do I espouse? I paint pictures! You're the one who comes up with these fancy labels, people like *you*!

GRETE (*over "people like you"*): How can you talk about *the* truth? Mr. Waxman, how can you talk about truth when your own sense of morality . . .

JONATHAN: What do you know about morality?

GRETE: . . . when your own sense of morality is so compromised and so—

JONATHAN: Huh? What do you know with your sneaky little Jew-baiting comments?

GRETE: I beg your pardon.

JONATHAN: Don't give me this innocence shit. You know exactly what I'm talking about.

GRETE (*over "what I'm talking about"*): No, I am sorry, I have no idea.

JONATHAN: You think I haven't picked up on it? Huh? You think I don't know what this is all about?

GRETE: Mr. Waxman, this is all in your imagination.

JONATHAN: My imagination?! I'm imagining this?! I'm imagining you've been attacking me from the word go?

GRETE: Mr. Waxman!

JONATHAN: You have, Miss, don't deny it. You expect me to sit here another minute? What do you take me for? Huh? What the fuck do you take me for?

> *He abruptly goes.*

GRETE: Mr. Waxman . . .

> *Pause. She presses a button on the tape recorder. We hear the tape rewind.*

Scene 7: The farmhouse, a few hours after the end of Scene 5

It is the middle of the night, but Jonathan is awake and fully dressed, brewing himself some tea, writing Patricia a message and leaving six 50-pound notes. The painting is wrapped in newspaper and stacked against the kitchen table. Nick has been watching this from the shadows and finally emerges, startling Jonathan. Neither of them could sleep, they found, and Jonathan has decided to make an early start back to London, without the planned breakfast and visit to the dig.

Nick reminds Jonathan that Patricia will be most disappointed to wake up and find him gone, then launches into a confidence that Jonathan really doesn't want to hear: Nick and Patricia don't make love to each other very often. They did a couple of times before Nick asked her to marry him, and not occasionally Patricia will respond to Nick's loving gestures. Last night was one of those times, Nick confesses: "It was brilliant."

Nick is distracted from this subject when he sees the 300 pounds. He is not exactly offended—he says—by this generous gesture, but Jonathan sees that he is somehow taking it the wrong way.

JONATHAN: Nick. Jesus. I can't win with you, can I. Please. Just accept my thanks.

NICK: Your thanks for what?

JONATHAN: For letting me spend the night.

NICK: Three hundred pounds? For "letting you?" Three hundred pounds for letting you spend the night? If I'd known there was a price, I'd have charged you considerably more than three hundred pounds. Considering the damages to my home and happiness. Yes, like German reparations after the war. I should thank *you*. Your proximity served as a welcome marital aid. Interesting going at it like that. Each for his or her own reasons, yet mutually satisfying just the same. It *is* kind of like war, isn't it?

JONATHAN: I never meant you any harm.

NICK: Never meant me . . .?

JONATHAN: You act as if I'm to blame for your unhappiness. I'm sorry if you're unhappy. I never meant you any harm. We only met this afternoon . . .

NICK: Have I spoiled the surprise?

JONATHAN: What surprise?

NICK: Were we to awaken to find you gone but three hundred pounds in your stead, under the honey pot? Economic aid, is that it? Jonathan Waxman: Our American Cousin. Our Jewish uncle.

JONATHAN: Enough with the "Jewish," Nick.

NICK: You're right; cheap shot. A Robin Hood for our time, then. Stealing from the rich and giving to the poor. Hey, not entirely off the mark, is it?, stealing from the rich and giving to the—You are quite the charlatan, as it turns out.

JONATHAN: Am I?

NICK: Oh, yes. You shit on canvas and dazzle the rich. They oo and ah and shower you with coins, lay gifts at your feet. The world has gone insane. It's the emperor's new clothes.

JONATHAN (*reaching for it*): Look, if you don't want my money . . .

NICK: Uh uh uh. Don't get me wrong: I will take your money. Gladly. *And* insult you. I will bite your hand. With relish. Your money is dirty, Wax Man. Hell, I don't care; I could use a few quid.

Patricia enters in her robe and discovers what's taking place. Nick unobtrusively removes himself from the room, as Patricia states to Jonathan, "You have this incredible knack for dismissing me whenever I've finished serving whatever purpose you've had in mind for me. Just incredible." Jonathan protests that he enjoyed seeing her again, that he felt he absolutely had to come here and face her—but she notices the painting wrapped up and immediately protests that it's hers and she doesn't want it removed. Jonathan explains that he only wants to borrow it to fill in a gap in his career at the retrospective. It can be exhibited anonymously. But Patricia doesn't want the painting she sat for on the day they met to be exhibited for all eyes to see. She views Jonathan's intention of borrowing it without asking, even though leaving a note of explanation, as something pretty close to outright theft.

PATRICIA: God, Jonathan, the arrogance! So you just take what you want now, hm? Is that what fame entitles you to? I don't understand what's happened to you, Jonathan, what's happened to your conscience? You had a conscience, I know you did. Guilt did wonders for you. It made you appealing. Now I don't *know*. You've lost your goodness or something. Your spirit.

Nick has slipped back in.

JONATHAN: You're right; I have. I *have* lost something. I've lost my way somehow, I don't know. I thought maybe if I retraced my steps . . . If I went back . . .

You were there, at the beginning, Patty . . . I'm nobody's son any more. They're all gone now, all the disappointable people. There's no one left to shock with my paintings. I didn't realize . . . All along I was painting for *him*, to get a rise out of *him*. The whole time my father was dying . . . I've been trying to remember where I came from. When I saw this painting . . . There's a kind of purity to it, you know?, before all the bullshit. Patty, I just need to hold onto it.

NICK: How much is it worth to you?

JONATHAN: What?

NICK (*gets the painting*): Start the bidding. What's it worth?

PATRICIA: Nick. For God's sake . . .

JONATHAN: I'm only talking about borrowing it.

NICK: Borrowing it is no longer an option. Either you buy it outright . . .

JONATHAN: You're not serious.

PATRICIA: Nick! This is none of your business!

NICK: None of my—? It most certainly is my business.

PATRICIA: It isn't yours to sell!

NICK: Oh, let him have the bloody painting and let's be on with it.

PATRICIA: No!

NICK: Please, love. Let him take it out of our home. At long last, please. (*To Jonathan.*) Well?

PATRICIA: It isn't for sale!

NICK: *Let* him, Patricia. Let him take it to London. Let him buy it. Doesn't it make sense, love? Think of it: This one painting . . .

PATRICIA: No, Nick!

NICK: We'll make some money, love. Tens of thousands.

PATRICIA: This isn't about money!

NICK: It's about our future, love! Our future was sitting on the wall all along. Think of it: We can save some money, we can pay our debts. We can get on with it, Patricia. (*Pause. Softly.*) Let him buy the painting, love.

After a long pause in which Patricia and Nick look at each other, Patricia gives the painting to Nick, who passes it to Jonathan with a "There you go." Nick goes out while Patricia remains to see Jonathan off.

PATRICIA: I can't describe the pleasure I had being your muse. The days and nights I sat for you. It thrilled me, watching you paint me. The connection. The connection was electric. I could see the sparks. I never felt so alive as when I sat naked for you, utterly still, obedient. I would have done anything for you, do you know that?

JONATHAN: Patty . . .

PATRICIA: Isn't that shameful? A girl so devoid of self? I would have done anything. (*A beat.*) You know, even after that last time in Brooklyn, I never actually believed that I'd never see you again.

JONATHAN: No?

PATRICIA: No. I always held out the *possibility*. But *this* time . . . (*A beat.*) We won't be seeing each other again. Will we. (*A beat. He shakes his head. A beat.*) Hm. I wonder what that will be like.

They continue looking at each other as the lights fade.

Scene 8: A painting studio at a New York art school, 17 years earlier

Class is over, but there is a model dressing behind a screen while Jonathan, a straggler, continues to paint. Finally the model emerges—it's Patricia—who persuades him to show her what he's doing, then looks at it without comment. "It's purposefully distorted," Jonathan explains. "I'm trying something. You see how it looks like I'm looking *down* at you and *at* you at the same time? That's why the figure, your figure, looks a little . . ."

"Huge," Patricia completes Jonathan's remark, resolving to put herself on a diet. Jonathan is the most talented member of the class, she tells him, and he in turn praises her skill as a model, her steadiness in holding the pose. Patricia's mother wouldn't approve of her daughter sitting naked and being stared at, but Jonathan reassures her that there's no sexual implication in her nakedness under these circumstances, in which the artist maintains a psychic distance.

Patricia offers to undress and work overtime so that Jonathan can continue painting, but he can keep going for a while from memory. She would have to cut her film history class—she describes herself as a "dilettante" who has no major but wants to dabble in many of the courses the college has to offer: American Film Comedy from Chaplin to Capra, Women in Faulkner's South, Poetry Workshop and Introduction to Archeology. In contrast to Jonathan, who's known he wants to be an artist ever since he was little, Patricia declares, "I see myself as a student of the world. A student of the world. I'm young, I have time. I want to try a lot of things."

Patricia has noticed a mannerism of Jonathan's while he's painting. To her, his form of intense concentration is sexy, she tells him, and on impulse she suddenly kisses him on the mouth.

JONATHAN (*surprised, he recoils*): Hey!

PATRICIA: Sorry. I'm sorry . . . Look, why don't you just paint . . .

Quickly gathers her things.

JONATHAN: No, wait . . . I didn't mean "Hey!" I meant "Oh!" It came out "Hey!"

PATRICIA: Are you gay or something?

JONATHAN: No . . . surprised. I'm not used to having girls . . .

PATRICIA: What.

JONATHAN: I don't know. Come on so strong.

PATRICIA: Sorry. It won't happen again.

She goes.

JONATHAN: Oh, great . . .

Patricia returns.

PATRICIA: Let me ask you something: If I hadn't kissed you, would you have kissed me?

JONATHAN: No.

PATRICIA: What is it with you?! We're staring at each other all day . . . I'm *naked*, totally exposed to you . . . your tongue is driving me insane—the attraction is mutual, wouldn't you say? I mean, wouldn't you say that?

JONATHAN: Yeah . . .

PATRICIA: Then what is it?

Pause.

JONATHAN: You . . . scare me a little.

PATRICIA: I scare you.

JONATHAN: You do. You scare me . . . a lot, actually . . .

PATRICIA: How could I scare you? I'm the scaredest person in the world.

JONATHAN: Oh, boy.

Takes a deep breath. A beat.

You scare me . . . 'cause of what you represent. I know that sounds . . .

PATRICIA (*over "I know that sounds"*): For what I r— What do I represent? Dilettantism? Nudity? Film studies?

JONATHAN (*a beat*): You aren't Jewish.

He smiles, shrugs. A beat.

PATRICIA: You're kidding. And all these years I thought I was?

JONATHAN: Look, this is hard for me. It's a major thing, you know, where I come from . . .

PATRICIA: What, your mother?

JONATHAN: Not just my mother. It's the six million! It's, it's the diaspora, it's the history of the Jewish people! You have no idea, the *weight*. You got to remember I come from Brooklyn. People where I come from, they don't like to travel very far, let alone intermarry. They've still got this ghetto mentality: safety in numbers, and stay put, no matter what . . . . . ."

Jonathan insists he can't become involved with Patricia, who reminds him they're only becoming involved to the extent of one kiss and then maybe a cup of coffee and a night together. Would this be an offense against the natural order of things or merely an adventure?

PATRICIA: I come from a tribe too, you know. Maybe not one with the same history as yours, but still . . . You're as exotic to me as I am to you! You're an artist! An artist has to experience the world! How can you experience the world if you say "no" to things you shouldn't have to say "no" to?!

JONATHAN (*a beat; he smiles*): Do me a favor?, get my mother on the phone?

He gestures to the easel with his brush, meaning: "I should get back to work." A beat. She kicks off her shoes.

(*Quietly*) No, no, don't, really . . . What are you doing?

> PATRICIA: Don't paint from memory. I'm here, Jonathan. (*A beat.*) Paint me.
> *They're looking at one another. As she slowly unbuttons her blouse, and he approaches, lights fade to black. Curtain.*

CONVERSATIONS WITH MY FATHER

A Play in Two Acts

BY HERB GARDNER

Cast and credits appear on pages 306-307

HERB GARDNER was born in Brooklyn December 28, 1934 and was educated at New York's High School of the Performing Arts (where he wrote his first play, the one-acter The Elevator), *Carnegie Tech (where he studied playwriting along with sculpture) and Antioch. He soon switched visual arts from sculpture to drawing, doing parts of TV commercials and creating the cartoon characters "The Nebbishes," which earned him the wherewithal to concentrate on writing his play* A Thousand Clowns, *based partly on his 1956 short story "The Man Who Thought He Was Winston Churchill" and partly on his own life experiences. It was produced on Broadway April 5, 1962 for 428 performances and was named a Best Play of its season.*

Gardner continued his outstanding playwriting career with The Goodbye People *(Broadway, 1968 and 1979),* Thieves *(Broadway, 1974),* Love and/or Death *(off off Broadway, 1979) and the book and lyrics for the musical* One Night Stand *(Broadway, 1980). His second Best Play was* I'm Not Rappaport, *produced off Broadway June 6, 1985 for 181 performances before moving to Broadway November 19 for a continuing 890-performance run. This play won him the best-play Tony, Outer Critics Circle and John Gassner Awards and has since been pro-*

duced in dozens of countries all over the world. His third Best Play, Conversations With My Father, *opened on Broadway this season on March 29.*

Gardner is also the author of the one-acters How I Crossed the Street for the First Time All by Myself, The Forever Game *and* I'm With Ya, Duke; *the screenplays of* A Thousand Clowns *(winning the best-screen-play award of the Screenwriters Guild and Academy nominations for best screenplay and best picture),* The Goodbye People *(which he directed),* Thieves *and* Who Is Harry Kellerman and Why Is He Saying Those Terrible Things About Me? *(based on a Gardner short story that was chosen for inclusion in* The Best American Short Stories of 1968*); and a novel,* A Piece of the Action. *He is married, with two children, and lives in New York City..*

Time: Between 1936 and 1976

Place: Canal Street in New York City

ACT I

Scene 1: July 25, 1976, early evening

SYNOPSIS: The Homeland Tavern (which, under the same management, will be known as Eddie Goldberg's Golden Door Tavern, The Flamingo Lounge and the Twin-Fifties Cafe) features a bar along the wall at stage left next to the entrance door downstage, booths along the wall stage right, and, upstage, a door to living quarters upstairs and the door to the kitchen on either side of a juke box. A few tables and chairs furnish the center of this barroom, a genuinely old structure on which has been superimposed an Olde Tavern atmosphere: "*The original tin-patterned ceiling is there, the pillared walls, the scarred oak bar, the leaded glass cabinets, the smoked mirror behind the bar, the high-backed wooden booths with their cracked leather seats, the battered and lumbering ceiling fans . . . . . a large, dusty moose head has been placed above the mirror, its huge eyes staring into the room; an imitation antique Revolutionary War musket and powder horn hangs on the wall over one of the booths, and over three others are a long-handled fake-copper frying pan, a commander's sword in a rusty scabbard and a cheaply framed reproduction of* Washington Crossing the Delaware," and there is other Americana in evidence, including photos of prize fighters and other prominent persons.

The voice of Aaron Lebedeff singing "Rumania, Rumania" accompanied by a Klezmer band is coming from the juke box, evoking memories of Yiddish Music Hall. The place has obviously been closed for some time and looks run-down here and there. Charlie—"*early 40s, casually dressed*"—enters through the street door, reaches for the vodka and pours himself a drink. His son Josh—"*about 20 . . . . . carrying an old folded baby-stroller, an antique samovar and a dusty framed photograph of a World War II destroyer*"—enters from the family quarters upstage, enthusiastic about the treasure trove of family history he's found in the photos and other objects stored here. Charlie tells Josh he can take whatever he wants, even Moe the moose, anything except the basic fixtures which are to be part of the sale.

JOSH: I don't get it, only a month since she died, why does the place have to be sold so fast?

CHARLIE: Leave a bar closed too long, it loses its value. Customers drift away. You bring your stock certificate with you?

JOSH: With me? I've had it in my pocket since I was nine.

CHARLIE: Ten percent, kid, that's seventy-two hundred dollars; there's your trip to Italy, there's your—

JOSH: I keep thinking Grandpa didn't want me to sell those shares . . .

CHARLIE: He wanted them to be valuable to you, Josh, to be worth something some day, that's all.

JOSH (*going upstairs*): I don't get it, I just don't get it, what's the *hurry*, what's the *hurry* here . . . ?

Josh exits into the apartment. Charlie goes to the juke box and puts on "Columbia, the Gem of the Ocean," with blaring marching band and full chorus.

Scene 2: July 4, 1936, early morning

The lights come up in the barroom to reveal "*an image of rampant patriotism*" that wasn't fully perceptible before: American flags and bunting all over the place. "*Eddie Goldberg, a man in his early 40s who moves like an ex-boxer, bursts out of the kitchen, a swath of bunting furled over his arm, a three-foot-high flag in one hand, a strip of holiday bunting and a small flag in the other,*" dressed in white shirt with black bow tie, black pants and polished shoes. Charlie stations himself on one of the booths while his father, Eddie, acts out his memory, placing the decorations, polishing this and that in preparation for opening his bar for the day, conducting the soaring patriotic music as the record comes to an end.

Eddie now concentrates on his infant son Charlie in the stroller, trying to make him say "moose" but giving up and taking out a wooden duck to inspire the infant to say "duckie"—as the infant did the previous Saturday—but to no avail. Eddie puts the duck on the bar.

EDDIE (*silence for a moment; he leans against the bar*): You lost it. You lost "duckie." You had it and you lost it. Now we're losin' what we *had*, we're going *back*wards, Charlie. (*Starts to pace in front of bar.*) Kid, you're gonna be two; we gotta get movin' here. Goddamn *two*, kid. I mean, your brother Joey—your age he *opened* with "Mama," "Papa," "bunny," threw that shit away at the *top* and moved right into to "Hi, there," "Joey go out," "Beer on tap," "Eat cracker," "Gimme bagel" and many others. Eight years ago sittin' right there in that stroller we had twenty-two pounds of *talkin' baby*! (*Silence for a moment.*) Charlie, Charlie, you got any idea how much heartache you're givin' us with this issue, with this Goddamn vow of *silence* here? Six words in two years and now *gornisht*, not even a "Mama" or a "Papa." (*Pacing tensely in front of the stroller, controlling himself, quietly.*) Frankly, I'm concerned about your mother. Granted the woman is not exactly a hundred percent in the Brains Department her*self*, also a little on the wacky side, also she don't hear a Goddamn word anybody says so why should you want to talk to her in the first place—nevertheless, on this issue, my heart goes out to the woman. She got a kid who don't do shit. She goes to Rutgers Square every morning with the other mothers, they sit on the long bench there—in every stroller, right down the line, we got talkin', we got singin', we got tricks; in *your* stroller we got *gornisht*. We got a kid who don't make an *effort*, a boy who don't *extend* himself. (*Leaning down close to the stroller.*) That's the *trouble* with you, you don't *extend* yourself. You never *did*. You don't *now*, you never *did*, and you never *will*. (*Suddenly, urgently, whispering.*) Come on kid, gimme something, what's it *to* ya? I open for business in an hour, every morning the regulars come in, you *stare* at them; I tell 'em you're sick, I cover for you. It's July Fourth, a special occasion, be American, make an effort.

    Grabs the duck off the bar, leans down to the stroller with it.
Come on: "duckie," just a "duckie," one "duckie" would be Mitzvah . . .

Sound begins to emerge from the stroller, but it's only an unintelligible babble. Furious, Eddie throws the toy duck across the room, smashing it against Charlie's booth. Charlie picks up the duck and tries to put it back together, commenting that this isn't the only toy that Eddie has smashed this year in one of his rages, and that "*gornisht*" means "nothing." "I *did* finally learn to talk," Charlie declares, "last year I even started using the word 'duck' without bursting into tears."

The sound of crying comes from the stroller, and Eddie calls for his wife Gloria to come change the baby's diaper.

    EDDIE (*turns towards stairway*): Gloria, why don't you *answer* me?!

    GUSTA'S VOICE (*from upstairs*): Because I only been Gloria two and a half weeks and I was Gusta for thirty-eight years; I'm waiting to recognize.

    EDDIE: I thought you liked the name.

    Gusta appears in open doorway . . . . . small, about 40, very busy, a
    strong Russian accent.

    GUSTA: I liked it till I heard it hollered. Meanwhile, Toots Shor, I'm scouring the rusty sink of some very poor people I know. She's very slow, this Gloria.

    EDDIE: Hey, what about the *kid* here? I gotta get the bar open!

    GUSTA (*graciously*): *A shaynim dank, mit eyn tokhes ken men nit zayn oyf tsvey simkhes.* (*She exits.*)

    CHARLIE (*to audience*): Roughly, that's: "Thank you, but with one rear end I can't go to two parties."

    EDDIE: English! Say it in *English*, for Chrissakes!

GUSTA'S VOICE: You can't say it in English, Eddie, it don't do the job.

His mother is right, Charlie observes, English is a weakling of expression compared to Yiddish. Eddie switches on the light in the entrance of Eddie Goldberg's Golden Door Tavern, which in the past has borne the names Cap'n Ed's Place, The Cafe Edward, Eduardo's Cantina and Frisco Eddie's Famous Bar and Grill. Living upstairs are Eddie (formerly Itzik) with his wife and their sons Charlie and Joey (formerly Chaim and Jussel) and a boarder, Prof. Anton Zaretsky, who enters *"carrying his 70 years like an award, his unseasonably long, felt-collared coat draped cape-like over his shoulder,"* a veteran performer in the Marinsky Theater in Odessa and now the last vestige of the Second Avenue Yiddish Classic Art Players, performing solo. Automatically, Eddie serves him a tumbler half full of vodka. He downs it in one gulp, gives forth a cry of pain which is apparently part of the ritual because it startles no one, not even the baby, and then goes to a table and sits to read in his *Jewish Daily Forward* about the plight of Jews in Hitler's Reich.

Eddie's anger at the baby has cooled. He approaches the stroller and advises the infant not to let anyone, not even his father, push him around: "Charlie Goldberg don't take shit from nobody." Still talking to the baby, he expresses his hope that he can earn and save enough with this bar to move uptown some day where the symbol of success is the mixed drink—the cocktail—in a place that has "frosted mirrors with silver frames, the bar is ten yards of mahogany." He has dropped a slug into the juke box and set it to playing "America the Beautiful" while he continues his stream of advice to the infant, explaining, "Now there's two ways a Jew *gets* uptown; wanna get outa here, kid, you gotta punch your way out or talk your way out. Bein' Jewish, very dicey; they give you *a lot* of enemies and only *one* God. You're Jewish you gotta be smarter than everybody else; or cuter or faster or funnier. Or tougher. Because, basically, they want to kill you; this is true maybe thirty, thirty-five hundred years now and is not likely to change next Tuesday. It's not they don't want you in Moscow, or Kiev, or Lodz, or Jersey City: it's the earth they don't want you on, the earth is the problem, so the trick is to become necessary. If they need you they don't kill you. Naturally, they're gonna hate you for needing you, but that beats they don't need you and they kill you. Got it?" He concludes, "This, kid . . . is the whole story," as the record comes to its crescendo, " . . .From sea to shining sea!"

Eddie reminds Zaretsky to call him "Eddie" when instead he calls Eddie "Itzik." Zaretsky views the sudden emphasis on red, white and blue in this bar's decor with skepticism and sarcasm. Gusta comes in making a joke about the moose head. Grown-up Charlie comments from his booth and perspective of 40 years later in memory that his mother seems to have had a great sense of humor but his father never laughed at her jokes. Gusta annoys Eddie by making another joke about one of his idols, F.D.R. She leans into the stroller and sings part of a Jewish lullaby to the infant Charlie, then exits to the kitchen from which she supplies food for the bar's customers. When Eddie asks for today's menu specials, she tells him such dishes as "brisket Tzimmes," which Eddie translates onto the blackboard as "Mulligan Stew."

Zaretsky further provokes Eddie by singing a line or two from "Danny Boy," as though yielding to Eddie's urging that he and Gusta drop their Jewish words and mannerisms in favor of corresponding Americanisms. Eddie scoffs at Zaretsky's specialty of presenting Yiddish-theater characters in his solo act, for which there is no longer much of an audience. Their argument over these matters is apparently a ritual which they perform daily.

Eddie has a sudden qualm that the infant Charlie might not be smart enough to succeed. "There's two kinda guys come off the boat," he observes, "go-getters and ground-kissers." His father was one of the latter, he remembers, "Nine hundred miles we walk to get to the boat, just him and me, I gotta handle all the bribes. Ten years *old*, I gotta grease my way across the Russian Empire," while his father, Solomon, was concerned only with fine points like refusing to eat non-kosher food even if it meant starving and kissing everything around him in gratitude, from the boat that brought them to America to an Ellis Island Immigration officer. Eddie's father opened a small tavern but insisted on obeying the law when Prohibition came in, tried to persuade other tavern owners to do the same and was beaten to death in an alley by gangster bootleggers. Eddie gets a card from the Sons of Moses every year reminding him to light a candle and do the Kaddish for his father. Eddie kicks one of his tables over in anger, but Zaretsky raises his glass in a toast: "To Solomon Goldberg . . . who I saw speak in Rutgers Square against drinking and crime to an audience of drunks and criminals. Completely foolish and absolutely thrilling. We need a million Jews like him."

Eddie reminds Zaretsky of the atrocities they all endured in their European communities, brutal acts of violence inflicted on Eddie's grandfather, brother and mother. "You wanna run around bein' Mr. Jewish—that's *your* lookout—but you leave me and my kids *out* of it. I got my own deal with God." His family will continue to "stay on His good side" by observing the rituals, but Eddie announces—proudly—that he has changed his name legally and officially from Goldberg to Ross and has changed the sign outside.

Zaretsky remembers the pogroms, all right; he remembers a poor fellow named Grillspoon who knelt in an imitation of Christian prayer to try to placate those who then beat him to death with shovels. He warns Eddie that changing his name will only cause him to "reap the disaster of a second-rate Christian-imitation."

Zaretsky picks up his carpetbag and prepares to exit, when Joey Goldberg ("*a tough-looking ten-year-old*") enters from the apartment carrying his Hebrew school books and a stack of tablecloths. The actor shows Joey all the symbols of Jewish characterization and drama he carries in this valise—swords, hats and other props—and tells the admiring youth about a conference with a Hollywood producer (Mike Marshall, formerly Mendl Meyerberg) just the other day. Zaretsky was offered a job playing Spaniards, Asians, Polynesians, etc. and was shown a Western in which a former Yiddish theater colleague was playing an Indian villain.

Zaretsky views this as still another dreadful form of alienation; it makes him "hear the hoof-beats of Cossack horses clattering on cobblestones." He turned down the job offer. He finishes with a declaration in Yiddish (translated for the audience by Charlie): "A Jew I am, pal, and a Jew I shall remain." As he exits carrying his carpetbag, he tells Eddie, "Good morning to you, Mr. Ross, and, of course, my regards to your wife, Betsy."

Eddie sends Joey for the day's mail. Passing the stroller and looking in at his sleeping brother, Joey reassures Eddie that the infant is very smart and is taking in everything that is said. He goes out and comes back in with the mail, having seen "Eddie Ross" on the sign outside, learning that his name is now Joe Ross.

Joey claps on his yarmulkeh and heads for the door.

EDDIE: *Wait* a minute— (*Points to yarmulkeh.*) Where ya goin' with *that* on your head? What're ya, crazy? Ya gonna go eight blocks through Little Italy and Irishtown, passin' right through Goddamn *Polack* Street, with *that* on your head? How many times I gotta tell ya, kid—that is *not* an outdoor garment. That is an indoor garment *only*. Why don't ya wear a sign on your head says, "Please come kick the shit out a me"? You put it on in Hebrew School, where it belongs.

JOEY: Pop, I don't—

EDDIE: I'm tellin' ya *once* more—stow the yammy, kid. *Stow* it.

JOEY (*whips yarmulkeh off, shoves it in his pocket*): O.K., O.K. (*Starts toward door.*) I just don't see why I gotta be ashamed.

EDDIE: I'm not askin' ya to be ashamed. I'm askin' ya to be smart. (*Sees something in the mail as Joey opens the door.*) *Hold* it—

JOEY: Gotta go, Pop—

EDDIE: *Hold* it right there—

JOEY: Pop, this Tannenbaum, he's a real Torah nut, another five minutes he's gonna smite me with the jaw-bone of an ass.

EDDIE (*looking down at the mail*): I got information here you ain't *seein'* Tannenbaum this morning. I got information here says you ain't even headed for Hebrew School right now.

    Silence for a moment. Joey remains in the doorway.
C'mere, we gotta talk.

JOEY: No whackin', Pop. It leaves marks. I get embarrassed with my friends.

EDDIE: I don't whack nobody.

JOEY: You don't—?

EDDIE: I got this note here says—

    Takes small piece of cardboard from his mail, reads.
"Dear Sheenie Bastard. Back of Carmine's, remind you, Jewshit Joe, eight o'clock a.m., be there. Going to make Hamburger out of Goldberger—S.D." Bastard is spelled here b-a-s-t-i-d: this and the humorous remarks I figure the fine mind of the wop, DeSapio.

    After a moment, looks up, slaps bar.

An I wanna tell ya *good* luck, *glad* you're goin', you're gonna *nail* 'im, you're gonna *finish* 'im, you're gonna *murder* 'im—

JOEY (*relieved*): It's O.K? Really—

EDDIE: —and here'a couple pointers how to do so.

JOEY: Pointers, pointers—I need a *shot*gun, Pop; DeSap's near twice my size, fourteen years *old*—

EDDIE: Hey, far *be* it! Far be it from me to give pointers—a guy got twenty-six bouts under his belt, *twelve* professional—

JOEY: Yeah, but this DeSapio, he really *hates* me, this kid; he hated me the minute he *saw* me. He says we killed Christ, us Jews . . .

EDDIE: They was *all* Jews there, kid, everybody; Christ, His mother, His whole crowd—you tell him there was a buncha Romans there, too, makes him *directly related* to the guys done the actual hit!

JOEY: I *told* him that, Pop—that's what *really* pissed him off, Mary bein' a Jewish mother; he says, "Get outa here with that *Jewish* shit, I'm just gettin' used to the idea she was a virgin"; and then he whacked me.

EDDIE: And I bet you whacked him back, which is appropriate; ya stuck to your *guns*, kid—

JOEY: So why're we hidin' then? How come we're "Ross" all of a sudden? (*With an edge.*) Or maybe Ross is just our *out*door name, and Goldberg's still our indoor name.

EDDIE: Trouble with you, ya never learned the difference between smart and smart-ass—

JOEY: If we didn't do anything, what're we ashamed of? Joey Ross, Joey Ross, who's that? I don't get it, this means we're not Jewish any more?

EDDIE: Of *course* we're still Jewish; we're just not gonna push it.

Eddie happened to see the last part of Joey's last street scrap, and he approves the boy's technique of going for the belly. Eddie advises Joey to get in the first blow, up from the ground with all his weight behind it, right in the middle of his chin, then jump back so that when DeSapio falls he won't land on Joey and hurt him (Joey, who believes DeSapio will kill him, thinks his father's optimism is crazy.) Eddie explains that one of his bouts in the ring was with a fighter named DiGangi who was so overjoyed at knocking Eddie out in the first round that he swore eternal friendship there and then. If Joey finds they're ganging up on him (Eddie advises), shout "DiGangi's my *brother*, call him!" DiGangi is now a man of tremendous influence, which is the reason why the protection thugs leave Eddie's bar alone. Joey exits in a hurry, putting on his yarmulkeh to "drive 'em crazy."

Entering through the now-open door are Hannah di Blindeh ("Hannah the Blind") and Nick, "*a matching pair of ragged, aging alcoholics*" to whom Eddie refers as "Fred and Ginger." Hannah ("*near 60, Russian, and obviously sightless, wears faded, oddly elegant, overly mended clothing that may have been fashionable 30 years earlier*") and Nick ("*bushy white beard and matted hair make it hard to read his age, anywhere between early 50s and late 60s . . . . . he has a soiled, ill-fitting suit and shirt, what once had been a tie, a noticeably red nose and a clear case of the pre-first drink shakes*") go through their daily ritual with Eddie pouring and Hannah and Nick sitting at their regular places at the bar and quickly downing their first shots of the day.

Charlie explains to the audience that after his sixth drink Nick becomes preoccupied with his fantasy that he is, in reality, Santa Claus. Actually, he's a former police sergeant forcibly retired after shooting out street lamps with his revolver: "He carried this famous Smith and Wesson with him every day to Pop's bar, which allowed them *both* to think of him as a kind of guard-bouncer for the place." As for Hannah, "She'd been blinded somehow on the second day of the October Pogrom; Hannah didn't remember what she saw that second day, but what she heard still woke her up every morning like an alarm clock . . . . . The noise didn't go away till she finished her first vodka."

Blind though she may be, Hannah immediately notices that Eddie has changed the character of his place; she can't hear the chuck-a-luck wheel of what used to be called "Frisco Eddie's."

Finney the Book ("*a tight tiny bundle of 40-year-old Irish nerves under a battered fedora*") enters and goes right to a wall phone upstage. He has a problem: today is July 4, so everybody is betting 776 in the numbers. If it hits, he's a ruined

Tony Gillan as Joey and Judd Hirsch as Eddie in a scene
from Herb Gardner's *Converstaions With My Father*

man, no numbers bank will take layoff bets on 776 today. And even if it doesn't hit, he'll have to reduce the amount he pays Eddie for the use of one of his booths till post time. Meanwhile, Nick is performing his routine task of reading the Racing Form entries to Hannah so that she can select her wagers.

Blue ("*large, Irish, about 50, slow-moving, powerful*") enters, followed by Jimmy Scalso ("*sleekly Italian, just 30, wiry, a smiler, wearing the kind of carefully tailored silk suit that demands a silver crucifix on a chain about his neck*"). Blue checks out the juke box while Scalso sits at the bar and asks, "You got Daitch on tap, fellah?" "I got it," Eddie replies, serving with his customary comment, "now *you* got it." But almost at once Eddie recognizes that Scalso is a gangster. Eddie insults Scalso, calling him boring and demanding that he shut up, drink up and leave the premises.

EDDIE: I got a private club here, pal. I got my own rules. You just had a free beer; goodbye.

SCALSO: This ain't no private club.

EDDIE (*indicating barroom*): Right, this ain't no private club; but this . . .
> *Takes billy-club out from under bar, places it on bar.*
. . . this is a private club. It's called The Billy Club. Billy is the president. He wants you to leave.

SCALSO (*after a moment*): Ya mean you're willin' to beat the shit outa some guy just because ya think he's *borin'*?

EDDIE (*taps the club*): Self-defense, pal. Death against death.
> *Scalso suddenly starts to laugh; Finney is wringing his fedora like a wet bathing suit.*

BLUE: Come on, Jimmy; tell him we got a long day comin'.

SCALSO: Hey, Blue, I like this guy, I like this guy . . . *I like this guy!*
> *Still laughing; Eddie regarding him stonily, tightening grip on club.*
You are *great*, Goldberg . . . you are *some*thin', baby . . . "A private *club*, The *Billy* Club" . . . great, great . . .

BLUE (*impatient with him*): Enough now; we got alotta *work* here, boy.

SCALSO (*still chuckling*): Absolutely right, babe. Goldberg . . . Goldberg, Goldberg, *Goldberg*; you are cute, you are some cute Jew, you are the cutest Jew I ever saw. And tough; I never seen such a tough Jew, I include the Williamsburg Boys.
> *Eddie, the club at the ready, waiting him out.*
I'm Jimmy Scalso; maybe you don't hear, various internal problems, Vito had an appointment with the Hudson River, which he kept, Seranno gimme alla his stops; bye-bye, Big Vito, bon jour, Jimmy.
> *Eddie absorbing this, lowers club to his side.*
Y'know, I seen ya box, barkeep, Stauch's Arena, I'm sixteen—hey, Blue, this was *some*thin', The East Side Savage against Ah Soong, The Fightin' Chinaman—

BLUE: Move it along, boy; move it *along*, will ya?

SCALSO: Absolutely right, babe. O.K., business, Goldberg; Vito's got fifty-four stops, fifty-three is solid—some reason he lets one of 'em slide; yours. I'm checkin' the books, ya got no *butt* machine here, ya don't got our *defense* system, you got a box should be doin' two and a half a month, you're doin' seventy. *Our* records, selected *hits*, *thirty* top tunes a month—you take only *two*. Blue, what's he *got* on there?

> *Slaps his head.*

Shit, where's my fuckin' manners—Mr. Goldberg, this is Blue, for Blue-Jaw McCann; called such because the man could shave five times a day, he's still got a jaw turns gun-metal blue by evenin', same color as the fine weapon he carries. A man, in his prime, done hench for Amato, Scalisi, Carafano . . .

> *Scalso pauses a moment, letting this sink in. Eddie puts his club down on the bar. Scalso nods, acknowledging Eddie's good sense.*

Blue reports that the juke box holds mostly archaic oldies, plus the Aaron Lebedeff record. Scalso expresses his mock despair at such a non-profitable inventory, while Finney whispers to Eddie to tell them about DiGangi—but Eddie hushes him.

Scalso tells Eddie he'll send in a cigarette machine the next day, put him on the protection list and replace the "funeral music" in the juke box with 40 selected hits. What's more, he puts $1,000 in $100 bills on the bar as a good will advance for Eddie. But then he refers to a number of unpleasant things that might happen to Eddie's establishment if Eddie doesn't agree to the deal.

Eddie asks Hannah to push the infant in his stroller into the kitchen, leans over the bar and repeats to Scalso that he is still boring him to death.

EDDIE (*calmly, evenly*): I want your nose and your ass, and everything you got in between, *outa* my business. Still only two things you gotta remember: first is goin' away, and second is never comin' back. I don't want your butt machine, your records, your advice, and I want your Goddamn angel off my shoulder. I give you the same deal I give Vito on the box, and that's *it*. And now I want you and your over-the-hill hench outa my joint instantaneous. Goodbye and good luck.

> *He picks up the club, raps it sharply on the bar like a gavel.*

Conversation over; end of conversation.

> *Scalso remains quite still, Blue takes a small step forward from the juke box, Charlie rises tensely in his booth.*

HANNAH (*very softly, wheeling stroller into kitchen*): Pogrom . . . pogrom . . . pogrom . . .

SCALSO (*points to his silver crucifix; quietly*): This here J.C., my pop give it to me; remind me of Our Savior, but mostly, he says, to do things peaceful before I do 'em hard; this has been my approach with you here. But you know what comes to me, I listen to you? Sooner or later, tough or chicken, lucky, unlucky, Jews is Jews. Ain't this the way, Blue? Ain't this the way? Fuckin' *guests* in this country, they are—they're here ten minutes, they're tellin' ya how to *run* the place . . .

> *He puts his hand on Eddie's arm.*

I pride myself, makin' friends with you Jews—but sooner or later, every *one* of ya—

> *Eddie reaches forward, gets a firm grip on Scalso's crucifix and chain and pulls him across the bar with it, Scalso still half-seated on barstool.*

EDDIE: You was holdin' my arm . . .

SCALSO: Hey, my J.C., my J.C.—

EDDIE: You know us Jews, we can't keep our hands off the guy.

SCALSO: *Blue, Blue* . . .

> *Blue thrusts his hand into his gun pocket.*

EDDIE (*retaining firm grip on Scalso*): Here's the situation: Mr. Blue, whatever you got in mind right now, a fact for ya: Nick here, an ex-cop, got two friends with him, Mr. Smith and Mr. Wesson; there's some say his aim ain't what it used to be, but a target your size he's bound to put a hole in it somewheres; 'sides which, he don't care if he kills ya, he thinks Donder and Blitzen gonna take the rap for him anyway.

That's the situation, Eddie emphasizes, and he suggests "We all go for a safe and sane Fourth." Nick, his hand in his pocket has assumed his Santa Claus persona: "I see you when you're sleepin', I know when you're awake; I know if you've been bad or good, so be good for goodness sake . . ." Eddie releases Scalso, goes to the juke box and puts on Aaron Lebedeff's "In Odessa" with the Klezmer Band. Scalso orders Blue to attack Eddie (Scalso is armed with a knife), but nobody moves—it's a stand-off.

At this moment, Zaretsky enters grandly, his arm around a somewhat battered Joey, declaring "Not since David and Goliath have I seen such!" Eagerly, Joey tells his father, "He went *down*, Pop, he went *down*," though his bloody nose is witness to the fact that DeSapio got up again. Firmly, Eddie orders Joey to go out and pick up the bread order. Joey, finally realizing that things in this barroom aren't as they should be, obeys, and Zaretsky also senses that there's something amiss.

SCALSO (*grips Blue's arm, urgently*): Now, Blue *now*; place is fillin' up. Look, Blue, man wants to dance; help him dance, Blue—the feet, go for the feet. I want to see the man *dance*, make him nervous . . .

BLUE (*after a moment*): Nervous? You ain't gonna make *this* boy nervous. This boy don't *get* nervous; which is what's gonna kill him one fine day. Now *today*, Jimmy, here's how the cards lay down—

> *Reaching for Nick's bourbon bottle on bar, pouring a shot with his left hand, keeping his right firmly in his gun-pocket, his gaze never leaving Nick and Eddie.*

What you got here is an ol' shithouse and a crazy Jew. Two and a half on this box, boy? You give this Jew Bing Crosby in person, you give him Guy Lombardo appearing nightly, he don't pull in more'n a hundred. Now tell me, Jimmy-boy, you want me to go shoot Santa Claus for a hundred-dollar box?

SCALSO (*urgently, commanding*): We gotta leave a *mark*, Blue, on *some*body, on *some*thing. Fifty-four stops, this news travels; there gotta be *consequences* here, Blue, things happened here—

BLUE: *Consequences*? This Jew don't know consequences and don't care. Look at his eyes, Jimmy. He just wants to kill you, boy; don't care if he dies the next minute, and don't care who dies with him. Make it a rule, Jimmy-boy, you don't want to get into a fight, weapon or no, with a man ain't lookin' to live.

    Downs the shot of bourbon; starts towards front door.

SCALSO (*not moving, rubbing neck burn*): Things *happened* here, Blue—

BLUE: Seranno ain't gonna give a cobbler's crap about this place—fifty-three stops to *cover*, Jimmy-boy, let's go.

SCALSO (*silence for a moment; then, striding angrily towards Blue*): Hey, *hey*— how about you leave off callin' me "Jimmy-boy," huh? How about we quit that shit, right? Now on *in*.

BLUE (*patting Scalso's shoulder*): In the old Saint Pat's, y'know, over on Prince, we used t'make you Guineas have mass in the basement. Biggest mistake we ever made was lettin' you boys up on the first floor.

Blue exits, leaving Scalso in the doorway. Mocking Scalso, Eddie and Zaretsky go into a dance to the Klezmer Band's rhythm. Joey runs in, shouting that "*DiGangi e mio fratello*" works just as his father said it would. Scalso, unable to cope with all this any longer, exits. Joey confesses he didn't really win the fight, but Eddie declares him a winner anyhow. Hannah, seeing that the emergency is over, comes to join the dancing. But she stops them all cold by announcing that the infant Charlie has finally spoken.

HANNAH: Two statements, clear like a bell.

EDDIE: Come on, what?

HANNAH: The first, very nice, he touches my hand, he says, "Papa." The second statement, a little embarrassing to repeat . . .

EDDIE: *What*, Hannah . . . ?

HANNAH: A couple seconds later, he's got my hand again, this time a firm grip, he says—clear like a bell, I tell you—"No shit from nobody!"

    Eddie throws his head back, laughing triumphantly, Zaretsky applauds, Nick cheers, Joey leaping joyously in the air; Eddie grabs up his billy-club, whirling it above his head to the music, joining Zaretsky and Hannah again in the circling dance, the music faster and louder as the circle spins.

EDDIE (*shouting proudly above the music*): No shit from nobody! From nobody . . .

LEBEDEFF'S VOICE (*sings*):
> "In Ades, oh Ades,
> In Ades, oh Ades,
> Oh, Adesser Mama . . ."

> *Eddie starts dancing faster than the others now, his own rhythms, faster and faster, until he is whirling wildly, no longer circling his club above his head but striking sharp blows with it in the air, his triumph turning gradually to defiance and, finally, rage.*

EDDIE (*swinging his club with each shouted phrase*): From *no*body . . . from *no*body . . . *no*body.

> *A sharp silence as the music stops abruptly, lights suddenly fading except for the glow of the juke box; all quite still, watching Eddie, Charlie rising from his booth and moving slowly towards him, riveted by the sight of his fierce blows.*

(*A last blow, a final shout*): Nobody!

> *Eddie freezes, a sharp silhouette in the glow of the juke box, the club clenched in his hand, ready to strike another blow. Curtain.*

ACT II

Scene 1: July 3, 1944, early morning

It is eight years later in the memory of Charlie, who is posed as he was at the end of the previous act. But the juke box plays an Andrews Sisters record, and when the lights come up Eddie is busy changing his decor to tropical Caribbean dominated by a huge chandelier in the form of a flying flamingo. There are plastic pineapples instead of American flags at each table, and rum drinks are now featured. Eddie Ross's Golden Door Tavern is now the Flamingo Lounge.

Joey, now almost 18, is having coffee at the far end of the bar. Zaretsky is reading a newspaper. While screwing in light bulbs, Eddie is giving Joey advice about his boxing match this evening. Joey is fighting in the main event, which will be broadcast on the radio, looking for his 28th straight victory (23 by knockouts).

Zaretsky insists on calling to their attention a five-sentence item in the New York *Times* about 350,000 more Hungarian Jews being sent to Poland, in contrast to the paper's page one coverage of the holiday traffic situation. Eddie scoffs at the possible inaccuracy, but Joey is disturbed by this news. Eddie argues that even his hero F.D.R. has made no mention of such dire happenings: "If F.D.R. *believed* all that, he'd be doin' somethin' about it this *minute, guaranteed!*" Zaretsky replies, "He knows that no one believes the Jews are dying, only that somehow, they are making millions from the war and want it." But Zaretsky promises to behave himself at Joey's victory party here tonight: "The J-word will not be spoken." He exits.

Joey tells his father he thinks Zaretsky's tales of extraordinary persecution may be true. After all, things seem to be getting worse right here: "Pop, *Brooklyn*, they hit two cemeteries in one *week*. Around *here*, every synagogue in the neighborhood's been marked up, and it's only *July*. You been on Rivington lately?—Jewish stars with swastikas painted over 'em, they're poppin' up on the walls like Lucky Strike ads. The Gladiators, the Avengers—*boys* clubs, they call 'em—they're on the prowl every night beatin' the crap outa Hebrew School kids." Eddie's answer is, "I *heard* it all already; been goin' on since before you was born. But this stuff *Zaretsky's* talkin' about—not even in old Moldavanka was there ever such." It just can't be true.

Young Charlie (*"about 11, concerned, thoughtful and several worlds away"*) enters from the kitchen carrying a pile of papers and table set-ups on a tray. Noticing Young Charlie's worried look, Charlie tries to reassure his younger self (who of course cannot hear him) that better days are coming. As a matter of fact, Young Charlie is obsessed with getting votes for Peggy Parsons (whose picture is on the wall with those of the other contestants) in the Miss Daitch Contest. Charlie advises Young Charlie, "Love does *not* make the world go round, *looking* for it does."

Joey cautions his kid brother not to go out on the street by himself tonight, but Young Charlie has other things on his mind; he wants to know what Joey thinks of the letter he showed him.

YOUNG CHARLIE: If you got a criticism, tell me.

JOEY: Charlie, number one— (*Pointing to the Miss Daitch photos.*) Will you please tell me the difference between her and—see, I can't even find her—they all got the same smile, the same eyes—

YOUNG CHARLIE: I don't believe it, I don't believe you're my brother.

JOEY: O.K., tell me, what's the difference between her and—"Lovely, Lively, Laurie Lipton" here.

YOUNG CHARLIE: The difference? The *dif*ference? Why am I discussing this with a boxer?

JOEY: I got to go to Bimmy's—

YOUNG CHARLIE: Thirty seconds, Joey. The revised version; I changed key words.

JOEY (*leans against booth*): Twenty.

YOUNG CHARLIE (*reads from loose-leaf paper*): "Mr. Samuel Goldwyn, Metro-Goldwyn-Mayer Studios, Sixteen Hundred Melrose Avenue, Hollywood, California. Dear Sam; I am the C.E. Ross with perhaps whom you are unfamiliar, being mostly employed in the screen play field by Arthur Rank of London. Enclosed please find photo of Peggy Parsons. I think you will agree that this is the outstanding exquisiteness of a motion picture star. You may reach her by the Daitch's Beer distribution place in your area is my belief. If motion picture employment is a result you may wish to say to her who recommended her eventually. She or yourself can reach me by post at the Flamingo Apartments, Six Eighty-One Canal Street, New York City. In closing I think of you first-hand instead of Darryl or David because of your nation of origin Poland which is right near my father's original nation Russia. Yours truly, C.E. Ross."

> *Young Charlie does not look up from the letter, so concerned is he about his brother's response. Joey, sensing this, sits opposite him in the booth.*

JOEY: To begin with, that's an exceptionally well-put, well-written letter, Charlie . . .

YOUNG CHARLIE: I know what you're thinkin', but *wild things* happen out there, Joey; they're findin' stars in *drug*stores, *elev*ators—

JOEY: Right, and I'm sure the feeling you have for this Peggy is—

YOUNG CHARLIE: Peggo, she prefers to be called Peggo—

JOEY: Peggo, right—is genuine. So let's follow this through for a moment. Say, thousand to one shot, but Goldwyn, somebody in his office, sees the picture, say he gets ahold of her; say she's grateful, comes down here to Canal Street to see you, right?

YOUNG CHARLIE: Right, right.

JOEY: And you're eleven.

YOUNG CHARLIE: At that point I'll deal with the age problem.

JOEY (*after a moment; quietly*): Tell ya, sometimes the similarities, you and Pop, it scares the shit out of me, kid. (*Indicating Eddie, far left, putting last few bulbs into the flamingo.*) Look at 'im; ten years, and he still thinks Canal Street runs uptown.

Joey leaves for his workout at Bimmy's. Going over the mail, Eddie comes upon a letter from the Star of David School. It seems that Charlie has not been there for eight months and up until now has managed to intercept the letters of inquiry about his absence. Charlie pleads with his father: the school is "just this ratty place on Houston Street," conducted by two men with bad breath who use physical punishment. Young Charlie can't believe that God is anywhere near there, though Eddie assures Young Charlie He is, and it's advisable to maintain the connection, stay in touch, however casually. Young Charlie may need God someday.

Eddie explains that he was married "under God" by a rabbi to a woman whose raven hair shone as she ran down the beach. But immediately after they were pronounced man and wife, the light went out of her hair "like somebody turned off a switch," and gradually she became "the totally wacky deaf person we know in our home." Despite this seeming betrayal by the Almighty, Eddie maintains his connection with God, "Because there'll be a night when the heart attack comes and somebody'll have to call Dr. Schwartzman and the ambulance. And who will do it? The Wacky Ravenhead! In five minutes she covers a fifty-year bet . . . . . It's called a Coronary Marriage. And when you find a better reason for people staying together, let me know. Love; forget it." Eddie maintains lip service to his religion because "All God's gotta do is come through *once* to make Him worth your while."

Eddie and Young Charlie shake as a sign of agreement in this matter, and Eddie pours his son a seltzer. Young Charlie agrees with his father that his mother "is *some* wacky *deaf* person," and Eddie immediately smacks him in the face, a blow that sends the boy off his bar stool to the floor.

EDDIE (*shouting*): You will not mock your mother! Even in jest!

YOUNG CHARLIE (*half-mumbling, still on his knees, his head still ringing, shocked and hurt at once*): Hell with you, *hell* with you, don't make no sense . . .

EDDIE (*thundering, pointing down at him*): What's *that*? What do I hear? Gypsies! Gypsies! The Gypsies brought ya! This can't be mine!

YOUNG CHARLIE (*scrambling to his feet, gradually rising to full, screaming, arm-flailing rage*): Oh, I wish to God they had! I wish to God the Gypsies brought me! I don't wanna be from you! *Nothin'* fits together, nothin' ya *say*! Goddamn switche*roo* alla time! *Her*? *Her*? *You*! *You're* the crazy one, *you're* the deaf one, *you're* the one nobody can talk to! (*His arms wide, taking in the whole place.*) Goddamn *loser*! You're a Goddamn crazy *loser* in a Goddamn loser *shit*house here!

> Young Charlie is suddenly silent, seeing, as we do, that Eddie has picked up the vodka bottle by its neck, holding it like a weapon, and is now, slowly and deliberately, coming out from behind the bar. Charlie turns away, but Young Charlie holds his ground at center; speaking firmly, evenly, without tears, as Eddie approaches.

Come on, great, let's see ya do the one thing ya *can* do . . . (*Shouting, challenging.*) No. No more hitting this year. This is *it* . . . Come on, come on, Pop . . . just one more move, I'm the perfect height; just one more move and I kick you in the balls so hard ya don't straighten up for a *month* . . . (*Full power now; pointing.*) One more move, and it's right in the balls—right in the *balls*, Pop, I swear to God!

EDDIE: Swear to *who*?

YOUNG CHARLIE: God! I swear to *God*!

EDDIE (*after a moment, quietly*): See how He comes in handy?

Subdued, Eddie replaces the bottle and acts as though he had simply been trying to make his point about God and Hebrew School. Both big and little Charlie realize that this is one round they won. Gusta enters, announcing today's menu and stating her intention of going upstairs when the prize fight starts because she can't bear to listen to it. She notices the flamingo, then goes into the kitchen, followed by Eddie who is discussing the possibility of advertising his Flamingo Lounge.

Young Charlie sits down and takes this opportunity of peace and quiet to compose a letter on his favorite subject to Darryl Zanuck. The lights dim, as Charlie, in memory, hears a pack of boys singing the Marine Corps hymn with grossly anti-Jewish lyrics, causing Charlie to clench his fist and comment, "If Joey was here . . . if Joey was here they'd never get away with it . . ."

Scene 2: About 7 that evening

The boys' voices are drowned out by the sound of a cheering crowd at a preliminary bout coming from a Philco radio on the bar. As the lights come up, all the barroom regulars gather: Hannah, Nick, Finney and Zaretsky. Eddie brings in champagne from the kitchen. The bout being broadcast ends in a knockout, then the clothing-store sponsor, Big Mike Baskin (formerly Manny Buffalino) comes on to announce that he will give a silver-plated watch to the winner of the main event.

Nick shows them all that he's wearing his special shirt, never washed since it was stained with Barney Ross's blood when Nick saw Ross lose his welterweight title in "the greatest Loosin' Win I ever saw." Eddie opens one of the champagne bottles for a toast in honor of Ross, followed by a toast to Joey. But when Eddie turns the Philco up to full sound, the crowd is jeering and labeling Joey "chicken" because he hasn't shown up for the fight and is obviously not going to do so. Joey had left for the arena an hour ago, and Eddie is afraid he may have been waylaid and beaten up. In a few moments, though, Joey enters quietly with Young Charlie, goes to the radio and switches it off. Eddie is at first relieved to see that Joey is O.K., then wants to know what happened: "We got, among other things, Mr. Vince

William Biff McGuire (Nick), Marilyn Sokol (Hannah), Peter Gerety
(Finney the Book) with Judd Hirsh in *Conversations With My Father*

DiGangi sittin' over at Carmine's right now hearin' it broadcast how his son's a *chicken*." Joey announces, "No more fights. No more fights, Pop. Not here." He downs a shot of vodka, then explains.

JOEY (*firmly*): This mornin', workin' out with Bimmy, we're skippin', we're sparrin', my mind ain't there, Pop. I'm doin' math. Three hundred and fifty thousand Jews in twenty-one days, comes out seventeen thousand five hundred a day, *this* day, today—

EDDIE: I *told* ya, Joey, a lotta these stories—

JOEY (*turns to him*): Please, ya gotta be quiet, Pop. That's maybe two thousand just while I'm workin' out. Seventeen thousand five hundred a day. No, it's impossible, I figure; Pop's *right*, it's nuts. I keep punchin' the bag. I come back to pick up Charlie, we're headin' over, not seven yet; then I hear people hollerin', I look up, I see it. Top of the *Forward* Building, tallest damn buildin' around here, there's the *Jewish Daily Forward* sign, y'know, big, maybe thirty feet high and wide as the buildin', electric bulbs, ya can see it even deep into Brooklyn, *forever*, Pop. What they did is, they took out the right bulbs, exactly the right bulbs, gotta be hundreds of 'em, so the sign says: "Jew is For war"; gettin' brighter every second as the sky gets darker and darker, till it's Goddamn blazin' over the city, Pop, and Charlie and me start runnin' towards it, we're still maybe eight blocks away, we're passin' a lotta people and kids on Canal, pointin' up, laughin', some cheerin' "yeah, yeah" and we're runnin' to it like a fire; in the Square, in front of the buildin', maybe five hundred people and the thing's a torch, glowin', you can see it bouncin' off the river now, "Jew is For war," "Jew is For war" and the crowd Yeah-yeahin', yeah-yeahin', like ball-fans, Pop . . . . . I know that second for sure they are doin' seventeen thousand five hundred a day, somewhere, seventeen thousand five hundred a day and I'm a guy who spends his time boppin' kids for a sil-ver-plated watch from Big Mike, hockable for fifteen dollars; right now I wouldn't hock me for a dime. Point is, I'm goin' in, Pop. I'm gettin' into this war and I need your help, now. (*Eddie is silent.*) Army don't register me till next month, then it could be a year, more, before they call me. *Navy*, Pop, navy's the game: they take ya at seventeen with a parent's consent. Eight a.m. tomorrow I'm at Ninety Church, I pick up the consent form, you fill it out, sign it, ten days later boot camp at Lake Geneva, September I'm in it, Pop. Corvette, destroyer, sub chaser, whatever, *in* the Goddamn thing.

EDDIE (*after a moment*): Your mother will never—

JOEY: I just need you, Pop. One parent. One signature.

        Silence for a moment.

Do me a favor; take a look outside. Just turn left and look at the sky.

They all go out except Hannah, who is holding Joey's arm. Young Charlie believes there are enough enemies to fight right here—his brother doesn't have to leave. The others soon drift back into the bar, shocked by what they've seen, Eddie declaring, "Get me the Goddamn paper, I sign it *now*." All he asks is that Joey "show 'em how a Jew fights." The others also sincerely approve of Joey's decision, while Eddie pours the champagne to celebrate a much more important event than victory in a prize fight.

Gusta enters and is told what has happened. She goes to the bar, sets down the tray she's carrying and slaps Eddie across the face. The juke box blares the Paul Whiteman orchestra and chorus version of "Anchors Aweigh."

Scene 3: August 8, 1945, early morning

Thirteen months later, some changes have been made in the barroom, noticeably a black drape over the portrait of F.D.R. and a map of the Pacific theater of war, where Joey is serving on a destroyer, manning twin-fifty anti-aircraft guns. "He was gone and *I* was here," Charlie tells the audience, "the house was mine. People started *noticing* me. 'How's it *goin'*, Charlie?' 'What're ya *doin'*, Charlie?' Pop started *talking* to me, hangin' *around* with me, asking my *opinion* on things—he didn't listen to the answer, but he *asked* me; I was it: star of the show, Top of the Card, the Main Event. Civilians look for job-openings in wartime . . . and there was an opening here for Prince."

On the radio, President Truman is explaining about the use of the atom bomb, and in the bar Eddie is inventing the Atomic Cocktail. Zaretsky enters while Eddie is venting his spleen at Young Charlie for criticizing the oil painting behind the bar. The actor tells them he's expecting word of an engagement in Buenos Aires, then goes out to get the mail. Eddie takes out a poem Young Charlie wrote him for Father's Day and asks him to read it aloud. Charlie does so, while Zaretsky enters, puts the mail on the bar and goes into the apartment.

YOUNG CHARLIE (*reads*): "Father of the Flamingo; by C.E. Ross: he leadeth them beside distilled waters, he restoreth their credit . . . . . And yea, though I may walk through the valley of the shadow of Little Italy, I shall fear no goy or evil sound, 'cause my Pop has taught me how to bring one up from the ground."

EDDIE: O.K., very nice. (*Leaning forward on the bar, pleasantly.*) O.K., now all I'm askin' is a truthful answer: who helped ya out with that?

YOUNG CHARLIE: Nobody, Pop. I mean, it's a Twenty-Third Psalm take-off, so I got help from the *Bible*—

EDDIE: I *know* that, *besides* that—the thing, the ideas in there, how it come together there—you tellin' me nobody helped ya out on that, the *Actor*, nobody?

YOUNG CHARLIE: Nobody, Pop.

EDDIE (*after a moment*): O.K., there's times certain Jewish words is unavoidable, I give ya two: *narrishkeit* and *luftmensh*. *Narrishkeit* is stuff bey*ond* foolish— like what? your mother givin' English lessons, this would be narrish-work. Now, this *narrishkeit* is generally put out by *luftmensh*—meanin', literal, *guys* who live on the *air*—from which we get the term "no visible Goddamn means of support." Poem-writers, story-writers, picture-painters, we got *alotta* 'em come in here, what ya got is mainly y'fairies, y'bust-outs and y'souseniks—a blue *moon*, ya get a sober straight-shooter, breaks even.

Slaps the bar.

Now, I'm lookin' at this poem two months now, besides takin' note, numerous situations, how you *present* y'self, kid—first-class, flat-out *amazin'*, this poem.

Young Charlie smiles happily. Eddie taps his son's head.

It's Goddamn Niagara *Falls* in there—all we gotta do is point it the right way so you can turn on a coupla *light*-bulbs with it. The *answer?* Head like yours, ya know it already, don't ya?

YOUNG CHARLIE (*confused but flattered*): No; I don't, Pop.

EDDIE: I speak, of course, of the Legal Profession! Brain like that, how you get them words together, I'm talkin' *up*town, Charlie, I'm talkin' about the firm o' Ross, Ross, Somebody and *Some*body; you're gonna be walkin' through places the dollars stick to your *shoes*, y'can't *kick* the bucks off. Hey, looka the experience you al*ready* got—(*Arms wide, delightedly struck by the perfect illustration.*) Twelve years now you been pleadin' cases before the *bar*!

He laughs happily at his joke, slapping the bar, Young Charlie laughing with him, their laughter building with the sharing of the joke, Charlie joining them.

CHARLIE (*chuckling*): Not bad, not bad; one for *you*, Pop . . . (*Suddenly, frightened, remembering; he shouts.*) Now—it was *now*—

We hear Gusta scream from upstairs—a long, wrenching, mournful wail, like the siren of a passing ambulance . . . . .

Zaretsky enters and informs them that Gusta has just received a telegram (he delivered it to her and not to Eddie because it was addressed to her) from the Secretary of War stating that Joey was killed in action two days previously. An enclosed cable from the captain of Joey's destroyer explains that Joey was killed manning his guns during a kamikaze attack by Zeros. Charlie recites from memory: "With ample time to leave his position for safety, your son, to his undying honor, remained in defense of his ship and shipmates, as determined to hit his target as was the target to destroy his battle station." Joey had requested to be buried at sea, the Kaddish having been read for him as Jussel Solomon Goldberg, and he is to receive the Navy Cross.

The others dress the barroom for mourning, while Gusta can be heard singing a lullaby softly to herself. Zaretsky explains to Charlie that the Mourner's Kaddish is about faith, not death. Eddie muses to himself, his anger growing and his voice growing louder: "It's like the Mafia, Charlie . . . It's like talkin' to a Mafia chief after he does a hit, ya kiss the capo's ass so he don't knock *you* off too: 'Hey, God, what a great idea, killin' Joey Ross! Throwin' my cousin Sunny under a garbage truck—I thought *that* was great—but having some nutso Nip drop Joey, this is You at the top of Your *form*, baby. Oh yeah, magnified and sanctified be *you*, Don Guiseppi—' . . . . . Hey, Charlie, that's *it* for Hebrew School." He shouts to God that after 50 years of being a Jew, he is a Jew no longer. Finally Young Charlie rises and tells his father to shut up.

YOUNG CHARLIE: You really gonna hang this on *God*, Pop? Really? This is what you *wanted*, Pop; Mr. America, the toughest Jew in the Navy, and you got it; only he's dead. Every *letter, twice* on the phone with him I heard ya—"Kill, kill, *kill* 'em, kid!" Same as you screamed in the *ring*. And you want *God* to take the rap for this? All for *you*, Pop, the ring, the twin-fifties, he was fightin' for you. "Kill 'em, kid! *Get* 'em!" Well, ya finally did it, Eddie—if *anybody* could do it, *you* could— you *talked* somebody to death.

> *He goes quickly up the stairs, exits into apartment, slamming the door behind him. Silence for a moment, except for the sound of Gusta continuing softly to sing the lullaby; Eddie goes quickly up the stairs towards the door.*

EDDIE: Listen to me, kid; ya got it all wrong, I straighten it out for ya . . .

> *He tries to open the door, but it has clearly been locked from the inside; he raises his voice a bit, leans closer, trying to talk to Young Charlie through the door.*

Listen to me, Charlie; it's just my wacky pop, see. Just my wacky pop all over again. *Fine* points; it's the Goddamn *fine* points, kid. He *knows* this Nip fruitcake is comin' right *for* 'im, but he stays there behind his gun, because he thinks he's *supposed* to. It's my pop all over again, pal—*fine* points; Goddamn fine points. Wacky, the *both* o' them.

> *Silence. He tries the knob again.*

Come on, kid. Open up.

> *One bang on the door; sternly, evenly.*

Hey, Charlie; open up. (*Silence.*) Let's move it, Charlie; let me in.

> *Starts banging more forcefully on door.*

Let me in, Charlie; let me *in* there . . .

> *Now wildly, fiercely, pounding with all his strength, the door shaking from his blows.*

Charlie, Charlie, let me *in*, let me *in*!

> *Both fists together now, pounding rhythmically, shouting with each blow.*

Let me *in*, let me *in*, let me *in* . . .

> *He continues banging on the door, his shouting almost like a chant now; Hannah, Nick and Finney quite still at the bar, watching; Gusta, silent now, watches him from the kitchen doorway.*

ZARETSKY (*his head bowed, intoning softly*): "Yisgaddal v'yiskaddash shmey rabboh . . ."

> *All lights fading gradually down to a blackout in the barroom; the shouting, the pounding and Zaretsky's prayer fading with the light. Charlie alone now in a small spotlight at the far right of the darkened*

> *stage. Silence for a few moments; he looks out at us.*
> CHARLIE (*quietly*): Well . . . I guess I won *that* one too.

Scene 4: October 15, 1965, early morning

As the lights come up in the barroom, Charlie is remembering the sound of Bob Hope entertaining troops in Viet Nam; Lyndon Johnson talking of the Great Society. It is about 20 years later, Charlie is doing very well as a writer, producing about a novel a year whose central character is Izzy, "Tough but warm, blunt yet wise, the impossible and eccentric Bleecker Street tavern keeper who won not only your heart in the final chapter but the Mayor's special cultural award that year for 'embodying the essential charm and excitement of New York's ethnic street life.'" Charlie and Eddie only got together a few times a year because Eddie would never go near a synagogue again and thus was absent from any of the usual family occasions.

Hannah, Nick and Zaretsky are dead, and Finney is operating out of Boca Raton. As Eddie enters from the kitchen—still spry, though 20 years older—he's chuckling about a story on the front page of the *World Telegram*, headlined, "Vatican Absolves Jews of Crucifixion Blame." Charlie has come to visit after a call from his mother telling him something was wrong with Eddie (he'd had a heart attack the year before, but recovered swiftly). Eddie seems to be in good shape, chortling over a telegram he's sent to the Pope: "Thanks a lot, you greaseball putz."

Eddie claims he's feeling fine. The place has suddenly become a hit, mostly to Gusta's credit. The neighborhood, SoHo, is rapidly gentrifying, and the people moving into the neighborhood like Gusta's cooking as well as the generic Yiddish names for the dishes. No more "Mulligan stew"—Eddie has renamed the place "The Homeland" and jacked up the prices.

Eddie saw Charlie accepting the Mayor's award on TV. "You come in old," Eddie comments, maybe because Charlie was wearing a tuxedo. Charlie figures his father is O.K., his usual self, and starts to leave, but Eddie inquires about Charlie's wife Sally. "We were divorced three years ago. As you well know," Charlie reminds his father, and he's had another wife since then, Karen. Eddie notes that he hasn't seen his 10-year-old grandson, Josh, for a couple of months. Josh likes hanging around his grandfather's barroom only too well, as Charlie remarks, "He's the only ten-year-old at Dalton who drinks his milk out of a shot glass."

Eddie agrees that Josh is "a pisser." Charlie has his hand on the knob, leaving, when Eddie stops him with the comment that he has skimmed one of Charlie's books—the first one.

EDDIE (*chuckling*): That's some *sweet*heart, that guy. Who *is* that guy? Bartender, two sons, comes from Russia; who *is* that sweetie? Is that a *Jewish* gentleman? Got *all* sweeties in there, y'sweet blind lady, y'sweet ex-cop, y'sweet bookie—*three* pages, I got an attack o' diabetes.

CHARLIE: Pop, if I told the truth they'd send a *lynch*-mob down here for ya.

EDDIE: Always glad to see new customers, kid. (*Turns to newspaper.*) Point is, regardless, I wanna wish ya good luck with them "Dizzy" books.

CHARLIE: Izzy!

Closes door, turns to him.

Izzy, Izzy, Izzy. As you know damn *well*. O.K., that's it. I came down here, I was worried about you, but you're O.K. and that's it; I am never playing this Goddamn game again. That was *it*. (*Moving towards him.*) Izzy? You don't like him? Too sweet for ya? He's *your Jew*, Pop, you made him up. He's *your* Jew, and so am I; no history, no memory, the only thing I'm linked to is a chain of bookstores. *Vos vilst du*, Pop?—that means "What do you *want*?" That's Yiddish, Pop, some people you knew used to speak it; they were called "Jews." Put a sign up, Eddie: "No Yiddish Spoken." Also no truth. Also no love. God bothered you, we got rid of Him. Hugging bothers you, we do not touch. Here I am, Pop, just what the Rabbi ordered; only now you don't like it; now you don't want it. *Vos vilst du*?

Charlie pounds the table and declares to his father that he is now everything his father asked for: he is a "red, white and blue, star-spangled American millionaire" with a fire burning in him representing his father, a fire he can't put out. Eddie answers, "I don't see you rushin' down to City Hall, changin' your name back to Goldberg." Charlie's problems can't be blamed on him, Eddie is responsible only for his own achievements or shortcomings, no one else's. "Give yourself a rest," he advises Charlie, "you'll waste your life tryin' to catch me, you'll find y'self twenty years from now runnin' around a cemetery tryin' to put a stake through my heart . . . . . Meanwhile, currently, I admit I give ya a hard time—but, frankly, I never liked rich kids."

Suddenly Eddie feels faint, but the attack goes away after he takes a long swig from the vodka bottle. It's something to do with his heart valve closing up, called Smithfield's Disease. He's supposed to sit in a wheelchair (he pulls one out from behind the bar and sits in it) in case he falls asleep, and he can suffer an embolism almost any time, as he did a while ago. And Eddie shows Charlie tattoos on his arms, "Pistol Pete" (Joey's boxing name) and "King of the Twin-Fifties," then reminding Charlie that no one who has tattoos can be buried in a Jewish cemetery. Gusta, now deeply religious, wants them to be buried in the same place as Zaretsky, and Eddie gets Charlie to promise to bury him in a non-sectarian spot in Queens.

Most particularly, Eddie doesn't want to be buried anywhere near Zaretsky, knowing about him what he knows now. It seems that Zaretsky, at 93, had premonitions that his time might be up and made a will leaving an estate of $1.5 million. Eddie is flabbergasted that Zaretsky was able to save that much, and with such resources would live in these shabby surroundings, "Takin' shit from me." Charlie declares, "He *loved* it here, Pop, he even liked fightin' with *you*." But Eddie cannot contain his outrage: "A *millionaire*, Charlie! Workin' in a loser language! He did everything *wrong*—and he was a hit! This Goddamn *green*horn! Can you make *sense* of this, Charlie? Can you tell me what *happened*? I did everything *right*, nothin' worked, and now I'm gettin' saved by a pot fulla your mother's *holishkehs*! *Zaretsky*, why *him*—why *him* and not *me*? And, you'll forgive me—I wish ya all the best . . . (*Gripping Charlie's arm.*) . . . but why *you*, ya little putz, with your Goddamn *narrishkeit*—why *you* and not me? (*Starting to become drowsy again.*) Surrounded by Goddamn millionaires here . . . Can you make *sense* of this . . . the bucks, what happened? The big bucks, why did they avoid me? Wherever I was, the bucks never came, and when I went to where the bucks were they flew away like pigeons . . . like pigeons in the park . . ."

Eddie is describing his recurring nightmare of arriving at Ellis Island and not being admitted, when he falls deeply asleep. Gusta comes in carrying two pots of food. She explains that Eddie does this a lot, falling asleep in the middle of a sentence or abruptly changing the subject. Charlie is worried about whether his father is getting the best of care, raising the possibility of a hospice for him, and he's also concerned about Gusta's loss of hearing. Gusta comments, "These hospice people, it's like a good host after a long party, they see you to the door," and she reassures Charlie that her deafness is selective, she hears what she wants to hear. She started screening out the bad news 40 years ago when Eddie possessed his tremendous energy: "For me he was America, Charlie, if they had the expression then you would call him sexy." Now with his illness, "All is fine again; he wakes up, half the time it's forty years ago, I'm Gusta, he's Itzik; it's always the beginning."

Gusta turns Eddie's wheelchair around so he isn't facing the light (or the audience). She exits to the kitchen, laughing about the place's new name, "The Homeland."

Scene 5: About eight weeks later, early morning

"*The lights change only slightly*," and Charlie and Eddie have not changed positions, as Charlie explains that Eddie has had an embolism which has left him without the power of speech. He's learning to write with his left hand. After discussing the situation with the speech therapist, Eddie has come to tell his father—who has been discouraged from trying to regain speech because the child-like sounds he makes annoy him—that he should try something the therapist calls "automatic speech": "You are capable, right now, of saying, distinctly as ever, certain automatic phrases—ends of songs, if I do the first part . . . . . You hear yourself *do* that, and that'll get you to want to work at the whole talkin'-shot again, see?"

Charlie tries parts of "The Star-Spangled Banner," to no effect. But when he asks his father, "You got Daitch on tap, fella?" Eddie reflexively replies, "Like the choice; *I* got it, now *you* . . . got it."

With this success, Eddie nods in agreement that he will keep trying. Charlie has brought a stack of cards with pictures of animals and birds, with the word printed underneath the image. He selects one of them and shows it to his father, saying, "'Duck.' We'll start with 'duck.' *Eddie does not move, then a soft chuckling sound, then silence. Then Eddie, rather forcefully, raises his left arm, the middle finger of his hand jabbing upward, giving Charlie 'The Finger.' Eddie continues to hold his hand up firmly, Charlie smiles and the lights come down, one single light remaining on 'The Finger" as Charlie moves downstage to far end of bar."*

Scene 6: June 25, 1976, early evening

The room is in darkness except for light on Charlie at the bar sipping vodka and remembering that Eddie died seven months later, talking again and making plans. "I wish I could tell you that he won my heart in the final chapter," Charlie tells the audience, "but he did not. I light his Yahrzeit candle every year, though. Trouble is, I can't seem to get halfway through the prayer without shouting, 'Go to hell, Pop.' (*After a moment.*) It's a month now since Mom died, joking as she closed her act. 'I'm thinking of becoming a Catholic,' she says, that last night. 'And why's that, Ma?' I say, feeding her the straight line like a good son. (*Gusta's accent.*) 'Well, Charlie, I figure better one of them goes than one of us.'"

The lights come up on the barroom as it was in Scene 1—stroller at center and juke box playing "Columbia, the Gem of the Ocean." Charlie tells the audience he misses his mother, he buried his father as requested and never forgets his Yahrzeit because his father paid the Sons of Moses $50 to remind Charlie every year—another piece of Eddie's puzzling personality which Charlie can't fit with the rest.

Charlie is glad to get rid of this place, but not his son Josh, who comes in to tell his father he can't bear to pack up the bar things, he knows he could keep the place going himself. The one thing he's always wanted was to be here, behind this bar.

JOSH (*leans forward, his arms wide, his hands on the bar*): Like Grandpa said, you're the host at a party that never ends. My own place, Dad, my *own*—people coming to *my* place, working for *myself*, nobody telling me what to *do* . . . (*Smiling to Charlie.*) Another vodka, pal?
    Picks up bottle and glass with a flourish.
I got it—
    Pours drink for Charlie.
Now *you* got it. (*Charlie looks up blankly at him.*) It all fits, it all makes sense, Dad, don't you see? Great-Grandpa, Grandpa, and now me . . .
    Taking folded stock certificate from pocket.
I can't give you this, Dad, I can't give you these shares. Look, I'm aware of the position this puts you in, but I can't let you sell this place. Grandpa had a *reason* for giving me these shares, I knew it when I couldn't pack the stuff, this is what he wanted; this is what *I* want.
    CHARLIE (*quietly, evenly*): Oh, I'm sure he had a reason . . .
    JOSH (*leans toward him*): Dad, Bicen*tennial's* next week, the *crowds* down here, the fireworks, *that's* when I re-*open*—the old sign's in the basement: "Eddie Ross' Golden Door"—July *Fourth*, Statue of *Liberty*, perfect—all I gotta do is build up the food volume, build up the food volume to match the liquor volume—
    Charlie suddenly grabs Josh by his shirt collar with both hands and

pulls him violently across the bar.

CHARLIE (*shouting fiercely*): Give me the Goddamn *shares*, kid, give them to me *now, now*!

      Shaking Josh violently.

You *hear* me, you hear what I'm *sayin'* to ya?

JOSH (*choking*): Dad—

CHARLIE (*tightening his grip; louder, wilder*): *Keep* them, *keep* them then, keep the Goddamn shares—I close it up and let it die—outa *my* life and outa *yours,* *dead, finally, over, over*—

      Suddenly sees the terror in his son's eyes, stops shouting; then slowly, carefully releases him.

(*Whispers.*) Oh my God, Josh . . . Oh my God . . . sorry, I'm sorry . . . I . . .

      Josh backs away from Charlie, warily, as though from a stranger, trembling, his stock certificate falling to the floor; near tears, whispering, his hand on his throat.

JOSH: You looked like you were gonna kill me, Dad . . .

Charlie apologizes, but Josh continues backing away, even after his father picks up the stock certificate, hands it to him and tells him it's his, he can open the bar if he chooses. While Charlie is still trying to explain, Josh goes out to wait in the car. Charlie turns off the overhead lights but sits at the bar in the semi-darkness with the juke box alit and playing the Lebedeff "Rumania."

      The old bar-lights fade quickly up, the colorful lights of the 1930s and 1940s, and Eddie enters briskly from the kitchen—the younger Eddie with his fine white shirt, black bow tie and sharp black pants. Eddie goes directly behind the bar, takes a glass and a bottle from the shelf, pours with his usual flourish and sets a drink down next to Charlie; Charlie looking off as the Lebedeff music fills the room, Eddie leaning forward with his hands on the bar, looking at the front door, waiting for customers. Curtain.

CRAZY FOR YOU

A Musical in Two Acts

BOOK BY KEN LUDWIG

MUSIC BY GEORGE GERSHWIN

LYRICS BY IRA GERSHWIN

CO-CONCEIVED BY KEN LUDWIG AND MIKE OCKRENT

INSPIRED BY MATERIAL BY GUY BOLTON AND JOHN McGOWAN

Cast and credits appear on pages 303-305

KEN LUDWIG (book, co-conception) was born in York, Pa. March 15, 1950. "I was your typical stagestruck, starstruck kid," he remembers, going to the theater whenever possible—A Visit to a Small Planet *was a particular favorite—and experimenting with writing plays as early as high school days. He was pointed firmly in the direction of college and law school, however, getting his B.A. from Haverford in 1972, his Ll.M. from Trinity College, Cambridge, England and finally his J.D. from Harvard in 1976. He kept at his playwriting too and arrived at Theater Row off off Broadway with* Divine Fire *in the early 1980s, and then with* Postmortem, *both also produced in regional theater.*

OOB saw a production of Ludwig's Sullivan and Gilbert *in December 1984.*

This script was later produced by the Kennedy Center for the Performing Arts and the National Arts Center of Canada and was voted 1988's best play by the Ottawa critics. His Lend Me a Tenor *was produced in London by Andrew Lloyd Webber, premiering at the Globe Theater June 3, 1986; was nominated for the Olivier Award for Comedy of the Year; was subsequently produced in a Pierre Barillet and Jean-Paul Gredy French translation in Paris; opened February 27, 1989 for a Broadway run of 481 performances in which it was cited as its author's first Best Play and was nominated for seven Tony Awards, four Drama Desk Awards and three Outer Critics Circle Awards; and has gone on to round-the-world production in 16 languages. Ludwig's second Best Play citation now goes to the book and co-conception of the hit musical* Crazy for You *which opened on Broadway February 19, 1992, this season's Tony winner for best musical and nominee for best book.*

Ludwig's other literary activities have included the screen play Heartbreaker, *the 1990 Kennedy Center Honors TV script (an Emmy nominee) and the screen play of* Lend Me a Tenor. *As a practicing lawyer (of counsel to the firm of Steptoe & Johnson), he serves as secretary of the board and general counsel of the Shakespeare Theater at the Folger, and he is a member of the artists committee of Kennedy Center Honors and of the Dramatists Guild. He and his wife have a daughter, and they live in Washington, D.C.*

MIKE OCKRENT (co-conception) was born in London in 1946 and educated in Edinburgh, earning a degree in physics from its University and returning to that Scottish city while pursuing his theatrical career as artistic director at the Traverse Theater. It is as a director that he made his mark on both sides of the Atlantic, having staged productions in London for the Royal Court Theater, the Royal Shakespeare Company and the National Theater and recently Michael Frayn's Look Look *at the Aldwych Theater and* Just So *and the multi-prizewinning revival of* Follies *for Cameron Mackintosh; and on Broadway* Once a Catholic, Atkinson *at the Atkinson and* Me and My Girl. *He received a Tony nomination for his direction of* Crazy for You, *which he also co-conceived. He widened his creative horizons last year with the direction of his first feature film, Willy Russell's* Dancin' Thru the Dark, *and this year with the publication of his first novel,* Running Down Broadway. *He is a proud parent of daughters and resides in London.*

GEORGE GERSHWIN, IRA GERSHWIN, GUY BOLTON, and JOHN McGOWAN provided essential elements of the creative foundation of Crazy for You *and inspired what they did not directly provide. Their lives and distinguished theater careers are a matter of extensive public record and need not be re-summarized here. The score of this musical is a collection of 18 outstanding theater songs with music by George Gershwin and lyrics by Ira Gershwin (plus one lyric each by Gus Kahn and Desmond Carter), five of them from* Girl Crazy. *And the Messrs. Bolton and McGowan are credited with inspiration, no doubt with their book of* Girl Crazy, *which like* Crazy for You *is about a New Yorker sent West by a rich parent*

and summoning a Broadway chorus to keep him company there. Girl Crazy *opened
at the Alvin Theater on October 14, 1930 with a cast including Allen Kearns,
Ginger Rogers and Ethel Merman, playing 272 performances. The elements which
have been included in* Crazy for You *are its first New York stage reappearance in
any form.*

    Our method of synopsizing Crazy for You *in these pages differs from that of the
other Best Plays. In order to illustrate the distinctly theatrical "look" of its characters, setting and in particular its Tony-winning Susan Stroman choreography, the
musical is represented here in photographs with captions giving a sketch of its continuity. These Joan Marcus photos of* Crazy for You *depict scenes as produced on
Broadway February 19, 1992 by Roger Horchow and Elizabeth Williams and as
directed by Mike Ockrent, with scenery by Robin Wagner, Tony-winning costumes
by William Ivey Long and lighting by Paul Gallo.*

    *Our special thanks are tendered to the producers, Roger Horchow and
Elizabeth Williams, and their press representatives, Bill Evans & Associates and
Jim Randolph, for making available these excellent photographs of the show.*

1. Bobby Child (Harry Groener, *above*) is the scion of a banking family—but he wants to dance. In the Zangler Theater on Broadway, the final number of the closing night of *Zangler's Follies* is in progress to the tune of "K-ra-zy for You." Bobby tries to get an audition with Bela Zangler after the show, but the impresario is chasing one of the girls, Tess, and brushes Bobby off.

2. Outside the theater, Bobby's mother and his fiancee, Irene, are waiting to pull him in opposite directions—Irene towards marriage, Mother towards his neglected banking duties. Mother hands him a property deed and threatens to cut off his allowance unless he goes to Deadrock, Nevada, immediately and forecloses on a defunct theater the bank has mortgaged there.

3. Bobby tunes mother and fiancee out of his mind and imagines a chorus line of Follies girls emerging from the roof of his mother's limousine and joining him in the number "I Can't Be Bothered Now" (*above*). When the number ends, Irene demands that Bobby choose between his banking obligations and her. To Bobby's mother's satisfaction, Bobby heads for Deadrock.

4. In Deadrock, which features a saloon and the old Gaiety Theater, the locals describe their existence as "Bidin' My Time." The theater, owned by Everett Baker and his pretty daughter Polly (Jodi Benson, *above*) is due to be foreclosed by Bobby's bank. Lank Hawkins, the saloon owner, offers to buy the Gaiety to expand his business, but Baker refuses.

Bobby staggers into town, exhausted by the desert heat. He spies Polly and decides "Things Are Looking Up." Cowboys help him into the saloon, where usual Western activities are in progress—a poker game, piano music, drinking, a quarrel followed by gunfire—but it turns out they're only rehearsing Famous Gunfights of the Old West to attract tourists.

5. While being revived, Bobby manages to steal a kiss from Polly. He appeals to her ("Could You Use Me?") and pursues her into the street, where he persuades her to join him in a dance ("Shall We Dance?," *below*) which ends in another kiss before the scene blacks out.

6. Visiting the theater with Polly, Bobby suggests they could put on a show to pay off the mortgage—the Follies girls are on vacation and would love to come to Deadrock. Then Polly recognizes Bobby as the banker who's come to take over the theater. She slaps him and departs. Mapping a new strategy, Bobby decides to vanish and then return disguised as Bela Zangler with beard, accent, and cane and put on the show.

Three days later, the showgirls (*above, right*) arrive in Deadrock with jazzy versions of "K-ra-zy for You" and "I'll Build a Stairway to Paradise." Bobby arrives pretending to be Zangler. Polly's father "recognizes" and welcomes "Zangler." Polly, attracted by the impresario, is left to consider her situation in "Someone to Watch Over Me."

Two weeks later, with rehearsals going badly under "Zangler's" direction, Lank, antagonistic, is determined to disrupt the show. But the amateur performers begin to shape up with "Slap That Bass." The romantic plot thickens as Irene arrives and recognizes her fiancee Bobby in his disguise, and Polly confesses her feelings for "Zangler" with the number "Embraceable You" which ends in a passionate kiss.

7. The show's cast sings "Tonight's the Night" as they prepare for their opening. Irene meets Lank, and they hit it off in an aggressive sort of way as she tries to explain Bobby's masquerade.

"Zangler" is glum because the show hasn't attracted a single ticket-buyer. Hopes are raised when the Fodors arrive in town, but it turns out that they weren't drawn here by the show but by Lank's saloon which they wish to cover for their latest guide book.

Polly and the Company try to cheer "Zangler" up, urging him to join them in looking on the bright side with "I Got Rhythm" (*below*, with Bobby, *at center*, in his Zangler disguise). As the song comes to an end, the real Bela Zangler staggers out of the desert. *Curtain; end of Act I.*

ACT II

8. In Lank's saloon, customers whoop it up with "The Real American Folk Song (Is a Rag)." Bobby—without his Zangler makeup—asks Polly to marry him. She refuses, declaring her love for "Zangler," not believing Bobby when he confesses his masquerade. At this moment the real Zangler enters. Polly kisses him passionately. Bobby disappears upstairs with a bottle.

But Zangler is looking for his beloved Tess, who spurns him when he refuses to help promote their show, driving him to drink. Two cowboys fight over Tess in a riproaring takeoff of Western bar brawls, which turns out to be just a rehearsal of The Dalton Boys Meet The Clanton Gang.

When the others drift outside, Bobby comes down, drunk, as "Zangler" and confronts the real Zangler, who is also drunk, in a mirror-image pantomime which includes the song "What Causes That?" As the song ends, they both pass out.

The next morning the two are still asleep when Polly enters with a telegram ordering Bobby back to New York. Bobby's impersonation is now exposed. Polly exits, humiliated and angry.

Irene (Michele Pawk, *below*) hears from Bobby that he now loves someone else. But as Bobby exits, Lank (John Hillner, *below*) comes in. Irene studies him, kisses him and then seduces him with the song "Naughty Baby."

9. Bobby and Polly continue quarreling at a cast meeting. The actors resolve "Stiff Upper Lip" in song but vote to discontinue their show. Bobby heads for New York after assuring Polly he'll always remember Deadrock: "They Can't Take That Away From Me." Then Zangler enters, having decided to promote the show. Polly now realizes it's Bobby she loves and sings her feelings in "But Not for Me."

10. In New York, Bobby's mother makes him a birthday present of the theater on which Zangler, preoccupied in Deadrock, has neglected to pay the mortgage. Bobby fantasizes (*above*) about dancing with Follies girls in his theater, with "Nice Work If You Can Get It." But realizing what Polly means to him, Bobby tears up the deed to Zangler's theater (*right*) and heads for Deadrock.

11. Bobby's mother (Jane Connell, *above right*) arrives in Deadrock and learns that Irene is no longer Bobby's fiancee but has married Lank, whose saloon is now a cafe catering to the hordes who have come to see the show, which has paid off the Gaiety's mortgage.

12. Follies girls have taken Polly offstage, and her costume is brought to her. When she reappears, it is on the arm of her father (Ronn Carroll, *bottom of opposite page*) like a bride being escorted down the aisle. Bobby and Polly embrace, kiss, then start to dance.

The main street of Deadrock becomes a stage for Bobby and Polly as the stars (*above*) of a lavish Follies number (*below*). *Curtain.*

TWO TRAINS RUNNING

A Play in Two Acts

BY AUGUST WILSON

Cast and credits appear on page 308

AUGUST WILSON was born in 1945 in Pittsburgh, where his father worked as a baker and his mother determinedly introduced her son to the written word and had him reading at 4 years old. Despite his early acquaintance and continuing fascination with words, he didn't long pursue a formal education, leaving Central Catholic High School before graduating. He can clearly remember when he began to approach writing as a profession: it was April 1, 1965; he had just earned $20 writing a term paper for his sister, and he bought a typewriter which, he remembers, "represented my total commitment" because it took every penny he had. Lacking bus fare, he carried it home.

Wilson started with poetry. By 1972 he was writing one-acts. His first production was Jitney, *staged in 1978 by Black Horizons Theater, a group which he himself had founded in 1968.* Jitney *was repeated in 1982 by Allegheny Repertory Theater; meanwhile his* Black Bart and the Sacred Hills *was produced in 1981 by Penumbra Theater in St. Paul. After a staged reading at the O'Neill Theater Center in Waterford, Conn. in 1982 and production by Yale Repertory Theater April 3, 1984 (both organizations and the play itself being directed by Lloyd Richards), Wilson's* Ma Rainey's Black Bottom *was brought to Broadway October*

*11, 1984 for 275 performances, becoming its author's first full New York produc-
tion, first Best Play, first Tony nominee and the winner of the New York Drama
Critics Circle citation as the season's best play.*

*All five of Wilson's New York productions have been named Best Plays and all
have been directed by Richards.* The second, Fences, *was also developed at the
O'Neill and premiered at Yale Rep on April 25, 1985, receiving the first annual
American Theater Critics Association New Play Award, as recorded in* The Best
Plays of 1985-86. *It was produced on Broadway March 26, 1987 for 526 performances and carried off its author's second Critics citation, the Pulitzer Prize and
the Tony Awards for both best play and direction.* Fences *was still running on
Broadway a year later when Wilson's* Joe Turner's Come and Gone *opened March
27, 1988 after previous productions at Yale Rep and at Huntington Theater,
Boston (two groups which also presented Wilson's* The Piano Lesson *in regional
theater productions during the 1987-88 season after an O'Neill tryout, then followed by a Goodman Theater, Chicago production cited by the American Theater
Critics Association for its fourth annual New Play Award).* Joe Turner *won Wilson
his third Best Play citation, third New York Drama Critics Circle Award and third
Tony nomination, playing 105 performances. When it finally arrived on Broadway
April 16, 1990 for a run of 329 performances,* The Piano Lesson *won Wilson his
fourth round of laurels in all three of these categories, plus the Pulitzer Prize.* Two
Trains Running *had already received ATCA's fifth annual New Play Award before
opening on Broadway this season and becoming its author's fifth straight Best
Play.*

Wilson is a member of New Dramatists (which presented his The Mill Hand's
Lunch Bucket *in staged readings in 1983 and 1984) and the Playwrights' Center
in Minneapolis. He has been a recipient of Bush, McKnight, Rockefeller and
Guggenheim fellowships in playwriting and a Whiting Writer's Award. He is married, with one daughter, and lives in St. Paul.*

The following synopsis of Two Trains Running *was prepared by Sally Dixon
Wiener.*

Time: 1969

Place: Memphis Lee's restaurant in the Hill District of Pittsburgh

ACT I

Scene 1: Saturday morning

SYNOPSIS: The yellow ochre-lit setting for the play is a dingy restaurant with a
sooty pressed tin ceiling. Across the street from West's Funeral Home and Lutz's

Meat Market, it is a home away from home to its regulars, who are as encapsulated in this ambiance as flies in amber. There are windows at stage right behind two worn leatherette booths. The door to the street is upstage, next to a large old-fashioned wooden phone booth. A table, with chairs, is upstage also, and upstage left is a passageway leading to the back of the restaurant and a visible door to the kitchen. Stage left is an angled counter with five stools, and behind the counter with its cash register is a wide pass-through space to the kitchen. Downstage left is a big juke box. Old photographs, postcards and soft drink signs are here and there on the walls. Prominently displayed behind the counter is a blackboard with the specials of the day chalked in on it—meat loaf, collard greens and mashed potatoes, $1.85, navy beans and corn muffins, 65 cents. Also on the blackboard, and revised daily, like the menu, is the winning number of the previous day—651.

As the play begins, Wolf is in the telephone booth. He comes out with his paperwork. He's on the younger side of middle age, moves quickly, wears a black hat and dark shirt, jacket and trousers. No sooner has he come out of the booth than the phone rings and he goes back to answer it, just as the proprietor, Memphis, comes on from the back. Memphis is energetic, edgy, a shirt-and-tie man whose hair and well-trimmed beard and mustache are just beginning to grizzle. He is very much the boss and is resentful of Wolf tying up his phone taking numbers bets.

Memphis notes that for the second time in a week 651 has hit. Wolf has been calling for Risa, the combination cook and waitress, to bring him some sugar for his coffee. Risa is a very pretty young woman with big saucer eyes, but there is an extraordinary poignancy about her, as if she were engaged in an ongoing dialogue with some interior pain. Her walk is just this side of paralyzingly slow, and her attitude is an admixture of alertness and detachment. She is both comic and endearing, with a stubborn quality of a self-protective nature, and her voice only seems to come alive when she's truly concerned or aroused about something or someone. Periodically when not busy she languidly reads a magazine. She wears a short skirt and light print blouse and an apron into the waistband of which she tucks a towel and her order pad. Her low shoes and white socks make one instantly aware of scars on each leg.

It seems Memphis's "old lady," after 22 years, walked out on him a couple of months ago. She's been at her sister's, Memphis tells Wolf in answer to his question. Memphis doesn't understand it. He'd treated her like a queen, he insists, and then when she left she wouldn't even shake hands with him. But all he'd done was to ask her to get up and make him some bread, Memphis insists, and she'd walked out. Said she was tired.

Holloway, in his mid-60s and of a philosophical bent, comes in, describing the lineup of people waiting to get into the funeral home to see the body of Prophet Samuel. It seems he'd had a stroke, but Memphis thinks one of his "sandalfoot" women poisoned him in a fit of jealousy. The funeral's not to be until Tuesday. The report is that Prophet Samuel has got hundred dollar bills, diamonds on every finger, and that the casket's all roped off. Memphis assures them West won't bury the man with all that money and jewelry. He thinks West sometimes takes the body out and resells the casket, but Risa doesn't believe he would.

Wolf wonders who had more money, West or Prophet Samuel. Holloway thinks West: "More people dying than getting saved." Wolf surmises Prophet Samuel has been cheating and fooling people for a long time. Risa defends Prophet Samuel as telling the truth. Memphis believes West has more money, West owns a lot of property. Memphis was lucky and got this building he owns, and West was angry about that and hasn't forgotten it. Memphis had gone to the hospital and made a deal with the owner the week before he died to buy it for $5,500. Later he'd found $1,200 was owing in back taxes, but Memphis didn't care. West had offered him $8,000 the next day. Now the city's about to tear down the whole block, and Memphis is to go downtown Tuesday to see how much he'll be paid for the property. He's going to insist on getting $25,000.

Memphis puts $1 on 764 in hopes that it'll come out and hold him until he gets the money. He might buy some new shoes. He doesn't want to wear a pair three years like West, even though West has never been seen without his shoes polished. Wolf remarks West's never been seen without gloves on his hands. And everything West wears, except for his white shirt, is black, Wolf complains. Wolf admits that West does make the bodies look natural. West gets the cars there on time and people like him for that, Holloway adds. And he is polite—after he's been paid his fee. Memphis mocks those who would pay West extra for a 20-year guarantee on a leak-proof casket. How would anyone know 20 years later that the expensive casket had lived up to its guarantee?

WOLF: I don't want West to bury me. I'll go anywhere else. Charles. McTurner. Harris. I'll let anybody bury me but West. Hell, I'm liable to do like the white folks do and get cremated.

MEMPHIS: What you got against West?

WOLF: I ain't got nothing against him. I just don't want him standing over me when I'm dead. I'd rather have a stranger standing over me.

HOLLOWAY: You ain't gonna know nothing about it. What you care who be standing over top of you? You talk foolish. West don't care nothing about you. The last person West buried that he cared about was his wife. He don't care nothing about you. You just be another dead nigger to him. I doubt if West can tell one nigger from another. Man got four or five viewing rooms and don't have no trouble keeping somebody in all of them. I remember one time he had two niggers laid out in the hallway and one on the back porch. Most of them had welfare caskets, but West don't care cause the government pay on time. He might have to worry his money out of some of them other niggers, but the government pay quicker than the insurance companies.

MEMPHIS: Wasn't nothing but a pine box with some cloth stretched over it. That's what the welfare casket was.

WOLF: They ain't changed. That's what they is now.

Hambone comes in, big, heavyset. *"He is in his late 40s. He is self-contained and in a world of his own. His mental condition has deteriorated to such a point that he can only say two phrases, and he repeats them idiotically over and over."* Risa is relieved to see him, reminding him that whether or not he has money he should come and have something to eat. She gives him a bowl of beans and corn-bread. Hambone throughout is saying "He gonna give me my ham" or varying it with "I want my ham."

It seems Risa has not been over to see Prophet Samuel and is not going to go. Memphis chides her for following him, giving him money and talking about him, and then not wanting to pay her respects. But she is adamant. Wolf offers to go with her. It is obvious that Wolf is interested in Risa. He gives her two quarters for the jukebox, but it's broken. Now Memphis is impatient with Risa and wants her to get the chicken ready, but Memphis's ordering her around rolls off Risa's back like water off a duck's back.

"Sterling enters. He is a young man of 30. He wears a suit, dress shirt without a tie. . . . . He has been out of the penitentiary for one week and the suit is his prison issue. Sterling appears at times to be unbalanced, but it is a combination of his unorthodox logic and straightforward manner that makes him appear so." He is nice-looking, appealing, eager to make it and get on with life. He's realistic enough to see it's not easy.

Memphis calls to Risa to come out and wait on Sterling, that he wants to eat. But things are not in great order in the kitchen. There's no chicken, no meat loaf and no hamburger, either. Memphis insists there's hamburger. Risa says it's frozen. All she's got is beans and cornbread. Beans is what Sterling doesn't want. He's had five years of beans. The sign out there says home style cooking. Where's the food? he wonders. He'll have a cup of coffee, and Risa brings it. Sterling recognizes her as Clarissa Thomas, the once-skinny sister of a close friend of his, Rodney, who apparently moved to Cleveland.

STERLING: Me and him had some fun times together. You remember I used to come up to the house and eat all the time? That was you that was doing all the cooking. Rodney say, "Come on man my sister got something to eat." Then we used to come up there. You used to be skinny.

RISA: I wasn't all that skinny.

STERLING: I don't know how skinny you were but you sure grown up now. What's your phone number?

RISA: I ain't gone none.

STERLING: Well, what's the address? If I can't walk I'll crawl up there.

When Memphis orders Risa to get on back to frying chicken, Sterling mutters that if you can't talk to anybody on the job, who would want the job, likening it to being in school.

Sterling frankly admits he's just out of the penitentiary and asks if anybody knows about a job he might get. Wolf suggests Hendricks who has a construction company, but it seems that's where Sterling's just been for a week. Then Hendricks claimed he didn't have enough business to keep him on. Memphis suggests the steel mill. So had Hendricks, Sterling reveals. But J & L Steel told him he'd have to join the union before he could work, and the union said he'd have to be working before he could join, and that he should get the steel mill to put him on a waiting list. His landlady isn't about to, though—if Sterling doesn't pay up by Friday Sterling can wait in the street. Holloway suggests Boykins who has a junkyard. Sterling thanks him. Sterling tries to sell someone his watch, but there are no takers, and he decides to go across the streeet and line up with the others to try to get his luck changed. A man across the street had said you could get good luck by rubbing Prophet Samuel's head. Somebody had found $20 on the street when he came out. Sterling might even go through the line two or three times. Holloway advises him it would be much better to go see Aunt Ester, "She give you more than money. She make you right with yourself." She lives not far away, at 1839 Wylie, in the back. There's a red door, he informs Sterling. Then they are interrupted by Hambone, suddenly calling out again.

HAMBONE: He gonna give me my ham. I want my ham.

STERLING: Somebody got his ham. (*To Hambone.*) Who got your ham, man? Somebody took your ham?

HOLLOWAY: He talking about Lutz across the street. He painted his fence for him nine . . . almost ten years ago and Lutz told him he'd give him a ham. After he painted the fence Lutz told him to take a chicken. He say he wanted his ham. Lutz told him to take a chicken or don't take nothing. So he wait over there every morning till Lutz come to open his store and he tell him he wants his ham. He ain't got it yet.

MEMPHIS: That ain't how it went. Lutz told him if he painted his fence he'd give him a chicken. Told him if he do a good job he'd give him a ham. He think he did a good job and Lutz didn't. That's where he went wrong. Letting Lutz decide what to pay him for his work. If you leave it like that, quite naturally he gonna say it ain't worth the higher price.

HAMBONE: He gonna give me my ham. He gonna give me my ham. I want my ham.

MEMPHIS (*to Hambone*): All right! I told you . . . That's enough of that.

HAMBONE (*to himself*): He gonna give me my ham. He gonna give me my ham.

Holloway is sure that all he would have to do is go see Aunt Ester. She could straighten him out. Sterling wonders if she could help him get a job. He wants to open a nightclub. It doesn't make any difference to her what the problem is, just knock on the door and say you've come to see Aunt Ester. You have to pay, Holloway cautions him, but she doesn't take the money. She'll tell him to go and throw it in the river, that it will come to her. It must be the truth, Holloway believes, because Aunt Ester doesn't want for anything, and the people who take care of her don't either.

Memphis asks Sterling to find out how old she is. She's 322 years old, Holloway insists. Memphis doesn't believe she's that old. Sterling thinks people lived that long in the Bible. Holloway goes to see her once in a while, "Get my soul washed." He claims when she puts her hands on your head, everything about your life seems calm and peaceful. Holloway admits she looks like she's 500 years old: "Look like death scared of her." He suggests asking West about her, he's been there and told the people there he'd bury her for free. Memphis doesn't believe she's changed anybody's luck. If it was so easy, everybody'd be rich.

HOLLOWAY: See? There you go talking about being rich. I ain't talking about that. I ain't said nothing about getting rich. I'm talking about getting your luck changed. You go up there with the wrong attitude and come out with worse luck than you had before. That's what the problem is now. Aunt Ester don't buy into that. She don't make people rich. You go up there talking about you wanna get rich, and she won't have nothing to do with you. She send you to see Prophet Samuel . . . and you see how far that'll get you. Most people don't know Prophet Samuel went to see Aunt Ester. He wasn't always a prophet. He started out he was a reverend. Had him a truck and he'd stand on that back of that truck . . . had him a loudspeaker and he'd go out and preach the word of the gospel and sell barbecue on the side. Everybody knew Reverend Samuel. He even went where the white folks lived and tried to preach to them. They seen him with that truck and thought he come out here to steal their furniture. Called the police on him. Many a time. He go on and pay his fifty-dollar fine for preaching without a permit and go on back out here. They had him in big trouble one time. He had all his money going to his church, and they arrested him for income tax evasion. That's when he went to see Aunt Ester. He walked in there a reverend and walked out a prophet. I don't know what she told him. But he went down to see the mayor. Say if they arrested him they had to arrest Mellon too. Say God was gonna send a sign. The next day the stock market fell so fast they had to close it early. Mellon called the mayor and told him to drop the charges. The next day the stock market went right on back up there. Except for Gulf Oil, which Mellon owned. That went higher than it ever went before. Mellon was tickled pink. He sent Prophet Samuel a five-hundred-dollar donation and a brochure advertising his banking services. Had his picture taken with him and everything. That's when Prophet Samuel went big. The police didn't bother him no more. Wouldn't even give him a parking ticket. If he hadn't started walking around in them robes going barefoot and whatnot . . . ain't no telling how big he would have got. A lot of people didn't like him wearing them robes . . . baptizing people in the river and all that kinda stuff.

MEMPHIS: That's the damnest thing I ever heard of.

HOLLOWAY: Don't take my word for it. Go on up there and see for yourself.

Go knock on the door. You don't have to be scared.

Again Memphis declares he doesn't believe all that, but Sterling is going to go see Aunt Ester. Before he leaves he calls to Risa to cook him some chicken to have when he gets back. "I wanna eat what you been eating. See if I can get nice and healthy too."

Scene 2: Monday morning

Wolf is looking out, across the street, at Hambone who is waiting for Lutz to come along. Memphis joins Wolf as he looks. Holloway is outside watching, waiting to hear what they'll say. Risa comes on from the back to ask what they're looking at. Memphis complains that she's been there half an hour and there's no coffee and that she should also get the grits cooked.

Wolf mentions that somebody had tried breaking into West's during the night to steal Prophet Samuel's money and jewelry, and West had been awakened by the burglar alarm.

Holloway comes in to report that the only exchange out on the street had been "I want my ham" and "Take a chicken." Memphis wonders how many days it's been, after all these years of days, that Hambone's been thinking he's going to get his ham. Hambone isn't in his right mind, Wolf reminds him, but Holloway isn't sure. "He might have more sense than any of us." Would Holloway stand there every morning for all that time, Wolf wonders. Holloway wouldn't, he admits, but that doesn't mean that he might not have as much sense as Hambone.

MEMPHIS: You tell me how that make sense. You tell me what sense that make?

HOLLOWAY: All right. I'll tell you. Now you take me or you. We ain't gonna do that. We gonna go ahead and forget about it. We might take a chicken. Then we gonna go home and cook that chicken. But how it gonna taste? It can't taste good to us. We gonna be eating just to be eating. How we gonna feel good about ourselves? Every time we even look at a chicken we gonna have a bad taste in our mouth. That chicken's gonna call up that taste. It's gonna make you feel ashamed . . . . . That's why I say he might have more sense than me and you. Cause he ain't willing to accept whatever the white man throw at him. It be easier. But he say he don't mind getting out of the bed in the morning to go at what's right. I don't believe you and me got that much sense.

MEMPHIS: That's that old backward Southern mentality. When I come up here they had to teach these niggers they didn't have to tip their hat to a white man. They walking around here tipping their hat, jumping off the sidewalk, talking about, "Yessir Captain, how do Major."

WOLF: How long you been up here, Memphis?

MEMPHIS: I been up here since Thirty-six. They ran me out of Jackson in Thirty-one. I hung around Natchez for three or four years, then I come up here. I was born in Jackson. I used to farm down there. They ran me out in Thirty-one. Killed my

Roscoe Lee Browne (Holloway), Cynthia Martells (Risa) and
Al White (Memphis) in August Wilson's *Two Trains Running*

mule and everything. One of these days I'm going back and get my land. I still got
the deed.

HOLLOWAY: I got an uncle and a bunch of cousins down in Jackson.

MEMPHIS: When I left out of Jackson I said I was gonna buy me a V-8 Ford and
drive by Mr. Henry Ford's house and honk the horn. If anybody come to the window I was gonna wave. Then I was going out and buy me a Thirty-oh-six, come on
back to Jackson and drive up to Mr. Stovall's house and honk the horn. Only this
time I wasn't waving. Only thing was it took me thirteen years to get the Ford. Six
years later I traded that in on a Cadillac. But I'm going back one of these days. I
ain't even got to know the way. All I got to do is find my way down to the train
depot. They got two trains running every day. I used to know the schedule. They
might have changed it . . . but if they did they got it posted up on the board.

When Risa leaves to get a pie, Memphis, Holloway and Wolf discuss her. A
man could be happy to get a woman like Risa, except for her having taken a razor
to her legs. She isn't "right with herself" is the way Memphis sees her. If she could

do that, she might cut your throat. But not wanting a man isn't natural.

In Holloway's opinion, Risa matured early, and every man since she was 12 has been after her, so she thought making her legs look ugly would force them to see her differently. Memphis wouldn't want a woman who had done that to herself. He wouldn't know what she might do to him. Risa had been at Western Psych, Holloway explains, but they found nothing wrong with her, even though they'd tried different counselors. Wolf doesn't believe she needs a counselor, she just needs a good man, somebody who will make her "feel like a woman," Wolf insists, noting that Sterling's been eyeing her. Maybe Sterling's a better man than he is, Wolf ponders, but he truly doesn't think so.

The talk turns to the numbers, but Holloway's not participating. He's waiting until he has a good dream, he tells Wolf before Wolf leaves.

Memphis has just found out that Sterling was the boy who robbed a bank and "was out spending the money ten minutes later." And now Hendricks had given him a job to help him out and Sterling had quit after a week. Memphis claims Sterling doesn't want to work. Holloway wouldn't blame Sterling if he did quit. Why would anybody haul bricks for a dollar and a quarter an hour? What can anybody do with ten dollars a day? Memphis claims it's more than Sterling has, and that his grandaddy worked for three dollars a day. And his great grandaddy worked for nothing, Holloway wryly remarks. Sterling could make two or three hundred a day gambling, if he were lucky. If he doesn't, somebody else will. Everybody around here has somebody else's money in their pocket, and they just trade it off, Holloway insists, until eventually somebody takes it and gives it to the white man . . . "bingo it's gone." That's why the ten won't do any good. "A nigger with a hundred dollars in his pocket around here is a big man," but out at Squirrel Hill, Holloway points out, they walk around with five thousand trying to turn it into five hundred thousand.

MEMPHIS: Ain't nothing wrong in saving your money and do like they do. These niggers just don't want to work. That boy don't want to work. He lazy.

HOLLOWAY: People kill me talking about niggers is lazy. Niggers is the most hard working people in the world. Worked three hundred years for free. And didn't take no lunch hour. Now all of a sudden niggers is lazy. Don't know how to work. All of a sudden when they got to pay niggers, ain't no work for him to do. If it wasn't for you the white man would be poor. Every little bit he got, he got standing on top of you. That's why he could reach so high. He give you three dollars a day for six months, and he got him a railroad for the next hundred years. All you got is six months' worth of three dollars a day. Now you can't even get that. Ain't no money in niggers working. Look out there on the street. If there was some money in it . . . if the white man could figure out a way to make some money by putting niggers to work, we'd all be working. He ain't building no more railroads. He got them. He ain't building no more highways. Somebody done already stuck the telephone poles in the ground. That's been done already. The white man ain't stacking no more niggers. You know what I'm talking about stacking niggers, don't you? Well, here's how that go. If you ain't got nothing . . . you can go out here and get you a nigger. Then you got something, see. You got one nigger. If that one nigger get out there and plant something . . . get something out the ground . . . even if it ain't nothing but a bushel of potatoes . . . then you got one nigger and one bushel of potatoes. Then you take that bushel of potatoes and go get you another nigger. Then you got two niggers. Put them to work and you got two niggers and two bushels of potatoes. See, now you can go buy two more niggers. That's how you stack a nigger on top of a nigger. White folks got to stacking . . . and I'm talking about they stacked up some niggers! Stacked up close to fifty millions niggers. If you stacked them on top of one another they make six or seven circles around the moon. It's lucky the boat didn't sink with all them niggers they had stacked up there. It take them two extra months to get here cause it ride so low in the water. They couldn't find you enough work back then. Now that they got to pay you they can't find you none. If this was different time, wouldn't be nobody out there in the street. They'd all be in the cotton fields.

West comes in. He's in his early 60s and is wearing only black, with the exception of his white shirt (black gloves as well). He greets Risa, who has returned, and she gives him his coffee and goes to get him a piece of the pie. "Let me get a little bit of sugar here, Risa," West requests.

Memphis mentions that people are lined up out on the street. West reports he's finally gotten Prophet Samuel laid out the way they wanted him to do it. People are trying to rub his head, West complains. He roped off the casket, but people go under the rope. Memphis asks about the jewels and the hundred dollar bills, and West states there's only a couple of rings, his gold cross and two hundred dollar bills—one in his breast pocket, the other glued around his finger. Memphis doesn't believe West has glued the money to Prophet Samuel's hand, but West assures him it's true.

Memphis is sure West won't put the money in the ground, but West says he'll bury anything with anybody. He's buried people with Bibles, canes, crutches, guitars, radios, baby dolls—even some tomatoes a lady brought from her sister's garden. Not only had she wanted to tell him where to put them in there, but she kept changing her mind, West recalls. But he doesn't care, as long as he can get the casket closed. Again Memphis repeats his doubts about whether that money is going in the ground. The family usually comes and gets it before you close the casket, West reveals, the rings and other things. He hates to lay people out with jewelry, he confides, because the family comes daily to remind him that it shouldn't go in the ground.

West wants to know what they are saying downtown to Memphis about paying for his property. Memphis is to go down there the next day, and he's not going to take less than $25,000. West is sure they'll only give him double what he paid for it—ten, eleven or twelve thousand at best. But West will give Memphis fifteen for it. They can go to the bank right now, West suggests, but Memphis refuses. West reminds him that they have the right of eminent domain and they do not care what Memphis thinks about what he should get for having to close up his business. They continue arguing until West leaves.

Sterling comes back on with some flyers for a rally for Malcolm X's birthday, to be held at the Savoy Ballroom. Memphis isn't having anything to do with it: "Malcolm ain't having no more birthdays. Dead men don't have birthdays." As far as Memphis is concerned, he'd rather celebrate Sterling's birthday. He'll buy cake and liquor and they'll have a party.

Holloway recalls Malcolm X coming to the Mosque when he had only 12 followers. Sterling wonders why Holloway didn't make the 13th. Memphis asks where Holloway would have followed him to—Malcolm X was only going to the graveyard. Holloway claims he didn't follow him because he knew where to find Aunt Ester. If it hadn't been for her, he's not sure what he might have done.

STERLING: I would have followed him. He was the only one who told the truth. That's why they killed him.

MEMPHIS: Niggers killed Malcolm. Niggers killed Malcolm. When you want to talk about Malcolm, remember that first. Niggers killed Malcolm . . . and now they want to celebrate his birthday.

HOLLOWAY: Malcolm got too big. People call him a saint. That's what the problem was. He got too big, and when you get that big ain't nothing else you could do. They killed all the saints. St. Peter. St. Paul. They killed them all. When you get to be a saint there ain't nothing else you can do but die. The people wouldn't have it any other way.

MEMPHIS: You right about that. They killed Martin. If they did that to him you can imagine what they do to me or you. If they kill the sheep you know what they do to the wolf.

STERLING: That's why they having the rally. They rallying for Black Power. Stop them from killing the sheep.

MEMPHIS: That's what half the problem is . . . these Black Power niggers. They got people confused. They don't know what they doing themselves. These niggers talking about freedom, justice and equality and don't know what it mean. You born free. It's up to you to maintain it. You born with dignity and everything else. These niggers talking about freedom. But what you gonna do with it? Freedom is heavy. You got to put your shoulder to freedom. Put your shoulder to it and hope your back hold up. And if you around here looking for justice you got a long wait. Ain't no justice. That's why they got that statue of her and got her blindfolded. Common sense would tell you if anybody need to see, she do. There ain't no justice. Jesus Christ didn't get justice. What makes you think you gonna get it? That's just the nature of the world. These niggers talking about they want freedom, justice and equality. Equal to what? Hell I might be a better man than you. What I look like going around here talking about I want to be equal to you? I don't know how these niggers think sometimes.

The only real power is a gun, Memphis continues, it's certainly the only kind of force the white man understands. As for being black and beautiful, "You got to think you ugly to run around shouting you beautiful," Memphis finishes. Sterling adds a comment that they're all supposed to attend the rally.

Hambone comes in. Memphis is out of patience and doesn't want Risa to give him anything. He doesn't feel like hearing Hambone today. Risa gives Hambone coffee anyway, but Memphis takes the coffee, throws it out, and then pushes Hambone toward the door. Risa points out Hambone wasn't bothering anybody, and Memphis replies that Hambone was bothering him. After about ten years he's tired of hearing Hambone talking about the same thing. He slams the restaurant door shut.

Scene 3: Tuesday afternoon

Risa and Sterling are alone. As he eats, he reports he's been to ask Boykins about a job, but Boykins didn't need anyone and suggested he go to the steel mill, not knowing they have a waiting list. Sterling also has seen Hambone, and they are developing a relationship. Risa claims people don't realize Hambone understands what's going on. Memphis has gone downtown, Risa says, explaining that this building is going to be torn down. It doesn't surprise Sterling. They tore the orphanage down, too. He was born an orphan, his mother gave him away to Mrs. Johnson, and when she died they put him in the orphanage. Now he's been on his own for 12 years, since he was 18, and has done pretty well except for a term in prison. He robbed a bank; he wanted some money, everybody else seemed to have it, and he thought he'd get some where Mellon got his.

Sterling wonders if Risa wasn't frightened of bleeding to death when she cut her legs to make scars on them, but apparently they didn't bleed all that much. He'd be scared to do that, he says, recalling a boy at the orphanage who'd cut his wrists and bled to death. They were about 13. When Sterling had tried to wake him in the morning the bed was filled with blood.

Sterling wants Risa to come with him to the rally for Malcolm X. There might be dancing, and does she like to dance? "If it be with the right person," she allows. Sterling admits he can't dance, but figures he could slow dance at least. But not fast dance. She can't believe he can't dance. Once he asked a girl to dance who refused him, he admits, and another time he almost asked a woman to dance, then changed his mind. He just didn't ask the right person, Risa tells him. Sterling is looking at the rally flyer.

STERLING: You ought to hang that announcement up there. Somebody might wanna go. It say come one come all. You ought to come and go with me.

RISA: I don't want to go down there with all them people. I stay away from all that kind of stuff. You never see me hanging around a bunch of people.

STERLING: People don't pay you half as much mind as you think they do. That just be in your head. Most people so busy trying to live their own lives, they ain't got time to pay attention to nobody else. I found that out. I used to think everybody cared what I did. I robbed that bank and thought people would be mad at me. Half of them didn't even know I was gone. Five years and ain't nobody missed me. They didn't even think about me till they saw me again. You can go down there with me and won't nobody even notice.

RISA: I don't care if they notice or not. I don't want to go down there with them niggers. There might be a riot or something.

STERLING: If a fight break out you just get behind me. I won't let nobody hurt you. Not when you with me.

Sterling is convinced that if he can't get a job he must keep playing the numbers. Even though Risa doesn't approve, she suggests he play 781 when he needs a good number to win. (She has seven scars on one leg and eight on the other, and, as for the one, that's her business, and that's all she'll tell him.) Sterling doesn't have any money now, but as soon as he gets $5, he plans to put it on 781, and if he wins they'll get married.

Sterling tells Holloway when he comes in that he's been looking at the fence Hambone painted for Lutz so long ago. Even though some of the paint's chipped off now, anyone can see Hambone had done a good job. It was a big job, too, Sterling remarks, and Hambone should have had two hams. Sterling was about to go over to Lutz's and get Hambone's ham for him, but then Hambone wouldn't have anything to do in the morning. He imagines Lutz could shock Hambone to death if one day he said "Here, take your ham!"

"Let me get some sugar, Risa," Holloway asks, and Sterling is curious as to why Risa never gives it to customers in the first place. Risa, unflappable, just claims, "All they got to do is ask." And she points out that West, for instance, asks for it and then seldom uses it.

Wolf comes in with a gift of stockings for Risa and some cologne for Memphis. Risa asks what she owes him. Wolf says nothing, but that if he'd brought a fur coat they could do some negotiating. Sterling asks Wolf to loan him $2, but Wolf claims he doesn't have it. Sterling wants to hit the numbers and buy Risa a present and then get a Buick Electra 225. Holloway reminds him he needs to find a job. Sterling wishes he had a good-paying white folks' job, but Holloway reminds him he hasn't had a white folks' education. This sets Sterling to bragging about how he can do anything, how he told a judge he could do his job. He can sit up there and can tell right from wrong, and knows when someone's getting railroaded and when the lawyer talks too much. Sterling can do anything the white man can do, he insists, and most things he can do better.

HOLLOWAY: You sit around talking about you want this . . . you want the other . . . you want a job . . . you want a car. What you don't know is everybody that want one got one. You talking about you want one and ain't done nothing to get one. The people that have them is the people that wanted them. You don't do nothing but sit around and talk about what you ain't got. The more you sit around and talk about what you ain't got, the more you have to talk about. Wait two or three years and see what you have to talk about then.

STERLING: I know what I'm doing. I'm gonna get me two or three Cadillacs and everything that go with them. If I can't find no job I might have to find me a gun. Hey Wolf, you know anybody got a gun they want to sell?

WOLF: What you looking for?

STERLING: Something that shoot straight. I don't care what it is. I don't want no twenty-two. A thirty-eight too big and heavy. Everybody can see it bulging out under your coat. I'll take me a snub-nosed thirty-two if I can get one. I don't want no silver gun that shine in the dark. I'll take a black one. Other than that I don't care what it is.

WOLF: Tony Jackson got an army forty-five he trying to sell.

STERLING: I don't want no forty-five. He probably got the same one I had. You liable to end up shooting yourself with that. I was shooting at some birds one time and couldn't even hit the tree.

WOLF: I'll ask around. Let me get some sugar, Risa.

HOLLOWAY: I see where you want to go back down the penitentiary. I thought you was trying to stay out.

STERLING: You subject to end up there anyway. You don't have to do nothing to go to jail.

WOLF: You right about that. I know. You can walk down there . . . just walk down the street and ask people . . . every nigger you see done been to jail one time or another. The white man don't feel right unless he got a record on these niggers. Walk on down there . . . I'll give you a dollar for every nigger you find that ain't been to jail. Ain't that right, Sterling. I been to jail. Stayed down there three months. Tried to make bond and couldn't do it. They kept me in the county jail for three months. Ain't done nothing but walk down the street. I was walking down Centre Avenue . . . . . police chasing somebody and wasn't looking where he was going, and I wasn't looking where I was going either . . . he ran into me so hard it knocked us both down. I started to get up and there was two three policemen with their guns pointed at my head. Told me not to move. They arrested me for obstructing justice. Kept me down there for three months before the judge had a chance to throw it out. But I learned a lot from that. I learned to watch where I was going at all times. Cause you always under attack.

STERLING: That's why I said if I was going I was going for something.

Sterling turns his attention to Hambone, who had come in earlier with his usual lament and is eating a bowl of beans. Risa thinks he's teasing Hambone, but Sterling insists he isn't, he's trying to get Hambone to trust him, to connect with him. He's teaching Hambone to say "Black is beautiful," saying the words to Hambone and having him repeat them one by one. Hambone does so and is obviously proud of his accomplishment but soon reverts to "He gonna give me my ham."

Memphis returns. He has been told downtown that they can pay him whatever they want for his building because of a clause in the deed. They offered $15,000 and Memphis hit the ceiling claiming he has a clause, too. He "raised so much hell" the judge postponed things, telling him to talk to his lawyer. Memphis did, and the lawyer said they were right, so Memphis fired him and got a white lawyer, admitting he should have gotten one in the first place.

STERLING: You got insurance? If you got insurance you could burn it down.

MEMPHIS: Nigger is you crazy! Insurance cost five times what the building is worth. That's why I keep me some good tenants upstairs. I don't put none of them fools up there that's liable to get drunk and burn down the place. When Mr. Collins died I let it set empty three months till I got somebody up there that was responsible. Look back in the kitchen . . . ask Risa . . . I got four or five fire extinguishers back there . . . and you talking about burning down the place. That's the one thing I am scared of. If it burn down I don't get nothing. I don't even get the $15,000. See, they don't know. The half ain't never been told. I'm ready to walk through fire. I don't bother nobody. The last person I bothered is dead. My mama died in 54. I said then I wasn't going for no more draws. They don't know I feel just like I did when my mama died. She got old and gray and sat by the window till she died. She must have done that cause she ain't had nothing else to do. I was gone. My brother was gone. Sister gone. Everybody gone. My daddy was gone. She sat there till she died. I was staying down on Logan Street. Got the letter one day and telegram the next. They usually fall on top of one another . . . but not that close. I got the letter say, if you wanna see your mother you better come home. Before I could get out the door the telegram came saying it's too late . . . your mother gone. I was trying to borrow some money. Called the train station and found out the schedule, and I'm trying to borrow some money. I can't go down there broke. I don't know how long I got to be there. I ain't even got the train fare. I got $12.63. I got the telegram and sat down and cried like a baby. I could beat any newborn baby in the world crying. I cried till the tears all run down in my ears. Got up and went out the door and everything looked different. Everything had changed. I felt like I had been cut loose. All them years something had a hold of me and I didn't know it. I didn't find out till it cut me loose. I walked out the door and everything had different colors to it. I felt great. I didn't owe nobody nothing. The last person I owed anything to was gone. I borrowed fifty dollars from West and went on down to her funeral. I come back and said everybody better get out of my way. You couldn't hold me down, it look like then I had somewhere to go fast. I didn't know where but I damn sure was going there. That's the way I feel now. They don't know I got a clause of my own.

I'll get up off the canvas if I have to. They can carry me out feet first . . . but my clause say . . . they got to meet my price!

The lights go down on the scene. Curtain.

ACT II

Scene 1: Wednesday morning

Sterling comes into the restaurant with a handful of flowers and a five-gallon gas can. The flowers are for Risa, but she's suspicious about where he got them. Actually, they are from the funeral home, but Sterling overrides her objections to having flowers stolen from a dead man by pointing out that he doesn't mind. There are so many flowers over there that West doesn't know where he can put them all. Sterling wanted her to have the flowers and doesn't see what's such a big deal about it, as they'll be dead in two or three days even if she puts them in water. As for the gas can, Sterling claims he found it in back of an alley, just sitting there. Nobody was around, so he took it. It's got five gallons of gas in it, but he didn't steal it—he found it.

Risa has put the flowers in a glass with water. Holloway, who has come in, suggests she put them in a bigger glass and put a little salt into it, his grandmother's system for making flowers last longer.

Sterling wonders if Aunt Ester is well yet, because he wants to ask her about Risa, if Risa's the woman God was going to send him. If she is, he warns Risa, they're "gonna make all kinds of babies."

When Hambone comes in, Sterling teaches him to say "United we stand, divided we fall," which Sterling learned in the penitentiary. The lesson disintegrates into a shouting match with both Hambone and Sterling yelling out "I want my ham" alternately, and then Sterling changing his yell to "Malcolm lives!" Memphis arrives and is very annoyed at the shouting—this is not a schoolyard, it's a business, and he doesn't want hollering inside the restaurant.

Sterling sells the gas to Memphis for $2. He's going to put it in Memphis's car and hopes Memphis will let him drive it around the block. Memphis refuses in no uncertain terms, and Sterling backs off. When Sterling's gone, Memphis wants to know if Hambone paid for the beans he's eating, and Hambone laboriously dredges up three quarters from out of his pocket. Memphis gives him his change and tells Risa to give Hambone another muffin.

When Wolf arrives he has the gun Sterling said he'd wanted, and the price is $20. Sterling only has two and claims it isn't worth more than fifteen. Wolf offers to loan him the money. Sterling takes the bag with the gun in it and sticks it in his pants.

Sterling puts his $2 on 781. He goes off with the gas can, and Memphis pronounces that within three weeks Sterling will be "laying over there across the street" or back in jail.

The phone rings again, to Memphis's annoyance, and he beats Wolf to it. He doesn't want Wolf taking numbers in the place. Wolf leaves after he and Memphis argue. Meanwhile, the spareribs everybody's been smelling as they cook are about to burn, and Memphis is impatient now with Risa.

West comes in, complaining that someone has broken his large window. He doesn't care how many more people want to see Prophet Samuel—he's leaving West's place the next day. And it's going to be expensive to replace the glass. He could put up a board there, Risa suggests, but West won't do it. He spent 12 years doing that, and it's a matter of principle with him now. "Let them cut a piece of glass and bring it out and bill me." The days are over when they wouldn't do that, or it would take two weeks to fix a broken toilet.

West and Memphis are talking about Memphis's dealings downtown, and West says he'll give Memphis $20,000 for the building. They can go to the bank right now, and West will give him fifteen now and the other five thousand after West sells it to the city. West has to leverage it with his other property, he explains to Memphis. Memphis doesn't like West's way of doing business. He doesn't think it's right. It's the only way to do business, West insists. He's trying to help Memphis and has to look for all the advantages he can. Memphis should be able to understand that.

MEMPHIS: I understand it. That's why I'm going downtown to the city and get my $25,000. Just like I'm going back to Jackson and get my land one of these days. I still got the deed. They ran me out of there but I'm going back. I got me a piece of farm down there. Everybody said I was crazy to buy it cause it didn't have no water on it. They didn't know my grandaddy knew how to find water. If there was water anywhere under the ground he'd find it. He told me where to dig and I dug a well. Dug sixty feet down. You ain't got no idea how far that is. Took me six months hauling dirt out this little hole. Found me some water and made me a nice little crop. Jim Stovall who I bought the land from told me my deed say if I found any water the sale was null and void. Went down to the Court to straighten it out and come to find out he had a bunch of these fellows get together to pick on me. He try to act like he ain't had nothing to do with it. They took and cut my mule's belly out while it standing there. Just took a knife and sliced it open. I stood there and watched them. They was laughing about it. I look and see where they got me covered. There's too many of them to fool around with. I didn't want to die. But I loved that old mule. Me and him had been through a lot together. He was a good old mule. Remind me of myself. He only do so much amount of work and that was it. He didn't mind working. He liked to get out there and exercise. Do anything you asked him. He didn't like you to half work him. If you gonna work him . . . he want you to work him. Or else let him lay. He didn't like to stop and start work. That wasn't to his suiting. Don't tell him you gonna do one thing and then do something else. He'd lay down and tell you. "Goddam it make up your mind!" I used to take him down there and let him mate with Jimmy Hollis' mule. I figure I get mine, let him get his. A man like a woman after a hard day's work. I stood there and watched them cut his belly open. He kinda reared back, took a few steps and fell over. One of them reached down, grabbed hold of his dick and cut that off. I stood there looking at them. I say, okay. I know the rules now. If you do that to something that ain't never done nothing to you . . . then I know what you would do to me. So I tell you what. You go on and get your laugh now. Cause if I get out of this alive I know how to play as good as anyone. Once I know the rules. Whatever they are. I can play by them. Went in there saw the judge and he say the deed was null and void. Now I got to walk home. I was looking for them to try something. But I didn't see nobody. Got home and they had set fire to my crop. To get to my house I'd have to walk through fire. I wasn't ready to do that. I turned around and walked up the hill to Natchez. Called it a draw. Said I was going back. Got up there and got tied up with one of them Mississippi gals, and one year led to two led to five. Then I come up here in Thirty-six. But I'm going back one of these days.

Sterling returns and tries to persuade West to give him a job driving one of his seven Cadillacs. Sterling claims to be good at driving. He drove a getaway car one time—and they got away, he reports proudly—but West has enough drivers. Sterling even offers to wash West's cars, more carefully than they are done at present, but West doesn't need anybody for that job either.

Sterling's been back up to try to see Aunt Ester but was told she was asleep. Holloway urges him to return when she's rested. He's going himself, and it seems West's been up there, too. It was 22 years ago, and "She look like she was half dead then," according to West. Holloway says she looks the same. West had gone to see Aunt Ester to find out if his wife had gone to heaven. He'd buried many people, but his wife was the first person he'd wondered about. He hadn't understood until then that death lasted forever. "You'll never have a greater moment than when you breathe your last breath," West muses. "You become a part of everything that come before." If anyone knew whether she was in heaven it would be Aunt Ester, but when Aunt Ester told West to throw $20 in the river, he wouldn't, just couldn't do it. So that's why he still doesn't know, Holloway explains.

Holloway went to see Aunt Ester to get rid of an urge to kill his grandfather, which went away after he threw $20 in the river every week for a month. So his grandfather died a natural death, though Holloway remembers, "That was the worst Negro I ever known. He think if it wasn't for white people there wouldn't be no daylight. If you let him tell it, God was a white man who had a big plantation in the sky and sat around drinking mint juleps and smoking Havana cigars. He couldn't wait to die to get up in heaven to pick cotton. If he overheard you might wanna go down and get you some extra meat out the white man's smoke house . . . he'd run and tell him. He see you put a rabbit in your sack to weigh up with the cotton, he'd run and tell. The white man would give him a couple pounds of bacon. He's bring that home and my grandmother would throw it out with the garbage. That's the kind of woman she was. I don't know how she got tied up with him. She used to curse the day she laid down with him. That rubbed off on me. I got a little older to where I could see what kind of man he was . . . I figure if he want to go to heaven to pick cotton I'd help him. I got real serious about it. It stayed on me so didn't nobody want to be around me cause of the bad energy I was carrying. Couldn't keep me a woman. Seemed like nothing wouldn't work out for me. I went up to see Aunt Ester and got that bad energy off me. And it worked too. Ask West. He died in his sleep. Caught pneumonia and laid down and died. They wouldn't let him in the hospital cause he didn't have any insurance. He crawled up in the bed in my grandmother's house and laid there till he died. March 5, 1952. So can't nobody tell me nothing about Aunt Ester. I know what she can do for you."

After West leaves, Sterling proposes to Memphis that all he'd need is a truck and to have Risa fry up the chicken for chicken sandwiches and they could make money selling them down at the steel mill at lunchtime. There are hundreds of people there. Memphis isn't interested. He's in business already. Sterling shrugs off the rejection, claiming that if 781 comes out he won't need to go into business, and he and Risa will get married—"Ain't that right, Risa?" When she doesn't answer, Sterling says she's being shy. If he finds any more gas he'll be back, he tells Memphis before going off. Memphis opines to Holloway that he makes it two weeks, not three, before Sterling will be laid out at West's or back in the penitentiary.

Scene 2: Thursday, mid-morning

It is the day of Prophet Samuel's funeral, but in Memphis Lee's restaurant there is more concern at this hour about the whereabouts of Hambone. It seems nobody has seen him, and even Lutz was wondering where he was. He used to live on Arcena Street, but now nobody knows where he's been staying. Risa wonders if he just got tired of waiting for Lutz to give him his ham, but Holloway doubts that. Hambone hasn't missed a day in nine and a half years over there, even Sundays, in case Lutz were to show up. Wolf comes in, claiming nobody's seen Hambone since yesterday.

It's reported the Prophet Samuel's funeral was immense, that the hearse had arrived at the cemetery while some of the cars were still in front of the funeral home. The boulevard was backed up for two miles, and people lined up on both sides of the street.

When Memphis comes in, it seems he hasn't seen Hambone either. Memphis is annoyed when Wolf asks him if it's all right if he takes Holloway's number. Memphis just doesn't like him using his phone, he reiterates. Wolf is concerned because Sterling "hit for two dollars" yesterday on 781, but the number's been cut in half. Nobody likes it when they do that, but Sterling "ain't gonna like it especially." Wolf wants Holloway to do him a favor and explain to Sterling before he sees him that it isn't Wolf's fault.

HOLLOWAY: If I know him like I think I do he gonna wanna know why everybody play his number instead of their own. Then he gonna come to understand that he don't care how many people played it . . . the Alberts still owe him all his money . . . and since you work for the Alberts if you don't get him his money then you all in cahoots and the Alberts is splitting it with you and you gonna buy a Cadillac next week with his money . . . therefore you gonna need your pistol. And if it go that way . . . West is gonna get a chance to bury one of you. If he go up there and mess with the Alberts then West gonna have to bury him in a closed casket. Now . . . I'm sixty-five years old and I got that way by staying out of people business, so no . . . I ain't gonna tell him nothing. If he come in here right now I'd walk out. Come back tomorrow, and Risa will have to tell me what happened.

WOLF: Well, I ain't gonna pay him out my pocket. The hell with it. You right. I got to go to the pawn shop and get my pistol. Hey Risa, I'll be back. If Sterling comes tell him I was looking to see him. (*Exits*).

HOLLOWAY: I don't know why I play the numbers. The Alberts want all the advantages. They got 600-to-1 odds, but that ain't enough for them. If thirty or forty niggers get lucky enough to hit the numbers the same day they don't even want them to enjoy their luck. They want to take that away from them. They don't say nothing about cutting the numbers when six thousand niggers guess wrong.

MEMPHIS: They been cutting numbers for the past hundred years. That's part of the game. You supposed to understand that when you play your money.

Larry Fishburne as Sterling and Cynthia Martells
as Risa in a scene from *Two Trains Running*

Memphis notices the flyer for the Malcolm X rally posted on the wall and angrily tears it down. He doesn't believe in rallies, which come along one after another but with no significant action in between. "That's the Sterling boy bringing that stuff in here," Memphis says, "He ain't gonna do nothing but end up right back down there in the penitentiary."

Holloway agrees Memphis could be right. And now Sterling's got a gun: "A nigger with a gun is bad news. You can't even use the word 'nigger' and 'gun' in the same sentence . . . . . The white man panic. Unless you say, 'The policeman shot the nigger with his gun.'" But Memphis concedes that Sterling needs to carry one, "As young and as crazy as that boy is . . . . ."

Sterling comes in, looking for Wolf. He's been at the cemetery and had hoped to see Risa there. She's disdainful about everyone going to see Prophet Samuel when he was dead rather than when he was alive, and Sterling hastens to agree with her. People don't care till you're dead. Then they say to everyone that they knew the person very well and it makes them feel "special," he philosophizes. That's what she's talking about, Risa points out. Half of those people are hypocrites, and that doesn't count with God. "He wants you all the time."

Risa shows Sterling her card that states she's a paid-up tithing member of the church, signed by Prophet Samuel. "God sent him to help the colored people get justice," Risa believes, but Memphis disagrees. He thinks that the people that lined up there were thinking of justice second and thinking of money first, like Prophet Samuel. People were paying Prophet Samuel's way in the hopes of getting a financial blessing. What did it get Risa? he asks her. Risa feels he takes that attitude because he doesn't believe in anything. But she believes that whatever Prophet Samuel prophesied came true. Sterling admits to believing that the world's about to end and wonders if Prophet Samuel said anything about that. It seems he'd only said God was going to send a sign, but "only the wise men would know what it meant." Sterling thinks the sign might be that the moon seems to him to be getting closer and closer. Memphis considers it a waste of time worrying about the end of the world instead of figuring out how to solve the situation they're now in. Sterling isn't worried. When he finds Wolf he won't have any more problems, he remarks, going off again.

Risa has exited into the back, and Memphis calls to her from near the cash register.

MEMPHIS: Come here, woman. (*Pause.*) If you want your pay you better get out here.
     Risa enters.
I owe you $46 with the ten you took.

RISA: I don't owe you but seven.

MEMPHIS: You ain't counting the $3 you got the other day to buy some hair grease. You ain't counting that.

RISA: I told you I put the $3 back cause they ain't had the kind I wanted.

MEMPHIS: Well, write a note saying you put it back. How in the hell I'm supposed to know you put it back. Here . . . take this $49. I got some business to take care of . . . don't forget to put the bread in the refrigerator when you lock up. Put the bread in the refrigerator and make sure you pull the shade down on the door. I got to go to the courthouse in the morning . . . make sure you got enough eggs before you leave out of here. Well, Holloway . . . I was talking to my lawyer . . . Joseph Bartoromo . . . I was talking to him on the phone. He said let him handle it. I'm ain't gonna let him handle it so far. I told him like I tell you . . . I ain't going for no more draws . . . and I ain't taking a penny less than $25,000.

He starts to exit and stops at the door.

What's that address?

HOLLOWAY: 1839 Wylie. In the back. Knock on the red door.

Scene 3: Thursday afternoon

Holloway is going over the details of Hambone's death for Risa and Wolf, who is sitting at a table doing his bookkeeping. Hambone had been living on Herron Avenue. The landlady found him dead, lying across the bed fully clothed. West, who has a contract with welfare, was contacted to get the body from the morgue. Hambone didn't have any people. He was from Alabama, but nobody even knew his real name. Holloway's told Lutz because Lutz asked him to let him know when he heard anything about Hambone. And Lutz had just looked at him.

Risa is sweeping, and when her broom accidentally sweeps Wolf's feet he is very upset. To him it means he'll end up in jail. Didn't Risa's mother ever teach her anything? Then he'd better move his feet, Risa advises, sweeping them again. Holloway comments that people don't know what causes trouble these days, and they break mirrors and open umbrellas in the house. He recalls a story about a man driving a truckful of mirrors who had an accident. He wasn't hurt but all the mirrors broke, and after the man saw 200 years of bad luck he had to be carried away in a straitjacket.

West comes in. He's finally got Prophet Samuel buried, and he's going to lay out Hambone tomorrow and bury him Saturday. Hambone had many scars on his back, his chest, and his legs. "I ain't never seen nothing like that," West tells them.

Risa doesn't want Hambone to be put in a welfare casket, as if his life hadn't meant anything. He wouldn't look right in a bronze or silver one, West points out, and welfare only pays $350. And West is laying him out for free. A bronze casket is $700 more. Risa wishes she had it. In fact she'd like him laid out in a gold casket. That would be a seventeen-hundred-dollar difference. He doesn't get them for nothing, and his overhead is high.

Sterling comes in and hears that Wolf was looking for him. Wolf owes him $1,200, Sterling announces, and now he's got a grubstake.

STERLING: Say, Mr. West . . . you ever been to Vegas? You ought to let me take you to Vegas and teach you how to gamble. We can make us some money.

WEST: I was gambling before you was born. Give me some sugar, Risa. I ran two or three crap games. Sold bootleg liquor and ran numbers too. The only thing you get out of that is an early grave. I know. I seen it happening. I looked up one day, and so many people was dying from that fast life I figured I could make me some money burying them and live a long life too. I figured I could make a living from it. I didn't know I was gonna get rich. I found out life's hard but it ain't impossible.

STERLING: That's what I figure. I get my money from Wolf . . . get in one of them white folks' crap games it be impossible to stop me. I'm gonna get me two or three Cadillacs like you. Get Risa to be my woman, and I'll be all right. That's all a man need is a pocketful of money, a Cadillac and a good woman. That's all he need on the surface. I ain't gonna talk about that other part of satisfaction. But I got sense enough to know it's there. I know if you get the surface it don't mean nothing unless you got the other. I know that, Mr. West. Sometimes I think I'll just take the woman part. And then sometimes that don't seem like it's enough.

WEST: That's cause you walking around here with a ten-gallon bucket. Somebody put a little capful in and you get mad cause it's empty. You can't go through life carrying a ten-gallon bucket. Get you a little cup. That's all you need. Get you a little cup, and somebody put a little bit in, and it's half full. That ten-gallon bucket ain't never gonna be full. Carry you a little cup through life, and you'll never be disappointed. I'll tell you what my daddy told me. I was a young man just finding my way through life. I told him I wanted to find me a woman and go away and get me a ranch and raise horses like my grandaddy. I was still waiting around to find the woman. He told me to get the ranch first and the woman would come. And he was right.

STERLING: That's what I'm gonna do, Mr. West. You hear that, Risa? Soon as I get my money we going to Vegas, and I'm gonna get me enough money to buy us a ranch. You like horses? I ain't never seen a real horse. I wouldn't know how to act around one. But if that's what it takes to get a woman to like you I'm willing to do that. What's the matter? Don't you wanna go to Vegas with me?

Risa's mind is still on Hambone and his casket, and she argues with West again about a different casket. Wolf comes in, and Sterling is eager to get his money so he and Risa can get married—the reverend wants $50, the cake man fifty, and the jewelry man wants two hundred. The date isn't set, but he wants the money now. Wolf reluctantly explains that the number has been cut, and he'll only get six hundred. Sterling is enraged and is going to the Alberts. He's not going to kill anybody, "just put them in a wheelchair," and he'll start with Wolf. Everybody is mad, Wolf claims, but it's not his fault. Wolf does what they tell him. Sterling takes the six hundred and starts to leave. He's going there and give the money back to them, to old man Albert himself. He'll carry a big sign saying that the game is cancelled.

As he goes out, Risa is suddenly galvanized into action for the first time in the play, almost flying to the door to call out after Sterling to try to stop him.

Scene 4: Thursday night

Risa is sweeping the floor, obviously hoping for Sterling's return. He finally shows up. Risa, painstakingly slowly, pulls up the blind on the door and unlocks it. He wants to know if she'll go to the rally with him. They won't be too late. Risa reminds him he'd left to go to the Alberts, and she didn't know if they'd be seeing him again. He didn't know it mattered to anybody, but he wondered why she'd call after him. She hadn't wanted to see him get killed. He did go to old man Albert, and told him to give him back his $2, that he was calling off the bet. He got his $2 back, but then Albert asked for the six hundred and Sterling told him that he was going to keep it: "That way I have something that belong to him for a change." He'd just looked oddly at Sterling and told him to leave.

Then, when he was walking by Aunt Ester's, he'd gone in to see her, and they'd talked a long time. He'd told her his life story and thought she was very nice, with a calm and sweet manner. When he asked her her age, she told him 349. Nobody ever talked to him quite like she did, he reveals. She'd told him, "Make better what you have and you have best." She'd written something on a paper which she placed in a small envelope. Sterling was to put it in his shoe and walk around on it for three days. When he offered to pay her, she told him to take $20 and throw it in the river, saying she'd get it. So he did.

She'd also told Sterling that, yes, Risa was the one God sent when he'd told him he could not send an angel. "Sterling, you crazy," Risa tells him. Sterling thinks they ought to get a place together. Risa doesn't. She's taking care of herself. Sterling wants to take care of her. He sings to her and continues his wooing. He compliments her, calling her everything a man needs. She cooks, pays "nice attention" to herself—except for her legs. Why did she do that? he asks. He wouldn't understand, she claims. He thinks he would. Aunt Ester had told him, before he even had said anything to her, that he had good understanding. Why is he looking at her legs anyway? Risa wonders. He's looked at her legs, her hips, her breasts and everything else, Sterling confesses. If she wanted ugly legs, she's got them. That's why she did it—"To make them ugly." God made them pretty, she made them ugly.

Sterling tries to make Risa see that she's here in the world and should make the best of things. Of course men are going to try to get her into a bed, "That's common sense." But she should take that as a compliment rather than being upset. All she has to do is say no. She has, Risa insists. Sterling knows that, and knows he should be talking to somebody else. He's tried, but he came back because when he was talking to somebody else he found he was thinking of Risa.

RISA: You ain't got no job. You going back to the penitentiary. I don't want to be tied up with nobody I got to be worrying is they gonna rob another bank or something.

STERLING: When I was living with Mrs. Johnson before she died I used to watch her husband. He get up every morning at six o'clock. Sunday too. Six thirty he out the door. Now . . . he ain't coming back till ten o'clock at night. He going down to J & L and lift hundred-pound slabs of steel till three o'clock. Then he going over after they close the fish market and clean up over there. Now what he got? He got six kids of his own, not to mention me. He got a raggedy house with some beat-up furniture. Can't buy no house cause he can't get a loan. Now that sound like a hard-working man. Good. Clean. Honest. Upright. He work thirty years at the mill and ain't even got a union card. You got to work six months straight. They lay him off for two weeks every five and a half months. He got to call the police after he clean up the fish market so they can let him out of the building. Make sure he don't steal anything. What they got? Two pound of catfish? There got to be something else. I ain't sure I want to do all that.

RISA: You got to do something.

Sterling backs down a little, and asks her, if she doesn't want to get married and have babies, could they be cousins, kissing cousins? He's cornering her, and Risa is trying to avoid him. Sterling says he's never met a woman like her. Risa admits she's never met a man like him, either, but she's not about to get tied up with him. Again he asks her to go to the rally, and she refuses. He can go alone, she tells him.

Risa walks over to the jukebox and puts a quarter in. An Aretha Franklin song begins playing.

STERLING: When did that get fixed?
RISA: Today.
STERLING (*hesitant*): You wanna dance?
RISA: Yeah.
> *They begin to dance. Sterling kisses her lightly.*
STERLING: How's that? You wanna be kissing cousins?
> *He kisses her passionately.*
Goddamn, baby!
RISA: Sterling.
STERLING: I didn't know it was gonna be like this. You can be my first cousin.
RISA (*between kisses*): I wanna be your only cousin.
STERLING: That too.
> *Sterling kisses her as the lights go down.*

Scene 5: Friday, late afternoon

The blackboard reads "Funeral For Hambone Saturday One O'Clock." Risa is cooking and Sterling stands at the window looking out as Holloway waxes philosophical about love and death. "Death will find you . . . it's up to you to find love" is what he's learned. As for love, he believes most people play at it, because the price is too high.

Wolf comes in, complaining about the number of people on the street. They are there because that's where the opportunities are, according to Holloway. Opportunities are not to be found if you sit at home.

Wolf's been over at the funeral home and tells them West laid Hambone out nicely, he looks as if he's sleeping. Sterling, who had been over there before Wolf, thought Hambone had looked dead. Only a few people had signed the book. Risa won't go over, as she doesn't want to see Hambone "like that."

Wolf and Sterling discuss the previous night's rally. There was a big crowd but no fighting. Sterling mentions the police had taken pictures of people there. They don't do that at white folks' gatherings, Wolf notes. There had also been a fire—a drugstore burned down. Wolf had been watching. There'd been nearly a dozen fire trucks and about a hundred police. Holloway insists that everyone knows the owner burned the store down for the insurance. When nobody wants to buy, the best thing to do is "sell it to the insurance company." But somebody will go to jail. The police will arrest somebody within a few days, Holloway predicts: "That way the insurance company pay quicker." And somebody will go to jail for two or three years. But the owner will be in Florida, and the fire inspector, too. That's the system in this country, Holloway instructs Wolf.

Wolf agrees, saying, "Did you all hear where Petey Brown killed his old lady last night? Caught her in the Ellis Hotel with his best friend. Killed him too. That's why I don't have no one woman. When I die every woman in Pittsburgh gonna cry. They ain't gonna know what to do with themselves. My woman come and told me she had another man. I told her say, all right baby, but he can't hear and he can't see. He can't see like I do. You got to be able to pull a whole lot of boxcars to keep up with me. I'm like Prophet Samuel . . . if a man can get him seven women . . . if he can find seven women want to be with him . . . let him have them seven and one or two more. Seven women wanna lay down with him must see something they like. Hell, it's hard to get one, let alone seven. It's hard to get one you can trust that far. See, when you lay down with her, you trusting her with your life. You lay down you got to close your eyes. It wouldn't be nothing for somebody to walk up and slit your throat. That's why you lock the door at night. You lock the door and it be just you and her. That's a whole lot of trust there. If I had that I wouldn't give it up for nothing. Other than that, when I die every woman in Pittsburgh gonna cry."

West arrives for coffee. The courthouse would be closed by now, and he's surprised Memphis hasn't returned. Sterling makes a special point of complimenting West on the job he did on Hambone. West reveals that Lutz came by to see Hambone after he'd closed the store. "Lutz gonna rot in hell," in Risa's estimation. "With a ham under each arm," Wolf adds.

Holloway and West are discussing Prophet Samuel's funeral when Sterling hands Wolf the $20 he owes him and then gives all the rest of his money to Risa, asking her to hold it for him. He'll be back soon, he tells her. When he goes off, Wolf tries to explain to Risa that he realizes there's something between her and Sterling; his attitude is live and let live. She claims she's not paying attention to what he's saying, but Wolf again assures her that Sterling's okay with him.

Memphis comes in, singing. He's been drinking. He met a barmaid at the Brass Rail near the courthouse who "can stand up right next to Risa." He's going back to meet her when she gets off work at seven. Now he needs Risa to fix him something to eat. He assures Holloway he took $20 and didn't just throw it in the river—he'd tied a rock around it and thrown it in. Aunt Ester told him if he threw the money in things would be all right, and she was right, he reports. She'd told him that if he couldn't fight the fire, he shouldn't mess around with it. Only now he's ready to fight it.

MEMPHIS: . . . . . Hey, West . . . look here . . . I went down there to the court-house ready to fight for that $25,000 I want for my property. I wasn't taking no fifteen. I wasn't taking no twenty. I want twenty-five thousand. They told me, "Well, Mr. Lee . . . we got a clause, and the city is prepared to put into motion . . . " that's the part I like, "prepared to put into motion" . . . "the securing of your property at 1621 Wylie Avenue" . . . they had the address right and everything . . . "for the sum of $35,000." I liked to fell over. The lawyer standing there, he know I'm mad and ready to fight it. I told him, "Don't you say a word. Don't you open your mouth." $35,000! I started to go up and tell my wife. She up there. She up there at the house. She come back to get her things and ended up staying. I moved out. She moved back in and I moved out. Told her I had something to do and if she be there when I get back . . . if I get back . . . then we can sit down and talk. You know what I'm gonna do? Aunt Ester clued me on this one. I went up there and told her my whole life story. She say if you drop the ball you got to go back and pick it up. Ain't no need to keep running cause if you get to the end zone it ain't gonna be a touchdown. She didn't say it in them words but that's what she meant. Told me . . . You got to go back and pick up the ball. That's what I'm gonna do. I'm going back to Jackson and see Stovall. If he ain't there, then I'm gonna see his son. He enjoying his daddy's benefits, he got to carry his daddy's weight. I'm going on back up to Jackson and pick up the ball . . . . .

When Memphis sees the sign about Hambone's funeral and realizes that he's died he begins to imitate Hambone's plaintive "He gonna give me my ham. He gonna give me my ham. I want my ham." Memphis gives Risa $50 to get flowers and to put on them that "it's from everybody . . . everybody who ever dropped the ball and went back to pick it up." He's waiting for Risa to bring him a plate of food and then he's going to celebrate with . . . "I forget her name." With all that money, when he gets back from seeing Stovall, he plans to open a big restaurant on Centre. There'll be two or three cooks, seven or eight waitresses. There'll be a jukebox.

"*The sound of glass breaking and a burglar alarm is heard.*" Memphis goes on despite the noise off, describing the big neon sign he'll have on the restaurant, and the menu. Maybe he'll even have a separate entrance for takeout, he's telling them, as Sterling comes on with a large ham. Sterling's grinning as he puts the ham on the counter. "Say, Mr. West . . . that's for Hambone's casket."

Curtain.

FIRES IN THE MIRROR

A Full-Length Program in One Act

BY ANNA DEAVERE SMITH

Cast and credits appear on pages 337, 339

ANNA DEAVERE SMITH was born in 1950 in Baltimore, where her father was self-employed in the coffee and tea business. She trained as an actress, receiving her M.F.A. from the American Conservatory Theater after graduating from Beaver College, and she became interested in "writing roles for multi-cultural casts and different representations of people in gender than we traditionally have seen." The Los Angeles Theater Center produced her play Piano, *which won her the 1991 Drama League Award in playwriting. Her New York professional stage debut as both actress and playwright, her first Best Play,* Fires in the Mirror, *was developed as part of a series called "On the Road: A Search for American Character." Its Crown Heights material was created for George C. Wolfe's* Moving Beyond the Madness: A Festival of New Voices *at the Joseph Papp Public Theater December 1. This material, together with other Smith sketches, was then presented on its own at the Public as* Fires in the Mirror *May 12, winning its author a special 1992 Obie citation.*

Smith has been commissioned by Crossroads Theater to collaborate with its artistic director, Ricardo Kahn, on an "On the Road" entitled Dream, *about the dreams of black Americans; and by the Berkeley Repertory Theater for a play. She is a fellow of Radcliffe College's Bunting Institute and an associate professor of drama at Stanford. She lives in San Francisco.*

SYNOPSIS: *Fires in the Mirror*, subtitled Crown Heights, Brooklyn and Other Identities, is a series of more than two dozen monologues, with writer-performer Anne Deavere Smith impersonating each of the male and female characters in a text taken from their own words in recorded interviews. Smith observes in a program note, "I am interested in where a person's unique relationship to the spoken word intersects with character . . . . . Often, the shows are built around a specific controversial and timely event or series of events."

Much of *Fires in the Mirror* is a connected series of character sketches of persons involved in the August 1991 confrontational events in Crown Heights, in which a black child was killed by an errant automobile driven by a Jew, causing a bitter disturbance in which an innocent Jewish student was wantonly stabbed to death in revenge. And *Fires in the Mirror* also includes a number of disconnected word portraits of other persons of special interest. In order to represent it as comprehensively as possible in these pages, we present six of the monologues in their entirety—the first two individual characterizations, the last four part of the Crown Heights continuity.

The Desert/Identity

NTOZAKE SHANGE (*playwright, seated to the side of a desk*):
Hummmm,
Identity
is is uh in a way it's um it's sort of it's uh
it's a psychic sense of place
u-m.
It's a way of knowing I'm not a rock or that tree?
I'm this other living creature over here?
And it's a way of knowing that no matter where I put myself
that I am not necessarily
what's around me
I become separate from that even though I'm a part of that
and it's being able to make those differentiations clearly
that lets us have an identity
and what's inside our identity
is everything that ever happened to us.
Everything that's ever happened to us as well as our
responses to it.
Sometimes if we are in trance states
or if we're alone someplace in the desert we begin to feel as
if we are part of the desert

which we are right at that minute
but we are not the desert
u-h
we are part of the desert
and when we go home
we take with us that part of the desert that the desert gave us
but we're still not the desert.
It's an important differentiation to make because you don't know
what you're giving if you don't know what you have and you don't
know what you're taking if you don't know what's yours and what's
somebody else's.

Hair

ANONYMOUS GIRL:
When I look in the mirror
I don't know
how did I find out I was black. (*Tongue sound.*)
When I grew up and I look in the mirror and saw I was black
when I look at my parents
that's how I knew I was black.
Look at my skin.
You black?
Black is beautiful.
I don't know
that's what I always say.
I think white is beautiful too
but I think black is beautiful too.
In my class nobody is white everybody's black
and some of them is Hispanic.
In my class if
you can't call any of them Puerto Ricans.
They despise Puerto Ricans I don't know why.
They think that Puerto Ricans are stuck up and everything
they say oh my gosh!
But they act like that themselves.
They act just like white girls.
Black girls is not like that.
Please you should be in my class.
Like they say that Puerto Ricans act like that
and they don't see they act like that themselves.
Black girls
they bite off of your clothes.
You don't know what that means?

Like cop, following
and last year they used to have a lot of girls like that
they come to school with a style right?
And if they see another girl with that style?
Oh my gosh look at her
she tryin to bite off of me in some way.
What she think she is.
No don't be bitin off of my sneakers
or something like that
and they be doin the same thing.
Or doin a hairstyle
I mean black people are into hairstyles.
Oh my gosh her hair look nice
I'm a get my hair done the same way
um hum
and they be
and they don't want people doin that to them
but they doin that to other people.
That's how black people are
yea/ah.
The Spanish girls don't bite off of us.
Some of the black girls follow them.
But they don't mind.
They don't care.
They follow each other.
Like there's three girls in my class
they from the Dominican Republic
they all stick together like glue
they all three best friends
they don't follow nobody
like there's none of them lead or anything.
They don't hang around us either.
They're
by theirselves.

No Blood in His Feet

> *9:30 a.m. Tuesday, November 12, 1991. A large home on President Street in Crown Heights. Only natural light, not very much. Dark wood. A darkish dining room with an enormous table, could seat 20. Rabbi Spielman sits at the head of the table. Lots of stuff on the table. He wears Hasidic clothing, a black fedora, and black jacket, and reading glasses. He slightly slides the tape recorder microphone which is in front of him at the table as he talks. The furniture in the dining room,*

including his chair, is for the most part very old, solid wood furniture.
There are children playing quietly in another room, and people come
in and out frequently, but always whispering and walking carefully not
to make noise, unless they speak to him directly.

RABBI JOSEPH SPIELMAN (*Chairman, Council of Jewish Organizations of Crown*
Heights):
　　Many people were on the sidewalk,
　　talking playing
　　drinking
　　beer or whatever
　　being that type of neighborhood.
　　A car
　　driven by a an individual
　　a Hasidic individual
　　went through the intersection
　　was hit by another car
　　and thereby causing it to go onto the sidewalk.
　　The driver on seeing
　　himself in such a position that he felt he was going to definitely hit
　　someone
　　because of the amount of people on the sidewalk,
　　he steered at the building
　　so as to get out of the way of the people.
　　Obviously for the most part
　　he was successful,
　　but regrettably
　　one child was killed
　　and another child
　　was
　　wounded.
　　Um
　　seeing what happened
　　he jumped out of the car
　　and realizing
　　there may be a child under the car
　　he tried to physically lift
　　the car
　　from the child.
　　Well, as he was doing this
　　the Afro Americans were beating him already.
　　He was beaten so much he needed stitches in the scalp and face
　　fifteen or sixteen stitches
　　and also

there were other passengers in the car
that were being beaten too.
One of the passengers was calling 911
on the cellular phone.
A black person
pulled the phone out of his hand and ran.
Just stole the, stole the telephone.
The Jewish community
has a volunteer
ambulance corps
which is funded totally from the nations.
There is not one penny of government funds.
And manned by volunteers and at many times at their expense
the equipment that they carry in order to save lives.
As one of the EMS ambulances were coming
one of the Hasidic ambulances or the Jewish ambulances came
on the scene.
The EMS responded with three ambulances on the scene.
They were there before
the Jewish ambulance
when the Jewish ambulance came
two or three police cars were already on the scene.
The police saw the potential for violence
and saw the occupants of the car
were being beaten and were afraid for their safety.
At the same time the EMS asked
the Hasidic ambulances for certain pieces of equipment that they
were out of
that they needed to take care of the Cato kid
and
um
in fact I was,
the Hasidic ambulance left leaving behind one of the passengers.
That passenger had a walkie-talkie and he requested that I
come down to pick him up.
And at that time there was a lot of screaming and shouting
and it was a mixed crowd Hasidic and Afro American.
The police said, "Rabbi get your people out of here."
I told them to leave and I left.
Now,
a few hours later
two and a half hours later
in a different part of Crown Heights

a scholar
from Australia (*Yankel Rosenbaum*)
who um
I think he had a doctorate or he was working on his doctorate
was walking on the street
on his own
I mean he was totally oblivious
and he was accosted by a group of young blacks
about twenty of them strong,
which was being egged on by a black
male approximately
fault (*sic*)
forty years old and balding
telling them,
"Kill all Jews
look what they did to the kid
kill all Jews."
and all the epithets that go along with it.
"Heil Hitler" and all of it.
They stabbed him
which later on the stab wounds were fatal
and he passed away in the hospital.
The mayor,
hearing that the Cato kid passed away
came to the Kings County Hospital
to give condolences to the family
at the meantime they had already wheeled in
Mr. Rosenbaum.
He was in the Emergency Room
and I was at the hospital at the same time
and the mayor,
expressed his concern
that a child
uh innocent child had been killed.
Where I explained to him
the fact
that
whereas the child was killed from an unfortunate accident
where there was no malicious intent,
here
there was an individual lying in the Emergency Room
who had been stabbed with malicious intent
and for the sole reason

Pictured above is Anna Deavere Smith playing two of the more than
a score of characters in the monologues of her *Fires in the Mirror*

not that he did anything to anyone
just from the fact that he happened to be Jewish.
And the mayor went with me to the Emergency Room
to visit Mr. Rosenbaum.
This was approximately one and a half hours before he passed away.
I noticed at the time that his feet
were
completely white.
And I complained to the doctor
on the scene,
"He's having a problem with blood circulation
because there's no blood in his feet."
And she gave me some assanine answer.
And the mayor asked her what his condition is.
"Serious but stable."
In the meantime he was screaming and in pain
and they weren't doing anything
subsequently they um
they started giving him anaesthesia in a time that
they weren't allowed to give him anaesthesia
and while he was anaesthesia
on anaesthesia he passed away.
So there was totally mismanagement in his case.
So whereas the mayor,

had been fed his people got
whatever information he got out of the black community was
that
the driver had run a red light
and also
and that the ambulance
the Hasidic ambulance
refused to take care of the black child that was dying and
rather took care of their own.
Nenh?
And this is what is fed amongst the black community.
And it was false
it was totally false
and it was done maliciously
only with the intent to get the riots
to start up the resulting riots.

My Brother's Blood

NORMAN ROSENBAUM:

My brother's blood cries out from the ground.
Let me make it clear
why I'm here and why I'm here.
In August of 1991
as you all have heard before today
my brother was killed in the streets of Crown Heights
for no other reason
than that he was a Jew!!!!
The only miracle was
that my brother was the only victim
who paid for being a Jew with his life.
When my brother was surrounded
each and every American was surrounded.
When my brother was stabbed four times
And as my brother bled to death in this city
while the medicos stood by
and let him bleed
to death it was the gravest of indictments against this country.
One person out of the twenty gutless individuals
who attacked my brother has been arrested.
I for one am not convinced that it is beyond the ability of the New
York police
to arrest others.
Let me tell you Mayor Dinkins

let me tell you Commissioner Brown
I'm here.
I'm not going home
until there is justice.

Rain

REV. AL SHARPTON:
  The D.A. came back with no indictment.
  Uh so then our only course
  was to ask for a special prosecutor
  which is appointed by the Governor
  who's been hostile
  and to sue civilly
  when we went into civil court
  we went to get an order to show cause
  the judge signed it and gave me a deadline of three days
  the driver left the country . . .
  No one even said "Why would he run?
  If he did no wrong."
  If you and I were in an accident we'd have to go to civil court.
  Why is this man
  above the law?
  So they said, "He's in Israel."
  So I said,
  "Well I'll go to Israel to show best effits."
  and the deadline
  was
  I had to serve him by Tuesday
  which was Yom Kippur
  that was the judge's decision not mine.
  So we went
  Alton Maddox and I
  got on a plane
  left Monday night
  landed Tuesday morning
  went and served the American Embassy uh
  so that
  if this man had any decency at all
  he could come to the American Embassy and receive service
  which he has not done to this day
  come back
  went to court
  and showed the judge the receipts

and the judge said, "You made best effits
therefore you are now permitted
by default
to go ahead
and sue the rabbi or whomever
because you cannot do the driver."
So it wasn't just a media grandstand
we wanted to show the world
1) this man *ran*
and was *allowed* to run and 2) we wanted to be able to legally go
around him
to sue the people he was working for so that we can bring them into
court and establish *why* and what happened
and it came out in the paper the other day
that the driver in the other car didn't even have a driver's license.
So we're dealing with a *complete* outrage here
we're dealing with a double standard
we're dealing with uh uh a a
situation where
blacks do not have equal protection under the law
and the media is used to castigate us
that merely asked for justice
rather than castigate those that would hit a kid
and walk away like he just stepped on a roach!
Uh
there also is the media
contention of the young Jewish scholar
that was stabbed that night
and they've even distorted
saying *my words at the funeral*
I *preached* the funeral
Uh
helped to to uh uh
spar or or or or or *inspire* or *incite* people to kill him
when he was dead the day before
I came out there.
He was killed the night
that the young man
was killed with the car accident.
I didn't even get a call
from the family
til eighteen hours later.
So there's a whole media distortion

to protect them.
Nobody is talking abut
"Why
is this guy
in flight?"
If *I* was a Rabbi
I am a ministuh
and my driver hit a kid
I would not let the driver *leave*
and I certainlih would give my condolences
or anything else I could
to the family
I don't care what race they are.
To this minute the Rebbe has never even uttered a word of
sympathy
to the family
not even sent 'em a *card*
a *flower* or *nothing*!
So it's treating us with absolute contempt
and I don't care how controversial it makes us
I *won't* tolerate being insulted.
If you *piss* in my face I'm gonna call it *piss*
I'm not gonna call it rain.

The Coup

ROZ MALAMUD:

Do you know what happened in August here?
You see when you read the newspapers.
I mean my son filmed what was going on
but when you read the newspapers
of course I was here
I couldn't leave my house
I only would go out early during the day
the police were barricading here.
You see
I wish
I could just like
go on television
I wanna scream to the whole world.
They said
that the blacks were rioting against the Jews in Crown Heights
and that the Jews were fighting back.
Do you know that the blacks who came here to riot were not my

neighbors?
I don't love my neighbors
I don't know my black neighbors
There's one lady on President Street
Claire
I adore her.
She's my girlfriend's next door neighbor.
I've had a manicure
done in her house
and we sit and kibbutz
and stuff
but I don't know them.
I told you we don't mingle socially
because of the difference
of food
and religion
and what you have here.
But
the people in this community
want exactly
what I want out of life
they want to live
in nice homes
they all go to work
they couldn't possibly
have houses here
if they didn't
generally they have
two
u-m
incomes
that come in
they want to send their kids to college.
They wanna live a nice quiet life.
They wanna shop for their groceries and cook their meals and go to
their Sunday picnics!
Theyu just want to have decent homes and decent lives!
The people who came to riot here
were brought here
by this famous
Reverend Al Sharpton
which I'd like to know who ordained him.
And he brought in a bunch of kids.

I wish you could see the New York *Times*.
Unfortunately it was on page twenty.
But
he brought in a bunch of kids who didn't have jobs in the
summertime.
When you don't have a job
and you're hanging out all day
I mean they interviewed
one of the black girls on Utica Avenue.
She said
the guys will make you pregnant
at night
and in the morning not know who you are.
(*Almost whispering.*) And if you're sitting on a front stoop and it's very very
    hot
and you have no money
and you have nothing to do with your time
and someone says come on you wanna riot.
You know how kids are.
The fault lies with the police department.
The police department did nothing to stop them,
I was sitting here in the front of the house
when bottles were being thrown
and the sergeant tells five hundred policemen
with clubs and helmets and guns
to duck.
And I said to him,
"You're telling them to duck?"
What should I do?
I don't have a club and a gun.
Had they put it.
Stopped it on the first night.
This kid who came from Australia. (*She sucks her teeth.*)
You know
his parents were Holocaust survivors he didn't have to die
he worked
did a lot of research in Holocaust studies.
He didn't have to die.
What happened on Utica Avenue
was an accident.
JEWISH PEOPLE
DO NOT DRIVE VANS INTO SEVEN-YEAR-OLD BOYS
YOU WANT TO KNOW SOMETHING BLACK PEOPLE DO NOT

DRIVE
VANS INTO SEVEN-YEAR-OLD BOYS
HISPANIC PEOPLE DON'T DRIVE VANS INTO SEVEN-YEAR-OLD
    BOYS
IT'S JUST NOT DONE
PEOPLE LIKE JEFFREY DAYMER MAYBE THEY DO IT
BUT AVERAGE CITIZENS DO NOT GO OUT AND TRY TO KILL
(*Sounds like a laugh but it's just a sound.*) SEVEN-YEAR-OLD BOYS.
It was an accident!
But it was allowed to fester and to steam and all that.
When you come here do you see anything that's going on riots?
No.
But Al Sharpton and the likes of him like Dowerty
who by the way has been in prison
and all of a sudden he became Reverend Dowerty
they once did an expose on him.
But
these guys live off of this
you understand?
People are not gonna give them money
contribute to their causes
unless they're out there rebble rousing.
My black neighbors?
I mean I spoke to them.
They were hiding in their houses just like I was.
We were scared.
I was scared!
I was really frightened.
I had five hundred policemen standing in front of my house
every day.
I had mounted police.
But I couldn't leave my block
because when it got dark I couldn't come back in
I couldn't meet anyone for dinner.
Thank God I told you my children were all out of town.
My son was in Russia.
The coup
was exactly the same day as the riot
and I was very upset about it,
he was in Russia running a camp
and I was very concerned when I had heard about that.
I hadn't heard from him.
That night the riot started.

When I did hear from him I told him to stay in Russia he'd be safer there than here.
And he was.

THE EXTRA MAN

A Play in Two Acts

BY RICHARD GREENBERG

Cast and credits appear on pages 333, 335-336

RICHARD GREENBERG was born in 1958 in East Meadow, Long Island, the son of an executive of a film theater chain. He was educated in local schools and went to college at all of the Big Three: Princeton (B.A. 1980), Harvard (in a Ph.D. course in English literature, abandoned after less than a year) and Yale (M.F.A. from the Drama School in 1985, where he won the Molly Kazan Playwriting Award). He began writing fiction at Princeton, including a novel for his thesis; but it was his first play, started after the Harvard experience and later submitted to Yale, that won him a place in the playwriting program under Oscar Brownstein.

Greenberg's first New York production took place while he was still at Yale: The Bloodletters *off off Broadway November 17, 1984 at Ensemble Studio Theater. It won him the 1985 Oppenheimer Award for best new playwright. His one-acter* Life Under Water *was produced by the same OOB group later that season and was published in the* Best Short Plays *volume of its year. Ensemble also mounted his one-acters* Vanishing Act *(1986) and* The Author's Voice *(1987, also a* Best Short Plays *selection). Also in 1987, his adaptation of a Martha Clarke performance work based on Kafka writing,* The Hunger Artist, *appeared OOB as a Music Theater Group/Lenox Arts Center showcase.*

Greenberg's first full off-Broadway production was The Maderati *at Playwrights Horizons February 19, 1987 for 12 performances. His first Best Play,* Eastern Standard, *opened October 27, 1988 at Manhattan Theater Club (after a run the previous season at Seattle Repertory Theater), played 46 off-Broadway performances, transferred to Broadway January 5, 1989 for 92 additional performances and was twice cited among the Outer Critics Circle nominees for the bests of the season. Greenberg's second Best Play,* The American Plan, *was produced at Manhattan Theater Club December 16, 1990 for 37 performances. For the third season in a row he has provided the New York stage with a a Best Play,* The Extra Man, *which opened a 39-performance run May 19 at Manhattan Theater Club. (Things were happening in threes at MTC;* The Extra Man *was not only their third Greenberg play but their third 1991-92 Best Play, with* Lips Together, Teeth Apart *and* Sight Unseen.*)*

Greenberg is also the author of Neptune's Hips *(1988, Ensemble Studio Theater OOB) and the TV scripts* Trying Times *and the adaptation of his own* Life Under Water. *He is a member of the Dramatists Guild and Ensemble Studio Theater, lives in New York City and almost always starts a new play while in rehearsal for the previous one (he is working on a new book for the Rodgers & Hart musical* Pal Joey*).*

Time: From fall to spring

Place: Various locations in New York City

ACT I

SYNOPSIS: Keith and Laura are inspecting an empty apartment, commenting on its features. Keith is a writer, Laura an editor married to a lawyer, Daniel, and trying to help Keith in his apartment-hunting. She comments that Keith is so set on seeing the best in everybody that he has acquired a group of mostly unattractive friends—one Randy, for example.

KEITH: He's a lovely person.
LAURA: He's a cretin.
KEITH: I know he can be difficult.
LAURA: He steals things at parties.
    Beat.
KEITH: What?
LAURA: He takes things. Whenever I invite him—which I only do because of you—he pilfers something. An ash tray or a picture or somebody's watch.
KEITH: My God! Why don't you say something?
LAURA: I do. I call him the next morning, and I say, "Randy, you idiot, give me back that Goddamn whatever-it-is-this-time, or I'm calling the cops."
KEITH: And he does?
LAURA: Yes.

KEITH: Well, there you are.

LAURA: But still he takes things—that he takes them in the first place—Also you can't say anything to him without his *singing* you some dire musical comedy selection in return, in this incredibly booming, flat, basso profundo—*why* are you friends?

KEITH: Because he really is a lovely person.

LAURA: . . . Exactly, just my point. Oh, by the way, we're having a party next week.

KEITH: Are you asking Randy?

LAURA: Of course.

KEITH: Why don't you not?

LAURA: It's not possible.

KEITH: Why?

LAURA: Because of you.

KEITH: God, that's terrible.

LAURA: No it's not—it's just the fact—we're all knit up in each other.

Laura suggests that Keith bring someone named Catherine to the party, but Keith is angry at her—Catherine left him "for my own good." Keith asks after Laura's husband Daniel, who of course will be at the party. Keith describes him as "a big sexy lawyer," but Laura comments that Daniel has "a terrible life" dealing with "the whole, crashing, ugly din of the world in vivid detail." She listens to her husband's tribulations, but she never seems to find the right thing to say about them except some routine exclamation or other.

LAURA: . . . . . I sit there feeling remarkably shallow for not having anything worse than your standard-issue urban malaise to offer . . . My little story of despair . . . whatever I've dredged up, falls flat. We hem and haw some more—nothing violent, nothing bitter, just . . . somehow . . . the death of rapport. I finish brushing my hair, and we go to bed.

KEITH: Do you have sex?

    Beat.

LAURA: Sometimes.

KEITH: I can't believe I said that.

LAURA: You did.

KEITH: I should be slapped.

LAURA: It's all right.

    Beat.

KEITH: You do love him don't you?

LAURA: I love him deeply. He's just not anyone I can have a conversation with.

Keith declares that he'd like to make Laura happy. His writing another book would do the trick (she tells him), but that's not what he means; he'd like to make her smile right now. He tells her that one of their friends—Laura's husband's friend, actually—named Jess told Keith that Laura is "The most beautiful woman he's ever known." "That's sweet," Laura replies, and it does make her smile. "It's a silly thing, but it's nice to know," she remarks, as the scene fades out.

The party is in full swing in Laura and Daniel's apartment, and in the kitchen Laura is putting food on a plate when Jess enters and tells her, "Not that I don't love you, but your party makes me want to open a vein." Apparently Randy is following Keith around singing into his ear, while others are holding forth on various subjects—including one would-be film maker casting aspersions on Jess's latest article in *Filmstream*. Laura's husband Daniel is wandering around contributing unfinished sentences to the party conversation.

Laura inquires about Jess's article (it's about "the abuse of holocaust imagery in contemporary American movies"). Laura sends Jess into a tizzy by observing that this subject may have already been covered. Meanwhile Keith comes in and sets about making another pot of coffee. They are gossiping about the guests when Daniel comes in with an empty platter which he proceeds to refill, while reporting that the film maker has been saying that he *likes* Jess's article. When Daniel returns to the party, Keith goes to keep him company.

LAURA: The greasy-haired Marxist *likes* your work.

JESS: Oh, you know, that's probably just a trick—Probably he just wanted to corner me to tell me how surprised he was that I'd written something so almost adequate, considering what the rest of my—

LAURA: You're insane—

JESS: Well . . . that's how it is. (*Beat. Defeated.*) Hmm. Well . . . (*Beat.*) Oh, screw it, might as well go back to the party.

LAURA (*to stop him*): Maybe we should do a collection.

JESS: What?

LAURA: Doesn't that sound fun?

JESS: Of what I write?

LAURA: Trade paperback.

JESS: Do you have that kind of power?

LAURA: I can suggest it; I'm taken more or less seriously.

JESS: That will stop if you suggest it.

LAURA: I love your stuff.

JESS: Great. Sure. Fine. We can call the whole collection "The Evil of Banality." "The Evil of Banality: A Case in Point."

LAURA: Stop.

JESS: It would be an excuse to have lunch together, anyway.

LAURA: Haven't we?

JESS: No.

LAURA: So let's.

JESS: That would be amazing.
LAURA: It's no big deal.
JESS: In my life? When?
LAURA: . . . Umm . . .
JESS: I'm free always. My schedule is clear till death.

They make a lunch date for a couple of weeks hence and are smiling at each other, reluctant to join the others, as the scene ends.

In Laura and Daniel's bedroom, Laura is seated at her dressing table, dressed in a robe, combing out her hair, as Daniel enters hunting high and low for his shoes. Laura declares herself exhausted. Daniel comments that Keith must be in love with Laura (which Laura denies) because he talks about her all the time, saying things like "Laura doesn't eat onions; they make her sick," which Daniel overheard at the party. But he trusts Keith. He sits, and Laura watches him in the mirror.

DANIEL: I'm sorry I'm such a . . . dodo with your friends.
LAURA: They're our friends.
DANIEL: I'm sorry I'm such a dodo with *our* friends.
LAURA: You're not.
DANIEL: I don't have anything to say to them.
LAURA: You do.
DANIEL: Name something. (*Pause.*) It's . . . they're all so . . . serious and . . . hectic. Are they . . . are they doing important things?
LAURA: . . . No.
DANIEL: I should . . . try to muster conversation, but . . . I'm not, I can be, I'm very . . . articulate in court.
LAURA: I know, I've seen you.
DANIEL: Not lately. (*Beat.*) I can be. Honest Injun. (*Beat. Sighs.*) Oh, well.
LAURA: . . . Randy took your shoes.
DANIEL: Huh?
LAURA: He'll bring them back tomorrow.
DANIEL: You saw him?
LAURA: No. But I know.
DANIEL: . . . He does that?
LAURA: It's something he does.

Randy is a law unto himself, Laura explains to a somewhat bewildered Daniel. Laura asks about her husband's present case, and Daniel says it's about a measles drug that was used improperly and has caused the deaths of 38 babies. Laura is appalled at this "corporate infanticide," as Daniel calls it. Daniel adds that he's been meeting with parents, and he is dazed at the recollection: "Their children are dead; they had *measles*. That could be considered . . . disappointing. (*Pause.*) The manufacturer . . . he thinks it's unfortunate, he doesn't understand . . . why the fuss. (*Beat.*) Oh . . . it's all just . . ."

Laura studies her husband, then mentions an author friend whose lover has AIDS, "So we don't mind when he rants any more." Daniel agrees that this is a terrible plague which has come upon them everywhere.

LAURA: I'm calling Randy first thing tomorrow morning and demand he return those shoes.

DANIEL: I'd appreciate it; people just, they shouldn't steal your shoes.

LAURA: I'm going to say that.

> *He crosses to her, stands behind her a moment, puts a hand on her head, smiles into the mirror, returns to the bed, starts to unbutton his shirt.*

It's just, really . . .

DANIEL: What?

LAURA: All those babies.

DANIEL: Yes . . .

> *He lies on the bed, still dressed, his body curling a little; his eyes wide open. She lays the brush on the dressing table. Fade out.*

On a bench, in an autumn afternoon, Keith and Laura are having lunch, commenting on the passers-by. Laura tells Keith of her plan to publish an anthology of Jess's writings, and Keith agrees that "Jess is probably the best writer on film this country has produced since James Agee." Laura confesses she's never read any of Jess's writings, expecting Keith to realize she would never read anything on a subject as mundane as the movies. Jess writes about everything, Keith explains, using film only as a starting point.

KEITH: Jess is one of those people who suddenly they're fifty years old and they're everywhere, and people ask where they came from, and it turns out they were there the whole time, only nobody noticed—But I can't believe you haven't—

LAURA: No . . . it's just . . . you know . . . *film* criticism . . .

KEITH: Then why did you say you wanted to do it in the first place?

LAURA: I don't know, I don't have the faintest idea. (*Pause.*) Because I wanted to keep him in the room . . . because he thinks I'm pretty.

> *Pause. Keith smiles.*

KEITH: You can't tell him you've changed your mind.

LAURA: I wasn't going to do that . . . I was just never going to bring it up again until he forgot.

KEITH: He won't forget.

Keith advises Laura to treat Jess gently—he's had a tough time lately—and disappointment would come hard, "especially from you." Laura picks up on that phrase, but Keith is slow to explain what he means by it. Is Jess madly in love with her? Laura asks in jest. Keith continues to tantalize her with innuendo. Jess's life is a sort of waste, he tells her.

KEITH: . . . . . He hides in the movies—as if some day there'll be a story—some story that will *include* him. But it never comes. He needs *someone* . . . to link him to things, somehow . . . and you were there. Anybody else and it wouldn't have mattered, but it was you . . . so there was no resisting it.

LAURA: That *is* insane.

KEITH: God—you say that, and I think you don't know him and you don't know yourself either!

LAURA: Keith—

KEITH: What's happened to you? When did you forget yourself? It's as if you fell asleep one night and never woke up. To be everything you are and not to know it—

LAURA: Look—

KEITH: You should be happy! If anyone should be, it's you. I feel so *helpless*. I stand here watching you fall further and further away from yourself, and I wonder

Laila Robins (Laura), Adam Arkin (Jess) and Boyd Gaines
(Keith) in a scene from Richard Greenberg's *The Extra Man*

who *did* this to you? How did it happen? Who's to blame? If only I could show you yourself *as you are*.

> *She looks at him, puts her hand tenderly to his face. She keeps it there a moment, then he puts his hand over it, holds it for a while, then gently removes it.*

Laura should go ahead with Jess's book no matter what, Keith advises her, before they part and the scene ends.

Laura and Jess are having their planned get-together for lunch in a restaurant. Laura borrows Keith's comparison of Jess's work to James Agee, but when Jess, knowledgeable on this subject, pursues it, Laura is forced to admit that she's never read any Agee.

Jess is eager to hear details of the forthcoming publication, like how many copies will be scheduled. He describes himself as a "marginal figure" in a department full of "*Cahiers du Cinema* types" who don't recognize him as a serious talent. Talking like this doesn't help the impression he'd like to make on his would-be publisher, he realizes, but Laura encourages him with a favorable comment on his reviews of Indian movies. Does she agree with his views in those reviews? Jess wonders, driving Laura to the edge of despair because she's never been to an Indian movie.

LAURA: Please don't talk to me about films. I don't go to films. If we could work together on this book without discussing the films involved, I'd be very grateful. I don't like films. I don't know anything about films. I—God, I feel like such an idiot with you! Ask me about Margaret Drabble, or, or *Brancusi*, I could discuss them with you at some length, but, not films, just *not films*.

> *Beat.*

JESS: Then why do you want to do the book?

> *Pause. The possible answers to that question are simultaneously tantalizing and deeply disappointing to Jess.*

LAURA: Well. I just do. You must think I'm the biggest dodo of an editor—

JESS: I know you're not—

LAURA: You've found me out—I'm completely out of my depth here—it's one of the topics I know almost nothing about—

JESS: I know you're one of the best young editors around—

LAURA (*blushing, if possible*): No, not that . . . not best, not young, but . . . (*Sees him looking.*) What?

JESS: You looked so pretty just then.

LAURA: . . . Umm . . .

JESS: Then especially, I mean. (*Beat.*) I shouldn't have said that.

LAURA: Don't say that.

It's time to order, and when Laura asks Jess what he's going to have, he can't help replying, "Sex sometime in the foreseeable future, I hope." Laura tells Jess that his writing sparkles, and his old-guard colleagues are probably just jealous of him. Jess confesses that for a long time he longed for "just a little serious attention." Sympathetically, Laura takes his hand, as the scene fades.

In another restaurant, Keith and Jess have a lunch date. Catching up on each other's activities, Jess learns that Keith has been spending his time reading a play by Hroswitha on a bench at The Cloisters. Keith has a message for Jess: Daniel wants Jess to phone him, as Jess has missed two months of their supposedly weekly lunches, busy with rewrites for his forthcoming book. Keith tells Jess that Laura's enjoying working on the book. But Jess has his doubts about the whole project, spending too much time together with Laura, his friend Daniel's wife.

JESS: I feel guilty as hell.
KEITH: I know.
JESS: For weeks.
KEITH: I know.
JESS: Ever since you told me—
KEITH: I shouldn't have told you—
JESS: No, I'm glad you did—
KEITH: It was the worst thing I've ever done—
JESS: I like knowing—
KEITH: It was evil; she didn't want me to. You haven't said—?
JESS: No, of course not, anyway, please don't, it's not you, you were just trying to cheer me up, it *worked*, but God! . . . She was always just . . . Daniel's wife. (*Beat.*) . . . She's so . . . beautiful, you know? (*Beat.*) And she loves me.
KEITH: She's said so?
JESS: Yes.
KEITH (*with great interest*): Really?
JESS: Yes. To *you*.
KEITH: Oh.
JESS: Not to me. Not *yet*. Not to me.
KEITH: Oh.
      Beat.
JESS: Of course nothing can come of it . . . . .

Jess is too fond of Daniel to carry things any further. Keith insinuates that Daniel works so hard, he's neglectful of other matters, such as a marriage "that has no warmth, no rapport, no conversation, no sex." Jess tells himself, "It's out of the question," as the scene ends.

Seated on a bench near a bus stop at twilight, Jess tells Laura he hasn't had sex for three years, and that time with someone who left him for his own good, "Like someone pitching you out of a window and telling you the fresh air will do you good." Jess refers to Laura's marriage as "dwindling." Laura admits that though she still loves Daniel, he's not someone she can talk to.

Jess feels that his life is aimless and lonely, and his work mediocre. He envies Laura's relationship with Daniel. He tells her, "I think you're a wonderful woman. And I think lately your life hasn't been worthy of you. And I wish I could change that." She kisses him and exits as the scene ends.

Daniel, on a pay phone, is calling Jess in his apartment. Jess pretends to be very busy, and Daniel senses his standoffishness but hopes to arrange a meeting. Daniel needs someone to talk to. Jess puts him off but promises to call him next week, as the scene ends.

Keith is looking at another empty apartment with Laura. Jess's book seems to be well accepted at her office, Laura tells him, but that's not what's on her mind just now. Keith tries to burrow conversationally under Laura's skin, accusing her of having too rigid a self-image at this early stage of her life; her clinging to marital fidelity, for example.

> KEITH: . . . . . And then you have what? A rotting marriage. A dying marriage. Your flag—your value—it's so narrow it leaves you faithful to a *corpse. Why?* Your husband—and don't get me wrong, I love Daniel, I really do—but your husband has been careless with your marriage, he's been somewhere else, doing something else, but you—
> LAURA: Who says that? What makes you think that?
> KEITH: They're your very own words, they're the things you've said yourself!
> LAURA: I've never said anything like that—
> KEITH: That's *exactly* what you've said. You don't listen when you speak. *I'm* the listener. *I'm* the one who listens. This is *what you say* . . . You've slipped your head into this noose of words, this phrase "A Faithful Wife," and I think—I can't help thinking—my God, what a mingy idea that is! What a tiny idea, what a crabbed way of looking at the world. The phrases we choose, the allegiances, the stupid, stifling, craven sentences we live inside—death sentences, *death* sentences—
> LAURA: So you're saying I should—
> KEITH: Oh God, how *much* I'm not saying anything! . . . Laura, I love you so much, so much, you're *what* I love in life . . . and it just seems to me that happiness—happiness is such a rare thing—when have we ever felt it?—We can check our diaries and list the *dates*—that to turn away from happiness—to turn away from it has to be . . . . . has to be . . . evil.
>> *Pause.*
> LAURA: But to choose someone else's happiness over your own?

KEITH: You can't choose someone else's happiness; it's impossible.

LAURA: . . . But to turn away happiness so as not to cause someone else's *unhappiness*?

KEITH: Is Daniel happy now?

LAURA: That's not the point.

KEITH: Is Daniel happy now?

LAURA: . . . No.

KEITH: Are you? Is Jess?

LAURA: No.

KEITH: Isn't the only point—isn't the only *decent* point—to allow as little unhappiness as possible? Isn't the aim—doesn't it have to be—an economy of pain?

> *Pause.*

LAURA: Yes. Yes.

KEITH: . . . I'm sorry, but I really don't like this apartment, either. All the onyx.

> *They look at each other. Fade out.*

Laura is showing the same empty apartment to Jess, who is nervous because he fears that Mrs. Warren, who let them in, will come back any minute. Laura assures him that she won't. She confides to Jess that Daniel didn't come home the previous evening, even though she'd cooked dinner. Laura characterizes this as "Quiet unkindness . . . disguised as distraction." Jess has noticed the bare simplicity of the way the former tenants have furnished this apartment.

LAURA: Uncluttered . . .

JESS: Warm and simple, that's what I—I'd imagined *sex* must be kind of uncomfortable on these bare wood floors, but otherwise . . .

LAURA (*suddenly*): We've brought our coats.

> *Long pause.*

JESS: Yes.

LAURA: She never pops in—Mrs. Warren—she waits for me to return the key— it's a pattern we've established . . . She's showing this place exclusively, no one else.

JESS: Why can't I breathe all of a sudden?

LAURA: Your place—you said it smells like dead insects—

JESS: It's impossible—

LAURA: And mine—

JESS: Oh God, no.

LAURA (*goes to door, locks it*): The lock works. (*Chains it.*) So does the chain.

JESS: I really can't breathe.

LAURA: I've been thinking about this a lot . . .

JESS: So have I . . .

LAURA: And I've decided . . . that we don't have anything left to lose.

Jess takes off his coat, lays it on the floor. She comes to him. They kiss, and he pulls her down. Fade out. Curtain.

ACT II

Keith and Laura are seated on a bench, Keith telling Laura that no one has seen much of her lately, Laura explaining that she's been "preoccupied." As a matter of fact, Laura happened to run into a friend, Paula, who chattered to her about adultery. Fortunately, Paula knows nothing of Laura's recent life, which has been so different from the usual that everything else "just seems like a kind of . . . old noise."

Keith assumes that Laura might be feeling a sort of guilt. Laura denies it but then admits, "Of course there's some of it all the time, every minute . . . but there's so much more." Probing for Laura's feelings and confidences, Keith tried to imagine what it must be like for Laura and Jess alone there in Jess's apartment.

KEITH: . . . . . I'd imagine the whole *first* part would be sort of . . . swirling and wonderful . . . and the next part, too—
LAURA: You mean the sex part.
KEITH: *Your* words—
LAURA: The sex part.
KEITH: . . . But then, these times . . . these moments . . . I've always felt were recesses . . . and after, there's that drop, that . . ."every animal is sad" . . . and especially where the context is so . . . prohibitive . . . it seems to me that . . . objects in the room . . . the baseball cap on his desk lamp—
LAURA: I thought you've never been there—
KEITH: I haven't, I haven't . . . but the baseball cap on his desk lamp . . . the woodcarved schooner in the window . . . and the strange smells the walls have trapped . . . old cooking . . . wet dust . . . paint . . . Do they begin to close in on you? . . . I wonder . . . Does that awful . . . presentness . . . of life seem . . . like a threat . . . or an accusation . . . or a sentence?
      Pause.
LAURA: When you see Catherine, do you ever want to whip out your dick and say, "Munch on my lovepole, slavechild?"
KEITH: Laura—
LAURA: Is that yes?
KEITH: I can't believe you said that.
LAURA: I thought we were asking personal questions.
KEITH: Your vocabulary has deteriorated—
LAURA: Maybe so—

Laura makes it clear that she doesn't want to share her emotions with Keith. He reproaches her for being reticent with a friend who cares, but she leaves without further discussion of her affair with Jess, as the scene ends.

In Jess's bedroom, Laura and Jess are in bed, naked under the sheets. They emerge and start collecting and donning their clothes. They converse about trivia until Jess notices his students' uncorrected papers on his desk and realizes he's been neglecting his duties. At this moment he should be showing them *Last Year at Marienbad*, but he decides they probably don't want to see it anyhow.

The subject of Keith and his "promising book of short stories" arises. That was six years ago, and Keith hasn't written anything since. Laura defends this lapse as a normal session of writer's block; besides, some of the fire went out of him when Catherine left him, she judges.

Jess and Laura are affectionately playful until the telephone rings, answered by machine, and Keith's voice comes from the speaker saying "Hi, guys!" and wishing them well. When the phone turns off, Laura comments that lately she finds Keith is "full of . . . . . literally, shit. Constipated." And Laura wonders how Keith would know they were here, together—neither of them had told him. And Keith keeps questioning her about the details of their relationship. Laura adds that she is fond of Keith, but she doesn't want any part of him right now.

JESS: Don't do that to *me*, okay?

LAURA: What?

JESS: Don't love me more than anybody for a little while, then just stop all of a sudden, okay?

LAURA (*sits down beside him; holds him*): I don't do that.

JESS: Oh.

>   *She keeps holding him.*

He's not so bad. You don't think he's so bad, really, do you?

LAURA: It's just a phase.

JESS: I mean, God, really, we should be grateful . . . if he hadn't told me you were so madly in love with me, we never would have—

LAURA: What?

JESS: I never would have given you a second—

LAURA: What did he say? What did he say?

>   *Pause.*

JESS: That was a mistake . . .

LAURA: When did he say that?

JESS: Why are you so—?

LAURA: When did he say that to you? Tell me.

>   *Pause.*

JESS: A long . . . a long time ago. (*Beat.*) Before anything . . . (*Beat.*) Look, it's no big deal.

>   *Pause. She looks at him, touches his cheek, runs her hand down.*

LAURA: . . . I think . . . I really do want to get back to the office.

JESS: Laura—

LAURA: I need to shower. I need to take a shower.

JESS: What's the matter, why are you—?

LAURA (*exiting to bathroom*): I have to take a shower.

> *She's gone. Jess is left alone.*

JESS: Shit.

> *He sits on the bed. He sees the panties she wore when she got there on the floor. He picks them up, looks at them, slips them into the pocket of his robe. Fade out.*

Keith, Jess and Laura meet for lunch in a restaurant. Their small talk includes having noticed that another person named Jess has been murdered, reported in tabloid headlines so that Jess's friends are leaving joking messages on his answering machine. Laura asks Keith about Catherine—he has no recent news of her. Keith tries to gossip about their friend Paula but senses a slight edge to the reactions of Laura and Jess.

Laura starts asking Keith questions about Catherine that embarrass him: "*Is* there a Catherine? Flesh, blood, cunt?" And furthermore, taking a close look at Keith with an editor's analytical eye, Laura concludes, "You are not a plausible character . . . . .The least we can ask of our friends is that they might logically exist!" Keith has no reply as the scene fades out.

Laura is drying herself off after a shower, when Daniel comes home, sits on the bed, gradually divulges to Laura that the case came to an end two days ago and his side won full damages. In her robe, Laura sits and brushes her hair, troubled that two whole days have passed and Daniel didn't tell her about the case's outcome.

Laura tells Daniel, in answer to his question, that she had lunch with Jess today, and the organizing of his anthology is very complicated. Daniel in turn tells Laura he lunched with Jess the day before, and afterward they happened to run into Randy with a girl. Randy completely ignored Jess.

DANIEL: But he was so unusually pleasant, otherwise. I didn't even—and the girl with him seemed . . . I didn't catch her function; they were acting like a couple, whatever *that* means, but still—

LAURA: Whatever.

DANIEL: But then—after completely refusing to acknowledge Jess's existence, you know—Randy turned to him, and without so much as a "hello," asked, "So, how's Laura?"

> *Pause.*

LAURA: That idiot.

DANIEL: Is that—?

LAURA: What an idiot.

DANIEL: Is that supposed to be *humor*?

LAURA: Well, of course that's what that's supposed to be. What did Jess say?

DANIEL: Well, Jess . . . Jess couldn't care less—he didn't mention it to you?

LAURA: No.

DANIEL: No. He couldn't care less, he just looked at him cross-eyed, and then Randy and the girl went off to have lunch with Keith—

As a matter of fact, Keith called Daniel at the office asking him to have Laura call him. Daniel wonders why Laura's friends talk so much, and Laura tells him, "They're just . . . idiots." Daniel agrees. Laura holds out the hairbrush to Daniel,

John Slattery as Daniel with Laila
Robins in a scene from *The Extra Man*

who rises and begins brushing her hair as the scene ends.

In a restaurant, Daniel joins Keith for lunch, a bit late because he's been consulting with a new client. In the middle of chatting about the menu, Keith asks Daniel, "Are you and Laura still together?", to Daniel's astonishment. Keith explains the reason for his question: people are talking, and he hasn't seen Laura for a long time—apparently she's been very busy. Keith pretends to be sympathetic and changes the subject, but now Daniel must know, are they talking about Laura and Jess? "They say nothing that bears repeating," Keith replies evasively, which nails it down for Daniel: Laura and Jess, it must be true.

DANIEL: Things hadn't been going well . . . but I'd hoped—
KEITH: It's all lies—
DANIEL: I don't know what she's told you—
KEITH: Daniel—
DANIEL: . . . I must have done something . . . I don't know what she's told you—
KEITH: Listen—
DANIEL: I . . . *love* her, you know.
    Beat. Daniel trying to piece it together.
. . . I must have . . . I must have *done* something—
KEITH: Daniel—
DANIEL: But what have I done? What have I done? What have I done?
    Grab's Keith's hand.
What have I done?
    Fade out.

In Laura's and Daniel's bedroom, Laura is in bed reading when Daniel comes in in his business clothes and undresses. Sitting on the edge of the bed, he begins to cry. When Laura notices this, it is a shock to her, "*Then she leans over and puts her arms around him. He rests his head against her cheek. She holds him tighter. Fade out.*"

At Jess's, Laura is collecting bits of clothing which she has left here from time to time, while Jess sits in a chair, trying to persuade her to stop. She sits on the bed, while telling Jess how she ran into Paula and Randy in the park yesterday and they all but brushed her off. And, Laura tells Jess, she is looking for another editor for his book. She rises, as does Jess, who helps her on with her coat and tells the departing Laura, "All right, but it happened. I had you. You belonged to me . . . . . It *did* happen," as the scene ends.

In their kitchen, Laura and Daniel are arranging the hors d'oeuvre trays for a party in progress which Daniel reports is "Fairly lively." Keith enters with an empty coffee pot and proceeds to make some more, while Laura exits with a reloaded tray.

Keith has heard that Daniel won his recent case. He did so, Daniel tells Keith, by means of a witness who finally told the truth after lying for almost fifty years. "Guilt and redemption," Keith comments, "The best kind of story." Keith asks Daniel how he is (he's fine), declaring that he cares about him. "You've been a very good friend," Daniel agrees, "When I was going crazy . . . when I had all those stupid ideas . . . you were so kind . . . I needed someone then. And you . . . . . listened." Keith assures him he never took "that stuff" seriously but then asks Daniel how Jess is doing. Daniel doesn't know, except that he's heard that Jess's manuscript won't be published.

Keith hints that there's a kind of information that, once acquired, sticks in the mind and is very difficult to dislodge. Daniel agrees but explains, "It's just . . . at the end of the day . . . you want a home to come to . . . so much," and exits.

Laura comes back to get another full tray. At first there is an awkward silence between herself and Keith, who is working on the coffee. Finally Laura observes, "Daniel's much happier not knowing," and Keith responds, "None of my business." Laura has heard that Jess has been spending a lot of time out of town, but she doesn't want to talk about Jess or his cancelled book, so Keith makes a remark about Paula.

LAURA: It's good having her around again.

KEITH: Isn't it? Isn't it fun?

LAURA: And all of them. I've . . . missed it.

KEITH: So have I. Terribly.

LAURA: Even Randy—

KEITH: I think his girl friend's a real knockout, don't you?

LAURA: And Daniel . . . and Paula . . . Even . . . all of it, all of them, the whole . . . thing. I wasn't sure I'd ever . . . have them again.

KEITH: They just had the wrong idea—

LAURA: I wasn't sure. I never realized how terrible it could be . . . it must be worse than anything . . . to lose . . . what's familiar . . .

> Pause.

KEITH: They just had to be given the right idea.

> Beat.

LAURA: Yes.

KEITH: . . . Hey, you know what we haven't done forever? Let's have lunch! And maybe hunt for an apartment after. You still have to find me some place to live, you know.

LAURA: . . . Sure.

KEITH: When?

LAURA: . . . Soon.

KEITH: How about the day after tomorrow?

LAURA: . . . I don't know; my book's at the office—

KEITH (*charmingly insistent*): Oh, come on—
LAURA: I may have an appointment—
KEITH: Cancel it—
LAURA: It may not be the kind I can cancel—
KEITH: Let's . . .
LAURA: I don't know if—
KEITH: *Let's.*
> *Beat.*

LAURA: Day after tomorrow. (*Looks at tray.*) Well. Finished. I'll take these out. (*Starts for door.*)

KEITH: Laura, I really do love you. You really are my best friend in the world, you know.

LAURA: Yes. I think that might as well be true.
> *She exits. He remains. Fade out. Curtain.*

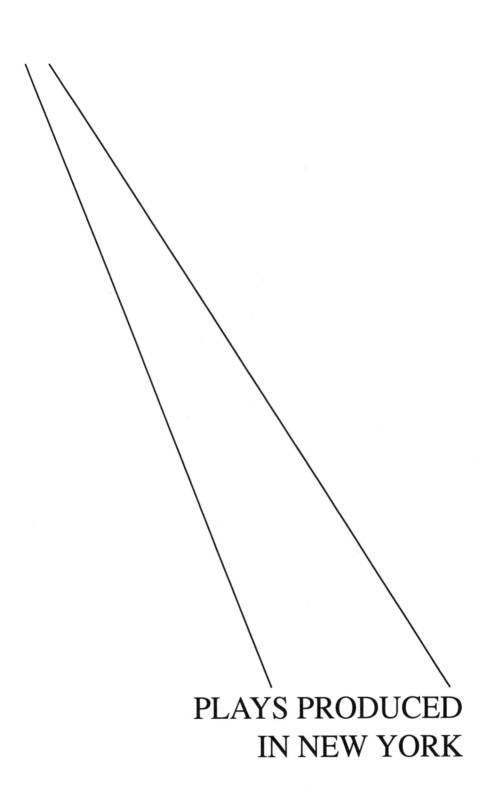

PLAYS PRODUCED
IN NEW YORK

PLAYS PRODUCED ON BROADWAY

Figures in parentheses following a play's title give number of performances. These figures are acquired directly from the production offices and do not include previews or extra non-profit performances. In the case of a transfer, the off-Broadway run is noted but not added to the figure in parentheses.

Plays marked with an asterisk (*) were still in a projected run June 1, 1992. Their number of performances is figured through May 31, 1992.

In a listing of a show's numbers—dances, sketches, musical scenes, etc.—the titles of songs are identified wherever possible by their appearance in quotation marks (").

HOLDOVERS FROM PREVIOUS SEASONS

Plays which were running on June 1, 1991 are listed below. More detailed information about them appears in previous *Best Plays* volumes of appropriate years. Important cast changes since opening night are recorded in the Cast Replacements section of this volume.

*Cats (4,029). Musical based on *Old Possum's Book of Practical Cats* by T.S. Eliot; music by Andrew Lloyd Webber; additional lyrics by Trevor Nunn and Richard Stilgoe. Opened October 7, 1982.

*Les Misérables (2,116). Musical based on the novel by Victor Hugo; book by Alain Boublil and Claude-Michel Schönberg; music by Claude-Michel Schönberg; lyrics by Herbert Kretzmer; original French text by Alain Boublil and Jean-Marc Natel; additional material by James Fenton. Opened March 12, 1987.

*The Phantom of the Opera (1,815). Musical adapted from the novel by Gaston Leroux; book by Richard Stilgoe and Andrew Lloyd Webber; music by Andrew Lloyd Webber; lyrics by Charles Hart; additional lyrics by Richard Stilgoe. Opened January 26, 1988.

Grand Hotel (1,077). Musical (subtitled The Musical) based on Vicki Baum's *Grand Hotel*; book by Luther Davis; songs by Robert Wright and George Forrest; additional music and lyrics by Maury Yeston. Opened November 12, 1989. (Closed April 26, 1992)

Gypsy (582). Revival of the musical suggested by the memoirs of Gypsy Rose Lee; book by Arthur Laurents; music by Jule Styne; lyrics by Stephen Sondheim; original production directed and choreographed by Jerome Robbins. Opened November 16, 1989. (Closed January 6, 1991 after 477 performances) Reopened in a return engagement April 28, 1991. (Closed July 28, 1991 after 105 additional performances)

City of Angels (878). Musical with book by Larry Gelbart; music by Cy Coleman; lyrics by David Zippel. Opened December 11, 1989. (Closed January 19, 1992)

Jackie Mason: Brand New (216). One-man show created, written and performed by Jackie Mason. Opened October 17, 1990. (Closed June 30, 1991)

Once on This Island (469). Transfer from off Broadway of the musical based on the novel *My Love, My Love* by Rosa Guy; book and lyrics by Lynn Ahrens; music by Stephen Flaherty. Opened off Broadway May 6, 1990 where it played 24 performances through May 27, 1990; transferred to Broadway October 18, 1990. (Closed December 1, 1991 matinee)

Six Degrees of Separation (485). Transfer from off Broadway of the play by John Guare. Opened June 14, 1990 off Broadway where it played 155 performances through October 28, 1990. Transferred to Broadway November 8, 1990. (Closed January 5, 1992)

Fiddler on the Roof (241). Revival of the musical based on Sholom Aleichem's stories; book by Joseph Stein; music by Jerry Bock; lyrics by Sheldon Harnick. Opened November 18, 1990. (Closed June 16, 1991)

Penn & Teller: The Refrigerator Tour (103). Magic show by and with Penn Jillette and Teller. Opened April 3, 1991. (Closed June 30, 1991 and transferred to off Broadway as *Penn & Teller Rot in Hell*; see its entry in the Plays Produced Off Broadway section of this volume)

***Lost in Yonkers** (532). By Neil Simon. Opened February 21, 1991.

I Hate Hamlet (80). By Paul Rudnick. Opened April 8, 1991. (Closed June 22, 1991)

***Miss Saigon** (475). Musical with book by Alain Boublil and Claude-Michel Schönberg; music by Claude-Michel Schönberg; lyrics by Richard Maltby Jr. and Alain Boublil; adapted from the original French lyrics by Alain Boublil; additional material by Richard Maltby Jr. Opened April 11, 1991.

***The Secret Garden** (457). Musical based on the novel by Frances Hodgson Burnett; book and lyrics by Marsha Norman; music by Lucy Simon. Opened April 25, 1991.

Our Country's Good (48). By Timberlake Wertenbaker; based on the novel *The Playmaker* by Thomas Keneally. Opened April 29, 1991. (Closed June 8, 1991)

***The Will Rogers Follies** (450). Musical with book by Peter Stone; music by Cy Coleman; lyrics by Betty Comden and Adolph Green. Opened May 1, 1991.

PLAYS PRODUCED JUNE 1, 1991-MAY 31, 1992

Circle in the Square Theater. 1990-91 season concluded with **Getting Married** (70). Revival of the play by George Bernard Shaw. Produced by Circle in the Square Theater,

Theodore Mann artistic director, Robert Buckley managing director, Paul Libin consulting producer, at Circle in the Square Theater. Opened June 26, 1991. (Closed August 25, 1991)

Mrs. Bridgenorth . . . . Elizabeth Franz	Hotchkiss . . . . Scott Wentworth
Collins . . . . Patrick Tull	Cecil . . . . J.D. Cullum
General . . . . Nicolas Coster	Edith . . . . Jane Fleiss
Lesbia . . . . Victoria Tennant	Soames . . . . Walter Bobbie
Reginald . . . . Simon Jones	Beadle . . . . Guy Paul
Leo . . . . Madeleine Potter	Mrs. George . . . . Linda Thorson
Bishop . . . . Lee Richardson	

Understudies: Messrs. Tull, Coster, Paul, Jones, Richardson—Burt Edwards; Misses Thorson, Franz, Tennant—Alexandra O'Karma; Messrs. Wentworth, Cullum, Bobbie—Guy Paul; Misses Potter, Fleiss—Alexandra Napier.

Directed by Stephen Porter; scenery, James Morgan; costumes, Holly Hynes; lighting, Mary Jo Dondlinger; production stage manager, William Hare; press, Maria Somma.

Time: Spring morning, 1908. Place: The Bishop's Palace. The play was presented in two parts.

The last major New York revival of *Getting Married* took place off Broadway in the season of 1959-60.

New York City Opera. Schedule of two revivals of Broadway musicals. **The Most Happy Fella** (10). Based on Sidney Howard's *They Knew What They Wanted*; book, music and lyrics by Frank Loesser. Opened September 4, 1991. (Closed October 18, 1991) **Brigadoon** (12). Book and lyrics by Alan Jay Lerner; music by Frederick Loewe. Opened November 7, 1991. (Closed November 17, 1991) Produced by New York City Opera, Christopher Keene general director, Donald Hassard managing director of artistic administration, at the New York State Theater.

THE MOST HAPPY FELLA

Cashier; Postman . . . . . . William Ledbetter	Joe . . . . Burke Moses
Cleo . . . . Karen Ziemba	Giuseppe . . . . Arthur Rubin
Rosabella . . . . Elizabeth Walsh	Pasquale . . . . Richard Byrne
Busboys . . . . Dean Dufford, Michael Langlois	Ciccio . . . . John Lankston
Tony . . . . Louis Quilico	Doctor . . . . Peter Blanchet
Marie . . . . Elaine Bonazzi	Priest . . . . Don Yule
Max . . . . Ron Hilley	Tessie . . . . Alice Roberts
Herman . . . . Lara Teeter	Gussie . . . . Zachary London
Clem . . . . Gregory Moore	Artie . . . . Jonathan Zwi
Jake . . . . David Frye	Station Attendant . . . . James Russell
Al . . . . Jonathan Guss	

Waitresses: Jean Barber, Joan Mirabella, Deidre Sheehan. Neighbors: Harry Davis, Michael Langlois, Louis Perry, Phillip Sneed, William Ward, Edward Zimmerman. Neighbor Ladies: Lee Bellaver, Esperanza Galan, Stephanie Godino, Rita Metzger.

Directed by Arthur Allan Seidelman; conductor, Chris Nance; choreography, Dan Siretta; scenery, Michael Anania; costumes, Beba Shamash; lighting, Mark W. Stanley; sound, Abe Jacob; orchestrations, Don Walker; chorus master, Joseph Colaneri; press, Susan Woelzl.

Act I, Scene 1: A restaurant in San Francisco, January 1953. Scene 2: Main Street, Napa, California in April. Scene 3: Tony's barn, a few weeks later. Scene 4: Tony's front yard, immediately following. Act II, Scene 1: The vineyards in May. Scene 2: Tony's yard in June. Scene 3: The barn. Scene 4: The vineyards in June. Act III, Scene 1: The barn, an hour later. Scene 2: Napa bus and train station, a short while later.

The last major New York revival of record of *The Most Happy Fella* took place on Broadway 10/11/79 for 52 performances. A second revival of this musical took place this season 2/13/92; see its entry in the Plays Produced on Broadway section of this volume.

The list of musical numbers in *The Most Happy Fella* appears on pages 366-7 of *The Best Plays of 1979-80*.

BRIGADOON

Tommy Albright . . . . John Leslie Wolfe	Archie Beaton . . . . William Ledbetter
Jeff Douglas . . . . Tony Roberts	Angus MacGuffie . . . . Don Yule
Maggie Anderson . . . . Joan Mirabella	Meg Brockie . . . . Joyce Castle

Stuart Dalrymple . . . . Richard Byrne   Fiona MacLaren . . . . Michele McBride
Sandy Dean . . . . Gregory Moore   Jean MacLaren . . . . Camille de Ganon
Harry Beaton . . . . Scott Fowler   Charlie Dalrymple . . . . David Eisler
Andrew MacLaren . . . . . . David Rae Smith   Mr. Lundie . . . . Ron Randell

Others: Joe Deer, Leslie Farrell, Stephen Fox, Stephanie Godino, Jonathan Guss, William Ward.

Directed by Gerald Freedman; conductor, Paul Gemignani; scenery and costumes, Desmond Heeley; lighting, Duane Schuler; Agnes de Mille's choreography re-created by James Jamieson.

The last major New York revival of *Brigadoon* took place on Broadway 10/16/80 for 133 performances.

The list of scenes and musical numbers in *Brigadoon* appears on pages 351-2 of *The Best Plays of 1980-81*.

Circle in the Square Theater. Schedule of four programs. **On Borrowed Time** (99). Revival of the play by Paul Osborn; based on the novel by L.E. Watkin. Opened October 9, 1991. (Closed January 5, 1992) **Search and Destroy** (46). By Howard Korder. Opened February 26, 1992. (Closed April 5, 1992) And *Salome,* revival of the play by Oscar Wilde in repertory with *Chinese Coffee* by Ira Lewis, scheduled to open June 28, 1992. Produced by Circle in the Square Theater, Theodore Mann artistic director, Robert A. Buckley managing director, Paul Libin consulting producer, at Circle in the Square Theater, in its 40th anniversary season.

ON BORROWED TIME

Pud . . . . Matthew Porac   Boy in Tree . . . . Matt White
Julian Northrup, Gramps. . . . . George C. Scott   Workmen . . . . Arnie Mazer, James Noah
Nellie, Granny . . . . Teresa Wright   Dr. Evans . . . . Conrad Bain
Mrs. Tritt . . . . Jennie Ventriss   Mr. Grimes . . . . George DiCenzo
Mr. Brink . . . . Nathan Lane   Mr. Pilbeam. . . . . Allen Williams
Marcia Giles . . . . Alice Haining   Sheriff . . . . Joseph Jamrog
Demetria Riffle . . . . Bette Henritze   Betty . . . . Marilyn

Understudies: Mr. Scott—Bill Severs; Mr. Lane—John LaGioia; Misses Wright, Henritze—Jennie Ventriss; Misses Haining, Ventriss—Katie Finnernan; Messrs. Williams, Jamrog—Arnie Mazer; Messrs. Bain, DiCenzo—James Noah; Messrs. Porac, White—Daniel Reifsnyder.

Directed by George C. Scott; scenery, Marjorie Bradley Kellogg; costumes, Holly Hynes; lighting, Mary Jo Dondlinger; production stage manager, William Hare; press, Maria Somma.

Time: A late summer's day before the Great War. Act I, Scene 1: Afternooon. Scene 2: A week later. Scene 3: Dusk, a week later. Act II, Scene 1: Two hours later. Scene 2: Ten o'clock that night. Scene 3: Dawn, the next morning. Scene 4: Dusk, the same day. Scene 5: Later that night.

The last major New York revival of *On Borrowed Time* took place on Broadway 2/10/53 for 78 performances.

SEARCH AND DESTROY

Martin Mirkheim . . . . Griffin Dunne   Hotel Clerk; Carling . . . . . Michael Hammond
Accountant . . . . James Noah   Security Guard; Nunez. . . . . . . Jerry Grayson
Lauren; Jackie; Radio Announcer. . . Jane Fleiss   Dr. Waxling . . . . Stephen McHattie
Robert . . . . T.G. Waites   Bus Driver; State Troooper . . . . . Mike Hodge
Kim . . . . Keith Szarabajka   Ron . . . . Paul Guilfoyle
Marie; Terry . . . . Welker White   Pamfilo . . . . Arnold Molina
Roger . . . . Gregory Simmons   Lee . . . . Thom Sesma

Directed by David Chambers; scenery, Chris Barreca; costumes, Candice Donnelly; lighting, Chris Parry; sound, David Budries; production stage manager, William Hare.

Time: The present. Place: The United States of America. The play was presented in two parts.

A man's cross-country pursuit of the American Dream in the form of producing movies. Previously produced in regional theater at South Coast Repertory, Costa Mesa, Calif. and Yale Repertory Theater.

Note: The Russian actor Vitaly Solomin played a single performance of Russian selections with English introduction and explanations on 1/12/92 at Circle in the Square as part of an exchange program with the Maly Theater, Moscow.

THE ROUNDABOUT ON BROADWAY—This season's series of revivals by Roundabout Theater Company included Harold Pinter's *The Homecoming* with Lindsay Crouse and Roy Dotrice, (photo *at left*) and Friedrich Duerrenmatt's *The Visit* with Jane Alexander (*right*) as Claire Zachanassian

Andre Heller's Wonderhouse (9). Variety revue adapted by Andre Heller; English adaptation by Mel Howard. Produced by Mel Howard in association with Jean D. Weill at the Broadhurst Theater. Opened October 20, 1991. (Closed October 27, 1991)

Igor	Billy Barty	Stagehand	Gunilla Wingquist
Olga	Patty Maloney		

Others: Carlo Olds, Macao, Baroness Jeanette Lips Von Lipstrill, Omar Pasha, Ezio Bedin, Marion and Robert Konyot; Rao, Milo and Roger.

Directed and designed by Andre Heller; stage curtain, Erté; costumes, Susanne Schmoegner; lighting, Pluesch; sound, T. Richard Fitzgerald; arrangements and orchestrations, Andrew Powell; conductor, J. Leonard Oxley; technical supervisor, Val Medina; executive producer, Norman E. Rothstein; production stage manager, Joe Lorden; press, Susan Bloch and Company, Kevin McAnarney.

Variety acts framed in a surprise 70th birthday party given by a husband for his wife, a retired performer. The show was presented without intermission. A foreign production previously produced in Vienna, Berlin and on tour in Europe.

*Dancing at Lughnasa (253). By Brian Friel. Produced by Noel Pearson in association with Bill Kenwright and Joseph Harris in the Abbey Theater production, Garry Hynes artistic director, at the Plymouth Theater. Opened October 24, 1991.

Michael	Gerard McSorley	Rose	Bríd Ní Neachtain
Chris	Catherine Byrne	Kate	Rosaleen Linehan
Maggie	Dearbhla Molloy	Gerry	Robert Gwilym
Agnes	Bríd Brennan	Jack	Donal Donnelly

Understudies: Misses Brennan, Byrne—Bernadette Quigley; Miss Linehan—Alma Cuervo; Misses Molloy, Neachtain—Selena Carey-Jones; Mr. Donnelly—Liam Gannon; Messrs. Gwilym,

McSorley—Kenneth L. Marks.

Directed by Patrick Mason; design, Joe Vanek; lighting, Trevor Dawson; sound, T. Richard Fitzgerald; choreography, Terry John Bates; production supervisor, Jeremiah J. Harris; production stage manager, Sally J. Jacobs; press, Shirley Herz Associates, Sam Rudy.

Place: The home of the Mundy family, two miles outside the village of Ballybeg, County Donegal, Ireland. Act I: A warm day in early August, 1936. Act II: Three weeks later.

The hopes and dreams of five unmarried sisters and their missionary brother, portrayed in the hustle and bustle of family life in rural Ireland during the traditional harvest festival of Lughnasa. A foreign play previously produced at the Abbey Theater, Dublin, and in London.

Kenneth L. Marks replaced Gerard McSorley, Jennifer Van Dyck replaced Catherine Byrne, Jacqueline Knapp replaced Dearbhla Molloy, Jan Maxwell replaced Bríd Brennan, Miriam Healy-Louie replaced Bríd Ní Neachtain, Patricia Hodges replaced Rosaleen Linehan, John Wesley Shipp replaced Robert Gwilym 3/3/92.

A Best Play; see page 100.

Roundabout Theater Company. Schedule of five revival programs. **The Homecoming** (49). By Harold Pinter. Opened October 27, 1991. (Closed December 8, 1991) **The Visit** (45). By Friedrich Duerrenmatt; adapted by Maurice Valency. Opened January 23, 1992. (Closed March 1, 1992) **Hamlet** (45). By William Shakespeare. Opened April 2, 1992. (Closed May 10, 1992) And *The Price* by Arthur Miller, scheduled to open June 10, 1992, and *The Real Inspector Hound* and *The Fifteen-Minute Hamlet* by Tom Stoppard, scheduled to open 8/13/92. Produced by Roundabout Theater Company, Todd Haimes producing director, Gene Feist founding director, at Criterion Center Stage Right.

THE HOMECOMING

Max	Roy Dotrice	Joey	Reed Diamond
Lenny	Daniel Gerroll	Teddy	Jonathan Hogan
Sam	John Horton	Ruth	Lindsay Crouse

Directed by Gordon Edelstein; scenery, John Arnone; costumes, William Ivey Long; lighting, Peter Kaczorowski; sound, Philip Campanella; dialect coach, Elizabeth Smith; fight director, David Leong; production stage manager, Kathy J. Faul; stage manager, Matthew T. Mundinger; press, Joshua Ellis, Susanne Tighe.

Place: The living room of an old house in North London. Act I, Scene 1: An evening in summer. Scene 2: Night. Scene 3: Morning. Act II, Scene 1: Afternoon. Scene 2: Evening.

The last major New York revival of record of *The Homecoming* was by Classic Stage Company off Broadway 10/2/76 for 34 performances.

THE VISIT

1st Man; Bobby; Camera Man	Richard Levine	Teacher; 5th Man	Tom Tammi
2d Man; Conductor; Loby; Athlete;		Priest; Dr. Nusslin; Egg Man	Paul Kandel
Truck Driver	Gordon Joseph Weiss	Anton Schill	Harris Yulin
3d Man; Pedro; Ottilie	Timothy Britten Parker	Station Master; Koby; Karl;	
4th Man; Schultz; Mayor's		Sound Man	Kelly Walters
Wife; Reporter	Jarlath Conroy	Claire Zachanassian	Jane Alexander
Painter; 1st Woman; Frau Schill;		Mike	John Jason
Sacristan	Ellen Lancaster	Max	Garry D. Williams
Mayor	Doug Stender		

Understudies: Messrs. Levine, Weiss, Stender, Tammi—Daniel P. Donnelly; Miss Alexander—Ellen Lancaster.

Directed by Edwin Sherin; scenery, Thomas Lynch; costumes, Frank Krenz; lighting, Roger Morgan; music composition and sound, Douglas J. Cuomo; masks, Michael Curry; assistant director, Cathie D. Quigley; production stage manager, Matthew T. Mundinger.

Time: Some time ago. Place: The town of Güllen. The play was presented in two parts.

The last major revival of *The Visit* was by New Phoenix Repertory on Broadway 11/25/73 for 32 performances.

HAMLET

Bernardo; Fortinbras's Captain . . . James Colby	Ghost of Hamlet's Father;
Francisco; Lucianus; Sailor . . . . . Bruce Faulk	Player King . . . . Robert Hogan
Horatio . . . . Michael Genet	Reynaldo; Priest . . . . Torben Brooks
Marcellus . . . . Thomas Schall	Rosencrantz . . . . Michael Galardi
Claudius . . . . Michael Cristofer	Guildenstern . . . . Michaeljohn McGann
Laertes . . . . Bill Campbell	Player Queen; Fortinbras . . . . David Comstock
Polonius . . . . James Cromwell	Gravedigger . . . . John Newton
Hamlet . . . . Stephen Lang	Osric . . . . Charles E. Gerber
Gertrude . . . . Kathleen Widdoes	Lady-in-Waiting . . . . Kathleen Christal
Ophelia . . . . Elizabeth McGovern	

Courtiers: Robert Driscoll, Joe Latimore, Tim McGee. Norwegian Soldiers: Robert Driscoll, Joe Latimore, Bruce Faulk.

Understudies: Messrs. Genet, Galardi—Torben Brooks; Miss McGovern—Kathleen Christal; Messrs. McGann, Newton—James Colby; Mr. Campbell—David Comstock; Mr. Comstock—Bruce Faulk; Mr. Lang—Michael Galardi; Mr. Gerber—Tim McGee; Mr. Cromwell—John Newton.

Directed by Paul Weidner; scenery, Christopher H. Barreca; costumes, Martin Pakledinaz; lighting, Natasha Katz; sound, Douglas J. Cuomo; fight direction, David Leong; vocal coach, Mary Lowry; literary advisor, Isaiah Sheffer; production stage manager, Kathy J. Faul; press, the Joshua Ellis Office, Susanne Tighe.

Place: In and near Elsinore Castle in Denmark. The play was presented in two parts.

The last major New York production of *Hamlet* took place off Broadway in New York Shakespeare Festival's Shakespeare Marathon 5/8/90 for 32 performances.

Moscow Circus (31). The Cirk Valentin, Valentin Gneushev artistic director; book by Bob Bejan; music by Bobby Previte. Produced by Steven E. Leber and Soyuzgocirk at the Gershwin Theater. Opened November 6, 1991. (Closed December 1, 1991)

Directed by Bob Bejan; choreography, Pavel Briun; production design, Stephen Bickford; costumes, Audrey Carter; lighting, Stephen Bickford; sound, Scott Rogers, Alexei Volkov; Soviet technical director, Andrey Streltsov; technical interpreter, Arsen Arsenian; press interpreters, Alla Savranskaya, Michael Evstafiev; stage manager, John Wismer; press, Peter Cromarty.

Visiting Russian troupe of circus acts adapted to theatrical presentation rather than the customary ring.

ACT I

Appearing Throughout the Program	Alexander "Sasha" Frish, Gennady Chizhov
Clown	Pavel Boyarinov
Prologue	Company
Russian Bars	Nikolai Zemskov, Yuli Babich, Igor Boitsov, Natalia Ioshina, Yuri Maiorov, Irina Mironova, Yelena Mironova, Valery Sychev
Equilibrium	Yelena Fedotova, Anatoly Stykan
Juggler on Ball	Yuri Borzykin, Yelena Larkina
Charlie	Serogia Loskutov Jr., Sergey Loskutov Sr.
Polarity	Nikolai Zehskov, Igor Boitsov, Yuli Babich, Sergey Kuznetsov, Slava Lunin, Yuri Odintsov, Nina Zemskova
Angel	Alexander "Sasha" Streltsov

ACT II

Chimes	Slava Lunin, Igor Boitsov, Andrey Ridetsky, Sergey Rudenko, Sergey Shipunov, Vladimir Sizov, Valery Sychev, Vladimir Zhih
Clowns	Pavel Boyarinov, Alexei Ivanov
Rattango	Gennady Chizhov
Primavera	Yelena Larkina
Frish	Alexander "Sasha" Frish
Finale	Company

Park Your Car in Harvard Yard (122). By Israel Horovitz. Produced by Robert Whitehead, Roger L. Stevens, Kathy Levin and American National Theater and Academy at the Music Box. Opened November 7, 1991. (Closed February 22, 1992)

Jacob Brackish. . . . . Jason Robards
Kathleen Hogan . . . . Judith Ivey

Understudies: Mr. Robards—Salem Ludwig; Miss Ivey—Kristin Griffith.
Directed by Zoe Caldwell; scenery, Ben Edwards; costumes, Jane Greenwood; lighting, Thomas R. Skelton; sound, John Gromada; produced in association with Baltimore Center for the Performing Arts; production stage manager, Jay Adler; stage manager, Dianne Trulock; press, Shirley Herz Associates, Glenna Freedman.
Time: From one winter to the next. Place: Gloucester, Mass. The play was presented without intermission.
Tough-minded, retired school teacher employs a live-in housekeeper who was one of his former pupils.

Radio City Music Hall. Schedule of two programs. **Christmas Spectacular** (176). Return engagement of the revised version of the spectacle originally conceived by Robert F. Jani. Opened November 15, 1991. (Closed January 7, 1992) **Easter Show** (24). Spectacle including *The Glory of Easter* pageant originally produced by Leon Leonidoff. Opened April 10, 1992. (Closed April 23, 1992) Produced by Radio City Music Hall Productions, David J. Nash producer, J. Deet Jonker executive producer, at Radio City Music Hall.

CHRISTMAS SPECTACULAR

Scrooge; Santa;
Narrator. . . . . Charles Edward Hall
Mrs. Santa . . . . Marty Simpson
Bob Crachit . . . . David Elder
Scrooge's Nephew . . . . James Darrah
Marley's Ghost . . . . Scott Spahr
Ghost of Christmas Past . Pascale Faye-Williams

Chost of Christmas Present . . Timothy Hamrick
Mrs. Crachit . . . . Leigh-Anne Wencker
Belinda Crachit . . . . Suzanne Phillips
(Sarah Crachit) . . Laura Bundy, Christen Tassen
(Peter Crachit) . . . . . Dean Dooley, Joey Rigol
(Tiny Tim). . . . Christopher Boyce, Arl Vernon
Poultry Man . . . . Todd Hunter

(Parentheses indicate roles in which the actors alternated)

Skaters: Laurie Welch & Randy Coyne, Alison Blake & Bruce Hurd.
Elves: Jiggle—Robert E. Lee; Squiggle—R. Lou Carry; Wiggle—John Edward Allen; Giggle—Michael J. Gilden; Bruce—Leslie Stump. Understudies—Elena Rose Bertagnolli, Phil Fondacaro.
The New Yorkers: Ellyn Arons, Leslie Bell, Michael Berglund, John Clonts, James Darrah, John Dietrich, Jack Hayes, Nanci Jennings, Keith Locke, Michelle Mallardi, Sharon Moore, Wendy Piper, Stephen Reed, Marty Simpson, Mary Jayne Waddell, Jim Weaver, Leigh-Anne Wencker, David Wood.
Dancers: Joe Bowerman, Tina DeLeone, David Elder, Pascale Faye-Williams, Christopher Gattelli, Steve Geary, Timothy Hamrick, Bill Hastings, Todd Hunter, Terry Lacy, Bonnie Lynn, Marty McDonough, Joan Mirabella, Suzanne Phillips, Scott Spahr.
Rockettes: Pauline Achilles, Carol Beatty, Linda Beausoleil, Dottie Bell, Kiki Bennett, Susan Boron, Julie Branam, Janice Cavargna, Stephanie Chase, Connie Cittadino, Eileen Collins, Lillian Colon, Linda Deacon, Susanne Doris, Dottie Earle, Prudence Gray, Susan Heart, Vicki Hickerson, Ginny Hounsell, Stephanie James, Jennifer Jones, Joan Peer Kelleher, Pam Kelleher, Debbie Kole, Dee Dee Knapp, Luann Leonard, Judy Little, Sonya Livingston, Setsuko Maruhashi, Lori McMacken, Mary McNamara, Lori Mello, Laraine Memola, Rosemary Noviello, Carol Paracat, Kerri Pearsall, Gerri Presky, Laureen Repp, Mary Six Rupert, Jereme Sheehan, Jane Sonderman, Terry Spano, Maureen Stevens, Pam Stacey, Lynn Sullivan, Susan Theobald, Darlene Wendy, Beth Nolan Woods, Eileen Woods.
Radio City Music Hall Orchestra: Don Pippin conductor; Bryan Louiselle associate conductor; Louann Montesi concert master; Andrea Andros, Gilbert Bauer, Carmine DeLeo, Joseph Kowalewski, Julius J. Kuntsler, Nannette Levi, Samuel Marder, Holly Ovenden violin; Barbara H. Vaccaro, Richard Spencer viola; Frank Levy, Sarah Carter cello; Dean Crandall bass; Kenneth Emery flute; Gerald J. Niewood, Richard Oatts, John Cippola, Joshua Siegel, Kenneth Arzberger reeds; George Bartlett, Nancy

Freimanis, French horn; Richard Raffio, Zachary Shnek, Norman Beatty trumpet; John D. Schnupp, Thomas B. Olcott, Mark Johansen trombone; Andrew Rogers tuba; Thomas J. Oldakowski drums; Mario DeCiutiis, Maya Gunji percussion; Anthony Cesarano guitar; Susanna Nason, Henry Aronson piano; Jeanne Maier harp; George W. Wesner III, Robert Maidhof organ.

Directed and choreographed by Scott Salmon; original direction, Robert F. Jani; original staging and choreography restaged by Violet Holmes and Linda Lemac; choreography for "Carol of the Bells," *A Christmas Carol,* and "We Need a Little Christmas," Scott Salmon; choreography for "Christmas in New York," Marianne Selbert; musical direction and vocal arrangements, Don Pippin; scenery, Charles Lisanby; original costumes, Frank Spencer; additional costumes, Jose Lengson; costumes for "Carol of the Bells" and "We Need a Little Christmas," Pete Menefee; lighting, Ken Billington; dance music arrangements, Marvin Laird; orchestrations, Michael Gibson, Danny Troob, Jonathan Tunick, Jim Tyler, Bob Wheeler; Rockette director, Violet Holmes; Rockette captain, Joyce Dwyer; production stage manager, Howard Kolins; stage managers, Janet Friedman, Peter Muste, Michael Pule, Mark Tynan, Zoya Wyeth; press, Sandra Manley, Kevin M. Brockman.

Special Music Credit: "Silent Night" arrangement by Percy Faith. Original Music: "They Can't Start Christmas Without Us" music by Stan Lebowsky, lyrics by Fred Tobias; "Christmas in New York" writ-

NICK & NORA & ASTA—The famous Dashiell Hammett characters were played by Riley (Asta), Barry Bostwick (Nick Charles) and Joanna Gleason (Nora Charles) in the Arthur Laurents-Charles Strouse-Richard Maltby Jr. musical

ten by Billy But. Original orchestrations: Elman Anderson, Robert N. Ayars, Michael Gibson, Don Harper, Arthur Harris, Bob Krogstad, Phillip J. Lang.

The Music Hall's annual Christmas show starring the Rockettes, with its famous Nativity pageant last offered 11/15/91 for 176 performances.

SCENES AND MUSICAL NUMBERS: Greeting (Herald Trumpeters). Scene 1: "We Need a Little Christmas" (Rockettes, Company). Overture (Radio City Music Hall Orchestra). Scene 2: *The Nutcracker*, A Teddy Bear's Dream. Scene 3: *Charles Dickens' A Christmas Carol* by Charles Lisanby. Scene 4: "Christmas in New York" (The New Yorkers, Rockettes, Radio City Music Hall Orchestra, Company). Scene 5: Ice Skating in the Plaza. Scene 6: The Story of Santa Claus. Scene 7: "They Can't Start Christmas Without Us" (Santa, Mrs. Claus, Elves). Scene 8: The Parade of the Wooden Soldiers (Rockettes). Scene 9: Beginning of Santa's Journey. Scene 10: "Carol of the Bells" (Rockettes, Company). Scene 11: The Living Nativity (*One Solitary Life*), "Silent Night," "O Little Town of Bethlehem," "Away in a Manger," "The First Noel," "We Three Kings," "O Come All Ye Faithful," "Hark, the Herald Angels Sing." Scene 12: Jubilant, "Joy to the World" (Radio City Music Hall Orchestra).

EASTER SHOW

Rabbit . . . . Joel Blum
Tortoise . . . . James Darrah

Dancers: David Elder, Jennifer Frankel, Chris Gattelli, Lori Hart, Bill Hastings, Jack Hayes, Todd Hunter, Bonnie Lynn, Suzanne Phillips, Ralph Ramirez, Sheri Ramirez, David Scala, Scott Spahr, Lynn Sterling, Susan Trainor, Valerie Wright.

Singers: Ellyn Arons, Leslie Bell, Michael Berglund, Joe Bowerman, Pamela Cecil, James Darrah, Andi Hopkins, Keith Locke, Karen Longwell, Sharon Moore, Clarence M. Sheridan, David A. Wood.

Singer/Dancer Swings: Steve Geary, Deborah Roshe.

Antigravity: Michael Ambrozy, Kimberlyn Anthony, Harrison Beal, Tony Flores, Debbie Fuhrman, Gary Giffune, Wendy Hilliard, Niahal Hope, Tiffanie Marie Lynn, Michele Maly, Jeanne-Marie Markwardt, Andrew Pacho, Juan Soto. Swings: C. Farrell Davis, Ronanne Comerford.

Rockettes: Pauline Achilles, Linda Beausoleil, Dottie Bell, Kiki Bennett, Julie Branam, Stephanie Chase, Connie Cittadino, Eileen Collins, Lillian Colon, Susanne Doris, Joyce Dwyer, Prudence Gray, Susan Heart, Vicki Hickerson, Ginny Hounsell, Stephanie James, Jennifer Jones, Joan Peer Kelleher, Pam Kelleher, Dee Dee Knapp, Judy Little, Sonya Livingston, Setsuko Maruhashi, Mary McNamara, Lori Mello, Laraine Memola, Lynn Newton, Carol Paracat, Kerri Pearsall, Gerri Presky, Laureen Repp, Mary Six Rupert, Jereme Sheehan, Terry Spano, Pam Stacey, Lynn Sullivan, Darlene Wendy, Beth Nolan Woods, Eileen Woods.

Radio City Music Hall Orchestra: Don Pippin conductor; Bryan Louiselle associate conductor; Louann Montesi concert master; Andrea Andros, Gilbert Bauer, Carmine DeLeo, Joseph Kowalewski, Julius J. Kuntsler, Nannette Levi, Samuel Marder, Holly Ovenden violin; Barbara H. Vaccaro, Richard Spencer viola; Frank Levy, Sarah Carter cello; Dean Crandall bass; Kenneth Emery flute; Gerald J. Niewood, Michael Migliore, John Cippola, Joshua Siegel, Frank Santagata reeds; George Bartlett, Nancy Freimanis, French horn; Bud Burridge, Zachary Shnek, David F. Rogers trumpet; John D. Schnupp, Thomas B. Olcott, Mark Johansen trombones; Andrew Rodgers tuba; Jeff B. Potter drums; Erik Charlston, Daniel Haskins percussion; Robert Kirshoff guitar; Jeanne Maier harp; Susanna Nason piano; George W. Wesner III organ; Robert Wendel keyboard.

Musical direction, Don Pippin; Antigravity director and choreographer, Chris Harrison; Antigravity rehearsal captain, Linda Talcott; Rockette director, Violet Holmes; Rockette dance captain, Joyce Dwyer; director of stage operations, Giles Colahan; director of costumes, Leanne Mitchell; scenic coordinator, Richard Ellis; flying by Foy; production stage manager, Howard Kolins; stage managers, Mimi Apfel, Andrew Feigin, Peter Muste, Zoya Wyeth; press, Sandra Manley, Kevin M. Brockman.

Original Music: "Put a Little Spring in Your Step" (music and lyrics by Jeffrey Ernstoff), "Think About That" (music by Larry Grossman, lyrics by Hal Hackaday), "I Know" (music by Larry Grossman, lyrics by Hal Hackaday), "How About Me" (music by Larry Grossman, lyrics by Hal Hackaday).

Special Music Credits: "Put on Your Sunday Clothes" (music and lyrics by Jerry Herman); "Friends" (music by Larry Grossman, lyrics by Hal Hackaday); "La Cage aux Folles" (music by Jerry Herman, arranged by Gordon Lowry Harrell); "Optical Race" (composed and performed by Tangerine Dream).

SCENES: Prologue, "The Glory of Easter" (return engagement of the pageant performed annually from 1933 to 1979); Overture (Radio City Music Hall Orchestra); Scene 1, Pure Imagination; Scene 2, Put a Little Spring in Your Step (Rabbit, Singers, Dancers; Rockettes in "Happy Feet"); Scene 3, Yesteryear (1890s Easter Parade); Scene 4, Bunny Revelry (with Antigravity); Scene 5, The Chase (Tortoise vs. Hare, with the Rockettes); Scene 6: With Gershwin (Singers, Dancers, Rockettes, Radio City Music Hall Orchestra, with George and Ira Gershwin numbers); Scene 7: Optical Race (with Antigravity); Scene 8: "Dancing in the Dark" (laser show and Rockettes); Scene 9: Hats (Dancers); Scene 10, Rainbow Follies (Finale).

Peter Pan (48). Return engagement of the revival of the musical version of the play by James M. Barrie; music by Moose Charlap; lyrics by Carolyn Leigh; additional music by Jule Styne; additional lyrics by Betty Comden and Adolph Green. Produced by Thomas P. McCoy and Keith Stava in association with P.P. Investments, Inc. and Jon B. Platt at the Minskoff Theater. Opened November 27, 1991. (Closed January 5, 1992)

Wendy Darling; Jane	Cindy Robinson	1st Twin	Janet Kay Higgins
John Darling	David Burdick	2d Twin	Courtney Wyn
Michael Darling	Joey Cee	Slightly	Christopher Ayres
Liza	Anne McVey	Tootles	Julian Brightman
Nana	Bill Bateman	Mr. Smee	Don Potter
Mrs. Darling;		Cecco	Calvin Smith
Wendy Grown	Lauren Thompson	Gentleman Starkey	Carl Packard
Mr. Darling; Capt. Hook	J.K. Simmons	Crocodile	Barry Ramsey
Peter Pan	Cathy Rigby	Tiger Lily	Michelle Schumacher
Curly	Alon Williams		

Orchestra: Brian Tidwell conductor; Mark Mitchell assistant conductor, piano; Craig Barna keyboards; Steve Bartosik drums; Tom Mendel bass; Ben Herman percussion; Chris Jaudes, Larry Lunetta, Domenic Derasse trumpet; Jon Taylor trombone; Allen Spanjer, French horn; Dan Gerhard flute, piccolo; Mark Thrasher flute, piccolo, baritone sax; Rick Heckman clarinet, tenor sax, English horn; John Winder clarinet, bass clarinet, bassoon; Paul Woodiel concertmaster; Marti Sweet, Lisa Brooke, Heidi Stubner, David Niwa, David Tobey violin; Roger Shell, Eliana Mendoza cello; Nina Kellman harp.

Understudies: Miss Rigby—Cindy Robinson; Mr. Simmons—Carl Packard; Miss Thompson—Anne McVey; Mr. Potter—Bill Bateman; Misses Robinson, Schumacher—Courtney Wyn; Mr. Burdick—Christopher Ayres; Mr. Cee—David Burdick; Messrs. Brightman, Ayres, Williams—Janet Kay Higgins; Ensemble Swing— Jim Alexander.

Original production conceived, directed and choreographed by Jerome Robbins; directed by Fran Soeder; restaged by Bill Bateman; choreography, Marilyn Magness; musical direction, Brian Tidwell; scenery, Michael J. Hotopp, Paul dePass; costumes, Mariann Verheyen; lighting, Natasha Katz; sound, Peter J. Fitzgerald; flying by Foy; Neverland scenery, James Leonard Joy; musical supervisor, Kevin Farrell; additional arrangements, M. Michael Fauss, Kevin Farrell; production stage manager, Frank Hartenstein; stage manager, Eric Insko; press, Shirley Herz Associates, Glenna Freedman.

The last major New York revival of *Peter Pan* was a return engagement of this production on Broadway last season, 12/13/90 for 45 performances.

The list of scenes and musical numbers in *Peter Pan* appears on page 370 of *The Best Plays of 1954-55.*

*Catskills on Broadway (205). Revue conceived by Freddie Roman. Produced by Kenneth D. Greenblatt, Stephen D. Fish and 44 Productions at the Lunt-Fontanne Theater. Opened December 5, 1991.

Dick Capri	Mal Z. Lawrence
Marilyn Michaels	Freddie Roman

Orchestra: Barry Levitt piano, Brian Brake drums, Gary Guzio trumpet, William Kerr saxophone, Mark Minkler bass, Robert Kirshoff electric guitar, Joseph Baker keyboard.

Production supervised by Larry Arrick; musical direction, Barry Levitt; scenery, Lawrence Miller; lighting, Peggy Eisenhauer; sound, Peter J. Fitzgerald; opening musical sequence arranged by Don

Pippin; projection design, Wendall Harrington; associate producer, Sandra Greenblatt; creative consultant, Richard Vos; production stage manager, Martin Gold; stage manager, David O'Brien; press, Shirley Herz Associates, Miller Wright.

Half-hour presentations by each of four comics, in the inimitable 1950s and 1960s Catskill resort-show style. The show was presented without intermission.

Nick & Nora (9). Musical based on the characters created by Dashiell Hammett and on the movie *The Thin Man*; book by Arthur Laurents; music by Charles Strouse; lyrics by Richard Maltby Jr. Produced by Terry Allen Kramer, Charlene and James M. Nederlander, Daryl Roth and Elizabeth Ireland McCann at the Marquis Theater. Opened December 8, 1991. (Closed December 15, 1991)

Asta . . . . Riley	Spider Malloy. . . . . Jeff Brooks
Nora Charles . . . . Joanna Gleason	Lorraine Bixby . . . . Faith Prince
Nick Charles . . . . Barry Bostwick	Edward J. Conners. . . . . Kip Niven
Tracy Gardner. . . . . Christine Baranski	Lt. Wolfe. . . . . Michael Lombard
Yukido . . . . Thom Sesma	Maria Valdez . . . . Yvette Lawrence
Mavis. . . . . Kathy Morath	Lily Connors. . . . . Debra Monk
Delli; Waitress . . . . Kristen Wilson	Selznick . . . . Hal Robinson
Max Bernheim . . . . Remak Ramsay	Msgr. Flaherty. . . . . John Jellison
Victor Moisa . . . . Chris Sarandon	Mariachi . . . . . . Tim Connell, Kris Phillips

Orchestra: Les Scott, Seymour Red Press, Charles Millard, Dennis Anderson, Wally Kane woodwinds; Brian O'Flaherty, Burt Collins, Kamau Adilifu trumpet; Bruce Bonvissuto, Earl McIntyre trombone; Roger Wendt, French horn; Elliot Rosoff, Ethel Abelson, Melanie Baker, Katsuko Esaki, Marion Guest, Robert Lawrence violin; Anne Callahan, Jeff Szabo cello; Francesca Corsi harp; Patrick Brady synthesizer; Raymond Kilday bass; Ronald Zito drums, percussion.

Standbys: Misses Gleason, Baranski—Kay McClelland; Messrs. Bostwick, Sarandon—Richard Muenz. Understudies: Messrs. Ramsay, Lombard—Hal Robinson; Misses Prince, Monk—Kathy Morath; Miss Lawrence—Kristen Wilson; Messrs. Brooks, Niven—John Jellison; Mr. Sesma—Kris Phillips; Asta—BJ.

Dance captain—Mark Hoebee; Swings—Mark Hoebee, Cynthia Thole.

Directed by Arthur Laurents; choreography, Tina Paul; musical and vocal direction, Jack Lee; scenery, Douglas W. Schmidt; costumes, Theoni V. Aldredge; lighting, Jules Fisher; orchestrations, Jonathan Tunick; dance and incidental music, Charles Strouse; dance and incidental music arrangements, Gordon Lowry Harrell; sound, Peter J. Fitzgerald; production stage manager, Robert Bennett; stage manager, Maureen F. Gibson; press, Jeffrey Richards Associates, David LeShay.

Time: 1937. Place: Hollywood.

Murder mystery with Dashiell Hammett's famous amateur detectives Nick and Nora Charles (played on the screen by William Powell and Myrna Loy) remodeled for a Broadway musical context.

ACT I

Scene 1: Nick & Nora's bungalow, The Garden of Allah
    "Is There Anything Better Than Dancing?" . . . . Nick, Nora, Tracy
Scene 2: The studio
    "Everybody Wants to Do a Musical" . . . . Tracy
Scene 3: Lorraine's (Max's version)
    "Not Me" . . . . Max, Lorraine, Connors
Scene 4: The studio
    "Swell" . . . . Nick, Spider, Nora, Victor
Scene 5: Nick & Nora's bungalow
    "As Long as You're Happy" . . . . Nick & Nora
    "People Get Hurt" . . . . Lily
Scene 6: Lorraine's (Victor's version)
    "Men" . . . . Lorraine, Victor, Connors, Tracy
Scene 7: Beverly Hills
    "May the Best Man Win" . . . . Nick, Nora, Tracy
    "Detectiveland" . . . . Company

Scene 8: Lorraine's
"Look Who's Alone Now". . . . . Nick

ACT II

Scene 1: Victor's villa
"Class" . . . . Victor
Scene 2: Nick & Nora's bungalow
"Let's Go Home" . . . . Nora
Scene 3: Lorraine's (Maria's version)
Scene 4: Lorraine's
"A Busy Night at Lorraine's" . . . . Nick, Nora, Spider, Suspects
Scene 5: The Big Tamboo
"Boom Chicka Boom". . . . . Maria, Mariachi
Scene 6: Tracy's terrace
"Let's Go Home" (Reprise) . . . . Nick, Nora

National Actors Theater. Schedule of three revivals. **The Crucible** (32). By Arthur Miller. Opened December 10, 1991. (Closed January 5, 1992) **A Little Hotel on the Side** (42). Translated by John Mortimer from *L'Hôtel du Libre Echange* by Georges Feydeau and Maurice Desvallières. Opened January 26, 1992. (Closed March 1, 1992) **The Master Builder** (45). By Henrik Ibsen; translated by Johan Fillinger. Opened March 19, 1992. (Closed April 26, 1992) Produced by National Actors Theater, Tony Randall founder and artistic director, at the Belasco Theater.

ALL PLAYS: Scenery, David Jenkins; costumes, Patricia Zipprodt; lighting, Richard Nelson; sound, T. Richard Fitzgerald; executive producer, Manny Kladitis; press, Springer Associates, John Springer, Gary Springer.

THE CRUCIBLE

Betty Parris.	Genia Sewell Michaela	Giles Corey	George N. Martin
Rev. Samuel Parris	Brian Reddy	Rev. John Hale.	Michael York
Tituba.	Carol Woods	Elizabeth Proctor	Maryann Plunkett
Abigail Williams	Madeleine Potter	Francis Nurse.	John Beal
Susanna Walcott	Nell Balaban	Ezekiel Cheever	John Fiedler
Ann Putnam.	Molly Regan	John Willard	Patrick Tull
Thomas Putnam	Peter McRobbie	Judge Hathorne.	Bruce Katzman
Mercy Lewis	Danielle Ferland	Deputy-Gov. Danforth	Fritz Weaver
Mary Warren.	Jane Adams	Sarah Good	Priscilla Smith
John Proctor	Martin Sheen	Hopkins	Andrew Hubatsek
Rebecca Nurse	Martha Scott		

Understudies: Messrs. Hubatsek, Katzman—Doug Adair; Misses Adams, Potter—Nell Balaban; Misses Regan, Plunkett—Priscilla Smith; Miss Woods—Trazana Beverley; Messrs. Sheen, McRobbie—Richard Ferrone; Misses Balaban, Michaela—Melissa Joan Hart; Messrs. York, Tull—Michael O'Hare; Misses Scott, Smith—Lucille Patton; Messrs. Reddy, Fiedler, Weaver—Martin Rudy.

Directed by Yossi Yzraely; musical direction, John Kander; incidental music supervision, David Loud; production stage manager, Glen Gardali; stage manager, Donna A. Drake.

Time: 1692. Place Salem, Mass. Act I, Scene 1: Spring, a bedroom in the home of Rev. Samuel Parris. Scene 2: The common room of John Proctor's house, eight days later. Act II, Scene 1: The vestry of the Salem meeting house, two weeks later. Scene 2: A cell in Salem jail, three months later.

The last major New York revival of *The Crucible* was by Roundabout off Broadway 3/29/90 for 53 performances.

A LITTLE HOTEL ON THE SIDE

Benoit Pinglet	Tony Randall	Maxime	Rob Lowe
Angelique Pinglet	Lynn Redgrave	Victoire.	Madeleine Potter
Marcelle Paillardin.	Maryann Plunkett	Mathieu	Paxton Whitehead
Henri Paillardin	George N. Martin	Head Porter.	John Beal

Violette . . . . Siobhan Tull	Ernest . . . . Brian Reddy
Paquerette. . . . . Kia Graves	Lady. . . . . Carol Woods
Pervenche . . . . Danielle Ferland	Chervet . . . . Zane Lasky
Marguerite . . . . Nell Balaban	Inspector Boucard . . . . John Fiedler
Bastien . . . . Patrick Tull	1st Constable . . . . Bruce Katzman
Boulot . . . . Alec Mapa	2d Constable . . . . Richard Ferrone

Porters: Doug Adair, Danny Burstein, Richard Ferrone, Andrew Hubatsek, Liam Leone. Constables: Doug Adair, Danny Burstein, Andrew Hubatsek. Hotel Guests: Leslie Anderson, Angela Baker, Karen Chapman, Heather Harlan, Liam Leone, Lisa Ann Li, Lucille Patton, Dennis Pressey, Brian Reddy, Steven Satta, Daisy White.

FOUR BABOONS ADORING THE SUN—James Naughton, Eugene Perry (*at top*) and Stockard Channing in John Guare's play at Lincoln Center

Understudies: Miss Potter—Nell Balaban; Messrs. Lowe, Mapa—Andrew Hubatsek; Mr. Randall—Brian Reddy; Messrs. Martin, Tull, Fiedler—Bruce Katzman; Miss Plunkett—Karen Chapman; Messrs. Lasky, Whitehead—Richard Ferrone; Miss Woods—Lucille Patton; Mr. Beal—Martin Rudy; Constable—Doug Adair, Danny Burstein.

Directed by Tom Moore; original music, Larry Delinger; production stage manager, Mitchell Erickson; stage manager, John Handy.

Time: Just after the turn of the century. Place: Paris. Act I: The Pinglets' house, a spring afternoon. Act II: Hotel Good Night. Act III: The Pinglets' house, the following morning. The play was presented in two parts with the intermission following Act II.

The only 20th century New York production of record of this Feydeau-Desvallières farce was under the title *Hotel Paradiso* on Broadway in a Peter Glenville adaptation starring Bert Lahr 4/11/57 for 108 performances. This Mortimer adaptation was previously produced by England's National Theater in 1984.

THE MASTER BUILDER

Kaja Fosli . . . . Maryann Plunkett	Mrs. Alvine Solness . . . . Lynn Redgrave
Knut Brovik . . . . John Beal	Dr. Herdal . . . . Patrick Tull
Ragnar Brovik . . . . Peter McRobbie	Hilde Wangel . . . . Madeleine Potter
Halvard Solness . . . . Earle Hyman	

Standby: Mr. Hyman—Robert Stattel. Understudies: Miss Plunkett—Nell Balaban; Mr. Beal—Martin Rudy; Messrs. McRobbie, Tull—Bruce Katzman; Miss Redgrave—Lucille Patton.

Directed by Tony Randall; production stage manager, Glen Gardali; stage manager, Joe McGuire.

Time: The turn of the century. Place: A Norwegian town. the play was presented in two parts.

The last major New York revival of *The Master Builder* was by Roundabout off Broadway 9/20/83 for 88 performances.

A Christmas Carol (14). One-man performance by Patrick Stewart; adapted by Patrick Stewart from Charles Dickens. Produced by Timothy Childs at the Eugene O'Neill Theater. Opened December 19, 1991 in a limited engagement. (Closed December 29, 1991)

Lighting, Fred Allen; associate producers, Kate Elliott, Creation Entertainment; production stage manager, Kate Elliott; press, Boneau/Bryan-Brown, Bob Fennell.

The Dickens Christmas tale, with Patrick Stewart playing all the roles. The play was presented in two parts. A foreign play first produced in 1988 and in a pre-Broadway tour of the U.S.

Lincoln Center Theater. Schedule of two programs. **Two Shakespearean Actors** (29). By Richard Nelson. Opened January 16, 1992. (Closed February 9, 1992) **Four Baboons Adoring the Sun** (38). By John Guare; music by Stephen Edwards. Opened March 18, 1992. (Closed April 19, 1992) Produced by Lincoln Center Theater; Gregory Mosher director, Bernard Gersten executive producer as of 1/16/92; Andre Bishop and Bernard Gersten directors as of 3/18/92; *Two Shakespearean Actors* at the Cort Theater, *Four Baboons Adoring the Sun* at the Vivian Beaumont Theater.

TWO SHAKESPEAREAN ACTORS

Actors at the Broadway Theater:
Edwin Forrest (Macbeth;
   Metamora) . . . . Victor Garber
Miss Jane Bass (1st Witch) . Jenifer Van Dyck
Miss Helen Burton (2d Witch;
   Goodenough) . . . . Judy Kuhn
Miss Anne Holland (3d Witch;
   Nahmeokee) . . . . Hope Davis
Tilton (Porter; Church) . . . . Tom Lacy
Thomas Fisher (Young Siward;
   Kaweshine) . . . . Graham Winton
Robert Jones (Banquo; Malcolm;

Anrawandah) . . . David Andrew Macdonald
Mr. Blakely (Duncan;
   Errington) . . . . Richard Clarke
Scott . . . . Jeffrey Allan Chandler
John Ryder (Macduff) . . . . . . Zeljko Ivanek
(Parentheses indicate the roles the "actors" play)
Actors at the Astor Place Opera House:
William Charles Macready
   (Macbeth) . . . . Brian Bedford
Mrs. Pope (Lady
   Macbeth) . . . . Le Clanché du Rand
Charles Clark (Macduff) . . . Alan Brasington

George Bradshaw (Banquo) . . Michael Butler
Frederick Wemyss (Siward;
  Old Man). . . . . Bill Moor
James Bridges (Young Siward;
  3d Witch; Ross) . . . . Tim Macdonald
John Sefton (1st Witch;
  Donalbain) . . . . James Murtaugh
Mr. Chippindale (2d
  Witch). . . . . Mitchell Edmonds

Peter Arnold (Malcolm) . . . . . . Ben Bodé
(Parentheses indicate the roles the "actors" play)
Friends and Family:
Catherine Forrest. . . . . . . Frances Conroy
Miss Wemyss . . . . Katie Finneran
Dion Boucicault . . . . Eric Stoltz
Agnes Robertson . . . . Laura Innes
Washington Irving . . . . Tom Aldredge

Other Actors and Servants: David Andrew Macdonald, Katie MacNichol, Susan Pellegrino, Thomas Schall.

Understudies: Mr. Garber—Michael Butler; Miss Van Dyck—Hope Davis; Misses Kuhn, Davis, Finneran—Katie MacNichol; Messrs. Lacy, Clarke—Mitchell Edmonds; Mr. Macdonald—Ben Bodé; Messrs. Winton, Bodé—David Andrew Macdonald; Mr. Chandler—James Murtaugh; Mr. Ivanek—Alan Brasington; Mr. Bedford—Jeffrey Allan Chandler; Messrs. Brasington, Butler, Murtaugh, Edmonds, Macdonald—Thomas Schall; Misses du Rand, Conroy, Innes—Susan Pellegrino; Messrs. Moor, Aldredge—Richard Clarke; Mr. Stoltz—Graham Winton.

Directed by Jack O'Brien; scenery, David Jenkins; costumes, Jane Greenwood; lighting, Jules Fisher; sound, Jeff Ladman; poster art, James McMullan; original score, Bob James; fight director, Steve Rankin; production stage manager, Alan Hall; stage manager, Deborah Clelland; press, Merle Debuskey, Susan Chicoine.

Time: Between May 3 and May 10, 1849. Place: Various locations in New York City, including the stages and backstages of the Broadway Theater and the Astor Place Opera House. The play was presented in two parts.

Rivalry between a British (Macready) and an American (Forrest) Shakespearean actor at the time of the Astor Place riots. An American play which was first produced by the Royal Shakespeare Company in England.

FOUR BABOONS ADORING THE SUN

Eros. . . . . Eugene Perry
Penny McKenzie . . . . . . Stockard Channing
Philip McKenzie . . . . James Naughton
Wayne. . . . . Wil Horneff
Lyle . . . . Michael Shulman
Sarah . . . . Ellen Hamilton Latzen

Teddy . . . . Alex Sobol
Halcy . . . . Angela Goethals
Jane . . . . Zoe Taleporos
Peter . . . . John Ross
Robin . . . . Kimberly Jean Brown
Roger. . . . . Zachary Phillip Solomon

Understudies: Miss Channing—Harriet Harris; Mr. Naughton—W.T. Martin; Mr. Horneff—Eddie K. Thomas; Misses Taleporos, Latzen—Kate Bernsohn; Messrs. Solomon, Brown, Sobol—Noah Fleiss; Miss Goethals—Zoe Taleporos; Mr. Ross—Matthew McCurley.

Directed by Peter Hall; scenery, Tony Walton; costumes, Willa Kim; lighting, Richard Pilbrow; sound, Paul Arditti; projections, Wendell K. Harrington; musical direction, Michael Barrett; poster art, James McMullan; production stage manager, Thomas A. Kelly; stage manager, Charles Kindl.

Time: A few years ago, a summer. Place: Sicily. The play was performed without an intermission.

Man and wife on an archeology dig, bringing with them their children from previous marriages and a longing for enhanced life and love.

Crazy He Calls Me (7). By Abraham Tetenbaum. Produced by Weissman Productions and Roger Alan Gindi under the auspices of the Broadway Alliance at the Walter Kerr Theater. Opened January 27, 1992. (Closed February 1, 1992)

Benny . . . . Barry Miller
Yvette . . . . Polly Draper

Understudies: Mr. Miller—Daniel Oreskes; Miss Draper—Susan Cella.

Directed by John Ferraro; scenery, Loren Sherman; costumes, Jennifer Von Mayrhauser; lighting, Dennis Parichy; sound, Raymond D. Schilke; production stage manager, Karen Armstrong; stage manager, Dan Hild; press, Shirley Herz Associates, Miller Wright.

Time: Between 1938-40. Place: In and around Brooklyn, N.Y. The play was presented in two parts. Attorney's romance with an eccentric ends up in court.

*The Most Happy Fella (125). Revival of the musical based on Sidney Howard's *They Knew What They Wanted*; book, music and lyrics by Frank Loesser. Produced by the Goodspeed Opera House, Michael P. Price executive producer, Center Theater Group/Ahmanson Theater, Gordon Davidson producing director, Lincoln Center Theater, Andre Bishop artistic director, Bernard Gersten executive producer, The Shubert Organization, Gerald Schoenfeld chairman, Bernard B. Jacobs president, and Japan Satellite Broadcasting/Stagevision at the Booth Theater. Opened February 13, 1992.

Cashier; Postman; Doctor . . . . . . Tad Ingram	Al . . . . Ed Romanoff
Cleo . . . . Liz Larsen	Marie . . . . Claudia Catania
Rosabella . . . . Sophie Hayden	Max; Priest . . . . Bill Badolato
Tony . . . . Spiro Malas	Joe . . . . Charles Pistone
Herman . . . . Scott Waara	Pasquale . . . . Mark Lotito
Clem . . . . Bob Freschi	Ciccio . . . . Buddy Crutchfield
Jake . . . . John Soroka	Giuseppe . . . . Bill Nabel

Folks of San Francisco and the Napa Valley: John Aller, Anne Allgood. Bill Badolato, Molly Brown, Kyle Craig, Mary Helen Fisher, Bob Freschi, Ramon Galindo, T. Doyle Leverett, Ken Nagy, Gail Pennington, Ed Romanoff, Jane Smulyan, John Soroka, Laura Streets, Thomas Titone, Melanie Vaughan.

Conductor/pianist, Tim Stella; assistant conductor/pianist, Michael Rafter.

Standby: Mr. Malas—Jack Dabdoub. Understudies: Messrs. Malas, Romanoff—T. Doyle Leverett; Miss Hayden—Anne Allgood; Miss Larsen—Melanie Vaughan, Molly Brown; Mr. Waara—John Soroka; Mr. Pistone—Ed Romanoff; Miss Catania—Jane Smulyan; Mr. Ingram—Bob Freschi; Messrs. Lotito, Crutchfield—John Aller; Messrs. Nabel, Freschi, Soroka—Thomas Titone; Mr. Romanoff—T. Doyle Leverett; Swings—Robert Ashford, Keri Lee.

Directed by Gerald Gutierrez; musical direction, Tim Stella; choreography, Liza Gennaro; scenery, John Lee Beatty; costumes, Jess Goldstein; lighting, Craig Miller; duo piano arrangements, Robert Page under the supervision of Frank Loesser; artistic associate, Jo Sullivan; poster art, James McMullan; production stage manager, Michael Brunner; stage manager, Kate Riddle; press, Merle Debuskey, Susan Chicoine.

Act I, Scene 1: A restaurant in San Francisco, 1927. Scene 2: Main Street, Napa, California, April. Scene 3: Tony's barn, a few weeks later. Scene 4: The front yard, later that night. Act II, Scene 1: A clearing at the edge of Tony's vineyard, one week later. Scene 2: The arbor, later in May. Scene 3: The clearing at the edge of Tony's vineyard, a month later. Scene 4: The barn. Scene 5: The clearing at the edge of Tony's vineyard, an afternoon in July. Act III, Scene 1: The barn, an hour later. Scene 2: Main Street, Napa, California, a little later. The play was presented in two parts with the intermission following Act I.

Compact version of this love story, with a two-piano accompaniment, this production originally presented at Goodspeed Opera House, East Haddam, Conn. The last major New York revival of *The Most Happy Fella* took place this season 9/4/91 for 10 performances at New York City Opera; see its entry in the Plays Produced on Broadway section of this volume.

The list of musical numbers in *The Most Happy Fella* appears on pages 366-7 of *The Best Plays of 1979-80*.

*Crazy for You (117). Musical with book by Ken Ludwig; co-conceived by Ken Ludwig and Mike Ockrent, inspired by material (in the musical *Girl Crazy*) by Guy Bolton and John McGowan; music by George Gershwin; lyrics by Ira Gershwin. Produced by Roger Horchow and Elizabeth Williams at the Sam S. Shubert Theater. Opened February 19, 1992.

Tess . . . . Beth Leavel	Susie . . . . Ida Henry
Patsy . . . . Stacey Logan	Louise . . . . Jean Marie
Bobby Child . . . . Harry Groener	Betsy . . . . Penny Ayn Maas
Bela Zangler . . . . Bruce Adler	Margie . . . . Salome Mazard
Sheila . . . . Judine Hawkins Richard	Vera . . . . Louise Ruck
Mitzi . . . . Paula Leggett	Elaine . . . . Pamela Everett

Irene Roth . . . . Michele Pawk	Jimmy . . . . Michael Kubala
Mother. . . . . Jane Connell	Billy . . . . Ray Roderick
Perkins . . . . Gerry Burkhardt	Wyatt . . . . Jeffrey Lee Broadhurst
The Manhattan Rhythm Kings:	Harry . . . . Joel Goodness
Moose . . . . Brian M. Nalepka	Polly Baker . . . . Jodi Benson
Mingo . . . . Tripp Hanson	Everett Baker . . . . Ronn Carroll
Sam . . . . Hal Shane	Lank Hawkins . . . . John Hillner
Junior . . . . Casey Nicholaw	Eugene . . . . Stephen Temperley
Custus . . . . Gerry Burkhardt	Patricia . . . . Amelia White
Pete . . . . Fred Anderson	

Ensemble: Fred Anderson, Jeffrey Lee Broadhurst, Gerry Burkhardt, Pamela Everett, Joel Goodness, Tripp Hanson, Ida Henry, Michael Kubala, Paula Leggett, Stacey Logan, Penny Ayn Maas, Jean Marie, Salome Mazard, Brian M. Nalepka, Casey Nicholaw, Judine Hawkins Richard, Ray Roderick, Louise Ruck, Hal Shane. Swings: Ken Lundie, Chris Peterson, Maryellen Scilla.

Orchestra: Suzanne Ornstein concert master; Martin Agee, Ann Leathers, Aloysia Friedmann, Laura Corcos, John Connelly violin; Scott Ballentyne, Deborah Assael cello; Charles Bageron bass; Les Scott, John Moses, Andrew Drelles, Charles Millard, John Campo woodwinds; Ronald Sell, Michael Ishii horns; Wilmer Wise, David Brown trumpet; Bruce Eidem, Dean Plank trombone; Pam Drews Phillips assistant conductor, keyboards; Paul Pizutti drums; Thad Wheeler percussion; Andrew Schwartz guitar, banjo.

Understudies: Messrs. Groener, Hillner, Adler—Michael Kubala; Miss Benson—Beth Leavel; Misses Pawk, White—Jessica Molaskey; Mr. Carroll—Gerry Burkhardt; Miss Connell—Amelia White; Miss Leavel—Paula Leggett; Mr. Temperley—Casey Nicholaw; Miss Logan—Penny Ayn Maas.

Directed by Michael Ockrent; choreography, Susan Stroman; musical direction, Paul Gemignani; scenery, Robin Wagner; costumes, William Ivey Long; lighting, Paul Gallo; sound, Otts Munderloh; dance and incidental music arangements, Peter Howard; musical consultant, Tommy Krasker; orchestrations, William D. Brohn; fight staging, B.H. Barry; associate producers, Richard Godwin, Valerie Gordon; production stage manager, Steven Zweigbaum; stage managers, John Bonanni, Mindy Farbrother; press, Bill Evans & Associates, Jim Randolph.

Gershwin numbers, many from *Girl Crazy*, in a new book about a young man who goes to close a bankrupt theater and remains to put on a show to save it.

A Best Play; see page 210.

ACT I

Scene 1: Backstage at the Zangler Theater, New York City, in the 1930s
"K-ra-zy for You" . . . . Bobby
Scene 2: 42d Street, outside the theater
"I Can't Be Bothered Now" . . . . Bobby, Girls
Scene 3: Main Street, Deadrock, Nevada
"Bidin' My Time" . . . . Mingo, Moose, Sam
"Things Are Looking Up" . . . . Bobby
Scene 4: Lank's Saloon
"Could You Use Me?" . . . . Bobby, Polly
Scene 5: In the desert
"Shall We Dance?" . . . . Bobby, Polly
Scene 6: The Gaiety Theater
Scene 7: Main Street, Deadrock, three days later
"Someone to Watch Over Me" . . . . Polly
Scene 8: The lobby of the Gaiety Theater, two weeks later
Scene 9: The stage of the Gaiety Theater
"Slap That Bass" . . . . Bobby, Moose, Tess, Patsy, Company
(orchestration by Sid Ramin)
"Embraceable You" . . . . Polly, Bobby
Scene 10: The Gaiety Theater dressing rooms, opening night
"Tonight's the Night" . . . . Company
(lyrics by Ira Gershwin and Gus Kahn)
Scene 11: Main Street, Deadrock
"I Got Rhythm" . . . . Polly, Bobby, Company

PARK YOUR CAR IN HARVARD YARD—Jason Robards and a friend in a scene from the play by Israel Horovitz

ACT II

Scene 1: Lank's Saloon, later that evening
"The Real American Folk Song (Is a Rag)". . . . . Mingo, Moose, Sam
"What Causes That?" . . . . Bobby, Bela
Scene 2: Lank's Saloon, the next morning
"Naughty Baby" . . . . Irene, Lank
    (lyric by Ira Gershwin and Desmond Carter)
Scene 3: The Gaiety Theater, backstage
Scene 4: The auditorium of the Gaiety Theater
"Stiff Upper Lip". Bobby, Polly, Eugene, Patricia, Company
"They Can't Take That Away From Me" . . . . Bobby
"But Not for Me" . . . . Polly
Scene 5: New York, six weeks later
"Nice Work If You Can Get It" . . . . Bobby, Girls
Scene 6: Main Street, Deadrock, six days later
Finale . . . . Company

Private Lives (37). Revival of the play by Noel Coward. Produced by Charles H. Duggan by arrangement with Michael Codron at the Broadhurst Theater. Opened February 20, 1992. (Closed March 22, 1992)

Sybil Chase . . . . Jill Tasker   Amanda Prynne . . . . Joan Collins
Elyot Chase . . . . Simon Jones   Louise. . . . . Margie Rynn
Victor Prynne . . . . Edward Duke

    Standbys: Miss Collins—Mary Layne; Messrs. Jones, Duke—Guy Paul.
    Directed by Arvin Brown; scenery, Loren Sherman; costumes, William Ivey Long; lighting, Richard Nelson; sound, Tom Morse; tango choreography, Michael Smuin; fight direction, Ellen Saland; stage manager, Judith Binus; press, the Pete Sanders Group.

Act I: The terrace of a hotel in France, mid-1930s, a summer evening. Act II: Amanda's flat in Paris, a few days later, evening. Act III: The same, the next morning. The play was presented in two parts with the intermission following Act I and a pause between Acts II and III.

The last major New York revival of *Private Lives* took place on Broadway 5/8/83 for 26 performances, starring Elizabeth Taylor and Richard Burton.

Bunraku—The National Puppet Theater of Japan (7). **The Love Suicides at Sonezaki** by Monzaemon Chikamatsu, presented in the Japanese language with simultaneous English commentary. Produced by the Mito Kikaku Corporation, Peter Grilli and Okamoto Tazuru in the Bunraku production at the City Center. Opened March 10, 1992 in a limited engagement. (Closed March 14, 1992)

CAST: Narrator—Rodayu Toyotake; Shamisen Musician—Seiji Tsuruzawa; Principal Puppeteers—Minosuke Yoshida, Itcho Kiritake.

Technical director, Hamatani Hitoshi; Hayashi music, Temekichi Mochizuku; scenery, Kanai Scene Shop; lighting, Mark Stanley.

Based on an actual incident which took place in Osaka in 1703, this play is known as "a Japanese *Romeo and Juliet.*"

*Death and the Maiden (88). By Ariel Dorfman. Produced by Roger Berlind, Gladys Nederlander and Frederick Zollo in association with Thom Mount and Bonnie Timmermann at the Brooks Atkinson Theater. Opened March 17, 1992.

Paulina Salas	Glenn Close	Roberto Miranda	Gene Hackman
Gerardo Escobar	Richard Dreyfuss		

Standbys: Miss Close—Lizbeth Mackay; Mr. Dreyfuss—David Goewey; Mr. Hackman—Jimmie Ray Weeks.

Directed by Mike Nichols; scenery, Tony Walton; costumes, Ann Roth; lighting, Jules Fisher; sound, Tom Sorce; associate producers, Hal Luftig, Ron Kastner, Peter Lawrence, Sue Macnair; production stage manager, Anne Keefe; stage manager, Steven Shaw; press, Bill Evans, Susan L. Schulman.

Time: The present. Place: A beach house in a country that is probably Chile, but could be any country that has given itself a democratic government just after a long period of dictatorship. The play was presented in two parts.

A woman victim of political violence kidnaps and interrogates her suspected torturer. A foreign (Chilean) play previously produced at the Royal Court Theater in London.

*Jake's Women (79). By Neil Simon. Produced by Emanuel Azenberg at the Neil Simon Theater. Opened March 24, 1992.

Jake	Alan Alda	Molly at 21	Tracy Pollan
Maggie	Helen Shaver	Edith	Joyce Van Patten
Karen	Brenda Vaccaro	Julie	Kate Burton
Molly at 12	Genia Michaela	Sheila	Talia Balsam

Standbys: Mr. Alda—Munson Hicks; Miss Shaver—Marsha Waterbury; Misses Vaccaro, Van Patten—Linda Atkinson; Miss Michaela—Beau Dakota Berdahl; Miss Pollan—Maura Russo; Misses Burton, Balsam—Ilana Levine.

Directed by Gene Saks; scenery, Santo Loquasto; lighting, Tharon Musser; sound, Tom Morse; production supervisor, Peter Lawrence; production stage manager, John Brigleb; stage manager, Greta Minsky; press, Bill Evans & Associates, Jim Randolph.

Place: In Jake's apartment and in his mind. The play was presented in two parts.

The six most important women in a writer's life, in his imagination and in reality. Previously produced in an early version in a pre-Broadway tryout at the Old Globe Theater, San Diego, 3/8/90.

*Conversations With My Father (73). By Herb Gardner. Produced by James Walsh at the Royale Theater. Opened March 29, 1992.

Charlie	Tony Shalhoub	Gusta	Gordana Rashovich
Josh; Joey	Tony Gillan	Zaretsky	David Margulies
Eddie	Judd Hirsch	Young Joey	Jason Biggs

Hannah Di Blindeh . . . . Marilyn Sokol　Jimmy Scalso . . . . John Procaccino
Nick . . . . William Biff McGuire　Blue . . . . Richard E. Council
Finney the Book . . . . Peter Gerety　Young Charlie . . . . David Krumholtz

Standby: Mr. Margulies—Sidney Armus. Understudies: Mr. Gillan—Robert Canaan; Mr. Procaccino—Richard E. Council; Misses Rashovich, Sokol—Cheryl Giannini; Mr. Shalhoub—John Procaccino; Messrs. McGuire, Council, Gerety—Michael M. Ryan; Messrs. Krumholtz, Biggs—Tristan Smith.

Directed by Daniel Sullivan; scenery, Tony Walton; costumes, Robert Wojewodski; lighting, Pat Collins; sound, Michael Holten; production stage manager, Warren Crane; press, Jeffrey Richards Associates, David LeShay, Ben Gutkin.

Time: Between 1936 and 1976. Place: Canal Street in New York City. Act I, Scene 1: June 25, 1976, early evening. Scene 2: July 4, 1936, early morning. Act II, Scene 1: July 3, 1944, early morning. Scene 2: About 7 o'clock that evening. Scene 3: August 8, 1945, early morning. Scene 4: October 15, 1965, early morning. Scene 5: About eight weeks later, early morning. Scene 6: June 25, 1976, early evening.

A son's reflections on life with his father, an immigrant and abrasive head of his Jewish family. The play was originally presented in regional theater at Seattle Repertory.

A Best Play; see page 183.

*Five Guys Named Moe** (61). Musical with book by Clarke Peters; music by various authors including Louis Jordan (see list of credits below). Produced by Cameron Mackintosh at the Eugene O'Neill Theater. Opened April 8, 1992.

Nomax . . . . Jerry Dixon　No Moe . . . . Kevin Ramsey
Big Moe . . . . Doug Eskew　Eat Moe . . . . Jeffrey D. Sams
Four-Eyed Moe . . . . . . Milton Craig Nealy　Little Moe . . . . Glenn Turner

Band: Reginald Royal musical director, piano; Joseph Joubert assistant musical director; Luico Hopper bass; Brian Kirk drums; Reggie Pittman trumpet, flugel horn; Gregory Charles Royal trombone; Mark Gross saxophone, clarinet.

Understudies: Mr. Dixon—Phillip Gilmore; Mr. Eskew—Michael-Leon Wooley; Mr. Nealy—Phillip Gilmore, W. Ellis Porter; Messrs. Ramsay, Turner—W. Ellis Porter; Mr. Sams—Phillip Gilmore, Michael-Leon Wooley.

Directed and choreographed by Charles Augins; scenery, Tim Goodchild; costumes, Noel Howard; lighting, Andrew Bridge; sound, Tony Meola/Autograph; vocal arrangements and musical supervision, Chapman Roberts; musical direction and supervision, Reginald Royal; orchestrations, Neil McArthur; executive producer, Richard Jay-Alexander; production stage manager, Marybeth Abel; stage managers, Gwendolyn M. Gilliam, Roumel Reaux; press, Merle Frimark, Mark Thibodeau.

Revue-style celebration of the life and works of Louis Jordan (1908-1975), saxophonist, composer and orchestra leader who made popular the songs of others as well as his own. A foreign play previously produced in England at the Theater Royal, Stratford East.

MUSICAL NUMBERS, ACT I: "Early in the Morning" (by Louis Jordan, Leo Hickman and Dallas Bartley); "Five Guys Named Moe" (by Larry Wynn and Jerry Breslen); "Beware, Brother, Beware" (by Morry Lasco, Dick Adams and Fleecie Moore); "I Like 'em Fat Like That" (by Claude Demetriou and Louis Jordan); "Messy Bessy" (by Jon Hendricks); "Pettin' and Pokin'" (by Lora Lee); "Life Is So Peculiar" (by Johnny Burke and Jimmy Van Heusen); "I Know What I've Got" (by Sid Robin and Louis Jordon); "Azure Té" (by Bill Davis and Don Wolf); "Safe, Sane and Single" (by Louis Jordan, Johnny Lange and Hy Heath); "Push Ka Pi Shi Pie" (by Joe Willoughby, Louis Jordon, Dr. Walt Merrick).

ACT II: "Push Ka Pi Shi Pie" (instrumental reprise); "Saturday Night Fish Fry" (by Ellis Walsh and Louis Jordan); "What's the Use of Getting Sober" (by Bubsy Meyers); "If I Had Any Sense" (by R. McCoy and C. Singleton); "Dad Gum Your Hide Boy" (by Browley Bri).

The Cabaret: "Five Guys Named Moe," "Let the Good Times Roll" (by Fleecie Moore and Sam Theard); "Reet, Petite and Gone" (by Spencer Lee and Louis Jordan); "Caldonia" (by Fleecie Moore); "Ain't Nobody Here but Us Chickens" (by Joan Whitney and Alex Kramer); "Don't Let the Sun Catch You Crying" (by Jo Greene); "Choo, Choo, Ch'boogie" (by Vaughn Horton, Denver Darling and Milton Gabler), "Look Out, Sister" (by Sid Robin and Louis Jordan).

Medley: "Hurry Home" (by Joseph Meyer, Buddy Bernier and Robert Emmerich), "Is You Is or Is You Ain't My Baby?" (by S. Austin and Louis Jordan), "Don't Let the Sun Catch You Crying" (reprise), "Five Guys Named Moe."

*A Streetcar Named Desire (57). Revival of the play by Tennessee Williams. Produced by Gregory Mosher, James Walsh, Capital Cities/ABC Inc., Suntory International Corp. and The Shubert Organization at the Ethel Barrymore Theater. Opened April 12, 1992.

Stanley Kowalski. . . . . Alec Baldwin	Harold Mitchell . . . . Timothy Carhart
Stella Kowalski . . . . Amy Madigan	Pablo Gonzales . . . . Lazaro Perez
Eunice Hubbell. . . . . Aida Turturro	Young Collector . . . . Matt McGrath
Negro Woman . . . . Edwina Lewis	Mexican Woman . . . . Sol Etcheverria
Blanche DuBois . . . . Jessica Lange	Man . . . . William Cain
Steve Hubbell . . . . James Gandolfini	Woman . . . . Susan Aston

Understudies: Miss Lange—Leslie C. Hendrix; Misses Madigan, Aston—Deborah La Coy; Messrs. Baldwin, Gandolfini, Perez—Don Yesso; Mr. Carhart—James Gandolfini; Misses Turturro, Etcheverria, Lewis—Susan Aston; Mr. McGrath—Michael P. Connor; Mr. Cain—Richard Thomsen.

Directed by Gregory Mosher; scenery, Ben Edwards; costumes, Jane Greenwood; lighting, Kevin Rigdon; music consultant, Michael Barrett; sound, Scott Lehrer; production stage manager, Michael F. Ritchie; stage manager, Sally J. Jacobs; press, Bill Evans & Associates, Susan L. Schulman, Jim Randolph.

Time: 1947. Place: New Orleans. The play was presented in two parts.

The last major New York revival of *A Streetcar Named Desire* was by Circle in the Square on Broadway 3/10/88 for 85 performances.

*Two Trains Running (56). By August Wilson. Produced by Yale Repertory Theater, Stan Wojewodski Jr. artistic director, Center Theater Group/Ahmanson Theater, Gordon Davidson producing director, and Jujamcyn Theaters with Benjamin Mordecai executive producer, in association with Huntington Theater Company, Seattle Repertory Theater and Old Globe Theater, in Lloyd Richards's Yale Repertory Theater production. Opened April 13, 1992.

Risa . . . . Cynthia Martells	Hambone . . . . Sullivan Walker
Wolf . . . . Anthony Chisholm	Sterling . . . . Larry Fishburne
Memphis . . . . Al White	West . . . . Chuck Patterson
Holloway . . . . Roscoe Lee Browne	

Understudies: Messrs. Browne, Patterson—Ed Cambridge; Messrs. White, Walker—Robinson Frank Adu.

Directed by Lloyd Richards; scenery, Tony Fanning; costumes, Chrisi Karvonides; lighting, Geoff Korff; production stage manager, Karen L. Carpenter; stage manager, Fred Seagraves; press, Jeffrey Richards Associates, David LeShay.

Time: 1969. Place: Memphis Lee's restaurant in the Hill District of Pittsburgh. Act I, Scene 1: Saturday morning. Scene 2: Monday morning. Scene 3: Tuesday afternoon. Act II, Scene 1: Wednesday morning. Scene 2: Thursday, mid-morning. Scene 3: Thursday afternoon. Scene 4: Thursday night. Scene 5: Friday, late afternoon.

A local preacher's funeral takes place on the same day as a rally in honor of Malcolm X's birthday. Winner of the 5th Annual American Theater Critics Association New Play Award in 1991 as an outstanding regional theater play, *Two Trains Running* has previously been produced at Yale Repertory Theater in New Haven, Conn., the Huntington Theater Company in Boston, the Seattle Repertory Company, the Old Globe Theater in San Diego, the Kennedy Center in Washington, D.C. and the Doolittle Theater in Los Angeles.

A Best Play; see page 222.

*Guys and Dolls (55). Revival of the musical based on a story and characters by Damon Runyon; book by Jo Swerling and Abe Burrows; music and lyrics by Frank Loesser. Produced by Dodger Productions, Roger Berlind, Jujamcyn Theaters/TV Asahi, Kardana Productions and the John F. Kennedy Center for the Performing Arts at the Martin Beck Theater. Opened April 14, 1992.

Nicely-Nicely Johnson . . . . . . Walter Bobbie	Calvin . . . . Leslie Feagan
Benny Southstreet . . . . J.K. Simmons	Martha . . . . Victoria Clark
Rusty Charlie . . . . Timothy Shew	Harry the Horse. . . . . Ernie Sabella
Sarah Brown . . . . Josie de Guzman	Lt. Brannigan . . . . Steve Ryan
Arvide Abernathy . . . . John Carpenter	Nathan Detroit. . . . . Nathan Lane
Agatha . . . . Eleanor Glockner	Angie the Ox; Joey Biltmore . . . . Michael Goz

Miss Adelaide . . . . Faith Prince		Gen. Matilda B. Cartwright. . . Ruth Williamson
Sky Masterson . . . . Peter Gallagher		Big Jule . . . . Herschel Sparber
Hot Box MC . . . . Stan Page		Drunk . . . . Robert Michael Baker
Mimi . . . . Denise Faye		Waiter . . . . Kenneth Kantor

Guys: Gary Chryst, R.F. Daley, Randy Andre Davis, David Elder, Cory English, Mark Esposito, Leslie Feagan, Carlos Lopez, John MacInnis, Scott Wise.

Dolls: Tina Marie DeLeone, Denise Faye, Pascale Faye, JoAnn M. Hunter, Nancy Lemenager, Greta Martin.

Orchestra: Edward Strauss conductor; Lawrence Yurman assistant conductor; Lawrence Yurman, Steve Tyler keyboards; Katsuko Esaki, Robert Lawrence, Andrew Stein, Melanie Baker violin; Juliet Haffner viola; Jeffrey Szabo cello; Joseph Bongiorno bass; Glenn Rhian, Eric Kivnick percussion; Brian O'Flaherty, Glenn Drewes, Kamau Adilifu trumpet; Bruce Bonvissuto, Earl McIntyre trombone; Roger Wendt, French horn; Seymour Red Press, Raymond Beckenstein, Dennis Anderson, Robert Steen, Wally Kane woodwinds.

Understudies: Messrs. Lane, Simmons, Sabella—Jeff Brooks; Mr. Gallagher—Robert Michael Baker; Messrs. Bobbie, Simmons, Lane—Larry Cahn; Mr. Sabella—Leslie Feagan; Mr. Sparber—Michael Goz; Mr. Ryan—Kenneth Kantor; Mr. Carpenter—Stan Page; Messrs. Bobbie, Ryan—Timothy Shew; Mr. Feagan—Steven Sofia; Mr. Shew—Scott Wise; Misses Glockner, Prince—Victoria Clark; Miss Williamson—Eleanor Glockner; Miss Faye—Tina Maria DeLeone; Miss Glockner—Denise Faye; Miss Clark—Nancy Lemenager; Swings—Randy Bettis, Larry Cahn, Susan Misner, Steven Sofia.

Directed by Jerry Zaks; scenery, Tony Walton; costumes, William Ivey Long; lighting, Paul Gallo; musical supervision, Edward Strauss; dance arrangements, Mark Hummel; sound, Tony Meola; orchestrations, George Bassman, Ted Royal, Michael Starobin; choreography, Christopher Chadman; production stage manager, Steve Beckler; stage manager, Clifford Schwartz; press, Boneau/Bryan-Brown, John Barlow.

The last major New York revival of *Guys and Dolls* took place on Broadway 7/21/76 for 239 performances.

The list of scenes and musical numbers in *Guys and Dolls* appears on page 329 of *The Best Plays of 1950-51.*

Metro (13). Musical with original Polish book and lyrics by Agata Miklaszewska and Maryna Miklaszewska; English book by Mary Bracken Phillips and Janusz Jozefowicz; English lyrics by Mary Bracken Phillips; music by Janusz Stoklosa. Produced by Wiktor Kubiak at the Minskoff Theater. Opened April 16, 1992. (Closed April 26, 1992)

Anka . . . . Katarzyna Groniec		Philip . . . . Janusz Jozefowicz
Jan . . . . Robert Janowski		Viola . . . . Violetta Klimczewska
Edyta . . . . Edyta Gorniak		Iwona . . . . Iwona Runowska
Max . . . . Mariusz Czajka			

Members of the Company (playing themselves): Krzysztof Adamski, Monika Ambroziak, Andrew Appolonow, Jacek Badurek, Alicja Borkowska, Michal Chamera, Pawel Cheda, Magdalena Depczyk, Jaroslaw Derybowski, Wojciech Dmochowski, Malgorzata Duda, Katarzyna Galica, Katarzyna Gawel, Denisa Geislerova, Lidia Groblewska, Piotr Hajduk, Joanna Jagla, Jaroslaw Janikowski, Adam Kamien, Grzegorz Kowalczyk, Andrzej Kubicki, Katarzyna Lewandowska, Barbara Melzer, Michal Milowicz, Radoslaw Natkanski, Polina Oziernych, Marek Palucki, Beata Pawlik, Katarzyna Skarpetowska, Igor Sorine, Ewa Szawlowska, Marc Thomas, Ilona Trybula, Beata Urbanska, Kamila Zapytowska.

Orchestra: Janusz Stoklosa conductor; Nicholas Archer assistant conductor; Kinny Landrum synthesizer I; Ted Baker synthesizer II; Jeff Klevit trumpet I; Larry Lunetta trumpet II; Dale Kirkland trombone; Scott Kreitzer saxophone; Vince Fay bass; Mark Sherman percussion; Miroslaw Kaczmarczyk guitar; Radoslaw Macinski drums; Wojciech Dmochowski accordion; Paul Woodiel violin I; Francisca Mendoza, Byung Kwak, Nina Simon, Susan Lorentsen, David Tobey violin; Susan Follari viola I; Judy Witmer viola II; Katherine Sinsabaugh viola III; Jennifer Langham cello I; Eliana Mendoza cello II.

Directed and choreographed by Janusz Jozefowicz; musical direction, vocal and orchestral arrangements, Janusz Stoklosa; scenery, Janusz Sosnowski; costumes, Juliet Polcsa, Marie Anne Chiment; lighting, Ken Billington; sound, Jaroslaw Regulski; laser effects, Mike Deissler; technical supervisor, Arthur Siccardi; musical coordinator, John Monaco; American dance supervisor, Cynthia Onrubia; executive producer, Donald C. Farber; production stage manager, Beverly Randolph; stage manager, Dale Kaufman; press, Bill Evans & Associates, Jim Randolph.

Young performers audition for a new musical. A foreign play previously produced at the Dramatyzny Theater in Warsaw.

ACT I

Scene 1: A theater somewhere in Europe—Philip, Jan, Company
Overture
Scene 2: A metro somewhere in Europe
  "Metro" . . . . Jan, Company
Scene 3: The theater—Klaus, Denisa, Alicja, Duda, Wojtek, Jaga, Basia, Monika, Magda, Max, Philip
    Anka, Company.
  "My Fairy Tale". . . . . Basia, Alicja, Denisa; (dancers) Iwona, Lidia, Violetta
Scene 4: The metro—Jan, Anka
  "But Not Me" . . . . Jan, Company
Scene 5: The theater—Max, Philip, Anka, Company
  "Windows". . . . . Anka; (dancer) Iwona
Scene 6: The metro—Jan, Anka
Scene 7: Audition results—Edyta, Piotr, Alicja, Denisa, Monika, Duda, Jaga, Magda, Anka
  "Bluezwis" . . . . Jan, Wijtek, Company
  "Love Duet" . . . . Anka, Jan
Scene 7: Tower of Babel
  "Tower of Babel". . . . . Company

ACT II

Scene 1: The metro
  "Benjamin Franklin, in God We Trust. . . . . Jan, Company
Scene 2: Philip's office—Philip, Max
Scene 3: Abandoned subway station—Anka, Jan, Edyta, Duda, Jaga, Klaus, Alicja, Basia, Wojtek.
  "Uciekali" (a Christmas carol). . . . . Jan, Company
Scene 4: The metro—Jan, Anka, Philip
Scene 5: The metro
  "Waiting" . . . . Edyta, Anka, Dancers
Scene 6: The metro—Anka, Jan, Max, Philip
Scene 7: Pieniadze
  "Pieniadze" . . . . Company
Scene 8: The metro—Edyta, Denisa, Jan, Wojtek, Duda, Basia, Magda, Piotr, Alicja, Grzegorz, Monika, Jaga
  "Love Duet II" . . . . Anka, Jan
Scene 9: The metro
  "Dreams Don't Die". . . . . Anka

The High Rollers Social and Pleasure Club (12). Musical revue conceived by Judy Gordon; music and lyrics by various authors including Allen Toussaint. Produced by Judy Gordon, Dennis Grimaldi, Allen M. Shore and Martin Markinson at the Helen Hayes Theater. Opened April 21, 1992. (Closed May 3, 1992)

CAST: Allen Toussaint; Wonder Boy #1—Keith Robert Bennett; Queen—Deborah Burrell-Cleveland; King—Lawrence Clayton; Jester—Eugene Fleming; Sorcerer—Michael McElroy; Enchantress—Vivian Reed; Princess—Nikki Rene; Wonder Boy #2—Tarik Winston; Dance Captain—Bruce Anthony Davis.
    High Rollers Band: Allen Toussaint conductor, piano; Carl Maultsby associate conductor; Frank Canino bass; Gary Keller saxophone; Joel Helleny trombone; Steve Johns drums; Darryl Shaw trumpet; Bob Rose guitar.
    Understudies: Messrs. Bennett, Winston—Bruce Anthony Davis; Misses Burrell-Cleveland, Reed, Rene—Mona Wyatt; Messrs. Clayton, McElroy—Frederick J. Boothe.
    Directed and choreographed by Alan Weeks; musical direction, arrangements and orchestrations, Allen Toussaint; scenery, David Mitchell; costumes, Theoni V. Aldredge; lighting, Beverly Emmons; sound, Peter J. Fitzgerald; music advisors, Jerry Wexler, Charles Neville; musical coordinator, John Miller; associate director, Bruce Heath; associate producers, Nicholas Evans, Mary Ellen Ashley, Donald Tick, Irving Welzer; stage manager, David H. Bosboom; press, John Springer, Gary Springer.

Time: Mardi Gras. Place: The High Rollers Social and Pleasure Club, New Orleans—with a side trip to the bayou. The show was presented in two parts.

Musical numbers presented in the festive mood of a Mardi Gras celebration, with side references to voodoo.

The Good Times: "Tu Way Pocky Way"—Jester; "Open Up"—Band; "Mr. Mardi Gras"—Company; Piano Solo—Allen Toussaint; "Chicken Shack Boogie"—Jester, Company; "Lady Marmalade"—Enchantress, Sorcerer, Company; "Don't You Feel My Leg"—Queen, King, Jester, Sorcerer; "You Can Have My Husband"—Enchantress; "Fun Time"—Wonder Boys; Rock Medley: "It Will Stand," "Mother-in-Law," "Working in a Coal Mine," "Lipstick Traces," "Rockin' Pneumonia," "Sittin' in Ya Ya"—Company; "Feet Don't Fail Me Now"—Wonder Boys; "Ooh Poo Pa Doo"—Jester; "Dance the Night"/"Such a Night"—King, Queen; "All These Things"—Enchantress, Sorcerer; "Mellow Sax"—Princess, Saxophone, Company; "Sea Cruise"—Enchantress, Queen, Princess; "Jambalaya"—Jester, Company.

More Good Times: "Tu Way Pocky Way"—Jester; "Bourbon Street Parade"—Company; "Jelly Roll"—Wonder Boys; "Heebie Jeebie Dance"—Princess, Queen, Enchantress; "I Like It Like That"—Jester, Company; "Fiyou on the Bayou"—Company; "Marie Leveau"—Enchantress; "Walk on Gilded Splinters"—Company; "Black Widow Spider"—King; "Tell It Like It Is"/"You're the One"—Queen, King; "Let the Good Times Roll"—Company; "Challenge Dance"—Jester, King, Sorcerer, Wonder Boys; "Mos Scoscious"—Sorcerer, Princess; "We All Need Love"—Enchantress; "Tu Way Pocky Way"—Jester; "Injuns Here We Come"—Wonder Boy #1, Company; "Golden Crown"—Company; "Jockomo"—Company; "Hey Mama"—Company; "Saints Go Marchin' In"—Company.

MAN OF LA MANCHA—Tony Martinez (Sancho), Raul Julia (Don Quixote) and Sheena Easton (Aldonza) in the 25th anniversary revival of the Dale Wasserman-Mitch Leigh-Joe Darion musical treatment of Cervantes

Gypsy Passion (15). Musical in the Spanish language by Tomas Rodriguez-Pantoja. Produced by the National Theater of the Performing Arts, Ltd., Stephen A. Rapaport president, in association with the Government of Andalucia, Spain at Town Hall. Opened April 22, 1992. (Closed May 3, 1992)

Estefania Aranda	Manuela Nuñez
Sara Baras	Juan Antonio Ogalla
Paco el Clavero	Antoniô el Pipa
Antonio Malena	Juana la del Pipa
Luis Moneo	Mercedes Ruiz
Manuel Moneo	Patricia Valdés
Manuel Morao	Concha Vargas
Antonio Moreno	

Directed by Tomas Rodriguez-Pantoja; artistic and musical direction, Manuel Morao; scenery, David Sumner; costumes, M. Muniz, M. Zarzana; production manager, Carlos Gorbes; stage manager, Antonio Moreno; press, Max Eisen.

Act I, Scene 1: The Patriarch. Scene 2: The forest outside Seville. Scene 3: Seville. Scene 4: Children at play. Act II, Scene 1: Falling in love. Scene 2: The wedding. Scene 3: Men at work in the blacksmith shop. Scene 4: Flamenco, a celebration of life.

With a score of traditional Flamenco music, Act I enacts a gypsy community's visit to Seville to trade their goods and Act II tells of the romance and early married life of a young gypsy couple.

ACT I

Scene 1: The Patriarch
"Toná". . . . . Manuel Morao
Scene 2: The forest outside Seville
"Villancico". . . . . Company
"Soleá" . . . . . . Juana la del Pipa, Concha Vargas, Manuel Morao, Luis Moneo, Antonio Moreno
"Cantiña" . . . . Antonio Malena, Antonio el Pipa, Morao, Luis Moneo, Moreno
"Tangos". . . . . la del Pipa
"Tanguillos" . . . . la del Pipa, Manuela Nuñez, Mercedes Ruiz, Patricia Valdés,
                                                    Estefania Aranda, Morao, Luis Moneo, Moreno
"Seguirillas". . . . . Manuel Moneo, Sara Baras, Morao, Luis Moneo, Moreno
Scene 3: In Seville, the next day
"Zapateado". . . . . Company
"Taranto" . . . . Paco el Clavero, Vargas, Juan Antonio Ogalla, Morao
Scene 4: Children at play
"Bulerias" . . . . Malena, la del Pipa, Nuñez, Ruiz, Valdés, Aranda, Luis Moneo, Moreno

ACT II

Scene 1: Falling in love in the Gypsy Village
"Alegrias". . . . . Malena, el Pipa, Baras, Vargas, Ogalla, Morao, Luis Moneo, Moreno
Scene 2: The wedding
"Alboreá". . . . . Company
"El Polo de Tobalo" . . . . Malena, el Pipa, Baras, Morao, Luis Moneo, Moreno
Scene 3: Men at work
"Martinetes" . . . . el Clavero, Manuel Moneo, el Pipa, Baras
Scene 4: Flamenco, a celebration of life
"Bulerias". . . . . Company

Shimada (4). By Jill Shearer. Produced by Paul B. Berkowsky, Richard Seader, Furuyama International, Inc. and Ellis and Mike Weatherly in association with Sally Sears at the Broadhurst Theater. Opened April 23, 1992. (Closed April 25, 1992)

Shimada; Toshio Uchiyama . . . . Mako
Eric Dawson. . . . . Ben Gazzara
Clive Beaumont; Mark Beaumont . . Robert Joy
Commandant Matsumoto;
   Samurai. . . . . Ernest Abuba

Denny. . . . . Estelle Parsons
Jan Harding; Wisteria Lady . . . . Tracy Sallows
Sharyn Beaumont . . . . Ellen Burstyn
Billy . . . . Jon Matthews

Standbys: Mr. Gazzara—Jack Davidson; Misses Parsons, Burstyn—Judith Barcroft. Understudies: Mako—Ernest Abuba; Messrs. Joy, Matthews, Abuba—Christopher Taylor; Miss Sallows—Pamela Stewart.

Directed by Simon Phillips; scenery, Tony Straiges; costumes, Judy Dearing; lighting, Richard Nelson; original score, Ian McDonald; sound, Peter J. Fitzgerald; production stage manager, Martin Gold; stage manager, John McNamara; press, Keith Sherman & Associates, Chris Day.

Time: The present. Place: A small town in Australia, with flashbacks to a Japanese prisoner-of-war camp in the Burmese jungle in 1945. The play was presented in two parts.

A Japanese and an Australian in business conflict which has its roots in the hostilities and cruelties of World War II. A foreign play previously produced by the Melbourne Theater Company in Australia.

*Man of La Mancha (44). Revival of the musical suggested by the life and works of Miguel de Cervantes y Saavedra; book by Dale Wasserman; music by Mitch Leigh; lyrics by Joe Darion. Produced by the Mitch Leigh Company at the Marquis Theater. Opened April 24, 1992.

Cervantes; Don Quixote . . . . Raul Julia
Aldonza; Dulcinea. . . . . Sheena Easton
Sancho . . . . Tony Martinez
Governor; Pedro; Head Muleteer . Chev Rodgers
Padre. . . . . David Wasson
Dr. Carrasco . . . . Ian Sullivan
Innkeeper . . . . David Holliday
Antonia . . . . Valerie De Pena
Housekeeper . . . . Marceline Decker
Barber . . . . Ted Forlow
Paco; Mule . . . . Hechter Ubarry

Juan; Horse . . . . Jean-Paul Richard
Manuel. . . . . Luis Perez
Tenorio . . . . Gregory Mitchell
Jose. . . . . Bill Santora
Jorge . . . . Chet D'Elia
Maria. . . . . Tanny McDonald
Fermina; Moorish Dancer. Joan Susswein Barber
Captain of the Inquisition . . . Jon Vandertholen
Guitarists . . . . . . Robin Polseno, David Serva
Guards . . . . Chet D'Elia, Darryl Ferrera

Orchestra: Bill Meade, Lucy Goeres, Helen Camp flute; Larry Guy clarinet; David Diggs oboe; Ethan Silverman bassoon; Richard Raffio, Larry Etkin trumpet; Dennis Elliot, George Moran, Jack Jeffers trombone; Ann Yarborough, Will Parker, Sue Panny, Kathy Morse, French horn; William Trigg, Steve Bartosik, Maya Gunji, David Yee percussion; Ray Kilday bass; Robin Polseno, David Serva, Cherie Rosen guitars.

Understudies: Messrs. Julia, Rodgers—David Holliday; Misses Easton, De Pena, McDonald—Joan Susswein Barber; Messrs. Martinez, Wasson, Forlow—Darryl Ferrera; Mr. Holliday—Chev Rodgers; Mr. Sullivan—Jon Vandertholen; Misses Decker, Barber—Tanny McDonald; Mr. Ubarry—Bill Santora; Mr. Vandertholen—Jean-Paul Richard; Swing—Rick Manning.

Directed by Albert Marre; musical direction, Brian Salesky; scenery, Howard Bay; costumes, Howard Bay, Patton Campbell; lighting, Gregory Allen Hirsch; sound, Jon Weston; dance arrangements, Neil Warner; executive producer, Manny Kladitis; assistant to the director, Ted Forlow; production stage manager, Patrick Horrigan; stage manager, Betsy Nicholson; press, Dennis Crowley.

Time: The end of the 16th century. Place: A prison in Seville and various other places in the imagination of Miguel de Cervantes. The play was presented without intermission.

The last major New York revival of *Man of La Mancha* took place on Broadway 9/15/77 for 124 performances.

The list of musical numbers in *Man of La Mancha* appears on page 387 of *The Best Plays of 1965-66*.

*Jelly's Last Jam (41). Musical with book by George C. Wolfe; music by Jelly Roll Morton; lyrics by Susan Birkenhead; musical adaptation and additional music by Luther Henderson. Produced by Margo Lion and Pamela Koslow in association with Polygram Diversified Entertainment, 126 Second Avenue Corp./Hal Luftig, Rodger Hess, Jujamcyn Theaters/TV Asahi and Herb Alpert at the Virginia Theater. Opened April 26, 1992.

Chimney Man . . . . Keith David
Jelly Roll Morton . . . . Gregory Hines
The Hunnies: Mamie Duncan-Gibbs, Stephanie
Pope, Allison M. Williams.
The Crowd: Ken Ard, Adrian Bailey, Sherry D.
Boone, Brenda Braxton, Mary Bond Davis, Ralph
Deaton, Melissa Haizlip, Cee-Cee Harshaw, Ted L.
Levy, Stanley Wayne Mathis, Victoria Gabrielle
Platt, Gil Pritchett III, Michelle M. Robinson.
The People of His Past:
Young Jelly . . . . Savion Glover
Sisters . . . . Victoria Gabrielle Platt,
Sherry D. Boone

Miss Mamie . . . . Mary Bond Davis
Buddy Bolden. . . . . Ruben Santiago-Hudson
Too-Tight Nora . . . . Brenda Braxton
Three Finger Jake. . . . . . . Gil Pritchett III
Gran Mimi . . . . Ann Duquesnay
Jack the Bear . . . . . . Stanley Wayne Mathis
Foot-in-Yo-Ass Sam. . . . . Ken Ard
Anita. . . . . Tonya Pinkins
Melrose Brothers . . . . Don Johanson,
Gordon Joseph Weiss
Ancestors: Adrian Bailey, Mary Bond Davis,
Ralph Deaton, Ann Duquesnay, Melissa Haizlip.

Jelly's Red Hot Peppers: Brian Grice drums, Ben Brown bass, Steve Bargonetti banjo, Virgil Jones trumpet, Britt Woodman trombone, Bill Easley clarinet.

Orchestra: Linda Twine conductor; Daryl M. Waters associate conductor; Brian Grice drums; Ben Brown bass; Steve Bargonetti banjo; Warren Smith percussion; Jerome Richardson, Jimmy Cozier, Bill Easley, George Barrow woodwinds; Byron Stripling, Stanton Davis, Virgil Jones trumpet; Britt Woodman trombone; Joe Daley tuba; Daryl M. Waters, Leonard Oxley piano.

Standby: Mr. Hines—Lawrence Hamilton. Understudies: Mr. David—Ken Ard; Mr. Glover—Jimmy W. Tate; Miss Pinkins—Stephanie Pope; Mr. Mathis—Ralph Deaton; Mr. Santiago-Hudson—Adrian Bailey; Misses Duquesnay, Davis—Clare Bathé; Hunnies—Melissa Haizlip; Melrose Brothers—Bill Brassea; Dance Captain/Swing—Ken Roberson; Women's Swings—Janice Lorraine-Holt, La-Rose Saxon.

Directed by George C. Wolfe; choreography, Hope Clarke; tap choreography, Gregory Hines, Ted L. Levy; musical direction, Linda Twine; scenery, Robin Wagner; costumes, Toni-Leslie James; lighting, Jules Fisher; musical supervision and orchestrations, Luther Henderson; music coordinator, John Miller; sound, Otts Munderloh; mask and puppet design, Barbara Politt; executive producer, David Strong Warner, Inc,; associate producers, Peggy Hill Rosenkranz, Marilyn Hall, Dentsu Inc., New York; production stage manager, Arturo E. Porazzi; stage managers, Bernita Robinson, Bonnie L. Becker; press, Richard Kornberg & Associates, Carol R. Fineman.

Time: The eve of Jelly Roll Morton's death. Place: The Jungle Inn—a lowdown club somewhere's 'tween heaven 'n' hell.

Reflections on the life and career of the noted jazz pioneer, including some of the special problems of being black and a prominent member of the jazz age.

ACT I

Scene 1: The jam
"Jelly's Jam". . . . . Hunnies, Crowd
(music by Jelly Roll Morton)
"In My Day" . . . . Jelly, Hunnies
(music by Jelly Roll Morton)
Scene 2: In the beginning
"The Creole Way". . . . . Ancestors, Sisters, Young Jelly
(music by Luther Henderson)
"The Whole World's Waitin' to Sing Your Song". . . . . Jelly, Young Jelly, Street Crowd
(music by Jelly Roll Morton)
"Street Scene" . . . . Jelly, Young Jelly, Street Crowd
(music by Luther Henderson)
Scene 3: Goin' uptown
"Michigan Water". . . . . Miss Mamie, Buddy Bolden
The Banishment
"Get Away, Boy". . . . . Gran Mimi, Young Jelly, Jelly
(music by Luther Henderson)
"Lonely Boy Blues" (traditional). . . . . Gran Mimi, Young Jelly, Jelly
Scene 4: The journey to Chicago
"Somethin' More" . . . . Jelly, Jack, Chimney Man, Hunnies, Crowd

(music by Jelly Roll Morton)
"That's How You Jazz". . . . . Jelly, Jack, Dance Hall Crowd
Scene 5: Chicago!
"The Chicago Stomp" . . . . Jelly, Red Hot Peppers, Chimney Man, Hunnies, Chicago Crowd
(music by Jelly Roll Morton)
Scene 6: Jelly 'n' Anita
"Play the Music for Me" . . . . Anita
(music by Jelly Roll Morton)
"Lovin' Is a Lowdown Blues" . . . . Hunnies
(music by Jelly Roll Morton)
Scene 7: The Midnite Inn
"Dr. Jazz . . . . Jelly, Crowd
(music by King Oliver and Walter Melrose, additional lyrics by Susan Birkenhead)

ACT II

Scene 1: The Chimney Man takes charge
Scene 2: The New York suite
"Good Ole New York" . . . . Chimney Man, Hunnies, Jelly, New York Crowd
(music by Jelly Roll Morton)
"Too Late, Daddy" . . . . Jelly, Harlem Crowd
(music by Luther Henderson)
"That's the Way We Do Things in New Yawk". . . . . Jelly, Melrose Brothers
(music by Jelly Roll Morton)
Jelly's Isolation Dance. . . . . Jelly, Young Jelly
Scene 3: The last chance
"The Last Chance Blues". . . . . Jelly, Anita
Scene 4: Central Avenue
Scene 5: The last rites
"The Last Rites" . . . . Jelly, Chimney Man, People of His Past
(music by Luther Henderson and Jelly Roll Morton)

A Small Family Business (48). By Alan Ayckbourn. Produced by Weissman Productions, Inc. (Walt K. and Beth Weissman) and MTC Productions, Inc., Lynne Meadow artistic director, Barry Grove managing director, at The Music Box. Opened April 27, 1992. (Closed June 7, 1992)

Jack McCracken	Brian Murray	Desmond	John Curless
Poppy	Jane Carr	Harriet	Patricia Conolly
Ken Ayres	Thomas Hill	Yvonne Doggett	Patricia Kilgariff
Tina	Barbara Garrick	Benedict Hough	Anthony Heald
Roy Ruston	Robert Stanton	Giorgio Rivetti, Orlando Rivetti,	
Samantha	Amelia Campbell	Vincenzo Rivetti, Lotario	
Cliff	Mark Arnott	Rivetti, Umberto Rivetti	Jake Weber
Anita	Caroline Lagerfelt		

Understudies: Misses Carr, Lagerfelt, Conolly, Kilgariff—Robin Moseley; Messrs. Stanton, Arnott, Heald, Weber—Edmund C. Davys; Mr. Murray—John Curless.

Directed by Lynne Meadow; scenery, John Lee Beatty; costumes, Ann Roth; lighting, Peter Kaczorowski; sound, Tom Sorce; incidental music, Jake Holmes; fight coach, J. Allen Suddeth; executive producer, Barry Grove; associate producer, Roger Alan Gindi; production stage manager, James Harker; stage manager, John M. Atherlay; press, Helene Davis, David Roggensack.

Time: Over one week. Place: The sitting room, kitchen, hall, landing, bathroom and bedroom in the houses of various members of the family. The play was presented in two parts.

The dark comic adventures of a family of thieves. A foreign play previously presented in London.

*Falsettos (37). Revival of the musicals *March of the Falsettos* and *Falsettoland*; book by William Finn and James Lapine; music and lyrics by William Finn. Produced by Barry and Fran Weissler at the John Golden Theater. Opened April 29, 1992.

Marvin . . . . Michael Rupert   Trina. . . . . Barbara Walsh
Whizzer . . . . Stephen Bogardus   Charlotte . . . . Heather Mac Rae
Mendel . . . . Chip Zien   Cordelia . . . . Carolee Carmello
Jason . . . . Jonathan Kaplan

Musicians: Scott Frankel piano; Ted Sperling synthesizer, associate conductor; Greg Landis percussion.

Understudies: Philip Hoffman, John Ruess; Jason alternate—Andrew Harrison Leeds.

Directed by James Lapine; musical direction, Scott Frankel; scenery, Douglas Stein; costumes, Ann Hould-Ward; lighting, Frances Aronson; sound, Peter J. Fitzgerald; musical arrangements, Michael Starobin; produced in association with James and Maureen O'Sullivan Cushing, Masakazu Shibaoka, Broadway Pacific; associate producer, Alecia Parker; stage manager, Karen Armstrong; press, the Pete Sanders Group.

Act I: 1979. Act II: 1981.

The complex emotional and family life of Marvin, who takes a homosexual lover, is divorced by his wife (who then joins up with Marvin's psychiatrist) and is deserted by the lover (in *March of the Falsettos*, first produced off Broadway 5/20/81 for 268 performances). Marvin is then reconciled with the lover, who contracts AIDS; at the same time, Marvin's son Jason is approaching his bar mitzvah (in *Falsettoland*, first produced off Broadway 6/28/90 for 215 performances and named a Best Play of its season). A third musical in the Marvin trilogy, *In Trousers*, the first in chronological order, was not revived in this production. These musicals are expressed almost entirely in song, without dialogue.

FALSETTOS—In the back row, Heather Mac Rae, Chip Zien and Michael Rupert; *in front row*, Carolee Carmello, Stephen Bogardus, Jonathan Kaplan and Barbara Walsh in a scene from the Broadway revival of two off-Broadway "Marvin" musicals by William Finn and James Lapine

ACT I

"Four Jews in a Room Bitching" . . . . Whizzer, Marvin, Jason, Mendel
"A Tight Knit Family" . . . . Marvin, Mendel
"Love Is Blind" . . . . Marvin, Jason, Whizzer, Mendel, Trina
"Thrill of First Love" . . . . Marvin, Whizzer
"Marvin at the Psychiatrist" (A Three Part Mini-Opera) . . . . Jason, Mendel, Whizzer, Marvin
"My Father's a Homo" . . . . Jason
"Everyone Tells Jason to See a Psychiatrist" . . . . Jason, Marvin, Trina, Whizzer
"This Had Better Come to a Stop" . . . . Marvin, Whizzer, Jason, Trina, Mendel
"I'm Breaking Down" . . . . Trina
"Please Come to My House" . . . . Trina, Mendel, Jason
"Jason's Therapy" . . . . Mendel, Trina, Whizzer, Marvin, Jason
"A Marriage Proposal" . . . . Mendel, Trina, Jason
"A Tight Knit Family" (Reprise) . . . . Marvin, Mendel
"Trina's Song" . . . . Trina
"March of the Falsettos" . . . . Mendel, Marvin, Jason, Whizzer
"Trina's Song" (Reprise) . . . . Trina
"The Chess Game" . . . . Marvin, Whizzer
"Making a Home" . . . . Mendel, Jason, Trina, Whizzer
"The Games I Play" . . . . Whizzer, Mendel, Trina, Jason
"Marvin Hits Trina" . . . . Marvin, Mendel, Jason, Trina, Whizzer
"I Never Wanted to Love You" . . . . Marvin, Mendel, Jason, Trina, Whizzer
"Father to Son" . . . . Marvin, Jason

ACT II

"Welcome to Falsettoland" . . . . Company
"The Year of the Child" . . . . Company
"Miracle of Judaism" . . . . Company
"Sitting Watching Jason (Play Baseball)" . . . . Company
"A Day in Falsettoland" . . . . Company
"Racquetball: How Was Your Day" . . . . Company
"The Fight" . . . . Jason, Marvin, Trina, Mendel
"Everyone Hates His Parents" . . . . Mendel, Jason, Marvin, Trina
"What More Can I Say" . . . . Marvin, Whizzer
"Something Bad Is Happening" . . . . Charlotte, Cordelia
"Second Racquetball" . . . . Marvin, Whizzer
"Holding to the Ground" . . . . Trina
"Days Like This I Almost Believe in God" . . . . Company
"Cancelling the Bar Mitzvah" . . . . Jason, Mendel, Trina
"Unlikely Lovers" . . . . Marvin, Whizzer, Charlotte, Cordelia
"Another Miracle of Judaism" . . . . Jason
"Something Bad Is Happening" (Reprise) . . . . Marvin, Charlotte
"You Gotta Die Sometime" . . . . Whizzer
"Jason's Bar Mitzvah" . . . . Company
"What Would I Do" . . . . Marvin, Whizzer

PLAYS PRODUCED OFF BROADWAY

Some distinctions between off-Broadway and Broadway productions at one end of the scale and off-off-Broadway productions at the other are blurred in the New York Theater of the 1990s. For the purposes of the *Best Plays* listing, the term "off Broadway" is used to distinguish a professional from a showcase (off-off-Broadway) production and signifies a show which opened for general audiences in a mid-Manhattan theater seating 499 or fewer and 1) employed an Equity cast, 2) planned a regular schedule of 8 performances a week in an open-ended run (7 performances a week in the case of solo shows) and 3) offered itself to public comment by critics at designated opening performances.

Occasional exceptions of inclusion (never of exclusion) are made to take in visiting troupes, borderline cases and nonqualifying productions which readers might expect to find in this list because they appear under an off-Broadway heading in other major sources of record.

Figures in parentheses following a play's title give number of performances. These figures do not include previews or extra non-profit performances.

Plays marked with an asterisk (*) were still in a projected run on June 1, 1992. Their number of performances is figured from opening night through May 31, 1992.

Certain programs of off-Broadway companies are exceptions to our rule of counting the number of performances from the date of the press coverage. When the official opening takes place late in the run of a play's regularly-priced public or subscription performances (after previews) we count the first performance of record, not the press date, as opening night—and in each such case in the listing we note the variance and give the press date.

In a listing of a show's numbers—dances, sketches, musical scenes, etc.—the titles of songs are identified wherever possible by their appearance in quotation marks (").

HOLDOVERS FROM PREVIOUS SEASONS

Plays which were running on June 1, 1991 are listed below. More detailed information about them appears in previous *Best Plays* volumes of appropriate date. Important cast changes since opening night are recorded in the Cast Replacements section of this volume.

*The Fantasticks (13,310; longest continuous run of record in the American theater). Musical suggested by the play *Les Romanesques* by Edmond Rostand; book and lyrics by Tom Jones; music by Harvey Schmidt. Opened May 30, 1960.

*Nunsense (2,680). Musical with book, music and lyrics by Dan Goggin. Opened December 12, 1985.

*Perfect Crime (2,091). By Warren Manzi. Opened October 16, 1987.

Other People's Money (990). By Jerry Sterner. Opened February 16, 1989. (Closed July 4, 1991)

*Forever Plaid (882). Musical by Stuart Ross. Opened May 20, 1990.

Smoke on the Mountain (368). Transfer from off off Broadway of the Gospel musical conceived by Alan Bailey; written by Connie Ray; musical numbers by various authors. Opened May 12, 1990 off off Broadway where it played 84 performances through August 11, 1990; changed to off-Broadway status August 14, 1990. (Closed June 30, 1991)

The Sum of Us (335). By David Stevens. Opened October 16, 1990. (Closed August 4, 1991)

Playwrights Horizons. The Substance of Fire (120). By Jon Robin Baitz. Opened March 17, 1991. (Closed June 30, 1991) **The Old Boy** (33). By A.R. Gurney. Opened May 5, 1991. (Closed June 2, 1991)

And the World Goes 'Round (408). Musical revue with music by John Kander; lyrics by Fred Ebb; conceived by Scott Ellis, Susan Stroman and David Thompson. Opened March 18, 1991. (Closed March 8, 1992)

*Song of Singapore (430). Musical with book by Allan Katz, Erik Frandsen, Michael Garin, Robert Hipkens and Paula Lockheart; music and lyrics by Erik Frandsen, Michael Garin, Robert Hipkens and Paula Lockheart. Opened May 23, 1991.

Mump & Smoot in "Caged"... With Wog (11). Written and created by Michael Kennard and John Turner. Opened May 29, 1991. (Closed June 9, 1991)

The Haunted Host (101) and **Pouf Positive** (55). By Robert Patrick. Opened April 19, 1991. (Closed July 14, 1991) *Safe Sex* replaced *Pouf Positive* on this bill for the final 46 performances of the run.

Pageant (462). Musical with book and lyrics by Bill Russell and Frank Kelly; music by Albert Evans. Opened May 2, 1991. (Closed June 7, 1992)

The Subject Was Roses (62). By Frank D. Gilroy. Opened May 15, 1991. (Closed July 7, 1991)

States of Shock (19). By Sam Shepard. Opened May 16, 1991. (Closed June 2, 1991)

Breaking Legs (401). By Tom Dulack. Opened May 19, 1991. (Closed May 10, 1992)

New York Shakespeare Festival Public Theater. The Way of the World (16). By William Congreve. Opened May 21, 1991. (Closed June 2, 1991) **Casanova** (8). By Constance Congden. Opened May 28, 1991. (Closed June 2, 1991)

The Good Times Are Killing Me (207). By Lynda Barry. Opened May 21, 1991. (Closed June 30, 1991) Reopened in this production, co-produced by David Mirvish at the Minetta Lane Theater, August 8, 1991. (Closed November 24, 1991)

PLAYS PRODUCED JUNE 1, 1991—MAY 31, 1992

Mambo Mouth (77). Return engagement of one-man performance by John Leguizamo; written by John Leguizamo. Produced by Island Visual Arts, Mark Groubert and Ellen M. Krass at the Orpheum Theater. Opened June 5, 1991. (Closed August 25, 1991)

Directed by Peter Askin; scenery, Philipp Jung; lighting, Natasha Katz; sound, Bruce Ellman; musical supervisor, Jellybean Benitez; silhouette, Theresa Tetley; executive producer, Elizabeth Heller; associate producers, Michael Scott Bregman, David Klingman; production stage manager, Joseph A. Onorato; press, Cromarty & Company, Peter Cromarty, David Lotz, David P. Katz.

Subtitled A Savage Comedy, a portrayal by John Leguizamo of Latino street personalities named Agamemnon, Angel Garcia, Loco Louie, Pepe, Manny the Fanny, Inca God and Crossover King. The play was performed without intermission. Previously produced off Broadway by American Place Theater 11/8/90 for 114 performances.

Safe Sex (46). Revival of the play by Harvey Fierstein. Produced by Lawrence Lane at Actors' Playhouse. Opened June 7, 1991 on the continuing program with *The Haunted Host*. (Closed July 14, 1991)

Mead. . . . . Jason Workman
Ghee. . . . . Harvey Fierstein

Directed by Eric Concklin; production stage manager, Joe McGuire; press, Shirley Herz Associates, Sam Rudy.

Safe Sex was produced on Broadway 4/5/87 for 9 performances and has been "reconceived" by its author in this version.

Lincoln Center Theater. 1990-91 season concluded with **Mr. Gogol and Mr. Preen** (55). By Elaine May. Produced by Lincoln Center Theater, Gregory Mosher director, Bernard Gersten executive producer, at the Mitzi E. Newhouse Theater. Opened June 9, 1991. (Closed July 28, 1991)

Mr. Gogol . . . . Mike Nussbaum   The Woman. . . . . Zohra Lampert
Mr. Preen . . . . William H. Macy

Directed by Gregory Mosher; scenery, John Lee Beatty; costumes, Jane Greenwood; lighting, Kevin Rigdon; sound, Serge Ossorguine; press, Merle Debuskey, Susan Chicoine.

Untidy, reclusive intellectual meets fastidious and pushy vacuum cleaner salesman. The play was presented in two parts.

Bergman on Stage. Schedule of three revivals in the Swedish language. **Miss Julie** (3). By August Strindberg. Opened June 10, 1991. (Closed June 12, 1991) **Long Day's Journey Into Night** (3). By Eugene O'Neill; Swedish translation by Sven Barthel. Opened June 14, 1991. (Closed June 16, 1991) **A Doll's House** (3). By Henrik Ibsen; Swedish translation by Klas Ostergren. Opened June 18, 1991. (Closed June 20, 1991) Produced in the Royal Dramatic Theater of Sweden production, Lars Lofgren artistic director, by the Brooklyn Academy of Music, Harvey Lichtenstein president and executive producer, in association with the New York International Festival of the Arts at the Majestic Theater.

ALL PLAYS: Directed by Ingmar Bergman; scenery and costumes, Gunilla Palmstierna-Weiss; press, Peter Carzasty.

MISS JULIE

Miss Julie . . . . Lena Olin	Kristin . . . . Gerthi Kulle
Jean . . . . Peter Stormare	

With Marie Richardson, Kicki Bramberg, Ingrid Bostrom, Per Mattson, Bjorn Granath, Jakob Eklund.

The last major revival of *Miss Julie* took place off Broadway at the Roundabout 9/22/81 for 196 performances. The play was presented without intermission.

LONG DAY'S JOURNEY INTO NIGHT

James Tyrone . . . . Jarl Kulle	Edmund Tyrone . . . . Peter Stormare
Mary Cavan Tyrone . . . . . . Bibi Andersson	Cathleen . . . . Kicki Bramberg
Jamie Tyrone . . . . Thommy Berggren	

Scene 1: Morning. Scene 2: Later the same morning. Scene 3: Afternoon. Scene 4: Evening. Scene 5: Late night. The play was presented in two parts with the intermission following Scene 4.

The last major New York revival of *Long Day's Journey Into Night* took place on Broadway 4/28/86 for 54 performances.

A DOLL'S HOUSE

Torvald Helmer . . . . Per Mattson	Mrs. Linde . . . . Marie Richardson
Nora . . . . Pernilla Ostergren	Krogstad . . . . Bjorn Granath
Dr. Rank . . . . Erland Josephson	Hilde . . . . Erika Harrysson

Act I: In the home of Torvald Helmer, Christmas Eve. Act II: The dining room, Christmas Day. Act III: The dining room, the day after Christmas. The play was presented in two parts with the intermission following Act II.

The last major New York revival of *A Doll's House* was on Broadway by New York Shakespeare Festival at Lincoln Center 3/5/75 for 56 performances.

Selling Off (13). By Harris W. Freedman. Produced by Takka Productions Ltd. at the John Houseman Theater. Opened June 13, 1991. (Closed June 23, 1991)

Leon Berkowitz . . . . Andrew Bloch	Harvey Schnorr . . . . Robert Stattel
Sydney O'Leary . . . . Deborah Cresswell	Arnold Handler . . . . John C. Vennema
Maurice Hughes . . . . John Braden	Muriel Berkowitz . . . . Sofia Landon
Ethel Berkowitz . . . . Dody Goodman	Bernie Weiner . . . . Larry Block
Sally Lowell . . . . Janet Zarish	

Directed by Gene Feist; scenery, James Youmans; costumes, David C. Woolard; lighting, Donald Holder; sound, Scott Lehrer; production stage manager, David Hyslop; press, Jeffrey Richards Associates, David LeShay.

An accountant attempts to escape from his profession and start life anew. The play was presented in two parts.

State Theater of Lithuania. Schedule of two programs in the Lithuanian language. **Uncle Vanya** (16). Revival of the play by Anton Chekhov. Presented June 13-16 and June 25-30, 1991. **The Square** (17). By Eimuntas Nekrosius. Presented June 19-23 and July 2-7, 1991. Produced by the Joyce Theater Foundation, Inc. and Lincoln Center in association with the New York International Festival of the Arts at the Joyce Theater.

BOTH PLAYS: Directed by Eimuntas Nekrosius; simultaneous English translation by Arunas Ciuberkis; artistic diretor, Ruta Wiman; lighting adaptation, Michael Blanco; production stage manager, Birute-Ona Jaruseviciene.

UNCLE VANYA

Alexandr Serebryakov . . . . . Vlada Bagdonas	Ivan Voynitsky . . . . Vidas Petkevicius
Yelena Andreyevna . . . . Dalia Storyk	Mihail Astrov . . . . Kostas Smoriginas
Soyfa Alexandrovna . . . . . . Dalia Overaite	Ilya Telyegin . . . . Juozas Pocius
Marya Vassilyevna . . . . Elvyra Zebertaviciute	Marina . . . . Irena Tamosiunaite

Servants: Rimgaudas Karvelis, Jurate Aniulyte, Vytautas Raukinaitis.

Scenery and costumes, Nadiezda Gultiajeva; lighting, Romualdas Treinys, Gintautas Urba; music, Faustas Latenas.

The last major New York revival of *Uncle Vanya* was by Circle in the Square on Broadway 6/4/73 for 64 performances.

THE SQUARE

He. . . . . Kostas Smoriginas	Doctor; Announcer; Prison	
She . . . . Dalia Overaite	Guard . . . . Remigijus Vilkaitis	
	Prisoner . . . . Gerardas Zalenas	

Scenery and costumes, Adomas Jacovskis; lighting, Gintautas Urba.

Abuse of a prisoner in the Communist political system.

Forbidden Broadway 1991½ (237). New edition of the musical revue with concept and parody lyrics by Gerard Alessandrini. Produced by Jonathan Scharer at Theater East. Opened June 20, 1991; see note. (Closed January 12, 1992)

Mary Denise Bentley	Herndon Lackey
Susanne Blakeslee	Jeff Lyons
Brad Ellis	

Understudies: Misses Bentley, Blakeslee—Leah Hocking; Messrs. Lyons, Lackey—Phillip George.

Directed by Gerard Alessandrini; costumes, Erika Dyson; wigs, Teresa Vuoso; musical direction, Brad Ellis; assistant director and dance captain, Phillip George; production consultant, Pete Blue; associate producer, Chip Quigley; production stage manager, Jerry James; press, Shirley Herz Associates, Glenna Freedman.

Ninth version of the revue taking off current New York stage attractions. The show was presented in two parts.

Music and lyrics for the songs "Forbidden Broadway 1991½," "Who Do They Know?" and "The Phantom of the Musical" by Gerard Alessandrini.

Note: The final weeks of this show's run consisted of a special edition entitled *Forbidden Christmas* for 56 performances November 19, 1991 to January 5, 1992 written, designed and staged by the same persons as in the previous run, with a cast comprising Susanne Blakeslee, Brad Ellis, Leah Hocking, Herndon Lackey and Michael McGrath.

New York Shakespeare Festival Shakespeare Marathon. Schedule of two revivals of plays by William Shakespeare (see note). **Othello** (21). Opened June 21, 1991 (see note). (Closed July 14, 1991) Produced by New York Shakespeare Festival, Joseph Papp producer, in association with New York Telephone and with the cooperation of the City of New York, David N. Dinkins mayor, Mary Schmidt Campbell commissioner of cultural affairs, Betsy Gotbaum commissioner of parks & recreation, at the Delacorte Theater in Central Park.

Also **Pericles, Prince of Tyre** (56). Opened November 5, 1991 (see note). (Closed December 22, 1991) Produced by New York Shakespeare Festival, Joseph Papp producer, JoAnne Akalaitis artistic director, Jason Steven Cohen managing director, Rosemarie Tichler associate artistic director, at the Public Theater (see note).

OTHELLO

Roderigo . . . . Jake Weber	Desdemona. . . . . Kathryn Meisle
Iago . . . . Christopher Walken	Montano . . . . Christopher McHale
Brabantio . . . . George Morfogen	1st Gentleman . . . . Jed Diamond
Othello. . . . . Raul Julia	2d Gentleman . . . . Robert Jimenez
Cassio . . . . Michel R. Gill	3d Gentleman . . . . Jeffrey Wright
Duke of Venice . . . . Frank Raiter	Emilia . . . . Mary Beth Hurt
Gratiano . . . . Daniel Oreskes	Bianca . . . . Miriam Healy-Louie
Senator of Venice . . . . Bruce Katzman	Lodovico. . . . . Tom Hewitt
Messenger; Herald. . . . . . . Michael Gaston	

Senators: David Borror, Eddie Bowz, Torben Brooks, Jed Diamond, Robert Jimenez, Jeffrey Wright.

Soldiers and Cypriots: David Borror, Eddie Bowz, Torben Brooks, Josh Fardon, Eric LaRay Harvey, Richard Holmes, Nancy Hower, Nina Humphrey, Royal Miller, Adam Trese.

ONE-PERFORMER SHOWS—*Left*, Julie Halston as herself in her *Lifetime of Comedy*; above, Stan Freeman as Oscar Levant in *At Wit's End*

Understudies: Mr. Julia—Geoffrey Owens; Mr. Walken—Daniel Oreskes; Mr. Raiter—Jed Diamond; Mr. Hewitt—Royal Miller; Mr. Weber—Richard Holmes; Mr. McHale—Michael Gaston; Miss Meisle—Nancy Hower; Misses Hurt, Healy-Louie—Nina Humphrey; Mr. Oreskes—Torben Brooks; Mr. Katzman—David Borror; Messrs. Gaston, Diamond—Eric LaRay Harvey; Mr. Jimenez—Josh Fardon; Mr. Wright—Adam Trese; Mr. Gill—Eddie Bowz; Mr. Morfogen—Bruce Katzman.

Directed by Joe Dowling; scenery, Frank Conway; costumes, Jane Greenwood; lighting, Richard Nelson; fight staging, David Leong; music, Peter Golub; associate producer, Jason Steven Cohen; production stage manager, Karen Armstrong; stage manager, Buzz Cohen; press, Richard Kornberg, Barbara Carroll, Carol Fineman.

The play was presented in two parts. The last major New York revival of *Othello* took place on Broadway 2/3/82 for 123 performances.

PERICLES, PRINCE OF TYRE

Chorus:
John Gower . . . . Don R. McManus
Antioch:
  Antiochus . . . . Byron Jennings
  Pericles. . . . . Campbell Scott
  Daughter of Antiochus . . . . Martha Plimpton
  Thaliard. . . . . Joseph Haj
  Messenger . . . . Arnold Molina
Tyre:
  Helicanus. . . . . Paul Butler
  Escanes. . . . . MacIntyre Dixon

Lords . . . . Dan Moran, Larry Block
Tarsus:
  Cleon . . . . Steve Mellor
  Dionyza. . . . . Saundra McLain
  Lord . . . . MacIntyre Dixon
Pentapolis:
  Fishermen . . . Larry Block, MacIntyre Dixon,
                            Robert Beatty Jr.
  Simonides . . . . Byron Jennings
  Thaisa. . . . . Cordelia Gonzalez
  Lords. . . . . Joseph Haj, Arnold Molina

Knights . . . . Dan Moran	Pirates . . . . Joseph Haj
Lychorida . . . . Bobo Lewis	Mytilene:
Ephesus:	Pandar . . . . Larry Block
Sailors . . . . Dan Moran, Joseph Haj	Bawd . . . . Bobo Lewis
Cerimon . . . . Larry Block	Boult . . . . Arnold Molina
Philemon . . . . Don R. McManus	Lysimachus . . . . Byron Jennings
Gentlemen . . . . MacIntyre Dixon,	Tyrian Sailor . . . . Dan Moran
Robert Beatty Jr.	Lord of Mytilene . . . . . . MacIntyre Dixon
Tarsus:	Tyrian Gentlemen . . . . Joseph Haj,
Marina . . . . Martha Plimpton	Robert Beatty Jr.
Leonine . . . . Dan Moran	Diana . . . . Don R. McManus

Musicians: Christine Gummere violoncello, recorder; Will Parker, French horn, guitar; Steve Silverstein woodwinds.

Directed by Michael Greif; scenery, John Arnone; costumes, Gabriel Berry; lighting, Frances Aronson; original music and musical direction, Jill Jaffe; sound, Mark Bennett; choreography, Kenneth Tosti; dramaturge, Barry Edelstein; film, Jonathan Rosenberg, Ed Fabry; production stage manager, Michele Steckler; stage manager, Lisa Buxbaum.

The last major New York revival of *Pericles, Prince of Tyre* was by the Acting Company off Broadway 4/19/83 for 8 performances. The play was presented in two parts.

Note: Press date for *Othello* was 6/27/91, for *Pericles, Prince of Tyre* was 11/24/91.

Note: In the Public Theater there are many auditoria. *Pericles, Prince of Tyre* played the Estelle R. Newman Theater.

Note: New York Shakespeare Festival's Shakespeare Marathon is scheduled to continue through following seasons until all of Shakespeare's plays have been presented. *A Midsummer Night's Dream, Julius Caesar* and *Romeo and Juliet* were produced in the 1987-88 season; *Much Ado About Nothing, King John, Coriolanus, Love's Labour's Lost, The Winter's Tale* and *Cymbeline* were produced in the 1988-89 season; *Twelfth Night, Titus Andronicus, Macbeth* and *Hamlet* were produced in the 1989-90 season, and *The Taming of the Shrew, Richard III* and *Henry IV, Part 1* and *Part 2* were produced in the 1990-91 season (see their entries in *Best Plays* volumes of appropriate years).

Red Scare on Sunset (101). Transfer from off off Broadway of the play by Charles Busch. Produced by Theater in Limbo (Manny Kladitis, Drew Bennett and Shaun Huttar) in the WPA theater production, Kyle Renick artistic director, at the Lucille Lortel Theater. Opened June 21, 1991. (Closed September 15, 1991)

Ralph Barnes; Sales Girl; R.G.	Mary Dale . . . . Charles Busch
Benson; Granny Lou . . . . . Mark Hamilton	Malcolm; Old Lady . . . . Andy Halliday
Harold; Bertram Barker . . . . . Roy Cockrum	Marta Towers . . . . Judith Hansen
Pat Pilford . . . . Julie Halston	Mitchell Drake . . . . Ralph Buckley
Frank Taggart . . . . Arnie Kolodner	

Understudies: Messrs. Cockrum, Halliday, Hamilton—Tom Aulino; Messrs. Buckley, Kolodner—Richard Cuneo

Directed by Kenneth Elliott; scenery, B.T. Whitehill; costumes, Debra Tennenbaum; lighting, Vivien Leone; sound, Aural Fixation; wigs, Elizabeth Katherine Carr; associate producers, Michael Cohen, Bill Repicci, Lyle Saunders; production stage manager, T.L. Boston; press, Shirley Herz Associates, Sam Rudy.

Time: 1951. Place: Hollywood, Calif. The play was presented in two parts.

Movie star obsessed with the idea that everyone she knows is a communist. Previously produced off off Broadway 3/19/91 in this production by WPA Theater.

Circle Repertory Company. 1990-91 season concluded with **The Balcony Scene** (33). By Wil Calhoun. Produced by Circle Repertory Company, Tanya Berezin artistic director, Terrence Dwyer managing director, at Circle Repertory Theater. Opened June 23, 1991. (Closed July 28, 1991)

Paul . . . . William Fichtner	Alvin . . . . Jonathan Hogan
Karen . . . . Cynthia Nixon	

Directed by Michael Warren Powell; scenery, Kevin Joseph Roach; costumes, Thomas L. Keller; lighting, Dennis Parichy; sound, Chuck London, Stewart Werner; fight director, Rick Sordelet; production stage manager, Fred Reinglas; press, Gary Murphy.

Romantic comedy, lonely neighbors meet on their adjoining high-rise balconies. The play was presented without intermission.

*Manhattan Theater Club. 1990-91 season concluded with ***Lips Together, Teeth Apart** (388). By Terrence McNally. Produced by Manhattan Theater Club, Lynne Meadow artistic director, Barry Grove managing director, at City Center Stage I. Opened June 25, 1991.

Chloe Haddock	Christine Baranski	John Haddock	Anthony Heald
Sam Truman	Nathan Lane	Sally Truman	Swoosie Kurtz

Directed by John Tillinger; scenery, John Lee Beatty; costumes, Jane Greenwood; lighting, Ken Billington; sound, Stewart Werner; fight staging, Jerry Mitchell; artistic associate, Michael Bush; stage manager, Craig Palanker; production stage manager, Pamela Singer; press, Helene Davis, Stephen Hancock.

Time: The present, a Fourth of July weekend. Place: A summer beach house. The play was presented in three parts.

Two married couples review their lives within the framework of a weekend at a beach frequented mostly by the gay community.

Deborah Rush replaced Christine Baranski 7/16/91. Roxanne Hart replaced Swoosie Kurtz 7/20/91. Jonathan Hadary replaced Nathan Lane 9/7/91. Hillary Bailey-Smith replaced Deborah Rush 10/8/91. Lee Brock replaced Roxanne Hart 2/7/92. Christine Baranski replaced Deborah Rush, Joanne Camp replaced Lee Brock and Brian Kerwin replaced Jonathan Hadary 2/18/92.

A Best Play; see page 77.

Prom Queens Unchained (57). Musical with book by Stephen Witkin; music by Keith Herrmann; lyrics by Larry Goodsight; conceived by Larry Goodsight and Keith Herrmann. Produced by PQU Productions Inc. at the Village Gate. Opened June 30, 1991. (Closed August 18, 1991)

Mr. Kelty; Roy Mackelroy.	Don Crosby	Brenda Carbello	Ilene Bergelson
Mr. Sloan; Mr. McIssac; Mr. Cornelius;		Richie Pomerantz.	Mark Traxler
Miss Carlson; Mr. Turk	Ron Kurowski	Violet O'Grady	Becky Adams
Grant Cassidy	James Heatherly	Myron "Hicky" Greenberg . . .	Gary Mendelson
Cindy Mackelroy	Dana Ertischek	Sherry Van Heusen	Connie Ogden
Louise Blaine.	Sandra Purpuro	Mr. Pike; Mario Lanza	David Brummel
Carla Zlotz	Susan Levine	Venulia	Natasha Baron
Frank "Switch" Dorsey	David Phillips	Mrs. Glick; Bunny	
Eddy "Wheels" Stevenson;		Mackelroy	Pamela Lloyd
Minka Lasky.	Mark Edgar Stephens		

Musicians: Stuart Malina conductor, keyboard; Steve Bargonetti guitar; Steve Mack bass; Bart McLaughlin drums; Scott Schacter saxophone, flute.

Understudies: Misses Ogden, Ertischek—Becky Adams; Misses Levine, Baron—Ilene Bergelson; Messrs. Traxler, Stephens—Gary Mendelson; Mr. Heatherly—Mark Edgar Stephens; Messrs. Crosby, Brummel, Kurowski—Chuck Muckle; Misses Lloyd, Bergelson—Judy Kaplan; Misses Purpuro, Adams—Trish Santini; Messrs. Phillips, Mendelson—Michael McElroy.

Directed and choreographed by Karen Azenberg; musical direction, Stuart Malina; scenery, Bob Phillips; costumes, Robert Strong Miller; lighting, Nancy Collings; sound, Richard Dunning; vocal and dance arrangements, Stuart Malina, Keith Herrmann; associate producer, Ric Kirby; production stage manager, Susan Whelan; stage manager, Denise Laffer; press, Cromarty & Company, David Lotz.

Time: Spring 1959. Act I, Scene 1: Various classrooms, Robert Underwood High School. Scene 2: A hallway. Scene 3: Vice-principal's office. Scene 4: The gymnateria. Scene 5: The Malt Shoppe. Act II, Scene 1: The Mackelroy home. Scene 2: The street. Scene 3: The Mackelroy home, Carla's home, Mr. Sloan's office, a parking lot. Scene 4: The prom.

A contest for queen of a 1950s high school prom.

ACT I

Overture. . . . . Band
"Down the Hall" . . . . Kelty, Company
"That Special Night" . . . . Students
"Dustbane: The Ballad of Minka" . . . . Kelty, Richie, Grant, Switch, Wheels, Hicky
"Eat the Lunch" . . . . Company
"Most Likely" . . . . Richie, Cindy, Glee Club
"The Venulia"/"Seeing Red". . . . . Venulia, Switch, Students
"That Special Night" (reprise) . . . . Company

ACT II

"The Perfect Family". . . . . Company
"Corsage". . . . . Bunny, Cindy, Grant, Hicky, Wheels.
"Seeing Red" (reprise) . . . . Switch
"Squeeze Me in the Rain" . . . . Carla, Minka, Cindy, Sloan, Bunny, Richie
"Going All the Way". . . . . Cindy, Carla, Sherry, Louise
"Sherry's Theme" . . . . Company
"Give Your Love" . . . . Company

New York Shakespeare Festival. Co-sponsorship of two Festival Latino (Oscar Ciccone and Cecilia Vega directors) offerings of revivals of plays by William Shakespeare. **A Midsummer Night's Dream** (12). Translated and adapted by Caca Rosset; the Teatro do Ornitorrinco of Brazil production in the Portuguese language. Opened July 30, 1991 (see note). (Closed August 11, 1991) **The Tempest** (12). Adapted by Ugo Ulive; the Fundacion Rajatabla of Venezuela production in the Spanish language. Opened August 27, 1991 (see note). (Closed September 8, 1991) Produced by New York Shakespeare Festival, Joseph Papp producer, in association with New York Telephone and with the cooperation of the City of New York, David N. Dinkins mayor, Mary Schmidt Campbell commissioner of cultural affairs, Betsy Gotbaum commissioner of parks & recreation, at the Delacorte Theater in Central Park.

A MIDSUMMER NIGHT'S DREAM

Theseus; Oberon	Jose Rubens Chacha	Helena	Carolina N. Riberiro
Hippolyta; Titania	Christiane Tricerri	Nick Bottom; Pyramus	Caca Rosset
Hermia.	Elaine Garcia	Francis Flute; Thisby.	Ary Franca
Lysander	Rubens Caribe	Puck	Augusto Pompeo
Demetrius.	Richard Homuth		

Directed by Caca Rosset; scenery and costumes, Jose De Anchieta Costa; lighting, Peter Kaczorowski; musical direction, Duca Franca; choreography, Val Folly; associate producer, Jason Steven Cohen; press, Richard Kornberg, Barbara Carroll, Carol Fineman.

Infused with music, and circus performance, this *A Midsummer Night's Dream* (Sonho de Uma Noite de Verao) was put on by the Brazilian troupe founded in 1977 by Caca Rosset, Maria Alice Verguerio and Luiz Robert Galizia, which visited New York in the summer of 1991 with a musical version of Moliere's *The Imaginary Invalid*. The last major New York revival of this Shakespeare play took place at the Public Theater 1/12/88 for 81 performances, the opening production of the Shakespeare Marathon.

THE TEMPEST

Ariel	Erich Wildpret	Adrian	Ramon Goliz
Prospero	Jose Tejera	Black Spirit	William Cuao
Miranda	Nathalia Martinez	Trinculo	Cosme Cortazar
Caliban.	Daniel Lopez	Estefano	Anibal Grunn
Fernando	Jesus Araujo	Old Spirits; Sailors	Ricardo Martinez,
Captain; Old Spirit	Rodolfo Villafranca		Hector Becerra
Boatswain; Spirit	Norman Santana	Young Spirits; Sailors	Ismael Monagas,
Alonso.	German Mendieta		Gregorio Milano
Antonio.	Francisco Alfaro	Goddesses; Nymphs.	Ivezku Celis
Gonzalo.	Hugo Marquez	Sailor	Alejandro Faillace
Sebastian	Aitor Gaviria		

Directed by Carlos Gimenez; scenery, Marcelo Pont-Verges, Augusto Gonzalez; costumes, Hugo Marquez, Marcelo Pont-Verges, Augusto Gonzalez; lighting, Trevor Brown, Carlos Gimenez; original music, Juan Carlos Nunez; sound, Eduardo Bolivar; artistic production, Jorge Borges, Andres Vazquez, Gabriel Flores; executive producer, William Lopez; associate producer, Jason Steven Cohen.

This version of *The Tempest* (La Tempestad) was put on by the Venezuelan troupe, founded by Carlos Gimenez, which visited New York in 1989 with *El Coronel No Tiene Quien le Escriba* (No One Writes to the Colonel) adapted from a Gabriel Garcia Marquez story. The last major New York revival of this Shakespeare play was by New York Shakespeare Festival at the Delacorte 6/26/81 for 24 performances.

Note: Press date for *A Midsummer Night's Dream* was 8/1/91, for *The Tempest* was 8/29/91.

Penn & Teller Rot in Hell (203). Magic show by and with Penn Jillette and Teller. Produced by Richard Frankel, Thomas Viertel, Steven Baruch, Tim Jenison and Paul Montgomery at the John Houseman Theater. Opened July 30, 1991. (Closed January 19, 1992)

Special Guest—Carol Perkins. Standby—Denise Krueger.

Scenery, John Lee Beatty; costumes, Peter J. Fitzgerald; lighting, Dennis Parichy; sound, T. Richard Fitzgerald; director of covert activities, Robert P. Libbon; director of internal affairs, Ken "Krasher" Lewis; associate producer, Marc Routh; production stage manager, Cathy B. Blaser; stage manager, Peter Wolf; press, Chris Boneau, Jackie Green.

Act I: Casey at the Bat, A Card Trick, Liftoff to Love/Ripoff of Love, Fakir Tricks, Quotation of the Day, Houdini Tricks.

Act II: Mofo, the Psychic Gorilla; By Buddha This Duck Is Immortal!, Burnin' Luv, Shadows, King of Animal Traps.

Transfer of some of the material performed on Broadway in *Penn & Teller: The Refrigerator Tour* for 103 performances last season beginning 4/3/91, plus some other Penn & Teller routines. "Liftoff/Ripoff of Love" written by Gary Stockdale, Penn Jillette and Teller, performed by Gary Stockdale; "Burnin' Luv" music by Gary Stockdale; ambient music by Yma Sumac.

Roundabout Theater Company. 1990-91 season concluded with **The Matchmaker** (32). Revival of the play by Thornton Wilder. Produced by the Roundabout Theater Company, Todd Haimes producing director, Gene Feist founding director, at the Haft Theater (see note). Opened August 27, 1991. (Closed September 22, 1991)

Mrs. Dolly Levi. . . . . Dorothy Loudon	Malachi Stack. . . . . Jarlath Conroy
Horace Vandergelder . . . . Joseph Bova	Ambrose Kemper; August . . . Michael Hayden
Cornelius Hackl. . . . . Jim Fyfe	Joe Scanlon; Cabman . . . . . . Theodore Sorel
Barnaby Tucker . . . . Rob Kramer	Rudolph . . . . Jack Cirillo
Irene Malloy . . . . Lisa Emery	Miss Flora Van Huysen. . . . Eileen Letchworth
Minnie Fay . . . . Lisa Dove	Gertrude; Cook. . . . . Mary Diveny
Ermengarde . . . . Wendy Lawless	

Understudies: Misses Dove, Lawless—Christine Champion; Mr. Conroy—Jack Cirillo; Miss Loudon—Mary Diveny; Messrs. Fyfe, Kramer—Michael Hayden; Miss Emery—Wendy Lawless; Messrs. Hayden, Sorel, Cirillo—David Ruckman; Mr. Bova—Theodore Sorel.

Directed by Lonny Price; scenery, Russell Metheny; costumes, Gail Brassard; lighting, Stuart Duke; sound, Philip Campanella; music, Claibe Richardson; production stage manager, Roy W. Backes; press, Joshua Ellis, Susanne Tighe.

Time: Just after the turn of the century. Act I: Vandergelder's house in Yonkers, N.Y. Act II: Mrs. Molloy's hat shop, New York City. Act III: The Harmonia Gardens Restaurant on the Battery, New York City. Act IV: Miss Van Huysen's house, New York City. The play was presented in two parts with the intermission following Act II.

The Matchmaker was produced on Broadway 12/5/55 for 486 performances and was named a Best Play of its season. Its only previous major New York revival of record (except in the form of the musical *Hello, Dolly!* which was adapted from it) took place off Broadway in the 1958-59 season.

Note: The Roundabout Theater Company's 1991-92 season of revivals took place at the Criterion Center Stage Right, a Broadway theater; see its entry in the Plays Produced on Broadway section of this volume.

Unidentified Human Remains and the True Nature of Love (86). By Brad Fraser. Produced by Michael Frazier, Richard Norton and Ted Snowdon at the Orpheum Theater. Opened September 19, 1991. (Closed December 1, 1991)

Benita . . . . Kimberley Pistone	Kane . . . . Michael Connor
David . . . . Scott Renderer.	Jerri . . . . Michelle Kronin
Candy . . . . Lenore Zann	Robert . . . . Sam Rockwell
Bernie . . . . Clark Gregg	

Directed by Derek Goldby; scenery and costumes, Peter Hartwell; lighting, Kevin Rigdon; original music and sound, Richard Woodbury; associate producer, Valerie Gordon; production supervisor, Frank Scardino; production stage manager, George Boyd; stage manager, Jeffrey Goodman; press, Edward Callaghan, Judith Young.

Time: The present. Place: Edmonton, Alberta, various locations. The play was presented in two parts.

Graphic sexual activities disturbed by the presence of a serial killer. A foreign play previously produced in Canada and in regional theater in Chicago.

*Playwrights Horizons. Schedule of four programs. **The 1991 Young Playwrights Festival** (30). Program of four one-act plays: *Secrets to Square Dancing* by Denise Maher, *I'm Not Stupid* by David E. Rodriguez; *Donut World* by Matthew Peterson and *Man at His Best* by Carlota Zimmerman; presented in the Foundation of the Dramatists Guild production, Nancy Quinn producing director, Sheri M. Goldhirsch managing director. Opened September 24, 1991. (Closed October 20, 1991) ***Marvin's Room** (206). By Scott McPherson; produced in association with the Goodman Theater and Hartford Stage Company. Opened December 5, 1991. **The End of the Day** (64). By Jon Robin Baitz. Opened April 7, 1992. (Closed May 24, 1992) And *Flaubert's Latest* by Peter Parnell scheduled to open June 21, 1992. Produced by Playwrights Horizons, Andre Bishop outgoing artistic director, Don Scardino artistic director, Paul S. Daniels executive director, at Playwrights Horizons.

THE 1991 YOUNG PLAYWRIGHTS FESTIVAL

Secrets to Square Dancing

Karl . . . . Louis Falk	Bruce . . . . Steve Hofvendahl
Veronica . . . . Anne Lange	Rhoda . . . . Olga Merediz
Mr. Pondence . . . . Ethan Phillips	Janet . . . . S. Epatha Merkerson
Mr. Lewis . . . . Peter Francis James	Brad . . . . Paul Bates
Gladys . . . . Mary Testa	

Directed by Gloria Muzio; dramaturge, Victoria Abrash; stage manager, Liz Small. Bureaucrats make a test case out of an 8th grader.

I'm Not Stupid

Roger . . . . Curtis McClarin	Margret Fletcher . . . . . . S. Epatha Merkerson
Dr. Green . . . . Peter Francis James	

Directed by Seret Scott; dramaturge, Paul Selig; stage manager, Liz Small. Mother and disabled son grapple with shattered lives and with a doctor who attempts to intervene.

Donut World

Bud . . . . Paul Bates	Lester . . . . Steve Hofvendahl
Sparky . . . . Ethan Phillips	Mavis . . . . Olga Merediz

Directed by Michael Mayer; dramaturge, Paul Selig; stage manager, Roy Harris. A man's preoccupation with matters of limited scope.

Man at His Best

Dean . . . . Seth Gilliam	Skyler . . . . James G. Macdonald

Directed by Mark Brokaw; fights, Rick Sordelet; dramaturge, Morgan Jenness; stage manager, Roy Harris. Sexual games leading inevitably to death.

ALL PLAYS: Scenery, Allen Moyer; costumes; Elsa Ward; lighting, Pat Dignan; sound, Janet Kalas; production manager, David A. Milligan; press, the Fred Nathan Company, Mark Thibodeau.

These four plays by young authors (Denise Maher 17, David E. Rodriguez 18, Matthew Peterson 17 and Carlota Zimmerman 17, at the time of submission) were selected from hundreds of entries in the Foundation of the Dramatists Guild's 10th annual playwriting contest for young people. The program was presented in two parts with the intermission following *I'm Not Stupid.*

MARVIN'S ROOM

Bessie	Laura Esterman	Dr. Charlotte; Retirement Home	
Dr. Wally	Tim Monsion	Director	Shona Tucker
Ruth	Alice Drummond	Hank	Mark Rosenthal
Bob	Tom Aulino	Charlie	Karl Maschek
Lee	Lisa Emery	Marvin	Adam Chapnick

Directed by David Petrarca; scenery, Linda Buchanan; costumes, Claudia Boddy; lighting, Robert Christen; music composition and sound design, Rob Milburn; production stage manager, David A. Milligan; stage manager, Jane Seiler.

Time: The present. Place: Various locations in Florida and a mental institution in Ohio. The play was presented in two parts.

Black comedy of the human struggle against disability and illness. Previously produced in regional theater at Victory Gardens and the Goodman Theater, Chicago and the Hartford, Conn. Stage Company.

A Best Play; see page 137.

THE END OF THE DAY

Graydon Massey	Roger Rees	Rosamund Brackett; Jocelyn	
Hilly Lasker; Swifty	Paul Sparer	Massey	Nancy Marchand
Jonathan Toffler; Young		Helen Lasker-Massey; Lady Hammersmith;	
Graydon	John Benjamin Hickey	Urbaine Supton Stoat	Jean Smart
Jeremiah Marton; Tellman	Philip Kerr		

Directed by Mark Lamos; scenery, John Arnone; costumes, Jess Goldstein; lighting, Pat Collins; sound, David Budries; production stage manager, M.A. Howard; stage manager, Thom Widmann.

Prologue: Malibu, 1986. Act I: San Cristobal Clinic, San Pedro, Calif., 1992. Act II: A town house on Belgrave Square, London, the next day; and San Christobal Clinic, the following day.

An English psychiatrist's disillusionment with modern life and values in two acts, the first in America and the second in England.

*American Place Theater. Schedule of two programs. **The Radiant City** (22). By Theodora Skipitares. Opened October 6, 1991. (Closed October 27, 1991) ***Zora Neale Hurston** (30). Return engagement of the play by Laurence Holder. Opened April 29, 1992. Produced by American Place Theater, Wynn Handman director, Dara Hershman general manager (*The Radiant City* in association with Skysaver Productions, Inc.) at American Place Theater.

THE RADIANT CITY

CAST: William Badgett, Charles W. Croft, Edward Greenberg, Cora Hook, John Jowett, Lisa Kirchner, Michael Preston, Jane Catherine Shaw, Christopher Thall.

Directed and designed by Theodora Skipitares; music, Christopher Thall; lyrics, Andrea Balis; lighting, F. Mitchell Dana; sound, David Wonsey; kinetics, Raymond Kurshals; technical design, Nir Lilach; dramaturge, Cynthia Jenner; production stage manager, Lloyd Davis Jr.; press, David Rothenberg.

Multimedia (slides, film clips, oratory, puppets, sculpture, live actors, etc.) based on the career of city-builder Robert Moses. The play was presented in two parts.

ZORA NEALE HURSTON

Zora Neale Hurston	Elizabeth Van Dyke
Herbert Sheen; Langston Hughes; Alain Locke; Richard Wright	Joseph Edwards

Directed by Wynn Handman; lighting, Shirley Prendergast.

Time: Christmas Eve, 1949. Place: A bus station, New York City. The play was presented without intermission.

Return engagement of the theater biography of "The Queen of the Harlem Renaissance," an important literary figure of the 1920s and 1930s, previously produced by American Place Theater 2/4/90 for 32 performances.

Circle Repertory Company. Schedule of four programs. **Babylon Gardens** (32). By Timothy Mason. Opened October 8, 1991. (Closed November 3, 1991) **The Rose Quartet** (16). By Thomas Cumella. Opened December 17, 1991. (Closed December 29, 1991) **The Baltimore Waltz** (39). By Paula Vogel; produced in association with AT&T: OnStage and the Alley Theater. Opened February 11, 1992. (Closed March 15, 1992) **Empty Hearts** (48). By John Bishop. Opened May 5, 1992. (Closed June 14, 1992) Produced by Circle Repertory Company, Tanya Berezin artistic director, Terrence Dwyer managing director, at Circle Repertory.

BABYLON GARDENS

Bill	Timothy Hutton	Jessica	Lea Floden
Molly	Bobo Lewis	Larry	Bruce McCarty
Jean	Mary-Louise Parker	Robin	Cordelia Richards
Opal	Cynthia Martells	Philippe	Robert Jimenez
Andrew	Steve Bassett	Hector	Hector M. Estrada

Directed by Joe Mantello; scenery, Loy Arcenas; costumes, Toni-Leslie James; lighting, Dennis Parichy, Michael J. Baldassari; sound, Scott Lehrer; production manager, Jody Boese; production stage manager, Denise Yaney; press, Bill Evans & Associates, Jim Randolph, Erin Dunn.

Time: The present. Place: New York City. The play was presented in two parts.

Young couples striving to adjust to a troubled and depressing city environment.

Tanya Berezin replaced Bobo Lewis 10/29/91.

THE ROSE QUARTET

Rose Brill	Joan Copeland	Jack Singer	Larry Keith
Helen Brauer	Ruby Holbrook	Lou Gold	Mason Adams

Directed by Tee Scatuorchio; scenery, Loren Sherman; costumes, Thomas L. Keller; lighting, Dennis Parichy; sound, Stewart Werner, Chuck London; production stage manager, Lori M. Doyle.

Time: Near present. Place: New York City, the Upper West Side. The play was presented in two parts.

Romantic comedy of urban life, two widows attempting to snare two bachelors.

Ruby Holbrook replaced Anne Pitoniak prior to the opening, owing to the latter's illness.

THE BALTIMORE WALTZ

Anna	Cherry Jones	Third Man	Joe Mantello
Carl	Richard Thompson		

Directed by Anne Bogart; scenery, Loy Arcenas; costumes, Walter Hicklin; lighting, Dennis Parichy; sound and score, John Gromada; production stage manager, Denise Yaney.

Time: The present. Place: Baltimore, Md. The play was presented without intermission.

A sister provides her brother, dying of AIDS, with imaginative distractions.

EMPTY HEARTS

Michael Shartel	Cotter Smith	Jan Horvath; Deidre	
Carol Shartel	Mel Harris	McCullough	Susan Bruce
Bob Hutchins; John Whalen	Edward Seamon	Mrs. Cambridge; Sara Kohler;	
Dave Ennis; Hank Sweetzer	John Dossett	Judge Ruth Denhardt; Minister;	
Tom Kyle; Earl Tracey;		Mrs. Shartel	Claris Erickson
Dr. Maxwell	Joel Anderson		

Directed by John Bishop; scenery, John Lee Beatty; costumes, Ann Roth, Bridget Kelly; lighting, Dennis Parichy; sound, Stewart Werner, Chuck London; concert sequence staging, Marcia Milgrom Dodge; incidental music, Robert Waldman; production stage manager, Leslie Loeb.

A murder case, husband is suspected of killing his wife. The play was presented in two parts.

A SEASON AT CIRCLE REP—
Above left, Joe Mantello, Richard Thompson and Cherry Jones in Paula Vogel's *The Baltimore Waltz*; *above right*, Claris Erickson (*background*) and Cotter Smith in John Bishop's *Empty Hearts*; *left*, Timothy Hutton and Mary-Louise Parker in Timothy Mason's *Babylon Gardens*; *below*, Mason Adams and Anne Pitoniak in Thomas Cumella's *The Rose Quartet*

At Wit's End (27). One-man musical play with Stan Freeman; by Joel Kimmel; based on *A Smattering of Ignorance, The Unimportance of Being Oscar* and *Memoirs of an Amnesiac* by Oscar Levant. Produced by Lawrence Kasha and Ronald A. Lachman in association with Warner/Chappell Music Group at Michael's Pub. Opened October 8, 1991. (Closed November 2, 1991)

Directed by Barbara Karp; lighting, Andrew Taines; scenic consultant, Alan Kimmel; associate producer, Richard T. Hart; production stage manager, Bob Thurber; press, Terry M. Lilly, David J. Gersten.

Stan Freeman portraying Oscar Levant, with piano and material based on Levant's three autobiographies. The play was presented in two parts. Previously presented in an extensive tour.

MUSICAL NUMBERS: "Rhapsody in Blue," "Second Rhapsody," "Prelude I, II and III," "An American in Paris," "Concerto in F" by George Gershwin; "Swanee" by George Gershwin and Irving Caesar; "Somebody Loves Me" by George Gershwin, B.G. DeSylva and Ballard McDonald; "Lady Play Your Mandolin" by Oscar Levant and Irving Caesar; "True Blue Lou" by Whiting, Spier & Coslow; "That Old Feeling" by Sammy Fain and Lew Brown; "Wacky Dust" by Oscar Levant and Stanley Adams; "Blame It on My Youth" by Oscar Levant and Edward Heyman; "That's Entertainment" by Howard Dietz and Arthur Schwartz.

*Beau Jest (269). By James Sherman. Produced by Arthur Cantor, Carol Ostrow and Libby Adler Mages at the Lamb's Theater. Opened October 10, 1991.

Sarah Goldman	Laura Patinkin	Joel	Larry Fleischman
Chris	John Michael Higgins	Miriam	Roslyn Alexander
Bob	Tom Hewitt	Abe	Bernie Landis

Directed by Dennis Zacek; scenery, Bruce Goodrich; costumes, Dorothy Jones; lighting, Edward R. F. Matthews; production stage manager, Jana Llynn; press, Arthur Cantor Associates.

Comedy, Jewish girl hires an actor to play what her parents would consider the ideal suitor. The play was presented in three parts. Previously produced by Victory Gardens Theater, Chicago.

Return to the Forbidden Planet (245). Musical written by Bob Carlton; songs by various authors (see listing below). Produced by Andre Ptaszynski and Don Taffner at the Variety Arts Theater. Opened October 13, 1991. (Closed April 26, 1992)

Captain Tempest	Robert McCormick	Chorus	James Doohan
Dr. Prospero	Steve Steiner	The Infant Miranda	Rebecca Ptaszynski
Ariel	Gabriel Barre	Damage Control Crew:	
Cookie	Louis Tucci	Ens. Betty Will	Allison Briner
Science Officer	Julee Cruise	Petty Officer Axel Rhodes	Chuck Tempo
Bosun Arras	James H. Wiggins Jr.	Ens. Harry Saul Spray	David LaDuca
Navigation Officer	Mary Ehlinger	Ens. Dane G. Russ	Michael Rotondi
Miranda	Erin Hill		

Understudies: Misses Ehlinger, Cruise—Allison Briner; Miss Hill—Mary Ehlinger; Messrs. Barre, Wiggins, Tempo, Rotondi—David LaDuca; Mr. Steiner—Robert McCormick; Messrs. McCormick, LaDuca, Miss Briner—Michael Rotondi; Mr. Tucci—Chuck Tempo.

Directed by Bob Carlton; musical direction, Kate Edgar; scenery, Rodney Ford; costumes, Sally J. Lesser; lighting, Richard Nelson; sound, Bobby Aitken for Autograph; special film effects, Gerry Anderson; Ariel costume, Adrian Rees; production stage manager, Bonnie Panson; stage manager, Victor Lukas; press, Boneau/Bryan-Brown, John Barlow.

Time: the year 2024. Place: D'Illyria, the Forbidden Planet. The play was presented in two acts.

Shakespeare's *The Tempest* fancifully adapted to 21st century space travel, loosely based on the 1956 M-G-M movie *Forbidden Planet*. A foreign musical previously produced in London.

MUSICAL NUMBERS: "Born to Be Wild" by Mars Bonfire; "Don't Let Me Be Misunderstood" by Gloria Caldwell, Sol Marcus and Bennie Benjamin; "Gloria" by Van Morrison; "Go Now" by Larry Banks and Milton Bennett; "Good Golly Miss Molly" by Robert Blackwell and John Marascalco; "Good Vibrations" by Brian Wilson and Mike Love; "Great Balls of Fire" by Otis Blackwell and Jack Hammer; "I Can't Turn You Loose" by Otis Redding; "I Heard It Through the Grapevine" by Barrett Strong and

Norman Whitfield; "I'm Gonna Change the World" by Eric Burdon; "It's a Man's World" by James Brown and Betty Newsome; "Mister Spaceman" by Roger McGuinn.

Also "Monster Mash" by Bobby Pickett and Leonard Capizzi; "Oh, Pretty Woman" by Roy Orbison and Billy Dees; "Only the Lonely" by Roy Orbison and Joe Melson; "Robot Man" by Sylvia Dee and George Goehring; "Shake, Rattle and Roll" by Charles Calhoun; "Shakin' All Over" by Johnny Kidd; "She's Not There" by Rod Argent; "Tell Her" by Bert Berns; "It's His Kiss (The Shoop Shoop Song)" by Rudy Clark; "Telstar" by Joe Meek; "Who's Sorry Now" by Bert Kalmar, Harry Ruby and Ted Snyder; "Why Must I Be a Teenager in Love?" by Doc Primus and Mort Shuman; "Wipeout" by Patrick Connolly, Robert Berryhill, James Fuller and Robert Wilson; "Young Girl" by Jerry Fuller.

The Baby Dance (61). By Jane Anderson. Produced by John A. McQuiggan, Lucille Lortel and Daryl Roth in association with Susan Dietz at the Lucille Lortel Theater. Opened October 17, 1991. (Closed December 8, 1991)

Wanda	Linda Purl	Richard	Joel Polis
Al	Richard Lineback	Ron	John Bennett Perry
Rachel	Stephanie Zimbalist		

Directed by Jenny Sullivan; scenery, Hugh Landwehr; costumes, David Murin; lighting, Kirk Bookman; sound, Brent Evans; associate producers, Chantpleure, Inc., James and Maureen O'Sullivan Cushing, Graconn, Ltd.; production stage manager, Tammy Taylor; stage manager, R. Wade Jackson; press, Boneau/Bryan-Brown, Susanne Tighe.

Time: The present, summer (highs are in the 90s and the humidity is 100 percent). Place: Act I, a trailer park in Northern Louisiana: Scene 1: A rainy night in April. Scene 2: An afternoon in July. Act II: A hospital room in Monroe, Louisiana, one month later.

Infertile couple attempting to have a child by buying one. Previously produced in regional theater at the Long Wharf Theater, New Haven, Conn., the Williamstown, Mass. Theater Festival and the Pasadena Playhouse.

Servy-n-Bernice 4Ever (39). By Seth Zvi Rosenfeld. Produced by Al Corley, Bart Rosenblatt and Marcy Drogin at the Provincetown Playhouse. Opened October 22, 1991. (Closed November 24, 1991)

Bernice	Lisa Gay Hamilton	Servy	Ron Eldard
Caria	Cynthia Nixon	Scotty	Erik King

Directed by Terry Kinney; scenery, Edward T. Gianfrancesco; costumes, Judy Dearing; lighting, Kenneth Posner; sound, Jeffrey Taylor; associate producer, Eugene Musso; production stage manager, M.A. Howard; press, Peter Cromarty, David B. Katz.

Interracial romance between a black model and a white home-town boy become a street-wise thief. The play was presented in two parts.

*Manhattan Theater Club. 20th anniversary season. Schedule of seven programs. **Beggars in the House of Plenty** (56). By John Patrick Shanley. Opened October 23, 1991. (Closed December 8, 1991) **A Piece of My Heart** (48). By Shirley Lauro; suggested by the book by Keith Walker; produced by special arrangement with Roger L. Stevens. Opened November 3, 1991. (Closed November 24, 1991) ***Sight Unseen** (150). By Donald Margulies. Opened January 20, 1992. **Boesman and Lena** (63). Revival of the play by Athol Fugard. Opened January 29, 1992. (Closed March 22, 1992) **Groundhog** (40). Musical composed and written by Elizabeth Swados. Opened April 14, 1992. (Closed May 17, 1992) **The Extra Man** (39). By Richard Greenberg. Opened May 19, 1992. (Closed June 21, 1992) And *The Innocents' Crusade* by Keith Reddin scheduled to open June 23, 1992. Produced by Manhattan Theater Club, Lynne Meadow artistic director, Barry Grove managing director, *Beggars in the House of Plenty, Sight Unseen* and *Groundhog* at City Center Stage II; *Boesman and Lena* and *The Extra Man* at City Center Stage I; *A Piece of My Heart* at Union Square Theater.

ALL PLAYS: Associate artistic director, Michael Bush; general manager, Victoria Bailey; press, Helene Davis, Deborah Warren.

BEGGARS IN THE HOUSE OF PLENTY

Johnny	Loren Dean	Sheila	Laura Linney
Ma (Noreen)	Dana Ivey	Joey	Jon Tenney
Pop	Daniel von Bargen	Sister Mary Kate	Jayne Haynes

Directed by John Patrick Shanley; scenery, Santo Loquasto; costumes, Lindsay W. Davis; lighting, Natasha Katz; sound, Bruce Ellman; production stage manager, Renee Lutz.

Resentful sons dominated by an overbearing father in a troubled, love-starved family. The play was presented without intermission.

A PIECE OF MY HEART

Martha	Annette Helde	Leeann	Kim Miyori
Maryjo	Cynthia Carle	Steele	Novella Nelson
Sissy	Corliss Preston	American Men	Tom Stechschulte
Whitney	Sharon Schlarth		

Directed by Allen R. Belknap; scenery, James Fenhagen; costumes, Mimi Maxmen; lighting, Richard Winkler; sound, John Kilgore; guitar and vocal arrangements, Cynthia Carle; production stage manager, Richard Hester; stage manager, Susan R. Fenty.

Time: The recent past. The play was presented in two parts.

The adventures of women, civilian and military, in Vietnam during the war, based on 26 true oral histories. Previously produced in regional theater at the Philadelphia Festival Theater for New Plays and the Actors Theater of Louisville.

SIGHT UNSEEN

Jonathan Waxman	Dennis Boutsikaris	Patricia	Deborah Hedwall
Nick	Jon De Vries	Grete	Laura Linney

Understudy: Misses Linney, Hedwall—Kayla Black

Directed by Michael Bloom; scenery, James Youmans; costumes, Jess Goldstein; lighting, Donald Holder; music and sound, Michael Roth; associate artistic director, Michael Bush; production stage manager, Harold Goldfaden.

Act I, Scene 1: A farmhouse in the English countryside. Scene 2: An art gallery in London, four days later. Scene 3: The farmhouse, an hour before the start of Scene 1. Scene 4: Jonathan's bedroom in Brooklyn, 15 years earlier. Act II, Scene 5: The farmhouse, a few hours after the end of Scene 1. Scene 6: The gallery, continued from the end of Scene 2. Scene 7: The farmhouse, a few hours after the end of Scene 5. Scene 8: A painting studio at a New York art school, 17 years earlier.

A gifted American painter's mid-life crisis in emotional and esthetic turbulence. Previously presented at South Coast Repertory, Costa Mesa, Calif.

A Best Play; see page 162.

BOESMAN AND LENA

Boesman	Keith David	Outa	Tsepo Mokone
Lena	Lynne Thigpen		

Directed by Athol Fugard; scenery and costumes, Susan Hilferty; lighting, Dennis Parichy; associate director, Susan Hilferty; production stage manager, Sandra Lea Williams.

Boesman and Lena was first produced in New York off Broadway 6/22/70 for 205 performances and was named a Best Play of its season. This is its first major New York revival, presented without intermission.

GROUNDHOG

CAST: Dr. R.T. Ebney, etc.—Stephen Lee Anderson; Gila—Anne Bobby; Judge Alex T. Waldman, etc.—Bill Buell; Zoe, etc.—Gilles Chiasson; Georgette Bergen—Nora Cole; D.A. Randall—Ula Hedwig; Weatherperson, etc.—Ann Marie Milazzo; Sandy, etc.—Lauren Mufson; Mayor of New York, etc.—Daniel Neiden; Lauree, etc.—Suzan Postel; Groundhog—David Schechter; Fez, etc.—Tony Scheitinger; Danilo Chelnik—Michael Sottile;

Musicians: Michael Sottile keyboards; Paul O'Keefe guitars, bass guitar; Lewis Robinson percussion.

Directed by Elizabeth Swados; musical direction and arrangements, Ann Marie Milazzo, Michael Sottile; scenery and costumes, G.W. Mercier; lighting, Natasha Katz; sound, Ed Fitzgerald; production stage manager, Richard Hester; stage manager, Elise-Ann Konstantin.

Time: Mid-1980's. Place: New York City. The play was presented in two parts.

A mentally disturbed homeless man vs. the system, reportedly based partly on the experiences of the author's late brother.

ACT I

"Weather Report #1" . . . . Meteorologists
"Cooper Square" . . . . Groundhog, Street People
"Project Heal" . . . . Mayor, Company
"One More Day" . . . . Groundhog, Company
"Willard Scott" . . . . Groundhog, Gila
"Abduction" . . . . Company
"Weather Report #2" . . . . Meteorologist Ann Marie
"Street People" . . . . Gila, Street People
"Groundhog Is Going to Trial" . . . . Street People
"My Movie of the Week" . . . . Judge, Company
"Who Will It Be?" . . . . Gila
"Flight to Health" . . . . Street People
"Bellevue and the Judge" . . . . D.A. Randall, Bergen
"Testimony" . . . . Dr. Chang, Dr. Schloss
"Experts" . . . . Groundhog, Company
"This Isn't How I Imagined a Trial To Be" . . . . Groundhog, Company
"Just Trust Me" . . . . Gila, Groundhog
"Yes/No" . . . . Gila, Groundhog
"Flight to Health" . . . . Street People
"Doctor's Canon" . . . . Drs. Davidkoff, Jakes, Giles, Green
"Bill and Willa" . . . . Bill Dajurian, Willa Dajurian
"Danilo's Rap" . . . . Danilo
"Sweet Bitter Candy" . . . . Groundhog, Gila, Company

ACT II

"Hey Groundhog" . . . . Groundhog, Company
"Why Did I Forget?" . . . . Gila, Groundhog, Company
"Ten Year Blues" . . . . Groundhog
"Harmonica Man" . . . . Groundhog
"Weather Report #3" . . . . Meteorologists Stephen and Suzan
"If I Am Released" . . . . Groundhog, Company
"Closing Arguments" . . . . Bergen, D.A. Randall, Groundhog
"The Judge's Decision . . . . Judge, Company
"Battle Hymn of Groundhog" . . . . Groundhog, Company
"Groundhog Has Won" . . . . Street People
"Lawyer's Lament" . . . . D.A. Randall, Bergen, Company
"Open the Door" . . . . Gila; Company
"Groundhog Is Becoming Important" . . . . Street People
"Hearing Voices" . . . . Company
"Pay Phone" . . . . Gila, Groundhog, Company
"Hearing Voices" . . . . Company
"ACLU" . . . . Groundhog, Company
"Rewrite Your Own Story" . . . . Company
"Hymn to Spring" . . . . Groundhog, Company
"Weather Report #4" . . . . Meteorologists Ann Marie, Lauren and Suzan
"What Could I Have Done?" . . . . Gila, Company
"Someone Is Discovering Something" . . . . Groundhog, Gila, Company

THE EXTRA MAN

Laura . . . . Laila Robins   Jess . . . . Adam Arkin
Keith . . . . Boyd Gaines   Daniel . . . . John Slattery

Directed by Michael Engler; scenery, Loy Arcenas; costumes, Jess Goldstein; lighting, Donald Holder; sound, Scott Lehrer; production stage manager, Robin Rumpf; stage manager, James Mountcastle.

Time: From fall to spring. Place: Various locations in New York City. The play was presented in two parts.

A mischief-maker and his victims as a microcosm of modern life, in a work commissioned by American Playwrights Project and South Coast Repertory Theater, Costa Mesa, Calif.

A Best Play; see page 267.

Cole Porter at the Kaufman (63). Revue with songs by Cole Porter and Noel Coward. Produced by Martin R. Kaufman at the Kaufman Theater. Opened November 5, 1991. (Closed January 6, 1992)

Julie Wilson   William Roy

Scenery, Phillip Baldwin; lighting, Douglas O'Flaherty; production stage manager, Eileen Toner; press, John Springer, Gary Springer.

Act I: The Songs of Cole Porter. Act II: The songs of Noel Coward.

Julie Wilson singing the Porter and Coward numbers, accompanied by William Roy on the piano (and occasionally in song), in a show designed for stage presentation.

RETURN TO THE FORBIDDEN PLANET—Steve Steiner and Gabriel Barre in the musical by Bob Carlton loosely based on Shakespeare's *The Tempest*

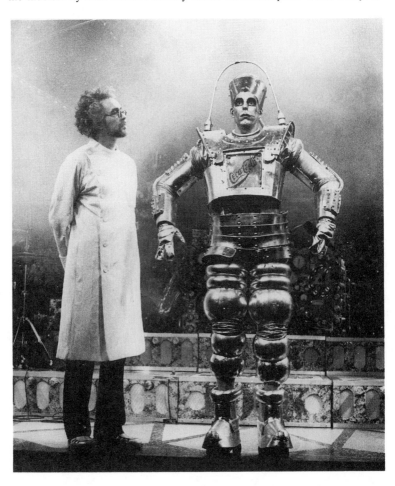

*New York Shakespeare Festival. Schedule of nine programs. **In the Jungle of Cities** (24). Revival of the play by Bertolt Brecht; co-produced by Mabou Mines, Jennifer Greenfield associate producer. Opened November 5, 1991. (Closed November 24, 1991) **Moving Beyond the Madness: A Festival of New Voices** (15). Multi-presentation program, George C. Wolfe curator. Opened December 1, 1991. (Closed December 15, 1991) **Reno Once Removed** (17). One-woman performance piece conceived, written and performed by Reno; produced in association with I.P.A. Presents. Opened December 18, 1991. (Closed January 5, 1992) **The Home Show Pieces** (24). Program of four one-act plays by David Greenspan: *Doing the Beat, Too Much in the Sun, Portrait of the Artist* and *The Big Tent.* Opened January 28, 1992. (Closed February 16, 1992) **Homo Sapien Shuffle** (24). By Richard Caliban; presented in the Cucaracha Theater production, Elizabeth J. Theobald producing director. Opened March 9, 1992. (Closed March 29, 1992) **Before It Hits Home** (16). By Cheryl L. West; presented in the Second Stage Production, Robyn Goodman and Carole Rothman artistic directors. Opened March 10, 1992. (Closed March 22, 1992) **'Tis Pity She's a Whore** (19). Revival of the play by John Ford. Opened April 5, 1992. (Closed April 19, 1992) ***Fires in the Mirror** (24). One-woman performance by Anna Deavere Smith; conceived and written by Anna Deavere Smith. Opened May 12, 1992. **Blood Wedding** (21). Revival of the play by Federico Garcia Lorca; translated by Langston Hughes. Opened May 14, 1992. (Closed May 31, 1992) Produced by New York Shakespeare Festival, Joseph Papp founder, JoAnne Akalaitis artistic director, Jason Steven Cohen managing director, Rosemarie Tichler associate artistic director, at the Joseph Papp Public Theater; see note.

IN THE JUNGLE OF CITIES

Mae; Mae Garga . . . . Ruth Maleczech	Jane Larry . . . . Karen Evans-Kandel
Skinny; Employee; Barman . . . . . Brian Jucha	Mary Garga . . . . Fanni Green
George Garga . . . . Mario Arrambide	Salvation Army Preacher; John
Shlink . . . . Frederick Neumann	Garga . . . . Raul Aranas
C. Maynes; Pat Manky;	Sinners . . Karen Evans-Kandel, Terry O'Reilly
Reporter. . . . . Terry O'Reilly	Loading Dock
Worm . . . . Greg Mehrten	Workers . . . . David McIntyre, Royston Scott
Baboon; Man . . . . Rene Rivera	

Directed by Anne Bogart; scenery, Donald Eastman; costumes, Gabriel Berry; lighting, Heather Carson; sound, Jacob Burkhardt/L.B. Dallas; composer, Judson Wright; production stage manager, Buzz Cohen; press, Richard Kornberg, Barbara Carroll, Carol Fineman, James Morrison.

This 1923 Brecht play was first produced off Broadway by the Living Theater 12/20/60 for 66 performances and the following season for 110 performances. This production is its first major New York revival, presented without intermission.

MOVING BEYOND THE MADNESS:
A FESTIVAL OF NEW VOICES

Festival schedule comprised the following programs:

Spic-o-rama by John Leguizamo, Dec. 1, one-person show about a six-person family (work-in-progress).

An American Griot by Ed Bullins and Idris Ackamoor, with Idris Ackamoor, Dec. 4 and 5, a jazz autobiography.

Big Butt Girls, Hard-Headed Women by and with Rhodessa Jones, Dec. 4 and 5, monologues about women behind bars.

Tokyo Bound by and with Amy Hill, Dec. 6 and 8, multimedia presentation about the complexities of Japanese women.

Hazelle! The Absolute Outrageous Truth 'Bout Us by and with Hazelle Goodman, Dec. 6 and 8, collage of characters.

Remembrances and Dedications: A Haphazard Cabaret, Part 1, conceived by Vernon Reid, Dec. 7, an evening of music.

Identities, Mirrors and Distortions by and with Anna Deveare Smith, Dec. 10 and 12, points of view on political and social issues.

Symposium in Manila by and with Han Ong, Dec. 10 and 12, exploding multiculturalism myths.

Science and Ritual with Derin Young, Dec. 11 and 13, an evening of music from early West African and Cuban to modern rhythm and blues.

Danitra Vance and the Mel-O-White Boys Revisited with Danitra Vance, Dec. 11 and 14, an evening of characters and music.

Fierce Love by and with Pomo Afro Homos (Postmodern African American homosexuals), Dec. 13, the contradictions of black gay life. A second Pomo Afro Homos appearance Dec. 14 previewed a new work-in-progress.

Relationships: Intimate and Not So Intimate with Blondell Cummings, Dec. 15, dance/theater piece portraying an interracial couple's similarities and differences.

ALL PROGRAMS: Technical coordinator, Bill Barnes; lighting, Dan Kotlowitz.

As described by George C. Wolfe, the Festival was a series of Black, Asian and Hispanic "voices of color" which "speak of being on the out—of trying to get in—of being in and wanting out. Men, women, ambisexual. American voices."

RENO ONCE REMOVED

Original music, Mike Yionoulis; lighting, Dan Kotlowitz.

Political and social comment in the form of Reno's one-woman performance program. The show was presented without intermission. Previously presented OOB in Lincoln Center's 1991 Serious Fun summer festival at Alice Tully Hall.

THE HOME SHOW PIECES

Doing the Beast

Character 1 . . . . David Greenspan

Too Much in the Sun

Character 3 . . . . Ron Bagden
Character 4 . . . . Tracey Ellis

Portrait of the Artist

Character 1 . . . . David Greenspan
Character 2 . . . . Ron Bagden

The Big Tent

Character 1 . . . . Tracey Ellis
Character 5; Character 2 . . . . Ron Bagden

Directed by David Greenspan; scenery, William Kennon; costumes, Elsa Ward; lighting, David Bergstein; production stage manager, Mark McMahon.

This material was previously produced off off Broadway at HOME for Contemporary Theater in September 1988. The play was presented in two parts with the intermission following *Too Much in the Sun*.

HOMO SAPIEN SHUFFLE

Wheeler	Vivian Lanko	Willa	Sharon Brady
Moon	Erica Gimpel	Bernadette	Lauren Hamilton
Stage Manager	Diana Ridoutt	Rocky	Glen M. Santiago
Stagehand	Mark Dillahunt	Cleo	Mollie O'Mara
Craven	Martin Donovan		

Directed by Richard Caliban; music composed and performed by John Hoge; scenery, Kyle Chepulis; marionettes and costumes, Yvette Helin; lighting, Brian Aldous; sound, John Huntington; associate producers, Alexander J. Racolin, Annette Moscowitz; production stage manager, Paul J. Smith; press, Bruce Campbell, Barbara Carroll, James Morrison.

Moving back in time to study the events leading up to a homicide.

BEFORE IT HITS HOME

Wendal	James McDaniel	Bailey	Frankie R. Faison
Simone; Miss Peterson . . .	Sharon Washington	Dwayne	James Jason Lilley
Douglas	Keith Randolph Smith	Nurse	Carol Honda
Reba	Yvette Hawkins	Dr. Weinberg	Beth Dixon
Maybelle	Marcella Lowery	Junior	Monti Sharp

Directed by Tazewell Thompson; scenery, Loy Arcenas; costumes, Paul Tazewell; lighting, Nancy Schertler; sound, Susan White; production stage manager, James Fitzsimmons; stage manager, Cathleen Wolfe.

Black family is devastated when they find out that their son is a homosexual and has contracted AIDS. The play was presented in two parts. Previously produced in regional theater at Arena Stage, Washington, D.C. and elsewhere.

'TIS PITY SHE'S A WHORE

Friar Bonaventure . . . . Wendell Pierce	Lt. Grimaldi . . . . Daniel Oreskes
Florio . . . . Frank Raiter	Poggio. . . . . Mark Kenneth Smaltz
Giovanni . . . . Val Kilmer	Richardetto. . . . . Rocco Sisto
Annabella . . . . Jeanne Tripplehorn	Philotis. . . . . Marlo Marron
Putana. . . . . Deirdre O'Connell	Hippolita . . . . Ellen McElduff
Soranzo . . . . Jared Harris	Cardinal . . . . Tom Nelis
Vasques . . . . Erick Avari	Banditti . . . . J. David Brimmer, Angel David,
Donado . . . . Helmar Augustus Cooper	Larry Grant Malvern
Bergetto . . . . Ross Lehman	

At the Wedding Party: Jugglers, Servants—Adrian Danzig, Doug Von Nessen; Girl Scouts—Soraya Butler, Joan Elizabeth, Giovanna Sardelli; Singer—April Armstrong.

Policemen, Nuns, Party Guests, Soldiers, Townspeople: April Armstrong, J. David Brimmer, Soraya Butler, Adrian Danzig, Angel David, Joan Elizabeth, Larry Grant Malvern, Tom Nelis, Giovanna Sardelli, Doug Von Nessen.

Directed by JoAnne Akalaitis; scenery, John Conklin; costumes, Gabriel Berry; lighting, Mimi Jordan Sherin; original music, Jan A.P. Kaczmarek; sound, John Gromada; fight direction, David Leong; choreography, Timothy O'Slynne; assistant director, Jonathan Rosenberg; dramaturge, Barry Edelstein; production stage manager, Pat Sosnow; stage manager, Liz Small.

Time: The early 1930s. Place: Parma, Italy. The play was presented in two parts.

Ford's 1624 play transposed to Fascist Italy. The last major New York revival of 'Tis Pity She's a Whore took place off Broadway in the 1958-59 season.

FIRES IN THE MIRROR

Directed by Christopher Ashley; scenery, James Youmans; costumes, Candice Donnelly; lighting, Debra J. Kletter; projections, Wendall K. Harrington, Emmanuelle Krebs; music, Joseph Jarman; production stage manager, Karen Moore.

Subtitled Crown Heights, Brooklyn and Other Identities, a study of the situation in Crown Heights in 30 monologues derived by Anna Deavere Smith from actual interviews with persons in that neighborhood. The play was presented without intermission. Portions previously produced at the Public Theater in Moving Beyond the Madness: A Festival of New Voices.

A Best Play; see page 251.

BLOOD WEDDING

Mother . . . . Gloria Foster	Child . . . . Marchand Odette
Groom . . . . Al Rodrigo	Father . . . . Mike Hodge
Neighbor; Servant . . . . Ivonne Coll	Bride . . . . Elizabeth Peña
Wife of Leonardo. . . . . . Cordelia Gonzalez	Moon . . . . Omar Carter
Mother-in-Law . . . . Phyllis Bash	Beggar Woman . . . . Fanni Green
Leonardo . . . . Joaquim de Almeida	

Bridesmaids, Girls: Gina Torres, Sara Erde, Marchand Odette. Youths, Woodcutters: Tim Perez, Michael Mandell, Omar Carter.

Musicians: Michele Navazio guitar; Rex Benincasa percussion; Erik Friedlander, Peter Sanders violoncello.

Directed by Melia Bensussen; scenery, Derek McLane; costumes, Franne Lee; lighting, Peter Kaczorowski; composer and musical director, Michele Navazio; choreography, Donald Byrd; production stage manager, James Bernardi; stage manager, Liz Dreyer.

The last major New York revival of record of Blood Wedding took place off Broadway in the 1957-58 season. This 1992 production, the world premiere of the Langston Hughes translation, was presented without intermission.

Note: In the Public Theater there are many auditoria. In the Jungle of Cities, The Home Show Pieces and *Blood Wedding* played Martinson Hall, *Moving Beyond the Madness* and *Reno Once Removed* played the Anspacher Theater, *Homo Sapien Shuffle* and *Fires in the Mirror* played the Susan Stein Shiva Theater, *Before It Hits Home* played LuEsther Hall, *'Tis Pity She's A Whore* played the Estelle R. Newman Theater.

Riverside Shakespeare Company. Schedule of two programs. **Iron Bars** (22). By Arpad Goncz; translated by Katherina M. and Christopher C. Wilson. Opened November 10, 1991. (Closed December 1, 1991) **Cinderella** (70). Musical with book by Norman Robbins; music by Dan Levy; lyrics by Amy Powers and Dan Levy. Opened December 19, 1991. (Closed February 23, 1992) Produced by Riverside Shakespeare Company, Gus Kaikkonen artistic director, Stephen Vetrano managing director, at Playhouse 91.

IRON BARS

Emmanuel . . . . Garry Goodrow	2d Plainclothesman . . . . Dan Daily
Dolores . . . . Alice White	1st Prisoner; Window Dresser;
Beata . . . . Lisbeth Bartlett	Police Minister . . . . . Bruce Edward Barton
Woman Doctor . . . . Maureen Clarke	2d Prisoner; 1st Handyman;
The President . . . . Richard Thomsen	2d Male Nurse. . . . . Brian Keane
Major; Upholsterer;	3d Prisoner; Errand Boy;
1st Plainclothesman. . . . . . David Lipman	Lackey . . . . James Matthew Ryan
Sergeant; 1st Delivery Man;	4th Prisoner; 2d Delivery Man;
1st Male Nurse . . . . Mark Young	1st Policeman . . . . Mikel Borden
1st Prosecutor; Telephone Company Man;	5th Prisoner; 2d Handyman;
Doctor . . . . Christopher Mixon	2d Policeman . . . . Peter Brown
2d Prosecutor; Gas Company Man;	

Understudies: Mr. Goodrow—Christopher Mixon; Misses White, Bartlett—Maureen Clarke; Miss Clarke—Alice White; Messrs. Young, Barton, Keane—James Matthew Ryan; Messrs. Thomsen, Mixon—Bruce Edward Barton; Messrs. Lipman, Daily—Brian Keane.

Directed by Andre De Szekely and Laszlo Vamos; scenery, Bob Barnett; costumes, Pamela Scofield; lighting, Stephen J. Backo; music composed and arranged, Tommy Vig; production stage manager, Matthew G. Marholin; stage manager, Rona Bern; press, Boneau/Bryan-Brown, Bob Fennell.

About iron bars that remain in the minds of free people after an authoritarian government has been overthrown, written by a past president of the Hungarian Writers Guild and the present president of Hungary, elected in 1990. The play was presented in two parts. A foreign (Hungarian) play in its world premiere in this production.

CINDERELLA

Buttons . . . . Mark Honan	Euthanasia . . . . John Keene Bolton
Dandini. . . . . Fredi Walker	Ammer . . . . Jim Fitzpatrick
Cinders . . . . Melanie Wingert	Tongs . . . . Jay Brian Winnick
Baron Hardupp . . . . Pat Flick	Prince Charming . . . . Anthony Stanton
Baroness Hardupp . . . . Diane Ciesla	Old Lady; Fairy Godmother . . . Lora Lee Cliff
Asphyxia. . . . . Robert Mooney	

Understudies: Mr. Honan—Scott Huston; Messrs. Flick, Mooney—Dale Fuller; Misses Wingert, Cliff—Jean C. Childers; Misses Ciesla, Walker—Ann Harvey; Mr. Stanton—Doug Ladendorf; Messrs. Fitzpatrick, Winnick—Peter Dinklage.

Directed by Laura Fine; scenery, Harry Feiner; costumes, Gail Baldoni; lighting, Stephen Petrilli; musical arrangements, Dan Levy; production stage manager, Paula Gray; stage manager, Rona Bern; press, Boneau/Bryan-Brown, Wayne Wolfe.

Free-wheeling British "Panto"-like comedy musicalization of the fairy tale.

ACT I

Scene 1: The village of Merrivale
   "Bright Spring Morn" . . . . Company
   "It's What You Do (That Makes Your Wishes Come True)" . . . . Cinders
Scene 2: The woods
Scene 3: A woodland glade

"His Highness" . . . . Company
"I Am a Prince" . . . . Prince, Dandini
"Your Sticks, Your Hat, Your Hand" . . . . Prince, Cinders
Scene 4: The kitchen of Stoneybroke Mansion
"Getting Ready for the Ball" . . . . Cinders, Asphyxia, Euthanasia, Baron, Baroness
"It's What You Do" (Reprise) . . . . Cinders
"Dance at the Ball Tonight" . . . . Fairy Godmother, Cinders, Buttons

ACT II

Scene 1: Outside Castle Glamoreuse
"Waitin' on the Women" . . . . Prince, Dandini, Baron, Ammer, Tongs, Buttons
Scene 2: The ballroom of Castle Glamoreuse and the kitchen of Stoneybroke Mansion
"Keep the Castle Warm" . . . . Buttons, Company
"La Petite Oiseau" . . . . Euthanasia, Company
"Delighted You Invited Me" . . . . Company
Scene 3: The kitchen of Stoneybroke Mansion
"It's What You Do" (Reprise) . . . . Cinders
"Happy Ending" . . . . Company

From the Mississippi Delta (218). By Endesha Ida Mae Holland. Produced by Susan Quint
Gallin, Calvin Skaggs, Susan Wexler, Judith Resnick and Oprah Winfrey at Circle in the
Square Downtown. Opened November 11, 1991. (Closed May 17, 1992)

Woman One . . . . Sybil Walker   Woman Three . . . . Cheryl Lynn Bruce
Woman Two . . . . Jacqueline Williams

Understudy: Misses Walker, Williams, Bruce—Faye M. Price.
Directed by Jonathan Wilson; scenery and costumes, Eduardo Sicangco; lighting, Allen Lee Hughes;
sound, Rob Milburn, David Budries; traditional music arranged and performed by Michael Bodeen and
Rob Milburn; associate producers, Ric Cherwin, Adrianne Cohen, Harlene Freezer, Bernard Friedman;
stage manager, Anthony Berg; press, Jeffrey Richards Associates, David LeShay.
Time: From the early 1940s to the mid-1980s. Place: The South and the Midwest. Act I, Scene 1:
Memories. Scene 2: Ain't Baby. Scene 3: Calm, balmy days. Scene 4: Second Doctor Lady. Scene 5:
The water meter. Scene 6: The Delta Queen. Act II, Scene 7: The whole town's talking. Scene 8: The
funeral. Scene 9: From the Mississippi Delta. Scene 10: A permit to parade. Scene 11: Letter to Alice
Walker.
Episodes in a black woman's rise from rural poverty. Previously produced off off Broadway at New
Federal Theater (in a one-act version) and in regional theater at the Northlight Theater, Evanston, Ill.,
the Goodman Theater, Chicago, the Arena Stage, Washington, D.C. and the Hartford, Conn. Stage
Company, from whose May 1991 production this one was adapted.
Tempestt Bledsoe joined the ensemble 4/28/92.

*Tubes (225). Performance piece by and with Blue Man Group. Produced by Mark Dunn
and Makoto Deguchi at the Astor Place Theater. Opened November 17, 1991.

Matt Goldman   Chris Wink
Phil Stanton

Directed by Marlene Swartz; artistic coordinator, Caryl Glaab; scenery, Kevin Joseph Roach; cos-
tumes, Lydia Tanji, Patricia Murphy; lighting, Brian Aldous; sound, Raymond Schilke; computer graph-
ic design, Kurisu-Chan; associate producers, Akie Kimura, Broadway Line Company; press, David
Rothenberg Associates.
Blue Man Group Band: Brian Dewan, Larry Heinemann, Ian Pai.
Performance art often involving the audience, with a great deal of comic comment on aspects of mod-
ern living, by a trio of performers known as Blue Man Group. Previously produced OOB at La Mama
E.T.C.

The Shadow of a Gunman (13). Revival of the play by Sean O'Casey. Produced by Sally
de Sousa in the O'Casey Theater Company production at Symphony Space. Opened in a lim-

FROM THE MISSISSIPPI DELTA—Cheryl Lynn Bruce, Sybil Walker and Jaqueline Williams in the play by Endesha Ida Mae Holland

ited engagement November 25, 1991. (Closed December 8, 1991)

Seumas Shields	Niall Buggy	Maguire	Richard Holmes
Tommy Owens	Risteard Cooper	Mrs. Henderson	Doreen Keogh
Minnie Powell	Michelle Fairley	Tenement Resident	Shauna Rooney
Donal Davoren	Ian Fitzgibbon	Mr. Grigson	Sean McCarthy
Mrs. Grigson	Pauline Flanagan	Mr. Gallagher; Landlord	George Vogel
Auxiliary	Stephen Gabis		

Directed by Shivaun O'Casey; scenery, Brien Vahey; costumes, Jan Bee Brown; lighting, Rory Dempster; sound, Paul Bull; music, Tommy Sands; production stage manager, Bryan Young; press, Patt Dale.

Time: The 1920s. Place: A Dublin tenement. The play was presented in two parts.

Irish troupe founded by O'Casey's daughter and based in Newry, Northern Ireland, touring this production in Ireland and in five U.S. cities. The last major revival of *Shadow of a Gunman* was a transfer by the Irish Arts Center from off off Broadway to off Broadway 5/2/84 for 47 performances.

Note: The O'Casey Theater Company also offered two matinee performances of *The Shadow of O'Casey*, a stage documentary compiled by Shivaun O'Casey and celebrating the achievements of her father, on 12/5 and 12/7/91.

The Dropper (15). By Ron McLarty. Produced by Miranda d'Ancona, Doris Kaufman and Zaluma, Inc. at the Intar Theater. Opened December 3, 1991. (Closed December 15, 1991)

Mo Polleni . . . . Wendy Scharfman	Bobby Horn . . . . John Dawson Beard
Jack Polleni . . . . Nick Giangiulio	Young Shoe Horn . . . . Richard Long
Old Shoe Horn . . . . Bob Horen	

Directed by Ron McLarty; scenery, Stephen Olson; costumes, Traci di Gesu; lighting, Michael Stiller; music, Wayne Joness; production stage manager, Scott Pegg; press, David Rothenberg, Terrence Womble.

Time: 1910 England and 1984 America. Place: English town of Warrington and Bridgeton, Me. The play was presented in two parts.

A family copes with a severely handicapped child. Previously produced at Mill Mountain Theater, Roanoke, Va. and OOB by Prima Artists.

Mad Forest (54). By Caryl Churchill. Produced off off Broadway in a limited engagement by New York Theater Workshop, James C. Nicola artistic director, Nancy Kassak Diekmann managing director, at the Perry Street Theater. Opened December 4, 1991. (Closed January 25, 1992)

Vladu Family:	Doctor; Priest; Vampire; Someone with
Bogdan . . . . Lanny Flaherty	Sore Throat . . . . Joseph Siravo
Irina . . . . Randy Danson	Dog . . . . Christopher McCann
Lucia . . . . Calista Flockhart	Soldiers in Rodica's
Florina . . . . Mary Mara	Nightmare . . . Joseph Siravo, Lanny Flaherty
Gabriel . . . . Tim Nelson	Act II:
Rodica; Grandmother . . . . . . Mary Shultz	Painter . . . . Garret Dillahunt
Wayne . . . . Christopher McCann	Girl Student . . . . Mary Mara
Grandfather; Old Aunt. . . . . Joseph Siravo	Boy Students . . . Rob Campbell, Tim Nelson
Antonescu Family:	Translator . . . . Lanny Flaherty
Mihai . . . . Christopher McCann	Bulldozer Driver . . . . . Christopher McCann
Flavia . . . . Mary Shultz	Securitate Officer . . . . Joseph Siravo
Radu . . . . Jake Weber	Soldier . . . . Jake Weber
Grandmother . . . . Randy Danson	Student Doctor . . . . Calista Flockhart
Ianos. . . . . Garret Dillahunt	Flowerseller . . . . Randy Danson
Securitate Man; Angel; Patient; Toma;	House Painter . . . . Mary Shultz
Ghost; Waiter . . . . Rob Campbell	Others . . . . Company

Directed by Mark Wing-Davey; scenery and costumes, Marina Draghici; lighting, Christopher Akerlind; sound, Mark Bennett; fight direction, David Leong; dialect coach, Deborah Hecht; production stage manager, Thom Widmann; press, Richard Kornberg.

Time: November 22 through December 29, 1990. Act I: Lucia's Wedding. Act II: December. Act III: Florina's wedding. The play was presented in two parts with the intermission following Act II.

Subtitled A Play From Romania, a dramatization of events in the recent political upheaval, and their effects on a working-class and an intellectual family. A foreign play previously produced at the Central School of Speech and Drama, London, the National Theater, Bucharest, and the Royal Court Theater.

A Best Play (in our policy of citing specified special cases of OOB production); see page 119.

Willie & Esther (83). By James Graham Bronson. Produced by Fontana Entertainment, Bern Nadette Stanis, Debbie Lytle, Kevin Fontana, Daniel Siegel producers, at the 47th Street Theater. Opened December 7, 1991. (Closed March 7, 1992)

Willie . . . . Hugh Dane
Esther . . . . Edwina Moore

Directed by Diann McCannon; sound, Tarsha Harvard; production stage manager, Trell; press, Francine L. Trevens.

Time: Three years ago. Place: Outside of Bank of America in south central Los Angeles. Act I: 1:45 p.m. Tuesday. Act II: 48 minutes later.

Comedy, a couple contemplates borrowing money from a bank by robbing it. Previously produced at Inner City Cultural Center, Los Angeles.

Bern Nadette Stanis replaced Edwina Moore and Emmett Thrower replaced Hugh Dane 12/91; Jeris Poindexter replaced Emmett Thrower 2/92.

I Won't Dance (70). Cabaret revue with text by Steve Ross and Michael Sommers; songs by various authors (see listing below). Produced by American Cabaret Theater, Peter Ligeti producing director, at Theater at St. Peter's. Opened December 12, 1991. (Closed February 9, 1992)

CAST: Steve Ross, Bruno David Casolari (second piano), Brian Cassier (bass).

Scenery, Jean Valente; lighting, Matt Berman; sound, Cynthia Daniels; musical arrangements, Wally Harper; additional arrangements, Steve Ross, Bruno David Casolari; production supervisor, Michael Sommers; press, Boneau/Bryan-Brown, Chris Boneau, Susanne Tighe.

Subtitled Steve Ross Sings Fred Astaire, a cabaret performance in a theatrical setting, with songs selected from the list which follows, interspersed with narrative excerpts from Fred Astaire's life and career. The show was presented in two parts.

MUSICAL NUMBERS: "All of You," "Begin the Beguine," "Night and Day," "Please Don't Monkey With Broadway" by Cole Porter; "Change Partners," "Cheek to Cheek," "A Couple of Swells," "Easter Parade," "It Only Happens When I Dance With You," "Let Yourself Go," "Let's Face the Music and Dance," "The Piccolino," "Puttin' on the Ritz," "Steppin' Out With My Baby," "Top Hat, White Tie and Tails" by Irving Berlin; "City of Angels" by Fred Astaire and Tommy Wolf; "The Continental" by Herb Magidson and Con Conrad; "Dancing in the Dark," "I Guess I'll Have to Change My Plan" by Howard Dietz and Arthur Schwartz; "Dream," "A Lot in Common With You" (with Harold Arlen), "Something's Gotta Give" by Johnny Mercer.

Also "Fascinating Rhythm," "Funny Face," "Lady, Be Good," "Shall We Dance?", "They All Laughed," "They Can't Take That Away From Me" by George and Ira Gershwin; "Flying Down to Rio," "Orchids in the Moonlight" by Vincent Youmans, Edward Eliscu and Gus Kahn; "Heigh-Ho! The Gang's All Here," "Let's Go Bavarian" by Burton Lane and Harold Adamson; "I Won't Dance" and "The Way You Look Tonight" (with Dorothy Fields), "You Were Never Lovelier" (with Johnny Mercer), "Waltz in Swing Time" by Jerome Kern; "My Sunny Tennessee," "Nevertheless," "So Long, Oo-Long," "Thinking of You," "Three Little Words" by Bert Kalmar and Harry Ruby; "Say, Young Man of Manhattan" by Vincent Youmans and Harold Adamson; "You're All the World to Me" by Burton Lane and Alan Jay Lerner.

Finkel's Follies (65). Musical revue conceived by Fyvush Finkel; adapted by Robert H. Livingston; music by Elliot Finkel; lyrics by Phillip Namanworth. Produced by Eric Krebs at the John Houseman Theater. Opened December 15, 1991; see note. (Closed March 8, 1992)

Mary Ellen Ashley	Fyvush Finkel
Avi Ber Hoffman	Laura Turnbull

Directed by Robert H. Livingston; musical staging, James J. Mellon; scenery and costumes, Mimi Maxmen; lighting, Bob Bessoir; musical direction, Mike Huffman; historian, Gertrude Finkel; production stage manager, Robert Lemieux; press, David Rothenberg.

Subtitled An American Musical Vaudeville, sketches and songs reminiscent of the Yiddish vaudeville shows from the 1920s to mid-century.

Note: *Finkel's Follies* was one of 1991-92's long previewers, having begun performing at the John Houseman 8/29/91. After 19 performances there 12/15/91-1/1/92, it transferred to the Westside Theater 1/30/92, continuing its run and inviting critics to the reopening.

ACT I

"Yiddish Vaudeville Tonight" . . . . Company
Dallas . . . . Fyvush Finkel, Avi Ber Hoffman
How It All Began. . . . . Finkel, Company
"Mom, I Want To Be in Yiddish Vaudeville" . . . . Laura Turnbull
Togetherness. . . . . Turnbull, Mary Ellen Ashley, Finkel
"You Were Meant For Me". . . . . Finkel, Ashley
A Look Back . . . . Finkel, Company
"A Kliene Soft Shoe" . . . . Finkel, Turnbull
The Landlord. . . . . Hoffman, Turnbull, Finkel
"Ringa Zinga". . . . . Ashley
"Tankhum". . . . . Finkel
    (by Solomon Golub)

"Mi-Komash Melon" (What Is the Meaning?) . . . . Hoffman
   (by A. Reisen and N.L. Saslavsky)
The Genuine Article . . . . Company
   "Rozinkes Mit Mandlen" (Raisins and Olives)
     (by Abraham Goldfaden)
   "Di Greene Kuzeene" (My Little Cousin)
     (by Abe Schwartz)
   "Yossel, Yossel" (Joseph, Joseph)
     (by Nellie Casman)
   "Ich Hob Dich Tzufil Lieb" (I Love You Too Much)
     (music by Alexander Olshanetsky)
   "Belz" (Wonderful Girl of Mine)
     (music by Alexander Olshanetsky)

ACT II

It Happened One Night . . . . Hoffman, Turnbull, Finkel
"Vaudeville, Kosher Style" . . . . Ashley, Hoffman, Turnbull
"Not on the Top" . . . . Finkel
   (by Abe Ellstein)
"That Something Special" . . . . Hoffman, Turnbull

FINKEL'S FOLLIES—Mary Ellen Ashley and Fyvush Finkel,
who conceived this production based on Yiddish vaudeville

The Farewell . . . . Finkel, Turnbull, Hoffman
The Shawl . . . . Ashley
    "Vee Zenen Meine Zibn Gute Yor" (Where Are My Seven Good Years?)
      (by David Meyerowitz)
    "Oy Mama"
      (music by Abe Ellstein, lyrics by Molly Picon)
    "Rozinkes Mit Mandlen" (Reprise)
    "The Fiddle"
    "Tzi Vus Darf Ich Zein Du?" (Why Do I Have To Be Here?)
"These Are the Jokes" . . . . Company
    Auditions . . . . Company
"Odenemya" . . . . Hoffman
    The Golden Wedding . . . . Finkel, Ashley
"Abi Tsu Zein Mit Dir" (As Long as I'm With You) . . . . Finkel, Ashley
Finale . . . . Company

Big Noise of '92 (1). Musical revue subtitled Diversions From the New Depression. Produced by Neilan Tyree at the Cherry Lane Theater. Opened and closed December 16, 1991.

CAST: Neilan Tyree, Mink Stole, Kit McClure and her all-girl orchestra, Joel Forrester (piano), Tim Michael, Tom Kosis.

Scenery, Ann Davis; costumes, Gregg Barnes; lighting, Douglas O'Flaherty; sound, Serge Ossorguine; choreography, Tony Musco; wigs, Elizabeth Katherine Carr; musical arrangements, Mario Sprouse; assistant producer, Gregg Wilcynski; press, David Rothenberg Associates.

Variety show of satirical vignettes and characterizations, presented in two parts.

Raft of the Medusa (30). By Joe Pintauro. Produced by Peggy Hill Rosenkranz at the Minetta Lane Theater. Opened December 19, 1991. (Closed January 12, 1992)

Tommy	Robert Alexander	Bob	David F. Louden
Cora	Annie Corley	Larry	Bruce McCarty
Nairobi	Brenda Denmark	Doug	Reggie Montgomery
Alec	William Fichtner	Michael	Patrick Quinn
Donald	Dan Futterman	Felicia	Abigael Sanders
Jimmy	Robert Jimenez	Alan	Cliff Weissman
Jerry	Steven Keats		

Understudies: Messrs. Alexander, Fichtner, Futterman, McCarty—Joseph Fuqua; Messrs. Keats, Quinn, Louden—Michael Gaston; Misses Corley, Sanders, Denmark—Madigan Ryan; Messrs. Jimenez, Montgomery, Weissman—J. Ed Araiza.

Directed by Sal Trapani; scenery, Phillip Baldwin; costumes, Laura Crow; lighting, Dennis Parichy, Mal Sturchio; sound, Chuck London; fight staging, Rick Sordelet; production stage manager, Marjorie Horne; stage manager, Anne Marie Paolucci; press, Keith Sherman & Associates.

Victims of a shipwreck clinging to a raft as a metaphor for AIDS. The play was presented without intermission. Previously produced OOB at HOME for Contemporary Theater and Art 7/90.

Chess (83). Revival of the musical with book and lyrics by Tim Rice; music by Benny Anderson and Bjorn Ulvaeus. Produced by The Artist's Perspective in association with Chess Players Ltd. at the Master Theater. Opened February 1, 1992. (Closed April 12, 1992)

Florence Vassy	Kathleen Rowe McAllen	Arbiter	Patrick Jude
Anatoly Sergievsky	J. Mark McVey	Svetlana Sergievsky	Jan Horvath
Frederick Trumper	Ray Walker	Alexander Molokov	Bob Frisch

Ensemble: Mark Ankeny, Michael Gerhart, Mary Illes, David Koch, Nita Moore, Ric Ryder, Carol Schuberg, Rebecca Timms.

Orchestra: Phil Reno conductor; Garth Roberts associate conductor; Jim Abbott, Phil Reno, Garth Roberts keyboards; Ray Grappone drums; Rich Prior reeds.

Understudies: Miss McAllen—Nita Moore; Mr. McVey—Michael Gerhart; Mr. Walker—Ric Ryder; Mr. Jude—David Koch; Miss Horvath—Nita Moore; Mr. Frisch—Mark Ankeny; Ensemble—Jill Patton.

Directed by David Taylor; musical supervision and direction, Phil Reno; choreographer and assistant director, Madeline Paul; scenery, Tony Castrigno; costumes, Deborah Rooney; lighting, John Hastings; sound, Creative Audio Design; new arrangements and orchestrations, Phil Reno; production stage manager, Doug Fogel; press, JR Public Relations, Judy Rabitcheff.

Abridged and somewhat revised version of the British musical that was produced on Broadway 4/28/88 for 68 performances.

ACT I: MERANO, ITALY, 1972

Prologue. . . . . Arbiter
Scene 1: Merano
"Merano" . . . . Arbiter, Freddie, Ensemble
Scene 2: Anatoly's hotel room
"Where I Want To Be" . . . . Molokov, Svetlana, Anatoly, Ensemble
Scene 3: Freddie's hotel room
"How Many Women" . . . . Florence, Freddie
Scene 4: The tournament arena
"US vs. USSR". . . . . Ensemble
"The Arbiter's Song" . . . . Arbiter, Ensemble
"Chess Game #1". . . . . Orchestra
"A Model of Decorum and Tranquility" . . . . Molokov, Florence, Arbiter, Anatoly
"Chess Hymn" . . . . Ensemble
Scene 5: Anatoly's hotel room
"Someone Else's Story". . . . . Svetlana
Scene 6: Freddie's hotel room
"Nobody's on Nobody's Side" . . . . Florence, Ensemble
Scene 7: The hotel lobby
"The Merchandisers' Song" . . . . Freddie, Ensemble
Scene 8: Mountain top meeting
"Mountain Top Duet" . . . . Florence, Anatoly
"Who'd Ever Guess It?" . . . . Freddie
Scene 9: The tournament arena
"Chess Game #2". . . . . Orchestra
"Florence Quits" . . . . Freddie, Florence
"Pity the Child". . . . . Freddie
"Where I Want To Be" (Reprise) . . . . Anatoly, Florence
"Anthem". . . . . Anatoly

ACT II: BANGKOK, THAILAND, ONE YEAR LATER

Prologue. . . . . Arbiter
Scene 1: Bangkok
"One Night in Bangkok" . . . . Arbiter, Ensemble
Scene 2: Anatoly and Florence's hotel room
"Heaven Help My Heart" . . . . Florence
"Argument" . . . . Florence, Anatoly
Scene 3: Molokov's hotel room
"The Confrontation" . . . . Anatoly, Molokov, Svetlana
Scene 4: The hotel lobby
"No Contest" . . . . Anatoly, Freddie
Scene 5: Florence and Svetlana's balconies
"I Know Him So Well". . . . . Florence, Svetlana
Scene 6: The deal
"The Deal" . . . . Company
Scene 7: The tournament arena
"Endgame" . . . . Company
"You and I/Epilogue" . . . . Florence, Anatoly

Julie Halston's Lifetime of Comedy (125). One-woman performance written and performed by Julie Halston. Produced by Drew Dennett at the Actors' Playhouse. Opened

February 2, 1992. (Closed June 7, 1992)

Scenery, B.T. Whitehill; lighting, Vivien Leone; associate producers, Dea Lawrence, Carmel Gunther; production stage manager, Allison Sommers; press, Shirley Herz Associates, Sam Rudy.

Autobiographical monologue as comedy. The play was presented without intermission.

Grandchild of Kings (97). Adapted by Harold Prince from the autobiographies of Sean O'Casey. Produced by The Irish Repertory Theater Company, Inc., Ciaran O'Reilly and Charlotte Moore artistic directors, and One World Arts Foundation in the Irish Repertory Theater Company production at Theater for the New City. Opened February 16, 1992. (Closed May 10, 1992)

The Family:	
Old Sean . . . . Chris O'Neill	Mrs. Saunders; Ensemble . . . . . Paddy Croft
Sean . . . . Patrick Fitzgerald	Headmaster; Ensemble. . . . . . Chris Carrick
Johnny (Young Sean) . . . . . Padraic Moyles	Woods; Ensemble . . . . Denis O'Neill
Sue . . . . Pauline Flanagan	Drunken Woman;
Ella; Ensemble . . . . Terry Donnelly	Ensemble. . . . . Georgia Southcotte
Archie; Ensemble . . . . Ciaran O'Reilly	Reverend; Ensemble. . . . Dermot McNamara
Tom; Ensemble . . . . Ciaran Sheehan	Middleton; Ensemble . . . . Brian F. O'Byrne
Michael; Ensemble. . . . . . . Michael Judd	Daisy Battles; Ensemble . . . . . Louise Favier
The Life of Dublin:	Alice; Ensemble . . . . Rosemary Fine
Tram Conductor; Ensemble. . Nesbitt Blaisdell	Drummer Benson; Ensemble . . Chris A. Kelly
	Jenny Clitheroe; Ensemble . . . Maeve Cawley

Musicians: Rusty Magee conductor, piano; Carmel Johnston fiddle; Mary Courtney guitar, bodhran; Marge Mulvehill tin whisle, flute.

Directed by Harold Prince; scenery, Eugene Lee; costumes, Judith Anne Dolan; lighting, Peter Kaczorowski; sound, James M. Bay; musical direction, Martha Hitch; choreography, Barry McNabb; assistant to Mr. Prince, Charlotte Moore; production stage manager, Kathe Mull; stage manager, Jonathan Arak; press, Boneau/Bryan-Brown, Susanne Tighe.

Time: 1880-1910. Place: Dublin. The play was presented in two parts.

Sean O'Casey growing from youth to manhood in Dublin, the first part of a projected two-part autobiography of the noted Irish playwright.

Just a Night Out (65). Musical by Richard and Susan Turner; score includes numbers by Cole Porter and Betty Comden and Adolph Green. Produced by Negro Ensemble Company, Douglas Turner Ward artistic director, at Top of the Village Gate. Opened February 16, 1992. (Closed April 12, 1992)

CAST: Zenzele Scott, Messeret Stroman, Bruce Butler, Chandra Simmons, Deborah Keeling.

Directed by Leslie Dockery; scenery, Lisa Watson; costumes, Gregory Clenn; lighting, Sandra Ross; press, Peter Cromarty, David B. Katz.

Jazz singing group performs in a small city, with romances between the leader and his backup singers.

*The Substance of Fire (110). Return engagement of the play by Jon Robin Baitz. Produced by Lincoln Center Theater under the direction (as of 2/27/92) of Andre Bishop and Bernard Gersten at the Mitzi E. Newhouse Theater. Opened February 27, 1992.

Sarah Geldhart . . . . . . Sarah Jessica Parker	Aaron Geldhart. . . . . Jon Tenney
Martin Geldhart . . . . Patrick Breen	Marge Hackett. . . . . Maria Tucci
Isaac Geldhart. . . . . Ron Rifkin	

Understudies: Mr. Rifkin—Stan Lachow; Miss Tucci—Lucy Martin; Miss Parker—Cordelia Richards; Messrs. Breen, Tenney—Drew McVety.

Directed by Daniel Sullivan; scenery, John Lee Beatty; costumes, Jess Goldstein; lighting, Arden Fingerhut; sound, Scott Lehrer; production stage manager, Roy Harris; stage manager, Jane E. Seiler; press, Merle Debuskey Associates, Susan Chicoine.

Act I: Spring 1987, a conference room, Kreeger/Geldhart publishers, New York City. Act II: Three and one-half years later, an apartment on Gramercy Park.

Return engagement of the play with the same cast as originally produced in New York by Playwrights

Horizons 3/17/91 for 120 performances (see its entry in the Plays Produced Off Broadway section of *The Best Plays of 1990-91*).

The Other Side of Paradise (21). By John Kane. Produced by Martin R. Kaufman at the Kaufman Theater. Opened March 5, 1992. (Closed March 22, 1992)

F. Scott Fitzgerald . . . . Keir Dullea

Directed by Susie Fuller; music composed and produced by Fred Hellerman; costumes, Mary Peterson; lighting, Michael Chybowski; sound, Raymond D. Schilke; vocals, Michael Duffy; set decorator, Pearl Broms; stage manager, Deborah Cressler; press, Howard J. Rubinstein Associates, Gary Zarr, Janice Addams.

Act I: A bungalow attached to the Ambassador Hotel in Hollywood, circa 1927. Act II: The living room of Sheila Graham's apartment in Hollywood, Dec. 20, 1940.

One-man performance by Keir Dullea as the noted writer. Previously produced at the White Barn Theater, Westport, Conn.

Bert Sees the Light (40). By R.A. White. Produced by Sito Productions and Dave Feldman in association with Gentlemen Productions at the 45th Street Theater. Opened March 10, 1992. (Closed April 12, 1992)

CAST: Jack Black, Molly Bryant, Michael Rivkin.

Directed by R.A. White; scenery, R.A. White; costumes, Virginia M. Johnson; lighting, Dave Feldman; production stage manager, Jill Cordle; press, David Rothenberg Associates.

Bertolt Brecht's years in Hollywood, with Messrs. Black and Rivkin playing Brecht and Miss Bryant playing the women in his life. Brecht poems included in this text (with translators' names in parentheses) are: *Awaiting the Second Five-Year Plan, Hollywood Elegies 1 & 3, Hounded Out by Seven Nations, Epitaph for M, I the Survivor* (John Willet); *Sonnet in Emigration* (Edith Roseveare); *Of Poor B.B., Hollywood* (Michael Hamburger); *In View of Conditions in This Town, Deliver the Goods* (Humphrey Milnes); *The Swamp* (Naomi Replansky). Previously produced in regional theater at Intersection for the Arts in San Francisco.

Shmulnik's Waltz (71). By Allan Knee. Produced by Daryl Roth at the John Houseman Theater. Opened March 11, 1992. (Closed May 10, 1992)

Shmulnik . . . . Steve Routman		Father . . . . Robert Katims
Friend; Captain; Zalman; Others . . . Jerry Matz		Minnie . . . . Marilyn Pasekoff
Rachel. . . . . Wendy Kaplan		Jonathan . . . . Rob Gomes
Feyla. . . . . Ilana Levine		

Understudies: Messrs. Routman, Gomes—Michael Ornstein; Messrs. Matz, Katims—Joel Rooks; Misses Kaplan, Levine—Rachel Black.

Musicians: William Schimmel accordian, Mary Rowell violin.

Directed by Gordon Hunt; scenery, Ray Recht; costumes, David Loveless; lighting, Betsy Finston; musical direction and adaptation, William Schimmel; production stage manager, D.C. Rosenberg; press, Jeffrey Richards Associates, Denise Robert.

Time: Turn of the century. Place: New York City. The play was presented in two parts.

Romantic comedy, a peddler strives to win the affections of his true love. Previously produced off off Broadway at the Jewish Repertory Theater.

*****Lotto** (89). By Cliff Roquemore. Produced by Lafayette Ltd., Barbara Lerman, C. Frazier Enlow in association with Dick Scott, Ashton Springer executive producer, in the Billie Holiday Theater production at the Hecksher Theater. Opened March 15, 1992.

Horace Benson. . . . . Earl Fields Jr.		Blaze Jaxon . . . . Otis Young Smith
Spike . . . . Karl Calhoun		Nett . . . . Elise Chinyere Chance
Pearline Benson . . . . Peace Roberts		Seth Goldberg . . . . John L. Bennett
Mildred Banks . . . . Jessica Smith		Nathan Stokes . . . . Steve Baumer
Junebug . . . . Bryan Roquemore		Rochelle Moten . . . . Bridget Kelso
Lester Franklin . . . . Maurice Fontane		

GRANDCHILD OF KINGS—Patrick Fitzgerald and Chris O'Neill portraying Sean O'Casey at two stages of his life in a biographical play adapted and directed by Harold Prince

Alternates: Mr. Fields—Billy Ward; Messrs. Calhoun, Roquemore—Frederick Kiah Jr.; Miss Chance—Bridget Kelso; Messrs. Smith, Fontane—Gordon Lee; Miss Roberts—Cyndi B. Galloway-O'Connor; Miss Smith—Beverly Bonner.

Directed by Cliff Roquemore; scenery and costumes, Felix E. Cochren; lighting, Shirley Prendergast; original music, Joe Zamberlin, Melvin Brannon; production stage manager, Avan; press, Peter Cromarty, David B. Katz.

Time: The present. Place: Los Angeles. Act I, Scene 1: Benson home, early evening. Scene 2: The next day. Scene 3: The next day, dusk. Act II, Scene 1: New Benson home, three months later. Scene 2: One month later. Scene 3: The next morning. Scene 4: Later that evening.

Subtitled Experience the Dream, comedy about a big lottery win and its effect on a family.

*Forbidden Broadway 1992 (64). Created and written by Gerard Alessandrini. Produced by Jonathan Scharer at Theater East. Opened April 6, 1992.

Brad Ellis	Michael McGrath
Leah Hocking	Patrick Quinn
Alix Korey	

Directed by Gerard Alessandrini; costumes, Erika Dyson; wigs, Teresa Vuoso; production consultant, Pete Blue; musical direction, Brad Ellis; assistant director, Phillip George; associate producer, Chip

Quigley; production stage manager, Jerry James; press, Shirley Herz Associates, Glenna Freedman.

10th anniversary edition of the revue sending up popular New York stage attractions. The show was presented in two parts.

Dancing on the White House Lawn (17). One-woman performance by Donna Blue Lachman; written by Donna Blue Lachman. Produced by the Ballroom at the Ballroom. Opened May 6, 1992. (Closed May 31, 1992)

> Directed by David Petrarca; presented by Tim Johnson; press, David Rothenberg.
> Autobiographical monologue, the adventures of an aspiring actress and playwright from the 1960s on. The play was presented without intermission.

*Ruthless! (31). Musical with book and lyrics by Joel Paley; music by Marvin Laird. Produced by Musical Theater Works, Anthony J. Stimac artistic director, Mike Teele managing director, at the Players Theater. Opened May 6, 1992.

Sylvia St. Croix . . . . Joel Vig	Myrna Thorn; Reporter . . . . . . Susan Mansur
Judy Denmark. . . . . Donna English	Louise Lerman; Eave . . . . Joanne Baum
Tina Denmark. . . . . Laura Bundy	Lita Encore . . . . Denise Lor

> Understudies: Misses Bundy, Baum (Louise Lerman)—Rebecca Bowen; Misses Mansur, Lor, Baum (Eave), Mansur, Mr. Vig—Judy Frank.
> Directed by Joel Paley; musical direction, Marvin Laird; scenery, James Noone; costumes, Gail Cooper-Hecht; lighting, Kenneth Posner; sound, Tom Sorce; production stage manager, Pam Edington; stage manager, Susan Selig; press, Jeffrey Richards Associates, David LeShay.
> Act I: Small Town, U.S.A., now. Act II: New York, N.Y., four years later.
> The would-be child star as monster.

> MUSICAL NUMBERS: "Tina's Mother," "Born to Entertain," "Talent," "To Play This Part," "Third Grade," "The Lippy Song," "Where Tina Gets It From," "Kisses and Hugs," "Tina, My Daughter," "I Hate Musicals," "Angel Mom," "Eave's Song," "Look at Me," "Ruthless!"

*Eating Raoul (23). Musical based on the film *Eating Raoul*; book by Paul Bartel; music by Jed Feuer; lyrics by Boyd Graham. Produced by Max Weitzenhoffer, Stewart F. Lane, Joan Cullman and Richard Norton at the Union Square Theater. Opened May 13, 1992.

Mary Bland . . . . Courtenay Collins	Cop; Inez (Raoulette) . . . . . Lovette George
Paul Bland. . . . . Eddie Korbich	Donna the Dominatrix; Tyrone;
Mr. Doberman; Ginger . . . . M.W. Reid	Yolanda . . . . Cindy Benson
Mr. Kray; James; Junior . . . . Jonathan Brody	Raoul . . . . Adrian Zmed
Mr. Leech; Howard; Bobby. David Masenheimer	Gladys (Raoulette) . . . . Susan Wood

> Tourists, Swingers, etc.: Cindy Benson, Jonathan Brody, Lovette George, Allen Hidalgo, David Masenheimer, M.W. Reid.
> Orchestra: Albert Ahronheim conductor, keyboards; Sid Cherry keyboards; Kerry Meads drums, percussion; Dale Thompson acoustic and electric bass; Kevin McCann guitars.
> Understudies: Mr. Korbich—David Masenheimer; Miss Collins—Susan Wood; Mr. Zmed—Allen Hidalgo; Miss Benson—Lauren Goler-Kosarin; Mr. Reid—Jonathan Brody; Swings—Lauren Goler-Kosarin, Allen Hidalgo.
> Directed by Tony Kotite; choreography, Lynne Taylor-Corbett; musical direction, Albert Ahronheim; scenery, Loren Sherman; costumes, Franne Lee; lighting, Peggy Eisenhauer; sound, Peter J. Fitzgerald; orchestrations, Joseph Gianono; vocal arrangements, Jed Feuer, Albert Ahronheim; production stage manager, Alan Hall; stage manager, Ruth E. Rinkin; press, Keith Sherman.
> Time: Mid 1960s. Place: Los Angeles.
> Sex, murder and cannibalism in satirical context.

ACT I

Scene 1: The Blands' bedroom
  "Meet the Blands" . . . . Company
  "A Small Restaurant" . . . . Paul, Mary

Scene 2: Freeway; hospital; Kray's Liquor Store; bank; street
  "La La Land". . . . . Ensemble
Scene 3: The Blands' hallway
  "Swing, Swing, Swing" . . . . Ensemble
Scene 4: The Blands' apartment
  "A Small Restaurant" (Reprise) . . . . Paul, Mary
  "Happy Birthday Harry". . . . . Musclemen
  "You Gotta Take Pains". . . . . Donna, Her Boys
  "A Thought Occurs" . . . . Paul, Mary
Scene 5: The Blands' apartment
Scene 6: Donna's TV show
  "Sexperts". . . . . Girls
Scene 7: The Blands' apartment
  "Empty Bed" . . . . Junior, Mary
  "Basketball". . . . . Tyrone
Scene 8: The Blands' apartment
  "Tool for You". . . . . Raoul, Raoulettes
  "A Thought Occurs" (Reprise) . . . . Raoul, Paul, Mary
  "Think About Tomorrow" . . . . Raoul, Paul, Mary

ACT II

Scene 1: The Blands' apartment
  "Opening" . . . . Ensemble
Scene 2: Yolanda's Nightclub
  "Hot Monkey Love". . . . . Raoul, Raoulettes
Scene 3: The Blands' apartment
  "A Small Restaurant" (Reprise) . . . . Paul, Mary
  "Momma Said". . . . . Ginger, Paul, Mary, Raoul
  "Lovers in Love" . . . . Raoul, Mary
  "Mary". . . . . Paul
Scene 4: Yolanda's Nightclub; Raoul's dressing room
  "Eating Raoul". Raoul, Raoulettes, Ensemble
  "Mucho Macho Trio" . . . . Raoul, Paul, Mary
Scene 5: Yolanda's Nightclub (after hours)
  "Eating Raoul" (Reprise). . . . . Raoul
Scene 6: The Blands' apartment
  "One Last Bop". . . . . Mary, Ensemble
Scene 7: Finale . . . . Company

*Hauptmann (6). By John Logan. Produced by Dowling Entertainment, John Walker and Pamela Gay, Hal "Corky" Kessler and Gintare Sileika Everett in association with Charles J. Scibetti, in the Victory Gardens Theater production, Dennis Zacek artistic director, at the Cherry Lane Theater. Opened May 28, 1992.

Richard Hauptmann . . . . Denis O'Hare   Anna Hauptmann . . . . Wendy Lucker
Charles Lindbergh. . . . . Gunnar Branson   Dr. Condon. . . . . Dev Kennedy
Anne Morrow Lindbergh . . . . . Donna Powers   Judge Trenchard . . . . Rod McLachlan
Prosecuting Attorney Wilentz. . . . Craig Spidle

Directed by Terry McCabe; scenery, James Dardenne; costumes, Claudia Boddy; lighting, Todd Hensley; sound, Galen G. Ramsey; choreography, Ann Hartdegen; production stage manager, Kristin Larsen; press, Boneau/Bryan-Brown, Cabrini Lepis, Craig Karpel.

Time: April 3, 1936. Place: Richard Hauptmann's prison cell on Death Row. The play was presented in two parts.

Dramatization of the case against convicted kidnapper Bruno Richard Hauptmann. Previously produced at Victory Gardens Theater, Chicago, and the Edinburgh International Theater Festival.

CAST REPLACEMENTS AND
TOURING COMPANIES

The following is a list of the major cast replacements of record in productions which opened in previous years, but were still playing in New York during a substantial part of the 1991-92 season; or were still on a first-class tour in 1991-92 (replacements in first-class touring companies of previous seasons which were no longer playing in 1991-92 appear in previous *Best Plays* volumes of appropriate years).

The name of each major role is listed in *italics* beneath the title of the play in the first column. In the second column directly opposite appears the name of the actor who created the role in the original New York production (whose opening date appears in *italics* at the top of the column). Indented immediately beneath the original actor's name are the names of subsequent New York replacements, together with the date of replacement when available.

The third column gives information about first-class touring companies produced under the auspices of their original New York managements. When there is more than one roadshow company, #1, #2, etc., appear before the name of the performer who created the role in each company (and the city and date of each company's first performance appears in *italics* at the top of the column). Their subsequent replacements are also listed beneath their names, with dates when available.

BREAKING LEGS

	New York 5/19/91
Lou Graziano	Vincent Gardenia
Angie	Sue Giosa
	Karen Valentine 1/21/92
Mike Francisco	Philip Bosco
Frankie Salvucci	Larry Storch

BUDDY: THE BUDDY HOLLY STORY

	New York 11/4/90	*Hartford, Conn. 9/10/91*
Buddy Holly	Paul Hipp	Joe Warren Davis

CATS

	New York 10/7/82
Alonzo	Hector Mercado
	Brian Sutherland
	Scott Taylor
	General MacArthur Hambrick

Michael Koetting
Scott Taylor
Stephen M. Reed

Bustopher Jones; Asparagus;   Stephen Hanan
   Growltiger   Timothy Jerome
                                     Gregg Edelman
                                     Bill Carmichael
                                     Stephen Hanan
                                     Paul Harman
                                     Dale Hensley
                                     John Dewar
                                     Jeffrey Clonts

Bombalurina   Donna King
                                     Marlene Danielle

Cassandra   Rene Ceballos
                                     Christina Kumi Kimball
                                     Nora Brennan
                                     Charlotte d'Amboise
                                     Jessica Northrup
                                     Roberta Stiehm
                                     Julietta Marcelli
                                     Leigh Webster
                                     Darlene Wilson

Coricopat   Rene Clemente
                                     Guillermo Gonzalez
                                     Joe Antony Cavise
                                     Johnny Anzalone
                                     Devanand Janki
                                     Johnny Anzalone

Demeter   Wendy Edmead
                                     Marlene Danielle
                                     Jane Bodle
                                     Patricia Ruck
                                     Beth Swearingen
                                     Brenda Braxton
                                     Meera Popkin
                                     Mercedes Perez

Grizabella   Betty Buckley
                                     Laurie Beechman
                                     Loni Ackerman
                                     Heidi Stallings
                                     Lillias White
                                     Laurie Beechman
                                     Diane Fratantoni
                                     Laurie Beechman

Jellylorum   Bonnie Simmons
                                     Nina Hennessey

Jennyanydots   Anna McNeely
                                     Cindy Benson
                                     Rose McGuire

Macavity   Kenneth Ard
                                     Scott Wise

Randy Wojcik
Robb Edward Morris

Mistoffelees

Timothy Scott
Herman W. Sebek
Jamie Torcellini
Michael Scott Gregory
Barry K. Bernal
Don Johanson
Kevin Poe
Todd Lester
Michael Barriskill
Michael Arnold
Gen Horiuchi
Kevin Poe
Gen Horiuchi

Mungojerrie

Rene Clemente
Steven Gelfer
Ray Roderick
Todd Lester
Roger Kachel

Munkustrap

Harry Groener
Claude R. Tessier
Mark Fotopoulos
Rob Marshall
Robert Amirante
Greg Minahan
Bryan Batt
Robert Amirante
Bryan Batt

Old Deuteronomy

Ken Page
Kevin Marcum
Clent Bowers
Larry Small
Ken Prymus
Larry Small
Ken Prymus

Pouncival

Herman Sebek
Ramon Galindo
Robert Montano
John Joseph Festa
Devanand Janki

Rum Tum Tugger

Terrence Mann
Jamie Rocco
Rick Sparks
Steve Yudson
Frank Mastrocola
Bradford Minkoff

Rumpleteazer

Christine Langner
Paige Dana
Kristi Lynes

Sillabub

Whitney Kershaw
Denise Direnzo

Teresa Dezarn
Susan Santoro
Dana Walker
Michelle Schumacher
Lisa Mayer
Joyce Chittick
Lisa Mayer

Skimbleshanks

Reed Jones
Michael Scott Gregory
Robert Burnett
Reed Jones
Richard Stafford
Eric Scott Kincaid
Michael Scott Gregory
George Smyros

Tantomile

Janet Hubert
Sundy Leigh Leake
Lisa Dawn Cave
April Nixon
Michelle Artigas

Tumblebrutus

Robert Hoshour
Jay Poindexter
Randy Bettis
Joey Pizzi
John Vincent Leggio

Victoria

Cynthia Onrubia
Valerie C. Wright
Claudia Shell

CITY OF ANGELS

	New York 12/11/89	*Los Angeles 6/4/91*
Stone	James Naughton Tom Wopat 12/31/90 Joel Higgins 8/27/91	James Naughton Jeff McCarthy Barry Williams
Stine	Gregg Edelman Michael Rupert 12/31/90	Stephen Bogardus Jordan Leeds
Oolie/Donna	Randy Graff Susan Terry 12/31/90 Carolee Carmello 10/10/91	Randy Graff Betsy Joslyn
Irving S. Irving/Buddy Fidler	Rene Auberjonois Richard Kline 4/23/91	Charles Levin

THE FANTASTICKS

New York 5/3/60

El Gallo

Jerry Orbach
Ken Kantor
Michael Scott

Michael X. Martin
Kim Moore 3/17/92

Luisa   Rita Gardner
                            Marilyn Whitehead 1/23/89

Matt   Kenneth Nelson
                            Kevin Wright
                            Christopher Scott

Note: Only this season's or the most recent cast replacements are listed above under the names of the original cast members. For previous replacements, see previous volumes of *Best Plays*.

A FEW GOOD MEN

	New York 11/25/89	*Hartford, Conn. 1/7/92*
Lt. j.g. Daniel A. Kaffee	Tom Hulce Timothy Busfield 5/14/90	Michael O'Keefe
Lt. Cmdr. Joan Galloway	Megan Gallagher Pamela Blair 6/25/90 Kathleen McNenny 1/7/91	Alyson Reed
Lt. Col. Nathan Jessep	Stephen Lang Ron Perlman Perry King 12/3/90	Scott Sowers
Capt. Julius Alexander Randolph	Paul Butler	Paul Winfield Paul Butler 4/14/92

FOREVER PLAID

	New York 5/20/90
Sparky	Jason Graae Dale Sandish 4/15/91 Michael Winther
Smudge	David Engel Greg Jbara
Jinx	Stan Chandler Paul Binotto
Francis	Guy Stroman Drew Geraci 4/30/91 Neil Nash

Note: Casts of two road companies appear in *The Best Plays of 1990-91*. Out-of-town stagings of *Forever Plaid* in 1991-92 were local productions.

GRAND HOTEL

	New York 11/12/89	*Tampa 11/27/90*
Otto Kringeline	Michael Jeter Chip Zien 9/12/90 Austin Pendleton	Mark Baker
Baron Felix Von Gaigern	David Carroll Brent Barrett 5/8/90	Brent Barrett

Rex Smith 5/29/90
David Carroll 12/2/90
John Schneider 3/4/91

Elizaveta Grushinskaya   Liliane Montevecchi   Liliane Montevecchi
Rene Ceballos 11/12/90
Cyd Charisse 1/92

Flaemmchen   Jane Krakowski   DeLee Lively
Lynnette Perry

LES MISÉRABLES

#1 Boston 12/5/87
#2 Los Angeles 5/21/88
New York 3/12/87   *#3 Tampa 11/28/88*

Jean Valjean   Colm Wilkinson   #1 William Solo
Gary Morris 11/30/87   Craig Schulman 4/88
Timothy Shew 5/30/88   J. Mark McVey
William Solo 7/3/89   Gary Morris
Craig Schulman 1/13/90   Mark McKerracher
J. Mark McVey 1/22/91   #2 William Solo
Mark McKerracher 11/19/92   Jordan Bennett
Rich Hebert
Kevin McGuire
Richard Poole
#3 Gary Barker
Richard Poole
Brian Lynch
Dave Clemmons

Javert   Terrence Mann   #1 Herndon Lackey
Anthony Crivello 11/30/87   Charles Pistone
Norman Large 1/18/88   Robert DuSold
Anthony Crivello 3/14/88   Richard Kinsey
Norman Large 7/19/88   #2 Jeff McCarthy
Herndon Lackey 1/17/89   Richard Kinsey
Peter Samuel 1/15/90   Tim Bowman
Robert Westenberg   #3 Peter Samuel
Robert DuSold   Paul Schoeffler
Richard Kinsey 11/19/92   David Jordan
Chuck Wagner

Fantine   Randy Graff   #1 Diane Fratantoni
Maureen Moore 7/19/88   Ann Crumb
Susan Dawn Carson 1/17/89   Hollis Resnik
Laurie Beechman 1/15/90   Kathy Taylor
Christy Baron   Susan Dawn Carson
Susan Dawn Carson 11/19/92   Laurie Beechman 1/89
Rachel York   Susan Gilmour
Anne Runolfsson
#2 Elinore O'Connell
Kelly Ground
#3 Hollis Resnik
Christy Baron
Lisa Vro man
Donna Keane
Jill Geddes

Enjolras	Michael Maguire Joseph Kolinski Joe Locarro 1/15/90 Joseph Kolinski Joe Mahowald	#1 John Herrera Joe Locarro Pete Herber Christopher Yates #2 Greg Blanchard Raymond Sarr Craig Oldfather #3 Greg Zerkle Jerry Christakos Aloysius Gigl Christopher Yates
Marius	David Bryant Ray Walker Hugh Panaro Matthew Porretta John Leone Eric Kunze	#1 Hugh Panaro John Ruess Peter Gunther #2 Reece Holland Peter Gantenbein Matthew Porretta John Ruess #3 Matthew Porretta Gilles Chiasson Ron Sharpe
Cosette	Judy Kuhn Tracy Shayne Jacqueline Piro Melissa Anne Davis	#1 Tamara Jenkins Melissa Errico Kimberly Behlman #2 Karen Fineman Jacqueline Piro Ellen Rockne #3 Jacqueline Piro Tamara Hayden Lisa Vroman Marian Murphy Tamara Hayden
Eponine	Frances Ruffelle Kelli James 9/15/87 Natalie Toro 7/88 Debbie Gibson 1/7/92 Michele Maika Debbie Gibson 3/29/92	#1 Renee Veneziale Jennifer Naimo Susan Tilson #2 Michelle Nicastro Michele Maika Candese Marchese Misty Cotton #3 Michele Maika Dana Lynn Caruso Candese Marchese
Thenardier	Leo Burmester Ed Dixon Drew Eshelman	#1 Tom Robbins Neal Ben-Ari 12/5/88 Drew Eshelman #2 Gary Beach #3 Paul Ainsley J.P. Dougherty
Mme. Thenardier	Jennifer Butt Evalyn Baron 1/15/90	#1 Victoria Clark Rosalyn Rahn #2 Kay Cole Gina Ferrall #3 Linda Kerns Diana Rogers Gina Ferrall

LETTICE & LOVAGE

	New York 3/25/90	*Toronto 4/14/92*
Lettice Douffet	Maggie Smith	Julie Harris
Lotte Schoen	Margaret Tyzack	Roberta Maxwell

LOST IN YONKERS

	New York 2/21/91	*Chattanooga 10/28/91*
Grandma Kurnitz	Irene Worth Mercedes McCambridge 8/26/91 Rosemary Harris 10/14/91 Anne Jackson 6/2/92	Mercedes McCambridge
Bella	Mercedes Ruehl Jane Kaczmarek 8/26/91 Lucie Arnaz 6/2/92	Brooke Adams Susan Giosa 2/23/92 Brooke Adams 5/24/92
Louie	Kevin Spacey Bruno Kirby 8/12/91 Alan Rosenberg 12/16/91	Ned Eisenberg

Jane Kaczmarek (Bella) and Rosemary Harris (Grandma Kurnitz) in the 1991 replacement cast of Neil Simon's *Lost in Yonkers*

MISS SAIGON

New York 4/11/91

The Engineer

Jonathan Pryce
   Francis Ruivivar 8/19/91
   Jonathan Pryce 9/30/91
   Francis Ruivivar 12/16/91

Kim

Lea Salonga
   Leila Florentino 3/16/92

Chris

Willy Falk
   Sean McDermott 12/16/91

ONCE ON THIS ISLAND

	N.Y. Off B'way 5/6/90	
	N.Y. B'way 10/18/90	*Chicago 3/31/92*
Ti Moune	La Chanze	Vanita Harbour
Daniel	Jerry Dixon	Darius de Haas

THE PHANTOM OF THE OPERA

	New York 1/26/88	*#1 Los Angeles 5/31/90* *#2 Chicago 5/24/90*

The Phantom	Michael Crawford
	  Timothy Nolen 10/10/88
	  Cris Groenendaal 3/20/89
	  Steve Barton 3/19/90
	  Kevin Gray
	  Mark Jacoby 2/21/91
		#1 Michael Crawford
		  Robert Guillaume 5/1/90
		  Michael Crawford
		  Davis Gaines
		#2 Mark Jacoby
		  Kevin Gray

Christine Daaé	Sarah Brightman
	  Patti Cohenour 6/7/88
	  Dale Kristien (alt.) 7/88*
	  Rebecca Luker (alt.) 3/89*
	  Rebecca Luker 6/5/89
	  Katherine Buffaloe (alt.)*
	  Karen Culliver
	  Luann Aronson (alt.) 6/92
		#1 Dale Kristien
		  Mary Darcy (alt.)*
		#2 Karen Culliver
		  Teri Bibb (alt.)*
		  Sarah Pfisterer (alt.)*
		  Teri Bibb
		  Sarah Pfisterer (alt.)

Raoul	Steve Barton
	  Kevin Gray 9/18/90
	  Davis Gaines 3/12/90
	  Hugh Panaro
		#1 Reece Holland
		  Michael Piontek
		#2 Keith Buterbaugh
		  Nat Chandler 8/92

*Alternates play the role of Christine Daaé Monday and Wednesday evenings.

THE PIANO LESSON

	New York 4/16/90	*San Francisco 10/12/91*
Boy Willie	Charles S. Dutton	Isaiah Whitlock Jr.
Lymon	Rocky Carroll	Michael Jayce
Berniece	S. Epatha Merkerson	Starletta DuPois

| *Wining Boy* | Lou Myers | Danny Robinson Clark |
| | Ernie Scott 7/15/90 | |

THE SECRET GARDEN

	New York 4/25/91	*Cleveland 4/28/92*
Mary Lennox	Daisy Eagan	Melody Kay
	Kimberly Mahon	
	Lydia Ooghe 3/92	
Archibald Craven	Mandy Patinkin	Kevin McGuire
	Howard McGillin 8/27/91	

SIX DEGREES OF SEPARATION

N.Y. Off B'way 6/14/90
N.Y. B'way 11/8/90

Ouisa	Stockard Channing
	Kelly Bishop 8/6/91
	Stockard Channing 12/10/91
Flan	John Cunningham
Paul	James McDaniel
	Courtney B. Vance

THOSE WERE THE DAYS

	New York 11/7/90	*Boston 10/15/91*
	Bruce Adler	Mike Borstyn
	Mike Borstyn	
	Mina Bern	Mina Bern
	Robert Abelson	Robert Abelson
	Eleanor Reissa	Eleanor Reissa
	Lori Wilner	Lori Wilner

THE WILL ROGERS FOLLIES

	New York 5/1/91
Will Rogers	Keith Carradine
	Mac Davis 5/18/92
Betty Blake	Dee Hoty
	Nancy Ringham 5/18/92
Ziegfeld's Favorite	Cady Huffman
	Susan Anton 12/9/91
	Cady Huffman 1/27/92

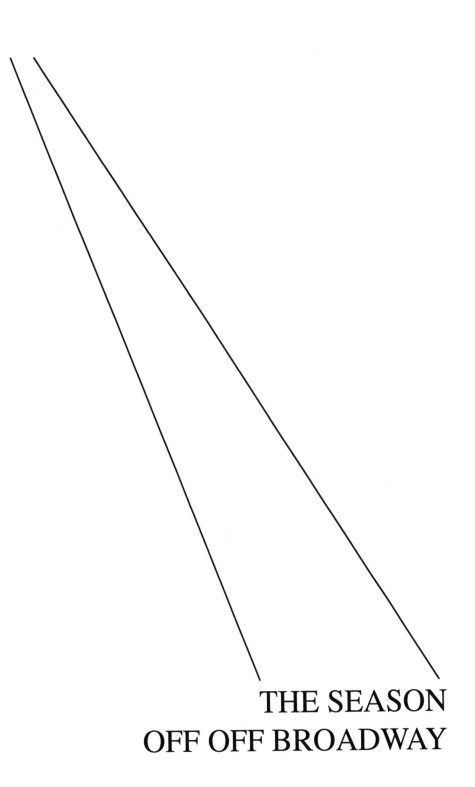

THE SEASON
OFF OFF BROADWAY

Mel Gussow Citations:
Outstanding
OOB Productions

Above, Steve Mellor (*foreground*) with Jan Leslie Harding, Lauren Hamilton, Anne O'Sullivan, William Mesnick and Tina Dudek in Mac Wellman's *A Murder of Crows* ("An apocalyptic comedy dealing with mankind's devastation of the environment"); *left*, Marin Hinkle and Peter Ashton Wise in Romulus Linney's *Ambrosio* ("A compelling exploration of obsessive love, both spiritual and temporal, during the Spanish Inquisition")

Right, Kristin Griffith, John Rotham, Lucille Patton and John Pankow in Percy Granger's *Scheherazade* ("Mirthful comedy about life confused with soap opera. . . . .Wittingly written and executed")

OFF OFF BROADWAY

By Mel Gussow

DESPITE the continuing economic emergency in the arts, off off Broadway had a productive season in 1991-1992, with a number of established playwrights, performers and companies reasserting their presence. There was a resurgence of work from, among others, Romulus Linney, Richard Foreman, the Ensemble Studio Theater and the Ridiculous Theatrical Company as well as the growth of new companies including the Atlantic Theater. Several theaters continued to be in jeopardy, and the Manhattan Punch Line, purveyors of laughter for 13 years, quietly closed down its operation. As usual, engagements were brief, and theatergoers had to be quick to catch a play or a performance piece before it closed or went on tour. Occasionally a show would move into an extended run, as was the case with plays as diverse as Ron McLarty's *The Dropper*, Todd Alcott's *One Neck* and Kevin Heelan's *Distant Fires*.

The Signature Theater Company fulfilled its admirable purpose by devoting an entire season to the work of one playwright, Romulus Linney, presenting premieres as well as revivals by this distinguished dramatist. Signature opened in the fall with a revival of Linney's historical drama *The Sorrows of Frederick*, with Austin Pendleton recreating the title role as Frederick the Great; and followed that with the New York premiere of *A Woman Without a Name* and a revival of *Heathen Valley*, two plays that are concerned with America's heartland. At the end of the season, Linney offered a new play, *Ambrosio* (cited here as an outstanding 1991-92 OOB produciton), a compelling exploration of obsessive love, both spiritual and temporal, during the Spanish Inquisition. James Houghton, head of the Signature company, will now choose other playwrights (presumably of Mr. Linney's stature) for succeeding festivals.

Richard Foreman, one of the most dedicated theatrical auteurs on the experimental scene, situated himself in a new space at St. Marks in the Bowery, one of the original sources of OOB. He opened in a darkly philosophical mood with *The Mind King*. Then, with Foreman's encouragement, two of his artistic associates, Paul Schiff Berman and Deborah Lewittes, staged *The Richard Foreman Trilogy*, drawn from previously unproduced work. Stylistically, this was Foreman in a non-Foreman manner, lush but filled with evocative stage pictures.

Theater for the New City continued to refurbish its home on Second Avenue and presented characteristically eclectic work, including an aberrant approach to Samuel Beckett in an evening entitled *Women in Beckett*. Needing money, Ellen Stewart threatened to close the doors of La Mama, but, in indomitable La Mama fashion, survived. Among this theater's contributions were John Jesurun's *Iron Lung*, a moody, elliptical visit to "Barton Fink" Country; and *Akin*, a new music-theater-dance piece by the virtuosic John Kelly (with Richard Peaslee as composer). In this co-production with the Music-Theater Group, Mr. Kelly looked back on the lives of medieval troubadours. The Performing Garage welcomed guest artists as well as the Wooster Group's Ron Vawter with *Roy Cohn/Jack Smith*, his correlation of the lives of this lawyer and filmmaker.

Everett Quinton, extending his range at the Ridiculous Theatrical Company, boldly revived *Bluebeard*, a signature piece of his predecessor and mentor Charles Ludlam, reinventing the title role in his own image. Later he did a star turn in a one-man version of that old melodrama, *The Bells*. Tisa Chang's Pan Asian Repertory turned to Japan for Kunio Shimizu's dreamlike backstage play *The Dressing Room*, then capped its season with Laurence Yep's *Fairy Bones*, about early Chinese settlers in the United States. While the Irish Repertory Company was busy with Sean O'Casey's autobiographies, the Irish Arts Center presented the New York premiere of Tony Kavanaugh's gritty *Down the Flats* and Judy GeBauer's docudrama, *Bobby Sands, M.P.*, about the Irish hunger striker. The American Jewish Theater slipped with Shelley Berman's creaky *First Is Supper* but regained its footing with a double bill of Charlie Schulman's *Angel of Death*, a lunatic comedy about Josef Mengele, and *Big Al*, a revival of the Bryan Goluboff comedy previously seen at the Ensemble Studio Theater. In the Schulman play, Daniel von Bargen gave one of the year's outstanding performances. In his poignant play, *The Dropper*, Ron McLarty looked back on emigration to America from rural England.

The Ensemble Studio Theater had an especially active year, principally because of its celebration of the anniversary of Columbus's discovery of America. Studying our nation's history and policies, Curt Dempster's troupe offered David Margulies in his own one-man show, *George Washington Dances*, in which a homeless person time-trips back to his days with our first president; *Deposing the White House*, drawn from documents about the Iran-Contra affair; a *New Living Newspaper*; and *Stars in Bars*, an amusing political cabaret prepared by Lew Black, Rusty Magee and others. *Big Frame Shakin'* was James G. Macdonald's autobiographical monologue about a rootless American, and Bill Bozzone's *Korea* was a wistful study about men at war but out of action. The Ensemble Studio Theater's annual Marathon of one-acts had its usual highs and lows. The rewarding work included *The Shallow End*, Wendy MacLeod's contemplation of adolescence; Bill Bozzone's *Fasting*, about a crisis in the lives of an older gay couple; Jon Shirota's sensitive cross-cultural *Ripples in the Pond*; Joyce Carol Oates's absurdist marital comedy, *Gulf War*; Frank D. Gilroy's Hollywood sendup, *Give the Bishop My Faint Regards*, and *Jenny Keeps Talking*, a madwoman's monologue written by Richard Greenberg under the pseudonym Lise Erlich. The choicest play of the 15 one-acts was Percy Granger's *Scheherazade*. Although this mirthful comedy about life confused with soap opera lasted only 30 minutes, it was so wittily written and executed (by a cast headed by John Rothman and John Pankow) that it earns a citation as an outstanding 1991-92 OOB production.

Mac Wellman, one of our most outspoken playwrights, was represented by two comedies. The first, the outrageously entitled *7 Blowjobs*, was a single-minded attack on government censorship of the arts; the second and more resonant work, *A Murder of Crows*, an apocalyptic comedy dealing with mankind's devastation of the environment. Cited as an outstanding OOB production, *A Murder of Crows* (at Primary Stages) raised an alarm about proliferating pollutants. It was given a sizzling production by Jim Simpson.

Puppetry was elevated in Janie Geiser's *When the Wind Blows/News Update*, two small chamber pieces by this Atlanta-based director, one a gathering of fairy tales, the other a spoof of television news. In *Invitations to Heaven (Questions of a Jewish Child)*, the puppeteer Eric Bass continued his autobiographical quest. Theodora Skipitares followed an uptown stint with *The Radiant City* at American Place Theater by returning to Theater for the New City for *Micropolis*, a compilation of highlights of her previous work. *Job: A Circus* was a vivid clown show from Elizabeth Swados.

In her final season at the CSC Repertory, Carey Perloff offered a varied menu, beginning with *Bon Appetit!*, Jean Stapleton's impersonation of Julia Child (and Ruth Draper). After that came the Weimar-style *Cabaret Verboten* and Len Jenkin's sprawling *Candide*. The most noteworthy event at the CSC was Perloff's staging of Strindberg's *Creditors*. The Jean Cocteau added Samuel Beckett and Vaclav Havel to its roster, and Jeffrey Horowitz's Theater for a New Audience invited the British director William Gaskill with a motley production of *The Comedy of Errors*.

While Caryl Churchill's *Mad Forest* was arresting audiences at the New York Theater Workshop, Theater Labrador/New Georges offered the first New York production of Churchill's *Vinegar Tom*, a provocative look at the suppression of women in England. *Approximating Mother* was Kathleen Tolan's discerning comedy about motherhood and adoption, a production of the Women's Project, which ended its season with Heather McDonald's *Dream of a Common Language*, about women Impressionist painters. On another stage, McDonald was represented by *The Rivers and Ravines*, a collage of stories about farmers and ranchers. The Home for Contemporary Theater and Art briefly set up home-keeping in Chelsea with Todd Alcott's *One Neck*, a comedy about a serial killer, starring the author. The Atlantic Theater Company proved to be at least semi-permanent, with the New York premiere of Kevin Heelan's *Distant Fires*, a probing look at the lives of construction workers, and Quincy Long's quirky service comedy, *The Virgin Molly*. Russell Davis's *Appointment With a High-Wire Lady* gave Victor Slezak a challenging role as a hospital patient suffering a memory loss.

A number of productions actively involved theatergoers in environments. In *As a Dream That Vanishes (A Meditation on the Harvest of a Lifetime)*, the team of Merry Conway and Noni Pratt mused about old age and death, as theatergoers walked through rooms lined with artifacts. In *Memento Mori*, an environmental installation at the Kitchen, Karen Finley commented on lost friends and drastically shortened lives. This was a more evocative piece than *Lamb of God Hotel*, a Finley play for other actors. Anne Hamburger's En Garde Arts trekked to Harlem for Laurie Carlos's collage, *Vanquished by Voodoo*, in which the site, an abandoned warehouse, proved to be far more interesting than the play. *Bernie's Bar Mitzvah* was the latest spinoff of the *Tony and Tina's Wedding* syndrome: invite people to a faux party, and they will come. Where *Tony and Tina* had a certain curiosity, *Bernie* was a bore. In any accounting of the OOB season, the Riverside Shakespeare Company's *Macbeth* merits a final footnote. Misconceived on a shoestring, the production lacked even a witch's cauldron and made Birnam Wood look like a potted plant.

PLAYS PRODUCED
OFF OFF BROADWAY

AND ADDITIONAL PRODUCTIONS

Here is a comprehensive sampling of off-off-Broadway and other experimental or peripheral 1991-92 productions in New York, compiled by Camille Croce. There is no definitive "off-off-Broadway" area or qualification. To try to define or regiment it would be untrue to its fluid, exploratory purpose. The listing below of hundreds of works produced by more than 100 OOB groups and others is as inclusive as reliable sources will allow, however, and takes in all leading Manhattan-based, new-play producing, English-language organizations.

The more active and established producing groups are identified in **bold face type**, in alphabetical order, with artistic policies and the names of the managing directors given whenever these are a matter of record. Each group's 1991-92 schedule, with emphasis on new plays and with revivals of classics usually omitted, is listed with play titles in CAPITAL LETTERS. Often these are works-in-progress with changing scripts, casts and directors, sometimes without an engagement of record (but an opening or early performance date is included when available).

Many of these off-off-Broadway groups have long since outgrown a merely experimental status and are offering programs which are the equal in professionalism and quality (and in some cases the superior) of anything in the New York theater, with special contractual arrangements like the showcase code, letters of agreement (allowing for longer runs and higher admission prices than usual) and, closer to the edge of the commercial theater, a so-called "mini-contract." In the list below, all available data on opening dates, performance numbers and major production and acting credits (almost all of them Equity members) is included in the entries of these special-arrangement offerings.

A large selection of lesser-known groups and other shows that made appearances off off Broadway during the season appears under the "Miscellaneous" heading at the end of this listing.

Amas Musical Theater. Dedicated to bringing all people, regardless of race, creed, color or economic background, together through the creation and development of new American musicals. Rosetta LeNoire founder and artistic director.

GUNMETAL BLUES (45). Book, Scott Wentworth; music and lyrics, Craig Bohmler and Marion Adler. April 4, 1992. Director, Davis Hall; scenery and costumes, Eduardo Sicangco; lighting, Scott Zielinski; musical director, Craig Bohmler. With Daniel Marcus, Michael Knowles, Marion Adler, Scott Wentworth.

JUNKYARD (workshop) (24). Book, Manuel Mandel and Michael Sahl; music, Michael Sahl;

lyrics, Manuel Mandel. May 14, 1992. Director, Avi Ber Hoffman; choreography, Barry Finkel; scenery, John Farrell; lighting, William Kradlak; costumes, Jessica Doyle. With Nicholas Augustus, Richert Easley, Julie Jirousek, Peter-Michael Kalin, Rick Leon, Susan Levine, Chris N. Norris, Obie Story, Natalie Toro, Darlene B. Young.

American Place Theater. In addition to the regular off-Broadway season, other special projects are presented. Wynn Handman director, Dara Hershman general manager.

FREE SPEECH IN AMERICA (59). Written and performed by Roger Rosenblatt. November 6, 1991. Director, Wynn Handman; lighting, Todd Bearden.

REALITY RANCH (27). Written and performed by Jane Gennaro. November 8, 1991. Director, Peter Askin; scenery and costumes, John Esposito; lighting, Natasha Katz; music, Daniel Schreier.

AND (19). By Roger Rosenblatt. March 8, 1992. Director, Wynn Handman; scenery, Kert Lundell; lighting, Brian MacDevitt. With Ron Silver.

American Theater of Actors. Dedicated to providing a creative atmosphere for new American playwrights, actors and directors. James Jennings, artistic director.

JAYHAWKS. Written and directed by James Jennings. June 12, 1991. With Tom Bruce, John Koprowski, Jim Shanley, Pati Sands, Tom O'Donoghue.

VOLLIES. By Robert Flannery. June 19, 1991. Director, Chris Olsen. With Chessie Roberts, Anne Flanagan, Mark Scherman, Kathy Durkin, Mike Roston, Belle Schneider.

WHAT'S A WOMAN TO DO? Written and directed by Andrea Fletcher. June 19, 1991. With Patrick Farrell, Janice Jenkins, Brenda Porter, Susann Singleton.

THE ARLES COUPLE. By T.J. Koshonski. July 10, 1991. Director, Mark Del Castillo Morante. With Jerome Richards, Lars Rosagher, Duane Boutte.

MOTHER'S LITTLE HELPER. Written and directed by Marilyn Seven. July 31, 1991. With Keith Heiman, Fred John, Helen Palladino, Donna Wynters.

BUTCHER OF BUDAPEST. Written and directed by Joseph King. September 25, 1991. With James Massey, Jerome Richards, Tom Bruce, Sandra Galati, Paul Dommermuth.

FOLKLIFE. Written and directed by James Jennings. October 9, 1991. With Keith Burns, Patrick Connelly, Greg Fox. Reopened November 5, 1991.

IN THE COUNTRY. By Walter Corwin. October 30, 1991. Director, James Jennings. With Jill Newman, Don Sheehan, Babrara Bayer, Norman Kruger, Donna Langen.

SAND PIES AND SCISSOR LEGS. By Mark Dunn. November 6, 1991. Director, Valerie Harris. With Matthew Healy, Lonnie Jones, Doris Reardon, Don Lowe, Jennifer Rosenberg, Dana Silverman.

WHERE THE ANGELS PLAY. By James O'Connor. November 20, 1991. Director, James Jennings. With John Borras, Ellen Bradshaw, Neil Dooley.

WATER FROM THE MOON. By Ray Stankovic. November 20, 1991. Director, Rosemary Hopkins. With David Lazzo, Kevin Baskette, Belle Maria Wheat, Tobey Hartman.

WHISPERS OF THE KOSHIRIS. Written and directed by James Jennings. December 16, 1991. With Tom Bruce, Patti Uhrich, Philip Scrima. Reopened February 19, 1992.

CRY FOR THE MOON. By Leland Blanchard. January 15, 1992. Director, James Jennings. With Kirsten Stammer, Doris Reardon, Ellen Bradshaw, Madelaine Schleyer.

LETHAL DOSE 100. By Stephen Jackson. February 5, 1992. Director, Jill Wisoff. With Traci

Daugs, Mark Drew, Courtney Everette, Tracy Lundell, Mark Krasnoff, Sarah Hauser.

PERFECT SON. By J.D. Madison. February 12, 1992. Director, Scott Sieffert. With Patrick Connelly, Barbara Bayer, Lou Lagalante, Ann Parker, Tony Dougherty, Jane Manning.

SONG OF SOLOMON. By Craig Sodaro. March 4, 1992. Director, Brian Feehan. With Claire Carter, Gregory Pekar, Tom O'Donoghue, Patti Uhrich, Belle Maria Wheat.

WELCOME HOME. By Richard Kannry. March 11, 1992. Director, Marc Bloomgarden. With Lonnie Jones, Joe Aycock, Anne Slattery, Madelaine Schleyer, Carrie Hall, Sally Graudons.

FACULTY MEETING. By Eugene Raskin. March 18, 1992. Director, Michael Rego. With Jerome Richards, Adam Schlesinger, Kent Sublette, Gary Fox, Ira Jaffe.

INSTANT KARMA. By James Cirinci. March 25, 1992. Director, Graham Chambers. With Rick Mowat, Mat Sarter.

SIMPLE PEOPLE. By Greg Fox. March 26, 1992. Director, James Jennings. With Greg Fox.

MONKEY'S WEDDING. Written and directed by Tom Labar. April 8, 1992. With Garry Williams, Tom Bruce, Annette Laskowski.

BOYS FROM KANSAS. Written and directed by James Jennings. May 6, 1992. With Michael DiMaggio, Ellen Bradshaw, Madelaine Schleyer, Larry Mitchell.

SUNSETS. By Robert Hodge. May 13, 1992. Director, James Jennings. With Tom Bruce, Greg Fox, Mat Sarter, Rick Mowat, Irv Butler.

THE WEDDING. By Joe Benjamin. May 27, 1992. Director, Peter Flynn. With Greg Fox, Ann Parker, Courtney Everette, Don Sheehan, Sidney Symington.

Circle Repertory Projects-in-Progress. Developmental programs for new plays. Tanya Berezin artistic director, Terrence Dwyer managing director.

CROSS DRESSING IN THE DEPRESSION (4). By Erin Cressida Wilson. February 17, 1992. Director, Kirsten Sanderson. With Erin Cressida Wilson, Barry Sherman, Edward Seamon.

ORPHEUS IN LOVE (2). Libretto, Craig Lucas; music, Gerald Busby. March 9, 1992. Director, Kirsten Sanderson; musical director, Jim May. With Steven Goldstein, Peter Samuel, Belinda Pigeon, Mary Beth Peil.

THE CHAIN (4). By Vittorio Rossi. May 4, 1992. Director, Joe Mantello. With George Dicenzo, Diane Martinelli, Stanley Tucci, Michael Imperioli, Lynn Cohen, Cathy Perry, Ken Johnson, Gus Rogerson.

Extended Readings:

INNOCENTS CRUSADE. By Keith Reddin. October 21, 1991. Director, Joe Mantello. With Christopher Shaw, Julie Halston, William Wise, Maggie Burke, Edmund Lewis, Welker White.
RESCUING GREENLAND. By Joan Ackermann. November 25, 1991. Director, Mark Ramont. With Robin Moseley, Michael Hume, Michael Warren Powell, Beau Berhahl, Scotty Bloch, Ashley Crowe, Peter Jacobson.
BRAILLE GARDEN. By Darrah Cloud. December 10, 1991. Director, Lynn M. Thompson. With Craig Bockhorn, Lily Knight, Michael Warren Powell, Melody Combs, Lynn Cohen.
MOE'S LUCKY SEVEN. By Marlane Meyer. May 18, 1992. Director, Roberta Levitow. With DiDi O'Connell, Brian Tarantina, Jack Wallace, J. Smith-Cameron, Barry Sherman, Bruce McCarty, Frank Lowe, Phyllis Somerville, Ed Seamon, Cliff Weissman, James Kissane, Jayce Bartok, Michelle Bosch.

CSC Repertory, Ltd. (Classic Stage Company). Aims to produce classics with a bold, contemporary sensibility. David Esbjornson, artistic director.

BON APPETIT! and THE ITALIAN LESSON (musical monologues) (27). By Julia Child and Ruth

Draper; music, Lee Hoiby. September 16, 1991. Director, Carey Perloff; scenery, Donald Eastman; lighting, Mary Louise Geiger; costumes, Jean Putch and Rita Riggs; musical director, Todd Sisley. With Jean Stapleton.

CABARET VERBOTEN (32). By Jeremy Lawrence, adapted from works by William Bendow, Bertolt Brecht, Hanns Eisler, Werner Finck, Fritz Grunbaum, Friederich Hollaender, Walter Mehring, Edmund Meisel, Rudolf Nelson, Marcellus Schiffer, Mischa Spoliansky, Konrad Tom, Kurt Tucholsky, Karl Valentin, translated by Kathleen L. Komar, Laurence Senelick, John Willet. October 23, 1991. Directors, Carey Perloff and Charles Randolph-Wright; scenery, Donald Eastman; lighting, Mary Louise Geiger; costumes, Gabriel Berry; musical director, Marjorie Poe. With Betsy Joslyn, Mark Nelson, John Rubinstein, Carole Shelley.

CREDITORS (42). By August Strindberg, translated by Paul Walsh. February 5, 1992. Director, Carey Perloff; scenery, Donald Eastman; lighting, Frances Aronson; costumes, Candice Donnelly. With Nestor Serrano, Zach Grenier, Caroline Lagerfelt, Elizabeth Beirne, Elena McGhee, Denis Sweeney.

CANDIDE (37). By Len Jenkin, adapted from Voltaire's work. April 22, 1992. Directors, David Esbjornson, Carey Perloff; scenery, Hugh Landwehr; lighting, Brian MacDevitt; costumes, Teresa Snider-Stein; music, David Lang. With Victor Mack, Edward Hibbert, Julia Gibson, Kent Gash, Dennis Reid, Michael Gaston, Rebecca Shull, Kimberly Pistone, William Keeler.

En Garde Arts. Dedicated to developing the concept of "site-specific theater" in the streets, parks and buildings of the city. Anne Hamburger founder and producer.

FATHER WAS A PECULIAR MAN (16). Reza Abdoh and Mira-Lani Oglesby. July 5, 1991. Director, Reza Abdoh; choreography, Maggie Rush, Ken Roht; scenery, Kyle Chepulis; lighting, Brian Aldous; costumes, Claudia Brown; music and sound, Eric Liljestrand. With Assurbanipal Babilla, Leyla Ebtehadj, Tom Fitzpatrick, Jan Leslie Harding, Meg Kruzewska, Ken Rhot, Irma St. Paule, Davidson Thomson.

ANOTHER PERSON IS A FOREIGN COUNTRY (19). By Charles L. Mee Jr. September 8, 1991. Director, Anne Bogart; scenery, Kyle Chepulis; lighting, Carol Mullins; costumes, Claudia Brown; music, Daniel Schreier. With Robert Beatty Jr., Victoria Boomsma, Rashid Brown, Christine Campbell, Maria Clarke, Bruce Hlibok, Marie Kalish, Terence Mintern, Tom Nelis, Jennifer Rohn, David Steinberg, Kelly Taffe.

VANQUISHED BY VOODOO. By Laurie Carlos. June 5, 1992. Directed by Laurie Carlos; with Avis Brown, Grisha Coleman, Dor Green, Dewarran Moses, Cynthia Oliver, Carl Hancock Rux.

Ensemble Studio Theater. Membership organization of playwrights, actors, directors and designers dedicated to supporting individual theater artists and developing new works for the stage. Over 250 projects each season, ranging from readings to fully-mounted productions. Curt Dempster artistic director, Christopher A. Smith associate artistic director, Dominick Balletta managing director.

OCTOBERFEST. Festival of 77 new plays by members. October 9-27, 1991.

A DREAM OF WEALTH. By Arthur Giron. November 21, 1991. Director, Melia Bensussen.

DEPOSING THE WHITE HOUSE. By Dan Isaac. November 23, 1991. Director, Christopher A. Smith. With Jay Barnhill, Stephanie Cannon, Chris Ceraso, Jude Ciccolella, Eric Conger, Sam Gray, David Konig, Pirie MacDonald, J.B. Martin, T.L. Reilly, Jaime Sanchez, Anders Wright.

BIG FRAME SHAKIN'. Written and performed by James G. Macdonald. November 29, 1991. Director, Shirley Kaplan.

STARS IN BARS (cabaret). November 29, 1991. Directors, Steve Rosenfield, Jason Fogelson. With Lew Black, Rusty Magee, Scott Blakeman, David Rasche, Kathy Rossetter, Rubber Feet (Julie Hays,

EN GARDE ARTS—Jennifer Rohn, David Steinberg and Tom Nelis in the site-specific staging of *Another Person Is a Foreign Country* by Charles L. Mee Jr.

Greg Pake, Ron Piretti, Kate Redway, Jo Winfield), Alarm Dog Rep (Marc Ashmore, Alan Ball, David Levine, Vicki March, Terri O'Neill, Connie Rotunda, Kevin Strader, Andrew Watts).

NEW VOICES '92 (staged readings): MOTHER EARTH by Martin Duberman; DARK HOURS by Jennifer Maisel; THE HEARTH by Alexander R. Scott; THE HOUSE OF PARADISE by Stuart Spencer. January 15-25, 1992.

HAMLET (workshop). By William Shakespeare; music and adapted by Shel Silverstein. January 29, 1992.

GEORGE WASHINGTON DANCES. By David Margulies. February 3, 1992. Director, Jack Gelber.

KOREA. By Bill Bozzone. February 14, 1992. Director, Kate Baggott; scenery, Sarah Lambert; lighting, Greg MacPherson; costumes, David Sawaryn. With Pete Benson, Bill Cwikowski, Zach Grenier, Josh Hamilton, Bai Ling, Kevin O'Keefe, Kevin Thigpen.

NEW LIVING NEWSPAPER. By Avery Hart. February 25, 1992. Director, Jeff Schechter; choreography, Janet Bogardus; music, Ray Leslee; additional music, Andrew Howard, Shel Silverstein; lyrics, Peter Moore, Shel Silverstein, Paul Mantell, Avery Hart, Carl Sandburg, Robert Creeley, Ray Leslee. With Polly Adams, Donald Berman, Stephanie Berry, Dominic Chianese, John-Martin Green, Baxter Harris, Gayle Humphrey, Paul Mantell, Les J.N. Mau, Julia McLaughlin.

LEGENDARY SIRENS. By Yvonne Adrian. March 6, 1992. Director, Margaret Mancinelli.

MARATHON '92 (festival of one-act plays). THROWING YOUR VOICE by Craig Lucas, directed by Kirsten Sanderson; THE SHALLOW END by Wendy MacLeod, directed by Susann Brinkley; WHAT IS THIS EVERYTHING? by Patricia Scanlon, directed by William Carden; FASTING by Bill Bozzone, directed by Kate Baggott; THE WILD GOOSE written and directed by John Patrick

Shanley; AWOKE ONE by Jack Agueros, directed by Curt Dempster; MY SIDE OF THE STORY by Bryan Goluboff, directed by Marcia Jean Kurtz; SCHEHERAZADE by Percy Granger, directed by Matthew Penn; GULF WAR by Joyce Carol Oates, directed by Christopher A. Smith; RIPPLES IN THE POND by Jon Shirota, directed by Ron Nakahara; THE ONLIEST WHO CAN'T GO NOWHERE by J.E. Franklin, directed by Woodie King Jr.; BLUE STARS by Stuart Spencer, directed by Jane Hoffman; ANGELS IN THE MEN'S LOUNGE by OyamO, directed by Kevin Confoy; GIVE THE BISHOP MY FAINT REGARDS by Frank D. Gilroy; JENNY KEEPS TALKING by Lise Erlich (a.k.a. Richard Greenberg), directed by Risa Bramon Garcia. April 29-June 7, 1992.

INTAR. Mission is to identify, develop and present the talents of gifted Hispanic American theater artists and multicultural visual artists. Max Ferra artistic director, Eva Brune managing director.

OUR LADY OF THE TORTILLA (22). By Luis Santiero. October 16, 1991. Director, Max Ferra; scenery, Charles McCarry; lighting, Michael Chybowski; costumes, Ellen McCartney. With Catherine Cobb Ryan, John Ortiz, Ilka Tanya Payan, Gary Perez, Carmen Rosario.

THE LADY FROM HAVANA by Luis Santiero. March 26, 1992. Directed by Max Ferra; with Lillian Hurst, Georgia Galvez, Feiga M. Martinez.

Interart Theater. Committed to producing innovative work by women theater artists and to introducing New York audiences to a bold range of theater that is non-traditional in form or theme. Margot Lewitin artistic director.

Schedule included:
THE HEMING'S FAMILY TRILOGY (reading). By Elsa Rael. June 12, 1991. Director, Margot Lewitin. With Frances Foster.

In Repertory:
970-DEBB (9). Written and performed by Deb Margolin. July 9, 1991.

ESTRELLA! WHO CAN YOU TRUST IN A CITY OF LIES? (17). Written and directed by Daniel Keene. July 10, 1991. Scenery, Christina Weppner; lighting, Joni Wong; music, Evan Lurie and Joan Lurie. With Rhonda Wilson.

CARTHAGINIANS (reading). By Frank McGuiness. March 23, 1992. Director, Rosey Hay.

Irish Arts Center. Provides a range of contemporary Irish drama, classics and new works by Irish American playwrights. Nye Heron artistic director.

Schedule included:
DAMIEN. By Aldyth Morris. October 1, 1991. With William Walsh.

DOWN THE FLATS. By Tony Kavanaugh. January 15, 1992. Director, Nye Heron; scenery, David Raphel; lighting, Jonathan Sprouse; costumes, Carla Gant; music, John Doyle. With Donald Creedon, Donal J. Sheehan, Caroline Winterson, Carmel O'Brien, Chris O'Neill, Marian Quinn, Susan McKeown, Jim Smallhorne.

BOBBY SANDS, M.P. By Judy GeBauer. May 30, 1992.

La Mama (a.k.a. LaMama) Experimental Theater Club (ETC). A busy workshop for experimental theater of all kinds. Ellen Stewart founder and artistic director.

Schedule included:
THE BAY OF NAPLES. Written and directed by Joel Dragutin. June 6, 1991. With Jean-Claude Bonnifait, Bernard Charnace, Joel Dragutin, Francoise D'Inca, Elisabeth Tual. (Theater 95)

THE DEAD CLASS. By Tadeusz Kantor. June 12, 1991. With Zbigniew Bednarczyk, Tomasz

Dobrowolski, Zbigniew Gostomski, Ewa Janicka, Leslaw Janicki, Waclaw Janicki, Maria Stangret Kantor, Maria Krasicaka, Jan Ksiazek, Bogdan Renczynski, Mira Rychlicka, Roman Siwulak, Lech Stangret, Teresa Welminska, Andrzej Welminski. Cricot 2 Theater. (Produced as part of the New York International Festival of the Arts.)

TODAY IS MY BIRTHDAY. By Tadeusz Kantor. June 18, 1991. With Cricot 2 Theater. (Produced as part of the New York International Festival of the Arts.)

FUTZ. By Rochelle Owens. October 18, 1991. Music, direction and sets, Tom O'Horgan; lighting, Howard Thies; costumes, Ellen Stewart. With Penny Arcade, John Bakos, Paul Beauvais, Peter Craig, Sheila Dabney, Kimberly Flynn, Tom Keith, John Moran, Doug von Nessen, Jonathan Slaff, Marilyn Roberts.

THEY CHAINED US TO A STAR. Written, composed and directed by Phelonise Willie. November 8, 1991. Lighting, Zdenek Kriz; sound, Dolores Allen. With Ron L. Cox, Ralph Guzzo, Damon White, Andrew Zenoff, Princess Wilson, Lata Chettri, Cecelia Waterman, Rima Otero, Kathena Bryant.

BASEMENT. Conception, text, space, costume, directed and performance by Denise Stoklos. November 28, 1991.

NOSFERATU: A SYMPHONY OF DARKNESS. Conceived and directed by Ping Chong, suggested by F.W. Murnau's film. December 5, 1991.

EXPLOSIONS. By Virlana Tkacz and Wanda Phipps. January 3, 1992. Director, Virlana Tkacz; choreography, June Anderson; scenery and lights, Watoku Ueno; costumes, Yuko Yamamura; music, Roman Hurko. With Richaro Abrams, Jessica Hecht, Ralph B. Pena, Jeffrey Ricketts, Sean Runette, Dawn Saito, Olga Shuhan, Jeff Sugarman. (Yara Arts Group)

IRON LUNG. Written, directed and designed by John Jesurun. January 16, 1992. Lighting, Jeff Nash. With Oscar De La Fe Colon, Rebecca Moore, Larry Tighe, Michael Tighe, Sanghi Wagner.

SHATTERHAND MASSACREE. Written and directed by John Jesurun. January 30, 1992. With Steve Buscemi, Rebecca Moore, Larry Tighe, Michael Tighe, Sanghi Wagner.

KAFKA: FATHER AND SON. By Mark Rozovsky, adapted from Franz Kafka's *Letter to His Father* and *Judgment*, translated by Elena Prischepenko. January 23, 1992. Directed and designed by Leonardo Shapiro. With Michael Preston, George Bartenieff.

FERN AND ROSE. Written and performed by Ellen Maddow and Rocky Bornstein; music, Ellen Maddow; choreography, Rocky Bornstein; director, Paul Zimet. A PERFECT LIFE by and with Paul Zimet; music, Harry Mann; director, Roger Babb. February 13, 1992. Lighting, Carol Mullins; costumes, E.G. Widulski.

THE GOLEM. Book and directed by Moni Ovadia and Danielle Abbado; music, Alessandro Nidi, Maurizio Deho and Gian Pietro Marazza. March 12, 1992.

THE FLIGHT OF CHUNG SOP. By Eui-Kyung Kim. March 26, 1992. Director, Youn-Taik Lee. With Hyundai Theater Company of Seoul.

EGYPT. By William Shakespeare, adapted by Douglas Langworthy and David Herskovits. April 16, 1992. Director, David Herskovits; scenery, Marsha Ginsberg; lighting, Lenore Doxsee; costumes, David Zinn; music, Thomas Cabaniss. With Will Badgett, Neil Bradley, Bradley Glenn, Eric Passoja, Mairhinda Groff, James Hannaham, Karl-Peter Hermann, Randolph Curtis Rand, Daniel Pardo, Gregor Paslawsky, Scott Rabinowitz, Steven Rattazzi, Thomas Jay Ryan, Greig Sargeant, Yuri Skujins.

PLUTO. By Sin Cha Hong. April 30, 1992. With Laughing Stone Theater Company.

IPHIGENIA IN TAURIS. By Euripides, adapted and directed by Yannis Houvardas from Richmond Lattimore's translation. May 7, 1992. Scenery and costumes, Dionyssis Fotopoulos; lighting, Howard Thies; music, Genji Ito. With Christina Alexanian, Paul Beauvais, Alyssa Bresnahan, Sandra Daley, Sarah Graham Hayes, Natalia Kapodistria, Akyllas Karazissis, Gregory Karr, Monica Koskey, George Kormanos, Anna Mascha, Randolph Curtis Rand, Laurie Galluccio, Ching Valdes-Aran.

GOD'S COUNTRY. By Steven Dietz. May 28, 1992. Director, Leonard Foglia; scenery, Michael McGarty; lighting, Russell H. Champa; costumes, Nina Canter. With Seth Barrish, Lee Brock, Marcia DeBonis, Tom Riis Farrell, Aaron Goodwin, Larry Green, Reade Kelly, Leigh Patellis, Wendee Pratt, Michael Elting Rogers, Stephen Singer. (The Barrow Group)

The Club

THE OPTIMISMO LOUNGE. Written and directed by Jim Neu. March 11, 1992. Music, Neal Kirkwood, Harry Mann, William Niederkorn. With Jim Neu, Deborah Auer, Roberta Levine, Carol Mullins, David Nunemaker, Terry O'Reilly, Bill Rice, Sue Sheehy.

THE (HAUNTED) HOUSE (chamber opera). By John Moran. April 2, 1992. Lighting, Howard Thies. With John Moran, Daniel Harnett, Rebecca Moore.

PHOTO OP (opera). Libretto, James Siena; music, Conrad Cummings. May 28, 1992. Director, Bob McGrath.

Lamb's Theater Company. Committed to developing and presenting new works in their most creative and delicate beginnings. Carolyn Rossi Copeland producing director.

Schedule included:

OPAL. Book, music and lyrics, Robert Nassif Lindsey. March 12, 1992. Director, Scott Harris; musical staging, Janet Watson; scenery, Peter Harrison; lighting, Don Ehman; costumes, Michael Bottari, Ron Case; musical director, Joshua Rosenblum. With Reed Armstrong, Mimi Bessette, Louisa Flaningham, Mark Goetzinger, Sarah Knapp, Alfred Lakeman, Judy Malloy, Marni Nixon, Tracy Spindler, Pippa Winslow.

PAN ASIAN REPERTORY THEATER—Keenan Shimizu and Raul Aranas in the one-acter *Fairy Bones* by Laurence Yep

Mabou Mines. Theater collaborative whose work is a synthesis of motivational acting, narrative acting and mixed-media performance. Collective artistic leadership.

IN THE JUNGLE OF CITIES. By Bertolt Brecht. November 5, 1991. Produced at the Joseph Papp Public Theater; see its entry in the Plays Produced Off Broadway section of this volume.

New Dramatists. An organization devoted to playwrights; member writers may use the facilities for anything from private cold readings of their material to public script-in-hand readings. Elana Greenfield director of artistic programming, Jana Jevnikar director of finance, Paul A. Slee, director of development.

Rehearsed readings:

RUNNING FOR BLOOD NO. 3. By Migdalia Cruz. July 2, 1991. Director, Marjorie Van Halteren. With J. Ed Araiza, Susan Finch, Dan Hagen, Karen Kohlhaas, DiDi O'Connell, John Seitz.

THE AMERICA PLAY. By Suzan-Lori Parks. July 23, 1991. Director, Liz Diamond. With Pamala Tyson, Rodney Hudson, Leon Addison Brown.

DISAPPEARED. By Phyllis Nagy. August 19, 1991. Director, Beth Schachter. With Rudy Caporaso, Paul Carlin, Lynn Cohen, Randy Danson, Mark Metcalf, Tom Nelis, Michael James Reed, Jacqueline Wolff.

AWAKE. By Phyllis Nagy. August 26, 1991. Director, Beth Schachter. With Adrienne Shelley, Pamala Tyson, Christopher Shaw, Alix Korey, Blanche Baker.

THE UNIVERSAL WOLF. By Joan Schenkar. August 28, 1991. Director, Liz Diamond. With Victoria Boothby, Alex Elias, Ron Faber, Robert Zuckerman.

THE REINCARNATION OF JAMIE BROWN. By Lynne Alvarez. September 16, 1991. Director, John Pynchon Holms. With Christine Burke, Doug von Nessen, Gary Dean Ruebsamen, Kitty Chen, Mel Duane Gionson, Sophie Maletsky, Richard Maynard, Leigh Dillon, Marvin Einhorn.

BLACK FOREST. By Anthony Giardina. September 27, 1991. Director, Doug Wagner. With John Christopher Jones, Mary Mara, Randy Danson, George N. Martin, Christopher McHale, Wyman Pendleton, Tom Tammi, Helen Stenborg, Elaine Bromka, Doug von Nessen.

WINDSHOOK. By Mary Gallagher. November 10, 1991. Director, Phil Soltanoff. With Gil Bellows, Allegra de Carpegna, Robert Fente, Rya Kihlstedt, Grayson McCouch, Kim Raver, Joe Taylor.

ACROSS A CROWDED ROOM. By Eduardo Machado. November 21, 1991. Director, Anne Bogart. With Joan MacIntosh, Mark Shannon, Sophie Maletsky, Olek Krupa.

GIRL BAR. By Phyllis Nagy. December 3, 1991. Director, Anne Bogart. With Cherry Jones, Lynn Cohen, Amelia Campbell, Jan Harding, Belynda Hardin, Terry McCarthy.

TO MY CHAGRIN. By Ben Siegler. December 9, 1991. With J. Smith-Cameron, John Dossett, Kevin Geer, Karen Trott.

CHAOS. Book and lyrics, Matthew Maguire; music, Michael Gordon. December 16, 1991. Director, Anne Bogart. With Susan Lambert, Hugo Munday, Natasha Lutov, Stephen Kalm, Tom Bogdan.

FUR. By Migdalia Cruz. December 18, 1991. Director, Stephen Pickover. With Barry Sherman, Jan Leslie Harding, Annie O'Sullivan.

ONCE REMOVED. By Eduardo Machado. December 18, 1991. Director, Mark Brokaw. With Joan MacIntosh, Christopher McCann, Diane Simms, Steve Rodriguez, Eileen Galindo, Eduardo Machado.

THE RIVER BOOK. By Erik Ehn. January 13, 1992. Director, Brian Mertes. With Amelia Campbell, Alyssa Bresnahan, Erin Wilson, Tom Gibson, Craig Ugoretz.

NACRE. By Erik Ehn. January 20, 1992. Director, Fritz Ertl. With Ariane Brandt, Erin Wilson, Amelia Campbell, J. Ed Araiza, Ed Baran, Peter Schmitz, Maja Hellmold, Sumer Mullen, Bill Christ.

THE YEAR OF MY MOTHER'S BIRTH. By Erik Ehn. January 22, 1992. Director, Fritz Ertl. With Ching Valdes-Aran, Anne O'Sullivan, Scott Renderer, Arabella Field, Rob Campbell.

THE OPIUM WARS. By Ana Maria Simo; music, Zena Parkins. February 28, 1992. Director, Linda Chapman. With Adriano Gonzalez, Lisa Cohen, Ching Valdes-Aran, J. Ed Araiza.

WELDON RISING. By Phyllis Nagy. March 19, 1992. Director, Lisa Peterson. With Becca Lish, Katie MacNichol, Barry Sherman, Richard Thompson, Henry Stram, David Egenberg.

THE CLOSER. By Willy Holtzman. April 13, 1992. Director, John Pynchon Holms. With Jane Kaczmarek, Brad Whitford, Julie Boyd, Paul McCrane.

SIN. By Wendy MacLeod. April 30, 1992. With Julie Boyd, Leslie Nipkow, Patrick Kerr, Barry

Sherman, Dwight Bacquie, Daniel von Bargen, Sam Robards, Ron Bagden.
HANNA. By Frank Gagliano. May 11, 1992. Director, Sara Romersberger. With Preston Mitchell, Holly McDonald, Leslie Ann Blauch, Catherine Ann Brown, Tammie L. Dauson, Kimberly Parrish.
THE DAY GOD DIED. By Bonnie Bluth. May 18, 1992. Director, Craig Lowy. With Tresa Hughes, Jean Korey, Jack R. Marks, Annette Hunt, Bob Adrian, Juanita Walsh, Dianne Stasi.

New Federal Theater. Dedicated to presenting new playwrights and plays dealing with the minority and Third World experience. Woodie King Jr. producer.

ZION! (19). By Beverly Trader. December 1, 1991. Director, Thomas Jones II; scenery and lighting, Richard Harmon; costumes, Gregory Glenn; musical director, Uzee Brown. With David Edwards, John D. Fitzgibbon, Lee James Ganzer, Roberta Illg, Maurice Langley, Kathleen J. Masterson, Ronald E. Richardson, Phyllis Y. Stickney, Michele-Denise Woods.

CHAIN and LATE BUS TO MECCA (Co-produced by the Women's Project; see its entry under Women's Project).

TESTIMONY (12). By Faiya Henderson-Holmes. May 1, 1992. Director, Raina von Waldenburg; scenery, Nathan Jones; lighting, Marty Liquori. With Sonita Surratt, Chris Kopp, Juli Bray-Morris, Mantee M. Murphy.

New York Shakespeare Festival Public Theater. Schedule of special projects, in addition to its regular off-Broadway productions. JoAnne Akalaitis producer.

FRAGMENTS (short pieces and works-in-process): SOLO by Rachelle Minkoff; FOOD by Neena Beber, directed by Beth Schachter; POSSESSED BY A DEMON by Elana Greenfield; TO DESIRE PEACEFULLY IS TO FALL ILL WITH LONGING by Maurya Wickstrom, directed by Joumana Rizk; BIRTH, BOOT AND SNEAKER written and directed by Dor Green; PORTRAIT OF THE ARTIST AS A SOUL MAN DEAD by Jake-Ann Jones, directed by Dennis Davis; REHEARSING THE GRANDA by Honour Molloy, directed by Julie Nichols; END OF HUMAN FRAILTY written and directed by John C. Russell; ABOUT THIS NECK WEAR THIS IDENTIFICATION by Juliann France, directed by Jessica Bauman; HOLD ME AND ROCK ME and MASOSONG by and with Evangeline Johns; LOVE LAKE written and directed by Lizzie Olesker; THE DARK written and directed by Harry Newman; INKTOMI by Charles Krezell, directed by Joumana Rizk; WHAT WILL BE by and with Sande Zeig, directed by Lizzie Olesker; BLUES IN A BUICK by Dennis Moritz. February 4-9, 1992.

New York Theater Workshop. Produces new theater by American and international artists and encourages risk and stimulates experimentation in theatrical form. James C. Nicola artistic director, Nancy Kassak Diekmann managing director.

MAD FOREST (A Best Play; see its entry in the Plays Produced Off Broadway section of this volume).

TIME FLIES WHEN YOU'RE ALIVE (21). Written and performed by Paul Linke. February 25, 1992. Director, Mark W. Travis; flag design, Anders Holmquist; lighting, Pat Dignan; music, Francesca Draper Linke.

LYPSINKA! A DAY IN THE LIFE (22). Created and performed by John Epperson. March 31, 1992. Director, Michael Leeds; scenery, James Schutte; lighting, Mark McCullough; costumes, Anthony Wong.

The Open Eye. Goal is to gather a community of outstanding theater artists to collaborate on works for the stage for audiences of all ages and cultural backgrounds. Jean Erdman founding director, Amie Brockway artistic director.

EAGLE OR SUN (Aguila o Sol) (12). By Sabina Berman, translated by Isabel Saez, edited, adapted and directed by Amie Brockway. October 12, 1991. Scenery, lighting, costumes, Adrienne J. Brockway. With Joey A. Chavez, John DiLeo, Ricky Genaro, Maria A. Merullo, Doug Jewell, Tara Mallen.

THE DEATH AND LIFE OF SHERLOCK HOLMES (16). By Susan Zeder. November 26, 1991. Director, Russell Treyz; scenery, Adrienne J. Brockway; costumes, Jane Trapnell; lighting, Spencer Moss. With Mitchell Greenberg, George Cavey, Kermit Brown, Amanda Gronich, Tara Mallen, Elton Beckett, Jim Helsinger, Arleigh Richards.

A WOMAN CALLED TRUTH (13). By Sandra Fenichel Asher. January 18, 1992. Director, Ernest Johns; choreography, Jamale Graves; scenery, lighting, costumes, Adrienne J. Brockway; musical director, Charles Brown. With Patricia R. Floyd, Ricky Genaro, Jen Wolfe, Joe Clancy, James Duane Polk, Alicia Rene Washington.

Pan Asian Repertory Theater. Strives to provide opportunities for Asian American artists to perform under the highest professional standards and to create and promote plays by and about Asians and Asian Americans. Tisa Chang artistic/producing director.

THE DRESSING ROOM (25). By Kunio Shimizu, translated by John K. Gillespie, adapted and dramaturgy by Chiori Miyagawa. November 2, 1991. Director, Kati Kuroda; scenery, Atsushi Moriyasu; lighting, Tina Charney; costumes, Eiko Yamaguchi; music, Bert Moon. With Constance Boardman, Carol A. Honda, Shizuko Hoshi, Mary Lee.

FAIRY BONES and PAY THE CHINAMAN (one-act plays) (21). By Laurence Yep. May 2, 1992. Director, Tina Chen; scenery, Atsushi Moriyasu; lighting, Deborah Constantine; costumes, Juliet Ouyong. With Raul Aranas, Keenan Shimizu, Lucy Liu, Christen Villamor.

Playwrights Horizons New Theater Wing. Full productions of new works, in addition to the regular off-Broadway productions. Don Scardino artistic director, Paul S. Daniels executive director.

14 performances each
BREAK, AGNES, EULOGY FOR MISTER HAMM and LUCKY NURSE (one-act operas). By Michael John LaChiusa. December 11, 1991. Director, Kirsten Sanderson; scenery, Derek McLane; lighting, Debra J. Kletter; costumes, David Sawaryn; musical director, Joshua Rosenblum. With Chuck Cooper, Joe Grifasi, Mary Beth Peil, Alice Playten.

MAN, WOMAN, DINOSAUR. By Regina M. Porter. January 29, 1992. Director, Melia Bensussen; scenery, Allen Moyer; lighting, Brian MacDevitt; costumes, Karen Perry. With Robinson Frank Adu, Jihmi Kennedy, Oni Faida Lampley, Sharif Rashed, Clarice Taylor.

LITTLE EGYPT. By Lynn Siefert. April 29, 1992. Director, Roberta Levitow; scenery, James Noone; lighting, Robert Wierzel; costumes, Mary Myer; music and sound, John Gromada. With Richard Gilliland, John Griesemer, J.R. Horne, Mary Shultz, J. Smith-Cameron, Phyllis Somerville.

Primary Stages Company. Dedicated to new American plays and new American playwrights. Casey Childs artistic director.

24 performances each
JOY SOLUTION. By Stuart Duckworth. November 24, 1991. Director, Seth Gordon; scenery, Bob Phillips; lighting, Allen D. Hahn; costumes, Martha Bromelmeier. With Daniel Ahearn, Justin Cozier, Leigh Dillon, Anne Newhall, Shareen Powlett.

MAKING BOOK. By Janet Reed. February 7, 1992. Director, Susan Einhorn; scenery and costumes, Bruce Goodrich; lighting, Spencer Mosse. With Daniel Ahearn, Catherine Curtin, Claudia Fielding, Percy Granger, Allison Janney.

A MURDER OF CROWS. By Mac Wellman. April 26, 1992. Director, Jim Simpson; scenery, Kyle

Chepulis; lighting, Brian Aldous; costumes, Bruce Goodrich. With Anne O'Sullivan, Jan Leslie Harding, William Mesnik, Lauren Hamilton, Steve Mellor, Reed Birney, Tina Dudek, Ray Xifo, David Van Tieghem.

Puerto Rican Traveling Theater. Professional company presenting bilingual productions primarily of Puerto Rican and Hispanic playwrights, emphasizing subjects of relevance today. Miriam Colon Valle founder and producer.

Schedule included:

THE OXCART (La Carreta) (62). By Rene Marques, translated by Dr. Charles Pilditch. March 18, 1992. Director, Alba Oms; scenery, H.G. Arrott; lighting, Brian Haynsworth; costumes, Mary Marsicano. With Eddie Andino, Miriam Cruz, Chris De Oni, Ebony Diaz, Jackeline Duprey, Norberto Kerner, Esther Mari, Iraida Polanco, Fernando Quinones, Victor Sierra, Jeanette Toro, Walter Valentin.

Quaigh Theater. Primarily a playwrights' theater, devoted to the new playwright, the established contemporary playwright and the modern (post-1920) playwright. Will Lieberson artistic director.

20 performances each

MY SON THE DOCTOR. By Marc J. Bielski. July 16, 1991. Director, Jeffrey B. Marx. With Matthew Boston, Colin Gray, Dan Gershwin, Joyce Renee Korbin, Bunny Levine, Sheila Sawney.

THE NERD by Larry Shue. August 9, 1991. Directed by Will Lieberson; with Paul Brandt, Kim Dickens, Derek Le Dain, Ron Roth, Cameron Foord, Jim Powderly, Ned Salisbury.

OUR LADY OF PERPETUAL DANGER. By Adam Kraar. October 3, 1991. Director, Joel Bishoff; scenery, Steve Carter; lighting, Matthew Frey; costumes, Amy Lenczewski. With Robert Arcaro, Arija Bareikis, Kevin Cristaldi, Nancy Kawalek, Mary Tahmin.

BROADWAY AFTER DARK. By Ward Morehouse III. May 18, 1992. Director, Will Lieberson; lighting, Joseph A. Goshert. With Steve Shoup.

Lunchtime Series. 10 performances each

TIME AFTER TIME. By John F. Bond. September 30, 1991. Director, P. Jenkins Scott. With Freida Washburn, Tom Hannen, Valerie Smythe.

SQUARE WHEELS. By Akiyo Furakawa. October 7, 1991. Director, Dennis Lieberson. With Helen Royce, Joyce Feldman.

THE LAST DEW. By Richard Round. October 21, 1991. Director, Alfred Brauer. With Tom Salisbury, Kim Roth, N. Acton.

TORNADO. By Sinclair Meegan. November 4, 1991. Director, Will Lieberson. With William Allen, Ed Varone, John Lynch, Ruth Wolf.

THE UNCOVERED TUNNEL. By Fred Shyer. November 18, 1991. Director, Mary Kelly. With Martin Rhodes, David Rubin.

THE HIDEAWAY. By Phillip Cohen. December 2, 1991. Director, Robert Fields. With David Rubin, Bob W. Weil, Pat Thomas, Amelia Jaffe.

A GIFT FOR EVELYN. By T.J. Elliot. January 6, 1992. Director, Lorna Sirrone. With George Harris, Lois Lawrence.

FEBRUARY 30TH. By Mark Richards. January 20, 1992. Director, Dennis Lieberson. With Veronica Blessing, Barbara Drury, Carl Schreiber.

THE POWER PEAK. By Jeff Engleman. February 3, 1992. Director, Janice Hannen. With Ben Ducore, Jon Lyman, K.C. Ball.

ICEBREAKERS FOR BAR MAIDS. By Fieldston Puckert. February 17, 1992. Director, Jeff Engleman. With Phil Roxbury, Sandy Curry.

FREEDOM IS JUST A WORD. By Jon Allen. March 2, 1992. Director, Sherwood Katz. With Betty Bliss, Elise Bell, Barbara Woll, Felicie Trayman.

THE YEAR ROUND SUMMER JOB. By Alec Fish. March 16, 1992. Director, Harold Gold. With Joyce Nass, Fred Bell, Bill Speaker.

TOO MANY WAYS OUT. By Veronica Nelson. March 30, 1992. Director, Robert Fields. With William Allen, Jonathan Lipman, Roberta Marx.

BALLOTS FOR BULLETS. By Rod Tracey. April 16, 1992. Director, Will Lieberson. With Don Gilbert, Tom Scott, Jane Stinger, Harris Feld.

Summer Reading Series
SUCCESS. By Jim Demarse. July 29, 1991.
HISTORY LESSON. By Dean Barrett. August 5, 1991.
LADIES IN WAITING. By Michael Palermo. August 12, 1991.
CAR WASH. By Jason Stahr. August 19, 1991.
A DAY IN THE PARK. By Louis Phillips. August 26, 1991.

QUAIGH THEATER—Robert Arcaro and Kevin Cristaldi
in *Our Lady of Perpetual Danger* by Adam Kraar

The Ridiculous Theatrical Company. The late Charles Ludlam's comedic troupe devoted to productions of his original scripts and new adaptations of the classics. Everett Quinton artistic director, Steve Asher managing director.

BLUEBEARD (84). By Charles Ludlam. October 31, 1991. Director, Everett Quinton; scenery, T. Greenfield; lighting, Richard Currie; costumes, Toni Nanette Thompson; music and sound, Jim Badrak. With Everett Quinton, Kevin Scullin, Eureka, Stephen Pell, Brian Neil Belovitch, Shawn Nacol, Lisa Herbold, Bill Graber, H.M. Koutoukas.

THE BELLS (74). Adapted and performed by Everett Quinton from Leopold Lewis's play. November 8, 1991. Director, Eureka; scenery, Richard Cordtz; lighting, Richard Currie; costumes, Toni Nanette Thompson; music, Mark Bennett. (Reopened February 8, 1992)

Second Stage Theater. Committed to producing plays believed to deserve another look, as well as new works. Robyn Goodman, Carole Rothman artistic directors.

HOME AND AWAY (42). Written and performed by Kevin Kling. July 23, 1991. Director and scenery, David Esbjornson; lighting, Frances Aronson.

DEARLY DEPARTED (42). By David Bottrell and Jessie Jones. December 16, 1991. Director, Gloria Muzio; scenery, Allen Moyer; lighting, Don Holder; costumes, Ellen McCartney. With Leo Burmester, Mary Fogarty, Sloane Shelton, Greg Germann, Jessie Jones, Dylan Baker, Linda Cook, J.R. Horne, Wendy Lawless.

RED DIAPER BABY (42). Written and performed by Josh Kornbluth. April 1, 1992. Director, Joshua Mostel; scenery, Randy Benjamin; lighting, Pat Dignan; costumes, Susan Lyall.

Signature Theater Company. Dedicated to the exploration of a playwright's body of work. James Houghton artistic director.

16 performances each

THE SORROWS OF FREDERICK. Written and directed by Romulus Linney. October 10, 1991. Scenery, E. David Cosier; lighting, Jeffrey S. Koger; costumes, Teresa Snider-Stein. With Kernan Bell, Bryant Bradshaw, Fred Burrell, James Coyle, Katina Commings, Claude D. File, Elliott Fox, Austin Pendleton, Garrison Phillips, Mitchell Riggs, T. Ryder Smith, Richard Thomsen, John Woodson.

HEATHEN VALLEY. By Romulus Linney. December 4, 1991. Directors, Romulus Linney, James Houghton; scenery, E. David Cosier; lighting, Jeffrey S. Koger; costumes, Teresa Snider-Stein. With Scott Sowers, Richard Bowden, Celia Howard, Jim Ligon, Peter G. Morse, Ann Sheehy.

A WOMAN WITHOUT A NAME. By Romulus Linney. January 30, 1992. Director, Thomas Allan Bullard; scenery, E. David Cosier; lighting, Jeffrey S. Koger; costumes, Teresa Snider-Stein. With Barbara Andres, Fred Burrell, Elisabeth Lewis Corley, Susan Eriksen, Marin Hinkle, Jim Ligon, Bernie McInerney, Peter G. Morse, Mark Niebuhr.

AMBROSIO. By Romulus Linney. April 24, 1992. Directors, Romulus Linney, James Houghton; scenery, E. David Cosier; lighting, Jeffrey S. Koger; costumes, Teresa Snider-Stein. With Craig Duncan, Mark Allan Gordon, Marin Hinkle, Garrison Phillips, T. Ryder Smith, Peter Ashton Wise.

Soho Rep. Dedicated to new, non-naturalistic plays. Marlene Swartz, Julian Webber artistic directors.

DANCENOISE: IT'S A CRIME (5). By Anne Iobst and Lucy Sexton. June 12, 1991. Scenery, James Vance. With Anne Iobst, Lucy Sexton, Ken Bullock, Stacy Grabert, Michael Iveson.

SITUATION ROOM (5). Text and directed by Jim Neu. June 19, 1991. Scenery, David Nunemaker; lighting, Carol Mullins; music, William Niederkorn. With Jim Neu, Roberta Levine, Terry O'Reilly, Bill Rice, Mary Shultz.

R&D (5). Conceived and performed by Matt Goldman, Phil Stanton and Chris Wink (Blue Man Group). June 26, 1991. (*Dancenoise: It's a Crime*, *Situation Room* and *R&D* were presented as part of the "Yes, But Is It Theater?" Festival.)

7 BLOWJOBS (16). By Mac Wellman. April 3, 1992. Director, Jim Simpson; scenery and lighting, Kyle Chepulis; costumes, Caryn Neman. With Valerie Charles, Kristen Harris, Melissa Smith, Reed Birney, Steve Mellor, John Seitz, John Augustine, Jon Tyler.

TONE CLUSTERS (one-act play) (20). By Joyce Carol Oates. May 14, 1992. Director, Julian Webber; scenery, Kyle Chepulis; lighting, Don Holder; costumes, Mary Myers. With Richard Adamson, Kathryn Langwell, John Nacco, Black-Eyed Susan.

Theater for the New City. Developmental theater and new American experimental works. George Bartenieff, Crystal Field artistic directors.

Schedule included:

MARY JEMESEN. By Toby Armour. June 6, 1991. Director, Muriel Miguel.

WATERMOTIONS. By Brian Keith Jackson. September 13, 1991.

ACCIDENT; A DAY'S NEWS. By Christa Wolf, adapted by Ninth Street Theater and Eileen Myles. September 19, 1991. Director, Joanne Schultz; lighting, Mark Sussman; music, Ralph Denzer. With Jody Moore, Stephen Kaplin, Joanne Schultz, Jack Sheedy, John Bell.

KILL. Written and directed by Bina Sharif. October 10, 1991. Scenery, Paula Sjoblom; lighting, Susan Shannon. With Hakim Anes, Hocine Bacha, Regina Bartkoff, Edmond Cahill, William Cook, Samuel Davis, Mohamed Djellouli, Leonora Fishbein, Marilyn Ghoulson, Kevin Martin, Dusten J. McCormick, Gary McNeil, Re'ha Mezoughi, Nadime Nader, Kate Nelson, Edd Preston, Sabah, Bina Sharif, Robert Walker, Noel Wilson, Naima Zouioueche.

JAMBOREE. By David Sedaris. October 10, 1991.

UNFORGETTABLE TOUR. By Terry King. October 13, 1991.

LIBRARY LOVE (one-act musical). By Arthur Abrams and Walter Corwin and THE BRIDE'S BOOK OF FLOWERS by Walter Corwin. November 7, 1991. Director, James Jennings; scenery, Mary Blanchard; lighting, Tony Angel. With Mary Cozza, Mark Elliott, Jill Newman, Donna Langen, Norman Kruger, Barbara Bayer, Don Sheehan, Laurie Lion.

THE BUNNY AND DORIS SHOW. By Sebastian Stuart. November 8, 1991.

LIFE'S TOO SHORT TO CRY. Written and directed by Michael Vasquez; music and lyrics, Joseph V. Banks. November 18, 1991. Choreography, Maria Rubinate, Terry Lee King, Cedrick Campbell; scenery, Myrna Duarte; lighting, Charlie Spickler, Tom Barker; costumes, Lolly Alejandro. With Carmine Alers, Laura Daye, Cheryl Gadsen, Inez Guzman, Terry Lee King, Wayne Steele, Dion Trott, Stephen Whitley.

HELLO, MRS. PRESIDENT. Written and directed by Phoebe Legere. November 21, 1991.

WOMEN IN BECKETT (short plays for women). By Samuel Beckett. November, 1991. Director, Moses Kaufman; scenery, Marsha Ginsberg; lighting, Jack Jacobs; costumes, David Zinn. With Rosemary Brady, Pat Kier Edwards, Mimi Feiner, Janet Gibson, Megan Hunt, Lilian Johnson, Anne C. Putnam, Nellie Zastawna.

TIMES SQUARE ANGEL: A HARD-BOILED CHRISTMAS FANTASY. By Charles Busch. November 29, 1991.

DOWNTOWN PSYCHOBROADS and ODE TO KEITH HARING. By Larry Myers. November 29, 1991. Directors, Brad Friedman and Mike Wills; scenery, Kim Stoddard; lighting, J. Michael Gottlieb; costumes, Loren Bevans. With Gretchen Claggett, Sean Cullen, Michelle Durning.

DREAMERS OF THE ABSOLUTE. By Phil Motherwell. December 12, 1991. Director, Lindzee

Smith; scenery, lighting, costumes, Tim Burns. With Lindzee Smith, Jonathan Mezzacappa, Robert Cooney, Frank Morales, Rhonda Wilson, Marc Parent, Jerry Jaffe, Andrew Atwater, Leonard Abrams.

SQUARING THE CIRCLE. By Guy Gsell. December 19, 1991. Director, Thomas Gilpin; scenery, Myrna Duarte; lighting, Charlie Spickler. With Tricia Curran, Jacqueline Knox.

THE FLOOD. Written and directed by Rosalyn Drexler. January 9, 1992. Scenery, Tom Moore; lighting, Zdenek Kriz; costumes, Lolly Alejandro. With Black-Eyed Susan, Tom Cayler, Sheridan Roberts, Michael Osano.

GOING TO IRAQ (staged reading). By Karen Malpede. January 16, 1992.

LONG JOURNEY HOME. By Laura Sims. January 19, 1992.

HUIPIL II. By and with Elvira and Hortensia Colorado. January 30, 1992. Scenery, Tom Moore; lighting, Zdenek Kriz; costumes, Soni Moreno-Primeau; music, Franc Menusan.

FELICIA. By Pat Cobey. February 21, 1992. Director, Robert Bresnick; music, Brian Johnson. With Adam Auslander, Theresa Della Valle, Philip Hackett, Scott Leonard, Cristina Sanjuan, Zoe Zimmerman.

HIGHER POWERS (one-act plays). By Stephen Fife. February 21, 1992. Director, Seth Gordon; scenery and lighting, Michael A. Mariano; music, Andy Bloor. With Lorraine Wochna, Shaler McClure, Joey L. Golden, Robin Selfridge, Barbara Ann Davison.

AN EVENING OF BRITISH MUSIC HALL. February 24, 1992. Director, Mark Marcante; musical director, Arthur Abrams. With Crystal Field, George Bartenieff, Michael Osano, Mark Marcante, Cora Hook, T. Scott Lilly, Craig Meade, Jonathan Slaff, Shirley Curtain.

THE RIVALRY OF DOLLS. By James Purdy. March 26, 1992. Director, John Uecker; scenery, Myrna Duarte; lighting, Zdenek Kriz; costumes, Delia Doherty. With William Alderson, Kitty Crooks, Crystal Field, Christine Langner, Gordon MacDonald, Paul Anthony Stewart.

THEATER FOR THE NEW CITY—Kitty Crooks, Gordon MacDonald and Crystal Field in *The Rivalry of Dolls* by James Purdy

DUST. By Gary Goldberg. April 2, 1992. With Taylor Mead, Bill Rice, Scott Heron.

CHARLOTTE IN WONDERLAND. By Stephen Lott. April 11, 1992. Director, Penny Rockwell; choreography, Jeni Breen; scenery, Jamie Leo, Catherine Dill; lighting, Tom Barker; costumes, Geff Rhian; musical director, Tom Judson. With Cameron Foord, Eva Heinemann, John Heys, David Hirsh, John Jiler, Tom Judson, Katie Krocodile, Agosto Machado, Penny Rockwell, Irene Shea, Chris Tanner, Edward Weiss, Mary Lou Wittmer.

MICROPOLIS (PORTRAITS OF A CITY, 1980-1992). Text by Theodora Skipitares, Sebastian Stuart, Garry Rich. April 30, 1992. Music, Virgil Moorefield. With Theodora Skipitares, Preston Foerder, Cora Hook.

ANGELINA'S PIZZERIA. By Eddie DiDonna. May 14, 1992. Director, Mark Marcante.

Ubu Repertory Theater. Committed to acquainting American audiences with new works by contemporary French-speaking playwrights from around the world. Francoise Kourilsky artistic director.

A TEMPEST (12). By Aime Cesaire, translated by Richard Miller. October 13, 1991. Director, Robbie McCauley; choreography, Marlies Yearby; scenery, Jane Sablow; lighting, Zebedee Collins; costumes, Carol Ann Pelletier; music and musical direction, Tiye Giraud. With Rafael Baez, Ron Brice, Leon Addison Brown, Leo V. Finnie III, Clebert Ford, Arthur French, Bryan Hicks, Lawrence James, Jasper McGruder, Sharon McGruder, Patrick Rameau, Robert G. Silverls, Kim Sullivan, Marlies Yearby.

ISLAND MEMORIES (5). By Ina Cesaire, translated by Richard Miller. November 1, 1991. Director, Dianne Kirksey Floyd; scenery, Jane Sablow; lighting, Zebedee Collins; costumes, Carol Ann Pelletier. With Carmen de Lavallade, Ernestine Jackson.

THE BEST OF SCHOOLS (8). By Jean-Marie Besset, translated by Mark O'Donnell. March 3, 1992. Director, Evan Yionoulis; scenery, Karen Ten Eyck; lighting, Greg MacPherson; costumes, Anky Frilles. With Gil Bellows, Jonathan Friedman, Fiona Gallagher, Mira Sorvino, Justin Scott Walker, Danny Zorn.

THE WHITE BEAR (8). By Daniel Besnehard, translated by Stephen J. Vogel. March 28, 1992. Director, Peter Muste; scenery, John Brown; lighting, Greg MacPherson; costumes, Carol Ann Pelletier. With Peter Bretz, Kathryn Rossetter, Nicolette Vajtay.

FAMILY PORTRAIT (8). By Denise Bonal, translated by Timothy Johns. April 18, 1992. Director, Shirley Kaplan; scenery, John Brown; lighting, Greg MacPherson; costumes, Carol Ann Pelletier. With Alice Alvarado, Paul Austin, Alison Bartlett, Robert Kerbeck, Joanna Merlin, Matthew Mutrie, Gareth Williams.

JOCK (8). By John-Louis Bourdon, translated by Timothy Johns. May 9, 1992. Director, Andre Ernotte; scenery, John Brown; lighting, Greg MacPherson; costumes, Carol Ann Pelletier. With Margaret Kleneck, Jim Abelee, Craig Wasson.

NOWHERE (8). By Reine Barteve, translated by Bruno Kernz and Lorraine Alexander. May 30, 1992. Director, Francoise Kourilsky; scenery, John Brown; lighting, Greg MacPherson; costumes, Carol Ann Pelletier; music, Genji Ito. With Julie Boyd, Stephen Mendillo, William Carden, Du-Yee Chang.

The Vineyard Theater. Multi-art chamber theater dedicated to the development of new plays and musicals, music-theater collaborations and innovative revivals. Douglas Aibel artistic director, Barbara Zinn Krieger executive director, Jon Nakagawa managing director.

THE DON JUAN AND THE NON DON JUAN (22). Book and lyrics, James Milton and David Goldstein, based on Marvin Cohen's writings; music, Neil Radisch. December 18, 1991. Director, Evan Yionoulis; scenery, William Barclay; lighting, A.C. Hickox; costumes, Teresa Snider-Stein;

musical director, Dale Reehling. With Joseph Adams, Karen Mason, Vicki Lewis, Polly Pen, Monica Carr.

The Women's Project and Productions. Nurtures, develops and produces plays written and, for the most part, directed by women. Julia Miles founder and artistic director.

APPROXIMATING MOTHER (28). By Kathleen Tolan. October 29, 1991. Director, Gloria Muzio; scenery, David Jenkins; lighting, Jackie Manassee; costumes, Elsa Ward. With Mia Dillon, Shawana Kemp, Deirdre O'Connell, Tonya Pinkins, Richard Poe, Steven Ryan, Ali Thomas.

CHAIN and LATE BUS TO MECCA (one-act plays) (25). By Pearl Cleage. February 28, 1992. Director, Imani; scenery, George Xenos; lighting, Melody Beal; costumes, Ornyece. With Claire Dorsey, Karen Malina White, Kim Yancey. (Co-produced by New Federal Theater.)

DREAM OF A COMMON LANGUAGE (24). By Heather McDonald. May 20, 1992. Director, Liz Diamond; scenery, Anita Stewart; lighting, Michael Chybowski; costumes, Sally J. Lesser; composer and sound, Daniel Moses Schreier. With Mary Mara, Joseph Siravo, Caris Corfman, Rocco Sisto, Mia Katigbak, J.R. Nutt.

WPA Theater. Produces new American plays and neglected musicals in the realistic idiom. Kyle Renick artistic director, Edward T. Gianfrancesco resident designer, Donna Lieberman managing director.

CLUB SODA (39). By Leah Kornfeld Friedman. June 23, 1991. Director, Pamela Berlin; scenery, Edward T. Gianfrancesco; lighting, Craig Evans; costumes, Deborah Shaw. With Dan Futterman, Aaron Harnick, Katherine Hiler, Patricia Mauceri, Alanna Ubach, Lenny Venito, Danny Zorn.

THE WHITE ROSE (35). By Lillian Garrett-Groag. October 29, 1991. Director, Christopher Ashley; scenery, Edward T. Gianfrancesco; lighting, Debra Dumas; costumes, Michael Krass. With J.D. Cullum, Melissa Leo, Roger Howarth, Victor Slezak, Larry Bryggman, Brad Greenquist, Michael Louden, Billy Morrissette.

BELLA, BELLE OF BYELORUSSIA (39). By Jeffrey Essmann. January 19, 1992. Director, Christopher Ashley; scenery, James Youmans; lighting, Debra Dumas; costumes, Anne C. Patterson; music, Michael John La Chiusa. With Claire Beckman, Harriet Harris, Becca Lish, Joe Grifasi, Willis Sparks, Ann Mantel, Jefferson Mays.

PEACETIME (25). By Elaine Berman. March 8, 1992. Director, Pamela Berlin; scenery, Edward T. Gianfrancesco; lighting, Craig Evans; costumes, Mimi Maxmen. With Stephen Mailer, Ken Garito, Barry Snider, Jessica Queller, Suzanne Costallos, Gordon Greenberg, Kelly Wolf, Sandra Laub.

York Theater Company. Specializing in producing new works, as well as in reviving unusual, forgotten or avant-garde musicals. Janet Hayes Walker producing director.

WHAT ABOUT LUV? (29). Book, Jeffrey Sweet; music, Howard Marren; lyrics, Susan Birkenhead. December 22, 1991. Director and choreographer, Patricia Birch; scenery, James Morgan; lighting, Mary Jo Dondlinger; costumes, Barbara Beccio; musical director, Tom Helm. With David Green, Judy Kaye, Austin Pendleton.

AFTER THE DANCING IN JERICHO (16). Written and directed by P.J. Barry. February 9, 1992. Choreography, Dennis Dennehy; scenery, Daniel Ettinger; lighting, Mary Jo Dondlinger; costumes, Barbara Beccio. With Pamela Burrell, James Congdon, Jack Davidson, John Kozeluh, Michelle O'Steen, Ginger Prince.

LITTLE ME. Book, Neil Simon, based on Patrick Dennis's novel; music, Cy Coleman; lyrics, Carolyn Leigh. March 26, 1992. Director, Jeffrey B. Moss. With Jo Ann Cunningham, Stephen Joseph, Denise Le Donne, Amelia Prentice, Jonathan Beck Reed, Russ Thacker, Ray Wills.

Miscellaneous

In the additional listing of 1991-92 off-off-Broadway productions below, the names of the producing groups or theaters appear in CAPITAL LETTERS and the titles of the works in *italics*. This list consists largely of new or reconstituted works and excludes most revivals, especially of classics. It includes a few productions staged by groups which rented space from the more established organizations listed previously.

ACTORS PLAYHOUSE. *The Jersey Girls* by Larry Manogue. August 30, 1991. Directed by Ken Lang; with William White, Kipling Berger, Kimberly Auslander, Suzanne Scott. *No Cure for Cancer* by and with Dennis Leary. October 23, 1991. Directed by Chris Phillips.

ALGONQUIN. *Jeff Harnar Sings the Warner Brothers Songbook* (cabaret). October, 1991.

ALICE'S FOURTH FLOOR. *Appointment With a High-Wire Lady* by Russell Davis. January 30, 1992. Directed by Michael Mantell; with Jayne Atkinson, Suzanne Shepherd, Victor Slezak. *Lovers* by Mario Fratti. March 22, 1992. Directed by Raymond Haigler; with Susan Egbert, Alexandra Napier, Gwen Torry-Owens, Brian Poteat.

AMERICAN JEWISH THEATER. *Rags* book by Joseph Stein; music by Charles Strouse; lyrics by Stephen Schwartz. December 2, 1991. Directed by Richard Sabellico; with Rachel Black, Ann Crumb, Philip Hoffman, Jonathan Kaplan, Crista Moore, Jan Neuberger, David Pevsner, Robert Tate, Alec Timerman. *Invention for Fathers and Sons* by Alan Brody. January 20, 1992. Directed by Jay E. Raphael; with Glynis Bell, Monica Bell, Elaine Grollman, Ben Hammer, Gordon MacDonald, Len Stanger, William Verderber. *First Is Supper* by Shelley Berman. March 15, 1992. Directed by Andre Ernotte; with Barbara Andres, Blaze Autumn Berdahl, Donald Christopher, Louis Falk, Nile Lanning, Patricia Mauceri, Marilyn Salinger, Mark Zimmerman. *Angel of Death* (one-act play) by Charlie Schulman, directed by Peter Maloney and *Big Al* (one-act play) by Bryan Goluboff, directed by Billy Hopkins; with Daniel von Bargen. April 25, 1992.

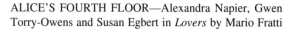

ALICE'S FOURTH FLOOR—Alexandra Napier, Gwen
Torry-Owens and Susan Egbert in *Lovers* by Mario Fratti

ATLANTIC THEATER COMPANY. *Distant Fires* by Kevin Heelan. October 11, 1991. Directed by Clark Gregg; with Giancarlo Esposito, Jordan Lage, Ray Anthony Thomas, Jack Wallace, Todd Weeks, David Wolos-Fonteno. *Five Very Live* (one-act plays): *Sure Thing* by David Ives; *Wonderful Party* by Howard Korder; *Five Very Live* by David Van Matre; *Call of the Wily* by Patrick Breen; *The Age of Pie* by Peter Hedges. January 8, 1992. *The Virgin Molly* by Quincy Long. March 25, 1992. Directed by Sarah Eckhardt; with Robert Bella, William Mesnik, Todd Weeks, Kevin Thigpen, Neil Pepe, Don Reilly.

BARROW GROUP. *Greetings* by Tom Dudzick. December 5, 1991. Directed by Seth Barrish; with Marcia DeBonis, Tom Riis Farrell, Aaron Goodwin, Vince O'Brien, Natalie Ross. *God's Country*. See La Mama entry.

BILLIE HOLIDAY THEATER. *Lotto: Experience the Dream*. Written and directed by Cliff Roquemore. December, 1991. With Steve Baumer, John L. Bennett, Karl Calhoun, Elise C. Chance, Earl Fields Jr., Maurice Fontane, Bridget Kelso, Frederick Kiah Jr., Cyndi B. Galloway-O'Connor, Bryan Roquemore, Jessica Smith, Otis Young Smith.

BLUE HERON THEATER. *Love in the Shadow of the Umbrella Bamboo* by Oana-Maria Hock. December 4, 1991. With Anna Vitkin, Andrea E. Davis.

BROOKLYN ACADEMY OF MUSIC. *Next Wave Festival*. Works included *Invitations to Heaven (Questions of a Jewish Child)* conceived and created by Eric Bass, written by Eric Bass, Richard Edelman, Alan Bern; music by Alan Bern. September 30, 1991. With Eric Bass, Alan Bern. *Maturando* conceived and directed by Marcos Caetano Ribas. October 9, 1991. With Marcos Caetano Ribas, Fernanda Amaral, Rachel Ribas, Alza Helena Alves. *1991 (A Performance Chronicle of the Rediscovery of America by the Warrior for Gringostroika)* written, directed and performed by Guillermo Gomez-Pena. October 15, 1991. *Israel: the Next Generation Festival*. Works included *Hamlet* by William Shakespeare, translated by Avraham Shlonski, adapted and directed by Rina Yerushalmi. January 22, 1992. With Shuli Rand, Dina Blei, Shlomo Sadan, Pnina Bradt. *Rosencrantz and Guildenstern Are Dead* by Tom Stoppard, translated into Hebrew by Joseph Brodsky. January 29, 1992. Directed by Yevgeny Arye; with Mark Ivanir, Yevgeny Terletsky. *Atlas* (opera) written and directed by Meredith Monk. May 13, 1992.

CHERNUCHIN THEATER. *Brotherly Love* by John Fedele. May 14, 1992. Directed by Frank Criscione; with John Fedele, Robert Arcaro, Jim Hance, Lynn Knight, Noemi Soulet.

COMEDY CELLAR. *Absolutely Rude* (musical revue) music and lyrics by Rick Crom. February 12, 1992. Directed by John McMahon; with Amy Ryder, Frankie Maio, Virginia McMath, Rick Crom, Carol McCann, Linda Gelman, Roger DeWitt.

COURTHOUSE THEATER. *When Lithuania Ruled the World, Part 3* written and directed by Kestutis Nakas. January 17, 1992.

CREATIVE TIME. *As a Dream That Vanishes (A Meditation on the Harvest of a Lifetime)* by Merry Conway and Noni Pratt. October, 1991. With Merry Conway, Noni Pratt, Albert Ratcliffe.

CUCARACHA THEATER. See New York Shakespeare Festival entry in the Plays Produced Off Broadway section of this volume.

DANCE THEATER WORKSHOP. *Uccelli, the Drugs of Love* (puppet theater piece) performed by Roman Paska. June 8, 1991. (Produced as part of the New York International Theater Festival.) *Sarrasine* by Neil Bartlett, based on Honore de Balzac's story; music by Nicolas Bloomfield. September 4, 1991. With Sheila Ballantine, Bette Bourne, Francois Testory, Beverley Klein. *When the Wind Blows* (puppet theater pieces) conceived and directed by Janie Geiser; *News Update* developed in collaboration with Judith Anderson, Kyle de Camp, Cathy Simmons, Janie Geiser. May 7, 1992.

DIPLOMAT HOTEL. *The Law of Remains* created and directed by Reza Abdoh. February 15, 1992. With Tom Pearl, Peter Jacobs, Sabrina Artel, Brenden Doyle, Anita Durst, Giuliana Francis, Stephan

Francis, Ariel Herrera, Priscilla Holbrook, Kwasi Boateng, Sardar Singh Khalsa, Veronica Pawlowska, Raphael Pimental, Tony Torn, Kathryn Walsh.

DOUBLE IMAGE THEATER. *Damon Runyon's Tales of Broadway*. Adapted and performed by John Martello. July 18, 1991.

DOWNTOWN ART COMPANY. *Canal Zone* by Roger Arturo Durling. April 23, 1992. Directed by Eduardo Machado; with John Billeci, Vicente Castellanos, Elzbieta Czyzewska, Nancy Franklin, Ryan Gilliam, George McGrath, Troy Michael Rowland, Paul Alexander Slee.

THE GLINES. *Body and Soul* written and directed by John Glines. June 30, 1991. With David Boldt, Martin Outzen, Eddie Cobb, Randall Denman, Douglas Gibson. *Get Used to It* (musical revue) by Tom Wilson Weinberg. March 22, 1992.

HAROLD CLURMAN THEATER. *Hour of the Lynx* by Per Olov Enquist, translated by Kjersti Board. March 29, 1992. Directed by Oeyvind Froeyland; with Rob Campbell, Heather Ehlers, Helen Harrelson, Jason Jacobs.

HOME FOR CONTEMPORARY THEATER AND ART. *Teenage Wedding* written and directed by John Steppling. July 10, 1991. With Michael Collins, Suzanne Fletcher, George Gerdes, Robin Ginsburg, Lola Glaudini, Michael Margotta. *Ready for the River* by Neal Bell. October 9, 1991. Directed by Joshua Astrachan; with Randy Danson, David Eigenberg, Kathleen O'Neill, Dylan Price, James Riordan. *One Neck* by Todd Alcott. May 9, 1992. Directed by Randy Rollison; with Frank Deal, Todd Alcott, David Thornton, Melissa Hurst, Allison Janney, Damian Young.

IMPROVISATION. *Short Shots* (one-act plays): *Norman* book and lyrics by Frank Jump, music by Lynn Portas; *Out of Focus* book and lyrics by Benita Green, music by David Tenney; *Poopsie* book and lyrics by Dan Clancy, music by Lynn Portas; *Room 1203* book and lyrics by Dan Clancy, music by Lynn Portas; *A Joinin' of the Colors* by Reena Heenan. July 28, 1991.

INTAR 2. *The Boxing Day Parade* by Clifford Mason. September, 1991. Directed by Jennifer Vermont-Davis; with Jeffrey Dobbs, Arthur French, Pam Hyatt, Carol London, Clifford Mason, Norman Matlock, Monica Parks, John Steber.

JEAN COCTEAU REPERTORY. *The Vanek Plays* (*Audience* and *Unveiling* translated by Jan Novak, *Protest* translated by Vera Blackwell) by Vaclav Havel. May 7, 1992. Directed by David Fishelson; with Craig Smith, William Charles Mitchell, Elise Stone, Grant Neale, Robert Ierardi.

JUDITH ANDERSON THEATER. *A Rendezvous with God* by Miriam Hoffman, translated by Miriam Hoffman and Rena Berkowicz. July 14, 1991. Directed by Sue Lawless; with Avi Hoffman. *Napalm the Magnificent* conceived and performed by David Craig. March 5, 1992. *Farther West* by John Murrell. April 17, 1992. Directed by Victoria Liberatori.

KAMPO CULTURAL CENTER. *The Wedding Portrait* by Gudmundur Steinsson. March 20, 1992. Directed by Rebecca Kreinen; with Peter Galman, Rod C. Hayes III, Atli W. Kendall, Paul Kielar, Stacie Linardos, Tracey Osborne, Brenda Smiley, Martha Thompson, Ann B. Wyma.

THE KITCHEN. *Vena Cava* by and with Diamanda Galas. February, 1992. *Lamb of God Hotel* written and directed by Karen Finley. April 22, 1992. With Helen Schumacher, Hapi Phace. *Memento Mori* by Karen Finley.

LINCOLN CENTER. *Serious Fun!* Schedule included *The Mysteries* and *What's So Funny* written and directed by David Gordon, music by Philip Glass, with Lola Pashalinski, Ralph Williams, Jane Hoffman, Karen Graham, Benjamin Bode, Norma Fire, Alice Playten; *It's a Girl* by DanceNoise with Anne Iobst, Lucy Sexton; *B-4-Sin* written and directed by Johanna Went; *Half Reel* by Rinde Eckert and Leonard Pitt; by and with Matt Goldman, Phil Stanton, Chris Wink (Blue Man Group); *Big Bad God* by and with Harry Kipper; *Pangaean Dreams* by and with Rachel Rosenthal; *Reno's New Show* by and with Reno; *Voices from the Beyond* by and with Laurie Anderson. July 9-30, 1991.

LIVING THEATER. *Waste (A Street Spectacle)*. Adapted by Hanan Reznikov; music by Michael Shenker. August 2, 1991. Directed by Judith Malina; with Alan Arenius, Bob Paton, Gary Brackett, Gene, Jerry Goralnick, Kristin Armstrong, Laura Kolb, Nomena Strusz, Robert Hieger. *We Should . . . (a Lie)* by Kenneth Bernard. January 22, 1992. Directed by Robert Press; with Joanie Fritz, Gene, Lois Kagan, Kevin D. Mayes,Victoria Murphy, Joe Pichette, Michael St. Clair.

MANHATTAN CLASS COMPANY. *Manhattan Class One-Acts: A Therapeutic Moment* written and directed by Ethan Silverman; *Mixed Babies* by Oni Faida Lampley, directed by Jennifer Nelson; *A.M.L.* by Jacquelyn Reingold; *St. Stanislaus Outside the House* by Patrick Breen, directed by Ethan Silverman. March 9-21, 1992. *A Snake in the Vein* by Alan Bowne. March 30, 1992. Directed by Jimmy Bohr; with Gil Bellows, Charles Cragin.

TRIPLEX—Timothy Chipping and Karen Bowlas in David Mowat's *The Guise*

MARYMOUNT MANHATTAN THEATER. *The Complete Works of William Shakespeare (Abridged)* by Jess Borgeson, Adam Long, Daniel Singer, with additional material by Reed Martin. June 13,1991. With Reed Martin, Jess Borgeson, Adam Long. (Produced as part of the New York International Festival of the Arts.)

NAKED ANGELS THEATER. *Hot Keys* by and with Jeff Weiss. February, 1992.

NAT HORNE THEATER. *Currents Turned Awry* (one-act plays): *Meet Doyle MacIntyre* and *Dining Out Alone* by D. L. Coburn. June 20, 1991. Directed by Philip Galbraith; with Michael Cannis, Larry Collins, Robert Lindley Sutton, Nick Stannard. *Folks Remembers a Missing Page (The Rise and Fall of Harlem)* by J. E. Gaines. September 25, 1991. Directed by Andre Mtumi; with Sonny Jim Gaines. *The Mask* by Bill Elverman. February 11, 1992. Directed by Le Wilhelm; with Jeffrey J. Albright, Stephen Beach, Peter Bock, Jed Dickson, Carol Halstead, Katherine Parks, Jeff Paul, Scott Sparks, Dustye Winniford.

NEW YORK PUBLIC LIBRARY FOR THE PERFORMING ARTS. *Free Theater Productions.* Program of readings by and with Betty Comden and Adolph Green. February 7, 1992. *Harry Kondoleon's Nightmare Alley: The Poet's Corner* and *The Little Book of Professor Enigma* (one-act plays) by Harry Kondoleon. April 13, 1992. With Marian Seldes, Jeff Weiss, Jayne Haynes.

NEW YORK STATE THEATER INSTITUTE. *Beauty and the Beast* by Ray Bono. January 12, 1992. Directed by Ed. Lange; with Marlene Goudreau, David Bunce, Joel Aroeste, John Thomas McGuire III, Erika Johnson Newell, Etta Caren Fink, Skye McKenzie, Joseph Larrabee-Quandt, Betsy Riley, John Romeo, Mariye Inouye.

ONE DREAM THEATER. *The Dropper* written and directed by Ron McLarty. October 30, 1991. With John Dawson Beard, Nick Giangiulio, Bob Horen, Richard Long, Wendy Scharfman. *Like to Live/Tissue* by Louise Page. April 23, 1992. With Laurence Gleason, Meg Wynn Owen, Maria Radman.

ONTOLOGICAL-HYSTERIC THEATER AT ST. MARK'S. *The Mind King* written and directed by Richard Foreman. January 9, 1992. With David Patrick Kelly, Henry Stram, Colleen Werthmann. *The Richard Foreman Trilogy: Part I: In the Mind, Part II: My Father Was Already Lost, Part III: The Field of White Light* by Richard Foreman, adapted by Spin Theater. May 8, 1992. Directed by Paul Schiff Berman and Deborah Lewittes; with R. P. Brink, Carol Blanco, Antonia Chiodo, Betty Anne Cohen, Sean Eden, Kay Gayner, Elisabeth S. Rodgers.

PERFORMANCE SPACE 122. *Stitsha* written and directed by Cont Mhlanga. June 10, 1991. With Princess Dlamini, Doubt Dube, Sithembiso Gumpo, Patriciah Mhete, Alois Moyo, Andrew Moyo, Joyce Mpofu, Taurai Dumisani Muswere, Nomusa Ncube, Herebert Phiri, Pedzisai Sithole, Priscilla Sithole. *Citizen Mind* written and directed by Cont Mhlanga. June 14, 1991. (Both plays produced as part of the New York International Festival of the Arts.) *Caught Between the Devil and the Deep Blue Sea* by and with Peggy Pettit. October 17, 1991. *Roy Cohn/Jack Smith* conceived and performed by Ron Vawter. May 9, 1992. Directed by Greg Mehrten.

PLAYHOUSE 125. *A Fresh of Breath Air* by Dale Stein, original music by Charles Goldbeck and Dale Stein. May 28, 1992. Directed by Christopher Ashley; costumes, Sharon Lynch; lighting, Daniel MacLean Wagner; with Dale Stein.

PROVINCETOWN PLAYHOUSE. *A Terrible Beauty* written and directed by Kevin Breslin. April 9, 1992. With William Hickey, Tatum O'Neal, Holt McCallany, Fiona Hutchison, Michael A. Healy.

RAINBOW AND STARS (cabaret). *What a Swell Party! The Cole Porter Revue.* July 23, 1991. Directed by Fred Greene; with Ronny Whyte, Mary Cleere Haran, Helen Schneider, Bruce Coyle, Terri Klausner. *Varieties* conceived by Steve Paul and Gregory Dawson. November 24, 1991. Directed by Fred Greene; with Douglas Bernstein, Jason Graae, Marilyn Pasekoff, Sharon Douglas, Fred Wells, Christopher Durang and Dawne, Anne Francine, Tony Roberts, Brian O'Connor. *'S Wonderful, 'S Marvelous, 'S Gershwin!* conceived by Gregory Dawson and Steve Paul. March 31, 1992. With Jo Anne Worley, Judy Blazer, Carol Woods, Peter Reardon.

ST. BARTHOLOMEW'S CHURCH. *The Tragedy of Macbeth* by William Shakespeare. June 14, 1991. Directed by Stephen Rayne; with Bhasker, Burt Caesar, David Case, Trevor Gordon, Mona Hammond, Caroline Lee-Johnson, John Matshikiza, Desmond McNamara, Patrick Miller, Clara Onyemere, Indra Ove, Alex Tetteh-Lartey. (Produced as part of the New York International Festival of the Arts.)

SALAMANDER REPERTORY THEATER. *Frankenstein* by Mary Shelley, adapted by Joel Leffert and Nancy Nichols. September 16, 1991. Directed by Ted Davis; with James L. Walker, Timothy Wheeler, Jean Tafler, Barry Craig Friedman, Jenn Thompson, Larry Swansen.

SCANDALOUS MINDS. *I Can't Stop Screaming* by Andy Halliday. November 17, 1991. Directed by Jeff Mousseau; with Andy Halliday, Thomas Bolster, Jay Corcoran, Linda Evanson, Charles Kelly, Matt Lenz, Alan Pratt, Elaine Rinehart, Louis Silvers, Bill Tripician.

SINGERS FORUM. *Perpetrator* by Tedd Smith. March 10, 1992. Directed by Tom Ferriter; with Stephen Bradbury, Thomas Barbour, Robert Mason Ham, Anne Marie Campbell, Mark Doerr, Dennis Jordan, Oscar Koch, Frank Medrano, Sarah Taylor.

SOUPSTONE PROJECT. *Natural Selection* (one-act plays): *Genius Loci* by Neal Brilliant, directed by Eric Concklin; *Women Who Love Science Too Much* by Kathleen Cahill, directed by Neile Weissman; *Fast!* by A.E.O. Goldman, directed by Neile Weissman; *Dead Voices* by Noel Madlansacay, directed by Chris Mack. July 17-August 3, 1991.

SYMPHONY SPACE. *Women Observed* (readings from Leo Tolstoy's *Anna Karenina*, Henry James's *The Turn of the Screw* and Virginia Woolf's *A Room of One's Own* and *Mrs. Dalloway*) created and performed by Claire Bloom. September 27-29, 1991.

THEATER FOR A NEW AUDIENCE. *The Comedy of Errors* by William Shakespeare. January 18, 1992. Directed by William Gaskill; with Al Carmines, Peter Schmitz, Jeffrey Guyton, Elizabeth Meadows Rouse. *The New Americans* written, composed and directed by Elizabeth Swados. March 28, 1992.

THEATER LABRADOR. *Vinegar Tom* by Caryl Churchill. April 12, 1992. Directed by Marjorie Ballentine; with Susan Bernfield, James Rutigliano, Greer Goodman, Carolyn Baeumler, Charlotte Colavin, Colleen McQuade, Deborah Kampmeier, Patrick McCarthy, Sally Ramirez, Erik Tieze.

THEATER ROW THEATER. *Sublime Lives* by Paul Firestone. September 12, 1991. Directed by William E. Hunt; with Pamela Cecil, Jordan Charney, Susan Farwell, Hans Friedrichs, Ron Keith, Lenny Singer, William Verderber. *The Novelist* by Howard Fast. October 20, 1991. Directed by Sam Schacht; with Gretchen Walther, Will Lyman. *Nebraska* by Keith Reddin. May 27, 1992. Directed by Graf Mouen; with Michael Griffiths, Michael Hayden, Paula Mann, Robert North, Cathy Reinheimer, Anne Torsiglieri, Jon Patrick Walker.

TRIANGLE THEATER COMPANY. *Salt-Water Moon* by David French. February 9, 1992. Directed by Charles R. Johnson; with Kimberly Topper, Steve Dane. *More Fun Than Bowling* by Steven Dietz. April, 1992. Directed by John Seibert; with Fred Burrell, T. Cat Ford, Sue Kenny, Kimberly Topper, Alexander Webb.

TRIPLEX. *The Guise* by David Mowat. November 17, 1991. Directed by Brian Astbury; with Tania-Jane Bowers, Karen Bowlas, Timothy Chipping, Karl Collins, Michael Hodgson, Carine Sinclair, Andrew Weale. *Havoc in Gold Mountain* (collaborative multi-media work) by Ming Fay, Fred Wei-Han Ho, Jia Lu Hu, Corky Lee, Siu Fai Pun, Liang Xing Tang, Liang Tee Tue. April 24, 1992.

T.W.E.E.D. *Atomic Opera* by Kevin Malony, Michele Elliman, John O'Malley; music, Douglas J. Cuomo. October 25, 1991. Directed by Kevin Malony; with Torrin Cummings, Michele Elliman, Audrey Fort, Lisa Gillette, Peggy Gould, Renate Graziadei, Mia Kim, David McGrath, John O'Malley, Colleen O'Neill, Craig Victor. *Nervous Splendor—The World of Ludwig Wittgenstein* by Perry Souchuk. February 28, 1992. Directed by Rebecca Holderness.

24 KARAT CLUB. *Bernie's Bar Mitzvah* written and directed by Howard Perloff. March 3, 1992. With

Ian Bonds, Carolyn Beauchamp, Benjamin Blum, Barney Cohen, Laura Covello, Tiffany Garfinkle, Bob Garman, S. Rachel Herts, Marjorie F. Orman, Louis Levy, Howard Segal.

29th STREET PLAYHOUSE. *Rutherford and Son* by Githa Sowerby. February 13, 1992. Directed by Michael Hillyer; Saylor Creswell, John Hillyer, Holly Hawkins, Annette Hunt, Mark Edward Lang, Gwendolyn Lewis, Miller Lide, Joan Matthiessen. *The Duck Blind* by Peter Maeck. May 13, 1992. Directed by David Dorwart; with Alison Lani Bronda, Tim Corcoran, Leo Farley, David Mogentale, Richard Sachar.

UNDER ONE ROOF. *Job: A Circus* conceived, composed and directed by Elizabeth Swados. January 9, 1992. With Mary Dino, J. Tori Evans, Jeff Hess, Ann Marie Milazzo, Alan Mintz, Daniel Neiden, Paul O'Keefe, Stephen Ringold, Michael Sottile. *Jungle Movie* by and with Ridge Theater. March 8, 1992.

VILLAGE GATE. *The Real Live Brady Bunch* from the series created by Sherwood Schwartz; music by Faith Soloway. Directed by Jill and Faith Soloway; with Andy Richter, Jane Lynch, Pat Towne, Becky Thyre, Benjamin Zook, Melanie Hutsell, Tom Booker, Susan Messing, Mari Weis. *The Real Live Game Show* by Eric Waddell. September 26, 1991.

VILLAGE THEATER COMPANY. *The Rivers and Ravines* by Heather McDonald. November 6, 1991. Directed by Henry Fonte; with Barbara Bercue, Matthew Caldwell, Terrence Martin, Julia McLaughlin, Zeke Zaccaro. *Anima Mundi* by Don Nigro. January 29, 1992. Directed by Henry Fonte; with Michael Curran, Julia McLaughlin, Michelle Berke. *This One Thing I Do* by Claire Braz-Valentine and Michael Griggs. April 1, 1992. Directed by Gigi Rivkin; with Julia Flood, Marjorie Feenan.

WESTSIDE THEATER. *The Lunatic, the Lover and the Poet* (one-man show). April 21, 1992. Shakespeare anthology by and with Brian Bedford.

WORKING THEATER. *Working One-Acts '91: New Hope for the Dead* by John Sayles, directed by Earl Hagan; *Betting on the Dust Commander* by Suzan-Lori Parks, directed by Liz Diamond; *Abandoned in Queens* by Laura Maria Censabella. June 13, 1991. With Kevin N. Davis, Linda Marie Larson, Dean Nichols, Joseph Palmas, Roger Serbagi, Pamala Tyson. *Ascension Day* by Michael Henry Brown. February 12, 1992. Directed by L. Kenneth Richardson; with Kevin N. Davis, Andre De Shields, Novella Nelson, Arthur French.

WOW CAFE. *The Love Affairs of an Old Maid* written and directed by Lucinda Rhea Zoe. April 16, 1992. With Claire Olivia Moed, Joan Nestle, Donna Jean Evans, Carlyn Patierno.

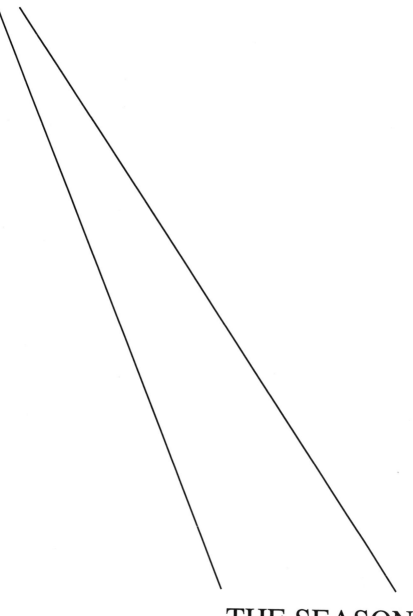

THE SEASON
AROUND
THE UNITED STATES

○
○
○

OUTSTANDING NEW PLAYS CITED BY AMERICAN THEATER CRITICS ASSOCIATION

and

A DIRECTORY OF NEW-PLAY PRODUCTIONS

○
○
○

THE American Theater Critics Association (ATCA) is the organization of 250 leading drama critics in all media in all sections of the United States. One of this group's stated purposes is "To increase public awareness of the theater as a *national* resource" (italics ours). To this end, ATCA has cited three outstanding new plays produced this season around the country, to be represented in our coverage of The Season Around the United States by excerpts from each of their scripts demonstrating literary style and quality. And one of these—*Could I Have This Dance?* by Doug Haverty—was designated the first-place play and received the 6th annual ATCA New Play Award of $1,000.

The process of selection of these outstanding plays is as follows: any ATCA member critic may nominate a play if it has been given a production in a professional house. It must be a finished play given a full production (not a reading or an airing as a play-in-progress). Nominated scripts were studied and discussed by an ATCA play-reading committee chaired by T.H. McCulloh of the Los Angeles *Times* and comprising Jeffrey Borak of the *Berkshire Eagle*, Richard Christiansen of the Chicago *Tribune*, Damien Jaques of the Milwaukee *Journal* and free-lance critics Porter Anderson, Dan Sullivan and Gerald Weales. The committee members made their choices on the basis of script rather than production, thus placing very much the same emphasis as the editors of this volume in making the New York Best Play selections. There were no eligibility requirements except that a nominee be the first full professional production of a new work outside New York City within this volume's time frame of June 1, 1991 to May 31, 1992. If the timing of nominations and openings prevents some works from being considered in any given year, they will be eligible for consideration the following year if they haven't since moved on to New York production, and their program listing will be included in our Directory. We offer our sincerest thanks and admiration to the ATCA members and their committee for the valuable insight into the 1991-92 theater season around the United States which their selections provide for this *Best Plays* record, in the form of the following excerpts from outstanding scripts illustrating their style and the nature of their content, with brief introductions provided by T.H. McCulloh (*Could I Have This Dance?*), Dan Sullivan (*Miss Evers' Boys* by David Feldshuh) and Jonathan Abarbanel (*American Enterprise* by Jeffrey Sweet, in his journalistic persona the associate editor of *Best Plays*).

COULD I HAVE THIS DANCE?

A Play in Two Acts

BY DOUG HAVERTY

Cast and credits appear on page 433

COULD I HAVE THIS DANCE?: At first glance, Doug Haverty's *Could I Have This Dance?* might seem like just another "disease of the week" play, but this bright young playwright skillfully avoids that trap by making the illness, in this case Huntington's Disease, a secondary force in his story. Haverty also uses an incisive and humane sense of humor to give breadth to his subject. The conflict arises from the psychological parrying between two sisters, Amanda and Monica, who may have inherited the illness from their mother, but aren't sure they want to take the tests which will confirm or deny the fact.

Jeannette, their mother, founded a back-porch public relations firm years earlier, which has grown into a highly visible Los Angeles enterprise, whose office is the play's setting. Jeannette's frustration with the tragic manifestation of her illness centers on her inability to continue the work she loves. (An inventive device is used to illustrate Jeannette's illness—she does not shake as Huntingon's victims do, but does a gentle waltz step, waving her arms in waltz rhythm.) Her husband Hank cares for her, while Amanda and Monica have successfully taken over the operation. While Monica juggles the possibly dangerous dream of having children, Amanda limits her relationships to one-night stands, the latest being 20ish Errol, a mailroom hustler looking for the next rung on his career ladder. He enters, joining Monica and Amanda.

ERROL: Hi. (*To Amanda.*) I'm here to set up our second date.

MONICA: What? A "second" date? This is fascinating. How'd you convince her?

ERROL: I threatened to wear my glasses, cut off my hair and pretend to be someone else.

MONICA: Well, that might have fooled her once.

ERROL: Then I'd dye my hair, wear an eye-patch and limp.

MONICA: No. That would remind her too much of her fourth husband.

ERROL (*to Amanda*): Fourth? You told me there was only three.

MONICA: She lied. Is "Errol" your real name?

ERROL: Yeah. My mom had a thing for old movie stars. My brothers are named: Spencer, Clark and Ronald.

MONICA: I can't believe you survived a date with man-eating-Mandy and had the tenacity to show up here.

AMANDA: He's an agent. He doesn't give up.

MONICA: You are? Which agency?

ERROL: William Morris. Only I'm not an agent yet.

MONICA: Oh. Still in the mail room, huh? How old are you?

AMANDA (*to Errol*): You see? You see? Now you know why I don't bring anyone home. My steply ugsister gives everyone the third degree.

ERROL: I'm twenty-three.

MONICA: Given up on seventeen-year-olds, have you? Going in for the more mature type, huh?

ERROL: Ten years may seem like a big difference now, but when we're sixty-seven and fifty-seven, no one will notice.

MONICA: Look out, Mandy.

AMANDA: Don't you have to write a press release or something?

> *Jeannette dances through carrying wilted flowers. She waves them at Monica and Amanda. She throws them down and stops to check out Errol. Casually, Monica wipes the saliva off Jeannette's chin. Then Jeannette waltzes out.*

MONICA: So, Errol, what did you major in at UCLA?

ERROL: How did you know I went to UCLA?

MONICA: That's where Mandy does all her shopping.

ERROL: Marketing.

MONICA (*to Amanda*): Why didn't you get her fresh flowers?

AMANDA: I overslept. (*To Errol.*) You kept me up too late.

ERROL: You kept me up too long. (*He laughs, then sees Monica is not amused.*) Right. (*Referring to Jeannette.*) Do you get fresh flowers for street people every day?

AMANDA: That wasn't a street person. It was my mother.

> *Errol looks at Amanda in amazement, then to Monica.*

MONICA: Mine, too.

ERROL: But you didn't say that she—she—

AMANDA: Don't you remember what I said last night about Huntington's Disease?

MONICA: Sometimes our retentive powers are not what they should be when all the blood is engorging other parts of our anatomy.

ERROL: No. I heard what you said, that it was a nervous disorder and I—

MONICA: Mandy, did Mac say why he's not at his hotel?

ERROL: Mac? You mean you guys do Mac, the rock star?

MONICA: Film star, poet, novelist, father, humanitarian, missing in Tokyo.

ERROL: God. He's one of my favorites. I've seen him in concert, and one time he just stopped playing and ripped off his shirt and dove into the audience. It was so cool. You—

MONICA: Excuse me. I'm certain it's a fascinating recounting, but I just remembered where I might have the promoter's home number. It was neat meeting you. (*She exits.*)

ERROL: Well. I sure had your family figured all wrong.

AMANDA: How so?

ERROL: Well. Your sister is the scary one. Not your mom.

AMANDA: Errol?

ERROL: Yeah?

> *Jeannette dances in again. Amanda looks away. Errol watches Jeannette, fascinated. Jeannette carries a child's plastic cup with cover and straw. She tries to hand it to Amanda, who reaches for it, but they don't connect. The cup falls. Errol reaches down and picks it up. He tries to hand it to Jeannette.*

AMANDA: She needs a refill. Mom, this is Errol. We met last night.

ERROL: Hey, there, Mrs. Glendenning.

> *He puts a hand out to shake. Jeannette just waltzes in place, looking suspicious.*

This is the shaking you were talking about?

AMANDA: This is why I don't do second dates.

ERROL (*yelling to Jeannette*): Mrs. G, it's nice to meet you.

AMANDA: She can hear you fine.

ERROL: Can she see me?

AMANDA: Yes. She just has occasional trouble focusing.

ERROL: Anyone would if they lurched around like they were being electrocuted. (*To Jeannette.*) Don't you get tired?

> *Jeannette appears to laugh, then looks at Amanda.*

AMANDA: She can't stop.

ERROL: Even, like, at night when she sleeps? (*Amanda shakes her head. To Jeannette.*) God. I'm so sorry.

> *Jeannette smiles at Amanda.*

ERROL: This is a put-on, right? Anybody tries to stretch the second date rule gets this jack-hammer dance?

> *Errol tries to hold Jeannette still. She continues waltzing, but he reacts as if he was touching a strong, trembling man in shock.*

God.

Jeannette smiles and exits.

Monica's on-and-off boy friend, by whom she learns she is pregnant, is free lance photographer Colin. Jeannette's self-preserving sense of humor and honesty is echoed not only in her family, but in those who surround them. In one scene Jeannette's husband Hank gives his daughters' boy friends a lesson in coping.

ERROL: How's it going?

HANK: I've had better decades.

ERROL: How long you been retired now, Mr. G?

HANK: Retired? I work seven days a week, fifty-two weeks a year.

ERROL: Oh. You mean helping with the business.

HANK: That and watching Jeannette. It's a full-time job.

COLIN: What would you be doing if you weren't committed—so to speak?

HANK: Camp. Bird-watch. I took Nettie with me one time, sort of a trial. Whew. What a mistake. She did not like it. She thrashed that tent within an inch of its life. Somebody thought a bear got to it. She scared the birds, too.

ERROL: I'll bet. Oh.

HANK: I'd just like to drive. Just get in the car with all my gear. No plans, no phone numbers, no check-in points. Just go. (*Beat.*) I'll get to it.

ERROL: Amanda told me you love looking after your Mrs. G; that you refused a nurse.

HANK: True. I didn't want a nurse, that was because of her. But "love" looking after Nettie? Nah.

ERROL: Is it hard?

HANK: Of course it is. What kind of question is that? If you're trying to make conversation, don't bother. It's not necessary. If you want to talk to me, ask something spicy.

ERROL: Okay. Do you still have sex with your wife?

HANK (*smiles*): What do you think?

ERROL: I don't know. I know old people do it.

HANK: We do, huh? You knew that?

ERROL: Yeah. My grandfather told me.

HANK: Yeah. Well—it's tricky.

ERROL: I'll bet. Oh. You mean tricky to talk about or do?

HANK: Both.

COLIN: Hank, you don't have to—

HANK: Ya see, the hard part is holding her still.

COLIN: I can imagine.

HANK: You got to hold her, see, and get into her rhythm.

ERROL: But does she like it? I mean, can you tell?

HANK (*to Colin*): He's obviously very inexperienced. (*To Errol.*) Son, I always know when a lady likes my lovemaking. You develop a sense for this. Yes. She likes it. You know the disease makes her arms and legs go like crazy, but she's still

Toni Sawyer as Jeannette and Elizabeth Norment
as Monica in Doug Haverty's *Could I Have This
Dance?* at Colony Studio Theater, Los Angeles

a person inside with needs and desires and love. And let me tell you, once you get
in rhythm with that buckin' bronco, it's like dancing with an epileptic hooker.
(*Beat.*) I don't mean any disrespect by that. It's just the only way I can describe it
and I'm not used to describing it. But you asked.
    ERROL: Right.

    Realizing that she needs room to breath and straighten out her thinking, Amanda
decides to take a vacation from the family, just as her conflict with Monica over

being tested for Huntington's begins to come to a boil.

Amanda starts to exit. Monica stops her.

AMANDA: Let me go.

MONICA: You're going on vacation. Isn't that enough?

AMANDA: No. They just issued me extra pages in my passport. And I'm going to fill them.

MONICA: Good for you! But what you do mean, "Let me go?" What's happened to us, Mandy? A few weeks ago—

AMANDA: Only little things have happened, Nick. I took a test and found out I have a life, you got yourself knocked up and insist on remaining in the dark.

MONICA: So? It's all my fault for not going through with—

AMANDA: You are carrying a child that could be faced with the same life we've had. If you had any guts you'd learn the results and deal with it. It's not fair to the baby—

MONICA: What about me?

AMANDA: What about you?

MONICA *(beat)*: Okay. I'm scared. I'm terrified of being alone. A month ago, you and I were in the same boat. It wasn't necessarily a great ride, but we were in it together. Then you rocked the boat by being so goddamn brave. I'm alone in here. (*Beat.*) And I want a baby, a family. Is that so terrible?

AMANDA: I just want you to think of the baby.

MONICA: I do. Constantly.

AMANDA: Would you wish your life on a child?

MONICA: Yes. Until Mother got sick, it was pretty decent. And since then, it's been up and down, but mostly up.

AMANDA: Then, no doubt you've considered that your child will not have the same luxury of ignorance that we did. He will know that this disease is a possible factor in his life. He'll have that question staring him in the face much sooner—and longer—than we did. Oh, what's the use? Nothing I say ever has an effect on you. I'll never change your mind.

MONICA: I change fifty times a day. If the seed has been passed on, then I will just have to have every faith that they'll come up with a cure in the baby's lifetime. Go shop.

Could I Have This Dance? *was produced at the Colony Studio Theater in Los Angeles May 11, 1991.*

MISS EVERS' BOYS

A Play in Two Acts

BY DAVID FELDSHUH

Cast and credits appear on page 442 of *The Best Plays of 1990-91*

MISS EVERS' BOYS: At what point does medical research become, in effect, murder? David Feldshuh's play concerns the infamous Tuskegee Study of Untreated Syphilis in the Male Negro, a 40-year study sponsored by the U.S. Public Health Service and the Tuskegee Institute. Midway through the project, in the 1940s, an actual cure for syphilis appeared: penicillin. Nonetheless the project's directors, white and black, decided that it would be bad science to cure the 400 men being observed. The experiment must proceed to end-point: 400 certified autopsies. Feldshuh, a physician himself, is fascinated by the arrogance of the public-health establishment, but this could be a study of any system that puts its own "needs" before those of human beings. Rather than a self-righteous docudrama, *Miss Evers' Boys* is a drama of conscience. Miss Eunice Evers, a district nurse, has administered the project in Macon County, Alabama, since its beginnings. Now that she sees the study's true aim, how can she pretend to her "boys" that her liniments and placebos are doing them any good? She has grown particularly fond of four ambitious fellows who intend to dance their way north to the Cotton Club. That's how she first talked them into giving her a blood sample.

EVERS: That spirochete germ can make trouble with your heart. And with your head. And with your muscles and movement.

WILLIE: You mean like how you walk or dance or something like that?

EVERS: It can make it so you don't know where your feet are going. You can hardly walk. You shuffle.

WILLIE: That's bad.

EVERS: It can kill you.

WILLIE (*quietly, to Caleb*): I told you we ought to get us some life insurance.

CALEB: You ain't sick. Not the way you dance.

    A dance suddenly erupts between the two men.

EVERS (*cutting them off*): But the sneaky thing about bad blood is that you all might have it right now and don't even know it.

HODMAN: I don't want my blood took. I'm still young. I've got a wife. I've got obligations. We all do. Even Ben.

BEN: What do you mean, "even Ben," Hodman?

EVERS: Obligations?

HODMAN: To my wife, I mean. You know . . . Family obligations. So I just can't have my blood took.

EVERS: Oh. Well, I think I understand your concern, Mr. Bryan. But I can assure you that taking your blood won't interfere with your obligations.

CALEB: That ain't what Willie's grandpa said. He said it interfered with his obligations for a week.

EVERS: You know Fred Milsen down by Alma?

CALEB: The sawmill foreman?

EVERS: Same one. Now he got seven children, going on eight. He been giving his blood for six years. His obligations been going fine. Both in the short run and the long run.

HODMAN: I hope you right.

EVERS: I am and I wouldn't say if it wasn't so. (*Ready to put down his name.*) Mr. Washington?

CALEB (*interrupting*): Why the government helping us all of a sudden? They got a war coming or something?

EVERS: No such thing. The government got a new point of view on things.

CALEB: What's that?

EVERS: A people point of view. They interested.

CALEB: The government interested in us?

EVERS (*challenging him*): The Public Health Service is interested and they part of the government. (*Ready to write down his name.*) Mr. Washington?

BEN: You be our nurse?

EVERS: Yes, sir.

CALEB (*sharply*): Ben.

BEN: What?

CALEB: Don't sign nothing until you know what you're signing.

BEN: I know.

CALEB (*interrupting before Ben can say anything else*): I don't remember getting nothing free before. And we all healthy, Nurse Evers.

EVERS: Well, you are going to get free doctorin', Mr. Humphries. Even if you're healthy.

HODMAN (*positive*): That sounds nice, Caleb.

EVERS: Well, how about you, Mr. Bryan?

CALEB: Hold on, Hodman.

EVERS (*direct, serious, strong*): This is a good thing. We don't get a lot of

Pictured in a scene from David Feldshuh's *Miss Evers' Boys* at the Illusion Theater in Minneapolis are (*back row*) T. Mychael Rambo as Ben, Lester Purry as Willie and Mark M. Cryer as Hodman and (*front row*) Dion Graham as Caleb and Denise Burse-Mickelbury as Miss Evers

chances around here to say "no" to a good thing.

     Pause. Silence.

BEN (*breaking the silence*): Where you from, Miss Evers?

EVERS: Originally from Reinart, Mr. Washington.

BEN: You gotta call me "Ben" or I won't know who you're talking to.

WILLIE: Me neither.

HODMAN: Same for me.

BEN: We can't all be "Ben."

EVERS (*laughing*): All right. That will be fine.

WILLIE: You got any kinfolks up there?

EVERS: All over Macon and Tuscaloosa. But no direct kin.

HODMAN: You ain't married?

EVERS: No. Been too busy.

CALEB: Doing what?

EVERS: Supporting myself, Mr. Humphries. Nursing school. Been working for the county until the really bad times hit in '30.

BEN: What you been doing since then?

EVERS: Domestic work when I could get it.

BEN: Domestic work? . . . You a nurse.

EVERS: That's what Dr. Eugene Brodus up at Tuskegee thinks too. So when the government started this program, he called me and now I'm back to nursing.

BEN: That's only right.

WILLIE (*an important connection*): Well. (*Addressing everyone in the room.*) Looks like we all got something in common.

EVERS: What's that?

WILLIE: Well, we a group. The four of us.

EVERS: What do you mean?

WILLIE (*doing a few quick steps, which the others support*): You looking at the next winners of the Macon County Gillee Competition come this Saturday.

EVERS: Saturday?

WILLIE: Yes. And you know why we're going to win?

EVERS: Because you all the best. I can tell that by looking at you.

WILLIE: I am and we are. That's true too. But see this here's why. (*Goes to the blackboard.*) Can you make this out?

EVERS: No, I can't.

WILLIE: I put this here. It say, "Aspiration." Like when you was doing that domestic cleaning 'cause you wanted to get back to your nursing. You had to work, right?

EVERS: Right.

WILLIE: Work hard. Real hard. That's "Aspiration." You got it. And we got it too. That's what we all got in common.

     The other men agree.

EVERS (*sincerely complimented*): Why, thank you. That's a good word.

CALEB: Willie is the best double-fly stepper around.

Willie does his step.

Ben play a mean washboard. Hodman slaps a beat. And I bend some notes.

EVERS: Well, you all are something I'll have to see.

BEN: I'd like that.

WILLIE: You're invited. Any time.

HODMAN: You watch that Gillee, just as soon as they turn those car headlights on us, you got to jump up and screech and scream so we win.

The men laugh, enjoying the thought.

EVERS (*laughing*): Lord, oh Lord.

Silence. Evers looks at the men.

You men are winners. But you got to stay healthy to win.

Pause.

BEN: Nurse Evers—

EVERS: Yes?

BEN (*proud*): Put me down.

The play's epilogue takes place in Miss Evers' conscience forty years later. Willie now uses a cane.

WILLIE: Nurse Evers . . . You was a friend to me.

EVERS: I am a friend to you.

WILLIE: What kind of friend could do what you did?

EVERS: Understand, Willie. You have to try to understand.

WILLIE: You try to understand me. That penicillin would have made it so I could walk without pain and maybe even jackspring. And they didn't give that to me in Birmingham because you pulled me out of that line so I could be a part of Miss Evers' Boys and Burial Society. So you all could do your watching while I wake up past midnight not feeling my legs or else feeling pain, burning pain like a hot iron pressin' on my skin, till I shout, "Take this pain away, Lord, please, take this pain away." My body was my freedom. You hear me? MY BODY WAS MY FREEDOM. (*He takes Victrola from Caleb, puts it down.*) You all wanna watch. Watch now. Watch and think what I used to do with my feet and what I could have done: how my feet sounded faster than this here music could have pushed them.

Willie puts the needle down on the record. The music starts. Caleb remembers the music. The two men enjoy the remembrance for a moment. But as Willie listens to the music and as he remembers the way he used to be able to dance, his rage increases. This memory becomes more vivid as he turns to Evers and recites the pattern he used to use.

"Drop over; double step; drop over, double step: drop over, step, step, strut." Lord, you remember that, Caleb?

The two men laugh.

"Drop over, double step"? (*To the others.*) You watchin'? "Gillee strut, down, drop; Gillee strut, down, drop, drop." Watch. You watch this now. "Gillee, drop, drop,

drop, drop, down, drop, down, drop, down . . . " Watch. (*Angry.*) "Drop, down, drop, drop, drop, down . . . " WATCH. "Drop, down, down, down, down . . . "
> *Evers moves to help Willie.*

NO. NO HELP.
> *Enraged, Willie uses his cane to stop the Victrola; silence.*

(*To Evers, tapping his cane*): . . . I can walk pretty good on this stick.

Miss Evers' Boys *was produced by the Illusion Theater at Hennepin Center for the Arts in Minneapolis May 3, 1991.*

AMERICAN ENTERPRISE

A Play in Two Acts

BY JEFFREY SWEET

Cast and credits appear on page 421

AMERICAN ENTERPRISE: Previously known for small-cast plays and musicals such as *Porch, The Value of Names* and *Love* (from Murray Schisgal's *Luv*), Jeffrey Sweet makes a radical change with *American Enterprise*, a large-cast pageant play bustling with songs, politics, famous heroes and villains of the late 19th century labor movement, and ironic humor. Making history both clear and entertaining is no small task, but Sweet accomplishes it through his quickly-paced narrative and use of story theater techniques. Almost all the characters and incidents in the play are taken from the record, as are many of the works themselves.

The title is, perhaps, the best note as to what the play is about. The word "enterprise" encompasses Yankee ingenuity, unbridled ambition, self-righteousness, vision, fixation; all qualities reflected in the life and career of George Pullman. Pullman's story, in turn, is an allegory for all that is best and worst about Americans as a people and the United States as a nation.

In his notes to the published text, Sweet says, "This is meant to be read as a proposal for an event rather than as a conventional script." The author encourages producers to experiment with casting, assignment of ensemble lines and inclusion of period music.

The opening scene of the play sets the tone, sets the pace, and tells you almost everything you need to know about the personality of its hero, George Pullman.

411

The play's ensemble gathers in a chorus arrangement and, led by a conductor with a pitch pipe, sings a song entitled "Shall We Plant a Tree." "This is the story of an American enterprise," one of the choristers declares, and the opening scene begins.

ALL: Chicago!

ENSEMBLE: And there's a fortune to be made—if you have the right idea.

FIRST BUSINESSMAN: Harvest time. The wheat stands tall and you have your choice. Hire six men or put this beauty to work in your fields.

ENSEMBLE: The reaper.

FIRST BUSINESSMAN: The McCormick Reaper.

ENSEMBLE: One hundred twenty dollars on the installment plan.

FIRST BUSINESSMAN: Don't be left behind.

ENSEMBLE: And Cyrus McCormick makes his fortune in—

ALL: Chicago!

ENSEMBLE: And there's a fortune to be made—if you have the right idea.

SECOND BUSINESSMAN (*advancing on a woman customer*): You have a fine house, and why not? You've earned it. But to make that house a home you need—

> *The Ensemble splits into two groups which, on their lines, advance on the woman.*

ENSEMBLE: Persian rugs.

SECOND BUSINESSMAN: And hand-painted china.

ENSEMBLE: And lace and tableware.

SECOND BUSINESSMAN: Courtesy and convenience at our State Street address.

ENSEMBLE: And Marshall Field makes his fortune in—

ALL: Chicago!

ENSEMBLE: And there's a fortune to be made—

> *Pullman steps forward.*

PULLMAN: This is what it means to travel overnight by railroad today.

> *Members of the Ensemble mime a very disagreeable rail journey. One of them plays a passenger, the others jostle and push and otherwise manhandle him, finally tossing him to the floor.*

Narrow, uncomfortable berths. Linen which is either filthy or non-existent. Noise, dust, smoke. Sleep is out of the question. The traveler arrives at his destination rumpled, exhausted, debilitated. He must rest a day, perhaps two, before pursuing his business. Result: loss of time and consequent income. I now have the pleasure of introducing the Pullman alternative.

> *During the following, the Ensemble again mimes a rail journey. This time, however, the passenger is pampered and caressed, at one point being hoisted on their shoulders as if sleeping comfortably in a berth. By the end, he has been set gently down on his feet and politely awakened. In short: a wonderful time.*

Twice the standard number of wheels, springs, shock absorbers. Cushioned seats that convert into real beds with clean sheets and pillow cases. Result: a smooth ride, a luxurious sleeping experience. The traveler arrives refreshed, ready to face the challenges of the day. I present to you the Pullman car—the railway car that makes travel a pleasure.

> *The Railroad Owner, a prosperous man with a stovepipe hat, steps into the car with his Assistant in tow. Pullman watches as the Railroad Owner looks around. In the meantime, the Assistant begins measuring dimensions unobtrusively. (Note: During the following, Pullman's attitude is consistently genial, if a little distant. If any of the things the Railroad Owner says to him upsets him, he takes care not to let it show.)*

RAILROAD OWNER (*after a beat*): Cherry wood?

PULLMAN: Yes.

RAILROAD OWNER (*nods appreciatively, looks at another detail*): Velvet?

PULLMAN: Yes.

RAILROAD OWNER (*nods again, looks around some more, then turns to Pullman*): Aren't you a little worried?

PULLMAN: About—?

RAILROAD OWNER: Some of our ridership are not—shall we say, very refined? Traveling salesmen and so forth. What's to keep them from climbing into your clean beds with their boots on, spattering mud on your sheets?

PULLMAN: The car will tell them not to.

RAILROAD OWNER: In addition to everything else, the car *talks*?

PULLMAN: It is my belief that people behave better when they are in a refined and esthetic environment.

RAILROAD OWNER: An interesting theory. What if you're wrong?

PULLMAN: I lose.

RAILROAD OWNER: What is it you want, exactly?

PULLMAN: A trial on the line between Chicago and Springfield.

RAILROAD OWNER: A trial—on what terms?

PULLMAN: Three months. You collect the basic fare, I collect an additional fare when a passenger chooses to ride in my car.

RAILROAD OWNER: And the advantage to me is—?

PULLMAN: More people will ride your train. The more people ride your train—

RAILROAD OWNER: —the more basic fares I collect.

PULLMAN: That's the idea.

RAILROAD OWNER: And if it doesn't work out that way? If I'm not happy at the end of three months—

PULLMAN: I unhook my car, we shake hands, and that's the end of it.

> *A beat as the Railroad Owner considers this for a second. Then he nods.*

RAILROAD OWNER: You may have yourself a deal.

ASSISTANT: Uh, sir—

RAILROAD OWNER: Bennett?

ASSISTANT: Perhaps you should take a look at this—

> *The Assistant shows the Railroad Owner some figures he's marked*

down.

RAILROAD OWNER (*to Assistant*): You're sure?

ASSISTANT: I double-checked.

RAILROAD OWNER: We seem to have run into a little problem here, Mr. Pullman.

PULLMAN: Oh?

During the following, Pullman continues to smile politely, dealing with the owner's objections with slightly condescending patience. The Railroad Owner, too, gives a great show of geniality tinged with condescension. The politeness masks the impatience they both feel having to deal with what each considers to be the other's denseness.

RAILROAD OWNER: Station platforms are built on the assumption that all railroad cars conform to a standard width.

PULLMAN: Yes.

RAILROAD OWNER: Mr. Bennett here tells me your car is wider than that standard.

ASSISTANT: By a good two feet.

PULLMAN: Yes.

RAILROAD OWNER: You're aware of this?

PULLMAN: I am aware.

RAILROAD OWNER: You knew that the car you were building was two feet wider than the standard, and you built it anyway.

Pictured below in Jeffrey Sweet's *American Enterprise* at Chicago's Organic Theater are (*foreground*) Paula Harrigan as Florence Pullman with Gary Houston as George Pullman; (*background*) Chris Farrell (Heathcote), Jamie O'Reilly (Mrs. Kelsey) and Juan Ramirez (Eugene V. Debs)

PULLMAN: I needed these dimensions to accommodate all the features I'd designed. The pulleys, the plumbing—

RAILROAD OWNER: Yes, yes, but how do you expect the train to come into the station? If the car is too big—

PULLMAN: You have saws.

RAILROAD OWNER: Saws?

PULLMAN: I assume your platforms are made of wood.

RAILROAD OWNER: Oh, cut back the platforms?

PULLMAN: As you point out, my car won't fit otherwise.

>   *A beat.*

RAILROAD OWNER: How much did it cost you to build this?

PULLMAN: Twenty thousand dollars more or less.

RAILROAD OWNER: Investors?

PULLMAN: No.

RAILROAD OWNER: Your own money.

PULLMAN: Yes.

RAILROAD OWNER: Why would somebody spend twenty thousand dollars of his own money to build a railroad car that can't run?

PULLMAN: It *can* run.

RAILROAD OWNER: All I have to do is—

PULLMAN: —cut back the—

RAILROAD OWNER (*overlapping*): —the platforms, yes, I know. But why would I want to do that?

PULLMAN: It's a good car.

RAILROAD OWNER: It's a beautiful car. What I'm trying to understand is why you didn't build this beautiful car so as to conform to the standards.

PULLMAN: I wouldn't have been able to accommodate all the special features I had envisioned. The pulleys, the plumbing—

RAILROAD OWNER: But even if you had to give up one or two of the things you "envisioned," it still would have been a better car.

PULLMAN: "Better" is not necessarily good.

RAILROAD OWNER: It might just be good *enough.*

PULLMAN: My name is on what I build. When people see my name, I don't want them to think, "Oh, that's George Pullman. What he builds is good *enough.*"

RAILROAD OWNER: Have you ever heard of the word "compromise?"

>   *A beat.*

PULLMAN: (*a little steel glinting through the smile*): Our conversation appears to be over.

RAILROAD OWNER: If you ever build a practical version of this, do let me know.

PULLMAN: I have built what I intended.

>   *The Railroad Owner shakes his head, and he and his Assistant exit the car. The Railroad Owner moves onto a platform—an area we will later identify as the Chicago Club—where he joins three other Businessmen.*

THIRD BUSINESSMAN: So what is Pullman doing with it?

SECOND BUSINESSMAN: His precious car?

RAILROAD OWNER: He's got it sitting on a siding gathering dust.

SECOND BUSINESSMAN: The man won't bend.

PULLMAN (*to audience*): Why should I compromise? One compromises when one is wrong or when one is compelled to. I am not so compelled. And I am not wrong.

RAILROAD OWNER: Pigheaded. Just plain pigheaded.

PULLMAN: I prefer to call it determined. When I first arrived here—this was in 1855—Chicago was one big muddy swamp.

SECOND BUSINESSMAN: Oh, Christ, here comes that story again.

> *During the following speech, the Businessmen and Railroad Owner, shaking their heads, exit, leaving Pullman alone onstage addressing the audience.*

FIRST BUSINESSMAN (*anticipating*): "People were in such a rush—"

PULLMAN (*blithely continuing*): People were in such a rush to throw up buildings, they didn't bother to notice that they hadn't built them on proper foundations. They built too low. At times, Lake Michigan was practically lapping at the doorsteps. The cellars were constantly flooded. A proper drainage system was impossible. The answer was obvious—raise the buildings. Raise the buildings? No, no, I was told, that was impossible. I said, let me see what I can do. We agreed on a test case: the Tremont Hotel. I calculated it needed to be raised eight feet. I engaged twelve hundred men, positioned them by forty-eight hundred jackscrews. I won't go into the mechanics of it. But, at my signal, each man turned four jackscrews. And the building rose. Within the hour, it was raised by eight feet, and without spilling a single drop of tea from a cup in the tearoom. After that, I had all the work I wanted. I had arrived in Chicago with next to nothing in my pocket. Within a year, I was worth—well, let's just say neither I nor my family has wanted for anything since. This is the power of determination.

> *A beat.*

I am right about my car. They may not see it now, but that's all right. If something has value, it will find its time. I have confidence.

ENSEMBLE: April Fifteen, Eighteen Sixty-five—This morning, despite the best efforts of attending surgeons, President Abraham Lincoln died of an assassin's bullet—Mrs. Lincoln accompanies her husband's body on its journey home.

WOMAN: When she arrives in Chicago, she is on the verge of physical collapse.

ENSEMBLE: There are doubts as to whether she will be able to bear up under the strain of the final ride to Springfield.

> *Pullman steps forward, locates Mrs. Lincoln beyond the proscenium.*

PULLMAN: Mrs. Lincoln, may I offer you the use of my car?

> *Railroad Owner turns to the Assistant.*

RAILROAD OWNER: Where do we keep the saws?

ASSISTANT: The saws?

RAILROAD OWNER: The saws. The goddamn saws, goddamn it.

ASSISTANT: All of the platforms?

RAILROAD OWNER: Between here and Springfield.

ASSISTANT: But we can't do that.

RAILROAD OWNER: Would you like to tell that to Mrs. Lincoln?

Railroad Owner gives Pullman a disgruntled look. Pullman nods.

WOMAN: Mrs. Lincoln expresses her gratitude to Mr. Pullman for the comfort of his car.

ENSEMBLE (REPORTER): And suddenly everyone seems to want to ride in it.

PULLMAN: And so the Pullman Palace Car Company is born.

FIRST TRAVELER: Dear Mr. Pullman: I had the very great pleasure of riding in one of your sleepers on the twelfth of this month, and may I say I have never enjoyed a trip by rail more.

SECOND TRAVELER: Dear Mr. Pullman: There was a time when I would have scheduled two days to recover from a railway journey, but I arrived refreshed and ready to do business. You have my thanks and my congratulations.

The speeches below are contrapuntal. After each "Dear Mr. Pullman" and the first few words, the next speaker joins in until all are speaking at once.

THIRD TRAVELER: Dear Mr. Pullman: I cannot begin to tell you how very much I enjoyed riding in your lovely car. The service was exemplary and the hygiene impeccable. I shall certainly commend it to those friends of mine planning to travel.

FOURTH TRAVELER: Dear Mr. Pullman: I had heard from friends of your extraordinary car and the comfort it affords, but was not prepared for the joy of the actual experience. I use the word "joy," and that is exactly what I mean, for that is the only word to describe the sensation.

FIFTH TRAVELER: Dear Mr. Pullman: I had always thought the phrases "railway travel" and "comfort" to be mutually exclusive till I rode in your commodious car. It was worth every penny of the two-dollar surcharge.

As the above ends, the First Traveler chimes in.

FIRST TRAVELER: It's a godsend!

ENSEMBLE: And so George Pullman, too, makes his fortune in—

ALL: Chicago.

American Enterprise *was produced (with a Kennedy Center-American Express Fund for New American Plays Grant) by the Organic Theater in Chicago March 6, 1992.*

A DIRECTORY OF NEW-PLAY PRODUCTIONS

Compiled by Sheridan Sellers

Professional 1991-92 productions of new plays by leading companies around the United States that supplied information on casts and credits at Sheridan Sellers's request, plus a few reported by other reliable sources, are listed below in alphabetical order of the locations of the 60 producing organizations. Date given is opening date, included whenever a record was obtained from the producing management. All League of Resident Theaters (LORT) and other Equity groups were queried for this comprehensive Directory. Those not listed here either did not produce new or newly revised scripts in 1991-92 or had not responded by press time. Most of the productions listed—but not all—are American or world premieres. Some are new revisions, second looks or scripts produced previously but not previously reported in *Best Plays*.

Albany: Capital Repertory Company

(Artistic director, Bruce Bouchard)

PEACETIME. By Elaine Berman. January 3, 1992. Director, Pamela Berlin; scenery, Edward Gianfrancesco; costumes, Mimi Maxmen; lighting, Craig Evans; sound, David Wiggall.

Adela	Suzanne Costallos
Jake	Ken Garito
Ben	Gordon Greenberg
Blossom	Sandra Laub
Morris	Stephen Mailer
Frannie	Jessica Queller
Hyman	Barry Snider
Mimi	Kelly Wolf

Baltimore: Center Stage

(Artistic director, Irene Lewis; managing director, Peter W. Culman)

POLICE BOYS. By Marion Isaac McClinton. April 1, 1992. Director, Marion McClinton; scenery, Donald Eastman; costumes, Paul Tazewell; lighting, James F. Ingalls; sound, Mark Bennett.

Christopher "Comanche" Chileogus	David Alan Anderson
Royal Boy	Bobby Bermea
Jabali Abdul Jackson	Ron Richardson
Ruth "Babe" Milano	Faye M. Price
Cross "Superboy" Beauchamp	Jacinto Taras Riddick
Miller "High Life" Cummings	Eric A. Payne
Meredith Fellows; Lady in White	Liann Pattison
Benjamin Bowie	Terry E. Bellamy
Deejay	Paul Emmanuel Morgan
Dancer	Isaiah Davis, Francesca Nock

One intermission.

Berkeley, Calif.: Berkeley Repertory Theater

(Artistic director, Sharon Ott; managing director, Susan Medak)

THE ILLUSION. By Pierre Corneille; freely adapted by Tony Kushner. June 26, 1991. Director, Sharon Ott; scenery, Chris Barreca; costumes, Susan Hilferty; lighting, Stephen Strawbridge; sound, Jon Gottlieb; original music, Steve Moshier.

Pridament	Jarion Monroe
Amanuensis; Geronte	Yusef Bulos

Alcandre . . . . Wayne Ballantyne
Calisto; Clindor; Theogenes . Morgan Strickland
Melibea; Isabelle;
  Hippolyta . . . . Domenique Lonzando
Elicia; Lyse; Clarina . . . . Emile Talbot
Pleribo; Adraste; Prince
  Florilame . . . . Victor Talmadge
Matamore . . . . Charles Dean
One intermission.

McTEAGUE: A TALE OF SAN FRANCISCO.
Adapted by Neal Bell from the novel by Frank
Norris. Director, Sharon Ott; scenery, George
Tsypin; costumes, Lydia Tanji; lighting, James F.
Ingalls; sound, Stephen LeGrand.
McTeague . . . . Jeffrey King
Marcus . . . . Charles Dean
Miss Baker . . . . Barbara Oliver
Maria . . . . Mia Katigbak
Trina Sieppe . . . . Melissa Fraser Brown
Zerkow . . . . Steven Anthony Jones
Trina's Mother . . . . Ronnie Gilbert
Grannis . . . . Mark Isaac Epstein
Fancy Dentist; Ticket Seller; Lottery Agent;

Postman; Old Miner . . . . . L. Peter Callender
Time: The 1890s. Place: San Francisco. One
intermission.

DREAM OF A COMMON LANGUAGE. By
Heather McDonald. March 25, 1992. Director,
Sharon Ott; scenery, Kate Edmunds; costumes,
Susan Hilferty; lighting, Kent Dorsey; sound,
Stephen LeGrand.
Mylo . . . . Sebastian de Raadt
Clovis . . . . Lorri Holt
Victor . . . . James Carpenter
Dolores . . . . Judith Marx
Pola . . . . Amy Hill
Marc . . . . Victor Talmadge
Time: 1874. Place: A garden behind a country
house outside Paris. One intermission.

THE CONVICT'S RETURN. By Geoff Hoyle.
Director Anthony Taccone; scenery, Kate
Edmunds; costumes, Susan Hilferty; lighting,
Kent Dorsey; sound, Stephen LeGrand.
With Geoff Hoyle, Sharon Lockwood.

Cambridge, Mass.: American Repertory Theater

(Artistic director, Robert Brustein; managing director, Robert J. Orchard)

OLEANNA. By David Mamet. May 1, 1992 (presented by the Back Bay Theater Company).
Director, David Mamet; scenery, Michael Merritt;
costumes, Harriet Voyt; lighting, Kevin Rigdon.

John . . . . William H. Macy
Carol . . . . Rebecca Pidgeon
One intermission.

Cambridge, Mass.: Poets' Theater

(Producing director, Andreas Teuber)

JACKIE: AN AMERICAN LIFE. By Gip Hoppe.
January 9, 1992. Director, Gip Hoppe; scenery,
Dan Joy; costumes, Susan Santoian; lighting,
John Malinowski; choreography, Glenda
Medeiros; original music, J. Hagenbuckle.
Jackie . . . . Susan Winslow
Bobby Kennedy . . . . Diego Arciniegas

Teddy Kennedy . . . . Jeremiah Kissel
Marilyn Monroe . . . . Chloe J. Leamon
Lee Radziwill . . . . Jeanne Montano
JFK . . . . Kevin Rice
Aristotle Onassis . . . . Richard Snee
Janet Bouvier Auchincloss . . . Bobbie Steinbach
One intermission.

Chicago: Body Politic Theater

(Artistic director, Albert Pertalion; managing director, Kim Patrick Bitz)

WILD MEN. Musical with book by Peter Burns,
Mark Nutter, Rob Riley and Tom Wolfe; music
and lyrics by Mark Nutter. May 11, 1992 (presented by James Stern and Wildmen, Inc.).
Director, Rob Riley; scenery, Mary Griswold;
costumes, John Paoletti; lighting, Geoffrey
Bushor; musical director, Lisa Yeargan; choreog-

raphy, Jim Corti.
Stuart Penn . . . . Rob Riley
Bonnie Lodge . . . . David Lewman
Ken Finnerty . . . . George Wendt
Greg Neely . . . . Peter Burns
Artie Bishop . . . . Joe Liss
One intermission.

Chicago: Center Theater

(Artistic director, Dan LaMorte)

INSIDE GEORGE. By Dan LaMorte. February 27, 1992. Director, Kevin Rigdon; scenery, Daniel Ostling; costumes, Dawn DeWitt; lighting, Chris Phillips; sound, Joe Cerqua.
George . . . . R.J. Coleman
Woman . . . . Kathy Scambiatterra

Man. . . . . Andrew Leman
Pamela . . . . Marie Jagger
Lawrence . . . . John J. Dalesandro
The Crowd . . . . . Dan Primer, Elizabeth Porter
    One intermission

Chicago: Court Theater

(Executive director, Nicholas Rudall)

THE MYSTERY CYCLE—CREATION. Adapted from *English Mystery Plays* by Bernard Sahlins. January 10, 1992. Directors, Nicholas Rudall and Bernard Sahlins; scenery and costumes, Mary Griswold and John Paoletti; lighting, Michael Philippi; choreographer, Timothy O'Slynne; sound, Robert Neuhaus.
God. . . . . Matt De Caro
Lucifer . . . . Johnny Lee Davenport
Gabriel . . . . William D. King
Adam; Isaac . . . . John Schroeder
Eve . . . . Rebecca MacLean
Cain; Joseph. . . . . Tom Amandes
Abel; Herod's Son . . . . Kyle Colerider-Krugh
Noah; Herod . . . . Rob Riley
Noah's Wife . . . . Kate Buddeke
Abraham . . . . Daniel Mooney
Mary . . . . Tanya White
    Three Kings: Johnny Lee Davenport, Michael Raimondi, Craig Ricci Shaynak.
    Three Shepherds: Tom Higgins, Dan Mooney,

Gavin Witt.
    One intermission.

COMEDIANS. By Trevor Griffiths. April 10, 1992. Director, Barney Simon; scenery and costumes, Jeff Bauer; lighting, Rita Pietraszek.
Caretaker; M.C. . . . . Faith McKinney
Gethin Price. . . . . . Ramon Melindez Moses
Phyllis Murray. . . . . Ched Bendsen
George McBrain. . . . . Reg E. Cathey
Sammy Santiago . . . . Juan A. Ramirez
Mick Connor . . . . . . Johnny Lee Davenport
Eddie Waters . . . . Lex Monson
Jenny Murray . . . . Karol Kent
Mr. Patel . . . . Horatio Sanz
Bert Chance . . . . Peter Siragusa
    Place: Act I, A classroom in a junior college on the south side of Chicago; Act II, The Punch Line, a comedy club, later that evening; Act III, The classroom, after the performance.

Chicago: Goodman Theater

(Artistic director, Robert Falls; producing director, Roche Schulfer)

BOOK OF THE NIGHT. By Louis Rosen and Thom Bishop. June 24, 1991. Director, Robert Falls; choreographer, Marcia Milgrom Dodge; scenery, Michael S. Philippi; costumes, Gabriel Berry; lighting, James F. Ingalls.
Jill . . . . Hollis Resnik
Jill's Husband . . . . David Studwell
Wishing Man . . . . Keith Bryon-Kirk
Wishing Woman. . . . . Vicki Lewis
Woman from Room 220 . . . . Jessica Molaskey
Gypsy . . . . Adrian Bailey
Streetsinger; Juanita . . . . Ora Jones
Cop; Desk Clerk . . . . John Herrera

Young Widow . . . . Paula Newsome
Young Widow's Son . . . . . Christian Dornseif
Dealer. . . . . Jim Corti
Carolos . . . . David Bedella
Juanita . . . . Ora Jones
Jack's Wife . . . . Charlotte Maier
    Time: From dusk until dawn. Place An American city.

DOWN THE SHORE. By Tom Donaghy. February 16, 1992. Director, David Petrarca; scenery and costumes, Linda Buchanan; lighting, Robert Christen; sound, Rob Milburn.
MJ. . . . . Bruce MacVittie

Luke. . . . . Hynden Walch
Phippsey. . . . . Robert Mohler
Stan Man. . . . . Rick Snyder
Time: Just about summer. Just about night. Place: A hill behind a large church, somewhere between the actual city "Philly" and the suburban "Philadelphia."

ON THE OPEN ROAD. By Steve Tesich. March 23, 1992. Director, Robert Falls; scenery, George Tsypin; lighting, Michael Philippi; sound, Rob Milburn.

Al . . . . Jordan Charney
Angel. . . . . Steve Pickering
The Little Girl . . . . Denisha Powell
The Monk . . . . Christopher Pieczyniski
Jesus. . . . . Andy Taylor
Time: A time of Civil War. Place: A place of Civil War. One intermission.

Work-in-Progress

SPIC-O-RAMA. Written and performed by John Leguizamo. January 16, 1992. Director, Peter Askin.

Chicago: The Organic Theater

(Artistic director, Richard Fire)

A FEW SIMPLE TRUTHS: A CONTEMPLA-TION WITH MUSIC. Conceived by Richard Fire; written by Anne McGravie, Samantha Bennett, Julia Fabris, Richard Fire, Michael J. Gellman, Dale Heinen, Diana Jordon, Geoffrey MacKinnon, Anna Markin, Mark Mysliwiec, Nancy Seifried, Lizanne Wilson. Director, Michael J. Gellman; musical directors, Chris Farrell, Nate Herman; scenery and lighting, Robert G. Smith; costumes, Vicki Justice.
Maggie; Didi; Dana;
  Woman #1 . . . . Samantha Bennett
Beverley; Olivia. . . . . Tucker Brown
Doctor; Ruth . . . . Patrice Fletcher
Too Sweet; Officer; Charlie;
  Father Tom; Doctor #1 . . . Donn Carl Harper
Brother; Dave; Young Man. . . Charlie Hartsock
Deb; Kerry . . . . Anna Markin
Father; Mitch; Pastor J.;
  Doctor #2 . . . . Mark Mysliwiec
Laura; Leeta. . . . . Krista Strutz
Caroline . . . . Pamela Vear
Joan; Woman #2 . . . . Lizanne Wilson

AMERICAN ENTERPRISE. By Jeffrey Sweet. March 6, 1992. Director, Wesley Savick; scenery, Richard and Jacqueline Penrod; costumes, Yslan Hicks; lighting, Kevin Snow; music and lyrics for original songs, Jeffrey Sweet: music director and sound, Michael Vitali.
George Pullman . . . . Gary Houston
J. Patrick Hopkins . . . . Larry Russo
George Jr.; Rev. E.C. Oggel . Michael A. Krawic
Eugene V. Debs . . . . Juan Ramirez
Gov. John P. Altgeld; Mayor
  Carter Harrison; Supervisor . . . . Phillip East
Stephens; Harahan; Wright . . . . . L.D. Barrett
Thomas Wickes; Commissioner
  Worthington . . . . Peter Garino
Jackson; Beman . . . . Edmund Wyson
Richard T. Ely. . . . . Colin K. Jones
Heathcote . . . . Chris Farrell
Clayton . . . . McKinley Johnson
Jennie Curtis . . . . Tonray Ho
Florence Pullman . . . . Paula Harrigan
Mrs. Kelsey; Soloist . . . . . . Jamie O'Reilly
One intermission. (An ATCA selection; see introduction to this section.)

Chicago: Remains Theater

(Artistic director, Larry Sloan)

LAUGHTER IN THE DARK. Adapted by Mary Zimmerman from the novel by Vladimir Nabokov. March 1, 1992. Director, Mary Zimmerman; scenery, John Musial; costumes, Sarah J. Holden; lighting, Kenneth Moore; sound and original music, Michael Bodeen.
Axel Rex . . . . Christopher Donahue
Albinus . . . . Gerry Becker

Elisabeth . . . . Martha Lavey
Irma. . . . . . Rebecca Melsky, Orianna Mastro
Paul . . . . Craig Spidle
Margot Peters . . . . Heidi Stillman
Otto . . . . David Catlin
Others: David Alan Novak, Thomas Carroll, Jim True, Marilyn Dodds Frank.
One intermission.

Chicago: Steppenwolf Theater

(Artistic director, Randall Arney; managing director, Stephen B. Eich)

EARTHLY POSSESSIONS. By Frank Galati; adapted from the novel by Ann Tyler. August 3, 1991. Director, Frank Galati; scenery, Kevin Rigdon; costumes, Erin Quigley; lighting, Robert Christen; slide projections, John Boesche; sound and music, Rob Milburn.

Charlotte . . . . Molly Regan

Mrs. Emory . . . . Joan Allen
Jake . . . . Kevin Anderson
Saul . . . . Randall Arney
Mindy . . . . Sally Murphy
    With Rick Snyder, Alan Wilder, Peggy Roeder, Ellen Beckerman, Kimberly Dal Santo.
    One intermission.

COURT THEATER, CHICAGO—Tanya White (*foreground*) as Mary in *The Mystery Cycle—Creation* by Bernard Sahlins, based on the 14th century Mystery Plays

A SUMMER REMEMBERED. By Charles Nolte. December 8, 1991. Director, Stephen Eich; scenery, Michael Merritt, Suzan Wexler; costumes, Nan Cibula-Jenkins; lighting, Kevin Rigdon; sound, Richard Woodbury.

Dr. Wasburn . . . . Robert Breuler
Mildred Washburn . . . . Lucina Paquet
Ollie . . . . Thomas Carroll
Flo Durham . . . . Barbara Robertson
Henry Durham . . . . Gary Cole
Ted . . . . Scott Benjaminson
Crawford . . . . Todd Spicer
Zan . . . . Amy Love
Betty . . . . Anne Tremko
Myrna Hammerine . . . . Diane Houghton
Rose Buckley . . . . Martha Lavey
Tom Denfield . . . . Jim True
Bea . . . . Kara Zediker
    Two intermissions.

A SLIP OF THE TONGUE. By Dusty Hughes. February 9, 1992. Director, Simon Stokes; scenery, Thomas Lynch; costumes, Kaye Nottbusch; lighting, Kevin Rigdon; sound Richard Woodbury.

Dominic Tantra . . . . John Malkovich
Uvana Brezhinski . . . . Clotilde Courau
Isabel Brezhinski . . . . Lizzy McInnerny
Theresa Kovac . . . . Kara Zediker
Katya Lipp . . . . Ingeborga Dapkunaite
    One intermission.

THE SONG OF JACOB ZULU. By Tug Yourgrau. April 12, 1992. Director, Eric Simonson; scenery, Kevin Rigdon; costumes, Erin Quigley; lighting, Robert Christen; sound, Rob Milburn.

Judge Neville . . . . Robert Breuler
John Dawkins; Dr. Shaw . . . . David Connelly
Jacob Zulu . . . . K. Todd Freeman
Marty Frankel . . . . John Mahoney
Rev. Zulu; Mr. X; Itshe . . . . . . Zakes Mokae
    Others: Ladysmith Black Mambazo, Pat Bowie, Patrick Clear, Leelai Demoz, Deanna Dunagan, Erika L. Heard, Danny Johnson, Gary DeWitt Marshall, Tania Richard, Alan Wilder, Nicholas Cross Wodtke, Cedric Young.
    One intermission.

Chicago: Victory Gardens Theater

(Artistic director, Dennis Zacek)

WORKING MAGIC. By Margaret Hunt. March 26, 1992. Director, Sandy Shinner; scenery, Jeff Bauer; costumes, Frances Maggio; lighting, Ellen Jones; sound Galen G. Ramsey.

Harry Houdini Grant . . . . . . Michael Varna
Lila Grant . . . . Carlton Miller
Charlene Maxwell . . . . Meg Thalken
Moses Booth . . . . Michael McKune
Malcolm Maxwell . . . . Tom Amandes
Vinnie; Leon; Lentz; Directors;
DiAngelo; Cooper . . Phillip Edward Van Lear
Roz; Waitress; Receptionist;
Frankie; Cristal . . . . Kate Buddeke
Kim; Nettie; Jackie; Mrs. King . . Kelly Anchors
Voice of Louie . . . . Deborah E. Barber
    One intermission.

THE SHOW HOST. By Rodolfo Santana; translated by Juan Pazos. April 16, 1992. Director, Edward F. Torres; scenery, Robert Martin; costumes, Sara Davidson; lighting, Dana Low, John Imburgia; sound, Jeff Webb.

Carlos . . . . Henry Godinez
Marcelo Giner . . . . John Carlos Seda
    Place: Venezuela. One intermission.

THIS OLD MAN CAME ROLLING HOME. By James Sherman. May 28, 1992. Director, Dennis Zacek; scenery, James Dardenne; costumes, Claudia Boddy, lighting, Robert Shook, sound, Galen G. Ramsey.

Benjamin . . . . Mitch Litrofsky
Louise . . . . Kathryn Jaeck
Nate . . . . Bryne Piven
Jack . . . . Rengin Altay
    Time: The present. Place: A modern two-bedroom apartment in a high-rise in the River North area of Chicago. One intermission.

Cincinnati: Cincinnati Playhouse in the Park

(Artistic director, David G. Kent)

THE MESMERIST. By Ara Watson. June 4, 1991. Director, Worth Gardner; scenery, Marjorie Bradley Kellogg; costumes, Laura Crow; lighting, Kirk Bookman; sound, David Smith.

With A.D. Cover, Steven Crossley, Tessie Hogan, Betty Miller, Alan Muraoka, Harsh Nayyar.
One intermission.

JAPANGO. By Richard Epp. January 9,1992. Director, Kent Stephens; scenery, Victor A. Becker; costumes, Susan E. Mickey; lighting, Kirk Bookman; composer/sound, David Smith.
Christopher Columbus. . . . . . . Curt Karibalis
Fra Juan Perez . . . . Herman Petras
The Boy . . . . Josh Brockhaus
Isabella, Queen of Castille . . . Monique Fowler
Ferdinand, King of Aragon . . . Kent Broadhurst
Beatrice . . . . Celeste Ciulla
Francisco Babadilla; Knight Commander;
    Luis Santangel; Receiver General . Russel Leib
The Indian . . . . Tim Perez
    Time and Place: The play begins and ends in Spain, May, 1506, and recalls the years preceding. One intermission.

PERFECT FOR YOU, DOLL. By Steven Sater. April 23, 1992. Director, Beth Schachter; scenery and costumes, Craig Clipper; lighting, Victor En Yu Tan; sound David Smith.
Beth . . . . Jane LeGrand
Barry . . . . William Verderber
Betty. . . . . Erica Mitchell
Barbara . . . . Nadja Stokes
Barone. . . . . Rita Gardner
Arnold . . . . David S. Howard
Bradley . . . . Ted Neustadt
Candi . . . . Constance Shulman
    Time and Place: The present, over several months of summer and fall. Beth's modern-day home on the outskirts of Carbondale, Illinois.

HOT 'N COLD. Music and lyrics by Cole Porter; devised by David Holdgrive, Mark Waldrop and George Kramer. May 19, 1992. Director and choreographer, George Kramer; scenery, James Leonard Joy; costumes, Mariann Verheyen; lighting, Kirk Bookman; sound David Smith; musical director, George Kramer.
    With Deb G. Girdler, Ameilia Prentice, Mark Martino, Jonathan Smedley, Pamela Myers, Mark Waldrop.

A CHRISTMAS CAROL. By Charles Dickens; adapted by Howard Dallin. Director, Howard Dallin; scenery, James Leonard Joy; costumes, David Murin; lighting, Kirk Bookman; composer and sound designer, David Smith.
Undertaker . . . . Ron Lee Savin
Undertaker's Assistant;
    Dick Wilkins . . . . Gregory Procaccino

Ebenezer Scrooge . . . . Yusef Bulos
Bob Cratchit; Man With Pipe . . Michael Haney
Fred; Tailor at Fezziwig's . . . . . Michael Brian
Mr. Cupp; Fezziwig's Lawyer;
    Man With Newspaper. . . . . . James Harris
Mr. Sosser; Schoolmaster;
    Percy . . . . Steve Hendrickson
Jacob Marley; Young Jacob;
    Old Joe . . . . Darryl Croxton
Ghost of Christmas Past;
    Martha Cratchit . . . . Shelley Delaney
Boy Scrooge; Simon. . . . . Derek Hake
Matthew; Rich Boy at Fezziwig's;
    First Urchin . . . . Andy Cullison
Gregory; Apprentice at Fezziwig's;
    Boot Black . . . . Daniel Hood
Charles; Boy Guest at Fezziwig's;
    Second Urchin . . . . Michael Ogley
Fan; Boy Baker; Rose . . . . . . Mara De May
Mr. Fezziwig;
    Ghost of Christmas Present . . Patrick Farrelly
Mrs. Fezziwig; Mrs. Peake . . . . . Dale Hodges
Young and Mature Scrooge;
    Ghost of Christmas Yet to Come . Tom Dunlop
Belle; Catherine Margaret . . . . . Sara Harris
Mrs. Cratchit . . . . Kathryn Gay Wilson
Belinda Cratchit;
    Young Girl at Fezziwig's . . . Hannah Reck
Peter Cratchit; Poulterer at
    Fezziwig's and Streets . . . T. Thomas Brown
Tiny Tim Cratchit . . . . Matthew Harris
Topper; Accountant at Fezziwig's;
    Man Getting Shoe Shine . . . Russell Goldberg
Patience; Scrubwoman at
    Fezziwig's; Mrs. Dilber . . . . . Bonnie Black
Fiddler . . . . Betsy Lippitt
Caroler; Rich Father at
    Fezziwig's . . . . George B. Smart, III
Caroler; Laundress at
    Fezziwig's . . . . Rebecca Finnegan
Caroler; Constable at Fezziwig's . . . Kyle Legg
Caroler; Rich Wife at Fezziwig's . Maria Whitley
Maid at Fezziwig's and Streets . . Sioux Madden
2d Girl at Fezziwig's
    and Streets. . . . . Maya Elaine Lilly
Rich Girl at Fezziwig's
    and Streets . . . . Greta Storace
Child at Fezziwig's and Streets . . . Katie Harris
Little Girl . . . . Rosie Harris
    Time: 1830, Past, and Future. Place: England. One intermission.

Cincinnati: Ensemble Theater of Cincinnati

(Managing director, John Vissman)

JACK AND THE BEANSTALK: A BRITISH PANTOMIME. December 4, 1991. Director, David A. White, III; composer and musical director, David B. Kisor; choreographer, Mark Diamond; scenery, Ronald A. Shaw; costumes, Gretchen H. Sears; lighting, Jeffrey Gress.

Little Bo-Peep . . . . Jeanne Blessing
Giant Blunderbore. . . . . . David Schaplowsky
Black Spider . . . . Mark Edwards
Vegetable Fairy . . . . Ginny Hoffman
Georgie Porgie . . . . Mark Mocahbee
Mary, Mary . . . . Shannon Rae Lutz
Little Boy Blue . . . . Robert B. Rais
Little Jack Horner. . . . . . . Michael G. Bath
Little Miss Muffet; Old Woman
Who Lived in a Shoe . . . . Lee Walsh
King Crumble . . . . Gordon C. Greene
Dame Trot . . . . Paul Kennedy
Jack Trot . . . . Claire Slemmer
Princess Apricot . . . . Julia F. White
Gertie the Cow . Donna Rubin, Christine Whitley

THE CHRONICLES OF PLAGUE. By Aralee Strange. February 5, 1992. Director, David A. White, III; scenery, Ronald A. Shaw; costumes, Gretchen H. Sears; lighting, Anne Barnes.
Miss Place . . . . Julia F. White
Supreme Old Broad; Map Maker;
Crow Knows . . . . Lee Walsh
Most Reverend Mister;
Fact Collector . . . . . Michael J. Blankenship

Mr. Fiscal; Sonny Deltoid . . . . . . Buz Davis
Medicine Man; Mo Mary. . . . . Brian C. Russo
Time Keeper; A Gent . . . . David Wiles
Police Man; Anchor Man . . . . . Rick Landrum
Feral Girl . . . . Regina Pugh
Sonny's Chick;
Annie Catastrophie . . . . . . Jeanne Blessing
Sonny's Dick; The Rapist. . . . Mark Mocahbee
Bebe Sees . . . . Shannon Rae Lutz
Metro Gnome. . . . . Nicole Callender
The Three Furies:
Blade . . . . David Wiles
Rune. . . . . Regina Pugh
Wit . . . . Shannon Rae Lutz
Sheeba Queen of the Scene . . . . Julia F. White
Poets' Pride:
Jack Whack . . . . Mark Mocahbee
Robbie Blah . . . . Buz Davis
Weasel Burrows . . . . Michael J. Blankenship
Mrs. Burrows . . . . Shannon Rae Lutz

LAKE STREET EXTENSION. By Lee Blessing. May 13, 1992. Director, Jeanne Blade; scenery, Michael J. Blankenship; costumes, Gretchen H. Sears; lighting, Jeff Gress.
Fuller . . . . Gordon C. Greene
Trace . . . . Keith Brush
Gregorio . . . . Enrique Munoz

Cleveland: The Cleveland Play House

(Artistic director, Josephine R. Abady; managing director, Dean R. Gladden)

DAVID'S MOTHER. By Bob Randall. November 24, 1991. Director, Josephine R. Abady; scenery, James Morgan; costumes, C.L. Hundley; lighting, Marc B. Weiss; sound, Jeffrey Montgomerie.
Sally. . . . . Ellen Greene
David . . . . Jamie Harrold
Gladys . . . . Pamala Tyson
Bea. . . . . Carol Locatell
Young Susan. . . . . Kendall Harvey
Phillip . . . . David Berman
Susan. . . . . Liza Snyder
John. . . . . Kevin Geer
Justine . . . . Lisa Dove

Time: The present. Place: The living room of an apartment on the West Side of New York City. One intermission.

A QUARREL OF SPARROWS. By James Duff. March 10, 1992. Director, Kenneth Elliott; scenery, David Potts; costumes, John Glaser; lighting, Mary Jo Dondlinger; sound, Jeffrey Montgomerie.
August Ainsworth. . . . . . . George Grizzard
Rosanna Ainsworth Jackson . . . . . Pat Carroll
Paul Palmer. . . . . Robert LuPone
Angela Mercer . . . . Susan Appel
Lynn Waters. . . . . Joseph R. Sicari

Martin Green. . . . . John C. Vennema
  Time: The present. Place: The living room of
August Ainsworth's country house in Sag Harbor
on the North Fork of Long Island. One intermission.

MAN OF THE MOMENT. By Alan Ayckbourn.
April 21, 1992 (American premiere). Director,
Josephine R. Abady; scenery, David Potts; costumes, Linda Fisher; lighting, Richard Winkler;
sound, Jeffrey Montogomerie.
  With Harley Jane Kozak, Charlotte Booker,
Albert Macklin, Manuel E. Santiago, David
Schramm, Howard Hesseman, Regina Fisher,
Patti Glowe, Michael Tauber, Maggie Goz,
Stephen Gabis, Tony Sias, Dawn Arnold, Danette
Baker, William Hoffman, Gregory Paul, Liza
Anne Snyder, Lewis Victor.
  One intermission.

DAYS OF WINE & ROSES. By J P Miller. May
5, 1992. Director, Jack Hofsiss; scenery, David
Jenkins; costumes, Julie Weiss; lighting, Peter

Kaczorowski; sound, Jeffrey Montogomerie.
Joe Clay. . . . . William Katt
Kirsten Arnesen Clay . . . . Mia Dillon
Ellis Arnesen . . . . . . Christopher Wynkoop
Fred Boyle. . . . . Robert Hoffman
  Time and Place: The action of the play takes
place in various locations in New York City and
Long Island in the early 1960s. One intermission.

DISCOVEReads '92: Staged Readings:

LOVE. By Graham Reid. May 14, 1992. Director,
Josephine R. Abady.
THE FRED ALLEN SHOW. By Arnold and Lois
Pyser. May 15, 1992. Directors, David F. Eliet
and Arnold Peyser.
THE JAPANESE FOREIGN TRADE MINISTER. By Murray Schisgal. May 16, 1992.
Director, Roger T. Danforth.
HOMEWARD BOUND. By Elliot Hayes. May
21, 1992. Director, Leslie Swackhamer.
MONTE CARLO. By Lydia Stryk. May 22,
1992. Director, Roger T. Danforth.

Cleveland: Cleveland Public Theater

(Artistic director, James A. Levin)

A DEVIL IN THE HEAD. By Michael D.
Sepesy. June 13, 1991. Director, Alec Rubin;
scenery, Andrew Kaletta; costumes, Vanne J.
Furlan; lighting, Tom Saltzman; sound,
Christopher Shimp.
Lorne Myers . . . . Donald J. Morrison

William Payne . . . . Allen Branstein
Joy Hyland . . . . Amanda Shaffer
Barb Kurtland. . . . . Linda Mason
Heckler. . . . . Jimi Majors
Drummer . . . . Dave McKenzie

Cleveland: Great Lakes Theater Festival

(Managing director, Mary Bill; artistic director, Gerald Freedman)

OHIO STATE MURDERS. By Adrienne
Kennedy. March 7, 1992. Director, Gerald
Freedman; scenery, Gerald Freedman, John Ezell;
costumes, Alfred Kohout; lighting, Cynthia
Stillings; sound, Stan Kozak.
Suzanne Alexander. . . . . Ruby Dee
Youn Suzanne . . . . Bellary Darden
David Alexander. . . . . Michael Early

Robert Hampshire . . . . Allan Byrne
Iris Ann . . . . Leslie Holland
Suzanne's Father . . . . Michael Early
Aunt Louise . . . . Irma P. Hall
Val. . . . . Rick Williams
  Time: The present, winter. Place: In the stacks
on O level beneath the library at Ohio State
University, night.

Columbia, Md.: Toby's Dinner Theater

(Artistic director, Toby Orenstein; general manager, David A. Shaffer)

IT'S A WONDERFUL LIFE, Musical based on
the film *It's a Wonderful Life*; book by Michael

Tilford; music and lyrics by David Nehls.
December 15, 1991. Director, Toby Orenstein;

musical direction, Ross Scott Rawlings; choreography, Ilona Kessel; scenery, Tom Width; costumes, Lynne Sigler; lighting, Ted Doyle.
Joseph . . . . Bill Krause
Clarence . . . . Michael Carruthers
George Bailey . . . . Stephen Schmidt

Mary Hatch . . . . Carole Graham Lehan
Mr. Potter . . . . Michael Tilford
Uncle Billy . . . . Andrew Ho rn
Harry Bailey . . . . Timothy J. Ownby
Sam Wainwright . . . . Ed Eaton
One intermission.

Costa Mesa. Calif: South Coast Repertory

(Artistic director, Martin Benson)

THE EXTRA MAN. By Richard Greenberg. October 25,1991. Director, Michael Engler; scenery, Philipp Jung; costumes, Candice Donnelly; lighting, Peter Maradudin.
Laura . . . . Kandis Chappell
Keith . . . . Peter Frechette
Jess . . . . Kario Salem
Daniel . . . . Jonathan Emerson
One intermission.

NOAH JOHNSON HAD A WHORE. By Jon Bastian. January 25, 1992. Director, Martin Benson; scenery, Cliff Faulkner; costumes, Shigeru Yaji; lighting, Paulie Jenkins; sound, Michael Roth.
Jeremiah Bentonville . . . . Jonathan McMurtry
Noah Johnson . . . . Dominic Hoffman
Lydia Dollner . . . . Melissa Weill
Maj. Frost; Col. Grass . . . . . . Ron Boussom
One intermission.

Dallas: Undermain Theater

(Artistic directors, Katherine Owens, Raphael Parry)

A MURDER OF CROWS. By Mac Wellman. November 30, 1991. Director, Katherine Owens; scenery and lighting, Robert McVay; costumes, Happy Yancey; sound, Bruce DuBose.
Nella . . . . Kateri Cale
Susannah . . . . Lisa Lee Schmidt
Andy . . . . John Caddell

Howard . . . . Robert Erwin
Georgia . . . . Laurel Hoitsma
Raymond . . . . Ivan Klousia
Crow #1 . . . . Stephen Seybold
Crow #2 . . . . Rhonda Boutte
Crow #3 . . . . Lanell Pena
No intermission.

Denver: The Changing Scene

(Executive producers, Al Brooks, Maxine Munt)

Summerplay: Series I (July 11-July 29, 1991)
BLUE MONDAY IN A SAD CAFE. By Terry Chris Distel. Director, Angeline MacCambridge.
Katherine . . . . Johnette Toye
Billie Sue . . . . Judy Phelan-Hill
Travis . . . . Joseph Miller

FISH TALE. By Brian Quinette. Director, Jennifer Thero.
Thrisp . . . . Charles Kolar
Jones . . . . Mark Morgan

CURTAINS. By Joan Emmitt. Director, Rochelle Obechina.
Constance . . . . Gray Grether
Michael . . . . Michael Gutzait

Summerplay: Series II (August 8-August 25, 1991)
ON YOUR MARK, GET SET . . . By Martin Cobin. Director, Stephen R. Kramer.
Male Warrior . . . . Roger Wadnal
Young Girl . . . . Nadine Freed
Boss . . . . Michael S. Robinson
Glutton . . . . Jeanne Varney
Go Player . . . . Charles Kolar
Female Warrior . . . . Carol Gartner
Old Man . . . . Robert W. DeSpain
Bodyguard . . . . Paul Blomquist
Stranger . . . . Candice E. Wessling
Prophetess . . . . Gina Wencel

INTERMISSION. By Mark Ogle. Director, Ken Grimes.
Man . . . . Keith L. Hatton

CLEVELAND PLAY HOUSE—Pat Carroll and George
Grizzard in *A Quarrel of Sparrows* by James Duff

Woman . . . . Kimberly Enard
Mack. . . . . Creston McKim
Greg . . . . Michael Vernard-Winn

VISION. By David Nuss. Director, Jeremy Cole.
Milt. . . . . Randall L. Diamon
John . . . . Craig Patton

GLAD GRACE. By Vincent Sessa. October 10,
1991. Director, Sara Wright; scenery, Randall
Hertzman; costumes, Marianne Reilly Appel;
lighting, Carol McDowell; music composer, Mark
Harris.
Penelope . . . . Kate Temma Susman
Jersey Coast . . . . David J. Read
Rosie Finney . . . . Sharon Kahn-Kahn
John, the Colander Man. . . . . . Steve Brown
Max Ferraro . . . . Eric D. Schleisman

UNITED STATES. By Robert Patrick. November
21, 1991. Director, Jeffrey Pavek; scenery, John
Cunningham; costumes, Paula Harvey; lighting,
Angela Disbrow.
  With Michael Bruen, Tyrone Clark, Robert
Hainline, William H. Hunter, Kamalani Ishida,
Aaron Mason, Kevin Smith, Madrid St. Angelo.
  One intermission.

REPUBLICAN BLUE. By Stuart Boyce. January
23, 1992. Director, Kim Smith; scenery, Stuart
Boyce; costumes, Marianne Reilly Appel; light-
ing, Randall Hertzman; music composer, Chuck
Rhodes.
TZ. . . . . William H. Hunter
Rebo . . . . Eric Weber
Ed . . . . Grant LaMora
Sherri . . . . Renye M. Ress
Rob . . . . Theodore Dawson
Nan Wheeler . . . . Leslie Cullen
Zip . . . . Dan Driver
Senator Strong. . . . . Joe McDonald
Todd Strong . . . . Aaron Mason
  One intermission.

THE SPLIT. By Pat Gabridge. March 19, 1992.
Director, Trace Oakley; scenery, Jay Blodgett;
costumes, Marianne Reilly Appel; lighting, Scott
Hasbrouck.
Jack . . . . Creston McKim
Marilyn . . . . Nancy Portnoy
Jack . . . . Stephen Sealy
Jack. . . . . Lori Herbst
Sam . . . . Phil Boardman
  One intermission.

Denver: Denver Center Theater Company

(Artistic director, Donovan Marley)

U.S. West Theaterfest: April 27-June 28

WOLF-MAN. By Elizabeth Egloff. Director, Evan Yionoulis; scenery, lighting and costumes, Pavel M. Dobrusky; sound, Joel Underwood.

Oskar	Henry Stram
Dido	Tessie Hogan

Time: March, 1938. Place: Vienna. One intermission.

UNCERTAINTY. By Garrison Esst. Director, Anthony Powell; scenery, lighting and costumes, Pavel M. Dobrusky; sound, Joel Underwood.

Werner Heisenberg	Douglas Harmsen
Albert Einstein	Tony Church
Pierre	Paul Borrillo
Claire	Katherine Heasley
Depardieu	Frank Georgianna
Gaganov	Jim Baker
Pascale; Eva; Dasha	Jacqueline Antaramian
Chambermaid	Suzanne Fountain
Bellhop	Yuri Brusilovsky

Time: October, 1927. Place: The Hotel de L'Avenir, Brussels, shortly before the Fifth Solvay Congress.

THEY SHOOT HORSES DON'T THEY? Musical with book and lyrics by Nagle Jackson; music by Robert Sprayberry; based on the novel by Horace McCoy. May 16, 1992. Director, Alan Bailey; musical direction, Deborah R. Lapidus; choreography, Edie Cowan; scenery and costumes, Andrew V. Yelusich; lighting, Charles R. MacLeod; sound, Jim Kaiser.

Paul	Thomas Nahrwold
Gloria	Kathy Morath
Rocky	Jeff McCarthy
Rollo	Pi Douglass
Ruby	Corliss Preston
James	Brad Kindall
Vi	Cynthia Carle
Bucky	Bobby Clark
Stan	Michael Hartman
Bertha	Kathleen Brady-Garvin
Alyson	Blair Ross
Alex	James Puig
Mario	Mark Hardy
Jackie	Mimi Bessette
Max	Kipp Lockwood
Doris	Rosie Waters
Jill	Lise Simms
Herbie	Alan Onickel
Mrs. Layden	Dee Maaske
Detective Murphy	Michael Kevin
Charlie	Darren Davis
Maxine	Gabriella Cavallero
Reverend Gomez	Gail P. Luna
Cop	Mark Rubald

Attendants: Gabriella Cavallero, Darren Davis, Kay Doubleday, Gail P. Luna, Mark Rubald

Time: 1934. Place: Surfside Ballroom, Venice Beach, California. One intermission.

EVIL LITTLE THOUGHTS. By Mark D. Kaufmann. Director, Israel Hicks; scenery, Bill Curley; costumes, Nancy Bassett; lighting, Robert A. Keosheyan; sound, Jim Kaiser.

Douglas Jensen	John Hutton
Anna Jensen	Wendy Radford
Landy Harold	Patricia Jones
Lloyd Price	Randolph Mantooth
Herbert Tooney	Ron Headlee
Bo Riverton	James Michael Connor
Rusty Riverton	William M. Whitehead

Place: Concert hall lobby; office supply room; the Jensen solarium; Rusty's apartment; the Jensen bedroom. One intermission.

Staged Readings:

MONTE CARLO. By Lydia Stryk. June 2, 1992. Director, Jennifer McCray Rincon.

THE SIRENS. By Darrah Cloud. June 2, 1992. Director, Molly Smith.

BUSTER COMES THROUGH. By Phil Bosakowski. June 3, 1992. Director, Jamie Horton.

THE LIVING. By Anthony Clarvoe. June 3, 1992. Director, Nagle Jackson.

ALABAMA RAIN. By Heather McCutchen. June 4, 1992. Director, Bruce K. Sevy.

CHRYSANTHEMUM. By Eugene Lion. June 4, 1992. Director, Anthony Powell.

SAIL AWAY. Book adapted by Jeffrey Hatcher from Noel Coward; music and lyrics by Noel Coward. Director, Alan Bailey.

Evanston, Ill.: Next Theater Company

(Artistic director, Harriet Spizziri)

BANG THE DRUM SLOWLY. Adapted by Eric Simonson from the novel by Mark Harris. January 14, 1992. Director, Eric Simonson; scenery, Robert G. Smith; costumes, Karis Simonson Kopischke; lighting, Peter Gottlieb; sound, Larry Hart.

Henry Wiggen . . . . David New
Bruce Pearson . . . . Paul Sandberg

Dutch Schnell . . . . Jeff Still
Others: W. Earl Brown, George Czarnecki, Anthony Diaz-Perez, Thomas Greene, Kymberly Harris, Andrew Hawkes, Reginald Hayes, Tracy Letts, Michael Ortiz, Daryl Schultz, Charlie Strater, Holly Wantuch, Eric Winzenried.
One intermission.

Evanston, Ill.: Northlight Theater

(Artistic director, Russell Vandenbroucke)

THREE WOMEN TALKING. By Arnold Wesker. January 15, 1992. Director, Russell Vandenbroucke; scenery, Michael Merritt; costumes, Nan Cibula-Jenkins; lighting, Linda Essig; sound and video, Stephan Mazurek.

Mischa Lowenthal . . . . Carmen Roman
Minerva Thompson . . . . . Mary Ann Thebus
Claire Hope. . . . . Margo Buchanan
Leo Lowenthal: Montcrieff Hardy;
    Vincent Ferguson . . . . David Downs
One intermission.

THE RHINO'S POLICEMAN. By Rick

Cleveland. April 15, 1992. Director, B.J. Jones; scenery and lighting, Michael S. Philippi; costumes, Mary Griswold; sound, David Zerlin.
Dr. Ian Booth . . . . Greg Vinkler
Peter Cahill . . . . Kevin Crowley
Stephen Kapanda ; Fidelis . . . . . Ron Dortch
Andy Tyler. . . . . Michael Nash
Willis Lungu . . . . Ed Wheeler
Daut Muyatwa. . . . . Byron Stewart
Lisa Wilson . . . . Johanna McKay
Gunda Muchisa. . . . . Ernest Perry Jr.
One intermission.

Fort Worth: Hip Pocket Theater

(Director, Diane Simons; artistic director, Johnny Simons)

THE BRIDE OF FRANKENSTEIN. Adapted by David Yeakle from the original screen play by William Hurlbut and John L. Balderston. Director, David Yeakle; scenery, John Leach; costumes, Barbara O'Donoghue Proska; lighting, John Leach; sound, Dwight Welsh.

Lord Byron . . . . Ed Landwehr
Percy Shelley; Henry Frankenstein . Thomas Orr
Mary Shelley . . . . Ellen Yeakle
Minnie . . . . Serena Pfeiffer

Burgonmaster . . . . Ric Swain
The Monster . . . . Bob Allen
Elizabeth. . . . . Cynthia Cranz
Dr. Pretorius . . . . Dick Harris
The Hermit. . . . . Gardner Williams
Ygor . . . . Dean Kavrakoff
    Ensemble: David Matthews, Shana Lynn Smith, Valari Spann Haney, Gardner Williams, Dean Kavrakoff, Kristi Ramos, Ed Landwehr, Ed Cannady, Melinda Wood.

Hartford, Conn.: Hartford Stage

(Artistic director, Mark Lamos; managing director, David Hawkanson)

HIDDEN LAUGHTER. By Simon Gray. February 15, 1992. Director, Mark Lamos; scenery, Christopher Barreca, costumes, Candice

Donnelly; lighting, Stephen Strawbridge; sound, David Budries.
Ronnie Chambers. . . . . . . James R. Winker

Louise Pertwee . . . . Judy Geeson
Harry Pertwee . . . . Simon Templeman
Ben Pertwee. . . . . Mark Hammer
Sam Draycott . . . . Jack Stehlin
Natalie Pertwee . . . . Penny Balfour

Nigel Pertwee. . . . . David Alford
Naomi Huchins . . . . Gloria Biegler
  Place: The country cottage and garden of Henry
and Louise Pertwee in Great Yarcombe. One
intermission.

Hollywood, Calif.: Theater West

(Producer, W. Kim Sullivan)

SURVIVAL OF THE HEART. By Dayton Callie.
Director, Mark W. Travis; scenery, Joanna Park;
lighting, Peter Cornford.
Danny . . . . Dayton Callie
C . . . . Pat DiStefano
DJ . . . . Albert Oaten
Alice . . . . Mary Van Arsdel
Mel . . . . Allison Winston
  Time: The present. Place: Danny's apartment,
Hell's Kitchen, New York City. One intermis-
sion.

Plays in Progress:

THE GIFT. By Marion Gallo. June 5, 1991.
Director, Daniel O'Connor.
APPLE STRUDEL. By Mary Jane Roberts. June
12, 1991. Director, Jerry Evans with Seemah
Wilder.
THE SENIOR. By Eugene Pack. June 12, 1991.
Director, Dale Rehfeld.
MOTHER. By Hilma Wolitzer. June 12, 1991.

Director, Norman Cohen.
BRENDA: A PORTRAIT OF A TEENAGE
ANOREXIC. By Stephen Oles. June 26, 1991.
Director, Michael Lilly.
ONCE A COWARD, ALWAYS A COWARD.
By Gino Conforti. July 10, 1991.
PLAYING WITH MATCHES. By Tom
Dahlgren. July 17, 1991. Directors, Norman
Cohen, Delores Mann.
SERMON. Adapted and directed by John
Gallogly. July 24, 1991.
I DO NOT BOW TO LITTLE TRUTHS. By
Drew Katzman. October 11, 1991. Director, Enna
Werd.
ANDRE'S WOMEN. By Marion Gallo. October
11, 1991. Director, Marion Gallo.
A LESSON FROM GAUGHIN AND VAN
GOGH'S EAR. By Matt Swan. October 18, 1991.
Director, David Sage.
LORETTA, I'M SORRY. By Barbara Nell
Beery. October 25, 1991. Director, Deborah
LaVine.

Houston, Tex.: Alley Theater

(Artistic director, Gregory Boyd; executive director, Stephen J. Albert)

MARRIAGE PLAY. By Edward Albee. January
2, 1992. Director, Edward Albee; scenery, Derek
McLane; costumes, Derek McLane; lighting,
Howell Binkley.
Gillian. . . . . Shirley Knight
Jack. . . . . Tom Klunis

THE KIDDIE POOL. By Michael Wilson.
January 16, 1992. Director, Ron Link; scenery,
Yael Pardess; costumes, David C. Woolard; light-
ing, Howell Binkley.
Virgil. . . . . Jason London
Penny . . . . Sharon Madden
Rose . . . . Robyn Lively
Chester. . . . . James Black
Betty Sue . . . . Robin Moseley
Lucretia. . . . . Malinda Bailey

Time and Place: Modern American South.

AMERICAN VAUDEVILLE. By Anne Bogart
and Tina Landau. March 26, 1992. Director,
Anne Bogart; scenery, Douglas Stein; costumes,
David C. Woolard; lighting, Howell Binkley;
musical director and orchestrator, Ted Sperling.
Al Jolson . . . . Adam Heller
George M. Cohan; Man . . . . Tom Cayler
Eva Tanguay; Kitty Doner . . . Diane Fratantoni
Eubie Blake; Ethel Waters;
  Tony Pastor. . . . . Sheryl Sutton
Fanny Brice;
  Woman; E.F. Albee . . . . . Annalee Jefferies
Bert Williams; Turkish Sultan . Vernel Bagneris
Harpo Marx; Wife . . . . Tina Shepard
George Jessel; German Senator. . . Jeffrey Bean

ALLEY THEATER, HOUSTON—Shirley Knight and Tom Klunis in *Marriage Play* written and directed by Edward Albee

Eddie Cantor. . . . . Barney O'Hanlon
June Havoc . . . . Gabrielle Turner
Harry Houdini . . . . Robert Aberdeen
W.C. Fields; Husband. . . . . . . James Black
Sophie Tucker; B.F. Keith . . . . . Patti Allison
Will Rogers; Oscar Hammerstein;
  Grandmother. . . . . Bettye Fitzpatrick
Nora Bayes; Martin Beck. . . . . . Lee Merrill
Buster Keaton; Young Son . . . . Andy Einhorn
Irving Berlin . . . . Jamie Callahan
Mae West. . . . . Tina Shepard
Troupers. . . Catherine Douglas, William Cruse,
Anne Marie Cummings

Son. . . . . Barney O'Hanlon
Trio . . . . William Cruse, Jamie Callahan,
Vernel Bagneris

THE BALTIMORE WALTZ. By Paula Vogel.
April 4, 1992. Director, Anne Bogart; scenery,
Loy Arcenas; costumes, Walker Hicklin; lighting,
Dennis Parichy; sound, John Gromada.
Anna . . . . Alma Cuervo
Carl. . . . . Willis Sparks
Third Man . . . . Arnie Burton
  Time: The present. Place: Baltimore.

La Jolla, Calif.: La Jolla Playhouse

(Artistic director, Des McAnuff; managing director, Alan Levey)

FORTINBRAS. By Lee Blessing. June 23, 1991.
Director, Des McAnuff; scenery, Robert Brill;
costumes, Susan Hilferty; lighting, Chris Parry;
music composer and performer, Michael Roth;

sound, Kenneth Ted Bible, Michael Roth.
Hamlet . . . . Don Reilly
Osric . . . . Jefferson Mays
Horatio . . . . Ralph Bruneau

Polonius; English Ambassador. . . William Cain
Fortinbras . . . . Daniel Jenkins
Norwegian Captain. . . . . Paul Gutrecht
Marcellus . . . . James Crawford
Barnardo . . . . James Kiernan
Polish Maidens . . Archer Martin, Kim C. Walsh
Ophelia . . . . Laura Linney
Claudius . . . . Jonathan Freeman
Gertrude . . . . Devon Allen
Laertes . . . . Josh Sebers
    One intermission.

ELMER GANTRY. Musical based on the novel by
Sinclair Lewis; book by John Bishop; music by Mel
Marvin; lyrics by Bob Satuloff. October 20, 1991.

Director, Des McAnuff; scenery, Heidi Landesman;
costumes, Susan Hilferty; lighting, Chris Parry;
sound, Scott Lehrer; choreography, Marcia
Milgrom Dodge; musical director, Ted Sperling.
    With Adrian Bailey, Stephen Breithaupt, James
Crawford, Lynette DuPre, Tom Flynn, Jody Gelb,
Mark Harelik, Gordon G. Jones, James Kiernan,
Bruce Ladd, Juliet Lambert, Heather Lee, Darlene
Love, Denneth Marshall, Judith Moore, Michael
Mulheren, Michael O'Gorman, Sharon Scruggs,
Josh Sebers, Douglass Sills, Barry J. Tarallo,
Ross Wachsman, Kim C. Walsh, Jennifer Leigh
Warren, Wade Williams.
    One intermission. (Presented at the Mandell
Weiss Theater, San Diego.)

Los Angeles: Colony Studio Theater

(Producing director, Barbara Beckley)

COULD I HAVE THIS DANCE? By Doug
Haverty. May 11, 1991. Director, Jules Aaron;
scenery, Susan Gratch; costumes, Fantella Boone;
lighting, Michael Gilliam; sound, Tom Rincker.
Jeannette Glendenning . . . . . . Toni Sawyer
Monica Glendenning . . . . . Elizabeth Norment
Hank Glendenning . . . . John Bluto
Amanda Glendenning . . . . . Bonita Friedericy

Errol Watkins . . . . Gil Johnson
Colin McCann . . . . Robert Stoeckle
    Time: 1988, spring. Place: A loft in downtown
Los Angeles, the home of the Glendennings as
well as the office of Grapegine Public Relations.
The play was presented in two parts. (An ATCA
selection; see introduction to this section.)

Los Angeles: Mark Taper Forum

(Artistic director and producer, Gordon Davidson; managing director, Stephen J.
Albert)

WIDOWS. By Ariel Dorfman. July 14, 1991.
Director, Robert Egan; scenery, Douglas Stein;
costumes, Dunya Ramicova; lighting, Natasha
Katz; sound, Jon Gottlieb.
Sofia Fuentes . . . . Novella Nelson
Alexandra . . . . Ivonne Coll
Yanina . . . . Natsuko Ohama
Fidelia . . . . Luchy Garcia
Alexis . . . . Robert Ray Jimenez
Alonso; The Doctor . . . . Robert Glaudini
Teresa Salas . . . . Lillian Hurst
Katherina . . . . Tantoo Cardinal
Rosa . . . . Cordelia Gonzalez
Mariluz . . . . Akuyoe
Amanda . . . . Lauri Souza
Lucia . . . . Elizabeth Fong Sung
Ramona . . . . Margaret Medina
Cecilia Sanjines . . . . Lorraine Toussaint
Captain . . . . Tony Plana
Lieutenant . . . . Robert Beltran
Emmanuel . . . . Luis Antonio Ramos
Father Gabriel . . . . Carlos Gomez

Philip Kastoria . . . . Ruben Sierra
Beatrice Kastoria . . . . Cordelia Gonzalez
Kastoria's Brother . Winston Jose Rocha-Castillo
The Prisoner . . . . Nelson Mashita
    Soldiers: Robert Crow, Carlos Gomez, Nelson
Mashita, Winston Jose Rocha-Castillo, Ruben
Sierra.
    Time: Now. Place: Too many countries in the
world. Two intermissions.
*Taper Lab '91 New Work Festival: October 23-
November 24, 1991.*

WILLA AND THE WHOLE DAMNED FAMI-
LY. By Ernest Joselovitz; director, Frank Dwyer.
THE BEAR FACTS. By Jo Carson; director,
David Schweizer.
REASONS TO LIVE. REASON TO LIVE
HALF. NO REASON. By Han Ong; director,
Brian Kulick.
THE LIVING. By Anthony Clarvoe; director,
Oskar Eustis.
ASCENSION DAY. By Michael Henry Brown;

director, L. Kenneth Richardson.

MOE'S LUCKY SEVEN. By Marlane Meyer; director, Roberta Levitow.

THE DREAM GONE WILD. By David Lee Lindsey; director, Elizabeth Bell-Haynes.

TAPDANCER. By Conrad Bishop and Elizabeth Fuller; director, Peter C. Brosius.

MOTHERS. By Kathleen McGhee-Anderson;

director, Shirley Jo Finney.

THE TEARS WILL TELL IT ALL. By Oliver Mayer; director, Robert Egan.

MOONCALF. By Leon Martell; director, Michael Arabian.

THE ADVENTURES OF POR QUINLEY. By Quincy Long; director Kathleen Dimmick.

Louisville: Actors Theater of Louisville

(Producing director, Jon Jory)

Pamela Brown Auditorium: 16th Annual Humana Festival of New American Plays, February 27-March 28, 1992.

D. BOONE. By Marsha Norman. Director, Gloria Muzio; scenery, Paul Owen; costumes, Pamela Scofield; lighting, Karl E. Haas; sound, Darron West.

Daniel Boone . . . . Gladden Schrock
Russell . . . . Rod McLachlan
Flo . . . . Catherine Christianson
Hilly . . . . Dave Florek
Blackfish . . . . Chekotah Miskenack
Indian . . . . Steve Willis
Mr. Wilson . . . . Mark Shannon
Rick . . . . Skipp Sudduth
Jemima Boone . . . . Kathryn Velvel
Squire Boone . . . . Eddie Levi Lee
One intermission.

EVELYN AND THE POLKA KING. By John Olive; music by Carl Finch and Bob Lucas; lyrics by Bob Lucas. Director, Jeff Hooper; scenery, Paul Owen; costumes, Pamela Scofield; lighting, Karl E. Haas; sound, Darron West.

Henry Czerniak . . . . Tom Ligon
Evelyn Starkweather . . . . Seana Kofoed
Margaret; Others . . . . Margo Skinner
Time: The present, during the summer. Place: Chicago and around the Midwest. One intermission.

THE CARVING OF MOUNT RUSHMORE. By John Conklin. Director, John Conklin; scenery, John Conklin; costumes, Pamela Scofield; lighting, Karl E. Haas; sound, Darron West.

Gutzon Borglum . . . . Eddie Levi Lee
Harold Ickes . . . . Dave Florek
Red Anderson . . . . Skipp Sudduth
Tourist . . . . Catherine Christianson
Lecturer . . . . Rod McLachlan
Pianist . . . . Scott Kasbaum

Victor Jory Theater: 16th Annual Humana

Festival of New American Plays, February 18-March 22, 1992.

HYAENA. By Ross MacLean. Director, Mladen Kiselov; scenery, Paul Owen; costumes, Laura A. Patterson; lighting, Mary Louise Geiger; sound, Darron West.

Hyaena . . . . William McNulty
Patient . . . . Michael Hartman
Nurse . . . . Sandra Sydney
Wife . . . . Kathryn Layng
Friend . . . . Mark Shannon
Aides: Christopher Franciosa, S. Scott Shina, Daryl Swanson.
One intermission.

THE OLD LADY'S GUIDE TO SURVIVAL. By Mayo Simon. Director, Alan Mandell; scenery, Paul Owen; costumes, Hollis Jenkins-Evans; lighting, Mary Louise Geiger; sound, Darron West.

Netty . . . . Lynn Cohen
Shprintzy . . . . Shirl Bernheim
Time: Now. Place: San Diego. One intermission.

BONDAGE. By David Henry Hwang. Director, Oskar Eustis; scenery, Paul Owen; costumes, Laura A. Patterson; lighting, Mary Louise Geiger; sound, Darron West.

Time: The present. Place: An S&M parlor on the outskirts of Los Angeles.

DEVOTEES IN THE GARDEN OF LOVE. By Suzan-Lori Parks. Director, Oskar Eustis; scenery, Paul Owen; costumes, Laura A. Patterson; lighting, Mary Louise Geiger; sound, Darron West.

Lily . . . . Margarette Robinson
George . . . . Esther Scott
Madame Odelia Pandahr . . . . . Sandra Sydney
Time and Place: Once upon a time way up there in a garden in the middle of nowhere.

MARISOL. By Jose Rivera. Director, Marcus

Stern; scenery, Paul Owen; costumes, Laura A. Patterson; lighting, Mary Louise Geiger; sound, Darron West.

Marisol . . . . Karina Arroyave
Man With Gold Club;
  Man With Ice Cream; Lenny;
  Man With Scar Tissue . . V Craig Heidenreich
Angel. . . . . Esther Scott
June. . . . . Susan Knight
Homeless Person. . . . . Carlos Ramos
  Time: The present, winter. Place: New York City. One intermission.

LYNETTE AT 3 A.M. By Jane Anderson. Director, Reid Davis; scenery, Paul Owen; costumes, Kevin McLeod; lighting, Rob Dillard; sound, Darron West.

Lynette . . . . Anne O'Sullivan
Bobby. . . . . V Craig Heidenreich
Estaban. . . . . Rafael Baez

Time: The time is 3 a.m. Place: Lynette's apartment in Brooklyn.

PROCEDURE. By Joyce Carol Oates. Director, William McNulty; scenery, Paul Owen; costumes, Hollis Jenkins-Evans; lighting, Casey Clark; sound, Darron West.

A . . . . Margarette Robinson
B . . . . Stacey Leigh Ivey
Body . . . . James Wright Jr.
  Time: The present. Place: A hospital room.

EUKIAH. By Lanford Wilson. Director, Jon Jory; scenery, Paul Owen; costumes, Hollis Jenkins-Evans; lighting, Matthew J. Reinert; sound, Darron West.

Butch . . . . Mark Shannon
Eukiah . . . . Shaun Powell
  Time: The present. Place: An abandoned private airplane hangar.

Miami, Fla.: Coconut Grove Playhouse

(Producing artistic director, Arnold Mittelman)

TOO SHORT TO BE A ROCKETTE! Conceived by Gary Smith; written by Buz Kohan and Bruce Vilanch. May 29, 1992. Director, Gary Smith; scenery, Roy Christopher; costumes, Roy Christopher; lighting, Ken Billington; sound, Philip G. Allen.

Pia . . . . Pia Zadora
Curt . . . . Curt Anthon
Julie . . . . Julie A. Delgado
Bernard . . . . Bernard Dotson
Judette . . . . Judette Warren
Kady . . . . Kady Zadora

Millburn, N.J.: Paper Mill Playhouse

(Executive producer, Angelo del Rossi; artistic director, Robert Johanson)

GREAT EXPECTATIONS. Adapted from Charles Dickens by Robert Johanson. February 12, 1992. Director, Robert Johanson; scenery, Michael Anania; costumes, Gregg Barnes; lighting, Timothy Hunter; music, Albert Evans; sound, David R. Paterson.

Pip . . . . Michael James Reed
Young Pip; Little Pip. . . Daren Edward Higgins
Abel Magwitch. . . . . John MacKay
Joe Gargery . . . . Michael O'Gorman
Mrs. Joe. . . . . Suzanne Toren
Compeyson . . . . Joe Ambrose
Uncle Pumblechook . . . . Jim Hillgartner
Mr. Hubble; Wemmick . . . . . Kermit Brown
Mrs. Hubble; Mrs. Belind
  a Pocket . . . . Linda Poser
Sergeant; Bentley Drummle . . . Jeff Woodman
Estella . . . . Jennifer Holmes
Miss Havisham. . . . . Elizabeth Franz
Mr. Jaggers . . . . Larry Grey

Relatives of Miss Havisham:
  Sarah Pocket . . . . Michael Lewis
  Camilla . . . . Jeff Woodman
  Raymond. . . . . Timothy Wheeler
Pale Young Gentleman. . . . . . Jeff Seelbach
Estella, as a Young Lady; Molly . . . Nancy Bell
Orlick . . . . Timothy Wheeler
Biddy . . . . Marceline Hugot
Trabb; Matthew Pocket;
  Aged Parent . . . . Robert Molnar
Trabb's Boy. . . . . Chris Rempfer
Jaggers' Clients . . . . Carina Andersson,
                                    Andrew Segal
Herbert Pocket . . . . Michael Lewis
Nursemaids:
  Flopson . . . . Jim Hillgartner
  Millers . . . . Timothy Wheeler
Startop; Officer on the Thames . . Kyle Saunders
  Pocket Children: Emily Blau, Dante Deiana, Daren Edward Higgins, Jennifer Holmes, Chris Rempfer, Jeff Seelbach.

Milwaukee: Milwaukee Repertory Theater

(Artistic director, John Dillon; managing director, Sara O'Connor)

ALL THE TRICKS BUT ONE. By Gilles Ségal, translated by Sara O'Connor. Director, Kenneth Albers; scenery, Victor A. Becker; costumes, Sam Fleming; lighting, Robert Jared.

German Colonel . . . . Tom Blair
Nelly. . . . . Catherine Lynn Davis
Maurice . . . . Troy Dunn
(Ludovic) . . . . Jeff Lee, Brady Moran
President of the Court . . . . . Michael W. Nash
Director . . . . James Pickering
Director's Wife . . . . Rose Pickering
Little Slam . . . . Will Rhys
Deputy Mayor . . . . Gregory Steres
  Stagehands; German Soldiers; Free French Soldiers: Ross Dippel, Stephen McCormick, Michael Monteleone, T. Patrick Walsh.
(Parentheses indicate role in which the actors alternated)
  Time: 1944. Place: Limoges, Vichy France. One intermission.

MOOT. By John Leicht. April 12, 1992. Director, John Dillon; scenery, John Story; costumes, Charles Berliner; lighting, Chester Loeffler-Bell; composer and sound, John Tanner.

Edward Hubbord; Columnist #1;
  Uncle Sam Clown . . . . Derek Craig
Helen . . . . Saralynne Crittenden
John Sibley; Federal Judge;
  Uncle Bucky . . . . James DeVita
Cop Clown. . . . . Ross Dippel

Charles Sober; Robert Quary . Richard Halverson
Jackson Kemper . . . . Anthony Lee
General Clown . . . . . . Stephen McCormick
Belinda; Doris . . . . Terry Merrill
Edward Smout . . . . Daniel Mooney
Operator; TV Announcer;
  Mary Quary. . . . . Rose Pickering
Scientist Clown; TV Reporter;
  Columnist #2; Messenger . . . Stephan Roselin
Jarvis Bywater . . . . Gregory Steres
Harold Chadwick;
  Judge Warren Venerable. . . . Adolphus Ward
Buckridge Sims;
  Columnist #3 . . . . C. Michael Wright
Videophone . . . . . . Liza Balestrieri, Jill Steeg
  Media Mass: Derek Craig, Ross Dippel, Stephen McCormick.
  Time: 1979. Place: From sea to shining sea. One intermission.

Stackner Cabaret

MOTHER JONES: THE MOST DANGEROUS WOMAN IN AMERICA. Musical with book by Ronnie Gilbert; music and lyrics by Si Kahn. April 3, 1992. Director, Norma Saldivar; scenery, Kate Henderson; costumes, Dawna Gregory; lighting, Chester Loeffler-Bell.

Mother Jones . . . . Ronnie Gilbert
  Musicians: Michael Dubay, Jack Forbes Wilson.
  One intermission.

Minneapolis: Cricket Theater

(Artistic director, William Partlan)

SACRED JOURNEY. By Matthew Witten. January 10, 1992. Director, William Partlan; scenery, Steven Krahnke; lighting, Tina Charney.
  Time: Now. Place: Minneapolis. One intermission.

Staged reading:

VOICE OF THE GENERATIONS. By Ronald Schultz. Director, Paul Meshejian.

New Brunswick, N.J.: Crossroads Theater Company

(Producer and artistic director, Ricardo Khan; managing director, Andre Robinson Jr.)

BLACK ORPHEUS. Musical conceived by Ricardo Khan; adapted from the legend by OyamO; music by Ray Holman. December 7, 1991. Director, Ricardo Khan; scenery, Dan Proett; costumes, Toni-Leslie James; lighting,

William H. Grant III; sound, Rob Gorton; choreography, Dianne McIntyre.

Apollo . . . . Marshall R. Factors
Dion . . . . Helmar Augustus Cooper
Eurydice . . . . Sandra Daley

Herman Geb . . . . Larry Marshall	
Mama Cli'pe . . . . Carol Jean-Lewis	
Mariella . . . . Kim Weston-Moran	
Myra . . . . Julia Aponte	
Orpheus . . . . Jesse Moore	
Ping . . . . Al'sin Adams, James Lockhart	
Rock One . . . . Ming-Na Wen	
Sanchez. . . . . Cameron Boyd, Coleman Butler	

Sweet Mout' Virgil. . . . . Jack Landron
Little Girl . . . . Siobhan McCarty,
Kimi Ann Stephenson
Tityus . . . . Akwesi Asante
Toogie. . . . . Theara Ward
Time: Carnival season. Place: Trinidad. One intermission.

New Brunswick, N.J.: George Street Playhouse

(Producing artistic director, Gregory S. Hurst)

THE ENGAGEMENT. By Richard Vetere. September 28, 1991. Director, Matthew Penn; scenery, Deborah Jasien; costumes, Barbara Forbes, lighting, Paul Armstrong.
Tom . . . . Joel Anderson
Jeffrey . . . . Richmond Hoxie
Pat . . . . Michael Countryman
Tony . . . . Joseph Siravo
Susan . . . . Melinda Mullins
Time and place: The present, during one evening in various locations in and around Queens. One intermission.

SEPARATION. By Tom Kempinski. January 4, 1992. Director, Susan Kerner; scenery, Deborah Jasien; costumes, Barbara Forbes, lighting, Michael Giannitti.
Joe Green . . . . Richard Poe
Sara Wise . . . . Jordan Baker
Time: The present. Place: London and New York. One intermission.

SARAH AND ABRAHAM. By Marsha Norman. February 2, 1992. Director, Jack Hofsiss; music composer, David Yazbek; scenery, David Jenkins; costumes, Julie Weiss, Gary Lisz; lighting, Beverly Emmons.
Abraham; Cliff . . . . William Katt
Tom . . . . John Hickok
Jack . . . . Steven Keats
Sarah; Kitty . . . . Tovah Feldshuh

Hagar; Monica. . . . . Christine Andreas
Virginia . . . . Lee Chamberlin
Issac . . . . Carlo Alban
Stage Crew . . . . Bryan Gill, Ted Nolan
Dressers . . . . Billy Duvall Jr., Kristina Scalone
Time and place: During the six-week rehearsal of a small improvisational theater company.

ZARA SPOOK AND OTHER LURES. By Joan Ackermann. April 28, 1992. Director, Pamela Berlin; scenery, Loren Sherman; costumes, Barbara Forbes; lighting, Donald Holder.
Talmadge. . . . . Matthew Bennett
Evelyn . . . . Calista Flockhart
Teale . . . . Shelley Rogers
Margery. . . . . Glynis Bell
Joe . . . . Tom Tammi
Ramona . . . . Carolyn McCormick
Place: Beckley, West Virginia; Highway 25, New Mexico, between Albuquerque and Truth or Consequences; Elephant Butte Campground; Elephant Butte Reservoir; the shore; Willow Canyon; Arroyo Seco Motel; Civic Center Auditorium. One intermission.

Staged Readings:
JUST BEFORE SLEEP. By James Still. May, 1992. Director, Susan Kerner.
A VISIT TO HOLIDAY PARK. By Alan Zweibel. June, 1992. Director, Gregory S. Hurst.

New Haven, Conn.: Long Wharf Theater

(Artistic director, Arvin Brown; executive director, M. Edgar Rosenblum)

BOOTH IS BACK. By Austin Pendleton. October 3, 1991. Director, Arvin Brown; scenery, John Lee Beatty; lighting, Dennis Parichy; costumes, Jess Goldstein.
Junius Brutus Booth . . . . Frank Langella
Edwin Booth . . . . Raphael Sbarge

Mary Ann . . . . Maureen Anderman
Asia Booth . . . . Isabel Rose
Johnny Booth. . . . . Alexander P. Enberg
Mrs. Hill . . . . Joyce Ebert
Page . . . . Ralph Williams
Baxter . . . . Bob Morrisey

LONG WHARF THEATER, NEW HAVEN—
Maureen Anderman and Frank Langella as Mary Ann
and Junius Booth in Austin Pendleton's *Booth Is Back*

Adelaide . . . . Beth Dixon
Place: The Booth farm; dressing room of a theater in Boston; hotel room, stage and dressing room in Louisville; saloon on a steamboat; dressing room in New Orleans; California. Two intermissions.

ADVENTURES IN THE SKIN TRADE. Musical adapted from Dylan Thomas's short stories by John Tillinger and James Hammerstein; music by Tom Fay; lyrics by James Hammerstein. November 12, 1991. Director, John Tillinger; scenery, John Lee Beatty; costumes, Jane Greenwood; lighting, Tharon Musser; choreography, Danny Herman.
Samuel Bennet . . . . Daniel Jenkins
Winnie; Singer; Rose;
    Woman on Train. . . . . Victoria Clark
Hermione; Woman in Fur Coat . Susan Antinozzi
Mr. O'Brien; Man in Buffet . . . . . Ian Trigger
Dave; George Ring . . . . Albert Macklin
Mr. Bennet; Allingham . . . . Thomas Hill
Mrs. Bennet; Woman in Buffet;

Bar Maid . . . . Paddy Croft
Peggy; Polly; Lola . . . . Lily Knight
Mrs. Bevan; Mrs. Dacey . . . . Victoria Boothby
Reverend Bevan; Walter;
    Ron Bishop. . . . . Michael Waldron
Lou; Lucy; Waitress . . . . . . Erin J. O'Brien
Harold; 1st Man on Train . . . . . William Parry
Tom; 2d Man on Train . . . . John Curless
    Patrons in the Club: Susan Antinozzi, John Curless, Scott Murphree, William Parry, Ian Trigger, Michael Waldron.

Workshop Series
APPOINTMENT WITH A HIGH WIRE LADY. By Russell Davis. December 13, 1991.
THE INNOCENTS' CRUSADE. By Keith Reddin. November 1, 1991. Director, Joe Mantello.
CRAZY HORSE AND THREE STARS. By David Wiltse. January 24, 1992. Director, Mark Brokaw.
THE DAY THE BRONX DIED. By Michael Henry Brown. March 6, 1992. Director, Gordon Edelstein.

New Haven, Conn.: Yale Repertory Theater

(Artistic director, Stan Wojewodski Jr.)

Winterfest: January 16-March 7, 1992.
FEFU AND HER FRIENDS. By Maria Irene Fornes. January 16, 1992. Director, Lisa Peterson; scenery, Michael Vaughn Sims; costumes, Maggie Morgan; lighting, Trui Malten; sound, Jon Newstrom.

Fefu	Joyce Lynn O'Connor
Cindy	Kim Yancey
Christina	Sarah Long
Julia	Pippa Pearthree
Emma	Julianna Margulies
Paula	Tonia Rowe
Sue	Mary Magdalena Hernandez
Cecilia	Camilia Sanes

Time: Spring 1935. Place: New England. One intermission.

THE DEATH OF THE LAST BLACK MAN IN THE WHOLE ENTIRE WORLD. By Suzan-Lori Parks. January 22, 1992. Director, Liz Diamond; scenery, Riccardo Hernandez; costumes, Caryn Neman; lighting, Glen Fasman; sound, Dan Moses Shreier.

Black Man With Watermelon	Leon Addison Brown
Black Woman With Fried Drumstick	Fanni Green
Lots of Grease and Lots of Pork	Darryl Theirse
Queen-Then-Pharaoh Hatshepsut	Pamala Tyson
And Bigger and Bigger and Bigger	Michael Potts
Prunes and Prisms	Karen A. Bishop
Ham	Reg E. Cathey
Voice on thuh Tee V	Reginald Lee Flowers
Old Man River Jordan	Ron Brice
Yes and Greens Black-Eyed Peas Cornbread	Melody J. Garrett
Before Columbus	Leo V. Finnie III

Time: The present.

DEMOCRACY IN AMERICA. By Colette Brooks. January 24, 1992. Director, Travis Preston; scenery, Christopher Barreca; costumes, Tom Broecker; lighting, Stephen Strawbridge; sound, David Budries.

With Christopher Bauer, Reg. E. Cathey, Marissa Chibas, Brendan Corbalis, Reginald Lee Flowers, Melody J. Garrett, Carl R. Hudson, Elina Lowensohn, Adina Porter, Corliss Preston, John Gould Rubin, Elaine Tse, Francine Zerfas. One intermission.

Pasadena, Calif.: Pasadena Playhouse

(Artistic director, Paul Lazarus)

SOLITARY CONFINEMENT. By Rupert Holmes. November 24, 1991. Director, Kenneth Frankel; scenery and art direction, William Barclay; costumes, Kathleen Detoro; lighting, Donald Holder; sound Jack Allaway; music, Deborah Grunfield.

With Stacy Keach.

KIRBYSOMETHING. Musical revue by Kirby Tupper. Opened May 29, 1992 (produced in association with Theater Corporation of America and David Galligan). Director, David Galligan; musical director, David Snyder; lighting, Kevin Mahan; sound, Frederick Boot.

With Kirby Tupper, David Snyder, Kimberle Baxter, Michael Heitzman, John Harvey.

No intermission.

Philadelphia: Philadelphia Festival Theater for New Plays

(Artistic and producing director, Carol Rocamora)

BOBBY, CAN YOU HEAR ME? By Judy GeBauer. January 10,1992. Director, Carol Rocamora; scenery, Phillip A. Graneto; costumes, Janus Stefanowicz; lighting, Curt Senie; sound, Connie Lockwood.

Bobby	Ron Bottitta
Youth No. 1; Student; Young Bobby	Peter Pryor
Youth No. 2; Youth; Neighbor; Padraic Pearse	John Heffron
Rosaleen	Carla Belver

Marcella . . . . Jan Leslie Harding
Geraldine . . . . Susan Knight
John; Silent Man; Neighbor. . . . Michael Toner
Prisoner; Volunteer; Bik. . . . . . Bryant Weeks
Dorcha; Interrogator;Warder No. 2;
  Father Murphy . . . . Charles S. Roney
Warder No. 1; O/C; RUC No. 2;
  Barker; Doctor . . . . Pearce Bunting
Orderly; RUC No. 1; Officer;
  Ward; Owen Carron. . . . . . James Riordan
Time and place: The year 1981 and earlier in
Long Kesh Prison, Northern Ireland, and in the
city of Belfast.

THE CHAMPAGNE CHARLIE STAKES. By Bruce
Graham. April 17, 1992. Director, James J. Christy;
scenery, James Wolk; costumes, Vickie Esposito;
lighting, Curt Senie; sound, Connie Lockwood.
Mary . . . . Anne Swift
Mary Lee . . . . Marcia Mahon
Jackie. . . . . William Wise
Charlie . . . . John MacKay
Paul. . . . . Geoffrey Wade
Time: Memorial Day, 1990. One intermission.

THE PLAY OF LIGHTS. By Chaim Potok. May
13, 1992. Director, Carol Rocamora; scenery,
Allen Moyer; costumes, Vickie Esposito; light-
ing, Karen Ten Eyck; sound, Connie Lockwood.
Gershon Loran . . . . Benjamin White
Arthur Leiden. . . . . Matt Servitto
Elizabeth Leiden . . . . Carla Belver
Charles Leiden . . . . Forrest Compton
Waiter; Alvert Einstein;
  Solomon; Geiger . . . . Don Auspitz
Toshie . . . . Ann Harada

Previewers (Readings), October, 1991:
THE CHAMPAGNE CHARLIE STAKES. By
Bruce Graham.
THE BIG NUMBERS. By Craig Wright.
DINOSAUR DREAMS. By Tom Szentgyorgyi.
THE PLAY OF LIGHTS. By Chaim Potok.
D.N.R. By Anthony Clarvoe.
GUN PLAY. By Tom Dunn.
MORNING, STEVE. By Cassi Harris.
HELL ON WHEELS. By Mary Lathrop.
ONE-ACTS. By Geraldine Aron.

Phoenix: Arizona Theater Company

(Artistic director, David Ira Goldstein; managing director, Robert Alpaugh)

MINOR DEMONS. By Bruce Graham. April 17,
1992. Director, Andrew Traister; scenery, Greg
Lucas; costumes, Francis Kenny; lighting, Rick
Paulsen; sound, Brian Jerome Peterson.
Deke Winters . . . . Jack Wetherall
Diane Sikorski . . . . Kathy Fitzgerald
Vice DelGatto . . . . John Dennis Johnston

Carmella DelGatto . . . . . . Evangelia Costa
Mrs. O'Brien . . . . Dean Thompson
Mrs. Simmonds. . . . . Diane Kobayashi
Mr. Simmonds . . . . Apollo Dukakis
Kenny Simmonds . . . . Aron Eisenberg
  One intermission.

Pittsfield, Mass.: Berkshire Public Theater

(Director, Frank Bessell)

MUSIC MINUS ONE. Musical with book and
lyrics by George Furth; music by Doug Katsaros.
January 24, 1992. Director, Frank Bessell;
scenery and lighting, Don Mandigo; costumes,

Katherine Lampro.
Lady . . . . Vikki True
  One intermission.

Princeton, N.J.: McCarter Theater

(Artistic director, Emily Mann; managing director, Jeffrey Woodward)

THE TRIUMPH OF LOVE. Adapted by Stephen
Wadsworth from Pierre Carlet de Marivaux.
March 24, 1992. Director, Stephen Wadsworth;
scenery, Thomas Lynch; costumes, Martin
Pakledinaz; lighting, Christopher Akerlind.
Dimas . . . . Tom Brennan
Leonide . . . . Katherine Borowitz

Corine . . . . Brooke Smith
Harlequin . . . . John Michael Higgins
Agis . . . . Mark Deakins
Leontine . . . . Mary Lou Rosato
Hermocrate . . . . Robin Chadwick
  Place: The gardens of Hermocrate's country
retreat. Two intermissions.

St. Louis: Repertory Theater of St. Louis

(Artistic director, Steven Woolf; managing director, Mark D. Bernstein)

ALMOST SEPTEMBER. Musical with book and lyrics by David Schechter and Steven Lutvak; music by Steven Lutvak. Director, David Schechter, scenery, John Ezell; costumes, John Carver Sullivan; lighting, Max De Volder; musical director, Wendy Bobbitt.

Eustace . . . . Scott Schafer
Theodora . . . . Nancy Opel
Alexander . . . . Philip Lehl
Herbert . . . . Skip Lackey
Hermione . . . . Debbie Laumand
Molly . . . . Amanda Butterbaugh

Alastair Mole . . . . Himself
Time: The last night of summer, 1909. Place: The attic-turned-sleeping-quarters in Gran'mama's house, situated by a river somewhere in the English countryside. One intermission.

Lab Project:

SAVAGES. By John B. Justice and Tommy Thompson. February 9, 1992.

San Diego, Calif.: Old Globe Theater

(Artistic director, Jack O'Brien)

NECESSITIES. By Velina Hasu Houston. July 10, 1991. Director, Julianne Boyd; scenery, Cliff Faulkner; costumes, Shigeru Yaji; lighting, Ashley York Kennedy; sound, Jeff Ladman.

Zelda Kelly . . . . Jennifer Savidge
Kale Smith . . . . Jonathan Nichols
Daniel Kelly . . . . William Anton
Christina . . . . Suzanna Hay
Tommy . . . . Bray Poor
Elizabeth . . . . Freda Foh Shen
Janine . . . . Tara Marchant
Mary . . . . Sue-Anne Morrow
Time: The present. Place: A day in July in a contemporary Los Angeles office. Another day, a week later, in an elegant Phoenix hotel room. One intermission.

PASTORELA '91: A SHEPHERDS' PLAY. By Raul Moncada. December 12, 1991. Director, William Virchis; musical director, Fredrick Bastien Lanuza; scenery, John Iacovelli; costumes, Mirian Laubert.

Lucifer . . . . Anasa Briggs-Graves
Satan . . . . Johnny Warriner
Moloch . . . . Patrick A. Garcia
Seven Deadlies . . . . Janine Lowe-Moretto
Archangel Michael . . . . . . Mauricio Mendoza
Archangel Gabriel . . . . . Juan Del Castillo Jr.
Star of Bethlehem . . . . Laura Preble
The Hermit . . . . George Weinberg-Harter
Bato . . . . Gregorio Ruiz Flores
Gila . . . . Linda Lutz
Blas . . . . Carlos A. Mendoza
Menga . . . . Alma Villegas
Bartolo . . . . Ruben D. Padilla

Julia . . . . Charisma Lynn Largey
Celfa . . . . Ria Carey
Fileno . . . . Manuel Camacho
Veruta . . . . Elizabeth E. Bauer
Lucindo . . . . David Edward Taboado
Arminda . . . . Lora Higginbotham
Griselda . . . . Nancy Jimenez-Taboada
Shepherdesses . . . Arminda Joyce, Laura Preble
Mary . . . . Frances K. Smith
Joseph . . . . Ruben A. Ramirez
Wise Men: Juan Del Castillo Jr., Isabel Leon, Mauricio Mendoza.

THE SCHOOL FOR HUSBANDS. By Molière. January 23, 1992. Translated by Richard Wilbur. Director, Edward Payson Call; scenery, Robert Andrew Dahlstrom; costumes, Michael Krass; lighting, David F. Segal; composer, Larry Delinger; sound, Jeff Ladman.

Ariste . . . . Richard Easton
Ergaste . . . . Tom Harrison
Sganarelle . . . . Gordon Paddison
Valere . . . . Robert Petkoff
Isabelle . . . . Susan Wands
Leonor . . . . Andrea D. Fitzgerald
Lisette . . . . Evangeline Fernandez
Magistrate . . . . Paul James Kruse
Zanies . . . . Alex Perez, Donald Sager
Place: Paris

BARGAINS. By Jack Heifner. March 19, 1992. Director, Jack O'Brien; scenery, Ralph Funicello; costumes, Robert Wojewodski; lighting, Ashley York Kennedy; sound, Jeff Ladman.

Mr. Mead . . . . Stephen Caffrey

Dennis . . . . Jeb Brown
Sally . . . . Linda Hart
Tish . . . . Kellie Overbey
Mildred . . . . Marcia Rodd
Lothar . . . . Gregory Grove
  Time and place: Act I, a downtown department
store in a Central Texas town of about 20,000
people; a summer morning shortly before 9. Act
II, Mildred's trailer, an evening two weeks later.
One intermission.

MR. RICKEY CALLS A MEETING. By Ed
Schmidt. May 9, 1992. Director, Sheldon Epps;
scenery, Ralph Funicello; costumes, Christina
Haatainen; lighting, Barth Ballard; sound, Jeff
Ladman.
  With Jeremiah Wayne Birkett, Ron Canada,
Willie C. Carpenter, Nick LaTour, Sterling Macer
Jr., Arlen Dean Snyder.
  No intermission.

A . . . MY NAME IS STILL ALICE. Conceived
and directed by Joan Micklin Silver and Julianne
Boyd. May 14, 1992. Musical director, Henry
Aronson; choreographer, Liza Gennaro; scenery,
Cliff Faulkner; costumes, David C. Woolard;
lighting, David F. Segal; sound, Jeff Ladman,
Tony Tait.
  With Roo Brown, Randy Graff, Alaina Reed
Hall, Mary Gordon Murray, Nancy Ticotin.
  One intermission.

Play Discovery Program

THE MAN WHO KILLED GOD. By Alann Jack
Lewis. February 24, 1992. Director, Ralph Elias.
SPITE FOR SPITE. By Agustin Moreto. March
30, 1992. Translated by Dakin Matthews.
Directors, Dakin Matthews, Anne McNaughton.
TIES THAT BIND. By David Hyslop. April 20,
1992.
MASTERS OF THE SEA. By Gardner McKay.
May 18, 1992. Director, David Ralphe.

San Diego: San Diego Repertory Theater

(Artistic director, Douglas Jacobs; producing director, Sam Woodhouse)

RUBY'S BUCKET OF BLOOD. By Julie
Hebert. February 22, 1992. Director, Sam
Woodhouse; composer and musical director,
Mark Bingham; scenery, Jane LaMotte, Robert
Brill; lighting, Ashley York Kennedy, Diane
Boomer; sound, Mark Bingham, Jim Brooks.
Ruby Delacroix . . . . Amanda White

Emerald Delacroix . . . . Natalie Turman
Alfred Billy Dupre . . . . Rick Sparks
Betty Dupre . . . . . Deborah Van Valkenburgh
Johnny Beaugh . . . . Antonio Johnson
  Ensemble: Ken Bryant, Tammy Casey, Cynthia
Hammond, Definique Juniel, Damon Lamont,
Morris White.

San Francisco: Lorraine Hansberry Theater

(Artistic director, Stanley E. Williams)

RE/MEMBERING AUNT JEMIMA. By Glenda
Dickerson and Breena Clarke. February 7, 1992.
Director, Glenda Dickerson; scenery, Alan
Curreri; costumes, Susan Anderson; lighting,

Jeffrey Kelly; sound, Adam Liberman.
  With Brandie Swann, Patricia A. Wright,
Cynthia Ruffin, Imani Harringon, Ayana,
Winifred H. Cabiness, Hallyne Harris.

San Francisco: Magic Theater

(General director, Harvey Seifter)

MOZART'S JOURNEY TO PRAGUE WITH
DETOURS, DIVERSIONS AND AN EPI-
LOGUE IN NEW YORK CITY. By James Keller.
June 4, 1991. Director, Albert Takazauckas; scenery,
Barbara Mesney; costumes, Sandra Woodall;
lighting, Kurt Landisman; sound, Barney Jones,
Kerry Rose.

Eugenie; Zerlina; Frau Colonel . Signe Albertson
Constanze; Donna Anna . . . . . . Julia Elliott
Gardener; Garcia; Ottavio;
  Postillion . . . . Rick Hickman
Mozart; Don Giovanni . . . . . . Robin Karfo
Maria Theresa; Donna Elvira;
  Countess . . . . Anni Long

Max, the Libretto-Seller; Masetto. . . Art Manke
Child Mozart; Karl . . . . . Michael Michalske
Leopold Mozart; Count;
   da Ponte. . . . . Kurt Reinhardt

FAT MEN IN SKIRTS. By Nicky Silver.
December 10, 1991. Director, R.A. White;
scenery, Jeff Rowlings; costumes, Allison Connor;
lighting, Dirk Epperson; sound, Andy Murdock.
Bishop . . . . Sean Blackman
Phyllis. . . . . Susan Brecht
Pam; Popo . . . . Molly Bryant
Howard; Dr. Nestor . . . . Geoff Shields
   Two intermissions.

OSCAR AND BERTHA. By Maria Irene Fornes.
March 10, 1992. Director, Maria Irene Fornes;
scenery, Sandra Woodall; costumes, Sandra

Woodall; lighting, Jennifer Norris; sound, Kim
Foscato.
Roe . . . . Dennis Ludlow
Pea. . . . . Patrick Morris
Stephen . . . . Regina Saisi

Springfest 1992
ANGEL OF DEATH. By Charlie Schulman.
Director, David Dower.
REASONS TO LIVE. REASON TO LIVE
HALF. NO REASON. By Han Ong. Director,
Bruce Kulick.
XXX LOVE ACT. By Cintra Wilson. Director,
Rick Corley.

Staged Reading:
ADORING THE MADONNA. By Allan Havis.
May 18, 1992. Director, David Ford.

Sarasota: Florida Studio Theater

(Artistic director, Richard Hopkins)

ONE FOOT IN SCARSDALE. By Jack Fournier.
Director, Steven Ramay; scenery, Jeffrey W.
Dean; costumes, Vicky Small; lighting, Paul D.
Romance.

Dorothy Parker. . . . . Carolyn Michel
   Time: Wednesday, June 7, 1967. Place: The
Algonquin Hotel, New York City. One intermission.

Seattle: A Contemporary Theater

(Founding director, Gregory Falls; artistic director, Jeff Steitzer)

TEARS OF RAGE. By Doris Baizley. July 11,
1991. Director, Steven Dietz; staged by Lori
Sullivan Worthman; costumes, Laura Crow; lighting, Rick Paulsen; sound, Steven M. Klein.
Mimi . . . . Linda Emond
Anne . . . . Karen Meyer
Lou . . . . Stephanie Kallos
Monk . . . . David P. Whitehead
Petey . . . . Torrey Hanson
Pete . . . . John Aylward
Ginger. . . . . Cristine McMurdo-Wallis
   One intermission.

WILLI (AN EVENING OF WILDERNESS AND
SPIRIT). By and with John Pielmeier; based on
the speeches of Willi Unsoeld. September 19,
1991. Director, Ira Goldstein; scenery, Scott
Weldin; costumes, Carolyn Keim; lighting, Rick
Paulsen.

TRUST. By Steven Dietz. Director, Steven Dietz;
scenery, Michael Olich; costumes, Carolyn Keim;
lighting, Rick Paulsen; sound, Jim Ragland.

Gretchen . . . . Meg Judson
Becca . . . . Kristie Dale Sanders
Cody . . . . Louis A. Lotorto
Leah . . . . Geraldine Librandi
Holly . . . . Olga Sanchez
Roy . . . . Charley McQuary
   Time: The present. Place: An American City.
One intermission.

HALCYON DAYS. By Steven Dietz. Director,
Jeff Steitzer; scenery, Vicki Smith; costumes,
Sam Fleming; lighting, Rick Paulsen; sound,
Steven M. Klein.
Eddie . . . . Laurence Ballard
Tommy. . . . . Mark Chamberlin
Blonigen. . . . . Peter Silbert
Ruby . . . . Novel Sholars
Linda. . . . . Stephanie Shine
Raper . . . . Michael Winters
Patricia . . . . Linda Emond
Alex . . . . Andrew DeRycke
   Time: October, 1983. Place: Washington, D.C.
and St. George's, Grenada. One intermission.

Seattle: Empty Space Theater

(Artistic director, Kurt Beattie; managing director, Melissa Hines)

DR. TERROR'S 3-D HOUSE OF THEATER. Created by the Empty Space Ensemble: Kurt Beattie, Katie Forgette, Rex McDowell, David Pichette, Peter Silbert, Jeff Steitzer, R. Hamilton Wright; scenery, Charlene Hall; costumes, Paul Chi-Ming Louey; lighting, Rick Paulsen; sound, David Pascal.

Dr. Terror	Kurt Beattie
Katie	Katie Forgette
Kit	Kit Harris
Rex	Rex McDowell
Melissa	Melissa Parkerton
David	David Pichette
Chris	Christopher Shanahan
Peter	Peter Silbert
Jeff	Jeff Steitzer
Bob	R. Hamilton Wright

BLOOD ORGY OF THE BERMUDA TRIANGLE ZOMBIE ASSASSINS. Musical with book and lyrics by Eddie Levi Lee and Larry Larson; music by Peter Silbert, David Pascal and John Engerman. Scenery, Charlene Hall; costumes, Paul Chi-Ming Louey; lighting, Rick Paulsen; sound, David Pascal.

Eurethra Maalox	Katie Forgette
Eva	Kit Harris
Buckbill	Rex McDowell
Zombies	Melissa Parkerton, Christopher Shanahan
Chalmers	David Pichette
Dr. Mengele	Peter Silbert
Rufus	Jeff Steitzer
Rod Lance	R. Hamilton Wright

JAR THE FLOOR. By Cheryl L. West. Director, Gilbert McCauley; scenery, Don Yanik; costumes, Sarah Campbell; lighting, Brian Duea; sound, David Pascal.

Lola	Crystal Laws Green
MaDear	Tamu Gray
MayDee	Jacqueline Moscou

EMPTY SPACE THEATER, SEATTLE—David Pichette, Katie Forgette, R. Hamilton Wright and Jeff Steitzer in a scene from *Dr. Terror's 3-D House of Theater* created by the Empty Space Ensemble

Raisa . . . . Laurie Thomas
Vennie . . . . Mari-lynn

DARK RAPTURE. By Eric Overmyer. Director,
Kurt Beattie; scenery, Peggy McDonald; cos-
tumes, Paul Chi-Ming Louey; lighting, Michael
Wellborn; sound, David Pascal.
Julia . . . . Katie Forgette
Napoleon House Waiter . . . . . . Hunt Holman

Renee; Waitress . . . . Jessica Marlowe
Danny; Tony; Mr. Souza;
    Lounge Singer . . . . Rex McDowell
Babcock; Nizam. . . . . David Mong
Lexington; Scones . . . . David Pichette
Ron; Waiter . . . . Christopher Shanahan
Ray. . . . . Peter Silbert
Max. . . . . Sally Smythe
Vegas; Mathis; Bartender . . R. Hamilton Wright

Seattle: Intiman Theater Company

(Artistic director, Elizabeth Huddle; managing director, Peter Davis)

THE KENTUCKY CYCLE. By Robert
Schenkkan. June 1, 1991. Director, Warner
Shook; scenery, Michael Olich; costumes,
Frances Kenny; lighting, Peter Maradudin; sound,
Jim Ragland.
    With Patrick Broemeling, Lillian Garrett-
Groag, Demene Hall, Charles Hallahan, Ronald

Hippe, Gregory Itzin, Anthony Lee, Scott
MacDonald, Tuck Milligan, Randy Oglesby,
Jeanne Paulsen, Jillayne Sorenson, Michael
Winters.
    Presented in two parts and nine acts. (Winner of
the 1991-92 Pulitzer Prize.)

Seattle: Seattle Repertory Theater

(Artistic director, Daniel Sullivan)

INSPECTING CAROL. By Daniel Sullivan in
collaboration with the resident acting company.
December 11, 1991. Director, Daniel Sullivan;
scenery, Andrew Wood Boughton; costumes,
Robert Wojewodski; lighting, Rick Paulsen;
music composer, Norman Durkee; sound Michael
Holten.
M.J. McMann . . . . Barbara Dirickson
Wayne Wellacre. . . . . . . R. Hamilton Wright
Zorah Bloch . . . . Marianne Owen
Luther Radley . . . . Daniel Spiegelman
Dorothy Three-Hapgood . . . . . Jeannie Carson
Sidney Carolton. . . . . . William Biff McGuire
Phil M. Small . . . . Ethan Phillips
Walter E. Parsons . . . . . Mark Kenneth Smaltz
Kevin Emery. . . . . Larry Paulsen

Bart Jacob Frances . . . . Alban Dennis
Lary Vauxhall . . . . John Aylward
Betty Andrews . . . . Mary Anne Seibert
    One intermission.

REDWOOD CURTAIN. By Lanford Wilson.
January 8, 1992 (co-produced with Circle
Repertory Company). Director, Marshall W.
Mason; scenery, John Lee Beatty; costumes,
Laura Crow; lighting, Dennis Parichy; original
music, Peter Kater; sound, Chuck London/Stewart
Werner.
Lyman. . . . . David Morse
Geri. . . . . Kimiko Cazanov
Geneva . . . . Debra Monk
    No intermission.

Stamford, Conn.: Stamford Theater Works

(Artistic director, Steve Karp)

ELAINE'S DAUGHTER. By Mayo Simon.
February 6, 1992. Director, Steve Karp; scenery,
Jerry Rojo; costumes, Chris Lawton; lighting and
sound, Rob Birarelli.
Beth . . . . Nela Wagman

Elaine . . . . Marilyn Rockafellow
Tom . . . . Stephen Grafenstine
Gus . . . . Ronn Munro
Eliot . . . . Eric Nolan
    One intermission.

Teaneck, N.J.: American Stage Company

(Artistic director, Paul Sorvino)

WHITE LIES. Revue with sketches and lyrics by Douglas Carter Beane; music by Douglas Carter Beane and Keith Thompson. November 27, 1991. Director, Greg Ganakas; scenery, Dennis C. Maulden; costumes and lighting, John Carver Sullivan; musical director, Keith Thompson; choreography, Greg Ganakis.

With Adinah Alexander, Randl Ash, Don Goodspeed, Cheryl Tern, Mary Testa.

No intermission.

Venice, Calif.: Theater Works

(Producing director, Susan Albert Loewenberg)

THE PLAY'S THE THING. By Kirsten Dahl. March 11, 1992. Director, Robert Robinson.

Erin Coffey	Valerie Landsburg
Cabbie; Nicholae; Bartender . Kevin McDermott Vagrant; Armando;	
Josh Levine	William Palmieri
Sam Levine	Joshua Rifkind
Donny Le Grand	Al Ruscio
Della Doucet	Elizabeth Ruscio
Angie	Brenda Varda

Washington, D.C.: Arena Stage

(Artistic director, Douglas C. Wager; executive director, Stephen Richard)

A WONDERFUL LIFE. Musical based on the film *It's a Wonderful Life*; book and lyrics by Sheldon Harnick; music by Joe Raposo. November 21, 1991. Director, Douglas C. Wager; choreography, Joey McKneely; musical director, Jeffrey Saver; scenery, Thomas Lynch; costumes, Jess Goldstein; lighting, Allen Lee Hughes; sound, Susan R. White.

George Bailey	Casey Biggs
Harry Bailey	Scott Wise
Mr. Potter	Richard Bauer
Sam Wainwright	James Hindman
Clarence	Jeffrey V. Thompson
Joseph	Ralph Cosham
Mr. Martini; Tom Bailey	Terrence Currier
Ernie	Michael W. Howell
Milly Bailey	Halo Wines
Uncle Billy	Henry Strozier
Violet Bick	Deanna Wells
Mary Hatch	Brigid Brady
Ruth Reynolds	Kiki Moritsugu

Others: Hannahlee Casler, Heather Casler, Tyler John Chasez, Gabrielle Dunmyer, Joel Eskovitz, Tracy Flint, Michael Forrest, Harriett D. Foy, Kari Lynn Ginsburg, M.E. Hart, Tana Hicken, David Marks, John McInnis, Embrey Minor, Pamela Nyberg, Benjamin H. Salinas, David Truskinoff, Wendell Wright.

TRINIDAD SISTERS. By Mustapha Matura; based on Anton Chekhov's *Three Sisters*. March 6, 1992. Director, Clinton Turner Davis; scenery, Charles McClennahan; costumes, Marjorie Slaiman; lighting, Nancy Schertler; sound, Susan R. White.

Olga	Franchelle Stewart Dorn
Irene	Saundra Quarterman
Marsha	Gail Grate
Charles	Wendell Wright
Taylor	Teagle F. Bougere
St. Clair	M.E. Hart
Floorie	Beatrice Winde
Version	Ralph Cosham
Andre	Marcus Naylor
Kelly	David Toney
Nova	Shona Tucker

Time: Act I: September, 1939. Act II: February, 1940. Act III: June, 1942. Act IV: April, 1944. Place: Port-of-Spain, Trinidad.

FORD'S THEATER, WASHINGTON, D.C.—Patrick Cassidy and Pamela Isaacs with younger members of the cast of *Conrack: A New Musical*, book by Granville Burgess, music by Lee Pockriss and lyrics by Anne Croswell

Washington, D.C.: Ford's Theater

(Producing director, Frankie Hewitt; managing director, Michael Gennaro)

CONRACK: A NEW MUSICAL. Book by Granville Burgess; lyrics by Anne Croswell; music by Lee Pockriss. February 29, 1992. Director, Lonny Price; choreographer, Gregg Burge; scenery, Ann Sheffield; costumes, Charlotte M. Yetman; lighting, Stuart Duke; musical direction, Tim Weil.

Pat Conroy	Patrick Cassidy
Prophet	Joran Corneal
Kate	Tina Fabrique
Cindy Lou	Natalia Harris
Dr. Jackie Brooks	Pamela Isaacs
Top Cat	Cory King
Mary	Nicole Leach
Anna	LaShayla Logan
Quik Fella	Larry Marshall
Sam	Norman Matlock
Mr. Hudson	Roy Meachum
Edna Graves	Ella Mitchell
Doug Deese	Kevin Reese
Mrs. Brown	Myra Taylor
Dr. Henry Piedmont	Evan Thompson
Richard	Baakari Wilder

Time: 1969. Place: Various locations in Beaufort, South Carolina and on Yamacraw, one of the Sea Islands off the coast of South Carolina. One intermission.

Waterford, Conn. Eugene O'Neill Theater Center

(Artistic director, Lloyd Richards; president, George C. White)

National Playwrights Conference, July 11-27, 1991.

WELLER by Gannon Kenney, directed by Amy Saltz.

DINOSAUR DREAMS by Tom Szentgyorgyi, directed by William Partlan.

WASHINGTON SQUARE MOVES by Matthew Witten, directed by Clinton Turner Davis.

ANGEL OF DEATH by Charlie Schulman, directed by Amy Saltz.

HOME GROWN by Rick Cleveland, directed by William Partlan.

PIGS AND BUGS by Paul Zimmerman, directed by Walter Dallas.

VANDALS by Jeffrey Hatcher, directed by Clinton Turner Davis.

AND FAT FREDDY'S BLUES by P.J. Barry, directed by Amy Saltz.

CHARISMA by John Darago, directed by William Partlan.

Williamstown, Mass.: Williamstown Theater Festival

(Artistic director, Peter Hunt)

DEFYING GRAVITY. By Jane Anderson. July 17, 1991. Director, Jenny Sullivan; scenery, Hugh Landwehr; costumes, David Murin; lighting, Arden Fingerhut; sound, Martin Desjardins; aerialistics, Andre Simard; flying by Foy.

Monet	Tom Tammi
Elizabeth	Genie Francis
Teacher	Kate Burton
Edith	Audra Lindley
Ed	Joe Ponazecki
Donna	Kecia Lewis-Evans
C.B.	Kevin Geer
Man of Many Faces	Bruce Faulk
Jason	Owen Broch
Matthew	Eris Johnson-Smith
Bradley	Ryan Luczynski
Patricia	Amy Hunt
Jennifer	Schuyler Montgomery-Nassif
Heather	Maria Perry
2d Teacher	Alison Laslett
Degenerate Ground Crew	Barry Tropp
Aerialists/Astronauts	Esther Fally, Alain Veilleux

Class: Alexander Elvin, Kendall Johnson-Smith, Brianan Kassin, Pete Ticconi, Andrew Tynan.

One intermission.

FACTS AND
FIGURES

LONG RUNS ON BROADWAY

The following shows have run 500 or more continuous performances in a single production, usually the first, not including previews or extra non-profit performances, allowing for vacation layoffs and special one-booking engagements, but not including return engagements after a show has gone on tour. In all cases, the numbers were obtained directly from the show's production offices. Where there are title similarities, the production is identified as follows: (p) straight play version, (m) musical version, (r) revival.

THROUGH MAY 31, 1992

(PLAYS MARKED WITH ASTERISK WERE STILL PLAYING JUNE 1, 1992)

Plays	Number Performances	Plays	Number Performances
A Chorus Line	6,137	Ain't Misbehavin'	1,604
Oh! Calcutta! (r)	5,959	Mary, Mary	1,572
*Cats	4,029	Evita	1,567
42nd Street	3,486	The Voice of the Turtle	1,557
Grease	3,388	Barefoot in the Park	1,530
Fiddler on the Roof	3,242	Brighton Beach Memoirs	1,530
Life With Father	3,224	Dreamgirls	1,522
Tobacco Road	3,182	Mame (m)	1,508
Hello, Dolly!	2,844	Same Time, Next Year	1,453
My Fair Lady	2,717	Arsenic and Old Lace	1,444
Annie	2,377	The Sound of Music	1,443
Man of La Mancha	2,328	Me and My Girl	1,420
Abie's Irish Rose	2,327	How to Succeed in Business	
Oklahoma!	2,212	Without Really Trying	1,417
*Les Misérables	2,116	Hellzapoppin	1,404
Pippin	1,944	The Music Man	1,375
South Pacific	1,925	Funny Girl	1,348
The Magic Show	1,920	Mummenschanz	1,326
*The Phantom of the Opera	1,815	Angel Street	1,295
Deathtrap	1,793	Lightnin'	1,291
Gemini	1,788	Promises, Promises	1,281
Harvey	1,775	The King and I	1,246
Dancin'	1,774	Cactus Flower	1,234
La Cage aux Folles	1,761	Sleuth	1,222
Hair	1,750	Torch Song Trilogy	1,222
The Wiz	1,672	1776	1,217
Born Yesterday	1,642	Equus	1,209
The Best Little Whorehouse in		Sugar Babies	1,208
Texas	1,639	Guys and Dolls	1,200

LONG RUNS OFF BROADWAY

Plays	Number Performances	Plays	Number Performances
*The Fantasticks	13,310	True West	762
*Nunsense	2,680	Isn't It Romantic	733
The Threepenny Opera	2,611	Dime a Dozen	728
Forbidden Broadway 1982-87	2,332	The Pocket Watch	725
Little Shop of Horrors	2,209	The Connection	722
Godspell	2,124	The Passion of Dracula	714
*Perfect Crime	2,091	Adaptation & Next	707
Vampire Lesbians of Sodom	2,024	Oh! Calcutta!	704
Jacques Brel	1,847	Scuba Duba	692
Vanities	1,785	The Foreigner	686
You're a Good Man Charlie Brown	1,597	The Knack	685
The Blacks	1,408	The Club	674
One Mo' Time	1,372	The Balcony	672
Let My People Come	1,327	Penn & Teller	666
Driving Miss Daisy	1,195	America Hurrah	634
The Hot l Baltimore	1,166	Oil City Symphony	626
I'm Getting My Act Together and Taking It on the Road	1,165	Hogan's Goat	607
Little Mary Sunshine	1,143	Beehive	600
Steel Magnolias	1,126	The Trojan Women	600
El Grande de Coca-Cola	1,114	The Dining Room	583
Tamara	1,036	Krapp's Last Tape & The Zoo Story	582
One Flew Over the Cuckoo's Nest (r)	1,025	The Dumbwaiter & The Collection	578
The Boys in the Band	1,000	Forbidden Broadway 1990-91 (r)	576
Fool for Love	1,000	Dames at Sea	575
Other People's Money	990	The Crucible (r)	571
Cloud 9	971	The Iceman Cometh (r)	565
Sister Mary Ignatius Explains It All for You & The Actor's Nightmare	947	The Hostage (r)	545
Your Own Thing	933	What's a Nice Country Like You Doing in a State Like This?	543
Curley McDimple	931	Forbidden Broadway 1988-89	534
Leave It to Jane (r)	928	Frankie and Johnny in the Clair de Lune	533
*Forever Plaid	882	Six Characters in Search of an Author (r)	529
The Mad Show	871	The Dirtiest Show in Town	509
Scrambled Feet	831	Happy Ending & Day of Absence	504
The Effect of Gamma Rays on Man-in-the-Moon Marigolds	819	Greater Tuna	501
A View From the Bridge (r)	780	A Shayna Maidel	501
The Boy Friend (r)	763	The Boys From Syracuse (r)	500

NEW YORK DRAMA CRITICS CIRCLE AWARDS, 1935-36 to 1991-92

Listed below are the New York Drama Critics Circle Awards from 1935-36 through 1991-92 classified as follows: (1) Best American Play, (2) Best Foreign Play, (3) Best Musical, (4) Best, regardless of category (this category was established by new voting rules in 1962-63 and did not exist prior to that year).

1935-36—(1) Winterset

1936-37—(1) High Tor

1937-38—(1) Of Mice and Men, (2) Shadow and Substance

1938-39—(1) No award, (2) The White Steed

1939-40—(1) The Time of Your Life

1940-41—(1) Watch on the Rhine, (2) The Corn Is Green

1941-42—(1) No award, (2) Blithe Spirit

1942-43—(2) The Patriots

1943-44—(2) Jacobowsky and the Colonel

1944-45—(1) The Glass Menagerie

1945-46—(3) Carousel

1946-47—(1) All My Sons, (2) No Exit, (3) Brigadoon

1947-48—(1) A Streetcar Named Desire, (2) The Winslow Boy

1948-49—(1) Death of a Salesman, (2) The Madwoman of Chaillot, (3) South Pacific

1949-50—(1) The Member of the Wedding, (2) The Cocktail Party, (3) The Consul

1950-51—(1) Darkness at Noon, (2) The Lady's Not for Burning, (3) Guys and Dolls

1951-52—(1) I Am a Camera, (2) Venus Observed, (3) Pal Joey (Special citation to Don Juan in Hell)

1952-53—(1) Picnic, (2) The Love of Four Colonels, (3) Wonderful Town

1953-54—(1) Teahouse of the August Moon, (2) Ondine, (3) The Golden Apple

1954-55—(1) Cat on a Hot Tin Roof, (2) Witness for the Prosecution, (3) The Saint of Bleecker Street

1955-56—(1) The Diary of Anne Frank, (2) Tiger at the Gates, (3) My Fair Lady

1956-57—(1) Long Day's Journey Into Night, (2) The Waltz of the Toreadors, (3) The Most Happy Fella

1957-58—(1) Look Homeward, Angel, (2) Look Back in Anger, (3) The Music Man

1958-59—(1) A Raisin in the Sun, (2) The Visit, (3) La Plume de Ma Tante

1959-60—(1) Toys in the Attic, (2) Five Finger Exercise, (3) Fiorello!

1960-61—(1) All the Way Home, (2) A Taste of Honey, (3) Carnival

1961-62—(1) The Night of the Iguana, (2) A Man for All Seasons, (3) How to Succeed in Business Without Really Trying

1962-63—(4) Who's Afraid of Virginia Woolf? (Special citation to Beyond the Fringe)

1963-64—(4) Luther, (3) Hello, Dolly! (Special citation to The Trojan Women)

1964-65—(4) The Subject Was Roses, (3) Fiddler on the Roof

1965-66—(1) The Persecution and Assassination of Marat as Performed by the Inmates of the Asylum of Charenton Under the Direction of the Marquis de Sade, (3) Man of La Mancha

1966-67—(4) The Homecoming, (3) Cabaret

1967-68—(4) Rosencrantz and Guildenstern Are Dead, (3) Your Own Thing

1968-69—(4) The Great White Hope, (3) 1776

1969-70—(4) Borstal Boy, (1) The Effect of Gamma Rays on Man-in-the-Moon Marigolds, (3) Company

1970-71—(4) Home, (1) The House of Blue Leaves, (3) Follies

1971-72—(4) That Championship Season, (2) The Screens, (3) Two Gentlemen of Verona (Special citation to Sticks and Bones and Old Times)

1972-73—(4) The Changing Room, (1) The Hot l Baltimore, (3) A Little Night Music

1973-74—(4) The Contractor, (1) Short Eyes, (3) Candide

1974-75—(4) Equus, (1) The Taking of Miss Janie, (3) A Chorus Line

1975-76—(4) Travesties, (1) Streamers, (3) Pacific Overtures

1976-77—(4) Otherwise Engaged, (1) American Buffalo, (3) Annie

1977-78—(4) Da, (3) Ain't Misbehavin'

1978-79—(4) The Elephant Man, (3) Sweeney Todd, the Demon Barber of Fleet Street

1979-80—(4) Talley's Folly, (2) Betrayal, (3) Evita (Special Citation to Peter Brook's Le Center International de Créations Théâtrales for its repertory)

1980-81—(4) A Lesson From Aloes, (1) Crimes of the Heart (Special citations to Lena Horne: The Lady and Her Music and the New York Shakespeare Festival production of The Pirates of Penzance)

1981-82—(4) The Life & Adventures of Nicholas Nickleby, (1) A Soldier's Play
1982-83—(4) Brighton Beach Memoirs, (2) Plenty, (3) Little Shop of Horrors (Special citation to Young Playwrights Festival)
1983-84—(4) The Real Thing; (1) Glengarry Glen Ross, (3) Sunday in the Park With George (Special citation to Samuel Beckett for the body of his work)
1984-85—(4) Ma Rainey's Black Bottom
1985-86—(4) A Lie of the Mind, (2) Benefactors (Special citation to The Search for Signs of Intelligent Life in the Universe)
1986-87—(4) Fences, (2) Les Liaisons Danger-euses, (3) Les Misérables
1987-88—(4) Joe Turner's Come and Gone, (2) The Road to Mecca, (3) Into the Woods
1988-89—(4) The Heidi Chronicles, (2) Aristocrats (Special citation to Bill Irwin for Largely New York)
1989-90—(4) The Piano Lesson, (2) Privates on Parade, (3) City of Angels
1990-91—(4) Six Degrees of Separation, (2) Our Country's Good, (3) The Will Rogers Follies (Special citation to Eileen Atkins for her portrayal of Virginia Woolf in A Room of One's Own)
1991-92—(4) Dancing at Lughnasa, (1) Two Trains Running

NEW YORK DRAMA CRITICS CIRCLE VOTING, 1991-92

The New York Drama Critics Circle voted Brian Friel's *Dancing at Lughnasa* the best play of the season on a first-ballot majority of 11 votes (John Beaufort, *Christian Science Monitor*; William A. Henry III, *Time*; Melanie Kirkpatrick, *Wall Street Journal*; Howard Kissel, New York *Daily News*; Michael Kuchwara, The Associated Press; Jacques le Sourd, Gannett newspapers; Edith Oliver, *The New Yorker*; William Raidy, Newhouse newspapers; Jerry Tallmer, New York *Post*; Douglas Watt, New York *Daily News*; Edwin Wilson, *Wall Street Journal*), against 3 votes for Donald Margulies's *Sight Unseen* (Michael Feingold, *The Village Voice*; Mimi Kramer, *The New Yorker*; John Simon, *New York*), 2 for August Wilson's *Two Trains Running* (Jeremy Gerard, *Variety*; Linda Winer, *Newsday*) and 1 each for Herb Gardner's *Conversations With My Father* (Julius Novick, *Newsday*), Terrence McNally's *Lips Together, Teeth Apart* (Jan Stuart, *Newsday*) and Scott McPherson's *Marvin's Room* (Clive Barnes, New York *Post*). In addition to the 19 voting members, Jack Kroll of *Newsweek* and David Patrick Stearns of *USA Today* were absent, and Mel Gussow and Frank Rich of the New York *Times* are non-voting members of the Circle, per their paper's policy against its critics participating in award-giving.

The Critics having selected a foreign play as best regardless of category, they then proceeded to select a best American play. No play received a majority of the votes on the first ballot, so the Circle proceeded to a second ballot on which, again no play receiving a majority, the top three vote-getters (four plays, actually, since there was a tie for third place) went on to a third ballot where, according to this year's Circle voting rules, a simple plurality sufficed to determine a winner. *Two Trains Running* was declared the winner of the Critics Award for best American play on this third ballot with 6 votes (Beaufort, Gerard, Henry, Raidy, Watt, Winer) against 5 for *Marvin's Room* (Barnes, Kirkpatrick, Kuchwara, le Sourd, Stuart) and 4 each for *Conversations With My Father* (Kramer, Novick, Tallmer, Wilson) and *Sight Unseen* (Feingold, Kissel, Oliver, Simon).

After a discussion of this season's musicals including *Crazy for You*, *Falsettos* and *Jelly's Last Jam*, the Critics voted not to award a best-musical citation this year because none of the major candidates was a completely new work.

CHOICES OF SOME OTHER CRITICS

Critic	Best Play	Best Musical
Alvin Klein New York *Times* Regional, WNYC	Dancing at Lughnasa	Falsettos
Stewart Klein WNYW-TV	Dancing at Lughnasa	Guys and Dolls Crazy for You
Jeffrey Lyons WPIX-TV/CBS Radio	Conversations With My Father	Crazy for You
Leida Snow WNEW-AM	Lips Together, Teeth Apart	Jelly's Last Jam
Allan Wallach *Newsday*	Dancing at Lughnasa	Falsettos Crazy for You

PULITZER PRIZE WINNERS, 1916-17 TO 1991-92

1916-17—No award
1917-18—Why Marry?, by Jesse Lynch Williams
1918-19—No award
1919-20—Beyond the Horizon, by Eugene O'Neill
1920-21—Miss Lulu Bett, by Zona Gale
1921-22—Anna Christie, by Eugene O'Neill
1922-23—Icebound, by Owen Davis
1923-24—Hell-Bent fer Heaven, by Hatcher Hughes
1924-25—They Knew What They Wanted, by Sidney Howard
1925-26—Craig's Wife, by George Kelly
1926-27—In Abraham's Bosom, by Paul Green
1927-28—Strange Interlude, by Eugene O'Neill
1928-29—Street Scene, by Elmer Rice
1929-30—The Green Pastures, by Marc Connelly
1930-31—Alison's House, by Susan Glaspell
1931-32—Of Thee I Sing, by George S. Kaufman, Morrie Ryskind, Ira and George Gershwin
1932-33—Both Your Houses, by Maxwell Anderson
1933-34—Men in White, by Sidney Kingsley
1934-35—The Old Maid, by Zoë Akins
1935-36—Idiot's Delight, by Robert E. Sherwood
1936-37—You Can't Take It With You, by Moss Hart and George S. Kaufman
1937-38—Our Town, by Thornton Wilder
1938-39—Abe Lincoln in Illinois, by Robert E. Sherwood
1939-40—The Time of Your Life, by William Saroyan
1940-41—There Shall Be No Night, by Robert E. Sherwood
1941-42—No award
1942-43—The Skin of Our Teeth, by Thornton Wilder
1943-44—No award

1944-45—Harvey, by Mary Chase
1945-46—State of the Union, by Howard Lindsay and Russel Crouse
1946-47—No award
1947-48—A Streetcar Named Desire, by Tennessee Williams
1948-49—Death of a Salesman, by Arthur Miller
1949-50—South Pacific, by Richard Rodgers, Oscar Hammerstein II and Joshua Logan
1950-51—No award
1951-52—The Shrike, by Joseph Kramm
1952-53—Picnic, by William Inge
1953-54—The Teahouse of the August Moon, by John Patrick
1954-55—Cat on a Hot Tin Roof, by Tennessee Williams
1955-56—The Diary of Anne Frank, by Frances Goodrich and Albert Hackett
1956-57—Long Day's Journey Into Night, by Eugene O'Neill
1957-58—Look Homeward, Angel, by Ketti Frings
1958-59—J.B., by Archibald MacLeish
1959-60—Fiorello!, by Jerome Weidman, George Abbott, Sheldon Harnick and Jerry Bock
1960-61—All the Way Home, by Tad Mosel
1961-62—How to Succeed in Business Without Really Trying, by Abe Burrows, Willie Gilbert, Jack Weinstock and Frank Loesser
1962-63—No award
1963-64—No award
1964-65—The Subject Was Roses, by Frank D. Gilroy
1965-66—No award
1966-67—A Delicate Balance, by Edward Albee

1967-68—No award
1968-69—The Great White Hope, by Howard Sackler
1969-70—No Place To Be Somebody, by Charles Gordone
1970-71—The Effect of Gamma Rays on Man-in-the-Moon Marigolds, by Paul Zindel
1971-72—No award
1972-73—That Championship Season, by Jason Miller
1973-74—No award
1974-75—Seascape, by Edward Albee
1975-76—A Chorus Line, by Michael Bennett, James Kirkwood, Nicholas Dante, Marvin Hamlisch and Edward Kleban
1976-77—The Shadow Box, by Michael Cristofer
1977-78—The Gin Game, by D.L. Coburn

1978-79—Buried Child, by Sam Shepard
1979-80—Talley's Folly, by Lanford Wilson
1980-81—Crimes of the Heart, by Beth Henley
1981-82—A Soldier's Play, by Charles Fuller
1982-83—'night, Mother, by Marsha Norman
1983-84—Glengarry Glen Ross, by David Mamet
1984-85—Sunday in the Park With George, by James Lapine and Stephen Sondheim
1985-86—No award
1986-87—Fences, by August Wilson
1987-88—Driving Miss Daisy, by Alfred Uhry
1988-89—The Heidi Chronicles, by Wendy Wasserstein
1989-90—The Piano Lesson, by August Wilson
1990-91—Lost in Yonkers, by Neil Simon
1991-92—The Kentucky Cycle by Robert Schenkkan

THE KENTUCKY CYCLE—Charles Hallahan (*top*) and Tuck Milligan in the world premiere production at Intiman Theater, Seattle, of the play by Robert Schenkkan, winner of the 1992 Pulitzer Prize

THE TONY AWARDS, 1991-92

The American Theater Wing's Antoinette Perry (Tony) Awards are presented annually in recognition of distinguished artistic achievement in the Broadway theater. The League of American Theaters and Producers and the American Theater Wing present the Tony Awards, founded by the Wing in 1947. Legitimate theater productions opening in eligible Broadway theaters during the Tony eligibility season of the current year—May 2, 1991 to April 29, 1992—are considered for Tony nominations.

The Tony Awards Administration Committee appoints the Tony Awards Nominating Committee which makes the actual nominations. The 1991-92 Nominating Committee consisted of Jerry Bock, composer; Ted Chapin, theater executive; Alvin Colt, costume designer; Arthur Gelb, foundation president and journalist; Martin Gottfried, author; Mary Henderson, theater historian; George S. Irving, actor; Fran Kumin, theater administrator; Stuart Little, theater executive; Carole Rothman, producer-director; Suzanne Sato, arts executive; Howard Stein, theater educator.

The Tony awards are voted from the list of nominees by the members of the governing boards of the five theater artists' organizations: Actors' Equity Association, the Dramatists Guild, the Society of Stage Directors and Choreographers, the United Scenic Artists and the Casting Society of America, plus the members of the designated first-night theater press, the board of directors of the American Theater Wing and the membership of the League of American Theaters and Producers. Because of fluctuations within these boards, the size of the Tony electorate varies from year to year. In the 1991-92 season, there were 651 qualified Tony voters.

The list of 1991-92 nominees follows, with winners in each category listed in **bold face type.**

BEST PLAY (award goes to both author and producer). *Dancing at Lughnasa* by **Brian Friel**, produced by **Noel Pearson, Bill Kenwright, Joseph Harris**; *Four Baboons Adoring the Sun* by John Guare, produced by Lincoln Center Theater, Andre Bishop, Bernard Gersten; *Two Shakespearean Actors* by Richard Nelson, produced by Lincoln Center Theater, Gregory Mosher, Bernard Gersten; *Two Trains Running* by August Wilson, produced by Yale Repertory Theater, Stan Wojewodski Jr., Center Theater Group/Ahmanson Theater, Gordon Davidson, Jujamcyn Theaters, Benjamin Mordecai, Huntington Theater Company, Seattle Repertory Theater, Old Globe Theater.

BEST MUSICAL (award goes to the producer). *Crazy for You* produced by **Roger Horchow, Elizabeth Williams**; *Falsettos* produced by Barry and Fran Weissler; *Five Guys Named Moe* produced by Cameron Mackintosh; *Jelly's Last Jam* produced by Margo Lion, Pamela Koslow, PolyGram Diversified Entertainment, 126 Second Avenue Corp./Hal Luftig, Roger Hess, Jujamcyn Theaters/TV Asahi, Herb Alpert.

BEST BOOK OF A MUSICAL. *Crazy for You* by Ken Ludwig; *Falsettos* by **William Finn** and **James Lapine**; *Five Guys Named Moe* by Clarke Peters; *Jelly's Last Jam* by George C. Wolfe.

BEST ORIGINAL SCORE (music & lyrics) WRITTEN FOR THE THEATER. *Falsettos*, music and lyrics by **William Finn**; *Jelly's Last Jam*, music by Jelly Roll Morton and Luther Henderson, lyrics by Susan Birkenhead; *Metro*, mucic by Janusz Stoklosa, lyrics by Agata and Maryna Miklaszewska and Mary Bracken Phillips; *Nick & Nora*, music by Charles Strouse, lyrics by Richard Maltby Jr.

BEST LEADING ACTOR IN A PLAY. Alan Alda in *Jake's Women*, Alec Baldwin in *A Streetcar Named Desire*, Brian Bedford in *Two Shakespearean Actors*, **Judd Hirsch** in *Conversations With My Father*.

BEST LEADING ACTRESS IN A PLAY. Jane Alexander in *The Visit*, Stockard Channing in *Four Baboons Adoring the Sun*, **Glenn Close** in *Death and the Maiden*, Judith Ivey in *Park Your Car in Harvard Yard*.

BEST LEADING ACTOR IN A MUSICAL. Harry Groener in *Crazy for You*, **Gregory Hines** in *Jelly's Last Jam*, Nathan Lane in *Guys and Dolls*, Michael Rupert in *Falsettos*.

BEST LEADING ACTRESS IN A MUSICAL. Jodi Benson in *Crazy for You*, Josie de Guzman in *Guys and Dolls*, Sophie Hayden in *The Most Happy Fella*, **Faith Prince** in *Guys and Dolls*.

BEST FEATURED ACTOR IN A PLAY. Roscoe Lee Browne in *Two Trains Running*, **Larry Fishburne** in *Two Trains Running*, Zeljko Ivanek in *Two Shakespearean Actors*, Tony Shalhoub in *Conversations With My Father*.

BEST FEATURED ACTRESS IN A PLAY. **Brid Brennan** in *Dancing at Lughnasa*, Rosaleen Linehan in *Dancing at Lughnasa*, Cynthia Martells in *Two Trains Running*, Dearbhla Molloy in *Dancing at Lughnasa*.

BEST FEATURED ACTOR IN A MUSICAL. Bruce Adler in *Crazy for You*, Keith David in *Jelly's Last Jam*, Jonathan Kaplan in *Falsettos*, **Scott Waara** in *The Most Happy Fella*.

BEST FEATURED ACTRESS IN A MUSICAL. Liz Larsen in *The Most Happy Fella*, **Tonya Pinkins** in *Jelly's Last Jam*, Vivian Reed in *The High Rollers Social and Pleasure Club*, Barbara Walsh in *Falsettos*.

BEST DIRECTION OF A PLAY. Peter Hall for *Four Baboons Adoring the Sun*, **Patrick Mason** for *Dancing at Lughnasa*, Jack O'Brien for *Two Shakespearean Actors*, Daniel Sullivan for *Conversations With My Father*.

BEST DIRECTION OF A MUSICAL. James Lapine for *Falsettos*, Mike Ockrent for *Crazy for You*, George C. Wolfe for *Jelly's Last Jam*, **Jerry Zaks** for *Guys and Dolls*.

BEST SCENIC DESIGN. John Lee Beatty for *A Small Family Business*, Joe Vanek for *Dancing at Lughnasa*, Robin Wagner for *Jelly's Last Jam*, **Tony Walton** for *Guys and Dolls*.

BEST COSTUME DESIGN. Jane Greenwood for *Two Shakespearean Actors*, Toni-Leslie James for *Jelly's Last Jam*, **William Ivey Long** for *Crazy for You*, Joe Vanek for *Dancing at Lughnasa*.

BEST LIGHTING DESIGN. **Jules Fisher** for *Jelly's Last Jam*, Paul Gallo for *Crazy for You*, Paul Gallo for *Guys and Dolls*, Richard Pilbrow for *Four Baboons Adoring the Sun*.

BEST CHOREOGRAPHY. Terry John Bates for *Dancing at Lughnasa*, Christopher Chadman for *Guys and Dolls*, Hope Clarke, Ted L. Levy and Gregory Hines for *Jelly's Last Jam*, **Susan Stroman** for *Crazy for You*.

BEST REVIVAL OF A PLAY OR MUSICAL (award goes to the producer). *Guys and Dolls* produced by **Dodger Productions, Roger Berlind, Jujamcyn Theaters/TV Asahi, Kardana Productions, The John F. Kennedy Center for the Performing Arts**; *The Most Happy Fella* produced by The Goodspeed Opera House, Center Theater Group/Ahmanson Theater, Lincoln Center Theater, The Shubert Organization, Japan Satellite Broadcasting/Stagevision; *On Borrowed Time* produced by Circle in the Square Theater, Theordore Mann, Robert Buckley, Paul Libin; *The Visit* produced by Roundabout Theater Company, Todd Haimes, Gene Feist.

TONY HONOR. *The Fantasticks* for excellence in the theater. The long-running musical is currently in its 33d year.

SPECIAL TONY AWARD. **The Goodman Theater of Chicago.**

TONY AWARD WINNERS, 1947-1992

Listed below are the Antoinette Perry (Tony) Award winners in the categories of Best Play and Best Musical from the time these awards were established until the present.

1947— No play or musical award

1948— Mister Roberts; no musical award

1949— Death of a Salesman; Kiss Me, Kate

1950— The Cocktail Party; South Pacific

1951— The Rose Tattoo; Guys and Dolls

1952— The Fourposter; The King and I

1953— The Crucible; Wonderful Town

1954— The Teahouse of the August Moon; Kismet

1955— The Desperate Hours; The Pajama Game

1956— The Diary of Anne Frank; Damn Yankees

1957— Long Day's Journey Into Night; My Fair Lady

1958— Sunrise at Campobello; The Music Man

1959— J.B.; Redhead

1960— The Miracle Worker; Fiorello! and The Sound of Music (tie)

1961— Beckett; Bye Bye Birdie

1962— A Man for All Seasons; How to Succeed in Business Without Really Trying

1963— Who's Afraid of Virginia Woolf?; A Funny Thing Happened on the Way to the Forum

1964— Luther; Hello, Dolly!

1965— The Subject Was Roses; Fiddler on the Roof

1966— The Persecution and Assassination of Marat Performed by the Inmates of the Asylum of Charenton Under the Direction of the Marquis de Sade; Man of La Mancha

1967— The Homecoming; Cabaret

1968— Rosencrantz and Guildenstern Are Dead; Hallelujah, Baby!

1969— The Great White Hope; 1776

1970— Borstal Boy; Applause

1971— Sleuth; Company

1972— Sticks and Bones; Two Gentlemen of Verona

1973— That Championship Season; A Little Night Music

1974— The River Niger; Raisin

1975— Equus; The Wiz

1976— Travesties; A Chorus Line

1977— The Shadow Box; Annie

1978— Da; Ain't Misbehavin'

1979— The Elephant Man; Sweeney Todd, the Demon Barber of Fleet Street

1980— Children of a Lesser God; Evita

1981— Amadeus; 42nd Street

1982— The Life & Adventures of Nicholas Nickleby; Nine

1983— Torch Song Trilogy; Cats

1984— The Real Thing; La Cage aux Folles

1985— Biloxi Blues; Big River

1986— I'm Not Rappaport; The Mystery of Edwin Drood

1987— Fences; Les Misérables

1988— M. Butterfly; The Phantom of the Opera

1989— The Heidi Chronicles; Jerome Robbins' Broadway

1990— The Grapes of Wrath; City of Angels

1991— Lost in Yonkers; The Will Rogers Follies

1992— Dancing at Lughnasa; Crazy for You

THE OBIE AWARDS

The *Village Voice* Off-Broadway (Obie) Awards are given each year for excellence in various categories of off-Broadway (and frequently off-off-Broadway) shows, with close distinctions between these two areas ignored. The 37th annual Obies for the 1991-92 season, listed below, were chosen by a panel of judges chaired by Ross Wetzsteon and comprising *Village Voice* critic C. Carr and guest judges Linda Winer and Max Ferra.

PLAYWRITING. Donald Margulies for *Sight Unseen*, Robbie McCauley for *Sally's Rape*, Paula Vogel for *The Baltimore Waltz*.

SUSTAINED EXCELLENCE IN PLAY-

WRITING. Neal Bell, Romulus Linney.

PERFORMANCE. **Dennis Boutsikaris, Deborah Hedwall** in *Sight Unseen*, **Laura Esterman** in *Marvin's Room*, **Cherry Jones** in *The Baltimore*

Waltz, **James McDaniel** in *Before It Hits Home,* **S. Epatha Merkerson** in *I'm Not Stupid,* **Roger Rees** in *The End of the Day,* **Lynne Thigpen** in *Boesman and Lena.*

SUSTAINED EXCELLENCE IN PERFOR-MANCE. **Larry Bryggman, Randy Danson, Ofelia Gonzales, Nathan Lane.**

DIRECTION. **Anne Bogart** for *The Baltimore Waltz,* **Mark Wing-Davey** for *Mad Forest.*

DESIGN. **John Arnone** for sustained excellence in set design; **Marina Draghici** for the sets and costumes of *Mad Forest.*

SUSTAINED ACHIEVEMENT. **Athol Fugard.**

SPECIAL CITATIONS. **Gerard Alessandrini** for *Forbidden Broadway;* **David Gordon** for *The Mysteries* and *What's So Funny?;* **New York International Festival of the Arts** for producing the plays of Ingmar Bergman, Tadeusz Kantor and Eimuntas Nekrosius during the 1991-92 season; **Public Theater** for producing *'Tis Pity She's a Whore;* **Anna Deavere Smith** for *Fires in the Mirror;* **Jeff Weiss** for *Hot Keys.*

VILLAGE VOICE GRANTS: **Downtown Art Company, Franklin Furnace. Soho Repertory Company.**

ADDITIONAL PRIZES AND AWARDS, 1991-92

The following is a list of major prizes and awards for achievement in the theater this season. In all cases the names and/or titles of the winners appear in **bold face type.**

1991 ELIZABETH HULL-KATE WARRINER AWARD. To the playwright whose work dealt with controversial subjects involving the fields of political, religious or social mores of the time, selected by the Dramatists Guild Council. **Scott McPherson** for *Marvin's Room.*

7th ANNUAL ATCA NEW PLAY AWARD. For an outstanding new play in cross-country theater, voted by a committee of the American Theater Critics Association. *Could I Have This Dance?* by Doug Haverty. Also cited: *Miss Evers' Boys* by David Feldshuh; *American Enterprise* by Jeffrey Sweet.

14th ANNUAL KENNEDY CENTER HONORS. For distinguished achievement by individuals who have made significant contributions to American culture through the arts. **Roy Acuff, Betty Comden and Adolph Green, Fayard and Harold Nicholas, Gregory Peck, Robert Shaw.**

11th ANNUAL WILLIAM INGE AWARD. For lifetime achievement in the American theater. **Peter Shaffer.**

MARGO JONES MEDAL. For lifetime achievement in theater. **Otis L. Guernsey Jr.**

1992 AMERICAN THEATER WING DESIGN AWARDS. For design originating in the U.S., voted by a committee comprising Tish Dace (chair), Henry Hewes, Michael Sommers and Julius Novick. Scenic design, **John Arnone** for *Pericles.* Costume design, **Toni-Leslie James** for *Jelly's Last Jam.* Lighting, **Jules Fisher** for *Two Shakespearean Actors.* Noteworthy unusual effects (puppets), **Ralph Lee** and **Casey Compton** for *Wichikapache Goes Walking* (by the touring Mettawee River Company).

1992 ALAN SCHNEIDER AWARD. For a director who has exhibited exceptional talent through work in a specific community or region. **Charles Newell.**

8th ANNUAL GEORGE AND ELISABETH MARTON AWARD. To an American play-wright, selected by a committee of the Foundation of the Dramatists Guild. **David Hirson** for *La Bête.*

THEATER HALL OF FAME. Annual election by members of the profession of nominees selected by a vote of the American Theater Critics Association. **Stella Adler, Anne Bancroft, Cy Coleman, Charles Gilpin, Theresa Helburn, Hanya Holm, Gene Kelly, Harold Rome, Gene Saks, Patricia Zipprodt.** L. Arnold Weissberger Award for outstanding contribution to the theater: **James M. Nederlander.** Special tributes: **Joseph Papp, Colleen Dewhurst.**

1992 COMMON WEALTH AWARD. For

distinguished service in dramatic arts. **Arthur Miller**.

13th ANNUAL GEORGE OPPENHEIMER/-NEW YORK NEWSDAY AWARD. For the best new American playwright whose work is produced in New York City or on Long Island. **David Hirson** for *La Bête*.

WEXNER PRIZE. For an individual in any artistic field whose consistently innovative work has had significant impact on the arts, selected under the aegis of Ohio State University. **Peter Brook**.

JOSEPH KESSELRING PRIZE. Selected under the aegis of the National Arts Club, by a committee comprising John Guare, Anne Cattaneo and John Lahr. *Angels in America: A Gay Fantasia on National Themes* by Tony Kushner. Honorable mention: *Marvin's Room* by Scott McPherson, *Virgin Molly* by Quincy Long.

1991 JUJAMCYN THEATERS AWARD. Honoring outstanding contribution to the development of creative talent for the theater. **New York Shakespeare Festival**.

LUCILLE LORTEL AWARDS. For achievement off Broadway, voted by a committee comprising Clive Barnes, Jeremy Gerard, Howard Kissel, Alvin Klein, Edith Oliver, Allan Wallach, Edwin Wilson and Lucille Lortel. Body of work, **Terrence McNally**. Play, *Lips Together, Teeth Apart* by Terrence McNally. Musical, *And the World Goes 'Round*, music by John Kander, lyrics by Fred Ebb. Revival, *Boesman and Lena* by Athol Fugard. Direction, **Daniel Sullivan** for *The Substance of Fire*. Performer (tie), **Eileen Atkins** for *A Room of One's Own*, **Ron Rifkin** for *The Substance of Fire*. Special award, **Blue Man Group** for *Tubes*. Lifetime achievement, **Ellen Stewart** as founder of La Mama Experimental Theater Club.

56th ANNUAL DRAMA LEAGUE AWARDS. Distinguished performance, **Glenn Close** for *Death and the Maiden*. Musical theater, **Agnes de Mille**.

GEORGE JEAN NATHAN AWARD. For dramatic criticism. **Jonathan Kalb**.

GEORGE FREEDLEY MEMORIAL AWARD. Presented by the Theater Library Association.

Robert C. Allen for *Horrible Prettiness: Burlesque and American Culture*. Honorable mention, **Norris Houghton** for *Entrances and Exits: A Life in and Out of the Theater*.

48th ANNUAL CLARENCE DERWENT AWARDS. For the most promising male and female actors on the metropolitan scene during the 1991-92 season, sponsored by Actors' Equity Association. **Tonya Pinkins** in *Jelly's Last Jam*; **Patrick Fitzgerald** in *Grandchild of Kings*.

48th ANNUAL THEATER WORLD AWARDS. For outstanding new talent in Broadway and off-Broadway productions during the 1991-92 season, selected by a committee comprising Clive Barnes, Douglas Watt and John Willis. **Talia Balsam** and **Helen Shaver** in *Jake's Women*, **Lindsay Crouse** in *The Homecoming*, **Griffin Dunne** in *Search and Destroy*, **Larry Fishburne** and **Al White** in *Two Trains Running*, **Mel Harris** in *Empty Hearts*, **Jonathan Kaplan** in *Rags* and *Falsettos*, **Jessica Lange** in *A Streetcar Named Desire*, **Laura Linney** in *Sight Unseen*, **Spiro Malas** in *The Most Happy Fella* (Broadway), **Mark Rosenthal** in *Marvin's Room*.

1992 ASTAIRE AWARDS. For achievement in Broadway dance, administered by the Theater Development Fund, voted by a committee comprising Clive Barnes, Howard Kissel, Jack Kroll, Michael Kuchwara, Edith Oliver, Richard Philp, William Raidy and Douglas Watt. **Gregory Hines** of *Jelly's Last Jam*; **Christopher Chadman**, choreographer of *Guys and Dolls*.

42d ANNUAL OUTER CRITICS CIRCLE AWARDS. For outstanding achievement in the 1991-92 New York theater season, voted by an organization of critics on out-of-town periodicals and media. Broadway play, *Dancing at Lughnasa*. Performance by an actor, **Judd Hirsch** in *Conversations With My Father*. Performance by an actress, **Laura Esterman** in *Marvin's Room*. Broadway musical, *Crazy for You*. Actor in a musical, **Nathan Lane** in *Guys and Dolls*. Actress in a musical, **Faith Prince** in *Guys and Dolls* and *Nick & Nora*. Off-Broadway play, *Marvin's Room*. Off-Broadway musical, *Song of Singapore*. Book, music and lyrics of an off-Broadway musical, *Song of Singapore*. Comedy, *Catskills on Broadway*. Revival of a play, *The Visit*. Revival of a musical, *Guys and Dolls*. Director, **Patrick Mason** for *Dancing at Lughnasa*. Choreography, **Susan Stroman** for

Crazy for You. Scenic design, **Robin Wagner**; costume design, **William Ivey Long**; lighting design, **Paul Gallo**, for *Crazy for You.* Debut of an actor, **Larry Fishburne** in *Two Trains Running.* Debut of an actress, **Cynthia Martells** in *Two Trains Running.*

John Gassner Playwriting Award, **Scott McPherson** for *Marvin's Room.* Special awards: **Ellen Stewart** and **La Mama E.T.C.** for 30 years of achievement in theater; **Tony Randall** for the creation of his National Actors Theater.

37th ANNUAL DRAMA DESK AWARDS. For outstanding achievement, voted by an association of New York drama reporters, editors and critics. New play, *Marvin's Room* by Scott McPherson. New musical, *Crazy for You.* Director of a play, **Patrick Mason** for *Dancing at Lughnasa.* Director of a musical, **Jerry Zaks** for *Guys and Dolls.* Actor in a play, **Brian Bedford** in *Two Shakespearean Actors.* Actor in a musical (tie), **Gregory Hines** in *Jelly's Last Jam,* **Nathan Lane** in *Guys and Dolls.* Actress in a play, **Laura Esterman** in *Marvin's Room.* Actress in a musical, **Faith Prince** in *Guys and Dolls.* Featured actor in a play, **Larry Fishburne** in *Two Trains Running.* Featured actor in a musical, **Scott Waara** in *The Most Happy Fella* (Broadway). Featured actress in a play, **Christine Baranski** in *Lips Together, Teeth Apart.* Featured actress in a musical, **Tonya Pinkins** in *Jelly's Last Jam.* Music, **Erik Frandsen, Michael Garin, Robert Hipkens, Paula Lockheart** for *Song of Singapore.* Lyrics, **Susan Birkenhead** for *Jelly's Last Jam.* Orchestration and musical adaptation, **Luther Henderson** for *Jelly's Last Jam.* Book of a musical, **George C. Wolfe** for *Jelly's Last Jam.* Choreography, **Susan Stroman** for *Crazy for You.* Revival, *Guys and Dolls.* Set design, **Tony Walton** for *Guys and Dolls.* Lighting design (tie), **Jules Fisher** for *Jelly's Last Jam,* **Paul Gallo** for *Guys and Dolls.* Costume design, **William Ivey Long** for *Guys and Dolls.* Solo performance, **Patrick Stewart** in *A Christmas Carol.* Sound design, music in a play, **Paul Arditti** for *Four Baboons Adoring the Sun.* Music in a play, **Jan A.P. Kaczmarek** for *'Tis Pity She's a Whore.* Unique theatrical experience, **Blue Man Group** in *Tubes.* Ensemble performance, *Dancing at Lughnasa.*

1992 Special awards: **Andre Bishop** for artistic leadership at Playwrights Horizons; **The Irish Repertory Theater** for excellence in presenting distinguished Irish drama; **Broadway Cares/Equity Fights AIDS** and **Suzanne Ishee** for mobilizing the theater community in the fight against AIDS.

10th ANNUAL ELLIOT NORTON AWARDS. For distinguished contribution to the theater in Boston, selected by a committee of critics including Elliot Norton. Elliot Norton Medal, **David Wheeler** of the American Repertory Theater. Lifetime achievement, **Jason Robards.** 10th Anniversary Award, **Tommy Tune.** Otis Skinner Prize for best actor, **Jeremy Geidt.** Charlotte Cushman Prize for best actress, **Frances West.** Henry Jewett Prize for best director, **Tina Packer.** Special honors: **De Ama Battle**, founder and director, Art of Black Dance and Music; **Fernando Bujones**, permanent guest artist, Boston Ballet; **Elma Lewis**, artistic director, National Center of Afro-American Artists; **Jon B. Platt**, president, American Artists; **Ron Ritchell** and **Polly Hogan**, artistic director and producing director, the Lyric Stage.

8th ANNUAL HELEN HAYES AWARDS. In recognition of excellence in Washington, D.C. theater. Resident shows—Musical, *Sweeney Todd* by Hugh Wheeler and Stephen Sondheim. Play, *My Children! My Africa!* by Athol Fugard. Actor in a musical, **Pedro Porro** in *Sweeney Todd.* Actress in a musical, **Donna Lillard** in *Sweeney Todd.* Actor in a play, **Floyd King** in *A Tale of Two Cities.* Actress in a play, **Nancy Robinette** in *Fat Men in Skirts.* Supporting actor, **Ted Van Griethuysen** in *Saint Joan.* Supporting actress, **Marilyn Coleman** in *Jar the Floor.* Director of a musical, **Eric Schaeffer** for *Sweeney Todd.* Set design, **Lou Stancari** for *Sweeney Todd.* Costume design, **Barbara Kravitz** for *Pygmalion.* Lighting design, **Daniel MacLean Wagner** for *When I Was a Girl I Used to Scream and Shout.* Sound design, **David Crandall** for *Hamlet.*

Non-resident shows—Best show, *Crazy for You* by Ken Ludwig, George Gershwin and Ira Gershwin. Actor, **Robert Morse** in *Tru.* Actress, **Mercedes Ruehl** in *Lost in Yonkers.* Director **Lloyd Richards** for *Two Trains Running.* Supporting performer, **Roscoe Lee Browne** for *Two Trains Running.*

Charles MacArthur Award for outstanding new play, *Before It Hits Home* by Cheryl L. West. American Express Tribute for outstanding achievement in the performing arts, **Jason Robards.** KPMG Peat Marwick Award for distinguished service, **AT&T** for its corporate sponsorship of the arts. Washington *Post* Community Service Award, the **Shakespeare Theater** for its free summertime performance program.

23d ANNUAL JOSEPH JEFFERSON AWARDS. Citations for achievement in Chicago Theater during the 1990-91 season. New work or adaptation: *Still Waters* by Claudia Allen; *Deep in a Dream of You* by David Cale; *Sylvia's Real Good Advice* by Nicole Hollander, Arnold Aprill, Tom Mula, Cheri Coons and Steve Rashid; *The Golem* by Tom Mula; *American Enterprise* by Jeffrey Sweet. Production of a play, *The Iceman Cometh* at the Goodman Theater. Production of a musical, *Woody Guthrie's American Song* at Northlight Theater. Production of a revue, *Forbidden Broadway 1990* at Halstead Theater Center (Cochran Productions). Director of a play, **Robert Falls** for *The Iceman Cometh*. Director of a musical, **Peter Glazer** for *Woody Guthrie's American Song*. Director of a revue: **Gerard Alessandrini** for *Forbidden Broadway 1990*; **Barbara Wallace** for *We Made a Mesopotamia Now You Clean It Up*. Actor in a principal role, play, **Albert Finney** in *Another Time*. Actress in a principal role, play, **Maureen Gallagher** in *The Belle of Amherst*. Actor in a principal role, musical, **Gene Weygant** in *Me and My Girl*. Actress in a principal role, musical, Paula **Scrofano** in *On the Twentieth Century*. Actor in a revue: **Peter Burns** in *We Made a Mesapotamia, etc.*; **Kevin Ligon** in *Forbidden Broadway 1990*. Actress in a revue, **Rose Abdoo** in *We Made a Mesopotamia, etc.* Actor in a supporting role, play, **Jerome Kilty** in *The Iceman Cometh*. Actress in a supporting role, play, **Molly Regan** in *Another Time*. Actor in a supporting role, musical, **Dale Benson** in *Little Me*. Actress in a supporting role, musical, **Alene Robertson** in *Annie*. Ensemble, *Peepshow*. Original music: **Evan Chen** for *Coriolanus*; **Roy Nathanson** for *Deep in a Dream of You*. Musical direction, **Malcolm Ruhl** for *Woody Guthrie's American Song*. Choreography: **Mark S. Hoebee** for *Sweet Charity*; **Rudy Hogenmiller** and **James Harms** for *A Chorus Line*. Scenic design, **John Conklin** for *The Iceman Cometh*. Costume design: **Nan Cibula-Jenkins** for *Much Ado About Nothing*; **Jack Kirkby** for *Little Me*. Lighting design, **James F. Ingalls** for *The Iceman Cometh*. Sound design: **Jim Dawson** for *Artist Descending a Staircase*; **Rob Milburn** for *The Visit*.

23d ANNUAL LOS ANGELES DRAMA CRITICS CIRCLE AWARDS. For distinguished achievement in Los Angeles Theater during 1991. Production: *Avenue A* at Cast-at-the-Circle

Theater; *Heartbreak House* at South Coast Repertory; *The Most Happy Fella* at Doolittle Theater. Writing, **David Henry Hwang** for *M. Butterfly*. Direction: **Martin Benson** for *Heartbreak House*; **Gerald Gutierrez** for *The Most Happy Fella*; **Jim Holmes** for *Avenue A*. Lead performance: **Eileen Atkins** in *A Room of One's Own*; **Jeff Doucette** in *Rage!*; **Richard Frank** in *Kiss of the Spider Woman*; **Jane Krakowski** in *Henceforward...*; **Robert Morse** in *Tru*. Featured performance: **Loretta Devine** in *The Rabbit Foot*; **David Steen** in *Avenue A*. Ensemble performance: **Stan Chandler**, **David Engel**, **Larry Raben** and **Guy Stroman** in *Forever Plaid*; Scenic design: **John Iacovelli** for *Heartbreak House*; **Robin Wagner** for *City of Angels*. Lighting design, **James F. Ingalls** for *Jelly's Last Jam*. Costume design: **Ann Bruice** for *You Can't Take It With You*; **Florence Klotz** for *City of Angels*; **Shigeru Yaji** for *Happy End*. Sound design, **John Gottlieb** for *Henceforward...*. Hair and makeup design, **Kevin Haney** for *Tru*. Musical direction: **Steven Freeman** for *Forever Plaid*; **Tim Stella** for *The Most Happy Fella*; **Linda Twine** for *Jelly's Last Jam*. Musical arrangement and orchestration: **Robert Page** and **Frank Loesser** for *The Most Happy Fella*; **James Raitt** for *Forever Plaid*. Choreography, **Tommy Tune** for *Grand Hotel*; **Gregory Scott Young** for *Club Indigo*.

Margaret Harford Award, **Paul Verdier** and the **Stages Theater Center**. Ted Schmitt Award, **David Steen** in *Avenue A*. Angstrom Award, **Paulie Jenkins**. Special award: **Los Angeles Theater Center** (1985-1991), **Bill Bushnell** artistic director and **Diane White** producing director.

BAY AREA THEATER CRITICS AWARDS. In recognition of outstanding San Francisco area theater. Original script: **Tony Kushner** for *Angels in America*; **Dorothy Bryant** for *Dear Master*. Production: *Angels in America* at Eureka Theater; *Dear Master* at Sunseed. Director, **David Esbjornson** for *Angels in America*. Male performance: **John Belluci** and **Stephen Spinella** in *Angels in America*; **Ken Ruta** in *Cat on a Hot Tin Roof*. Female performance: **Anne Darragh** in *Angels in America*; **Barbara Oliver** in *Dear Master*; **Ingrid Gerstmann** in *O Pioneers!*. Lighting, **Jack Carpenter** and **Jim Cave** for *Angels in America*.

1991-92 PUBLICATION OF
RECENTLY-PRODUCED PLAYS

Assassins. Stephen Sondheim and John Weidman. Theater Communications Group (also paperback).
Chess: Libretto. Richard Nelson with Benny Andersson, Bjorn Ulvaeus, Tim Rice. Samuel French.
Coup, The. Mustapha Matura. Methuen (paperback).
Dancing at Lughnasa. Brian Friel. Faber & Faber (paperback).
Death and the Maiden. Ariel Dorfman. Penguin (paperback).
Dejavu. John Osborne. Faber & Faber (paperback).
Grapes of Wrath, The. Frank Galati. Penguin (paperback).
It's Ralph. Hugh Whitemore. Amber Lane.
Lettice & Lovage. Peter Shaffer. Harper & Row (paperback).
Lost in Yonkers. Neil Simon. Random House.
Murmuring Judges. David Hare. Faber & Faber (paperback).
Revengers' Comedies, The. Alan Ayckbourn. Faber & Faber (paperback).
Road to Nirvana. Arthur Kopit. Noonday Press/Hill & Wang.
Safe Sex. Harvey Fierstein. Atheneum (also paperback).
Shadowlands. William Nicholson. Plume/New American Library (also paperback).
Shimada. Jill Shearer. Currency (also paperback).
Spunk. Zora Neale Hurston. Theater Communications Group (paperback).
Tango at the End of Winter. Kunio Shimizu, adapted by Peter Barnes. Amber Lane (paperback).
Three Birds Alighting on a Field. Timberlake Wertenbaker. Faber & Faber.
Unidentified Human Remains and the True Nature of Love. Brad Fraser. Blizzard (Canada).

A SELECTED LIST OF OTHER PLAYS
PUBLISHED IN 1991-92

Baby Doll and Tiger Tail. Tennessee Williams. New Directions (also paperback).
Best American Short Plays 1990, The. Howard Stein and Glenn Young, editors. Applause (also
    paperback).
Black Thunder: An Anthology of Contemporary African-American Drama. William B. Branch, editor.
    Mentor/New American.
Bolsheviks and Other Plays, The. Mikhail Shatrov. Nick Hern Books (paperback).
Brand. Henrik Ibsen, translated and adapted by Robert David MacDonald. Oberon Books (England).
Collected Plays of Neil Simon, The, Volume 3. Random House.
Drama Contemporary: Hungary. Eugene Brogyanyi, editor. PAJ Publications.
Enrico Four. Luigi Pirandello. Oberon Books (England).
Four Plays. Beth Henley. Heinemann/Methuen (paperback).
Hey Little Walter and Other Prize-Winning Plays from the 1989 and 1990 Young Playwrights Festivals.
    Dell (paperback).
Imagination Dead Imagine. Samuel Beckett. Riverrun (paperback).
Love & Science: Selected Music-Theater Texts. Richard Foreman. TCG (paperback).
New American Plays—1. Lisa Barnett, editor. Heinemann (paperback).
New American Plays—2. Lisa Barnett, editor. Heinemann (paperback).
New Norwegian Plays. Janet Garton and Henny Sehmsdorf, editors. Norvik.
New Woman Plays. Linda Fitzsimmons and Viv Gardner, editors. Metheun (paperback).
Philanthropist and Other Plays, The. Christopher Hampton. Faber & Faber (paperback).
Pirandello's Major Plays. Luigi Pirandello. Northwestern University Press (paperback).
Plays: One—Nichols. Peter Nichols. Methuen (paperback).
Plays: Two—Nichols. Peter Nichols. Methuen (paperback).

Plays: One (Calderon). Calderon de La Barca, translated by Gwynne Edwards. Methuen (paperback).

Plays: One—Louise Page. Louise Page. Methuen (paperback).

Plays: Three—David Edgar. David Edgar. Methuen (paperback).

Plays: Three—Strindberg. August Strindberg. Methuen (paperback).

Professional Frenchman, The. Mac Wellman. Corner Books (Sun and Moon Press). Paperback.

Ray Bradbury on Stage: A Chrestomathy of His Plays. Ray Bradbury. Primis (paperback).

Recent Puerto Rican Theater: Five Plays. John Antush, editor. Arte Publico Press.

Rough Crossings/On the Razzle. Tom Stoppard. Faber & Faber (paperback).

Six Plays by Matura. Mustapha Matura. Methuen (paperback).

Stirrings Still. Samuel Beckett. North Star Line (paperback).

Three Plays: August Wilson. August Wilson. University of Pittsburgh Press.

Three Sisters, The. Anton Chekhov, adapted by David Mamet. Grove Weidenfeld.

12 Plays. Joyce Carol Oates. Dutton.

Unbalancing Acts: Foundations for a Theater. Richard Foreman. Pantheon/Random House.

Who Do I Have the Honour of Addressing? Peter Shaffer. Andre Deutsch (paperback).

Wind in the Willows, The. Alan Bennett. Faber & Faber (paperback).

Woman Alone and Other Plays, A. Franca Rame and Dario Fo, Stuart Hood, editors, translated by Gillian Hanna, Ed Emery and Christopher Cairns. Methuen (paperback).

NECROLOGY

MAY 1991—MAY 1992

PERFORMERS

Alison, Dorothy (66)—January 17, 1992
Allen, Ronald (54)—June 18, 1991
Allman, Elvia (87)—March 6, 1992
Alzado, Lyle (43)—May 14, 1992
Anderson, Judith (94)—January 3, 1992
Andor, Lotte Palfi (87)—July 8, 1991
Andor, Paul (90)—June 26, 1991
Arthur, Jean (98)—June 19, 1991
Ash, Walter Thompson (78)—February 1, 1992
Ashcroft, Peggy (83)—March 28, 1992
Ashe, Martin (80)—April 15, 1992
Assad, James Wilson (62)—April 14, 1992
Astor, Philip (47)—October 19, 1991
Aubuchon, Jacques (67)—December 28, 1991
Audley, Eleanor (86)—November 25, 1991
Ballard, Michael (49)—November 10, 1991
Barker, Margaret (83)—April 3, 1992
Bartholomew, Freddie (67)—January 23, 1991
Baruch, André (83)—September 15, 1991
Beatty, Robert (82)—March 3, 1992
Bellamy, Ralph (87)—November 29, 1991
Bender, Chris (19)—November 3, 1991
Bennett, Tracy (39)—October 18, 1991
Berti, Dehl (70)—November 26, 1991
Bertram, Bert (97)—October 31, 1991
Blaire, Sallie (68)—February 17, 1992
Boardman, Eleanor (93)—December 12, 1991
Booth, Edwina (86)—May 18, 1991
Bossard, Andres (47)—March 25, 1992
Bostwick, Dorothy Davis—May 25, 1991
Bourrelly, Henri (86)—July 20, 1991
Brand, Neville (71)—April 16, 1992
Brodie, Steve (72)—January 9, 1992
Brown, James (72)—April 11, 1992
Browne, Coral (77)—May 29, 1991
Bruni, Peter (60)—May 3, 1992
Brunner, Howard (51)—November 12, 1991
Bryceland, Yvonne (66)—January 13, 1992
Burke, Brendan (63)—October 1, 1991
Callaway, Joe A. (77)—December 15, 1991
Campbell, Evelyn (96)—May 9, 1992
Cantor, Michael (32)—October 3, 1991
Carey, Robert (32)—June 27, 1991
Carroll, David (41)—March 11, 1992
Caulfield, Joan (64)—June 18, 1991
Christi, Panos (54)—April 25, 1992

Clarke, Mae (81)—April 29, 1992
Clifford, Yvonne (60)—February 2, 1992
Colby, Anita (77)—March 27, 1992
Convy, Bert (56)—July 15, 1991
Cook, Charles (77)—August 8, 1991
Cook, Olga (100)—December 15, 1991
Coston, Ann Sorg (62)—December 6, 1991
Couper, Barbara (89)—Winter 1992
Cravens, Kathryn (92)—August 29, 1991
Cuevas, Jose Louis (34)—May 2, 1992
Daniels, Yvonne (53)—June 21, 1991
Danova, Cesare (66)—March 19, 1992
Danton, Ray (60)—February 11, 1992
Davis, Brad (41)—August 8, 1991
Dehner, John (76)—February 4, 1992
Dennis, Sandy (54)—March 2, 1992
Derr, Richard (74)—May 8, 1992
DeRusso, Richard (45)—September 16, 1991
Devlin, James G. (84)—October 17, 1991
De Vore, Maxine (86)—August 8, 1991
Dewhurst, Colleen (67)—August 22, 1991
Dheigh, Khigh (75)—October 25, 1991
Dietrich, Marlene (90)—May 6, 1992
Dixon, Adele (83)—April 11, 1992
Dixon, Willie (76)—January 29, 1992
Dubbins, Donald Gene (63)—August 17, 1991
Duggan, Gerry (82)—March 27, 1992
Dunbar, Dixie (72)—August 29, 1991
Dunnock, Mildred (90)—July 5, 1991
Dyer-Bennett, Richard (78)—December 14, 1991
Eisler, David (36)—February 16, 1992
Elkins, Lenore (James) (77)—August 6, 1991
Ellis, Karl Joseph (41)—July 24, 1991
Emery, Rick (39)—April 7, 1992
Engler, Arthur P. (71)—September 28, 1991
Evans, John Morgan (49)—December 27, 1991
Falat, Stephen J. (34)—October 10, 1991
Faye, Frances (late 70s)—November 8, 1991
Ferrer, Jose (80)—January 26, 1992
Ffrangcon-Davies, Gwen (101)—January 27, 1992
Field, Filip J. (67)—May 11, 1991
Field, Virginia (74)—January 2, 1992
Fisher, Maria (87)—July 11, 1991
Ford, Tennessee Ernie (72)—October 17, 1991
Foss, Harlan (50)—August 17, 1991
Foxx, Redd (68)—October 11, 1991
Franciscus, James (57)—July 8, 1991
Frommer, Ben (78)—May 1992

Gaudio, Joseph (79)—February 3, 1992
Gavert, Paul (76)—March 11, 1992
Geil, Corky (Joe) (64)—January 1, 1992
Gerry, Toni (65)—July 25, 1991
Gerson, Jeanne (87)—February 7, 1992
Grice, Winifred Wellington (97)—May 10, 1992
Griffith, Byron Q. (73)—December 23, 1991
Hall, Ed (60)—July 30, 1991
Hall, Kate (82)—June 21, 1991
Hamilton, Frank (66)—April 25, 1991
Hamilton, Patrick (45)—November 8, 1991
Hammond, Ruth (96)—April 9, 1992
Hannan, Thomas A. (40)—May 29, 1991
Hardin, Ken (62)—October 30, 1991
Harman, Esther (69)—August 2, 1991
Harris, Cassandra (Brosnan) (39)—December 28, 1991
Harris, Gene (late 30s)—January 27, 1992
Harris, Geraldine Delaney (67)—May 29, 1992
Hartley, Clyde (68)—April 26, 1992
Hayes, Christopher—November 12, 1991
Heath, Gordon (72)—August 28, 1991
Heider, Frederick (75)—May 17, 1992
Henreid, Paul (84)—March 29, 1992
Hill, Avon Jaeger (44)—January 6, 1992
Hill, Benny (67)—April 20, 1992
Hill, Elaine (52)—October 11, 1991
Hopkins, Bruce (44)—May 15, 1992
Houston, Donald (67)—October 12, 1991
Hoving, Jane Pickens (83)—February 21, 1992
Howerd, Frankie (70)—April 19, 1992
Hoyt, John (87)—September 15, 1991
Hubbard, Bruce (39)—November 12, 1991
Hunt, Richard (40)—January 7, 1992
Hyde, Jacquelyn (61)—February 23, 1992
Ireland, John (78)—March 21, 1992
Irwin, Bob (88)—June 9, 1991
James, Ralph (67)—March 14, 1992
Jones, Gib (34)—April 1, 1992
Jones, June (72)—May 13, 1991
Jones, Victor Charles (82)—November 25, 1991
Keen, Keith (34)—June 15, 1991
Kelley, Edward (82)—June 15, 1991
Kelly, Paula (72)—April 2, 1992
Kert, Larry (60)—June 6, 1991
Kinison, Sam (38)—April 10, 1992
Kinski, Klaus (65)—November 23, 1991
Kobal, John (51)—October 28, 1991
Kolb, Glenn (39)—July 13, 1991
Kramer, Sy (59)—April 4, 1992
Kressen, Sam (73)—December 26, 1991
Kusell, Maurice L. (89)—February 2, 1992
Lamont, Deni (59)—November 10, 1991
Landon, Michael (54)—July 1, 1991
Lantz, Gracie (88)—March 17, 1992
Lawrence, John (60)—March 21, 1992

Lawrence, Mary (73)—September 24, 1991
Lawrence, Sarah Sally (61)—October 10, 1991
Leaming, Chet (66)—February 19, 1992
Lederman, Victoria Kellem (52)—April 23, 1992
Lee, Billie (89)—May 30, 1991
Lee, Vanessa (71)—March 15, 1992
Leentvaar, Jeanette (41)—September 2, 1991
Le Gallienne, Eva (92)—June 8, 1991
Leighton, Merrill (51)—July 5, 1991
Lemkov, Tutte (73)—November 19, 1991
Lewis, Robert Q. (71)—December 11, 1991
Liddell, Laura (83)—February 5, 1992
Liss, Ted (72)—March 3, 1992
Lombardi, Paul Michael (31)—September 9, 1991
Loring, Kay (late 70s)—February 24, 1992
Lunchbox, Deacon (41)—April 19, 1992
Lund, John (81)—May 10, 1992
MacMahon, Aline (92)—October 12, 1991
MacMurray, Fred (83)—November 5, 1991
Magginetti, William Shaw (98)—February 21, 1992
Marrero, Ralph (33)—November 16, 1991
Martineau, Catherine (31)—July 29, 1991
Massey, Curt (81)—Fall 1991
Mauro, Joe (60)—March 6, 1992
Maxwell, Paul (70)—Winter 1992
McCallion, James (72)—July 11, 1991
McCum, James Patrick (32)—July 8, 1991
McDowell, Mitch—January 21, 1992
Mell, Marisa (53)—May 16, 1992
Merrill, Joan (74)—May 10, 1992
Messerer, Asaf (88)—March 7, 1992
Miles, Bernard (83)—June 14, 1991
Millar, Alan (62)—June 4, 1991
Minz, Alexander (51)—April 30, 1992
Monica, Maria A.G. (92)—October 29, 1991
Montand, Yves (70)—November 9, 1991
Moore, Eleanor (84)—August 28, 1991
Moore, Herbert R. (77)—June 13, 1991
Morrison, Barbara (84)—March 12, 1992
Murphy, George (89)—May 3, 1992
Nalder, Reggie (80s)—November 19, 1991
Nelson, Mervyn (76)—August 17, 1991
Newman, Thomas (60)—December 20, 1991
Nighswander, Mary Fluhrer (83)—Summer 1991
Nijinska, Irina (77)—July 2, 1991
Novello, Roselle (95)—January 16, 1992
Nute, Don (56)—August 25, 1991
Ocko, Daniel (78)—August 29, 1991
O'Connor, Kevin (56)—June 22, 1991
O'Toole, Ollie (79)—February 25, 1992
Oulton, Brian (84)—April 13, 1992
Padilla, Ruben Dario Sr. (81)—June 16, 1991
Parks, Bert (77)—February 2, 1992
Pettyjohn, Angelique (48)—February 14, 1992
Picon, Molly (94)—April 5, 1992

Preston, Wayde (62)—February 6, 1992
Provenza, Salvatore D. (45)—December 25, 1991
Rasulala, Thalmus (55)—October 9, 1991
Reading, Beatrice (50s)—June 8, 1991
Redcoff, Karl (67)—Winter 1991
Reed, Robert (59)—May 12, 1992
Reed, Vernon William Sr. (73)—January 25, 1992
Remick, Lee (55)—July 2, 1991
Remme, John (56)—January 19, 1992
Riley, Alice Mary (51)—April 19, 1992
Ritz, Annette (88)—January 30, 1992
Roman, Paul Reid (55)—November 17, 1991
Roman, Stella (87)—February 12, 1992
Rosenblatt, Martin (74)—June 24, 1991
Rossitto, Angelo S. (83)—September 21, 1991
Ruffin, David (50)—June 1, 1991
Russell, Andy (72)—April 16, 1992
Sabbey, Russel J. (74)—July 20, 1991
Samuel, Andrew (82)—March 5, 1992
Sanderson, Joan (79)—May 24, 1992
Scott, Daniel Simon (71)—December 11, 1991
Shurr, Gertrude (88)—January 2, 1992
Spessivtzeva, Olga (96)—September 16, 1991
Stanley, Helene (62)—December 27, 1991
Steel, Pippa (44)—May 29, 1992
Stevens, Fran (72)—November 2, 1991
Storey, June (73)—December 19, 1991
Stracke, Win (83)—June 29, 1991
Strange, Bill (62)—February 6, 1992
Sylvia, Margo J. (55)—October 25, 1991
Syms, Sylvia (74)—May 20, 1992
Talton, Alix (72)—April 7, 1992
Tarlow, Florence (70)—February 10, 1992
Thomas, Wilfrid (87)—August 16, 1991
Thompson, Marshall (66)—May 25, 1992
Thomson, Ian (61)—March 13, 1992
Tierney, Gene (70)—November 6, 1991
Tippet, Clark (37)—January 28, 1992
Toomey, Regis (93)—October 12, 1991
Touchstone, John (59)—January 25, 1992
Tree, Dorothy (85)—February 12, 1992
Tryon, Thomas (65)—September 4, 1991
Tully, Lee—September 16, 1991
Uehara, Ken (82)—November 23, 1991
Ulis, H. Jay (98)—January 15, 1992
Uris, Dorothy (85)—February 13, 1992
Valentino, Frank (84)—June 14, 1991
Vitto, Lawrence (69)—October 18, 1991
Vosseler, Heidi (74)—March 9, 1992
Walker, Bill (95)—January 27, 1992
Walker, Nancy (69)—March 25, 1992
Wallack, Roy Homer (64)—March 10, 1992
Walsh, James (68)—June 20, 1991
Walters, Casey (75)—December 3, 1991
Ward, Ken (37)—April 10, 1992
Washburn, Jack (64)—March 15, 1992

Webster, Byron (58)—December 1, 1991
Weist, Dwight (81)—July 16, 1991
Welford, Nancy (87)—September 30, 1991
Wheatley, Alan (84)—August 30, 1991
White, Glenn (42)—May 27, 1992
Williams, Pearl (77)—September 18, 1991
Wilson, John (64)—February 24, 1992
Wilson, Theodore (47)—July 21, 1991
Wolfe, Ian (95)—January 23, 1992
Wright, Clarence (84)—March 13, 1992
Yarbrough, Nancy (84)—June 17, 1991
Yarmy, Dick (59)—May 5, 1992
Yevstigneev, Yevgeny (65)—March 5, 1992
York, Dick (63)—February 20, 1992
Yupanqui, Atahualpa (84)—May 23, 1992
Zimmerman, Donald (70)—February 5, 1992

PLAYWRIGHTS

Alison, Joan (91)—March 30, 1992
Billetdoux, Francois (64)—November 26, 1991
Bovasso, Julie (61)—September 14, 1991
Bruno, Anthony (46)—June 14, 1991
Busch, Niven (88)—August 25, 1991
Catto, Max (84)—March 12, 1992
Churchill, Donald (60)—October 29, 1991
Davis, Donald (88)—March 28, 1992
Deutsch, Helen (85)—March 15, 1992
Dinelli, Mel (79)—November 28, 1991
Donovan, John (63)—April 29, 1992
Douglas, Felicity (81)—February 1, 1992
Dunne, Philip (84)—May 26, 1992
Elliott, Sumner Locke (73)—June 24, 1991
Eyen, Tom (50)—May 26, 1991
Fairchild, Mark Scott (34)—October 13, 1991
Freeman, Dexter (53)—April 11, 1992
Havers, Michael (69)—April 1, 1992
Idris, Yusuf (64)—August 1, 1991
Irwin, Ben (79)—June 12, 1991
Lord, Robert (45)—January 7, 1992
MacGrath, Leueen (77)—March 27, 1992
Marsh, Edward (79)—November 7, 1991
Marshall, Armina (96)—July 20, 1991
Menzies, Archie N. (87)—September 7, 1991
Merriam, Eve (75)—April 11, 1992
O'Neil, Russell (64)—December 18, 1991
Paris, Ronnie (66)—February 4, 1992
Phillips, Wendell K. (83)—October 6, 1991
Piazza, Ben (58)—September 7, 1991
Poiret, Jean (65)—March 14, 1992
Powers, Tim (34)—August 23, 1991
Reines, Bernard (84)—August 6, 1991
Roberts, Meade (61)—February 10, 1992
Russell, Robert W. (79)—February 11, 1992

Sakellarios, Alekos (78)—August 29, 1991
Whedon, John Ogden (86)—November 21, 1991
Yao, Hsin-Nung (86)—December 18, 1991

COMPOSERS, LYRICISTS, SONGWRITERS

Alexander, Joseph (84)—February 28, 1992
Cooper, Louis (79)—November 21, 1991
Cowan, Stanley Earl (73)—December 14, 1991
Darby, Ken (82)—January 24, 1992
Delerue, Georges (67)—March 20, 1992
DeVries, John (76)—April 17, 1992
DiMatteo, Robert (43)—August 16, 1991
Friedman, Lewis M. (47)—January 3, 1992
Goldsmith, Cliff (66)—June 14, l991
Grossman, Steven—June 23, 1991
Hastings, Ross R. (76)—July 5, 1991
Kaye, Sylvia Fine (78)—October 28, 1991
Kellem, Milton (81)—April 17, 1992
Krenek, Ernst (91)—December 23, 1991
Kresa, Helmy (86)—August 19, 1991
Latimer, Jack (78)—November 14, 1991
Lawrence, Mark (70)—August 24, 1991
Leventhal, Herbert (76)—November 2, 1991
Low, James R. (65)—August 16, 1991
Maltby, Richard (77)—August 19, 1991
Moore, Marvin (72)—April 26, 1992
Morali, Jacques (44)—November 15, 1991
North, Alex (81)—September 8, 1991
Oliver, Stephen (42)—April 29, 1992
Panufnik, Andrzej (77)—October 27, 1991
Ragni, Gerome (48)—July 10, 1991
Robbins, James Phillip (52)—July 3, 1991
Robinson, Earl (81)—July 20, 1991
Schaffner, Nicholas (38)—August 28, 1991
Schuman, William (81)—February 15, 1992
Sharpe, Emma Kapiolani (87)—September 20, 1991
Schuman, Mort (52)—November 3, 1991
Stevens, Mort (62)—November 11, 1991
Welin, Karl-Erik (58)—May 31, 1992

CONDUCTORS

Adrian, Louis (93)—August 26, 1991
Aliferis, James (79)—May 22, 1992
Barnet, Charlie (77)—September 4, 1991
Beveridge, Lowell P. (86)—June 18, 1991
Irving, Robert (78)—September 15, 1991
Jaffa, Max (79)—July 30, 1991
Korn, Michael (44)—August 29, 1991
Love, Geoff (73)—July 8, 1991
Ma, Hiao-Tsium (80)—August 28, 1991

Pflugradt, William (48)—December 22, 1991
Raph, Ted (86)—December 20, 1991
Rosenstock, Milton (74)—April 24, 1992
Schenck, Andrew (51)—February 19, 1992
Smith, Henry (86)—August 10, 1991
Strickland, W.R. (77)—November 17, 1991
Thomson, Bryden (63)—November 14, 1991
Vaughn, Billy (72)—September 26, 1991
Vernon, Vinton B. (91)—June 27, 1991
Welk, Lawrence (89)—May 17, 1992
Yates, Sterling (65)—July 11, 1991

CRITICS

Brooks, Elston (61)—May 22, 1991
Byron, Stuart (50)—December 13, 1991
Cartey, Wilfred (60)—March 21, 1992
Chase, Gilbert (85)—February 22, 1992
Crosby, John (79)—September 7, 1991
Eaton, Quaintance (90)—April 12, 1992
Heyworth, Peter—October 1, 1991
Hobson, Harold (87)—March 13, 1992
Howlett, John (41)—September 24, 1991
Huffhines, Kathy (48)—July 19, 1991
Jurrist, Charles (46)—June 22, 1991
Knight, Arthur (74)—July 25, 1991
Lang, Paul Henry (90)—September 21, 1991
McMillan, A.W. (91)—September 7, 1991
Nathan, Norma (65)—November 9, 1991
Primus, Francesca (45)—January 27, 1992
Simon, Alfred E. (83)—May 27, 1991
Sturdy, Jack R. (42)—August 16, 1991
Supree, Burt (51)—May 1, 1992
Williams, Martin (67)—April 13, 1992
Williams, Whitney (91)—March 14, 1992

MUSICIANS

Aronson, David (32)—August 19, 1991
Arrau, Claudio (88)—June 9, 1991
Balderas, Jimmy (88)—July 13, 1991
Barrett, Benjamin (86)—April 16, 1992
Blakeney, Andrew (93)—February 12, 1992
Blume, Theodore (75)—February 4, 1992
Brennand, James (69)—April 11, 1992
Briggs, Arthur (92)—July 17, 1991
Bushell, Garvin Payne (91)—October 31, 1991
Callender, Red (76)—March 8, 1992
Clayton, Buck (80)—December 8, 1991
Cook, Herman (57)—February 4, 1992
Davis, Miles (65)—September 28, 1991
Davis, Thunderbird (James) (53)—January 24, 1992
Docker, Robert (73)—May 9, 1992

Dupress, Chamion Jack (82)—January 21, 1992
Fishelson, Stanley (66)—September 3, 1991
Foldes, Andor (78)—February 9, 1992
Follari, Gregorio (51)—September 26, 1991
Frager, Malcolm (56)—June 20, 1991
Francescatti, Zino (89)—June 17, 1991
Getz, Stan (64)—June 6, 1991
Gideon, Israel (43)—November 7, 1991
Goldsand, Robert (80)—September 16, 1991
Hafford, Mary Louise (89)—January 3, 1992
Harris, William G. (55)—December 22, 1992
Hayward, Lance (75)—November 9, 1991
Hutchenrider, C.B. (83)—August 18, 1991
Jackson, Allen (51)—March 29, 1992
Johansen, Gunnar (85)—May 25, 1991
Kimmelman, Seth (40)—December 5, 1991
Kirkpatrick, John (86)—November 8, 1991
Laporte, Lucien Kirsh (91)—July 4, 1991
Lewis, Al (87)—April 12, 1992
Mangiapane, Sherwood (79)—Winter 1992
Marsh, Ozan (71)—March 15, 1992
Moorman, Charlotte (58)—November 8, 1991
Murray, Dee (45)—January 15, 1992
Osborne, Mary (70)—March 4, 1992
Papa, Tony (65)—April 5, 1992
Pepper, Jim (50)—February 10, 1992
Pessl, Yella (85)—December 8, 1991
Price, Sammy (83)—April 14, 1992
Raver, Leonard (65)—January 29, 1992
Rupp, Franz (91)—May 27, 1992
Russell, Arthur (40)—April 4, 1992
Schor, Ernestine B. (60)—May 30, 1991
Shapiro, Constantine (95)—May 25, 1992
Tuttle, John Williams (41)—August 12, 1991
Ventura, Charlie (75)—January 17, 1992
Walcha, Helmut (83)—August 11, 1991
Wallace, Norman (69)—January 16, 1992
Waters, Edward H. (85)—July 27, 1991
Wilson, Ernesto A. (35)—September 21, 1991

DESIGNERS

Abbott, Tony (68)—March 10, 1992
Astor, Ana I. (73)—January 3, 1992
Bardon, Henry (68)—July 19, 1991
Dodd, John P. (50)—July 14, 1991
Evans, Charles II (84)—January 15, 1992
Fox, Frederick (81)—September 11, 1991
Galster, Robert (68)—October 21, 1991
Levitt, Ruby (84)—January 18, 1992
Mastrogiovanni, Vito (39)—May 15, 1991
Moorcroft, Judy (56)—December 13, 1991
Schissler, Jeffrey M. (42)—June 22, 1991
Turner, Ethel (92)—June 13, 1991

PRODUCERS, DIRECTORS, CHOREOGRAPHERS

Adoue, Jean Baptiste III (81)—August 2, 1991
Alexander, William (75)—November 19, 1991
Allen, Irwin (75)—November 2, 1991
Antoon, A.J. (47)—January 22, 1991
Arnold, Jack (75)—March 17, 1992
Baldschum, Clyde H. (70)—November 22, 1991
Ball, William (60)—July 30, 1991
Brown, Lutcher Slade (68)—June 29, 1991
Cahan, George M. (72)—June 12, 1991
Capra, Frank (94)—September 3, 1991
Chambers, Kathy L. (41)—July 20, 1991
Chapman, Ben (83)—July 8, 1991
Chase, Richard G. Jr. (46)—April 7, 1992
Clore, Leon (73)—February 9, 1992
Cohen, Arthur W. (69)—October 16, 1991
Collins, Richard (46)—September 12, 1991
Cree, George (55)—March 4, 1992
DeLaurentis, Luigi (75)—March 30, 1992
Dinehart, Alan (74)—March 14, 1992
Dodds, Eddie (69)—April 24, 1992
Dowell, Clifton (44)—May 20, 1992
Doyle, Roz (49)—November 24, 1991
Dreyfus, Richard C. (70)—July 29, 1991
Emr, Roland Jon (45)—July 11, 1991
Epstein, Jerome (69)—November 16, 1991
Eyre, Ronald (62)—February 22, 1991
Feldman, Phil (69)—October 6, 1991
Field, John (69)—August 3, 1991
Frankovich, M.J. (83)—January 1, 1992
Fraser, Tom (60)—February 10, 1992
Gardner, William T. (57)—April 24, 1992
Gladstein, Robert (49)—May 5, 1992
Glasser, Steven B. (33)—April 29, 1992
Goodman, Martin (77)—January 5, 1992
Golden, Murray (79)—August 5, 1991
Gregory, Michael Scott (29)—February 23, 1992
Griffin, Rodney (46)—December 26, 1991
Haber, John (46)—January 29, 1992
Harris, Lou (85)—December 6, 1991
Herzberger, Jack L. (75)—April 23, 1992
Jaffe, Herb (70)—December 7, 1991
Kaplan, Paul Alan (36)—November 25, 1991
Laird, Jack (69)—December 3, 1991
Lerman, Oscar S—March 2, 1992
Levy, Benno—October 12, 1991
Levy, Franklin R. (43)—March 17, 1992
Loew, Sonja—August 12, 1991
Lorentz, Pare (86)—March 4, 1992
Love, Edward M. Jr. (43)—December 27, 1991
Lowenstein, Lynn Gendron (38)—October 9, 1991
Mann, Daniel (79)—November 21, 1991
Markle, Fletcher (70)—May 23, 1991

Marshall, Herbert P.J. (85)—May 28, 1991
Marton, Andrew (87)—January 7, 1992
Marx, Samuel (90)—March 2, 1992
Musilli, John (55)—August 17, 1991
O'Byrne, Robert (75)—June 18, 1991
Orezzoli, Hector (38)—November 4, 1991
Papp, Joseph (70)— October 31, 1991
Pasternak, Joe (89)—September 13, 1991
Peixoto, Mario (83)—February 3, 1992
Popkin, Harry M. (85)—October 7, 1991
Powell, Joe M. (73)—June 1991
Pratt, James C. (86)—October 10, 1991
Ray, Satyajit (70)—April 23, 1992
Richardson, Tony (63)—November 14, 1991
Roosevelt, James (83)—August 13, 1991
Rubinstein, Carol (51)—July 20, 1991
Schafranek, Franz (61)—June 3, 1991
Schlossberg, Jerry (55)—October 10, 1991
Sergeyev, Konstantin (82)—April 1, 1992
Sheppard, Harry (47)—February 21, 1992
Sherman, Emilia—February 28, 1992
Simpson, Robert Charles (65)—January 1, 1992
Stein, Robert M. (40)—June 13, 1991
Swerdlow, Stanley (72)—September 16, 1991
Sonntag, Jack (77)—September 22, 1991
Tucker, Paul (40)—May 25, 1991
Wachsberger, Nathan (75)—February 1, 1992
Willard, Charles Andrew (48)—August 11, 1991
Zampa, Luigi (86)—August 15, 1991

OTHERS

Aberbach Joachim (81)—May 27, 1992
  Music publisher
Allen, John E. Jr. (58)—February 25, 1992
  Founder, Freedom Theater
Anderson, Vivienne (77)—September 1, 1991
  Kennedy Center, Lincoln Center
Ashley, George (66)—September 9, 1991
  Publicist
Asimov, Isaac (72)—April 6, 1992
  Writer
Bardy, H. Wayne (49)—April 21, 1992
  Agent
Bartelme, Joe (61)—August 31, 1991
  NBC News
Baxter, Walter E. (53)—January 5, 1992
  Majestic Entertainment
Bercovici, Julian (71)—March 16, 1992
  ABC-TV
Bernardi, Harriet D. (74)—April 25, 1992
  Cleveland Opera Association
Bliss, Anthony A. (78)—August 10, 1991
  Metropolitan Opera, Joffrey Ballet

Bodne, Ben B. (88)—May 12, 1992
  Algonquin Hotel
Carroll, Mary Beth (47)—January 19, 1992
  The Acting Company
Chaplin, Oona (66)—September 27, 1991
  Charles Chaplin's widow
Colloff, Roger (46)—February 6, 1992
  WCBS-TV
Cork, Sir Kenneth (78)—October 13, 1991
  Royal Shakespeare Co.
diDonato, Pietro (80)—Winter 1992
  Novelist
Dow, Ian (76)—April 1, 1992
  Stage manager
Dudich, John T. (51)—June 9, 1991
  Publicist
Eastman, Lee V. (81)—July 30, 1991
  Lawyer
Feller, Fred (64)—December 4, 1991
  Set builder
Friedman, Jerome Meyer (97)—April 27, 1992
  Opera usher
Geisel, Theodor Seuss (87)—September 25, 1991
  Children's author
Gewirtz, Paul P. (87)—January 18, 1992
  Music Sales Corporation
Gershwin, Leonore S. (90)—August 20, 1991
  Widow of Ira Gershwin
Goody, Sam (87)—August 8, 1991
  Store owner
Goodyear, Tom (74)—January 7, 1992
  Glimmerglass Opera Theater
Haley, Alex (70)—February 10, 1992
  Author
Hall, Frances Stillman (72)—March 7, 1992
  Publicist
Hayes, J. William (70)—March 30, 1992
  Lawyer
Herman, Bob (66)—August 19, 1991
  Metropolitan Opera
Herman, Mary Ann (79)—March 23, 1992
  Folk dance teacher
Joel, Lydia (77)—May 24, 1992
  Dance Magazine
Kendall, Lester (73)—March 19, 1992
  Agent
Kiker, Douglas (61)—August 14, 1991
  Journalist
Lash, Irving (82)—July 29, 1991
  Music teacher
Lashwood, Hall—March 26, 1992
  Australian Actors' Equity
Lehman, Gary A. (34)—April 10, 1992
  Lawyer
Lewis, Joseph D. (69)—July 29, 1991
  Archivist

MacDonald, Mildred (79)—January 14, 1992
    NY Shakespeare Festival
Mardus, Richard (87)—June 25, 1991
    American Publicists Guild
Marton, Elisabeth (90)—May 18, 1992
    Agent
Maxwell, Robert (60)—November 5, 1991
    Media executive
McElroy, Howard D. Jr. (69)—September 4, 1991
    Agent
Mills, Cyril (89)—July 20, 1991
    Bertram Mills Circus
Mulberger, Charles (42)—January 5, 1992
    Dresser
Nederlander, Sarah Applebaum (97)—December 18, 1991
    Theater executive
O'Connell, Bill (41)—May 6, 1992
    Publicist
Offermans, David (46)—July 1, 1991
    Variety
Otelsberg, Martin (64)—April 10, 1992
    Agent
Patelson, Joseph (80)—April 3, 1992
    Patelson's music store
Philips, John F. (76)—May 21, 1991
    Restaurateur
Porter, Thomas Nelson (59)—December 1, 1991
    Stage manager
Powell, Charles M. (57)—June 14, 1991
    Motion Picture Academy
Rackmil, Milton R. (89)—April 2, 1992
    Decca Records, Universal Pictures
Raison, Robert (69)—May 19, 1992
    Agent
Reasoner, Harry (68)—August 5, 1991
    Journalist
Reisfeld, Bert (85)—July 1, 1991
    Hollywood Foreign Press Association

Rhodes, Willard (91)—May 15, 1992
    Music professor
Rosenberg, Jack B. (84)—November 30, 1991
    Agent
Rosenstock, Milton (74)—April 24, 1992
    Music director
Rubinstein, David (39)—November 24, 1991
    Stage manager
Rylander, Al (82)—April 30, 1992
    Publicist
Singer, Isaac Bashevis (87)—July 24, 1991
    Novelist
Smith, J. Welton (54)—April 7, 1992
    Publicist
Stark, Frances Brice (72)—May 31, 1992
    Fanny Brice's daughter
Stern, Noel (33)—March 22, 1992
    Stage manager
Swire, Willard (81)—November 13, 1991
    Actors' Equity Association
Weintraub, Louis (69)—September 19, 1991
    Publicist
Weissel, William L. (80)—January 29, 1992
    NY Philharmonic
Werblin, David A. (81)—November 21, 1991
    Madison Square Garden
West, Bill (62)—February 22, 1992
    Electrician
Wiesner, Theodora (83)—May 2, 1992
    American Dance Festival
Williams, Tom (65)—April 1, 1992
    Amargosa Opera House
Wyle, Clement J. (88)—October 31, 1991
    Publicist
Ziffren, Paul (77)—May 31, 1991
    Lawyer

THE BEST PLAYS, 1894-1991

Listed in alphabetical order below are all those works selected as Best Plays in previous volumes of the *Best Plays* series. Opposite each title is given the volume in which the play appears, its opening date and its total number of performances. Two separate opening-date and performance-number entries signify two separate engagements off Broadway and on Broadway when the original production was transferred from one area to the other, usually in an off-to-on direction. Those plays marked with an asterisk (*) were still playing on June 1, 1992 and their number of performances was figured through May 31, 1992. Adaptors and translators are indicated by (ad) and (tr), the symbols (b), (m) and (l) stand for the author of the book, music and lyrics in the case of musicals and (c) signifies the credit for the show's conception.

476

INDEX

INDEX

Play titles appear in **bold face**. *Bold face italic* page numbers refer to those pages where complete cast and credit listings for productions may be found.